Tourism on the Verge

Series editors
Pauline J. Sheldon
University of Hawaii, Honolulu, Hawaii, USA

Daniel R. Fesenmaier
University of Florida, Gainesville, Florida, USA

More information about this series at http://www.springer.com/series/13605

Roman Egger • Igor Gula • Dominik Walcher
Editors

Open Tourism

Open Innovation, Crowdsourcing and
Co-Creation Challenging the Tourism
Industry

 Springer

Editors
Roman Egger
Innovation & Management in Tourism
Salzburg University of Applied Sciences
Puch Urstein, Austria

Igor Gula
MODUL University Vienna
Wien, Austria

Dominik Walcher
School of Design and Product Management
Salzburg University of Applied Sciences
Salzburg-Kuchl, Austria

Tourism on the Verge
ISBN 978-3-642-54088-2   ISBN 978-3-642-54089-9   (eBook)
DOI 10.1007/978-3-642-54089-9

Library of Congress Control Number: 2015957965

Springer Heidelberg New York Dordrecht London
© Springer-Verlag Berlin Heidelberg 2016

Printed on acid-free paper

Springer-Verlag GmbH Berlin Heidelberg is part of Springer Science+Business Media
(www.springer.com)

Preamble and Acknowledgements

The tourism and leisure industry is characterized by a high level of dynamic change. The entire sector is now facing even greater challenges resulting from the enormous complexities, global competition, rapidly changing structures, processes and products, altered values and standards among customers, social change, and many other factors. This market dynamism is further accelerated by the great share of information and communication technologies used in the sector, a factor which is also responsible for establishing an entirely new balance of power between the customers and the providers. Add to this that the increasing expectations on the demand side coupled with the new empowered self-image of the customers, who can or wish to take on a new and more active role throughout the value generation chain in future, call for an innovative approach to be adopted by the entire industry. The tourism industry has, however, always been relatively rigid in its attitude to innovations. And despite the fact that innovative approaches to business are now firmly anchored in many industries, the service sector is significantly behind in this development, and new approaches are only taken up in a very slow and delayed manner. When reading the scientific literature on the subject a point that is immediately apparent is how few and far between technical and innovative approaches are in the tourism context and how very little discussion they receive. Actually there are many approaches of openness and collaboration in the field of tourism. Interestingly, there is no systematic collection and overview of these approaches. The book "Open Tourism" aims to bridge this gap by focusing on reports and case studies of Open Innovation, Crowdsourcing, and Co-Creation in the tourism industry. Therefore methods, theories, and models are discussed and examined regarding their practical applicability in tourism.

The process by which a book of this kind is written is often laborious and long drawn-out, but frequently beginning with a pleasant or amusing anecdote. This also applies in the present case. Many years ago and long before we ever even thought about bringing out a book on the subject of *Open Tourism*, Roman visited a small hotel not far from Salzburg. The hotel has 80 beds, and despite the close proximity to the provincial capital city it is somewhat remote and off the map in a tourism weak valley. During a discussion, the hotelier explained that over many years he had offered a special week for regular guests in October. The week concerned is always the one in which the hotel is prepared for the winter. This all began when a number of the regulars asked the hotelier if they might not be able to lend a hand during this winter preparation work. This included tasks such as harvesting the last of the apples, raking the autumn leaves, putting the pot plants away for the winter, helping out in the kitchen, and a great many other seasonal chores. Over the years, lists of the help work were compiled and the guests asked on arrival when and where they could make themselves useful and enter their names in the list. A very warm and social atmosphere developed as a result, and over the years these guests became more and more firmly integrated in this hotel process. Tasty snacks to keep them all going, the gratitude and appreciation they received for their work and the pleasant feeling of being a part of something of value and importance was a welcome reward for the effort. We still find this a very pleasing and successful example of innovation and especially convincing through its simplicity. One could, of course, make a crowdsourcing case study out of this, by describing each detail and episode in full, by analyzing all the various facets of the project and by coming up with a whole range of different theoretical references. But we do not intend to do this here. Our aim is for the reader to let this account sink in and take its effect; with all its simplicity, clarity, and in the knowledge that it all functions simply because someone was prepared to give free reign to the group dynamics of the guests and also provided the framework conditions required for this to flourish.

Years later, Igor Gula wrote his master thesis "Crowdsourcing in the Tourism Industry; Using the Example of Idea Competitions in Tourism Destinations" in Roman's "Innovation und Management in Tourism" course at the Salzburg University of Applied Sciences. Igor had worked his way carefully through all the theories and models and brought them all in with outstanding skill in his work. While Igor was presenting his thesis during the finals, Roman had the idea of editing a book with him on the subject. Dominik, who is also a Professor at the Salzburg University of Applied Sciences, MIT Associate, and a leading expert in the field of mass customization, was also brought in and this is how we ended up working as a trio on the book concept. A few months and numerous workshops later, a suitable framework was developed (contribution–utilization matrix), which in addition to its theoretical contribution was also structurally determining for the way the book developed. The closely linked thematic issues *Open Innovation, Crowdsourcing*, and *Co-Creation* were subsumed and brought into a relationship with each other under the basket term *Open Tourism*. Ultimately, 36 chapters were identified, selected, and edited for inclusion, and 74 authors worked on them.

As with every book, numerous people have been involved in the working process. First and foremost we would like to thank the authors for their contributions. It is their knowledge and the high quality of the essays they have written that brings this book to life. Christian Rauscher from Springer adopted the project and helped us to develop the book. He was a constant support throughout and gave us a free hand even at the most difficult times, ensuring that the work could be published as we had intended. Finally, of course, we would like to express our gratitude to our families and loved ones for the endless support and encouragement they have given us.

It is our hope this book will prove to be of value for the scientific community, students, and also for professionals and achieve a widespread echo.

Autumn, 2014   Roman Egger
                                                                   Igor Gula
                                                             Dominik Walcher

Contents

List of Contributors

Roman Egger is Professor of Tourism at the Salzburg University of Applied Sciences. He graduated in Communications Sciences and gained his Doctorate from the University of Salzburg, where he specialized in the fields of Information- and Communication Technologies in Tourism. He worked at the Tourism Board of Salzburg as a marketer. Roman is senior researcher and lecturer at the Salzburg University of Applied Sciences at the department of Innovation and Management in Tourism and divisional head of eTourism. He has written and coedited 14 books, published a number of articles in books and journals, and is coeditor of the scientific Journal "Zeitschrift für Tourismuswissenschaft." He is a Member of the International Federation of Information Technology for Travel and Tourism (IFITT), ÖGAF, DGT, and AIEST.

Igor Gula is a graduate of a Bachelor's degree program in tourism business studies of the Management Center Innsbruck and of a Master's degree program in innovation and management in tourism of the Salzburg University of Applied Sciences. He completed his internship in the department of Marketing New Media at the headquarters of the Casinos Austria in Vienna. Igor wrote his Bachelor's thesis about the trends of the modern ICTs and their impacts on tourism, focusing on Dynamic Packaging, mTourism, and Social Semantic Web. For his Master's thesis, he analysed the aspects of Open Innovation and Crowdsourcing in tourism and conducted a web-based ideas competition in cooperation with the Slovak Tourist Board. Igor is currently in charge of the corporate customer service at the Hotel Zeitgeist Vienna and also studies business administration at the MODUL University in Vienna.

Dominik Walcher studied Architecture and Management at the University of Stuttgart, the Technical University Munich (TUM), and the University of California at Berkeley. After some years of gaining work experience, he joined Prof. Reichwald's chair for Management at TUM in 2001, where he was part of Frank Piller's newly founded Center for Mass Customization and Open Innovation. His doctoral thesis about Customer Integration at Adidas was awarded with several prizes. Since June 2006, he is professor for Marketing and Innovation Management at Salzburg University of Applied Sciences/School for Design and Product Management. He extended his field of research to Brand Management, Business Creation, and Sustainability Marketing. He was founder of a start-up company in the field of customizable and eco-intelligent products. Results from his practical experience and academic research are numerously published and part of his teaching and consultancy. Dominik Walcher is visiting professor at universities in Germany, Switzerland, and Italy. Since May 2010, he is Research Associate at Massachusetts Institute of Technology (MIT) directing the LivingLabs' "Customization 500" initiative.

Philipp Allerstorfer graduated from the Tourism Management program at IMC University of Applied Sciences in Krems and is currently enrolled in the Web Science program of Johannes Kepler University in Linz. Philipp is frequently attending scientific conferences and is currently researching in the field of virtual currencies. Furthermore, he is employed in the field of e-Tourism and implements e-commerce-projects for national and international hotel chains and tourism destinations.

Kathrin Parson Bakk is an innovation researcher at Salzburg Research. She studied sociology at the Karl-Franzens-University in Graz. Before she joined the InnovationLab of Salzburg Research, she worked on quantitative and qualitative evaluation, quality management, and assurance at the University of Music and Performing Arts Graz. Her research interests include online communities and the application of information and communication technologies in (open) innovation processes.

Michael Bartl is CEO for HYVE—the innovation company. Prior to HYVE, Michael worked for the carmaker AUDI in the R&D division. He started his academic career with a Bachelor of Science from the University of Westminster London, a Dipl.-Kfm. from the University of Munich (LMU), and a PhD from the Otto Beisheim Graduate School (WHU) on the topic of "Customer integration in NPD." Michael has authored numerous articles and papers on the subjects of Co-Creation, Open Innovation, Netnography, Community-based Innovation, and Future Developments in Innovation Management. He has published in leading international journals such as Journal of Product Innovation Management, Electronic Commerce Research Journal, Harvard Business Manager and is research fellow of the Peter Pribilla Foundation. He is the author of the E-Journal "The Making-of Innovation" (http://www.makingofinnovation.com) and a regular speaker and host at innovation and other industry conferences. Since 2011, Michael is as an elected member of the national executive committee of the German Association of Market and Social Research (BVM). In 2012, he was appointed as German senator to the Senat der Wirtschaft which is part of the Global Economic Network.

Volker Bilgram is Associated Researcher at the Technology & Innovation Management Group of RWTH Aachen University and Team Lead at HYVE, an Open Innovation company. His academic research interest is on distributed innovation systems, consumer empowerment, and co-creation and has been published in journals such as the International Journal of Innovation Management, Marketing Review St. Gallen, and Harvard Business Manager. Volker graduated in International Business Law at the University of Erlangen-Nuremberg with a focus on New Product Development and Open Innovation.

Paul Blazek is founder and CEO of the digital agency cyLEDGE Media in Vienna and founder and board member of several start-ups. He teaches social network marketing at the University of Applied Science in Salzburg and referral marketing at the Lucerne University of Applied Sciences and Arts, is scientific head of the annual Business Goes Social Media Conference in Austria, founding member of the International Institute on Mass Customization and Personalization (IIMCP), research fellow of the Peter Pribilla Foundation, and is associated to the MIT's Smart Customization Group.

At cyLEDGE he developed CrowdCity (www.crowdcity.com) to generate knowledge about upcoming standards and success factors of crowdsourcing approaches.

www.twitter.com/PaulBlazek

Kim Boes is currently a PhD Researcher at the eTourismLab at Bournemouth University, UK, where she writes her thesis about Smart Tourism Destinations: Explore how smartness improves competitiveness in the context of tourism destinations. Kim holds a Bachelor's and a Master's degree in Innovation and Management in Tourism from the University of Applied Sciences Salzburg, Austria. Before joining Bournemouth University, she was working as a research assistant at the tourism research department at the University of Applied Sciences Salzburg in Austria.

Ulrich Bretschneider is a senior researcher at the department for Information Systems at University of Kassel, Germany. He received his PhD from the Technische Universität München, Germany, in 2011 with a dissertation about Open Innovation Communities. His research areas include Open Innovation, Crowdsourcing, and Crowdfunding. His work has been published in several academic journals, such as the Journal of Management Information Systems (JMIS), and international conferences, such as the Annual Meeting of the Academy of Management or the European Conference on Information Systems (ECIS). In 2013, he has been awarded with the Emerald Citation of Excellence Award for a research paper in the JMIS.

Sabine Brunswicker is an innovation researcher with a particular interest in open innovation and innovation ecosystems. She is an Associate Professor of Innovation and Director of the Research Center for Open Digital Innovation (RCODI) at Purdue University in West-Lafayette, United States. She is also affiliated with

Esade Business School, at Ramon Llul University in Spain, holds a role as Adjunct Professor at the School of Information Systems, Queensland University of Technology (QUT) in Australia, and is a strategic advisor for open innovation at the Fraunhofer Institute for Industrial Engineering, Germany. Sabine holds a Master in Engineering and Management Sciences (MSc, dual degree), a Master of Commerce with a Specialization in Marketing & Entrepreneurship, and a PhD in the area of innovation management. Sabine's general research interests lie in understanding collaborative models of innovation and value creation in today's global and digital economy. She maintains an active network of industry partners and foundations pioneering open and digital forms of innovation. Further, she closely interacts with the European Commission and is a member of the Open Innovation Strategy and Policy Group (OISPG) of DG Connect.

Sandra Bürcher studied geography and history at the University of Fribourg in Switzerland from which she has a Master's degree with focus on Sustainable Development. She wrote her Master's thesis about the reconstruction of decision-making processes in the Nature Park of Binntal. After her studies, she completed an internship in the network of Swiss Parks. She gained more work experience at the Swiss Centre for Mountain Regions and as an assistant at the Institute of Tourism of the University of Applied Sciences of Western Switzerland. Currently, she is doing her PhD on entrepreneurship in non-metropolitan Swiss regions at the University of Berne.

Francesca Cabiddu is Assistant Professor in Management in the Faculty of Economics of the University of Cagliari, Italy. Cabiddu's research interest has focused on strategy management, dynamic capabilities, customer service, and consumer behavior. She is currently pursuing a long-standing interest in Tourism and Information Technology.

Marut Doctor has a Master's degree in Natural Sciences /Geography from the Swiss Federal Institute of Technology in Zurich. As a meteorologist and a climatologist, he has been working since 2007 at the Institute of Tourism of the University of Applied Sciences of Western Switzerland. He has worked on the effects of weather and climate on the economy of a region, the optimization of artificial snow and of the skier flow, and other domains of tourism not linked with meteorology, especially the open innovation processes in tourism. He participated also in the Interreg project on the adaptation of Alpine tourism to climate change. Now, he works for a good part of his time on the Tourism Observatory of the Valais. This includes especially tourist frequentation (e.g., hotel overnight data) and the different economic and meteorological factors which influence this frequentation.

Robert A. Eckhoff is innovation researcher and consultant at the InnovationLab. He studied social sciences, management, and organizational psychology at Jacobs University Bremen (Germany) and the Free University of Amsterdam (Netherlands). His research interests include creativity, innovation management, team diversity, and diversity training. He advises companies with regard to their innovation management and innovation strategy and has published in journals such as Human Relations, The Journal of Intellectual Capital, and others.

Stefan Etzelstorfer is student of business economics and law at Johannes Kepler University Linz, Upper Austria, focusing on public management, knowledge management, and business law. For many years, he volunteered for the Austrian Student Union (ÖH) in Linz and was its head from 2010 until 2011. Currently, he is working on his diploma thesis on challenges of introducing open government at a local level with a focus on the City of Linz municipality.

Robert C. Ford is professor emeritus of management at the University of Central Florida. His research and teaching focus is on the management of service organizations. He has authored or coauthored numerous books and publications in both top research and practitioner journals and served as editor of *The Academy of Management Executive*. He has held numerous offices in his professional organizations including president of the Southern Management Association where he was elected as a Fellow and received its Distinguished Service Award. He also served as a founding member and Chair of the Accreditation Commission for Programs in Hospitality Administration.

Alexander Fritsch is an expert in online tourism. In addition to his work as a consultant, coach, and speaker, he is a lecturer for "eTourism" at the University of Applied Sciences in Chur, Switzerland.

Johann Füller holds the chair for Innovation and Entrepreneurship in the Department of Strategic Management, Marketing and Tourism, at the University of Innsbruck. Since his habilitation, he has been a senior lecturer of Marketing at the Innsbruck University School of Management. He is Fellow at the NASA Tournament Lab-Research at Harvard University and founder and CEO of HYVE AG, Europeans leading (open & user) innovation and community agency. From 2008 to 2010, Johann was a visiting scholar and research affiliate at MIT Sloan School of Management.

Oliver Gajda co-founded the European Crowdfunding Network and is acting Chairman & Executive Director and is an Executive Committee Member of CF50 Inc., the global think tank on Crowdfunding. As a business consultant, journalist, as well as start-up and buyout manager, Oliver worked with venture capital, microfinance, technology, and social entrepreneurship in commercial, nonprofit, and trade association settings in Europe and the USA. Oliver started his career in the early 1990s in the publishing and market research industries. He holds Masters degrees from Solvay Business School at the Université libre de Bruxelles and from the University of Hamburg; he also studied at SEESS, University College London, in London.

José Luis Galdón has a Bachelor's degree in Telecommunications Engineering from the Universidad Politécnica de Valencia (Spain) and a Bachelor in Business Administration from the Universidad Europea de Madrid. He has an MSc in Renewable Energies and has completed a course on business management at the IESE Business School in Barcelona. He has published articles in international books and journals in the areas of new technologies, tourism management, and knowledge management. He has taught and done research at universities in South America (Peru and Ecuador).

Thomas Gegenhuber is currently a doctoral student and recipient of a fellowship ("DOC-team") from the Austrian Academy of Sciences at the Institute for Organization and Global Management Studies at Johannes Kepler University, Linz. His research interests include crowdsourcing, (open) innovation, and organization theory. Furthermore, he is an open government advocate and contributes to such projects in Linz.

Barbara Gligorijevic has both academic and professional backgrounds in marketing. She holds an MBA in Marketing from the University of Sheffield. Her PhD research in media and communication and marketing at the Queensland University of Technology was funded by Smart Services Cooperative Research Centre (CRC). In a professional capacity, Barbara has worked as a market research consultant for major international brands in the retailing, finance, and telecom industries. Her research is focused on the use of electronic word-of-mouth marketing on social media platforms, specifically user-created reviews, ratings, and recommendations (across different industries: travel and tourism, consumer electronics, and retailing) and their impact on the purchasing decision-making process.

Robert Goecke is professor for information and service management at the faculty of tourism of the University of Applied Sciences Munich since 2006. From 1999 to 2006, he has been cofounder and CEO of segm@—service engineering & management AG which develops innovative internet-based services. Between 1996 and 1998, he worked as a consultant for major companies and lead a public funded interdisciplinary research project about new services for the twenty-first century. Robert Goecke received a diploma in computer science in 1991 and a doctorate of business administration in 1996 at Technische Universität München.

Frederic Gonzalo is passionate about marketing and communications, with over 19 years of experience in the travel and tourism sphere. Early 2012, he launched **Gonzo Marketing** and works as a strategic marketing consultant, professional speaker, and trainer in the use of new technologies (web, social media, mobile). He writes regularly about **e-tourism** on his blog fredericgonzalo.com and collaborates to influential sites such as Social Media Today, Business2Community, and ehotelier. In 2013, he was ranked most influential blogger for e-tourism and travel in the province of Quebec (Canada) and second most influential blogger for marketing & social media in the province of Quebec (Canada).

Ulrike Gretzel is Professor of Tourism at the University of Queensland, Australia. She received her PhD in Communication from the University of Illinois at Urbana-Champaign, USA. Her research interests focus on online consumer behavior, persuasion in online communication, social media marketing, and issues related to the development, adoption, and use of intelligent systems in tourism. She is Editor-in-Chief of the e-Review of Tourism Research and serves on the editorial boards of several other journals. She also served on the board of IFITT.

Christian Gülpen is head of the business development division at RWTH Aachen University Technology and Innovation Management Group (TIM Group). He has a background of multiple years in both management and strategy of academic executive education. At TIM Group, he is responsible for the development of new external education programs and corporate consulting.

Anita Hausen holds a Doctorate in Public Health from the Center for Social Policy, University of Bremen. She has a variety of research interests which include health services research, especially the quality assurance of healthcare, and workplace quality. Currently, she works as a research associate at the Institute of General Practice, University of Ulm. Before that, she worked in projects such as PiA (Professionalization of Interactive Work) and Talking Eyes. She studied Public Health at the Free University of Berlin and Health Management at the University of Applied Sciences of Magdeburg-Stendal.

Isabel Herms is an employee at the B·A·D GmbH (Munich), a company dealing with occupational health and safety and workplace health promotion. Prior to this, she was employed in various research projects at the Technical University of Munich, Technical University of Dresden, and at Aalen University. Furthermore, she is a freelancer, offering trainings and consulting. She holds a Diploma (2007, German master's-level degree) from the Technical University of Dresden. Her research and activities focuses on emotion work in human service work and occupational health.

Dennis Hilgers is professor of Public and Non-profit Management at the Johannes Kepler University Linz. His research focuses on managing innovation and performance in public administrations. One of the phenomena of his particular interest is open government, the application of open innovation methods for service innovation, and offerings in the public sector. He has been a coordinator on several large-scale project consortia in this field that receive funding from the European Union and the German Science Foundation.

Anne-Mette Hjalager is professor and research director at the Danish Center for Rural Research, University of Southern Denmark. Her areas of interest are among others local development, innovation, and labor market issues in tourism. She is involved in transnational research in the fields of rural wellbeing and ecosystems services and in the exploration of innovation issues in tourism. She is the cofounder of the INNOTOUR platform and the editor-in-chief of Journal of Gastronomy and Tourism.

Hindertje Hoarau is originally Dutch and since 2009 living and working in Northern Norway. She is a PhD candidate at the Bodø Graduate School of Business at University of Nordland. Her thesis about innovation in Nordic nature-based tourism is part of the research project Northern Insights (www.opplevelserinord. no). Hindertje got her bachelor in Environmental Management and Policy from the Radboud University in Nijmegen and her Master in International Development Studies from the Wageningen University and Research Centre (both Dutch

Universities). After working as a consultant and project manager in The Netherlands, she continues her Academic career in Norway. Her research interests are organizational change, knowledge, learning, tourism-SME's, sustainability, and corporate social responsibility.

Zsófia Horváth holds a Bachelor's degree in Tourism and Hospitality Management from the Budapest Business School, Hungary. Zsófia is currently finishing her master diploma at the Salzburg University of Applied Sciences in Austria. In her master thesis, she analysed the acceptance of Mobile Marketing in Tourism. In cooperation with the Salzburg State Theatre she developed a mobile application prototype to explore the potential of mobile marketing on a traditional institution.

Katja Hutter is Assistant Professor at the Innsbruck University School of Management and a research fellow at Harvard-NASA Tournament Lab at the Institute for Quantitative Social Science. Katja holds a doctorate degree in Social and Economic Sciences from the University of Innsbruck. Her research interest is in the field of open innovation, especially idea contests and online innovation communities.

Julia Jonas is research associate and doctoral student at the Chair for Information Systems I—Innovation & Value Creation at the FAU Erlangen-Nuremberg. She is researching on the integration of internal and external stakeholders in service innovation throughout the innovation process. She graduated from Karlstad University, Sweden, specializing on Service Management and Marketing and looks back at over 4 years of experience as a project manager in an innovation consultancy, where she assisted clients such as Beiersdorf, W.L. Gore or Symrise to plan and conduct open innovation projects.

Giordano Koch is currently working on his PhD at the University Hamburg. His research interests are open innovation and co-creation in the public as well as private sector including different forms of citizen participation. Furthermore, he is lecturer at the Johannes Kepler University of Linz (Austria) and an eligible speaker on topics of Open Government, Open Innovation within Public Administration, and Citizen Participation. Besides this, Giordano Koch is managing director at HYVE Innovation Community GmbH.

Thomas Kohler is Associate Professor of Marketing at Hawaii Pacific University and the founder of travel2change. The crowdsourcing platform travel2change is shaped by Thomas' research on how organizations can use crowdsourcing to create social innovation. His previous research has been published in journals such as the MIS Quarterly, Technovation, and the Harvard Business Manager.

Benjamin Kreitmeir works at the crowdsourcing software company innosabi. As a project manager, he is in charge of managing and guiding companies of all sizes through the concept and application of their open innovation projects and campaigns. He is a Masters graduate of Tourism and Entrepreneurship of the Management Center Innsbruck and holds a Bachelor's degree in Tourism Management from Munich University of Applied Sciences. Benjamin Kreitmeir wrote his Master's thesis on the application of open innovation and crowdsourcing in order to activate and support stakeholder participation in Alpine-Destinations. During his studies, he was working for an Online Marketing Agency, learning how to best utilize the economic possibilities of a digitalized world.

Yohei Kurata is an associate professor at the Department of Tourism Science, School of Urban Environmental Sciences, Tokyo Metropolitan University since 2010. He studied spatial information science and engineering at the University of Maine, USA, and got PhD there in 2007. His primary research interest is the use of geo-spatial information technologies in the tourism domain, especially for enriching the experience of self-guided travellers.

Sascha Langner is Assistant Professor of Marketing and Management at the Leibniz University of Hannover. His main research fields are Online Marketing, Consumer Behavior, and Neuroeconomics.

Markus Lassnig is head of the competence field e-tourism (http://etourism. salzburgresearch.at) and senior researcher at the InnovationLab at Salzburg Research. His scientific focus is on different aspects of internet economics, innovation management, business management, and strategy—especially in the tourism and leisure industries. In these fields, he is also teaching at Universities of Applied Sciences in Austria and Germany. Markus Lassnig studied communication research and political science at the University of Salzburg. He holds a degree in the field of media economics of audiovisual mass media and a PhD in the field of internet economics.

Jan Marco Leimeister joined St. Gallen University in 2012 as a professor at the Institute of Information Management (IWI HSG) and is also the Chair of Information Systems at Kassel University (Germany) since 2008. His research focuses on Service Engineering, Collaboration Engineering, IT Innovations, and Technology Management. He runs several research groups, and his research projects are funded by European Union, German Ministries, and DFG. Jan Marco Leimeister authored and/or edited more than 13 books as well as more than 300 scientific publications. His research has been published in a broad range of Journals such as Journal of Management Information Systems (JMIS) or Information Systems Journal (ISJ). In addition, Jan Marco Leimeister serves on the editorial board of the European Journal of Information Systems (EJIS), is a Senior Editor of the Journal of Information Technology (JIT), and is regularly member of programme committees of international conferences.

Janne J. Liburd is a Doctor in Philosophy, Associate Professor, and research director of the Centre for Tourism, Innovation and Culture, University of Southern Denmark. She is an anthropologist, and her research interests are in the fields of higher education and sustainable tourism development. She has published on epistemology, Open Innovation and Web 2.0, tourism education, quality of life, national park development, heritage tourism, tourism crisis communication, NGOs and the being of the university. Dr. Liburd has conducted a number of research projects relating to competence development for tourism practitioners and tourism educators. She is the cofounder of the INNOTOUR platform and serves on several editorial boards. Dr. Liburd is the past Chair of the B.E.S.T. Education Network (2005–2010).

Kurt Luger is Professor of Transcultural communication at the Department of Communication, Salzburg University, Chairman of EcoHimal, and UNESCO Chair of Cultural Heritage. Recent publications include: *Cultural Heritage and Tourism* (ed. with Karlheinz Woehler, 2010); *World Heritage and Tourism* (ed. with Karlheinz Woehler, 2007); *Searching for the place of eternal happiness—Culture, tourism and development in the Himalayas* (2007).

Tsz-Wai Lui is Assistant Professor at the International College at Ming Chuan University, Taiwan. Her research interests include customer service systems and virtual worlds. Her research has been published by the Center of Hospitality Research (CHR) at Cornell and in European Journal of Information Systems, The DATABASE for Advances in Information Systems, and Annals of Tourism Research.

Mark Markus is a senior researcher at the InnovationLab, a socioeconomic department at Salzburg Research, focusing on consulting and research in the front end of innovation management. He supports companies to identify and develop product and process innovations and teaches entrepreneurship and innovation at the University of Applied Sciences. Mark Markus has worked with companies like Atomic, KTM, ÖAMTC. He holds a doctorate in communication science at the University of Salzburg and has completed the education in innovation management at Management Centre Innsbruck, concentrating especially on how companies can generate innovations with users and customers.

Jennifer Menzel is Product Developer at the Online Hotel Search trivago GmbH. Prior to her current position, she graduated from the Management Center Innsbruck with a Master's degree in Entrepreneurship & Tourism. During her studies, she spent three semesters abroad studying the field of tourism in Switzerland, Costa Rica, and South Africa. Her Master thesis about Crowdsourcing as a tool for innovation in the hotel industry was one of the first scientific works researching the topic for small- and medium-sized hotels. It was awarded with the Austrian prize for tourism research in 2011.

Katsutoshi Murakami is a senior consultant and a general manager at Nomura Research Institute, Ltd in Japan. He received his Bachelor's degree in Law from Keio University and an MBA degree from the University of Michigan. He is a management consultant who has expertise in business strategy, innovation, and information technology. His consultation approach is providing hands-on solutions to implementing strategies and innovation concepts using IT. He has extensive consultation experience in a wide range of industries including travel agencies, global hotel chains, and theme parks.

Mihir Ignatius Nayak   attended the prestigious Salzburg Tourism School in Bad Hofgastein, where he graduated with Excellence. After completing his BA (Hons) at the University of Derby UK, he did his Masters in Innovation & Management in Tourism at the Salzburg University of Applied Sciences where Prof. Dr. Roman Egger was one of his Professors. Mihir is currently pursuing his PhD in UNESCO Heritage Communication and Tourism at the University of Salzburg, Austria with Prof. Dr. Kurt Luger as his PhD Supervisor. Mihir is currently a Visiting Lecturer at the elite IUBH Tourism University in Bavaria and also runs his own Heritage Hotel in Goa's Heritage Zone of Fontainhas.

Christian Papsdorf   is a lecturer at the Department of Sociology at the Chemnitz University of Technology. His research activities are focused on Internet sociology, industrial sociology, communications, and media sociology. In 2012, he was awarded a doctoral degree for his dissertation entitled "Internet and Society. On the relation between Online and Offline against the background of mediated communication."

Ignacio Gil Pechuán   is a Full Professor in the Business Organisation Department at the Universitat Politecnica de Valencia (Spain). He has a PhD in Computing. He also has Bachelor degrees in Business Administration, Library Science, and Market Research. He has an MSc in Information Technology Systems, from the Universidad Politécnica de Valencia (Spain), and has completed a business management programme at IESE Business School (UNAV). He has published articles in international books and journals, such as the Annals of Tourism Research, Tourism Management, the International Journal of Technology Management, the Journal of Knowledge Management, Small Business Economics, Management Decision, and The Service Industries Journal.

William P. Perry   is a senior hotel executive and Global Head of Hotel Asset Management for Cii Hotels & Resorts based in Johannesburg, South Africa. William's career spans more than two decades with major hotel brands including Ritz-Carlton, Marriott, Westin, Hilton, Courtyard, Hampton Inn & Suites, The St. Regis, and Radisson. His experience includes hotel operations, sales and marketing, revenue management, development, and asset management. William holds a BA from Stetson University, an MBA from Georgia College & State University, and an MHR degree from Rollins College. He is a member of Skal International and the Chaine des Rotisseurs.

Mike Peters   is Associate Professor at the Management Center Innsbruck, MCI Tourism. After finalizing his apprenticeship, he gained working experience in the hotel industry in Germany before he was studying social sciences at the Universities of Regensburg (Germany) and Innsbruck (Austria). He holds a doctoral degree and a professorship in the field of business management and published in well-known tourism journals.

Gabriele Piccoli   after earning tenure at the School of Hotel Administration at Cornell University Gabriele Piccoli is now Associate Professor at the University of Pavia. His research expertise is in strategic IS and the use of IT to support customer service in the hospitality and tourism sector. His research has appeared in MIS Quarterly, The Cornell Hospitality Quarterly, Harvard Business Review, Decision Sciences Journal, as well as other academic and applied journals.

Birgit Pikkemaat is Assistant Professor and founder of ifit—the Institute of Innovative Tourism, a research and consulting initiative focusing on the analysis of product development and innovation processes in tourism. Her academic work was published in a number of acquainted journals and covers empirical insights in small tourism business and destination innovation processes.

Frank T. Piller is a Professor of management and head of the Technology and Innovation Management Group (TIM Group) at RWTH Aachen University. After receiving his doctorate about production management, he habilitated about "Innovation and Value Co-Creation" at Technische Universität München (TUM). After that he was a research fellow at MIT Sloan School of Management, Massachusetts Institute of Technology, Cambridge, USA, where he is still head of the "Smart Customization Group."

Christiane Rau is Professor of Innovation Management at the Department for Innovation & Product Management (IPM) of the University of Applied Sciences Upper Austria. Her research focuses on organizational behavior in innovation processes and in particular on opportunities and challenges at the boundary between external and internal project partners. Her work has been presented at various scientific conferences and has been published in academic journals, such as R&D Management and Technology Analysis and Strategic Management. She did her PhD at the University Erlangen, Chair of Innovation and Value Creation, and has a background in industrial engineering.

Brendan M. Richard is a doctoral student at the University of Central Florida enrolled in the Methodology, Measurement, and Analysis program. He has taught several courses within the field of management at the college level including: strategic management, conflict resolutions and negotiations, human resources, and business ethics. He has authored or co-authored book chapters and journal publications in the fields of crowdsourcing, hospitality management, mentoring, and educational leadership. His research focus is on open innovation and crowdsourcing and its applications in the fields of management and hospitality management.

Kerstin Rieder is Professor for Health Sciences and Social Sciences at Aalen University, Department Health Care Management, Germany. Prior to this she was a professor at the University of Applied Sciences Northwestern Switzerland. She holds a Diploma (1992, German master's-level degree) and Doctorate (1998) from the Technical University of Berlin. Her research focuses on the psychology and sociology of interactive service work, occupational health, and the working customer. She is a cofounder and active member of the initiative Social Science Service Research (3sR).

Petra Ringeisen received a diploma in business administration, French and Spanish philology at the University of Mannheim, and a doctorate of business administration in 2011 at the University of Kassel. She is working for DB Rent since 2012.

Digna Roeffen works as a marketing controller at Swarovski in Zürich, Switzerland. She holds a degree in business administration from the University of Innsbruck School of Management. Digna specialized in controlling as well as service management and tourism. Her field of interest is especially within customer co-creation and its implications on the hospitality industry.

Emre Ronay started his career in the tourism industry in 2007. He graduated with a distinction award and received his Bachelor's degree in Tourism Management from the Dokuz Eylul University, a major university in Turkey. He continued his education at the Salzburg University of Applied Sciences in Austria, where he received scholarships for his studies. Since 2013, he holds a Master's degree in Innovation and Management in Tourism. Furthermore, he published several scientific articles and gave presentations at international conferences. Currently, he pursues his career in the tourism industry in Zurich, Switzerland.

Marc Schnyder holds a PhD in Economics of the University of Fribourg (Switzerland) and is a full-time professor since 2008 at the University of Applied Sciences of Western Switzerland/Valais (HES-SO Valais) in the field of tourism. He is also a Senior Researcher at the Institute of Tourism in Sierre. After a 1-year internship at the Swiss National Bank in Zurich, he worked as a researcher for the "Private Hochschule Wirtschaft" in Berne. His current research interests are in the areas of tourism innovation processes, international tourism, tourism policy, and regional economics.

Ursula Scholl-Grissemann is assistant professor at the Department of Strategic Management, Marketing, and Tourism at the University of Innsbruck School of Management. Ursula's primary research interest is in customer co-creation practices and their effects on financial and non-financial firm performance.

Marco Schröder works as a research assistant at the University of Augsburg. He studied Sociology at the University of Augsburg and Educational Science at the University of Education in Schwäbisch Gmünd. His research focuses on occupational choice and technical and economic education.

Fiona Schweitzer is Professor of Marketing and Market Research at the Department for Innovation & Product Management (IPM) of the University of Applied Sciences Upper Austria. Her academic research focuses on open innovation, customer integration into the innovation process, the front end of innovation, smart products, and technology acceptance. She has won three best paper awards and has presented and published her work at various scientific conferences and in academic journals, such as the International Journal of Innovation Management and Research Technology Management. She has a background of product management in profit and nonprofit organizations.

Marianna Sigala is Associate Professor at the University of the Aegean, Greece. Prior to her current position, she lectured at the Universities of Strathclyde and Westminster in the UK. She also has professional hospitality industry experience. Her interests include service management, Information and Communication Technologies (ICT) in tourism and hospitality, and e-learning. Her work has been published in several academic journals, books, and international conferences. She is currently the editor of the journal Managing Service Quality and the Journal of Hospitality & Tourism Cases. She is a past President of EuroCHRIE and has served on the Board of Directors of I-CHRIE, IFITT, and HeAIS.

Holger Sigmund works as a tourism consultant and coach. In addition, he is involved in his own travel business as an incoming and marketing expert.

Fernando José Garrigós Simón has a PhD in Management. He is an Associate Professor in the Business Organisation Department at the Universidad Politécnica de Valencia (Spain). He has an MSc in Tourism Management and Planning from Bournemouth University. He has a Degree in Economics from the University of Valencia. He has taught and done research at universities in France, the USA, the UK, Australia, Singapore, and Thailand. His primary areas of research include tourism management and knowledge management. He has published articles in international books and journals, such as the Annals of Tourism Research, Tourism Management, the International Journal of Technology Management, the Journal of Knowledge Management, Small Business Economics, Management Decision, and The Service Industries Journal.

Dorothée Stadler is a Senior Project Manager at HYVE Innovation Research GmbH. She supports clients such as W.L. Gore & Associates, Beiersdorf, and Procter & Gamble GmbH in various open innovation and market research projects. She holds a graduate degree in business administration from Ludwig-Maximilians Universität in Munich, majoring in "Market Oriented Management," "Strategic Management," and "Cross-Cultural Communication." Over the course of her studies, part of which she spent as a visiting student at Saint Mary's University in Halifax (Canada), Dorothée worked on several different projects in consumer research, applying both qualitative and quantitative techniques. In her thesis, she analyzed consumers' perception of different nutritional food labelling systems in Germany. Before joining HYVE, Dorothée worked at Happy Thinking People, a marketing research company.

Daniel Stieger is vice-president of travel2change and responsible for IT operations. He received his PhD in business administration at the Innsbruck University School of Management. He holds a Master's degree in economics and a degree in engineering. His previous research has been published in journals such as the Marketing Science, California Management Review, and the Harvard Business Manager.

Anna Stribl has recently completed her bachelor's degrees in Slavic Studies and Management & Economics at the University of Innsbruck, Austria, where her thesis examined the potential of crowdsourcing for business model innovation in volunteer travel. Anna's interest in volunteers and tourism draws upon her experience working as a volunteer traveller for a nature reserve on the Kamchatka Peninsula, Russia.

Nayeli Tusche In order to explore and research consumers, their behavior, attitudes, as well as their needs and motives, Nayeli Tusche (M.Sc.) combines online methods (e.g., social media and online community analyses) as well as offline research techniques (e.g., qualitative interviews and ethnographic research). Particularly in the context of international projects, Nayeli draws upon her international background and sophisticated language skills (five languages), which she constantly developed during her former international tennis career and various places of residence around the world.

Conny Weber is a project manager at ISN since 2007. She has conducted various strategy and innovation projects both in research and industry. She holds a degree in information science from Saarland University (Germany) and a PhD in business studies from Karl-Franzens University Graz (Austria). Her work and research topics are mainly related to innovative information systems supporting inter-organizational collaboration, realizing virtual factories, and enhancing productivity of knowledge work.

Klaus-Peter Wiedmann is a Full Chaired Professor of Marketing and Management and the Director of the Institute of Marketing and Management at the Leibniz University Hannover, Germany. He is also the German Representative of the Reputation Institute, New York et al., Deputy Chair of the Academy of Global Business Advancement (AGBA), and as a Visiting Professor at the Henley Business School faculty member of the University of Reading, UK. Moreover, Professor Wiedmann has many years of experience as a management consultant and top management coach and takes a leading position in different business organizations as well as public private partnerships—e.g., Chairman of the BDTEU-TIDAF (Union of European Turkish Entrepreneurs) and Chairman of WOB AG (No.1 Agency for B2B Brand Management in Germany).

Reinhard Willfort is educated as a communication engineer by Siemens Austria. After finishing his studies in Telematics and Economy at Graz University of Technology (TUG), he worked as a quality manager at Spengle. In 1997, he took up the career of an Assistant professor at the Institute of Industrial Economics and Management at the Technical University Graz. Since 2000, he holds his PhD and is managing director of the ISN—Innovation Service Network in Austria; Dr. Willfort has been working in numerous research and industrial projects; he holds several publications and is lecturer at different universities in Austria. He is an innovation expert, entrepreneur, and funder of several start-ups and open innovation and crowdfunding initiatives.

Kyung-Hyan Yoo is an Assistant Professor of Communication at William Paterson University in the United States. She received her PhD in Tourism from Texas A&M University, USA, focusing on Information Technology & Tourism. Her current research interests include electronic word-of-mouth, online trust, social media communication, online tourist information search, and tourist decision-making.

Part I
Theoretical Fundamentals and Concepts

Towards a Holistic Framework of Open Tourism

Roman Egger, Igor Gula and Dominik Walcher

1 Challenges for the Tourism Industry

The tourism industry is one of the biggest industries and its markets are highly saturated, with constantly falling profit margins on the one hand, and fast changing needs and customer demands on the other (Lohmann, 2004; Witt, Brooke, & Buckley, 2013). It seems that the growth of the industry has reached its environmental, social and economic limits, where boundaries can no longer be expanded. Products and services in tourism are becoming more and more similar and exchangeable. The tourism industry is predominantly organized in a traditional way. The main part of tourism companies are small and medium-sized (family) enterprises (Buhalis, 1998). Tradition, authenticity and adhering to time-tested principles are on the one hand, appreciated by most guests, while the risk of missing a timely adaption to far-ranging technological and societal transformations can be observed on the other. New approaches are needed to guarantee the survival of companies. The development of ICTs (Information and Communication Technologies), especially the Internet with its revolutionary impact on the value creation of companies, has resulted in an enormous increase on literature about how economy and business have to be managed in view of a global paradigm shift (Reichwald & Piller, 2009). Many of these publications focus on management, marketing and innovation in general, or on particular branches, such as IT or product management, while the tourism industry so far has been addressed insufficiently. Open Innovation, Crowdsourcing and Co-Creation have become the most researched and discussed innovation topics since their introduction by Prahalad and Ramaswamy (2000),

R. Egger (✉) • D. Walcher
Salzburg University of Applied Science, Salzburg, Austria
e-mail: roman.egger@salzburg.ac.at; dominik.walcher@salzburg.ac.at

I. Gula
MODUL University Vienna, Wien, Austria
e-mail: igor.gula@chello.at

© Springer-Verlag Berlin Heidelberg 2016
R. Egger et al. (eds.), *Open Tourism*, Tourism on the Verge,
DOI 10.1007/978-3-642-54089-9_1

Chesbrough (2003) and Howe (2006a). The fundamental considerations of integrating customers into corporate processes have attracted a lot of attention among academics and practitioners (Tapscott & Williams, 2010; Zhao & Zhu, 2014). The traditional conception of innovation management is based upon a goods-dominant logic, that focuses on the developing, producing and selling of products (Vargo & Lusch, 2004). With the rise of the software industry in the 1980s, theories and models were first applied to intangible products and subsequently to the service sector—giving rise to the service-dominant logic.

In the scientific literature, it is widely recognised that service innovations (especially in tourism) have been handled with kid gloves. One of the first researchers who examined the use of Open Innovation, Crowdsourcing and Co-Creation within the hospitality industry was Menzel (2011). Later, the studies of Doctor, Schnyder, and Stumm (2011), Hjalager and Nordin (2011) and Faullant, Krajger, and Zanker (2012) focusing on User-driven-Innovation and on identification of innovative users in tourism were published. Schemann (2012) concentrated on the relevance of these concepts in the cruise industry. In the tourism industry, the opening of corporate boundaries to accommodate external input is not limited to innovation processes but also comprises of other important functions, such as marketing, communication and the execution of services. The literature focusing on Co-Creation in tourism mainly discusses the generation of personalized customer experiences in services (Morgan, Lugosi, & Ritchie, 2010; Scott, Laws, & Boksberger, 2010; Binkhorst & Den Dekker, 2009).

According to Rifkin (2014), Open Innovation, Crowdsourcing and Co-Creation are only part of a much larger social change and the beginning of a completely new economy. A fundamental principle of our economic system is to achieve maximum productivity and to reduce marginal costs. Marginal costs are the costs of producing an additional unit of a good or service, after fixed costs have been absorbed. To produce the first cinematic travel report, several thousands or millions of dollars have to be spent on infrastructure, personnel, equipment etc. The costs of copying and duplicating the movie are comparatively marginal. The goal of a company will always be to lower the production costs as much as possible, to generate higher profits or to grant price reductions in order to remain competitive. The recent developments in the field of ICTs can be seen as drivers of economies of scale and scope, resulting in a progressive reduction of marginal costs. The Internet allows a myriad of small players to unite within decentralized peer-to-peer networks, the so-called "Collaborative Commons". These Collaborative Commons with their ability to reduce marginal costs, have already transformed the information goods industry, as consumers began to produce and share music, videos and knowledge for free. Toffler (1990) describes these people as "prosumers", being producer and consumer at the same time. The desire of consumers to play an active role in the creation of products and services in cooperation with companies has increased over the past years (Neuhofer, Buhalis, & Ladkin, 2013). In order to stay competitive, tourism companies have to handle these empowered customers strategically and apply the new technologies fruitfully (Neuhofer, Buhalis, & Ladkin, 2014). Outsourcing business tasks to customers is a double-edged sword.

It can be very enhancing on the one hand for users to produce and share content among themselves, in other words, to derive user-generated-content, peer-to-peer-production, and share economy. At the same time, these constitute potent challenges to the whole industry. On social media platforms like Facebook, Tripadvisor and Youtube, a steadily rising number of documented touristic experiences, ratings and recommendations, are continually published in an independent fashion by customers, without control from the affected destinations and service providers. The information seeking and decision making behaviour of modern customers is strongly influenced by these publications (Xiang & Gretzel, 2010). The provision of services such as renting out private rooms or offering car service to visitors, can easily be offered online and therefore, disrupts traditional processes in the tourism industry. The main transformations and challenges for the tourism industry triggered by new technologies can be summarized as follows:

- *Opening of operational boundaries (principle view):*
  The (online) provision and consumption of corporate or individual offers is mostly non-excludable and non-rivalrous as well as independent of time and space. Keywords: Public good/Any time, any place
- *Opening of economic boundaries (cost view):*
  Digital goods produced by companies or individuals are duplicated and distributed at near zero marginal costs, providing more and more offers (almost) for free, Keywords: Share economy/Free economy
- *Opening of institutional boundaries (ability view):*
  Companies on the one hand are able to integrate external sources into their value creation, individuals on the other can easily form affiliations with each other, substituting traditional business models. Keywords: Customer integration/Peer-to-peer production.
- *Opening of behavioural boundaries (motivation view):*
  Companies and individuals are willing to build partnerships for exchanging and sharing resources. Keywords: Co-Creation/Prosumer

The transforming processes are continuously expanding, thus affecting tourism and all other industries. The omnipresent modifications and paradigm shifts can therefore be seen as a "Third Industrial Revolution" (Rifkin, 2014).

2 Open Innovation, Crowdsourcing and Co-Creation

Open Tourism describes different manifestations of "opening-movements" in the tourism industry. Open Innovation, Crowdsourcing and Co-Creation, the most popular and well-researched occurrences, are explained in more detail in the following passages. Each of these terms share the common basis of bringing company's external resources into the formerly autonomous value creation process of the company.

The *Open Innovation* approach was firstly defined and described by Henry Chesbrough (2003). He defines Open Innovation as a new paradigm in contrast to the so-called Closed Innovation, described by Schumpeter (Schumpeter, 2006; Sobczak & Groß, 2010):

> Open Innovation is a paradigm that assumes that firms can and should use external ideas as well as internal ideas, and internal and external paths to market, as the firms look to advance their technology. (Chesbrough, 2003: XXIV)

The basic requirement for Open Innovation is "opening up the innovation process" (Huizingh, 2011: 1). Moreover, companies should cooperate with their periphery (e.g. universities, researchers and consultants) and exploit the knowledge and experience of their customers (Reichwald & Piller, 2009). Most often, Open Innovation describes the integration of consumers and users, or even competitors, to make use of the wisdom of crowds (Surowiecki, 2005). According to the new paradigm of interactive value creation, companies should not only listen to their customers, but also integrate them (Reichwald & Piller, 2009). Von Hippel (1988) established the Lead-User concept, which can be seen as a prime example of customer integration. Later on, he considered the growing number of user innovations and corporate opening processes as "Democratizing Innovation" (Von Hippel, 2005). Von Hippel describes users and communities as "increasingly able to innovate for themselves" (2005: 1), a phenomenon that flourishes "as a result of the steadily improving quality computer software and hardware" (2005: 13). The following Fig. 1 displays the differences between a Closed and Open Innovation process.

Stefan Lindengaard describes Open Innovation as a "two-way process":

> ...open innovation should be viewed as a two-way process in which companies have an inbound process in which they bring in ideas, technologies, or other resources needed to develop their own business and an outbound process in which they out-license or sell their own ideas, technologies and resources. This should take place during all stages of the innovation process. (Lindengaard, 2010: 4)

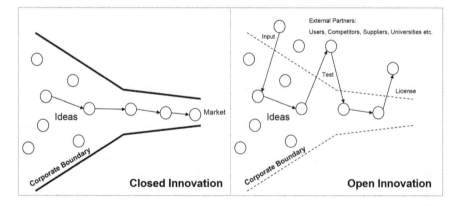

Fig. 1 Closed vs. open innovation model (*Source*: Adapted from Reichwald and Piller, 2009: 148)

Enkel, Gassmann, and Chesbrough (2009) conclude that there are different approaches of categorizing the theoretical developments in the field of Open Innovation, according to their purpose, process and the actors. Using the firm's perspective, they differentiate between three core processes in Open Innovation: an outside-in, an inside-out and a coupled process. Dahlander and Gann (2010) analysed 150 publications on Open Innovation and came to the conclusion that further research has to be done, taking into account the ambiguities and costs of Open Innovation initiatives. Gassmann et al. state that Open Innovation is still "a young research field" and currently "at an early stage". Moreover, developments in the field of "intellectual property and patents will play a core role" in the future (2010: 219). Huizingh predicts that within a decade, the term will become "business as usual" and will "fade away", because of its full integration into innovation management (2011: 6)

We understand Open Innovation as: *an organization's utilization of incoming and licensing of outgoing innovation knowledge from/to external partners (users, competitors, universities etc.) by opening up corporate boundaries.*

The term *Crowdsourcing* was developed by Jeff Howe in his article "The Rise of Crowdsourcing", published in the Wired magazine in June 2006 (Hopkins, 2011; Howe, 2006a). In his article, he describes the concept as a combination of the terms "crowd" and "outsourcing" and analyses examples such as Threadless, iStockphoto and InnoCentive (Howe, 2006a).

On his blog, Howe defines the concept of Crowdsourcing as follows:

> Simply defined, crowdsourcing represents the act of a company or institution taking a function once performed by employees and outsourcing it to an undefined (and generally large) network of people in the form of an open call. This can take the form of peer-production (when the job is performed collaboratively), but is also often undertaken by sole individuals. The crucial prerequisite is the use of the open call format and the large network of potential laborers. (Howe, 2006b)

In other words, Crowdsourcing can be understood as a special form of outsourcing processes to a dispersed audience via open call. It is an interactive form of performance by a large number of participants using information and communication technologies. Some authors date the rise of Crowdsourcing back to the development of peer production, which started with the introduction of the Open Source operating system Linux in 1991 (Tapscott & Williams, 2010). Open Innovation and Crowdsourcing can be seen as independent concepts, which have a common base. Howe discusses the circumstances which led to the birth, the state of the art and the future development of Crowdsourcing. Furthermore, he introduces different rules and categories of Crowdsourcing, such as Collective Intelligence (i.e. wisdom of the crowd) and Crowdfunding (Howe, 2008). Since the introduction of the term, more and more research on Crowdsourcing has been published (Gassmann, 2010; Muhdi, 2012; Brabham, 2013; Gegenhuber, 2013). Estellés-Arolas and González-Ladrón-de-Guevara (2012) collected and analysed 40 different definitions of Crowdsourcing and found out that the most frequently cited definitions are the ones proposed by Howe, Brabham and Wikipedia.

Brabham defines Crowdsourcing as follows:

> I define crowdsourcing as an online, distributed problem-solving and production model that leverages the collective intelligence of online communities to serve specific organizational goals. Online communities, also called crowds, are given the opportunity to respond to crowdsourcing activities promoted by the organization and they are motivated to respond for a variety of reasons. (Brabham, 2013: XIX)

We understand Crowdsourcing as: *a form of outsourcing process to a dispersed audience via open call. It is an interactive form of value creation by a large number of participants using information and communication technologies.*

Co-Creation was introduced by Prahalad and Ramaswamy (2000) and addresses the customer involvement in terms of corporate value creation processes. Ramaswamy and Gouillart define Co-Creation as "the practice of developing systems, products, or services through collaboration with customers, managers, employees, and other company stakeholders" (2010: 4). Piller et al. define Customer Co-Creation as "an active, creative and social process, based on collaboration between producers (retailers) and customers (users)" (2010: 9). Vaisnore and Petraite conclude that "co-creation activities imply an active role of customers and define their contributions to the value creation process" and that "Co-Creation can be reflected as a joint partnering activity between business, enterprise and customer" (2011: 66). Ramaswamy and Ozcan (2014) expand:

> Co-Creation is joint creation and evolution of value with stakeholding individuals, intensified and enacted trough platforms of engagements, virtualized and emergent from ecosystems of capabilities, and actualized and embodied in domains of experiences, expanding wealth-welfare-wellbeing. (Ramaswamy & Ozcan, 2014: 14)

We understand Co-Creation as: *a company's creation of value within an interactive collaboration process with external users and customers.*

The establishment of new technologies will have an enormous impact on the value creation process, especially the innovation process. This development will change whole sectors, including the tourism industry, and will bring about the creation of new business models (Gassmann, 2013; Brabham, 2013). It will become necessary for managers to take Open Innovation, Crowdsourcing and Co-Creation into consideration. It becomes more and more important to overcome the so-called "not invented here" phenomenon on the one hand and to find a balance between in-house and external resources on the other hand (Huff, Doz, & Lakhani, 2013). Tourism companies have to consider user communities as well as individuals as an important part of their business models.

3   The Contribution-Utilization-Matrix

The illustrated examples of Open Innovation, Crowdsourcing and Co-Creation accompanied by several other business model transformations in the tourism industry, represent the main part of this publication. In the last section, we look closer at the Contribution-Utilization-Matrix which allows one to classify all different occurrences within a singular framework. Frameworks can be of particular value for objectives of this kind. Pearce (2012) points out that "one of the biggest drivers to develop an explicit framework has been to organize, present and interpret large and complex bodies of ideas and material". Frameworks can furthermore be perceived from this perspective as having a fundamental role in the establishing of structures and also taking on conceptual functions among others (Pearce, 2001). Simultaneously, frameworks permit the establishment of a common understanding regarding the terminology and definitions, by making available both a common language and setting the necessary parameters for one to grasp the subject matter. This publication places tourism as a sector of the economy in the focus of analysis. It is an interdisciplinary field of research, which is a topic of interest to economists, sociologists, psychologists and geographers, and others. The respective lenses from the aforementioned various disciplines, through which the individual terms and phenomena can be examined in the context of their subjects, is in itself sufficient justification for the attempt to examine the entire issue in a structured and orderly manner.

According to economic theory, the starting point for any type of activity undertaken by a person or an institution is attributed to the lack of resources and therefore, a quest to satisfy certain needs (Picot, Dietl, & Franck, 1999). By way of example, we can think of a person who needs to gather information about a holiday destination or a company that is looking for creative contributions to improve its service offerings. These needy actors are called "seekers" in the Open Tourism structure. Their initiatives to satisfy their needs can take the form of an investigative search (e.g. to read an online recommendation, to watch a traveller's video clip etc.) or a concrete call (e.g. to announce an idea competition, to identify an innovative lead user). With the help of modern ICTs, formerly closed systems can now be opened (= open boundaries). Companies are able to integrate external sources into the value creation and individuals can form alliances with each other by building partnerships, exchanging and sharing resources. This technical transformation is accompanied by a social shift. The contemporary mindset and the desire for personalized and sustainable offers as well as the pursuit of happiness and memorable experiences, are more distinct and pronounced than ever before. Search and call activities are increasingly being enriched with multimedia elements, allowing for a multi-sensory-immersion. Need information is owned by seekers, solution information by "solvers" (i.e. individuals or institutions). It is no longer the case that only customers demand and companies supply. In this new system of open boundaries, there are enterprises that demand and users who provide. Basically, 1-to-1, 1-to-many, many-to-1 or many-to-many exchanges can be observed. Peer-to-peer transactions happen not only in private. Companies are still involved however, not as seekers or solvers, but as enablers and operators of the exchange platforms (e.g. Youtube run by Google). Due to the fact that using these platforms is mostly free of charge, companies do not make money directly by enabling these exchange activities, but have to rely on alternative earning channels, such as advertising, value added services and optional donations (cf. Wikipedia).

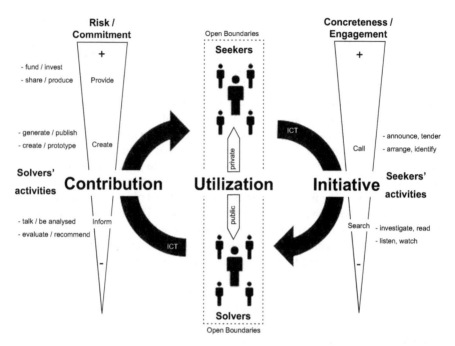

Fig. 2 Open tourism structure (*Source*: Own illustration)

Companies are interested in offering preferably interesting content on their sites, to generate high traffic and revenues (Fig. 2).

Contributions can take on different modes, informing, creating or providing, whereby the personal involvement of the solvers becomes respectively deeper. In the field of "informing" solvers describe, evaluate and comment upon certain touristic issues (cf. Tripadvisor). Likewise, informative contributions which have been posted freely online (e.g. in forums or communities of interest), are analyzed by companies. At this juncture, the effort and commitment of solvers is relatively low, respectively the solvers act completely passive and are analyzed. Netnography as an ethnographic research method for the observation of groups and their separate members, can be presented on an exemplary basis here. Poon (1993: 53) states: tourists' "experience is a source of tremendous wealth" and Williams and Shaw (2011: 15) are of the opinion that in this context, co-creation is to be understood as co-learning and furthermore in this respect, as an opportunity to innovate. In the next step, solvers develop more creative answers, by making elaborate text, graphic, design, music or film contributions, which requires a considerable high level of effort and skills. In the context of innovation, the user-generated content ranges from simple descriptions and sketches up to working mock-ups and prototypes. In the last step, solvers provide seekers with physical resources. The provision of capital and financial resources can be found in this field. On crowdfunding and crowdinvesting platforms, an increasing number of seekers are posting their ideas and articulating their capital needs. The scope ranges from small sponsorships for a symbolic reward to substantial investments in return for shares of the company. In addition, more and more individuals offer private belongings (e.g. a diving gear for a cruise holiday) on exchange platforms or provide their private accommodation to tourists, thus competing with hotels. The commitment of solvers is very high in this phase, due to the fact that they allocate personal resources or - as it is the case with some social network sites (e.g. Couchsurfing) - where they have to personally live together with the seeker, a complete stranger prior to the first meeting.

The degree of individual risk increases, across the "inform" to "provide" spectrum. The more memorable an experience is, the more a guest seems to be required to physically and psychologically integrate himself (e.g. Make-your-own-wine).

It is apparent that the level of experience also rises with increasing involvement (Prahalad & Ramaswamy, 2004). Here the supporters face the danger of becoming physically harmed, which has to be considered and actuarially managed by the tourism company. Beneficiaries of any contribution are the initiators of the activities, the seekers.

How the contributions are processed and who is allowed to utilize the outcomes, differs from initiative to initiative. The ideas collected within an innovation contest arranged by a company generally remain in possession of the initiator, who has the exclusive right to make use of them and to respectively grant licences. Contributions on public online platforms are basically non-excludable and are accessible to anyone using the internet. Moreover, its use is open-ended by nature and exclusivity cannot be enforced, thus allowing an unlimited number of users to get access anywhere at any time. The utilization of the contributions therefore can be divided into "private" and "public" - for a detailed description of intellectual property, see Sunstein (2008). The connection between the "Level of Contribution" and the "Level of Utilization" results in the "Contribution-Utilization-Matrix", which allows one to classify all Open Tourism occurrences within a common framework (Fig. 3).

3.1 Private Information Search

In this case, companies are searching for innovative input, which can be utilized privately. The exchange of experiences and ideas for improvement among users in online communities is growing, as well as its identification and analysis by companies (i.e. Netnography). In the field of tourism, numerous communities exist that provide abundant information virtually free of charge, which can be seen as a major challenge for the existing tourism industry.

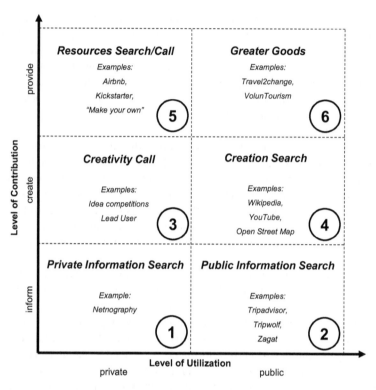

Fig. 3 Contribution-utilization-matrix (*Source*: Own illustration)

3.2 Public Information Search

In this case, seekers as well as solvers are individuals, who provide and retrieve information to/from online platforms. Professional companies run the infrastructure and potentially offer additional services. Thus, forthcoming users post evaluations, comments and recommendations on destinations and touristic products via social media networks or sites like Tripadvisor or Zagat. Interested users around the world are able to view these contributions for free. This direct, influential feedback from a critical mass audience is also a great challenge for the tourism industry (requiring special actions, such as Social Media Monitoring).

3.3 Creativity Call

Like Netnography, the methods in this field can be predominantly linked to Open Innovation principles. Companies inviting individuals to hand in creative contributions for detailed problems - at an ideas competition for example - are addressed here as well as the identification of innovative customers (lead users) with developing creative ideas in a following workshop. The results are utilized by the company exclusively.

3.4   Creation Search

In this case, solvers offer their contributions to seekers on online platforms mostly for free. These contributions, some of which are creative and elaborate, take the form of evaluations, recommendations and comments in field 2 "Public Information Search".,, Professional companies run the infrastructure for this peer-to-peer exchange. The most popular examples are Wikipedia, Youtube or Open Street Map, in which users around the world can hand in maps and pictures of their vicinity to finally create a complete map of the world. The whole Open Source movement is based on this principle: Creative programmers provide solutions for seekers. An increasing shift from the virtual to the physical world can be observed. On Thingiverse, users with design and coding literacy skills are able to provide digital models which can be downloaded and printed in 3D format by others. In tourism, merchandising items based on this technique can be found. Overall, these possibilities of exchanging creative contributions on a peer-to-peer level are challenging the tourism industry immensely.

3.5   Resources Search/Call

In this case, solvers are offering and seekers are looking or calling for (physical) resources. It is the central idea of the share economy (Botsman & Rogers, 2011). Accommodations, vehicles, equipment and capital (cf. Crowdfunding) constitute exchange resources. Contributing one's mental and physical resources to support a provider's value creation (e.g. make-wine, plant-trees, harvest-apples etc.) is also grouped under this category. Here, the former consumer takes the role of prosumer and co-producer.

3.6   Greater Good

More and more individuals travel to needy destinations around the world utilizing touristic offers in order to improve the social, economic or ecological situation on site. These tourists provide their personal time and engage in manual work to support the greater public good. This occurrence is called "VolunTourism", a combination of volunteering and tourism.

The contribution-utilization matrix attempts to demonstrate a continuum on both dimensions, from the traditional to the most varied, extreme, unorthodox Open

Tourism initiatives. It establishes relationships between the experience economy and the exploitation/risk index, and above all, presents itself as the basis in which to structure the book. The case studies presented in this book contain vastly different levels of contribution, as exemplified in the contribution-utilization matrix and are sequenced in accordance with it. Practitioners and researches all over the world are invited to apply, comment and further develop the matrix - we are thankful for all kinds of suggestions and improvements.

References

Binkhorst, E., & Den Dekker, T. (2009). Agenda for co-creation tourism experience research. *The Marketing of Hospitality and Leisure Experiences, 18*(2–3), 311–327.

Botsman, R., & Rogers, R. (2011). *What's mine is yours: How collaborative consumption is changing the way we live*. London: Collins.

Brabham, D. (2013). *Crowdsourcing*. Cambridge, MA: MIT Press.

Buhalis, D. (1998). Strategic use of information technologies in the tourism industry. *Tourism Management, 19*(5), 409–421.

Chesbrough, H. (2003). *Open innovation. The new imperative for creating and profiting from technology*. Boston, MA: Harvard Business School Press.

Dahlander, L., & Gann, D. (2010). How open is innovation? *Research Policy, 39*(6), 699–709.

Doctor, M., Schnyder, M., & Stumm, N. (2011). Potenziale von Open-Innovation-Modellen in der Tourismusbranche – Drei Fallbespiele (English: Potentials of open innovation models in the tourism industry – Three case studies). In P. Boksberger & M. Schuckert (Eds.), *Innovationen in Tourismus und Freizeit. Hypes, Trends und Entwicklungen (English: Innovation in tourism and leisure. Hypes, trends and developments)* (pp. 281–298). Berlin: Erich Schmidt.

Enkel, E., Gassmann, O., & Chesbrough, H. (2009). Open R&D and open innovation: Exploring the phenomenon. *R&D Management, 39*(4), 311–316.

Estellés-Arolas, E., & González-Ladrón-de-Guevara, F. (2012). Towards an integrated crowdsourcing definition. *Journal of Information Science, 38*(2), 189–200.

Faullant, R., Krajger, I., & Zanker, M. (2012). Identification of innovative users for new service development in tourism. In M. Fuchs, F. Ricci, & L. Cantoni (Eds.), *Information and communication technologies in tourism 2012. Proceedings of the international conference in Helsingborg, Sweden, January 25–27, 2012* (pp. 426–436). Vienna: Springer.

Gassmann, O. (2010). *Crowdsourcing. Innovationsmanagement mit Schwarmintelligenz (English: Crowdsourcing. Innovation management with collective intelligence)*. Munich: Carl Hanser.

Gassmann, O. (2013). *Crowdsourcing. Innovationsmanagement mit Schwarmintelligenz (English: Crowdsourcing. Innovation management with collective intelligence)* (2nd ed.). Munich: Carl Hanser.

Gassmann, O., Enkel, E., & Chesbrough, H. (2010). The future of open innovation. *R&D Management, 40*(3), 213–221.

Gegenhuber, T. (2013). *Crowdsourcing. Aggregation and selection mechanisms and the impact of peer contributions on contests*. Trauner: Linz.

Hjalager, A.-M., & Nordin, S. (2011). User-driven innovation in tourism – A review of methodologies. *Journal of Quality Assurance in Hospitality and Tourism, 12*(4), 289–315.

Hopkins, R. (2011). What is crowdsourcing? In P. Sloane (Ed.), *A guide to open innovation and crowdsourcing. Advice from leading experts in the field* (pp. 15–21). London: Kogan Page.

Howe, J. (2006a). *The rise of crowdsourcing*. Available under: http://www.wired.com/wired/archive/14.06/crowds.html. Accessed on November 01, 2014.

Howe, J. (2006b). *Crowdsourcing: A definition*. Available under: http://crowdsourcing.typepad.com/cs/2006/06/crowdsourcing_a.html. Accessed on November 01, 2014.

Howe, J. (2008). *Crowdsourcing. Why the power of the crowds is driving the future of business*. New York: Crown Business.

Huff, A., Doz, Y., & Lakhani, R. (2013). Epilogue: Learning to be more competitive, more cooperative, and more innovative. In A. Huff, K. Möslein, & R. Reichwald (Eds.), *Leading open innovation* (pp. 279–291). Cambridge, MA: MIT Press.

Huizingh, E. (2011). Open innovation: State of the art and future perspectives. *Technovation, 31* (1), 2–9.

Lindengaard, S. (2010). *The open innovation revolution. Essentials, roadblocks, and leadership skills*. Hoboken, NJ: Wiley.

Lohmann, M. (2004). *New demand factors in tourism*. Presentation at the European tourism forum in Budapest on the 15th October 2004.

Menzel, J. (2011). *Crowdsourcing: Neue Methode der Innovationsgenerierung in kleinen und mittleren Hotelbetrieben (English: Crowdsourcing: New method of innovation development in small and medium-sized hotels)*. Saarbrücken: Verlag Dr. Müller.

Morgan, M., Lugosi, P., & Ritchie, J. R. (2010). *The tourism and leisure experience. Consumer and managerial perspectives*. London: Channel View.

Muhdi, L. (2012). Understanding crowdsourcing – the process and the contributors: Based on the doctoral dissertation "Open Innovation and Collaboration for Innovation", Dr. Lousine Muhdi, ETHZ, 2011, Saarbrücken: Südwestdeutscher Verlag für Hochschulschriften.

Neuhofer, B., Buhalis, D., & Ladkin, A. (2013). *Experiences, co-creation and technology: A conceptual approach to enhance tourism experiences*. Available under: http://www.academia.edu/2703085/Neuhofer_B._Buhalis_D._and_Ladkin_A._2013._Experiences_Co-creation_and_Technology_A_conceptual_approach_to_enhance_tourism_experiences. Accessed on November 01, 2014.

Neuhofer, B., Buhalis, D., & Ladkin, A. (2014). Co-creation through technology: Dimensions of social connectedness. In Z. Xiang & I. Tussyadiah (Eds.), *Information and communication technologies in tourism 2014* (pp. 339–352). Cham: Springer.

Pearce, D. G. (2001). An integrative framework for urban tourism research. *Annals of Tourism Research, 28*(1), 926–46.

Pearce, D. G. (2012). *Frameworks for tourism research*. Wallingford, CT: CAB International Books.

Picot, A., Dietl, H., & Franck, E. (1999). *Organisation: Eine ökonomische Perspektive (English: Organization: An economic perspective)*. Stuttgart: Schäffer-Poeschel.

Piller, F., Ihl, Ch., & Voessen, A. (2010). *A typology of customer co-creation in the innovation process*. Available under: http://papers.ssrn.com/sol3/papers.cfm?abstract_id=1732127. Accessed on November 01, 2014.

Poon, A. (1993). *Tourism, technology and competitive strategies*. Wallingford: CAB International Books.

Prahalad, C., & Ramaswamy, V. (2000). Co-opting customer competence. *Harvard Business Review, 78*(1), 79–87.

Prahalad, C., & Ramaswamy, V. (2004). *The future of competition: Co-creating unique value with customers*. Boston, MA: Harvard Business School Press.

Ramaswamy, V., & Gouillart, F. (2010). *The power of co-creation. Build it with them to boost growth, productivity, and profits*. New York: Free Press.

Ramaswamy, V., & Ozcan, K. (2014). *The co-creation paradigm*. Stanford, CA: Stanford University Press.

Reichwald, R., & Piller, F. (2009). *Interaktive Wertschöpfung. Open Innovation, Individualisierung und neue Formen der Arbeitsteilung (English: Interactive value creation. Open innovation, individualism and new forms of labour division)* (2nd ed.). Wiesbaden: Gabler.

Rifkin, J. (2014). *The zero marginal cost society: The internet of things, the collaborative commons, and the eclipse of capitalism*. New York: Macmillan.

Schemann, B. (2012). User-driven innovation concepts and the cruise industry. In A. Papathanassis, T. Lukovic, & M. Vogel (Eds.), *Cruise tourism and society. A socio-economic perspective* (pp. 153–169). Berlin: Springer.

Schumpeter, J. (2006). *Theorie der wirtschaftlichen Entwicklung (English: The theory of economic development)*. Berlin: Duncker & Humblot.

Scott, N., Laws, E., & Boksberger, P. (2010). *Marketing of tourism experiences*. New York: Routledge.

Sobczak, S., & Groß, M. (2010). *Crowdsourcing: Grundlagen und Bedeutung für das E-Business (English: Crowdsourcing: Fundamentals and significance for e-business)*. Boizenburg: Werner Hülsbusch.

Sunstein, C. (2008). *Infotopia: How many minds produce knowledge*. New York: Oxford University Press.

Surowiecki, J. (2005). *The wisdom of crowds*. New York: Anchor Books.

Tapscott, D., & Williams, A. (2010). *Wikinomics. How mass collaboration changes everything*. Expanded Edition. New York: Penguin.

Toffler, A. (1990). *The third wave*. New York: Bantam Books.

Vaisnore, A., & Petraite, M. (2011). Customer involvement into open innovation process: A conceptual model. *Social Sciences, 73*(3), 62–73.

Vargo, S., & Lusch, R. (2004). Evolving to a new dominant logic for marketing. *Journal of Marketing, 68*(1), 1–17.

Von Hippel, E. (1988). *The sources of innovation*. New York: Oxford University Press.

Von Hippel, E. (2005). *Democratizing innovation*. Cambridge, MA: MIT Press.

Williams, A., & Shaw, G. (2011). Internationalization and innovation in tourism. *Annals of Tourism Research, 38*(1), 27–51.

Witt, S., Brooke, M., & Buckley, P. (2013). *The management of international tourism*. Oxon: Routledge.

Xiang, Z., & Gretzel, U. (2010). Role of social media in online travel information search. *Tourism Management, 31*(2), 179–188.

Zhao, Y., & Zhu, Q. (2014). Evaluation on crowdsourcing research: Current status and future direction. *Information Systems Frontiers, 16*(3), 417–434.

Innovation Through Co-creation: Towards an Understanding of Technology-Facilitated Co-creation Processes in Tourism

Barbara Neuhofer

1 Introduction

Numerous industries have undergone a substantial change with consumers no longer merely seeking to buy products and services but becoming increasingly active and involved in the consumption of their products and services. In line with this societal trend, the notion of consumer centricity has become a well-established concept in recent years. With intensified global competition, challenging markets and dynamic technologies, businesses have recognised the need for differentiating themselves by innovating at an accelerated pace. The empowerment of consumers as co-creators of their experiences has become a central notion companies strive to achieve. Several concepts have emerged to describe this trend. The notions of co-creation, co-production, crowdsourcing and open innovation all describe the underlying premise of integrating the customer as a key resource in consumer-oriented innovation processes. By recognising consumers in multiple roles as co-participants of the crowd, co-producers of products and services and co-creators of experiences and value, the literature has led to a rich diversity of terminologies, capturing the highly empowered nature of contemporary consumers.

The notion of consumer involvement has particularly been driven by one key facilitator. Information and communication technologies (ICTs) have transformed the role of consumers in product and service development, consumption and experience. The Internet and Web 2.0. platforms have become a catalyst of change that has not only impacted on the way businesses and consumers interact but has fundamentally transformed *the way how* and *by whom* tourism products, services and experiences are designed, created and consumed. The plethora of social media and networking tools has opened up unprecedented opportunities to engage

B. Neuhofer (✉)
Bournemouth University, Bournemouth, UK
e-mail: bneuhofer@bournemouth.ac.uk

© Springer-Verlag Berlin Heidelberg 2016
R. Egger et al. (eds.), *Open Tourism*, Tourism on the Verge,
DOI 10.1007/978-3-642-54089-9_2

consumers along the service value chain. While the conceptualisation and study of co-creation has received considerable attention in services marketing, its debate in the tourism and technology domain merits further exploration.

2   Purpose of the Chapter

It is with this premise in mind that the chapter aims to discuss innovation through co-creation, by interlinking the notion of consumer involvement and technology to explore how its combination can lead to innovation in the tourism industry. To advance the discourse in the literature, this chapter offers a holistic appraisal of consumer involvement and co-creation by accentuating differences and similarities of several processes when the factor technology comes into play. The chapter is divided into three main sections. The first part presents an overview of relevant theoretical developments within innovation and consumer empowerment. By examining the idea of consumer centricity, it sheds light on three types of customer involvement including crowdsourcing, co-production and co-creation to develop a differentiated understanding of these processes in the context of tourism. The second part offers a discussion and a classification of technology-facilitated co-creation processes. It outlines several key differences and similarities and presents best practice examples from the tourism industry. The third part discusses the theoretical implications of these developments and offers an outlook on the future agenda for open innovation in tourism management and practice. Overall, the chapter contributes to a more effective understanding of the role of consumers and technology as drivers of innovation in the future creation of competitive tourism services and experiences.

3   Theoretical Background

3.1   Innovation Through Customer Involvement

Travel and tourism businesses operate in a sphere of increased competitiveness globally. Intensified global competition, fluctuations in tourism demand and the increase of customer expectations capture some of the most powerful business challenges at present (Williams, 2012). To address these developments, businesses are forced to identify new means of developing competitive advantage (Walls, Okumus, Wang, & Kwun, 2011). This is particularly true for tourism firms which due to the dynamic and fast changing nature of tourism, are required to innovate at an accelerated pace (Zach, Gretzel, & Xiang, 2010). Exploring new ways of innovation has thus become an imperative.

The term *innovation* represents a complex concept with numerous definitional approaches contributing to its meaning. Generally it can be described as a process that introduces an idea to a problem that is perceived as new in a specific context. As such, it can be understood as the generation or implementation of new ideas, processes or services (Hjalager, 2010). Due to its complexity, the existing literature differentiates multiple levels, types and categories of innovation. For instance, it can range from radical innovation, introducing entirely new products and services, towards minor and incremental innovation, indicating an adaptation of pre-existing services (Ottenbacher & Harrington, 2010). Moreover, Hjalager (2010) emphasises the need to distinguish between product and service innovation, process innovation, managerial, management and institutional innovation.

Innovation has been established in production-dominant sectors, such as finance, transport and telecommunications (De Jong & Vermeulen, 2003), while innovation in the service sector has been lagging behind (Droege, Hildebrand, & Heras Forcada, 2009). This is also the case for tourism, an industry in which innovation efforts have been described as rather slow (Pikkemaat & Peters, 2006) in spite of their importance (Hjalager, 2010; Shaw, Bailey, & Williams, 2011; Zach et al., 2010). In recent years, it has become more important than ever before for tourism businesses to innovate effectively, as tourism offers and destination choices proliferate on a global scale (Hjalager, 2002; Ritchie & Crouch, 2003). However only more recently, the concept of innovation has received increasing attention, particularly in the field of new service development (Fitzsimmons & Fitzsimmons, 2000; Sigala, 2012b). In this growing body of literature, one of the key suggestions is the need for a proactive market orientation (Sanden, 2007) and a shift towards interaction-dense services (Ottenbacher & Harrington, 2010).

In this vein, the notions of *customer centricity*, *empowerment* and *involvement* have been highlighted as main driving forces of the new service development (Sigala, 2012b). New service orientation is about putting the consumer in the centre and being proactive by recognising consumers and addressing their needs before they emerge (Ramaswamy, 2009a). These developments have led to the wider acknowledgement of consumers and marked the beginning of a new paradigm in marketing, one that focuses on consumer centricity as a means to foster innovation, competitive advantage and growth (Shaw et al., 2011; Sigala, 2012a).

3.2   Customer Empowerment and the Rise of the Consumer

In today's society, consumers are more empowered than ever before. In the late 1990s, people have shifted from merely buying manufactured products and services towards a growing pursuit of interactive consumption experiences (Morgan, Lugosi, & Ritchie, 2010). In services and tourism marketing, the concepts of the experience economy have long provided a valuable vehicle to design, stage and deliver experiences to consumers, while fostering economic value and competitive advantage. Traditionally, the creation of services and experiences has been inspired by the underlying economic interest of how to increase turnover by selling experiences as new de-materialised commodities (Darmer & Sundbo, 2008; Stamboulis & Skayannis, 2003). However, the industrialisation, economic values and capitalist thinking primarily drove the business-focal perspective of producing *experiences for consumers*. With a radical shift in company-consumer relationships, the experience economy has therefore been raised to question, as an approach that does not sufficiently reflect the needs and wants of contemporary consumers (Boswijk, Thijssen, & Peelen, 2007).

In the past decade, society has undergone a transformation towards the centricity of individuals and their human experiences in quest for personal growth (Prahalad & Ramaswamy, 2004). This has led to the emergence of a '*prosumer society*' recognising consumers as being actively involved, not only in the consumption but also in the production of products, services and experiences (Ritzer & Jurgenson, 2010). This novel mind-set has especially been fostered by Prahalad and Ramaswamy (2004) who argue that consumers want to have a say in co-shaping their own experiences. They expect a sense of balance between themselves and the provider, who traditionally was the sole experience stager (Binkhorst, 2006; Ramaswamy & Gouillart, 2008). By doing so, consumers have become prosumers, protagonists, post-consumers or consum-actors actively involved in the entire value chain.

Consumers use their new power to share their opinions, complain, negotiate, endorse, interact and co-create experiences (Cova & Dalli, 2009). This means that the roles of companies and consumers are no longer distinct (Ramaswamy, 2011). The new principles of customer involvement foster consumers as empowered individuals to collaborate as a resource in processes traditionally performed by the company. Consumers want to contribute with their own resources, which allow them to transform a simple service encounter into an experience (Cova & Dalli, 2009). In this changed paradigm, the consumer as an individual, rather than the company, is regarded as the starting point (Sanden, 2007) and the central element driving the co-creation process (Binkhorst & Den Dekker, 2009).

3.3   Customer Centricity and the Co-creation Paradigm

The increased consumer involvement has opened a new era in marketing, widely acknowledged as the co-creation paradigm. Co-creation describes a collective and collaborative process, a joint value creation between the company and the consumer (Cova & Dalli, 2009; Payne, Storbacka, & Frow, 2008; Prahalad & Ramaswamy, 2004; Vargo & Lusch, 2006; Xie, Bagozzi, & Troye, 2008). While Prahalad and Ramaswamy (2004) were among the first to introduce the notion of co-creation. A wide body of literature has contributed to advancing the theoretical foundations and current understanding of experience co-creation (Binkhorst & Den Dekker, 2009; Edvardsson, Enquist, & Johnston, 2005; Huang & Hsu, 2010; Payne et al., 2008; Prahalad & Ramaswamy, 2004; Ramaswamy, 2009a, 2009b, 2011; Ramaswamy &

Gouillart, 2008; Vargo & Lusch, 2004). These studies have analysed the diverse roles of consumers in the consumption, production and interaction with businesses and have added to a more differentiated view of the concept.

In contributing to the wider debate on this paradigm, recent work has produced a wealth of terminologies, extending and refining co-creation. For instance, scholars have conceptualised prosumption (Ritzer & Jurgenson, 2010), co-creation (Prahalad & Ramaswamy, 2004), co-production (Etgar, 2008), service-dominant logic (Vargo & Lusch, 2004), customer-to-customer co-creation (Huang & Hsu, 2010), crowdsourcing (Geiger, Rosemann, & Fielt, 2011) as well as the notions of working consumers, collaborative innovation, consumer agency and consumer tribes (Cova & Dalli, 2009). Despite the emergence of new literature in the field, existing terminologies are rather fluid, often used interchangeably, while clear differentiations and boundaries between single concepts are difficult to define (Chathoth, Altinay, Harrington, Okumus, & Chan, 2013). Therefore, the following section aims to provide an overview to the reader of the dominant concepts to allow for a more differentiated understanding of co-creation processes. Next, the three concepts of crowdsourcing, co-production and co-creation are assessed.

3.3.1   Customer Involvement Process: Crowdsourcing

Crowdsourcing has been defined as a term that embraces a number of approaches based on the integration of a large and open crowd of people (Geiger et al., 2011). While the principal idea of crowdsourcing has existed for a long time, the term has only been coined in 2006 when it has emerged as a popular concept in numerous industries. Crowdsourcing can be described as an activity, traditionally company-led, that is now outsourced to a wider crowd, by openly calling individuals to participate (Geiger et al., 2011). Drawing upon the involvement of consumers it is a "crowd of people who help solve a problem that is defined by the system owners" (Doan, Ramakrishnan, & Halevy, 2011).

The crowd thus consists of people who are undefined or preselected, representing one large network of people who, to different extents, make an integrative and aggregated contribution to a defined purpose or goal (Howe, 2006). With the rise of the Web 2.0, crowdsourcing has reached its peak of application by opening numerous involvement processes, such as crowd wisdom and collective intelligence, user generated content, crowd voting and crowdfunding initiatives (Howe, 2006). Crowdsourcing has become an effective means for companies to outsource processes, which traditionally occurred internally, to a crowd of individuals aimed at performing specific goals.

3.3.2   Customer Involvement Process: Co-production

Co-production has become a widely used term, reflecting the notion of customer involvement (Chathoth et al., 2013). Co-production has been recognised as a key mechanism between companies and consumers in exchange (Bitner, Faranda, Hubbert, & Zeithaml, 1997) and defined as an interactive nature of services (Yen, Gwinner, & Su, 2004). Co-production has been applied in numerous industries, in which customers have become participants of service encounters, such as hairdressing, consultation or education. Essentially, co-production practices require the consumer to be physically present to receive the service, while being asked to provide information that is used to deliver the service more effectively (Yen et al., 2004). Co-production is thus a company-centric approach of customer involvement (Payne et al., 2008), in which the company retains the main role, while consumers are offered a limited choice in contributing to a pre-designed service bundle (Chathoth et al., 2013).

Examples in tourism include hotel personalisation, where customers can choose from a selection of defined options, such as pillows, meals or newspapers to best fit their personal needs and preferences. This approach allows for a-priori definitions of what "suits needs of what is available", while latent needs of consumers remain unmet. For instance, if a hotel offers hard and soft pillows, the hotel does not find idiosyncratic needs but only knows the customer's favourite choice of the available (Chathoth et al., 2013). As much potential of real consumer involvement is missed in co-production, co-creation allows for a more bottom-up approach.

3.3.3 Customer Involvement Process: Co-creation

In today's economy, companies and consumers are collaborating more and more (Romero & Molina, 2011). Co-creation is a customer-centric approach based on the principles of putting consumers first and recognising them as the starting point of experience and value creation (Vargo & Lusch, 2004). Co-creation, based on the underlying premise of value-in-use in the service dominant logic (S-D logic), suggests that experiences and value are created *with* the consumer rather than *for* the consumer (Vargo & Lusch, 2004). The concept is built on two main foundations as it (a) involves the consumer's participation in the creation of the core offering and (b) "value can only be created with and determined by the user in the 'consumption' process and through use" (Vargo & Lusch, 2006, p. 284).

This means that value does not automatically exist in products and services, but for value to emerge, experiences need to be co-created by consumers themselves (Payne et al., 2008). As a result, co-creation goes beyond co-production, which partially ignores the real potential of consumers, and recognises them as the main actor of co-creation. Moreover, due to the impact of ICTs, consumers are more connected than ever before. This has led to the emergence of co-creation as a collective, collaborative and dynamic process that occurs not only between companies and consumers but also among connected consumer communities and stakeholders (Baron & Harris, 2010; Baron & Warnaby, 2011; Huang & Hsu, 2010).

In outlining the main principles of crowdsourcing, co-production and co-creation, several key differences can be highlighted. Co-creation takes co-production one step further in that it allows for a predominantly consumer-centric approach. It not only facilitates dual company-consumer co-creation but also enables co-creation outside the company domain. In contrast to crowdsourcing, which serves a particular company purpose, co-creation puts the individual consumer in experience and value creation first. Crowdsourcing is distinct in that it mainly focuses on the collective rather than the individual, whereas co-production and co-creation primarily focus on the individual's involvement in and value of the service and experience creation. The increasing proliferation of ICTs has thereby played a key role. Technology has contributed to transforming the level of customer involvement in product and service development and the integration of consumers as a key resource in innovation processes. It is with this premise in mind that the chapter now turns to discuss innovation through technology-facilitated co-creation. Having reviewed the theoretical developments of different consumer involvement processes, the next section interlinks technology and co-creation and explores how it can be effectively used as a source of innovation and competitive advantage in the tourism and hospitality industry.

4 Innovation through Technology-Facilitated Co-creation

4.1 Impact of Technology on Tourism

One of the most far-reaching changes in the twenty-first century has been the proliferation of ICTs. The continuous developments in the sector of technology have led to the emergence of the Internet, which has triggered a knowledge-based economy of people transforming the ways in which information has become available and is used. Tourism, as one of the fastest growing sectors in the world, has always been at the forefront of technology, with information being the lifeblood of the travel industry (Sheldon, 1997). In this industry, ICTs have enabled increasing consumer independence and decreasing importance of traditional travel distributions by tour operators and travel agents. Technology has evolved into a powerful tool in the operation, structure and strategy of tourism organisations (Buhalis, 2003; Buhalis & Law, 2008) and become a central element in the innovation of products, processes and management (Hjalager, 2010).

The Internet serves as a platform for connection of people and businesses around the globe. The Web 2.0 and social media have represented one of the most critical technological developments over the past decade (Dwivedi, Yadav, & Venkatesh, 2012; Fotis, Buhalis, & Rossides, 2011; Hays, Page, & Buhalis, 2012; Sigala, 2009; Xiang & Gretzel, 2010), by turning the Internet into an immense space of social networking and collaboration (Sigala, 2009). Social media, such as networking sites, blogs, wikis, forums and folksonomies provide a wide range of tools for social engagement and participation of consumers, who are now able to interact, collaborate, share and create content, opinions and experiences with companies and among each other (Sigala, 2009; Xiang & Gretzel, 2010). The prevailing success is evident in many examples, such as Wikipedia in which people co-create a global knowledge database, TripAdvisor in which tourists rate, write and review tourist experiences, or YouTube and Pinterest as video and visual-image platforms in which users generate, share and co-construct content together.

4.2   Technology in the Co-creation Paradigm

The proliferation of social technologies has had a drastic impact, not only on tourism but also on the way services, experiences and value are created (Neuhofer, Buhalis, & Ladkin, 2012). Over the past decade, it has become apparent that consumer empowerment and co-creation have been fostered by one principal factor, namely technology. Emerging ICTs have triggered new levels of customer centricity and influenced how tourists and services providers interact. Due to the widespread use of Internet tools, constant connectivity and the engaging nature of social media, co-creation between individuals is maximised with interactions having "exploded on an unprecedented scale everywhere in the value creation system" (Ramaswamy, 2009a, p. 17). With new technologies predicted to emerge over the next years, experience co-creation opportunities are expected to expand further. It will thus become critical for tourism marketing to exploit the tools of the Web 2.0 to allow for more meaningful interrelations with tourists, by building platforms and spaces to interact and share experiences.

Therefore, the potential of ICTs needs to be assessed for innovation processes through co-creation (Chathoth et al., 2013). While the importance of co-creation has been introduced fairly recently, tourism businesses are urged to identify new sources to add value to co-creation experiences. One approach to facilitate more valuable co-creation and enhance the companies' competitiveness, is the implementation of technology (Neuhofer et al., 2012). In fact, the co-creation environment must embrace emerging ICTs (Van Limburg, 2012) to maximise consumer involvement and unfold new possibilities for tourists to proactively co-create experiences and value in every stage of the travel process (Neuhofer & Buhalis, 2013).

4.3   Technology for Innovation of Co-creation

In the dynamic tourism market environment, characterised by increased competition, businesses need to find ways for innovation and the creation of compelling experiences. In a response to this market force, tourism organisations have become highly competitive in order to reduce commodification and differentiate themselves by creating more valuable experiences. ICTs represent effective instruments to achieve this goal. Buhalis and Law (2008) argue that ICTs constitute a central element for the competitiveness of tourism businesses, which is supported by

Cetinkaya (2009) and Zach et al. (2010) who affirm that the adoption of technology provides a main source of competitive advantage.

Recent literature suggests that the range of ICTs available can support co-creation experiences in a number of different ways (Binkhorst & Den Dekker, 2009; Gretzel & Jamal, 2009; Tussyadiah & Fesenmaier, 2007, 2009). For instance, ICTs provide a system for interaction that (a) gives consumers more control, (b) empowers them to establish closer relationships with the company and (c) encourages them to actively co-create their experiences with each other. Moreover, Sigala (2012b) emphasises that the Web 2.0 can be used for active customer involvement in the development of new and relevant customer-centric services. As a collective space it allows tourists to become "co-marketers, co-producers and co-designers of their service experiences by providing them a wide spectrum of value" (Sigala, 2009, p. 1345).

For tourism organisations to take lead in experience offers, they need to implement ICTs as a source for innovation (Neuhofer et al., 2012). Innovation represents a strong decommoditiser to create something new, differentiated and valuable (Pine & Korn, 2011). In this sense, only those companies that make the leap to use technology for the innovation of co-creation processes could find a potential way to reduce commodification and gain competitive advantage long-term. Successful businesses will be the ones able to strategically use ICTs to facilitate customer involvement, co-production, co-creation and crowdsourcing. To employ these principles, it is critical to have a full understanding of the different processes that ICTs can support. Thus, the chapter now turns to discuss and classify the three highlighted customer involvement processes through the lens of technology.

4.4 Classification of Technology-Facilitated Co-creation Processes

Through the use of ICTs, co-creation can be taken to a whole new level. ICTs have enabled new processes of *how*, *when* and *where* consumers can play a role in the creation of their experiences. With ICTs in place, co-creation can occur anywhere throughout the customer journey and the service value chain. Recent studies point to a wide range of ICTs. For instance, virtual communities, such as Second Life (Binkhorst & Den Dekker, 2009), social networking platforms, blogs or micro-blogging, such as Twitter (Wang & Fesenmaier, 2004) and social networking sites, such as Facebook, YouTube or Wikipedia (Ramaswamy, 2009a) enable tourists to become engaged and contribute to both the tourist experience production and consumption. Tourists are able to connect with their social media networks to facilitate experiences (Kim & Tussyadiah, 2013), share and exchange information and latest updates. Through ICTs, consumers are connected to a vast network of stakeholders in which they can co-create experiences and value on multiple levels, extents and forms of engagement (Neuhofer et al., 2012).

4.4.1   Technology-Facilitated Crowdsourcing

Crowdsourcing has been a popular concept in a number of service industries and is becoming increasingly facilitated through ICTs in tourism. The technological developments of the past years have provided great opportunities for crowdsourcing by bundling crowd efforts through social media and networking channels online. For instance, AirBnB is a peer-to-peer platform of homeowners offering and renting their houses to tourists who want a place to stay with locals. The platform, entirely based on offers from the crowd, provides a variety of accommodation options, ranging from a shared flat in London to an entire castle in Edinburgh. Another prime example of crowdsourcing in the destination context represents VisitBritain. It facilitates crowdsourcing through a mobile travel application. The application UK Top 50 is entirely consumer-generated in that it lists the top 50 locations of the UK ranked by the accumulated number of tourists' Facebook check-ins. The more users check-in online, the higher the ranking of an attraction in the application (Neuhofer, Buhalis, & Ladkin, 2013).

This example demonstrates that VisitBritain, instead of controlling and predefining popular sites to visit, places its travel suggestions in the hands of the consumers, who determine the must-see places of a destination through their collective behaviour. Beyond AirBnB and VisitBritain, a number of best practice examples in tourism successfully demonstrate the potential of a bottom-up approach built on integrating the consumer as a resource for innovation. This means that consumers are not only considered as a source for contribution, but they become the main actor in the process. Consumers give businesses critical insights into understanding what they truly want by making them generate their experiences and own personal value obtained through this collective, participatory contribution.

4.4.2   Technology-Facilitated Co-production

Co-production in tourism and hospitality has been mainly focused on the idea of giving consumers choices. The personalisation of service encounters through ICTs can be mentioned as an example of application. Personalisation is achieved through the constant evaluation of consumers' preferences (Gupta & Vajic, 2000). Thus, it is essential not only to engage consumers but gather relevant information about their needs and preferences. This process can be facilitated through ICTs, which provide excellent tools to collect, store and retrieve information on an unprecedented scale in order to facilitate tailor-made experiences (Piccoli, O'connor, Capaccioli, & Alvarez, 2003). For instance, the best practice example Hotel Lugano Dante has introduced innovation processes through a system called HGRM, Happy Guest Relationship Management, to create enhanced experiences (Neuhofer et al., 2013).

The platform amalgamates all interactions of staff and guests throughout the entire guest journey. The hotel engages with consumers by collecting information pre-arrival, hotel stay and post-departure stage. The key is to gather information, such as name, buying patterns, pillow, mini-bar and newspaper preferences and other consumption behaviours to personalise the guest's stay based on individual preferences. A further example of co-production elements in the hospitality industry is the Inamo Restaurant in London. The eTable technology enables guests to adapt the colour scheme of the electronic table cloths, control the dining experience, manage the ordering process, waiters, bills and discover the local area, leading to a fully immersive, interactive and co-produced restaurant experience. Beyond the hospitality context, mobile services play an increasingly important role in tourism (Egger & Jooss, 2010), by supporting consumers with location based and context based services, gamification and augmented reality apps on the move (Buhalis & Wagner, 2013). These can be used to personalise settings, find relevant information in the tourist's current geographical location, context, including season, weather, time, and by doing so, create a personalised service and experience environment for the tourist.

4.4.3 Technology-Facilitated Co-creation

Social media tools, such as Facebook, Twitter, YouTube, TripAdvisor and more recently Pinterest or Vine, have allowed tourists to become generators of content. By being connected to their social networking sites, tourists can share experiences with friends, peers, tourism providers and other consumers, and co-create while still being in the travel location (Tussyadiah & Fesenmaier, 2009). Thus, tourists do not only co-create with their physical surroundings, e.g. destinations, hotels, attractions, sights or restaurants, but effectively extend their co-creation activities to the online space (Neuhofer et al., 2012). Numerous DMOs provide best-practice examples of how to foster co-creation with tourists. For instance, Sweden, Thailand and Puerto Rico have implemented innovative solutions for users to connect, upload and share images, stories and videos with the travel community (Buhalis & Wagner, 2013). By doing so, co-creation not only occurs with the DMOs but with consumer communities, who can create their pre- and post-holiday experiences together.

Moreover, the cutting edge example of Sol Melia's Sol Wave House successfully demonstrates the use of Twitter as a tool for extended co-creation. Being the world's first Twitter-Hotel, hashtags are used throughout the entire hotel to allow guests to co-create with employees, dedicated Twitter concierges (B2C co-creation) and other guests staying at the hotel (C2C co-creation). Additionally, KLM's initiative of social seating underlines the importance of encouraging customer-to-customer co-creation by using ICTs to facilitate that consumers connect, meet and can have an enhanced in-flight experience. In reviewing several different technology-facilitated examples of co-creation, it is evident that consumers are encouraged to actively engage in a number of co-creation efforts. Businesses need to adopt novel and unconventional approaches, which ICTs can support to foster

Table 1 Classification of technology-facilitated co-creation processes

Notion	Crowdsourcing	Co-production	Co-creation
Consumer Involvement	Active participation in idea generation, content generation, voting, funding	Active company-driven product or service exchange participation	Active consumer-centric experience and value co-creation
Role of the Consumer	One in many (Consumer in a crowd)	Two-way company-led involvement (Company and consumer)	Multi-level involvement (Company, consumer and consumer communities)
Role of the Company	Company defines crowdsourcing goal and leads activities	Company develops product/services and gives consumer a choice	Company facilitates co-creation of experiences and value
Experience Outcome	Crowd-generated, participatory experience	Customised, personalised co-creation experience	Rich, personalised, connected, co-constructed experience and value
Value for the Consumer	Value through participation in process, value through contribution to outcome	Value through customisation and personalisation of product and service	Value through co-created experiences and the co-creation process itself
Innovation through ICTs	Crowdsourcing activities through technology platforms and open calls	Co-production through technology-supported devices for personalisation	Co-creation of rich, meaningful experiences through social and mobile tools in the travel process

differentiation, innovation and competitiveness of tourist experiences. The classification in Table 1 provides an overview of the foregone review by synthesising distinct characteristics for a more differentiated understanding of technology-facilitated co-creation.

To provide tourism organisations and marketers with practical implications of how to innovate through technology-facilitated co-creation experiences, valuable insights can be gained by looking at existing examples across the tourism, hospitality and airline industry. For this purpose, Table 2 provides a summary of best-practice cases that apply innovative approaches of co-creation. In depicting these diverse organisations from a variety of industries, it becomes evident that customer involvement can take many different forms under the umbrella of co-creation. Specifically, this overview shall assist tourism practitioners to take a closer look at existing successful examples to understand (a) the various forms of consumer involvement, (b) the range of ICTs that can be used and (c) the various processes (crowdsourcing, co-production, co-creation) that can be applied. Whatever type of process is facilitated, several implications for companies can be defined. These include to (a) put the tourist consumer and his/her needs first, (b) allow for an active involvement in the co-creation process and (c) define which process, based on the particularities of the sector, is the most suitable one for a technology-enhanced experience.

Table 2 Tourism industry best-practice cases

Type of creation	Industry cases	Technology-facilitated innovation
Crowdsourcing		
	AirBnB	Crowd-based peer-to-peer platform of home-owners creating one of the largest private-house renting platforms for tourists
	Visit Britain	Crowd-sourced user generated content through tourist Facebook check-ins to attractions in order to generate the Top UK 50 Places mobile application
Co-production		
	Hotel Lugano Dante	Co-production by personalisation of the hotel stay, including mini-bar, pillows, newspapers, food and beverage through a customer-relationship platform
	Inamo Restaurant London	Co-production by personalisation of the dining experience including table ambience, order pace and bills through the eTable technology
Co-creation		
	Sol Melia's Sol Wave House	Co-creation through Twitter in the entire hotel through hashtags with employees, Twitter concierges and guests
	KLM	Co-creation through social media by facilitating a social seating in-flight initiative

5 Conclusion

The advances in customer involvement and the field of technology have contributed to new opportunities to innovate co-creation processes in tourism more effectively. In this light, the chapter had the aim to explore innovation through co-creation and, more specifically, to develop an understanding of how ICTs can be used to facilitate innovative co-creation processes. To this end, the chapter has started with a review of the rise of the consumer and the paradigm shift towards consumer empowerment, service dominant logic and co-creation. By recognising a multiplicity of existing terminologies, the chapter has then assessed three dominant processes, including crowdsourcing, co-production and co-creation and accentuated their differences and similarities in the context of tourism. The next part has discussed the impact of technology as a facilitator of co-creation, before developing a classification of technology-facilitated co-creation processes. The classification has contributed to the current understanding of co-creation by presenting distinct characteristics and mechanisms underlining ICTs-facilitated crowdsourcing, co-production and co-creation respectively. To complement the theoretical contribution with relevant practical implications, an overview of tourism best-practice cases was presented to highlight the potential of ICTs in tourism innovation practices.

This chapter draws several critical conclusions for tourism research and practice. Operating competitively in a fast-paced tourism industry first of all means recognising cutting-edge technological developments and being at the forefront of using them as a means for innovation and strategic competitive advantage. With co-creation flourishing over the years to come, the industry needs to capture its full potential by taking co-creation to the next level (Neuhofer et al., 2012). Only by adopting the technological solutions of the coming years that drive ever more social and mobile interactions and participatory behaviour, tourism businesses will have a great opportunity to empower tourists more effectively throughout all stages of travel. Involving the consumer does not only mean co-creating more meaningful experiences and value but does also provide the company with insights in better understanding their consumers and their inherent needs and wants.

The key to this process is the adoption of a co-creation philosophy that puts the consumer first. If this mind-set is established, there will be new opportunities to create socially dense and personal experiences together. The main chance for tourism businesses is to identify original, unique and innovative co-creation processes. For these to occur, businesses need to first identify the goal of the consumer involvement and then facilitate consumers with the necessary resources and tools to become a part of the innovation process. This can range from generating ideas, asking for opinions, personalising to co-creating experiences with companies, stakeholder and consumer communities. The more consumers are involved in the co-production, design or creation of their experiences, the more positive evaluations will they develop, leading to increased perceived value, loyalty and recommendation in the long-term. Thus, in order to keep up with the pace of dynamically moving markets, the use of ICTs for co-creation processes needs to become a strategic objective in new service development and innovation in tourism. Constant assessment and re-appraisal of current practices are needed to overcome technological challenges, seize opportunities and facilitate innovation that allows co-creating experiences with contemporary consumers most effectively.

References

Baron, S., & Harris, K. (2010). Toward an understanding of consumer perspectives on experiences. *Journal of Services Marketing, 24*(7), 518–531.

Baron, S., & Warnaby, G. (2011). Individual customers' use and integration of resources: Empirical findings and organizational implications in the context of value co-creation. *Industrial Marketing Management, 40*(2), 211–218.

Binkhorst, E. (2006). The co-creation tourism experience. In *XV international tourism and leisure symposium*, Barcelona.

Binkhorst, E., & Den Dekker, T. (2009). Agenda for co-creation tourism experience research. *Journal of Hospitality Marketing and Management, 18*(2/3), 311–327.

Bitner, M. J., Faranda, W. T., Hubbert, A. R., & Zeithaml, V. A. (1997). Customer contributions and roles in service delivery. *International Journal of Service Industry Management, 8*(3), 193–205.

Boswijk, A., Thijssen, T., & Peelen, E. (2007). *The experience economy: A new perspective.* Amsterdam: Pearson Education.

Buhalis, D. (2003). *eTourism: Information technology for strategic tourism management.* Harlow: Prentice Hall.

Buhalis, D., & Law, R. (2008). Progress in information technology and tourism management. 20 years on and 10 years after the internet. The state of eTourism research. *Tourism Management, 29*(4), 609–623.

Buhalis, D., & Wagner, R. (2013). E-destinations: Global best practice in tourism technologies and application. In L. Cantoni & Z. Xiang (Eds.), *Information and communication technologies in tourism 2012*. Austria: Springer.

Cetinkaya, A. S. (2009). Destination competitiveness through the use of information and communication technologies. In *European and Mediterranean conference on information systems*. Izmir, Turkey.

Chathoth, P., Altinay, L., Harrington, R. J., Okumus, F., & Chan, E. S. W. (2013). Co-production versus co-creation: A process based continuum in the hotel service context. *International Journal of Hospitality Management, 32*, 11–20.

Cova, B., & Dalli, D. (2009). Working consumers: The next step in marketing theory? *Marketing Theory, 9*(3), 315–339.

Darmer, P., & Sundbo, J. (2008). Introduction to experience creation. In J. Sundbo & P. Darmer (Eds.), *Creating experiences in the experience economy*. Cheltenham: Edward Elgar.

De Jong, J., & Vermeulen, P. (2003). Organizing successful new service development: A literature review. *Management Decision, 41*(9), 844–858.

Doan, A., Ramakrishnan, R., & Halevy, A. Y. (2011). Crowdsourcing systems on the world - wide web. *Communications of the ACM*.

Droege, H., Hildebrand, D., & Heras Forcada, M. (2009). Innovation in services: Present findings, and future pathways. *Journal of Service Management, 20*(2), 131–155.

Dwivedi, M., Yadav, A., & Venkatesh, U. (2012). Use of social media by national tourism organizations: A preliminary analysis. *Information Technology and Tourism, 13*(2), 93–103.

Edvardsson, B., Enquist, B., & Johnston, R. (2005). Cocreating customer value through hyperreality in the prepurchase service experience. *Journal of Service Research, 8*, 149–161.

Egger, R., & Jooss, M. (2010). Die Zukunft im mTourism: Ausblick auf Technologie- und Dienstentwicklung. In R. Egger & M. Jooss (Eds.), *mTourism: Mobile dienste im tourismus*. Wiesbaden: Gabler.

Etgar, M. (2008). A descriptive model of the consumer co-production process. *Journal of the Academy of Marketing Science, 36*, 97–108.

Fitzsimmons, J. A., & Fitzsimmons, M. J. (2000). *New service development: Creating memorable experiences*. Thousand Oaks, CA: Sage.

Fotis, J., Buhalis, D., & Rossides, N. (2011). Social media impact on holiday travel planning: The case of the Russian and the FSU markets. *International Journal of Online Marketing, 1*(4), 1–19.

Geiger, D., Rosemann, M., & Fielt, E. (2011). Crowdsourcing information systems - A systems theory perspective. In *ACIS 2011 proceedings*.

Gretzel, U., & Jamal, T. (2009). Conceptualizing the creative tourist class: Technology, mobility, and tourism experiences. *Tourism Analysis, 14*(4), 471–481.

Gupta, S., & Vajic, M. (2000). *The contextual and dialectical nature of experiences*. Thousand Oaks, CA: Sage.

Hays, S., Page, S. J., & Buhalis, D. (2012). Social media as a destination marketing tool: Its use by national tourism organisations. *Current Issues in Tourism, 16*(3), 1–29.

Hjalager, A.-M. (2002). Repairing innovation defectiveness in tourism. *Tourism Management, 23* (5), 465–474.

Hjalager, A.-M. (2010). A review of innovation research in tourism. *Tourism Management, 31*(1), 1–12.

Howe, J. (2006). Crowdsourcing: A definition. *Crowdsourcing: Tracking the rise of the Amateur* [Online].

Huang, J., & Hsu, C. H. C. (2010). The impact of customer-to-customer interaction on cruise experience and vacation satisfaction. *Journal of Travel Research, 49*(1), 79–92.

Kim, J., & Tussyadiah, I. P. (2013). Social networking and social support in tourism experience: The moderating role of online self-presentation strategies. *Journal of Travel & Tourism Marketing, 30*(1), 78–92.

Morgan, M., Lugosi, P., & Ritchie, J. R. B. (2010). *The tourism and leisure experience: Consumer and managerial perspectives*. Bristol: Channel View.

Neuhofer, B., & Buhalis, D. (2013). Experience, co-creation and technology: Issues, challenges and trends for technology enhanced tourism experiences. In S. Mccabe (Ed.), *Handbook of tourism marketing*. London: Routledge.

Neuhofer, B., Buhalis, D., & Ladkin, A. (2012). Conceptualising technology enhanced destination experiences. *Journal of Destination Marketing & Management, 1*(1–2), 36–46.

Neuhofer, B., Buhalis, D., & Ladkin, A. (2013). High tech for high touch experiences: A case study from the hospitality industry. In L. Cantoni & Z. Xiang (Eds.), *Information and communication technologies in tourism 2012*. Austria: Springer.

Ottenbacher, M., & Harrington, R. J. (2010). Strategies for achieving success for innovative versus incremental new services. *Journal of Services Marketing, 24*(1), 3–15.

Payne, A. F., Storbacka, K., & Frow, P. (2008). Managing the co-creation of value. *Journal of the Academy of Marketing Science, 36*, 83–96.

Piccoli, G., O'connor, P., Capaccioli, C., & Alvarez, R. (2003). Customer relationship management--A driver for change in the structure of the U.S. lodging industry. *Cornell Hotel and Restaurant Administration Quarterly, 44*(61), 61–73.

Pikkemaat, B., & Peters, M. (2006). Towards the measurement of innovation—A pilot study in the small and medium sized hotel industry. *Journal of Quality Assurance in Hospitality & Tourism, 6*(3–4), 89–112.

Pine, J. B., & Korn, K. (2011). *Infinite possibility: Creating customer value on the digital frontier*. San Francisco, CA: Berrett-Koehler.

Prahalad, C. K., & Ramaswamy, V. (2004). Co-creation experiences: The next practice in value creation. *Journal of Interactive Marketing, 18*(3), 5–14.

Ramaswamy, V. (2009a). Co-creation of value – Towards an expanded paradigm of value creation. *Marketing Review St. Gallen, 6*(11–17).

Ramaswamy, V. (2009b). Leading the transformation to co-creation of value. *Strategy & Leadership, 37*(2), 32–37.

Ramaswamy, V. (2011). It's about human experiences… and beyond, to co-creation. *Industrial Marketing Management, 40*(2), 195–196.

Ramaswamy, V., & Gouillart, F. (2008). Co-creating strategy with experience co-creation. *Balanced Scorecard Report, 10*, 1–3.

Ritchie, J. R. B., & Crouch, G. (2003). *The competitive destination: A sustainable tourism perspective*. Cambridge: CABI Publishing.

Ritzer, G., & Jurgenson, N. (2010). Production, consumption, prosumption. *Journal of Consumer Culture, 10*(1), 13–36.

Romero, D., & Molina, A. (2011). Collaborative networked organisations and customer communities: Value co-creation and co-innovation in the networking era. *Production Planning & Control: The Management of Operations, 22*(5–6), 447–472.

Sanden, B. (2007). *The customer's role in new service development*. Faculty of Economic Sciences, Communication and IT, Karlstad University, Karlstad.

Shaw, G., Bailey, A., & Williams, A. M. (2011). Service dominant logic and its implications for tourism management: The co-production of innovation in the hotel industry. *Tourism Management, 32*(2), 207–214.

Sheldon, P. (1997). *Tourism information technologies*. Oxford: CAB.

Sigala, M. (2009). E-service quality and Web 2.0: Expanding quality models to include customer participation and inter-customer support. *The Service Industries Journal, 29*(10), 1341–1358.

Sigala, M. (2012a). Social networks and customer involvement in new service development (NSD): The case of www.mystarbucksidea.com. *International Journal of Contemporary Hospitality Management, 24*(7), 966–990.

Sigala, M. (2012b). Web 2.0 and customer involvement in new service development: A framework, cases and implications in tourism. In M. Sigala, E. Christou, & U. Gretzel (Eds.), *Social media in travel, tourism and hospitality: Theory, practice and cases*. Surrey: Ashgate.

Stamboulis, Y., & Skayannis, P. (2003). Innovation strategies and technology for experience-based tourism. *Tourism Management, 24*(1), 35–43.

Tussyadiah, I. P., & Fesenmaier, D. R. (2007). Interpreting tourist experiences from first-person stories: A foundation for mobile guides. *15th European conference on information systems*. St. Gallen, Switzerland.

Tussyadiah, I. P., & Fesenmaier, D. R. (2009). Mediating the tourist experiences access to places via shared videos. *Annals of Tourism Research, 36*(1), 24–40.

Van Limburg, B. (2012). Visiting suriname, using DART to analyze a visitor's perspective in a cocreation environment. *Information Technology and Tourism, 13*(2), 119–132.

Vargo, S. L., & Lusch, R. F. (2004). Evolving to a new dominant logic for marketing. *Journal of Marketing, 68*(January), 1–17.

Vargo, S. L., & Lusch, R. F. (2006). Service-dominant logic: Reactions, reflections and refinements. *Marketing Theory, 6*(3), 281–288.

Walls, A. R., Okumus, F., Wang, Y., & Kwun, D. J.-W. (2011). An epistemological view of consumer experiences. *International Journal of Hospitality Management, 30*(1), 10–21.

Wang, Y., & Fesenmaier, D. R. (2004). Towards understanding members' general participation in and active contribution to an online travel community. *Tourism Management, 25*(6), 709–722.

Williams, A. (2012). *Understanding the hospitality consumer*. London: Routledge.

Xiang, Z., & Gretzel, U. (2010). Role of social media in online travel information search. *Tourism Management, 31*(2), 179–188.

Xie, C., Bagozzi, R., & Troye, S. (2008). Trying to prosume: Toward a theory of consumers as co-creators of value. *Journal of the Academy of Marketing Science, 36*(1), 109–122.

Yen, H. R., Gwinner, K. P., & Su, W. (2004). The impact of customer participation and service expectation on Locus attributions following service failure. *International Journal of Service Industry Management, 15*(1), 7–26.

Zach, F. J., Gretzel, U., & Xiang, Z. (2010). Innovation in web marketing programs of American convention and visitor bureaus. *Information Technology and Tourism, 12*(1), 47–63.

The Importance of Customer Co-creation of Value for the Tourism and Hospitality Industry

Digna Roeffen and Ursula Scholl-Grissemann

1 Introduction

The traditional system of value creation has focused on a firm centric perspective for many years. The roles of producers and customers were clearly defined and independent from each other. Today, this system does not meet market requirements anymore and shifts from a firm centric perspective to a customer centric perspective, through which value is co-created *with* the customer and not only *for* the customer (Prahalad & Ramaswamy, 2004; Michel, Brown, & Gallan, 2008). This development is a consequence of a change in the role customers play today. As such, individuals have undergone a transformation from isolated, uninformed, and passive actors to linked, well informed, and active participants in value creation processes (Prahalad & Ramaswamy, 2004).

Additionally, information and communication technology have empowered customers by increasing their information base, self-efficacy, and skills as well as enabling greater choice and more control (Füller et al., 2009). Due to these attributes, customers seek to take part in value creation themselves and influence business processes in various stages from product/service development to post-launch improvements (Füller et al., 2012). Vargo and Lusch (2004, 2008) follow the concept of value-in-use which implies the creation of value through the customer when he or she actually uses the product/service. This means, the customer actively participates in the value-creation process, whereas the firm provides the

D. Roeffen
Marketing Controller, Swarovski, Switzerland
e-mail: digna.roeffen@swarovski.com

U. Scholl-Grissemann (✉)
Department of Strategic Management, Marketing and Tourism, University of Innsbruck
School of Management, Innsbruck, Austria
e-mail: ursula.grissemann@uibk.ac.at

© Springer-Verlag Berlin Heidelberg 2016
R. Egger et al. (eds.), *Open Tourism*, Tourism on the Verge,
DOI 10.1007/978-3-642-54089-9_3

service and ideally co-creates value with the customer. In this case, one speaks about the co-creation of value between the customer and the firm.

Tourism research gains substantially from the idea that customers and companies are both resource integrators in the value creation process because tourism firms increasingly invite their customers to undertake activities that were initially tasks of the company, such as engaging in the service delivery process (e.g., using self-service technologies, such as online check-in services for flights, or fast check-in counters at hotels) or co-developing new services (e.g., developing mobile applications).

The purpose of this article is to provide the theoretical foundations of customer co-creation of value. We further highlight the importance of the co-creation concept for the tourism industry. Subsequently, we delineate implications for tourism and hospitality management.

2   The Relevance of Co-creation for the Tourism Industry

Grissemann and Stokburger-Sauer (2012, p. 1483) highlight the importance of co-creation for the tourism industry: First, in the emerging experience economy (Pine & Gilmore, 1999) creating unique and memorable experiences for customers is of paramount importance for tourism service providers to remain competitive. Creating a unique experience involves both customer participation and a connection which links the customer to the experience (Shaw, Bailey, & Williams, 2011). The concept of co-creation implies that value is created in the interaction process itself rather than exclusively in the provision of the service (Etgar, 2008). Therefore, involving customers in the creation of a travel arrangement helps tailoring the service to the customers' particular needs and hence creates a unique experience.

Second, the Internet has significantly changed the way of how customers allocate knowledge about hotels, flights or even destinations. Online booking engines and websites that allow customers to post their opinions and reviews about tourism service companies are not only a helpful co-creation tool for customers, but also an important source of marketing information about customer experiences for companies (Shaw et al., 2011).

Third, customers create value not only for themselves and the company, but also for other customers since they often share their travel experiences in online social media networks. This development has shifted considerable power to customers. Online communities operate as permanent agents of quality control and instantly report the shortcomings of service companies in online platforms. Thus, the travel experience of a single customer is accessible to multitudinous community members and, subsequently, shapes their future purchase behaviour (Grissemann & Stokburger-Sauer, 2012).

Fourth, online technologies such as booking engines and recommendation websites have shifted the competition of hotels form a destination level on an international level. High-quality holiday destinations such as the Alpine region in Europe are predominantly small- and medium sized family businesses having high labour costs and few opportunities to create economies of scale and scope (Pikkemaat, 2008). Thus they can hardly compete with the low-cost strategy of many hotels in the Mediterranean or Asian regions. As a consequence, their focus is predominantly on creating memorable experiences for customers and thus creating superior value for both customers and companies (Grissemann, Plank, & Brunner-Sperdin, 2012).

3 Service Dominant Logic

The purpose of Service Dominant Logic (S-D logic) is to provide a pre-theoretical foundation for a revised and transcending logic about exchange in marketing (Vargo & Lusch, 2011). In the traditional marketing view, companies create value and distribute value in the market through the exchange of money (i.e., value-in-exchange). Tangible goods were considered as the basic unit of exchange, whereas services were considered as somewhat intangible goods. This logic is what Vargo and Lusch (2004, 2006, 2008) call a Goods-Dominant Logic (G-D logic): "Producers" and "consumers" are distinct and value creation is considered as a series of company activities (Vargo, Maglio, & Akaka, 2008). As opposed to this paradigm, Vargo and Lusch (2004) introduced a Service-Dominant Logic (S-D logic) of value creation. S-D logic claims that marketing research has to shift the focus of marketing away from tangibles to the exchange of intangibles, such as skills, information, knowledge, or on-going relationships (Vargo & Lusch, 2004). Whereas the assumption of a G-D logic was that value is determined by the provision of output, the underlying assumption of S-D logic is that customers define what value is. The most crucial distinction between G-D logic and S-D logic is the conceptualization of service (Vargo & Lusch, 2008): G-D logic, defines services (plural) according to the traditional IHIP characteristics: Intangibility, heterogeneity, inseparability, and perishability (Parasuraman, Zeithaml, & Berry, 1988). Services are units of output of a special type of good, that is, an intangible good. S-D logic defines service (singular) as the application of competences for the benefit of another party. Service is a process and the foundational basis of exchange. It refers to assisting or helping someone through activities, tasks, or performances (Vargo & Lusch, 2011). Goods are sometimes involved in this exchange process and function as appliances for service provision.

Value and value creation are at the heart of service. This service centred view is customer centric and aims at collaborating with and adapting to customers. More specifically, involving the customer in co-creation is not an option but the only way to create value. Value is thus always value-in-use. Consequently, a firms' activity can be understood as input for the customer's resource integrating, value-creation activities (Vargo & Lusch, 2008, p. 214).

S-D logic further distinguishes between operant and operand resources. Operand resources are those that are acted upon. They are static and require other resources to make them useful. Operand resources are the primary focus of G-D logic, that is, the exchange of goods. Operant resources, alternatively, are often intangible (e.g., skills and knowledge) which makes them the primary focus of S-D logic.

Finally, because service is the basis for every exchange, S-D logic makes the traditional dichotomization between manufacturing and service industries obsolete. G-D logic is concerned with tangible or intangible output that a company produces (i.e., the creation of operand resources), while S-D logic focuses on the application of competencies and resources regardless of the type of output.

Service Dominant Logic raised a lively and controversial discussion about the customer's role in the value creation process. However, S-D logic contributed undeniably to a more customer centric debate in value research and therefore can't be disregarded when discussing the customer's role in value creation processes.

4 Customer Participation in the Value Creation Process

4.1 Dimensions of Customer Value

The concept of value creation is a key issue in tourism research as it is recognized as being vital in creating competitive advantage (Nasution & Mavondo, 2008; Sánchez et al., 2006) and should thus be considered in every marketing strategy. For tourism managers, this means that customer value plays an important role in developing market segmentation strategies, positioning policies or product differentiation strategies (Gallarza and Saura, 2006). Investigating the perceived value of customers also helps managers to identify dimensions where they perform well or poor and helps to better understand customers' decision making processes (Petrick, 2004).

For a long time, customer value was regarded as a one-dimensional construct mainly capturing value as value-for-money. Today, this view is rather outdated and customer value is considered being a multi-dimensional construct comprising several dimensions. Customers "assess products not just in functional terms of expected performance, value for money and versatility; but also in terms of the enjoyment or pleasure derived from the product and the social consequences of what the product communicates to others (Sweeney and Soutar, 2001, p. 216)."

In the context of hospitality research, Krasna (2008) found that solely price-strategies seem to be out-of-date. By contrast it is the "soul of the hotel" (p. 14) and the emotional experience that makes hotel guests return to the hotel and recommend it to others. This is confirmed by Gallaraza and Saura (2006) who study university students' travel behaviour and find that in the management of tourism experiences, there is a need to surpass pure utilitarian aspects and to focus on both the cognitive and affective nature of perceived value. Thus, our understanding of perceived value goes beyond a price-performance ratio concept and incorporates functional, hedonic, and social aspects.

Functional value has its roots in economic utility theory and is often suggested as being the primary force of customer choice. Sheth and Uslay (2007) define functional value as the perceived utility derived from an alternative's capacity for functional, utilitarian, or physical performance. Functional value is often evaluated by means of attributes such as price, reliability or durability. Woodruff (1997) identifies three key elements of functional value, that is, firstly, appropriate features, functions, attributes, secondly, appropriate performances, and thirdly, appropriate outcomes or consequences.

The hedonic (experiential) value dimension brings emotions into play and views the customer as more than just a thinker but also as feeler and doer. Holbrook and Hirschman (1982) were among the first dealing with these experiential aspects. Following their logic, value is not generated by the actual purchase but in the consumption experience. Within this view, other variables such as fun, pleasure, or emotions complement to the customer's value perception (Addis & Holbrook, 2001). Hedonic value is subjective and personal and often results from a fun experience rather than from purchasing or using a good or service. Hedonic value is filled with emotions, entertainment, freedom, and fantasy and can be influenced by atmosphere, employees' behaviour, crowding or other peripheral services (Holbrook & Hirschman, 1982).

The social value dimension emanates from a mind-set which is shared by a society and is determined by the social impact the purchase of the service constitutes (Sánchez et al., 2006). Drawing on social identity theory (Tajfel & Turner, 1979), social identification is a perception of oneness with a group of persons and leads to actions that are congruent with the group's identity and support institutions that embody this identity (Ashforth & Mael, 1989). Depending on a person's individual social value orientation he or she judges an entity for themselves and also for others. Thus, social value provides a basis for justification and acceptance when purchasing services. In tourism settings, purchase decisions often follow a social motivation which means that consumers want to belong or be accepted by a special group (Sánchez et al., 2006).

The conceptualization of consumer value is of particular importance for tourism products because they entail emotional value that goes beyond the functional utilities and provides more subjective, intangible benefits such as sensory pleasure, emotions, and excitement. Today, hospitality firms, for example, have to offer both impressive physical appearance and high-quality, personalized service offerings to their guests. Additionally, the chances of achieving competitive advantage solely through the provision of tangibles, such as exclusive hotel furniture, are rather short-lived (Cai & Hobson, 2004). Consequently, hotels achieve competitive advantage through creating symbolic, emotional, and intangible differences.

Beside the functional and hedonic benefits for the customer, which basically result from the purchase experience, the consumption of tourism services is also driven by customers' need to extend their own personality, that is, to enhance their self-concept and to achieve group affiliation. When guests feel comfortable at a hotel because it matches their way of living and enhances their feelings of belonging to a certain group of people, positive reactions, such as positive word of mouth can be expected.

4.2 Customer Co-creation of Value

Various strategies have been implemented by firms to use the customer as an external resource. In most cases, though, the benefits of the firm—increasing output and productivity—were at the very fore. However, this firm centred view is not in accordance with S-D logic. Nuttavuthisit (2010) takes a customer centric view and explores how and why individuals co-create and, additionally, derives four systematic categories of customer co-creation practices: participation-for-self, creation-for-self, participation-for-others, and creation-for-others. This categorization of practices should allow conclusions on the motive and the extent to which customers engage in co-creation.

Following Nuttavuthisit (2010) participation and creation are both elements of co-creation. Participation refers to the active involvement and cooperation of the customer, for instance, in the service development process. The extent to which customers are allowed to participate in this process is mainly predefined by the company. Creation, however, is controlled by the customer while he or she uses own or external resources to create individual value.

Participation-for-self aims at the fulfilment of specific needs demanded by the customer. The customer seeks to obtain a product or service which is tailored to his or her individual desires. The process to get to this stage is often cost intensive, as it needs to break free from standardization. Practices targeting at participation-for-self always actively involve the customer in business processes, whereas the advantages for the customer should compensate for possible risks s/he has to put up with (Nuttavuthisit, 2010). Participation-for-self activities can particularly be found in the sports and leisure industry, where skiers (e.g., http://www.wagnerskis.com/), sunglasses (http://www.customize-eyewear.com/), or bikes (e.g., http://www.kraftstoff-bikes.com/), are tailored to fit customers' unique needs with the help of mass customization tools.

Creation-for-self has been mainly influenced by the do-it-yourself concept. Customers use their individual skills and knowledge to create value by and for them. The firm supports customers by providing supportive surrounding conditions which allow them to apply and advance their skills. Both firm and customers are involved in the value creation process, whereas the customer plays an active role and the firm a rather passive but supportive role (Nuttavuthisit, 2010). Regarding the tourism industry, customers increasingly use online mix-and-match booking platforms to combine flights, hotels, and rental cars. These platforms have changed tourism substantially since they allow customers to easily compare different service providers and to find the most suitable offer for them.

Participation and creation-for-self obviously focus on benefits generated for the customer themselves and do not take any desires of other actors into account. Still, individuals feel the need for social affiliation, solidarity, and intercommunity, and therefore have to pay regard to benefits for other actors and society at large. The following two co-creation practices are aiming into this direction.

Participation-for-others refers to customers who make use of a company's resources and facilities in order to create value for others. A good example is sharing information with others for their benefit. This includes taking part in pre-tests of a product or writing reviews to share service experiences –whether positive or negative—with other potential customers and the company itself. This co-creation practice helps other customers in their buying decision and allows companies to make adjustments concerning the product or service.

Prominent examples from the tourism industry are online recommendation websites, such as Tripadvisor or Holidaycheck, where customers rate accommodations and share their experiences with other customers to help them in making their travel arrangements.

Creation-for-others takes the adherence of others even one step further as participation-for-others. Nowadays, information and communication technology allows fast, transnational, and low-cost interaction between customers. This technology enables individuals to share information with a whole community, improve creativity, and advance problem-solving capacities. Online communities, for example, are often based on values, interests or a belief which are shared amongst the community members. One example from the tourism industry is Wikitravel, a crowd-sourced travel guide, where users can contribute to existing articles or write new articles about travel destinations.

The four co-creation practices show different ways in which customers might co-create value with the firm or other actors. This classification is an attempt to clarify the various roles a customer can have when co-creating value. Nevertheless, it should also be clearly pointed out that all dimensions are strongly interrelated and cannot be dealt with independently. This framework, however, can help to develop strategies which foster co-creation (Nuttavuthisit, 2010).

Note that the extent to which a firm introduces co-creation practices mainly depends on the setting and on the discretionary policies a firm acts upon (Lengnick-Hall, Claycomb, & Inks, 2000). Once the willingness and opportunity to enable co-creation practices is existent, there are three factors which represent the key to successful and effective co-creation: *perceived clarity of the task*, *ability* or technical competence, and *motivation* (Bettencourt, Ostrom, Brown, & Roundtree, 2002; Lengnick-Hall et al., 2000). *Clarity of the task* means that customers exactly know what is required from them and which role they play in the service development process. According to Mills, Chase, and Newton (1983) a high level of task clarity increases the chance of better service outcome as the customer exactly knows what to do. Increased communication within the organization as well as between customers can help to enhance task clarity (Lengnick-Hall et al., 2000). Customers' *ability* to actually perform the task set by the firm is another key aspect of effective co-creation. They are required to act upon and deliver resources and make timely contributions to firm activities (Auh, Bell, McLeod, & Shih, 2007). When acting on the assumption that the task is clear for the customer and he also has the ability or technical competence to carry out the task, there is still one essential element missing, namely that of *motivation*. The customer must be willing to co-create and engage in organizational activities. Especially if customers have the feeling that their contribution improves the outcome, they will be motivated to reinforce co-creation (Lovelock & Young, 1979; Lengnick-Hall et al., 2000).

5   Implications for the Tourism and Hospitality Industry

Following the S-D logic mind-set, it is not the exchange of the service but customers' active involvement in the service development process that generates value. However, many practitioners in the tourism and hospitality industry seem to be trapped in a goods centred and value-in-exchange perspective. High quality services are produced within a hotel and supplied to the guests. However, the essence of S-D logic, namely that the customer is always a co-creator of value, points to the multidimensional relationship between customer and producer (i.e. the firm). The tourism industry mainly provides services, which are produced and consumed simultaneously and, therefore, the customer must always be involved in the service development process. S-D logic elaborates on this thinking as the engagement of the customer precedes the consumption stage, meets the consumption stage, and goes beyond the consumption stage.

In the *pre-consumption stage*, customers engage in co-creation practices by pre-arranging their service packages as opposed to consuming ready-made service packages offered by the tourism firm. Web technologies allow customers to collect information, connect with other people, and share information about specific travel experiences (Shaw et al., 2010). More specifically, customers use mix-and-match platforms to combine flights and accommodations tailored to their particular needs. In this regard, information and communication technology has contributed to a vast acceleration of co-creation practices (Füller et al., 2009; Füller & Matzler, 2007). As a result of the "digitization of content, high-speed wired and wireless networks, and new customer devices and appliances, there's an unprecedented number of touchpoints between the firm and the end-customer (Prahalad, Ramaswamy, & Krishnan, 2000, p. 1)". Recent research highlights that the more customers are involved in the pre-arrangement of their service package, the higher their willingness-to-pay for the package (Grissemann & Stokburger-Sauer, 2012). As such, offering service packages that are highly individualised can directly enhance firm performance.

In the *consumption stage*, the customer creates and determines value, whereupon the experience of using a good or service and the perception are essential for value determination (Vargo & Lusch, 2006). This notion is related to Pine and Gilmore's (1999) notion of an experience economy in which goods and services are seen as mechanisms to engage customers in a way that creates a memorable event. Nevertheless, their view is very much concentrating on the producer's perspective (Pine & Gilmore, 2002). Practitioners thus need to be aware of the eminent role of the customer in the consumption stage (Vargo & Lusch, 2004; Grönroos, 2009). In the consumption stage itself, the customer is virtually always present due to the nature of services. For example, when a service is provided in a hotel (e.g., a beauty treatment, a drink at the bar, or a dinner) the guest is always at hand. The challenge of a manager is to generate an even stronger involvement of the customer in order to build up a powerful and procreative relationship.

In the light of co-creation activities, the *post-consumption* phase gains particular importance. Similar to the "I designed it myself"-effect discussed by Franke, Schreier, and Kaiser (2010), customers get the feeling of being responsible for their successful holiday experience, which results in feelings of accomplishment and increased loyalty intentions. When customers return from their holiday trip, they frequently share their holiday experiences with friends and relevant others by uploading pictures on social networks such as Facebook or by writing reviews on online recommendation websites. In doing so, they create hedonic and social value for themselves but also for potential other customers. The post-consumption phase can be utilized by the customer to further engage in online communities and to reveal personal travel experiences. The hotel manager on the other hand should also try to stretch the co-creation process, for example, by inviting guests to engage in online communities. This makes customers reminisce about their holiday and gives the manager the possibility to build up an emotional relationship.

Also the nature of innovations change as firms can and should integrate the customer as an operant resource and use their skills and knowledge. By doing so, firms shift from production innovation to experience innovation. To enable such an innovation process to take place, the firm has to provide a platform for the customer that allows him or her to give his or her fancy full scope and create individual experiences (Prahalad, 2006). When giving customers the opportunity to create their own experiences and when they are willing to participate, diversification can be facilitated or even new markets discovered (Prahalad, 2006). For the customer, engaging in the co-creation process means to invest time and knowledge. Customers will be ready to invest in their resources when they gain psychological or monetary advantages. Skills and knowledge of the customer can be seen as an essential external resource for hotel managers. In some cases, customers are aware of their knowledge and the contribution they can make but often it is tacit knowledge which first needs to be extracted and further translated into action. The difficulty is the nature of tacit knowledge as it refers to "all intellectual capital or physical capabilities and skills that the individual cannot fully articulate, represent or codify (Hallin & Marnburg, 2008, p. 368)." Consequently, practitioners' challenge is to find ways of how to capture and exploit tacit knowledge. A possibility to obtain tacit knowledge from guests could be the organization of focus groups with selected key clients. Through lively and open discussions valuable explicit and implicit knowledge could be generated and further translated into action (Shaw et al., 2010). Furthermore, the establishment of an online community could be of great interest and importance—a community, in which only former hotel guests can become members. Generally, "through online community, companies can extend their customer relationship management initiatives to include interactions among customers, leveraging these interactions to attract and retain more customers, convert browsers to buyers, improve customer service, reduce support costs, increase revenue, and gain additional insight into their business (Wang & Fesenmaier, 2004, p. 710)." Within this social community, customers can exchange their holiday experiences, share precious information, point out critique, make suggestions on how to improve certain services, pinpoint services and amenities which are desirable but not offered by the hotel, and even make proposals for innovative ideas. Following the concept of social value, members of the community should feel like belonging to a special group together with people who share common interests and values. Guests who are participating should be rewarded with special offers, small presents, or vouchers. All these proactive approaches could help in establishing a broad community which is characterized by loyalty, satisfaction, progress and innovation.

Though, some customers are happy to engage in co-creation activities and others are not (Etgar, 2008). This might be a result of the presence or absence of psychological drivers. Moreover, the decision whether to engage in co-creation activities is also affected by a rational way of thinking. In most cases, customers participate in co-creation for their own benefit. Therefore, it is a manager's duty to provide sufficient information about the co-creation activities, which makes the customer aware of the benefits he is able to generate. The success of co-creation—whether it helps to uncover customers' needs and wants or accelerates the innovation rate—is always highly dependent on customers' commitment to actively participate in the co-creation process. Due to this fact customer and supplier (and possibly also other actors) are strongly interrelated, which leads to powerful trust and relationship building. As such, managers need to broaden their view on the innovation process. Due to the fact that the customer is always a co-creator of value (Vargo & Lusch, 2006) innovations either improve existing customers' value creation function or create new markets by making value propositions to non-customers (Michel et al., 2008). Within S-D logic, operant resources are a fundamental unit of exchange (Vargo & Lusch, 2004). But not only the available skills and knowledge from customers can contribute to innovations in the co-creation process but the knowledge transfer of all network partners is of high importance (Michel et al., 2008). Consequently, managers will need to collect, maintain, improve, and efficiently exploit all skills and knowledge available in their network system.

To conclude, this article aimed to provide the theoretical foundations of customer co-creation of value with regard to implications for tourism and hospitality management. Customers engage in value creating activities in various ways such as participation-for-self, creation-for-self, participation-for-others, or creation-for-others. The tourism industry can gain from these practices in form of increased spending behaviour, loyalty intentions, or positive word of mouth. Moreover, these value creating activities can take place in the pre-consumption stage, the consumption stage and the post-consumption stage. There clearly is considerable potential within the tourism industry when adopting a S-D logic perspective in a wide scope. In order to do so practitioners need to free their mind from a G-D mind-set, which they might not follow with intention but in a rather unconscious way. Nevertheless, the leading thought behind S-D logic might be a chance to push tourism into new and exciting directions.

References

Addis, M., & Holbrook, B. (2001). On the conceptual link between mass customization and experiential consumption: An explosion of subjectivity. *Journal of Customer Behaviour, 1*(1), 50–66.

Ashforth, B. E., & Mael, F. (1989). Social identity theory and the organization. *Academy of Management Review, 14*, 20–39.

Auh, S., Bell, S. J., McLeod, C. S., & Shih, E. (2007). Co-production & customer loyalty in financial services. *Journal of Retailing, 83*(3), 359–370.

Bettencourt, L. A., Ostrom, A. L., Brown, S. W., & Roundtree, R. I. (2002). Client co-production in knowledge-intensive business services. *California Management Review, 44*(4), 100–128.

Cai, L. A., & Hobson, J. S. P. (2004). Making hotel brands work in a competitive environment. *Journal of Vacation Marketing, 10*(3), 197–208.

Etgar, M. (2008). A descriptive model of the customer co-production process. *Journal of the Academy of Marketing Science, 31*(1), 97–108.

Franke, N., Schreier, M., & Kaiser, U. (2010). The "I designed it myself" effect in mass customization. *Management Science, 56*(1), 125–140.

Füller, J., & Matzler, K. (2007). Virtual product experience & customer participation – a chance for customer-centred, really new products. *Technovation, 27*(6/7), 378–387.

Füller, J., Matzler, K., Hutter, K., & Hautz, J. (2012). Consumers' creative talent: Which characteristics qualify consumers for open innovation projects? An exploration of asymmetrical effects. *Creativity and Innovation Management, 21*(3), 247–262.

Füller, J., Mühlbacher, H., Matzler, K., & Jawecki, G. (2009). Customer empowerment through Internet-based co-creation. *Journal of Management Information Systems, 26*(3), 71–102.

Gallarza, M., & Saura, I. G. (2006). Value dimensions, perceived value, satisfaction and loyalty: An investigation of university students' travel behaviour. *Tourism Management, 27*(3), 437–452.

Grissemann, U., Plank, A., & Brunner-Sperdin, A. (2012). Enhancing business performance of hotels: The role of innovation and customer orientation. *International Journal of Hospitality Management, 33*, 347–356.

Grissemann, U., & Stokburger-Sauer, N. E. (2012). Customer co-creation of travel services: The role of company support and customer satisfaction with the co-creation performance. *Tourism Management, 33*(6), 1483–1492.

Grönroos, Ch. (2009). *Towards service logic: The unique contribution of value co-creation.* Working paper, Hanken School of Economics.

Hallin, C. A., & Marnburg, E. (2008). Knowledge management in the hospitality industry: A review of empirical research. *Tourism Management, 29*(2), 366–381.

Holbrook, M. B., & Hirschman, E. C. (1982). The experiential aspects of consumption: Consumer fantasies, feelings & fun. *Journal of Consumer Research, 11*(2), 728–739.

Krasna, T. (2008). The influence of perceived value on customer loyalty in Slovenian hotel industry. *Turizam, 12*, 12–15.

Lengnick-Hall, C. A., Claycomb, V., & Inks, L. W. (2000). From recipient to contributor: Examining customer roles & experience outcomes. *European Journal of Marketing, 34*(3/4), 359–383.

Lovelock, C. H., & Young, R. F. (1979). Look to consumers to increase productivity. *Harvard Business Review, 57*(3), 168–178.

Michel, S., Brown, W. S., & Gallan, A. S. (2008). An expanded & strategic view of discontinuous innovations: Deploying a service-dominant logic. *Journal of the Academy of Marketing Science, 36*(1), 54–66.

Mills, P. K., Chase, R. B., & Newton, M. (1983). Motivating the client/employee system as a service production strategy. *Academy of Management Review, 8*(2), 301–310.

Nasution, H. N., & Mavondo, F. T. (2008). Customer value in the hotel industry: What managers believe they deliver and what customer experience. *International Journal of Hospitality Management, 27*(2), 204–213.

Nuttavuthisit, K. (2010). If you can't beat them let them join: The development of strategies to foster consumers' co-creation practices. *Business Horizons, 53*(3), 315–324.

Parasuraman, A., Zeithaml, V. A., & Berry, L. L. (1988). Servqual. *Journal of Retailing, 64*(1), 12–37.

Petrick, J. F. (2004). 'The roles of quality, value, & satisfaction in predicting cruise passengers' behavioural intentions. *Journal of Travel Research, 42*(4), 397–407.

Pikkemaat, B. (2008). Innovation in small and medium-sized tourism enterprises in Tyrol, Austria. *Entrepreneurship and Innovation, 9*(3), 1–11.

Pine, J. B., & Gilmore, J. H. (1999). Welcome to the experience economy. *Harvard Business Review, 76*(4), 97–105.

Pine, J. B., & Gilmore, J. H. (2002). Differentiating hospitality operations via experiences. *Cornell Hotel & Restaurant Administration Quarterly, 43*(3), 87–96.

Prahalad, C. K., & Ramaswamy, V. (2004). Co-creation experiences: The next practice in value creation. *Journal of Interactive Marketing, 18*(3), 5–14.

Prahalad, C. K., Ramaswamy, V., & Krishnan, M. S. (2000). Consumer centricity: The role of the consumer is being transformed from passive buyer to active participant in co-creating value. *Information Week* (April), 1–2.

Prahalad, C. K. (2006). The practice of co-creating unique value with customers: an interview with C.K. Prahalad. *Strategy and Leadership, 30*(2), 4–9.

Sánchez, J., Callarisa, L., Rodríguez, R., & Moliner, M. A. (2006). Perceived value of the purchase of a tourism product. *Tourism Management, 27*(3), 394–409.

Shaw, G., Bailey, A., & Williams, A. (2010). Aspects of service-dominant logic and its implications for tourism management examples from the hotel industry. *Tourism Management*, 1–8. Available online June 23, 2010.

Shaw, G., Bailey, A., & Williams, A. (2011). Aspects of service-dominant logic and its implications for tourism management examples from the hotel industry. *Tourism Management, 32*(2), 207–214.

Sheth, J. N., & Uslay, C. (2007). Implications of the revised definition of marketing: from exchange to value creation. *Journal of Public Policy and Marketing, 26*(2), 302–307.

Sweeney, J. C., & Soutar, G. N. (2001). Consumer perceived value: The development of a multiple item scale. *Journal of Retailing, 77*(2), 203–220.

Tajfel, H., & Turner, J. C. (1979). An integrative theory of intergroup conflict'. In W. G. Austin & S. Worchel (Eds.), *The social psychology of intergroup relations* (pp. 33–47). Monterey, CA: Brooks/Cole.

Vargo, S. L., & Lusch, R. F. (2004). Evolving to a new dominant logic for marketing. *Journal of Marketing, 68*(1), 1–17.

Vargo, S. L., & Lusch, R. F. (Eds.). (2006). *The service-dominant logic of marketing: Dialog, debate, & directions.* Armonk, NY: Sharpe.

Vargo, S. L., & Lusch, R. F. (2008). From goods to service(s): Divergences & convergences of logics. *Industrial Marketing Management, 37*(3), 254–259.

Vargo, S. L., & Lusch, R. F. (2011). Stepping aside and moving on: A rejoinder to a rejoinder. *European Journal of Marketing, 45*(7/8), 1319–1321.

Vargo, S. L., Maglio, P. P., & Akaka, M. A. (2008). On value and value co-creation: A service systems and service logic perspective. *European Management Journal, 26*(3), 145–152.

Wang, Y., & Fesenmaier, D. R. (2004). Towards understanding members' general participation in & active contribution to an online travel community. *Tourism Management, 25*(6), 709–722.

Woodruff, R. B. (1997). Customer value: The next source of competitive advantage. *Journal of the Academy of Marketing Science, 25*(2), 139–153.

IT-Enabled Value Co-creation in a Tourism Context: The Portale Sardegna Case

Francesca Cabiddu, Tsz-Wai Lui, and Gabriele Piccoli

1 Introduction

The value of information technology (IT) in a business's production process is still a highly debated issue among researchers. Most studies on business value have considered IT value from the individual firm perspective, which assume that IT investment by a single firm leads to value-creation for that firm (e.g., Hitt & Brynjolfsson, 1996). However, recent research has highlighted the importance of studying IT value beyond the level of individual firms and has developed the concept of IT-enabled co-creation value. This concept derives from the awareness that organizational boundaries are increasingly permeable and that emerging novel arrangements enable previously unattainable value propositions (Kohli & Grover, 2008). In particular, the co-creation of value is seen as occurring through the joint, voluntary actions of multiple parties, which include value network partners, customers, and even competitors (Kohli & Grover, 2008). Despite the importance of this subject, few studies have attempted to understand how IT-based value is co-created and shared among multiple partners (Sharaf, Langdon, & Gosain, 2007). Multi-firm IT implementations generally have been considered in the context of transactions in inter-organizational systems (Gebauer & Buxmann, 1999) or outsourcing arrangements (Dos Santos, 2003) in which the value research has

F. Cabiddu (✉)
Università degli Studi di Cagliari, Cagliari, Italy
e-mail: fcabiddu@unica.it

T.-W. Lui
Ming Chaun University, Taipei, Taiwan
e-mail: irislui@mail.mcu.edu.tw

G. Piccoli
Università di Pavia, Pavia, Italy
e-mail: gabriele.piccoli@unipv.it

© Springer-Verlag Berlin Heidelberg 2016
R. Egger et al. (eds.), *Open Tourism*, Tourism on the Verge,
DOI 10.1007/978-3-642-54089-9_4

focused primarily on how each firm benefits from such relationships. To address this gap, this study contains an analysis of the role played by IT in terms of value co-creation (Vargo & Lusch, 2004; 2008a, 2008b). The study examines how different companies with different ITs can join together and co-create value. It also explains why some companies can successfully capture more of the value co-created in the partnership while others are less successful. The setting is the tourism industry because it is inevitably influenced by IT and no player can escape its impacts (Werthner & Klein, 1999). The rapid development of both supply and demand makes IT an imperative for hospitality firms; they must rethink the ways in which they do business to satisfy tourism demands and survive in the long term (Buhalis, 1998).

We conducted an in-depth case study of an online tour operator (Portale Sardegna), which represents a remarkable case of travel innovation. Our objective was to demonstrate why comparable hotels showed different abilities in appropriating of value co-created. First, we investigate how customers and firms co-create value. Second, we explore why some organizations successfully capture a portion of the value co-created while others fail to do so.

The article is organized as follows: First, a review of the literature on Service-Dominant logic and IT-based value co-creation; second, an outline of the methodology and details about data collection; and finally, the presentation of the data analysis, discussion of results, managerial implications and concluding remarks.

2 Literature Review

Many past studies have demonstrated a relationship between IT and some aspects of firm value (Devaraj and Kohli, 2003; Santhanam & Hartono, 2003), and the business value of IT tackle different aspects of IT business value ranging from productivity benefits and customer surplus (Hitt & Brynjolfsson, 1996), market value, market share, sales, and assets (Sircar et al., 2000), and a firm's profits to cost reduction, competitive advantage, inventory reduction, and other measures of performance (Devaraj and Kohli, 2003). Melville et al. (2004) defined IT business value as "the organizational performance impacts of information technology at both the intermediate process level and the organization-wide level, and comprising both efficiency impacts and competitive impacts" (p. 287). In this study, we focused on a firm's financial performance (i.e. revenue) as the organizational performance affected by IT adoption.

3 IT-Enabled Value Co-creation

While the business value of IT is extremely important, only recently researchers have focused their attention on the co-creation of value through IT rather than on IT value alone. In this view, "co-creation represents the idea that (a) IT value is

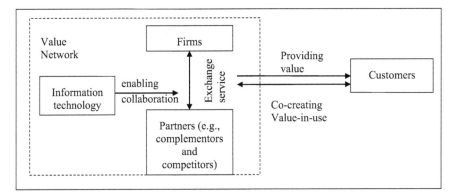

Fig. 1 The IT-enabled value co-creation network

increasingly being created and realized through actions of multiple parties, (b) value emanates from robust collaborative relationships among firms, and (c) structures and incentives for parties to partake in and equitably share emergent value are necessary to sustain co-creation" (Kohli & Grover, 2008, p. 28).

The notion of IT-enabled co-creation of value emerges from the realization that novel arrangements enable previously unattainable value propositions (Kohli & Grover, 2008). Looking through the lens of service dominant logic (S-D logic), a firm provides value proposition to its customers (i.e., other firms as the parties in the value co-creation actions), and IT enables such new arrangements and offers the potential to reshape how value can be created in collaborative relationships (Fig. 1). This co-created value exists when several firms, interacting with each other through IT, work together to create value that is greater than the sum of the value generated by single firms.

4 Methodology

4.1 Research Design and Data Collection

We adopted a theory-building case study methodology (Eisenhardt, 1989) to provide in-depth understanding of the IT-enabled value co-creation phenomenon in the tourism industry. We ground the discussion in a case history of Portale Sardegna, an Italian online tour operator on the island of Sardinia. In 2004, Portale Sardegna launched a new product, Open Voucher (OV), with the bold objective of prolonging the tourist season on the island, because Sardinia's tourism sector suffers from strong seasonal flux. The idea was conceptually simple—to create a Sardinian tourist product capable of attracting travellers to the island during the low season (autumn and winter). Our objective was to demonstrate why comparable hotels showed different abilities in appropriating of value co-created.

Table 1 Summary of the interviews administered to Portale Sardegna

Interviewee	Position
Interviewee A	Portale Sardegna's CEO
Interviewee B	Open Voucher's COO
Interviewee C	Portale Sardegna's Director of Group Travel

Table 2 Summary of the interviews administered to hotels

Star	Hotel	Performance	Number of hotel guests through OV	Number of room	Hotel guests/room
4	S1	Successful	749	29	25.8
4	U1	Unsuccessful	93	30	3.12
3	S2	Successful	168	12	14
3	U2	Unsuccessful	2	29	0.06
4	S3	Successful	749	58	12.91
4	U3	Unsuccessful	63	95	0.66
3	S4	Successful	429	20	21.45
3	U4	Unsuccessful	45	34	1.32
3	S5	Successful	459	22	20.86
3	U5	Unsuccessful	0	20	0.0

Portale Sardegna attempted this de-seasonalization through the development of an Internet-enabled network of affiliated hotels, providing availability of rooms year round, and offering its product through the OV platform at a low, fixed rate of 29,90€ per person, per day in a 3-star hotel for the autumn/winter season and 39,90€ in spring, including car rental. Unlike other online travel agents in Sardinia, OV allows tourists to plan a personalized itinerary in which they can change hotels daily to enjoy different parts of the island.

We collected data through interviews and secondary sources. The primary source was semi-structured interviews with individual respondents. Thirteen interviews were conducted over the telephone between July and October 2009, including three interviews with co-founders of Portale Sardegna and ten with the managements at the hotels participating in OV (Tables 1 and 2).

The sample hotels are selected based on a polar-type research design (Eisenhardt, 1989). With the help from Portale Sardegna, we identified hotels that, despite similar characteristics in terms of stars and the geographical locations, showed significant difference in performance (Table 2). We chose to select hotels based on the performance in 2008 instead of the most successful year (2006) because it was important to evaluate whether the good performance was due to the novelty of the product or the hotel's long-term appreciation by the market. Based on our definition of value in terms of financial performance, we used the number of hotel guests booked through OV, standardized by the size of the hotels (number of rooms), as a measure of value co-created. We divided these hotels into two groups based on financial performance: successful and unsuccessful ones. In this way, we were able to set up comparisons for five pairs of hotels.

To conduct the semi-structured interviews, two common protocols were adopted. The first protocol was employed for the interviews administered to Portale Sardegna's chief executive officer (CEO), OV's chief operating officer (COO), and Portale Sardegna's director of group travel. The second semi-structured interview protocol was adopted for the interviews with the officials from the hotels that had implemented OV. The interview script for the hotels was developed from one pilot interview. All interviews were recorded and transcribed. These data sources were supplemented with archival information from the OV's CEO.

5 Data Analysis and Findings

Qualitative data analysis was carried out using QSR Nvivo8, with no a priori hypotheses. We compared the hotels to identify the emerging constructs (Strauss and Corbin, 1998) and the number of references found for each in the source documents (Table 3) that would be relevant to the IT-based value co-creation. We then devised a case study for each hotel and used the method of within- and cross-case analysis (Eisenhardt, 1989) to analyze them. From within-case analyses, we gained a deeper understanding of the processes of value co-creation each organization underwent. The outcomes of the within-case analyses were then compared with the cross-case analysis to improve rigor and quality of results (Tables 4, 5, 6, and 7). This approach gave us the opportunity to highlight the similarities and differences among hotels and to indicate the factors important to IT-enabled value co-creation.

One foundational premise of S-D logic is that "the enterprise can only make value propositions" (Vargo and Lusch, 2004, p. 11). It is obvious that, in this case, Portale Sardegna does not deliver value, but only offers value propositions. Value is created by the interaction of a number of organizations (airlines, car rentals, hotels) and participation from travelers who customize their holiday package by choosing their own travel itinerary and hotels that best suit their accommodation needs. The novel arrangement of partnership is enabled by IT. The interviews performed with the executives of OV demonstrated that the launch of OV would not be possible without the Internet. More specifically, the CEO of OV stated:

> It would have been impossible to provide the same service without the Internet. It was the only way to sell Sardinia at a low price and with an itinerant package. The same product provided by a travel agency would have been more expensive and difficult to assemble.

Similarly, the COO of OV recalled:

> Internet is essential for us [. . .]. This technology allows us to satisfy the requirements of immediacy, simplicity, and low cost of our main customers.

Table 3 Number of references to co-creation of value	Nodes	Source	References
	Partner readiness	10	11
	Business alignment	10	15
	Strategic fit	10	17
	Synergy	10	17

Table 4 Matrix of cross-case analysis linking value co-creation and strategic fit

Hotels	Insights
S1	*"The OV product allows the hotel to have a reason to be open because it provides a continuous flow of incoming tourists."*
U1	*"They didn't make us work at all. They were interested in sending guests to other hotels."*
S2	*"The tourist season in Sardinia ends during the month of September. The collaboration with OV is an incentive to attract tourists to Sardinia during low season."*
U2	*"We decided to accept the OV offer in spite of the fact that the prices were low; we thought that we could recover some of the earnings with the meals. The results were totally unsatisfactory."*
S3	*"We have the same objective. With year-round opening, the proposal provided by OV, which enables guests to arrive during the low season, is like a ray of sunshine on a rainy day."*
U3	*"We decided to collaborate with OV only to increase our profits."*
S4	*"The out-of-season is our major objective. OV's offer was the answer to our needs: that is, to be able to keep the hotel opens year round."*
U4	*"We started to collaborate with OV because we thought that it could help us to keep the hotel open during the low season, but our expectations were not completely satisfied."*
S5	*"Operating with OV enables us to keep our hotels open during the low season."*
U5	*"[...] Our objectives differ from those of OV operators. They aren't interested in what months guests arrive. We are interested only in the low-season months."*

The above statements point out that the Internet allowed the followings: a quick and immediate response by all partners involved; immediate access to the OV package by travellers; completeness of the offer (hotel and car); and time-saving aspects for the travellers.

Originally, the sales in hotels in Sardinia were so low during winter that most hotels had to close during the low season. The launch on OV has generated business for Sardinia tourism industry. Indeed, the numbers grew rapidly, reaching 1287 bookings during the first year of activity (2005) and 2266 the next. Specifically, more OV packages were sold during the low seasons than during the high seasons because, during the high seasons (July and August), hotels can sell their rooms without the help of an intermediary at the highest price. This phenomenon is relevant to explain that co-creation of value during the low season was accomplished through the collaboration of different partners taking part in the OV initiative.

Table 5 Matrix of cross-case analysis linking value co-creation and synergy

Hotels	Insights
S1	*"The positive results obtained by using OV are determined by the consistent attitude of the hotels that joined the initiative and also by the professional expertise of Portale Sardegna in the management of collaboration among partners."*
U1	*"The element that created great resistance toward OV is that they requested our hotel's availability to achieve their personal interests."*
S2	*"Each partner involved in the selling of the OV product is responsible for 50 % of final results."*
U2	–
S3	*"The positive results are due to both players (hotels and OV), since it is important for both players to act in synergy."*
U3	*"OV is only an additional distribution channel for us; it allows for greater visibility and advertising opportunities."*
S4	*"All together (hotels, OV, car rental,) we contribute to reaching the final goal. None of us could have individually reached such positive results."*
U4	*"OV allowed us to complete our offer. By using OV we were able to have a 5 % increase in presences, which is no mean achievement for a small hotel as we are."*
S5	*"The hotels, car rentals, and the services provided by OV are all important for the success of this initiative. Indeed, customer satisfaction is generated by the entire holiday package."*
U5	*"We believe that the positive results obtained with the OV products are not synergistic. Those that have the best outcome are Portale Sardegna and Geasar."*

The hyphen (−) indicates that no statements were provided by interviewees

Table 6 Matrix of cross-case analysis linking value co-creation and process alignment

Hotels	Insights
S1	*"Use of the online booking system has become vital for our business. Traditional travel agencies are superseded."*
U1	*"We didn't understand to what point the technology was useful for the management of our business."*
S2	*"The control panel employed by OV for the bookings makes all our tasks much easier. It is not, however, a true innovation. Nowadays, it is become essential for the management of our business."*
U2	*[...] "Knowing how to use the technology is not of great help in our business."*
S3	*"OV's software has its advantages: You can access the Web site at any time and change accommodation availability. Furthermore, it allows you to make fewer mistakes. The more the system allows you to operate in the best possible way, the more this creates an advantage for your guests. "*
U3	–
S4	–
U4	–
S5	*"The control panel used by OV helped us to better manage our bookings and the services offered to our guests."*
U5	*"We use all major online channels such as Booking.com and Expedia. By using more than one channel, we can attract more guests to the island."*

The hyphen (−) indicates that no statements were provided by interviewees

Table 7 Matrix of cross-case analysis linking value co-creation and partner readiness

Hotels	Insights
S1	*"In order to create value by using the OV offer, flexibility is essential. This trait is of fundamental importance to manage the online booking system."*
U1	*"We are not well acquainted with the platform; nobody ever explained to us how accommodation availability should be entered online."*
S2	*"Even before starting our collaboration with OV, we knew how to use the software that allowed us to manage the booking of guests online."*
U2	*"Particular competencies are not at all useful in order to create value with OV. Being able to use the technology helps very little."*
S3	*"To create value by using OV, it is important to understand the importance of using the Internet."*
U3	*"I cannot underline any particular skill that could allow us to improve the value created by using OV."*
S4	*"We have never had any kind of problem in collaborating with OV and in interacting within the control platform."*
U4	*"Our hotel uses different booking channels, similar to OV. Interacting with the control panel utilized by OV didn't create any problems at all."*
S5	*"Some hotels are not able to create value with OV because they don't understand to what extent their Web site represents a showcase for guests. We have understood well how to interact with the Internet."*
U5	*"Customers were used, with other systems like booking.com, to receive immediate responses. [. . . second] customers increasingly ask to build their itinerary directly online [. . .] [this technology] helps us and helps them."*

6 Key Factors for Successful Co-creation of Value

While the above market responses illustrated the positive value co-creation, some of the hotels benefits more than the others through OV. Our objective was to demonstrate why comparable hotels showed different abilities in appropriating of value co-created. With this in mind, we structured the following section based on the key factors that emerged from the qualitative data analysis, as listed below: Strategic fit, Synergy, Process alignment, Partner readiness.

6.1 Strategic Fit

The concept of fit has received considerable attention in the literature. Studies (Chandler, 1962; Lawrence & Lorsch, 1967; Thompson, 1967; Smith & Reeceb, 1999) defined this concept as the synchronization between the organizational structure, strategy, and/or the wider environment (external fit) and the harmony among groups or units within the organization (internal fit). Based on the grounds on which this work was conceived, strategic fit may be defined as the degree to which the objectives of one company within the partnership are consistent with objectives of another company.

The evidence regarding strategic fit (Table 4) suggested that there were substantial differences in terms of strategic fit between successful (S) and unsuccessful hotels (U).

Successful hotels (S1, S2, S3, S4, S5) demonstrated a higher level of strategic fit compared to unsuccessful ones (U1, U2, U3, U4, U5). The former stated that their objectives were in line with those of OV; the latter, with one exception (i.e., U5), asserted that they have different goals or that their objectives were at least partially in line with those of OV. A relevant comment is from the director of Hotel S3: *"We have the same objective. With an opening year round, the proposal provided by OV, which allows for guests to arrive during the low season, is like a ray of sunshine on a rainy day."*

Another meaningful statement, which was given by an unsuccessful hotel director (U5), is the following: *"Our objectives differ from those of OV operators. They aren't interested in what months guests arrive. We are only interested in the low-season months."*

6.2 Synergy

One of the fundamental reasons why two firms combine their resources is to create value by pursuing the potential synergy existing between them. Synergy refers to the condition whereby the combination of two firms' resources is potentially more efficient than those of either firm operating independently. Usually, synergy exists when firm resources are different but interdependent and mutually supportive (Tanriverdi & Venkatraman, 2005). An example of synergy in a business context of service is elevated service offerings, "defined as a new or enhanced service offering that can only eventuate as a result of a collaborative arrangement, one that could not otherwise be delivered on individual organizational merits" (Agarwal & Selen, 2009, p. 432).

In our sample (Table 5), successful hotel managers acknowledge the higher value they were capable of attaining within their business because of the collaboration among different partners with different expertise and competence.

The statements provided by the director of Hotel S1 are quite meaningful in this sense: *"The positive results obtained by using OV are determined by the consistent attitude of the hotels that joined the initiative and also by the professional expertise of Portale Sardegna in the management of collaboration among partners."* The insights provided by the director of Hotel S4 are quite significant as well: *"All together (hotels, OV, car rental), we contribute to reaching the final goal. None of us could have individually reached such positive results."* At the same time, it is also clear that, among the unsuccessful hotels, there was not a full understanding of the increased value that could have been obtained by operating together, but rather the belief that they would have reached more or less the same goals without collaboration. In line with this issue, a particularly interesting comment by the director of Hotel U3 deserves to be highlighted: *"OV is only an additional distribution channel for us; it allows for greater visibility and advertising opportunities."*

It should also be pointed out that among unsuccessful hotels (i.e. U5) there was the strong idea that the collaboration did not create any type of synergy at all, but advantages for only a few partners and not all those involved in the initiative.

6.3   Process Alignment

We defined process alignment as the degree of fit between business processes and underlying technology assets to facilitate online transactions and sharing of, and access to, strategic and tactical information (Barua et al., 2004). By referring to the above-mentioned context, we can also pinpoint a number of differences between successful and unsuccessful hotels (Table 6).

The successful hotel owners clearly demonstrated that they understood the importance of IT in better managing their business, and they considered both the software and the control panel used by Open Voucher to be useful tools that allowed them to improve the management of bookings and offer higher quality services to guests.

Some of the statements provided by successful hoteliers were in line with the concept of process alignment, as in the case of the director of Hotel S3: *"OV's software has its advantages: You can access the Web site at any time and change accommodation availability. Furthermore, it allows you to make fewer mistakes. The more the system allows you to operate in the best of ways, the more this creates an advantage for your guests."*

The director of Hotel S2 had an opinion similar to that of the director of Hotel S3: *"The control panel employed by OV for the bookings makes all of our tasks much easier."*

On the other hand, the unsuccessful hotel operators demonstrated, with only one exception (U5), that they hadn't fully understood the importance of the use of technology to conduct their business as required by the market. An example of this view is provided by the director of Hotel U1: *"We didn't understand to what point the technology was useful for the management of our business."*

6.4   Partner Readiness

The management of information systems literature (Davis, 1989) has demonstrated that cognitive perceptions of technology, such as usefulness or ease of use, influence individuals' intent to use technology. In this paper, according to the literature, we used the concept of partner readiness to refer to the degree to which firms, customers, and suppliers are willing and ready to conduct business activities electronically (Barua et al., 2004).

The willingness of the hotels to use technology to operate their businesses is certainly an important element in understanding the ways in which IT can support the co-creation of value (Table 7). The hotels that refused to acknowledge the utility of technology to improve their business practices were, in fact, not able to completely take advantage of the opportunities of working within a partnership environment in which customer and partner relations of those involved were accomplished online.

As for this instance, it is important to highlight the statement provided by the director of Hotel U1: *"We are not well acquainted with the OV's platform. Nobody ever explained to us how accommodation availability should be entered online."*

Conversely, the hotels that took full advantage of the given opportunity were those that had a positive perception and that had fully acknowledged the use of technology. This can be seen from the statement provided by the director of Hotel S5: *"Some hotels are not able to create value with OV because they don't understand to what extent their Web site represents a showcase for guests. We have understood well how to interact with the Internet."*

7 Conclusion

Our goal in this paper was to explore the key successful factors of IT-enabled value co-creation within an inter-organizational context. In particular, the case study of Open Voucher has allowed us understand the fundamental role played by technology in the co-creation of value. When considering the statements provided by Portale Sardegna CEOs, it appears quite clear that the same results could not have been achieved without the use of IT. It is also clear that, in this case, IT was used as a tool for the creation of a travel product which in turn co-created business value (i.e., brought more tourists to the island).

Even though researchers (Devaraj & Kohli, 2002) have pinpointed a number of factors (IS-strategy alignment, organizational and process change, process performance, information sharing, IT usage) that are generally accepted as key conditions that lead to IT value creation, the key factors of IT-based value co-creation that emerged from this study provide new insights to the issues under investigation.

With regard to strategic fit, many past studies have examined the fit between a company's business strategic goals and its IS goals. In this paper, we demonstrated that the fit among the strategic goals of partnering hotels is achieved whenever the goals of one hotel can be reached only through the participation of all other hotels sharing the same project. However, when the participating firms have a different structure, strategy, or external environment, strategic fit is more difficult to achieve than the strategic fit involving only one firm. When the boundaries among companies become blurred by the advent of information technology, how can firms ensure that the objectives of one company within a partnership are consistent with the objectives of the other companies becomes an important issue. Second, as to synergy, our results were in line with existing literature (Tanriverdi &

Venkatraman, 2005; Nevo and Wade, 2010). It is evident from our work that market response was enhanced by the contributions of hotels, car rental companies, and airlines that make their resources available to all partners to attract tourists to Sardinia. The same results could not have been obtained without the involvement and contributions provided by all partners in the relationship. With the help of IT, there is more potential for different kinds of collaboration in terms of resources sharing to enhance synergy (Cabiddu & Piccoli, 2010; Cabiddu, Lui, & Piccoli, 2013).

When considering the third key factor, process alignment, our results pinpointed that the more the technology matches the business process that users must perform, the greater the positive impact on financial performance from its use. These findings are consistent with IS theory concerning task-technology fit (Goodhue and Thompson, 1995). However, the level of difficulty increases when multiple firms are involved. Each firm has its own way to conduct business. The underlying technology that aims to facilitate multiple firms' business processes will inherently produce a different fit with different firms. Therefore, how to optimize the degree of fit between business processes *in different firms* and the underlying technology that enables collaboration among these firms to facilitate transactions and the sharing of information should be studied.

Finally, with regard to partner readiness, our findings highlighted that the greater the perception of usefulness and ease of use of technology, the greater the propensity to embrace technology by the partners involved. The technology readiness index (Parasuraman, 2000), a key factor in adopting and embracing technologically innovative products and services, indicates the same result. In the case of OV, the successful hotels expressed *optimism* (the degree to which one believes that the technology offers increased control, flexibility, and efficiency) to OV, while the unsuccessful hotels (e.g., U2) showed *insecurity* (distrust of technology) by indicating that using the technology helps very little. Therefore, for a firm to take advantage of the IT-enabled value co-created, the employees have to be technology ready, which means that they need to understand the benefits delivered by the technology and be willing to act as a technology pioneer. Based on our results, we can assert that managers should find ways to implement the key factors highlighted in this paper to enhance the realization of the value co-created in inter-firm relationships. One core factor is the development of partner readiness. Managers should take advantage of partnership opportunities in which customer and partner relations are accomplished online.

This chapter has presented an exploratory study into how information technology may play a central role in terms of co-creation value within an inter-organizational context. The evidence from the 13 interviews suggested that the factors (strategic fit, synergy, process alignment, partner readiness) presented in this article are the elements enabling the co-creation value and are likely to be of interest to the researcher dealing with these issues. This study also has its limitations. The first limitation is related to the research context. The qualitative and empirical data analysis was undertaken with data collected from a single tourist service provider and its partner organizations. To further foster the multidisciplinary debate yet maintain a link with practice, future researchers may want to explore the gathering of data from the entire tourist industry sector and partner organizations and to consider other service sectors or cross-service industry collaborations, as well as those organizations for which collaboration is pivotal to success. This may also include additional data collection from the travellers' side. This further research could improve or expand our finding in several ways.

Acknowledgements Financial support from the Regional Law 7 August 2007, n., 41 "Promozione della ricerca scientifica e dell'innovazione tecnologica in Sardegna" is gratefully acknowledged.

References

Agarwal, R., & Selen, W. (2009). Dynamic capability building in service value networks for achieving service innovation. *Decision Sciences, 40*(3), 431–456.

Barua, A., Konana, P., Whinston, A. B., & Yin, F. (2004). An empirical investigation of net-enabled business value. *Mis Quarterly, 28*(4), 585–620.

Buhalis, D. (1998). Strategic use of information technologies in the tourism industry. *Tourism Management, 19*(5), 409–421.

Cabiddu, F., Lui, T., & Piccoli, G. (2013). Managing value co-creation in the tourism industry. *Annals of Tourism Research, 42*, 86–107.

Cabiddu, F., & Piccoli, G. (2010). Open voucher and the tourism season in Sardinia. *Communications of the Association for Information Systems, 27*(24), 437–454.

Chandler, A. D. (1962). *Strategy and structure*. Cambridge, MA: MIT Press.

Davis, F. D. (1989). Perceived usefulness, perceived ease of use, and user acceptance of information technology. *MIS Quarterly, 13*, 319–340.

Devaraj, S., & Kohli, R. (2002). *The IT payoff: Measuring business value of information technology investment*. Upper Saddle River, NJ: Financial, Times Prentice-Hall.

Devaraj, S., & Kohli, R. (2003). Performance impacts of information technology: Is actual usage the missing link? *Management Science, 49*(3), 273–289.

Dos Santos, B. L. (2003). Information technology investments: Characteristics, choices, market risk and value. *Information Systems Frontiers, 5*(3), 289–301.

Eisenhardt, K. M. (1989). Building theories from case study research. *Academy of Management Review, 14*(4), 488–511.

Gebauer, J., & Buxmann, P. (1999). Assessing the value of interorganizational systems to support business transactions. *International Journal of Electronic Commerce, 4*(4), 61–82.

Goodhue, D. L., & Thompson, R. L. (1995). Task-technology fit and individual performance. *MIS Quarterly, 19*, 213–236.

Hitt, L. M., & Brynjolfsson, E. (1996). Productivity, business profitability, and consumer surplus: Three different measures of information technology value. *MIS Quarterly, 20*(2), 121–142.

Kohli, R., & Grover, V. (2008). Business value of IT: An essay on expanding research directions to keep up with the times. *Journal of the Association of Information Systems, 9*(1), 23–39.

Lawrence, P. R., & Lorsch, J. W. (1967). *Organization and environment*. Boston, MA: Harvard Graduate School of Business Administration.

Melville, N., Kraemer, K., & Gurbaxani, V. (2004). Review: Information technology and organizational performance: An integrative model of IT business value. *MIS Quarterly, 28*(2), 283–322.

Nevo, S., & Wade, M. R. (2010). The formation and value of IT-enabled resources: Antecedents and consequences. *Management Information Systems Quarterly, 34*(1), 10.

Parasuraman, A. (2000). Technology readiness index (TRI) a multiple-item scale to measure readiness to embrace new technologies. *Journal of Service Research, 2*(4), 307–320.

Santhanam, R., & Hartono, E. (2003). Issues in linking information technology capability to firm performance. *MIS Quarterly, 27*(1), 125–153.

Sharaf, N., Langdon, C. S., & Gosain, S. (2007). IS application capabilities and relational value in interfirm partnerships. *Information System Research, 18*(3), 320–339.

Sircar, S., Turnbow, J. L., & Bordoloi, B. (2000). A framework for assessing the relationship between information technology investments and firm performance. *Journal of Management Information Systems, 16*, 69–97.

Smith, T. M., & Reeceb, J. S. (1999). The relationship of strategy, fit, productivity and business performance in a services setting. *Journal of Operations Management, 17*(2), 145–161.

Strauss, A., & Corbin, J. (1998). *Basics of qualitative research: Procedures and techniques for developing grounded theory*. Thousand Oaks, CA: Sage.

Tanriverdi, H., & Venkatraman, N. V. (2005). Knowledge relatedness and the performance of multibusiness firms. *Strategic Management Journal, 26*(2), 97–119.

Thompson, J. D. (1967). *Organizations in action*. New York: McGraw-Hill.

Vargo, S. L., & Lusch, R. F. (2004). Evolving to a new dominant logic for marketing. *Journal of Marketing, 68*(1), 1–17.

Vargo, S. L., & Lusch, R. F. (2008a). Service-dominant logic: Continuing the evolution. *Journal of the Academy of Marketing Science, 36*(1), 1–10.

Vargo, S. L., & Lusch, R. F. (2008b). From goods to service(s): Divergences and convergences of logics. *Industrial Marketing Management, 37*(3), 254–259.

Werthner, H., & Klein, S. (1999). *Information technology and tourism - A challenging relationship* (Springer computer science). New York: Springer.

Open Source Marketing in Tourism: Motivational Drivers and Practical Approaches

Klaus-Peter Wiedmann and Sascha Langner

1 Introduction

The Internet and its possibilities for interaction have a profound impact on consumer behavior. Initially driven by an information- and transaction-related focus, the World Wide Web increasingly reveals its true strength: social networking between individuals and organizations. The creation of communities is expanding, forums and weblogs are gaining considerable attention, and digital versions of social networks, such as Facebook.com, are maintaining billions of registered users. In the tourism sector, the networking of consumers is booming. Millions of people use and appreciate communities to make travel arrangements, including the exchange of feedback on platforms such as Tripadvisor.com and Oyster.com, or communities to plan and organize individual and group travel, such as Couchsurfing.com, Triporama.com, Globalzoo.de, Trippy.com, or Gogobot.com.

In the course of this development, network-related marketing has received growing attention in the tourism sector. A central question emerges: How can we effectively market products and services with the help of communities? In particular, how can the enormous marketing potential of thousands of community members be usefully integrated into the traditional marketing of tourism companies?

A promising approach is found in the "*veterans*" of social interaction on the Internet, the open source networks. Founded as a counterpart to classical software engineering (e.g., Windows vs. Linux or Internet Explorer vs. Firefox), these communities began the early implementation of collaborative development projects. Furthermore, the marketing of community results is organized and implemented collectively in open source networks with remarkable success.

K.-P. Wiedmann • S. Langner (✉)
Leibniz University of Hannover, Hannover, Germany
e-mail: wiedmann@m2.uni-hannover.de; langner@m2.uni-hannover.de

© Springer-Verlag Berlin Heidelberg 2016
R. Egger et al. (eds.), *Open Tourism*, Tourism on the Verge,
DOI 10.1007/978-3-642-54089-9_5

The browser Firefox, which was marketed only with community funds, has displaced Microsoft's long-time number-one browser, Internet Explorer, in browser rankings. Similarly, the independent third-party operating system Linux has become a global brand. The collaborative marketing approach of free communities is generally referred to as "*open source marketing*". Contrary to what one might expect, this form of marketing, which is based on the ideals of the open source movement, is suitable for many areas of commercial businesses as well as non-profit projects.

In this context, and with particular attention to research on motivation in open source communities in general and open source-marketing projects in particular, this article aims to present interesting approaches to open source-oriented marketing in the tourism market. Why do consumers participate in marketing-oriented open source networks? On which network characteristics is individual participation based? What are the underlying causes and motivational drivers that companies can specifically address to motivate consumers toward voluntary participation in marketing processes?

2 Open Source Networks and Marketing

In recent years, attention to open source networks has grown steadily. But what makes these networks so special? Founded spontaneously, open source networks recruit their members on a voluntary basis and avoid strict copyright standards in favor of more flexible usage rights for less restrictive use of their intellectual and creative work (see Perens, 1999; Open Source Initiative, 2006). Collaborative open source networks, such as Linux, Apache, or Typo 3, have shown that a large and complex system of software code can be built, preserved, and developed in a decentralized way through a worldwide network of programmers and that this system can grow and evolve continuously with the help of the network, even though most participants in the community do not receive payment (e.g., Lerner & Tirole, 2002; Weber, 2004; Feller & Fitzgerald, 2002; Raymond, 2001).

Today the open source movement is no longer confined to software. Many communities exist as collaborative networks in a variety of application areas, such as groups of creatives who generate texts, videos, images, or audio sources under public licenses (see e.g. creativecommons.org or youtube.com), as educational networks (e.g., MIT Open Courseware), as travel communities (e.g. Travellerspoint.com, Tripadvisor.com or Wikitravel.com) or as cooperative marketing communities (e.g., Mozilla's SpreadFirefox.com, P&G's Vocalpoint/ Tremor, or Converse's conversegallery.com). Open source networks are so promising that many companies, such as IBM and Red Hat, base their business models on them (e.g., the Linux kernel). It is therefore not surprising that businesses and large open source communities increasingly attempt to use open source principles for the efficient marketing of their products and/or services.

Fig. 1 SpreadFirefox.com—collaborative marketing headquarters of the open source browser (*Source*: SpreadFirefox.com, 2009)

A well-known company whose marketing efforts are completely based on an open source framework is the Mozilla Foundation. This non-profit company organizes, coordinates, and manages the development of the web browser Firefox. With a market share of ca. 20 %, Firefox is number two on the worldwide browser market today (source: Netmarketshare.com, July 2013) (Fig. 1).

The focus of Mozilla's innovative concept is the website "*SpreadFirefox.com*", the Internet headquarters of many global marketing activities that aim to increase the number of users (Lieb, 2004).

When Mozilla began marketing its browser Firefox in September 2004, its goal was to jointly plan and coordinate the marketing for Firefox by consistently using the rules of success in open source development (see Weber, 2004, pp. 128 ff.). The non-profit company founded a community, established the basis for a constructive exchange of ideas among members, and integrated mechanisms for their motivation and the selection of proposals. Mozilla accomplished this mainly through forums, blogs, and chats on SpreadFirefox.com.

In a next step, working groups of volunteers were formed whose task was to evaluate topic-specific ideas, to develop substantive details, and to coordinate practical implementation with the help of community members (see Mucha, 2004). Much of what Mozilla needed to plan in terms of the strategic framework or artwork for marketing activities was determined in working groups and allocated as work packages to appropriate community members.

Although this may sound bureaucratic, upon closer inspection, it was a vital evolutionary process. In its main phase from 2004 to 2009, the project established more than 150 different working groups with specific regional and international marketing foci.

The working groups organized themselves in extensive marketing activities (such as ways and means of disseminating the browser on CD-ROM and DVD media from computer magazines, promotion at trade shows, etc.). They also designed strategies and tactics that any webmaster could use to increase the awareness and distribution of Firefox (for example via banners, buttons, e-mail signatures, etc.).

The results were substantial. As a result of the collaborative marketing efforts, Mozilla's servers counted more than 100 million downloads in the first 12 months. Today, more than 450 million people worldwide use Firefox.

Thanks to their enormous passion for the project, members of the community even funded a costly two-page ad in the New York Times in 2004 ("*Firefox Advocacy Ad Campaign*") to promote the official launch of the Firefox 1 browser (see Kucuk & Krishnamurthy, 2006).

To motivate the individual members of the community in the long term, SpreadFirefox.com used simple reward systems. Every member of the community was assigned a unique ID. Members who integrated a button (with their specific ID) to the download page of the browser on their websites received one point for each triggered download. The attraction of new community members, working in the community, and even special services to the community were rewarded with points as well.

Based on the points, a ranking of all participants was formed. The websites of the 250 most active members were named and linked on the SpreadFirefox.com site (Google PageRank 8). To ensure that new members had a chance, developments in the previous 7 days, not the total number of points, was used for the ranking. There was also a second ranking that listed only the most dedicated new members.

In addition to the advantages of PageRank 8 links for search engine marketing, a high score served to attract new customers. The site views of SpreadFirefox.com (approximately 50,000–100,000 per day) ensured a continuous flow of visitors to the members' own websites. For those who did not like such rewards and gained a certain number of points, the community offered rewards such as merchandise items (e.g. limited editions of T-shirts, stuffed animals, etc.), an exclusive Firefox. com e-mail address, or the opportunity to win prizes, such as an iPod (Fig. 2).

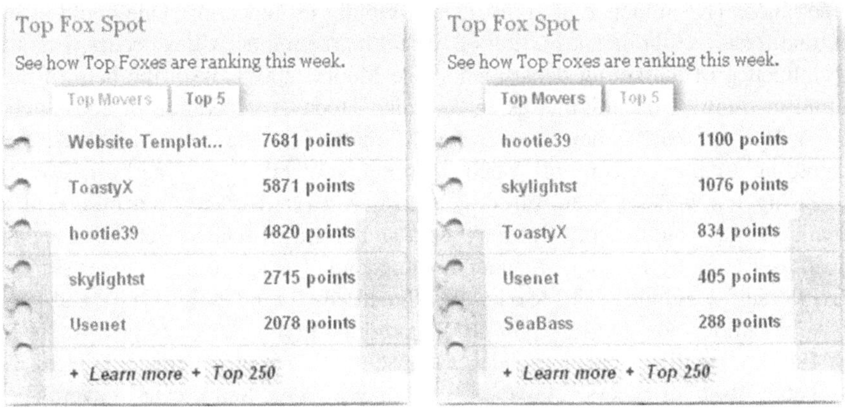

Top Fox Spot			Top Fox Spot		
See how Top Foxes are ranking this week.			See how Top Foxes are ranking this week.		
Top Movers	Top 5		Top Movers	Top 5	
Website Templat...	7681 points		hootie39	1100 points	
ToastyX	5871 points		skylightst	1076 points	
hootie39	4820 points		ToastyX	834 points	
skylightst	2715 points		Usenet	405 points	
Usenet	2078 points		SeaBass	288 points	
+ Learn more + Top 250			+ Learn more + Top 250		

Fig. 2 Top 5 members of the Firefox community (*Source*: SpreadFirefox.com, 2009)

Although a lot of development, planning, and implementation processes could be transferred to the community, there were still areas in which Mozilla had to act on its own. Many practical operations were therefore initiated and coordinated by the company's employees to ensure efficient results (see Mucha, 2004). For example, the adoption of some marketing elements by the community succeeded only partially. It was quite unlikely that one of the community members would have good contacts with national newspapers such as the *New York Times*. As part of its public relations, the *SpreadFirefox* community encouraged members to write reader's letters on thematically appropriate articles to draw attention to the new browser. However, this approach was questionable because it was uncertain whether responsible journalists saw this feedback as an incentive to write articles about the browser on their own. Many community ideas also lacked the necessary funding. Therefore, the open source project was dependent on donations to implement costly marketing ideas (e.g., placing advertisements online and offline).

Despite these limitations, from a marketing perspective, the following questions arise: What motivates consumers to participate in the joint development of marketing strategies and tactics? And: Do open source ideals provide alternative ways for companies to address their target groups in a more specific and authentic way through the active interaction of consumers in marketing processes?

3   Open Source Marketing: A Collaborative Marketing Approach

3.1   Theoretical Framework

Whether it involves product searches or the selection of a new merchant, in terms of consumer decisions, the exchange between customers has gained considerable importance. The influence of companies is rapidly disappearing. One could even say that today, a significant portion of typical marketing activities occurs without the influence of marketing departments (see Moore, 2003). With the help of the digital medium of the Internet as an *"enabler"*, today's generation of consumers increasingly practices their own types of marketing and product discussion. According to the concept of "open sourcing yourself" (see Cherkoff, 2005), increasing numbers of users offer their own generated content on community portals such as youtube.com and flickr.com and on travel-related websites such as tripadvisor.com, trippy.com, and couchsurfing.com. The spectrum includes simple reviews, self-developed sales texts and commercials (brand enthusiasm), and parodies of famous ads that misappropriate corporate brand messages (see Kahney, 2004). The positive consumer-side response to this user-generated content is evident in its high access rates (see Blackshaw, 2004). Self-created advertising materials are often exponentially distributed via the most highly linked communication media of consumers, such as blogs, forums, or fan pages on e.g. Facebook. com and it is not uncommon for these to gain media attention (see Cherkov, 2005). Compared with professional corporate campaigns, many consumers prefer "user-generated content" and semi-professional marketing ideas because they seem real and credible and because they are not suspected of having an economic motive (see Blackshaw, 2004).

The concept of open source-oriented marketing addresses these developments and links them with the ideas, ideals, and success factors of the open source movement. The purpose of this movement is the collaborative and authentic achievement of the objectives of traditional marketing management through community-organized processes. Through the active integration of consumers in the planning and implementation processes of marketing in the context of an open source network, the ongoing trend toward consumer empowerment is achieved, resistance toward marketing and advertising can be reduced, and, in a win-win situation, the creative human resources of consumers can be used efficiently (see Cherkoff, 2005; Christ, 2004).

Open source marketing encompasses normative, strategic, and operational levels. The normative level is of particular importance because open source marketing brings a fundamental change of attitude toward marketing, including fewer restrictions in the form of copyright in favor of a free exchange of ideas and less predictability in favor of improved customer orientation (see Brøndmo, 2004). That is, the customers of a company actively participate in the marketing of the company's products, and everyone working in the company is happy about the fact that customers are participating.

In terms of its strategic components, open source marketing refers to the collective and collaborative planning and specification of marketing objectives, strategies, and activities within an open source network. Based on its operational level, open source marketing includes the jointly organized, creatively designed implementation of marketing activities through the flexible use of copyright standards (Source: CreativeCommons.org, 2009).

More generally, open source marketing includes the following:

- Free access to marketing materials that are no longer protected by restrictive copyright standards but are available to consumers through a flexible license
- Permission for and promotion of derivatives for further developments of advertisements, text, and logos
- Free access to advertisements or banners as well as storyboards, animations, text, or sound recordings on the company's website
- The opportunity to discuss all relevant elements of collaborative marketing management in forums, chats, and blogs

To summarize, open source marketing primarily means "letting go". The target group is not only permitted but also prompted to improve the company's own marketing concepts with additions, enhancements, parodies, or criticism.

3.2   Motivation of Users in Open Source Marketing Projects

The project "Spread Firefox" by Mozilla is a good example of how open source marketing can work. However, a non-profit company has a great advantage: it does not follow a drive for profit maximization, as do most private companies. No one except the community itself benefits from the development and marketing of the browser. Is it conceivable that companies such as Expedia, Thomas Cook, or Orbitz could integrate open source ideas in their marketing under these conditions?

One thing is certain: no customer will voluntarily act in the interests of a private company whose only aim is to save money. This situation raises the question of whether and under what conditions consumers would participate in the marketing of products and services. To answer this question, it is useful to consider the motivating reasons for individuals to participate in an open source project as well as to provide a brief overview of the current technical opportunities for communication and participation.

A number of economic and non-economic approaches to explain the motives for participation in open source projects have been developed (see Weber, 2004, pp. 135–149; Lerner & Tirole, 2002; Ghosh, Glott, Krieger, & Robles, 2002 and part II Lakhani & Wolf, 2005; Hertel, Niedner, & Herrmann, 2003; Wiedmann, Langner, & Hennigs, 2007). Some of these are theoretically based, whereas others are based on initial empirical results. Numerous and occasionally very different motivational drivers for collaborative participation in open source marketing projects have been identified. These drivers can be reduced to three dimensions:

- *Pragmatic motivation*—This includes all motives resulting from a direct benefit to participating consumers, such as a specific reward for their work.
- *Social motivation*—These motives arise from the exchange relationships among community members, such as processes of identification or mutual aid and recognition.
- *Hedonic motivation*—This includes all subjects that result from emotional aspects, such as motives for the fun of group work or enthusiasm for a brand.

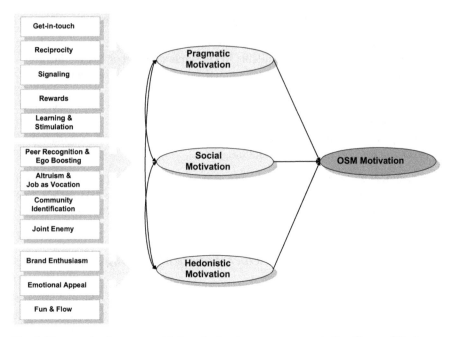

Fig. 3 Framework of consumer-sided motivation in open source marketing (*Source*: Wiedmann et al., 2007)

In the following, these three dimensions are briefly described (for details, see Wiedmann & Langner, 2006b; Wiedmann et al., 2007), and the individual motivational drivers of collaborative participation in open source marketing projects are illustrated and explained in more detail (see Fig. 3).

3.2.1 Pragmatic Motivation

Pragmatic incentives for an individual to actively participate in a marketing-related open source project arise from a number of factors. A reward in the form of free product samples or participation in a contest is one of the most important aspects (see Wiedmann & Langner, 2006a, pp. 143 ff. Lerner & Tirole, 2002; Lakhani & Wolf, 2005). Lucasfilm, normally a major advocate of copyrights, joined with atomfilms in 2002 and created the Star Wars Fan Film Awards. For 10 years thousands of amateur filmmakers competed to receive the prestigious award, to increase their reputation in the fan community, and to gain worldwide fame through the portal atomfilms.com. For Lucasfilm, the competition not only provided the opportunity to raise awareness of the Star Wars franchise (some posts reached over one million views) but also allowed the company to gain new ideas for its own film projects and for new marketing ideas.

Travel communities are also using customer contests as a first step toward open source marketing. The travel club Triphunter.de asked its users, in cooperation with the German newspaper "Der Freitag", to find the best travel photo in combination with the best travel story. Submissions were presented to the community and put to a vote. The best pictures and stories were then published once a month in the newspaper "Der Freitag". Through the interactive competition, TripHunter learned about new and interesting destinations and increased its customer loyalty through the active integration of its clients in its marketing activities (Source: triphunter. com, 2009).

However, it is not only rewards that drive people to participate. In particular, when well-respected companies creatively integrate their customers into their marketing activities, they motivate people to participate for a variety of other reasons. The opportunity to provide proof of their own skills to prospective employers (signaling), such as in the form of a self-created advertising spot or a self-created advertising idea, or the possibility of contacting key business representatives (getting in touch) are also seen as important motivators given the thousands of young job-seeking copywriters, PR strategists, and marketing managers (see Weber, 2004; Cherkoff, 2005; Raymond, 2001; Lakhani & Wolf, 2005; Lerner & Tirole, 2002).

3.2.2 Social Motivation

Relevant social motives include ideological reasons, such as the belief that creative work should be generally free, and intrinsic or psychological motives, such as self-confidence (peer recognition and ego boosting), participation in a community (community identification), selflessness (altruism and a job as vocation), or the fight for a common cause (or against a common or joint enemy) (see Lakhani & Wolf, 2005; Hertel et al., 2003; Lerner & Tirole, 2002; Weber, 2004; Bonarccorsi & Rossi, 2003).

The Australian company Blowfly shows how motivating the last aspect can be. The aim of the company, founded by Liam Mulhall, was to establish a new beer in the highly concentrated Australian beer market by creating an unconventional, grass-roots alternative to the impersonal mass production of large brewers. By using forums, chats, and voting on the Internet, Blowfly wanted to integrate potential buyers in the planning process from the very first moment of the beer. The idea paid off. As people heard about this user-integrating way of developing a new beer brand, many visited the Blowfly website and participated in the discussions and voting about the direction Blowfly should take. The logo, the shape of the bottle, and even the design of promotional materials were determined by the prospective customers of the beer. Even the flavor could be influenced by the consumers. At the end of the cooperative development phase, which lasted 13 weeks, thousands of users had participated in the votes and discussion, and approximately 10,000 users regularly followed the outcome of the voting as newsletter subscribers (see Langner, 2007) (Fig. 4).

Fig. 4 The community of travelpod.com shares travel feedback via travel blogs (*Source*: travelpod.com, 2013)

In the travel industry, travelpod.com is a good example of the use of social motivation to encourage people to participate. The online service was built around the specific social need to share one's travel experiences with others (peer recognition and ego boosting). The site focuses on providing users with an ideal platform for their own travelogues. Hence, the service includes weblog software with sophisticated map functionalities, picture and video galleries, and comment functions to interact with other travelers/trip followers (community identification). Most of the services are free. Advanced features are provided for a small fee, which forms the income stream of Travelpod.

3.2.3 Hedonistic Motivation

Hedonistic and emotionally colored reasons can also provide incentives for participation. Many consumers are so strongly associated with certain brands (love marks) that they can be regarded as fans (brand enthusiasm) (see Förster & Kreuz, 2003, pp. 74–83; Roberts, 2005). For example, in 2004, the American teacher George Masters created a completely independent commercial in honor of Apple's iPod. With the desire to be known as the author of the clip, he provided the film to a community of Apple fans. The commercial spread at an exponential rate over the Internet. Within a few days, more than 40,000 users viewed the clip. The quality of the spot was so good that many viewers thought it was the result of a major advertising agency (see Langner, 2006).

OpenstreetMap is a good example for a tourism related open source project that is based on a hedonistic motivation. The goal of the community is to create a free world map of all existing cities, streets, sights and so on. With the help of GPS-devices, Geo-information is collected worldwide and voluntary entered to OpenstreetMap by community participants. The completion, verification and correction of all data streams are also done by the community and represent a strong part of the project. The major advantage compared to proprietary map providers such as Google is, that everyone is allowed to use and process the data as desired and to use the maps for their purposes free of any licensing fees.

Another important subject is fun (fun & flow) (see Nakamura & Csikszentmihalyi, 2003; Voiskounsky & Smyclova, 2003; Lakhani & Wolf, 2005; Weber, 2004; Diamond & Torvalds, 2001). When the American beer producer Budweiser started its "Whassup" campaign in the early 2000s, it did not take long until the first fan-made derivatives of commercials found their way onto the Internet, such as spots in which Rabbis, English noblemen, superheroes, or South Park characters recreated the original spot. Although the creative works of the campaign were protected by copyright, Budweiser did not prevent the illegitimate use of their marketing material. Therefore, in a short time, a global community created new ideas for spots, discussed them online, and then (partially) transposed them jointly. The derivatives of the "Whassup" campaign still enjoy great popularity in social networks (source: AdCritic.com, 2007) (Fig. 5).

Fun as motivation also plays a major role in community marketing in the travel market. The community Couchsurfing.com, where people can offer their "couch" for travelers to stay for free anywhere in the world, has grown primarily due to this hedonistic motivation and the enthusiasm of its users, who love the idea of cultural exchange. Despite its global approach, the portal encourages users to form regional marketing groups, which actively seek new members online and offline to convince them of the community concept (Germann Molz 2007, pp. 65–77). Other activities include user-generated content. Therefore, couchsurfing.com encourages its users to publish videos of their experiences and self-made commercials on youtube.com. Since 2011, more than 3000 videos have been published that show, in the most authentic manner, what makes couchsurfing great and the issues people should consider when they decide to stay with strangers while travelling the world.

3.2.4 Technical Requirements

Consumers' ability to creatively participate and share their work is supported by the lack of a need for technical knowledge in these creative processes and online communication. Neither the creation of a video nor the dissemination of a video clip over the World Wide Web requires special skills, such as programming languages or communication protocols anymore. Tools, easy-to-understand

Fig. 5 The community of Couchsurfing.com makes travelling a cultural experience (*Source:* Couchsurfing.com, 2011)

programs, and online platforms allow almost anyone to create at least semi-professional work and to disseminate it effectively. As these reduced technical entry barriers for users are particularly important for an effective online dialogue, private companies still have to focus on well-established social platforms and should not try to use self-developed programs in order to have more control. Furthermore firms should not only consider technical requirements of platforms and programs themselves, but also of technical requirements related to the marketing tasks they want to work on collaboratively. A video with a mobile telephone is easily made and shared, whereas a new design of a product package needs knowledge of sophisticated graphic software and design skills, although the final picture of the product packaging itself can then be easily uploaded to almost all platforms.

3.2.5 Multi Channel Integration

Although internet based social media is the main platform for most collaborative marketing activities, open source marketing is not limited to online channels alone. This fact is evident in an idea by Mercedes Benz. In 2004, the U.S. automobile manufacturer invited its customers to send pictures via mail of themselves and their "beloved" Mercedes. Within a short time, the company had received hundreds of high-quality pictures, which became the core of a traditional ad campaign. However, rather than hiring a professional agency for the development of the ads, Mercedes integrated its customers into the development process of the campaign. The photos were put to a vote on the Internet. After the selection of the pictures, Mercedes customers were allowed to vote on the storyboard and the type of use in each of the advertising campaigns as well (see Cherkoff, 2005).

Airbnb.com represents an example of multichannel integration in the tourism sector. Airbnb.com is an online platform on which users are able to quickly and easily rent their private home to tourists. Around 60,000 accommodations are offered in more than 34,000 cities and 190 countries, ranging from simple apartments or rooms to luxurious villas. In total, over 15 Million people booked their accommodations through the platform so far (Airbnb, 2014). What makes the new idea/concept special is, that owners of the listed apartments and houses do not only publish a simple listing on Airbnb.com but they are directly marketing their accommodations over the platform via personal pictures and videos completed even with personal biographies and pictures of the owner. Multiple guidebooks on how to market one's own apartment or house via Airbnb.com written by users of Airbnb themselves are available under an open source license and are continuously extended.

4 Conclusion

Open source marketing has the potential to revolutionize conventional marketing. However, where there is light, there is shadow. The arguments against cooperative marketing are almost the same as those against open source software. The main point is reliability and quality. Opponents believe that open source marketing creates mediocrity at the expense of innovation. No company would take the risk of developing costly marketing ideas and materials when everyone—including its competitors—is allowed to simply copy, use, and possibly misuse them. Only legally secured competition between companies has the ability to produce innovations in the long term.

Proponents of open source, in contrast, argue that people hate closed systems and solutions. Whenever possible, they want to have freedom of choice. For example, people do not want an operating system that categorically excludes certain functions and providers. They simply do not want to be the last link in a chain and to be forced to accept what they are served. In the context of marketing, clients often reject advertising ideas because they have no influence on them (in terms of their ideas and form or their distribution). Even if marketing activities are oriented toward the expectations of the target group, they still lack a key success factor: authenticity. This disadvantage cannot be corrected by large market research efforts. However, the reality of open source marketing cannot be confirmed without empirical studies. The only certainty is that traditional marketing is changing. Ultimately, every company must keep in mind that the copying and parody of marketing materials cannot be prevented in the digital age.

Open source marketing does not simply mean giving up copyrights; rather, it involves knowing and appreciating the customer's opinion from the beginning. Open source means living the community's thoughts, even if this only involves the integration of an independent forum as a core functionality of a website without having to fear the opinions of the customers (e.g., AquaComputer.com).

Customers have always decided what works and what does not. Is it not time to integrate them in the creative marketing processes? Many experts preach greater interactivity and customer proximity. It is time to invest in a new era of communication and exchange with the customer.

References

Airbnb. (2014). *Information about Airbnb.* https://www.airbnb.de/about/about-us

Bergquiest, M., & Ljungberg, J. (2001). The power of gifts: Organizing social relationships in open source communities. *European Journal of Information Systems, 11*(4), 305–320.

Berkman, H. W., Lindquist, J. D., & Sirgy, J. M. (1997). *Consumer behavior.* Chicago, IL: NTC.

Blackshaw, P. (2004). *Buzz-informed predictions for 2005,* http://www.clickz.com/showPage. html?page=3446711

Blackwell, R. D., Miniard, P. W., & Engel, J. F. (2001). Consumer behavior (9 ed.), Fort Worth et al.

Bleh, W. (2005). *Bis zur Grenze des guten Geschmacks und weiter. . . .* http://www.intern.de/news/ 6368.html

Bonarccorsi, J., & Rossi, C. (2003). Why open source software can succeed. *Research Policy, 32* (7), 1242–1258.

Brøndmo, H.-P. (2004). *Open-source marketing.* http://www.clickz.com/experts/brand/sense/arti cle.php/3397411

Cherkoff, J. (2005). *End of the love affair. The love affair between big brands and mass media is over. But where do marketeers go next? The Open Source Movement has the answers. . . .* http:// www.collaboratemarketing.com/open_source_marketing/

Christ, P. (2004). *Can open development work for marketing activities?* http://www.knowthis. com/articles/marketing/collaboration.htm/

Csikszentmihalyi, M. (1975). *Beyond boredom and anxiety: The experience of play in work and games.* San Francisco, CA: Jossey-Bass.

Dalle, J. M., & David, P. A. (2003). *The allocation of software development resources in 'open source' production mode.* MIT working paper. http://opensource.mit.edu/papers/dalledavid. pdf

Deci, E. L., & Ryan, R. M. (1985). *Intrinsic motivation and self-determination in human behavior.* New York: Plenum.

Diamantopoulos, A., & Winklhofer, H. M. (2001). Index construction with formative indicators: An alternative to scale development. *Journal of Marketing Research, 38*(2), 269–277.

Diamond, D., & Torvalds, L. (2001). *Just for fun: The story of an accidental revolutionary.* New York: HarperCollins.

Feller, J., & Fitzgerald, B. (2002). *Understanding open source software development.* London: Addison-Wesley.

Förster, A., & Kreuz, P. (2003). *Marketing-Trends - Ideen und Konzepte für Ihren Markterfolg.* Wiesbaden: Gabler.

Franke, N., & Shah, S. (2003). How communities support innovative activities: An exploration of assistance and sharing among end-users. *Research Policy, 32*(1), 157–178.

Frey, B. (1997). *Not just for the money: An economic theory of personal motivation.* Brookfield, VT: Edward Elgar.

Germann Molz, J. (2007). Cosmopolitans on the couch: Mobile hospitality and the Internet. In J. Germann Molz & S. Gibson (Eds.), *Mobilizing hospitality: The ethics of social relations in a mobile world* (pp. 65–80). London: Ashgate.

Ghosh, R. A., Glott, R., Krieger, B., & Robles, G. (2002). *Survey of developers.* http://floss. infonomics.nl/report/FLOSS_Final4.pdf

Hars, A., & Ou, S. (2002). Working for free? Motivations for participating in Open -Source projects. *International Journal of Electronic Commerce, 6*(3), 25–39.

Hertel, G., Niedner, S., & Herrmann, S. (2003). Motivation of software developers in open source projects: An Internet-based survey of contributors to the Linux kernel. *Research Policy, 32*, 1159–1177.

Himanen, P. (2001). *The hacker ethic and the spirit of the information age.* New York: Random House.

Holmström, B. (1999). Managerial incentive problems: A dynamic perspective. *Review of Economic Studies, 66S*, 169–182.

Jarvis, C. B., MacKenzie, S. B., & Podsakoff, P. M. (2003). A critical review of construct indicators and measurement model misspecification. *Journal of Consumer Research, 30*(2), 199–218.

Kahney, L. (2004). *The cult of Mac.* Heidelberg: No Starch Press.

Klandersmans, B. (1997). *The social psychology of protest.* Oxford: Basil Blackwell.

Kretiner, R., & Kinicki, A. (1998). *Organizational behavior* (4th ed.). Boston, MA: Irwin McGraw-Hill.

Kucuk, U. S., & Krishnamurthy, S. (2006). An analysis of consumer power on the Internet. *Technovation, 27*, 47–56.

Lakhani, K. R., & von Hippel, E. (2003). How open source software works: "Free" user-to-user assistance. *Research Policy, 32*, 923–943.

Lakhani, K. R., & Wolf, R. G. (2005). Why hackers do what they do: Understanding motivation and effort in free/open source software projects. In J. Feller, B. Fitzgerald, S. A. Hissam, & K. R. Lakhani (Eds.), *Perspectives on free and open source software* (pp. 3–22). Cambridge, MA: MIT.

Lakhani, K. R., Wolf, B., Bates, J., & DiBona, C. (2002). *Hacker survey.* http://www.osdn.com/ bcg/

Langner, S. (2006). *Marketing 2.0 - Strategien und Taktiken für eine sozial vernetzte Welt.* http:// www.marke-x.de/deutsch/webmarketing/archiv/marketing_20.htm

Langner, S. (2007). *Viral Marketing – Wie Sie Mundpropaganda gezielt auslösen und Gewinn bringend nutzen.* Wiesbaden: Gabler.

Lerner, J., & Tirole, J. (2002). The simple economics of open source. *Journal of Industrial Economics, L:2*, 197–234.

Levy, S. (1994). *Hackers. Heroes of the computer revolution.* New York: Penguin.

Lieb, R. (2004). *Crazy like a firefox.* http://www.clickz.com/showPage.html?page=3434811

Maslow, A. (1943). A theory of human motivation. *Psychological Review, 50*, 370–396.

Maslow, A. (1954). *Motivation and personality.* New York: Harper.

McConnell, B., & Huba, J. (2002). *Creating customer evangelists*. Chicago, IL: Kaplan.

McVoy, L. (1993). *The sourceware operating system proposal*. http://www.bitmover.com/lm/papers/srcos.html

Mitchell, T. R. (1982). Motivation: New directions for theory, research, and practice. *Academy of Management Review, 7*, 80–88.

Moody, G. (2001). *Rebel code: Inside Linux and the open source revolution*. New York: Perseus.

Moore, R. E. (2003). From genericide to viral marketing: On 'brand'. *Language and Communication, 23*(3), 331–357.

Morrison, P. D., Roberts, J. H., & Von Hippel, E. (2000). Determinants of user innovation and innovation sharing in a local market. *Management Science, 46*(12), 1513–1527.

Mucha, T. (2004). *Firefox: Marketing's Borg - The new browser taps the power of the collective*. http://www.business2.com/b2/web/articles/0,17863,845562,00.html

Nakamura, J., & Csikszentmihalyi, M. (2003). The construction of meaning through vital engagement. In C. L. Keyes & J. Haidt (Eds.), *Flourishing: Positive psychology and the life well-lived*. Washington, DC: American Psychological Association.

Omoto, A. M., & Snyder, M. (1995). Sustained helping without obligation: Motivation, longevity of service, and perceived attitude change among AIDS volunteers. *Journal of Personality and Social Psychology, 68*, 671–686.

Open Source Initiative. (2006). *Open source definition*. http://www.opensource.org/docs/definition

Perens, B. (1999). The open source definition. In C. DiBona, S. Ockman, & M. Stone (Eds.), *Sources: Voices from the open source revolution* (pp. 171–196). Sebastopol, CA: O'Reilly.

Ramlall, S. (2004). *A review of employee motivation theories and their implications for employee retention within organizations* (pp. 52–63). Cambridge, MA: The Journal of American Academy of Business.

Raymond, E. S. (2001). *The cathedral and the bazaar: Musings on Linux and open source by an accidental revolutionary*. Sebastopol, CA: O'Reilly.

Riggs, W., & Von Hippel, E. (1994). Incentives to innovate and the sources of innovation: The case of scientific instruments. *Research Policy, 23*(4), 459–469.

Robbins, S. (1993). *Organizational behavior* (6th ed.). Englewood Cliffs: Prentice-Hall.

Roberts, K. (2005). *Lovemarks: The future beyond brands*. New York: PowerHouse Books.

Simon, B., Loewy, M., Stürmer, S., Weber, U., Freytag, P., Habig, C., et al. (1998). Collective identification and social movement participation. *Journal of Personality and Social Psychology, 74*, 646–658.

Solomon, M., Bamossy, G., & Askegaard, S. (2002). *Consumer behaviour: A European perspective*. Edinburgh: Pearson Education.

Stallman, R. (2002). *Free software, free society*. Boston, MA: GNU.

Steers, R., & Porter, L. (1983). *Motivation and work behavior* (3rd ed.). New York: McGraw-Hill.

Stephens, D. C. (Ed.). (2000). *The Maslow business reader*. New York: Wiley.

Torvalds, L., & Diamond, D. (2001). *Just for fun: The story of an accidental revolutionary*. New York: HarperCollins.

Voiskounsky, A., & Smyclova, O. (2003). Flow-based model of computer hackers' motivation. *CyberPsychology & Behavior, 2*(6), 171–180.

Von Hippel, E. (1988). *The sources of innovation*. New York: Oxford University Press.

Von Krogh, G., Spaeth, S., & Lakhani, K. R. (2002). Community, joining, and specialization in open source software innovation: A case study. *Research Policy, 32*, 1217–1241.

Vroom, V. H. (1964). *Work and motivation*. New York: Wiley.

Wayner, P. (2000). *Free for all: How Linux and the free software movement undercuts the high-tech titans*. New York: HarperBusiness.

Weber, S. (2004). *The success of open source*. Cambridge, MA: Harvard University Press.

Wiedmann, K.-P., & Langner, S. (2006a). Open source marketing - ein schlafender Riese erwacht. In B. Lutterbeck (Ed.), *Open source Jahrbuch*. Berlin: Lehmanns.

Wiedmann, K.-P., & Langner, S. (2006b). Understanding open source networks: Proposing a conceptual model of motivation. In *Proceedings of the IFSAM VIIIth world congress 2006.*

Wiedmann, K.-P., Langner, S., & Hennigs, N. (2007). The underlying motivation(s) of consumers' participation in open source oriented marketing projects – Results of an exploratory study. In J. Mohr & R. Fisher (Eds.), *Enhancing knowledge development in marketing* (2007 AMA Educators' Proceedings, Vol. 18, p. 167ff). Chicago, IL: American Marketing Association.

Crowdsourcing in the Lodging Industry: Innovation on a Budget

Brendan Richard, William P. Perry, and Robert C. Ford

1 Introduction

> For the longest time, hotel brands have followed the 'closed' model of innovation by creating amenities in-house and force feeding them to guests, with an increasingly dynamic marketplace, and the emergence of a younger and more sophisticated travel consumer, this model no longer works
>   Chekitan Dev, Cornell University

As the lodging industry challenges itself to develop new models to adapt to the ever-changing ways in which we work, travel, and experience leisure, it has found a willing partner in the crowd. By seeking to co-create solutions with a diverse crowd of potential customers, interested parties and experts, hotels are opening up their innovation process to the world. Hotels are hopeful that through this two-way dialogue they will be able to develop new models of service excellence, to provide a new level of authenticity and personalization, and position themselves to successfully adapt to future trends. One such firm recently announced the start of a campaign to collaboratively design the world's first 'cotel,' a crowdsourced hotel. This hotel will be designed and funded by a worldwide crowd of contributors and built in New York City's Downtown district. Seeking to infuse the industry with new ideas, and possessing the belief that the intelligence of the crowd is greater than that of any one expert, the company is offering up to thousands in prizes for design contributions. The design competitions, judged by a panel of experts, will seek out contributions in the areas of digital services to improve the guest experience, and designs for the suites and public spaces (Vivion, 2014).

B. Richard (✉) • R.C. Ford
University of Central Florida, Orlando, FL 32816, USA
e-mail: Brendan.Richard@ucf.edu; rford@bus.ucf.edu

W.P. Perry
CII Holdings (Pty) Ltd, Gauteng, South Africa
e-mail: William@CIIHoldings.com

© Springer-Verlag Berlin Heidelberg 2016
R. Egger et al. (eds.), *Open Tourism*, Tourism on the Verge,
DOI 10.1007/978-3-642-54089-9_6

The drive to partner with the crowd to co-create solutions is not limited though to just small and boutique hotels. As Marriott executives seek to shift their image from "a sea of sameness to a world of difference," and avoid as some younger guests have quipped "another beige room," (p. 1) they have sought to engage in a truly consumer-driven innovation process (Barnes, 2014). Eschewing the old corporate-centric method of innovation followed by a delayed process of guest validation, Marriott has instead constructed a new innovation lab at its headquarters where the idea starts with the consumer. Leaving traditional focus groups behind, hotels are taking advantage of social media, which acts as a real-time, worldwide focus group. Other prominent brands such as Starwood Hotels and Hyatt Hotels have recently taken similar steps including opening up innovation labs, seeking out contributions through social media, and partnering with open-innovation consultancy groups. Driving all of these efforts is the simple logic that in order to better understand what is most important to the customer, and how best the hotel can meet their needs, hotels need to seek out solutions from the customer (Trejos, 2013). To better appreciate why this new innovation technique is applicable to and beneficial for the lodging industry, we seek to first understand the current state of the industry, the challenges it's facing, and the opportunities that exist.

Lodging represents one of the oldest industries in existence. Originally little more than four walls, a roof and a bed; early forms of lodging existed solely to provide shelter for travelers. Yet, within the past century the industry has grown from relatively humble beginnings to playing a vital role in the development of trade, commerce and leisure travel on a global basis. In the U.S. alone, over one billion roomnights are sold each year, with revenues exceeding 150 billion (STR Analytics, 2013). Innovation over the past century has seen the development of amenities such as telephones originally introduced by Statler, wireless service and flat screen televisions to creating standards of opulence as pioneered by Ritz, financial innovations that created branded chains such as those forged by Conrad Hilton, and technological innovations such as the first central reservation system (Holodex) introduced by Kemmons Wilson (Bardi, 2006). In spite of all this innovative activity, however, the lodging industry is constantly challenged in its efforts to design products and provide services that meet the ever changing needs of the guest.

Chain hotels in the lodging industry typically operate with the support of multiple stakeholders, including: the institutional owners, the brand, and the management company. The institutional owners provide the capital that builds the properties and owns the land. The brand provides the marketing effort that seeks to provide a customer preference. The management company provides the operational expertise and capabilities that ensure that the investment of the institutional owners is maximized while protecting the brand promise for the brand and making money for the operator. Obviously, those goals can and do conflict as they do in any organizational arrangement where one function seeks to prioritize their own interests over those of other functions (Barney & Hesterly, 2009). Getz and Carlsen (2005) have suggested that this owner-manager structure could result in less specialization in management, less professional managers, and lesser resources.

Martínez-Ros and Orfila-Sintes (2009) further surmise that this relationship can ultimately lead to a decreased likelihood of hotels engaging in radical innovations.

The competing goals of financial stakeholders has been driven by the recent rise in institutional ownership. While the history of this industry has been characterized by sole proprietors, the success of investors in finding a consistent and sustainable yield in the 1990s led to the increased bundling of individual properties in financial packages that could be sold on Wall Street to individual investors or to cash heavy institutional investors looking for places to invest growing pools of retirement funds. The goal of these investors is consistent and predictable yield. Thus, they sought and found packages of properties that would yield a consistent percentage (Raleigh, 2012). While ownership seeks to drive profitability and value to the shareholders, the brand and management firms seek to maximize revenue per their contractual obligations. Given the conflicting goals of the stakeholders and the short-term investors perceived unwillingness to engage in a long-term innovation strategy, how can the industry generate the innovative activity that will allow it to sustain its ability to perform? In other words, what strategy can it find that is inexpensive, requires few resources, and consumes little time. We suggest the answer lies within open innovation, specifically crowdsourcing, which can yield the innovations the industry needs without incurring substantial costs, consuming resources, or utilizing dedicated employees.

Over the next 5 years the industry will begin to again experience expansion, with strong growth in boutique and extended-stay hotel, resorts and spas (IBIS, 2013). Institutional investment will increasingly turn its attention to international growth fueled by expansion in developing markets such as China, India, the Middle East and Africa and Latin America, with merging economies expected to account for 57 % of international arrivals by 2030 (UNWTO, 2011). Guests are demanding new facilities and amenity offerings such as: open lobbies, social spaces and distinctive designs. Guests are seeking authenticity, new experiences, personalization, all while maintaining simple and seamless service. In addition, over half of consumers in the lodging industry consider sustainability when making a purchasing decision. There is room for growth in leveraging consumer sentiment, engaging guests, leveraging social media and creating unique experiences.

It has been contended that core tourism actor's, such as hotels, possess limited resources for innovation (Hjalager, 2010). Adapting to new trends can be challenging, risky and ultimately costly. New trends require new knowledge, new ideas, new processes and procedures. New ideas will require new innovations in order to obtain practical, beneficial, implementable solutions. It is therefore imperative that the lodging industry considers and explores new innovation techniques—especially ones that are less costly, and produce solutions that are easily implementable. This chapter provides the readers with: an overview of innovation in the lodging industry and its impediments, strategies to overcome these impediments, a rationale for why crowdsourcing is an appropriate innovation technique, a crowdsourcing framework with examples of solutions for the industry, and the managerial implications of pursuing a crowdsourced strategy.

2 The Need for Innovation

In order to survive a company must be adaptable to the changing environment, not just adjusting to changes as they occur, but ultimately predicting them, and in doing so re-aligning operations accordingly ahead of the competition (Porter, 2008). In order to survive a company must invest in innovation. A meta-analysis of empirical studies examining the relationship between organization innovation and firm performance found that innovation had a significant, positive affect on organization performance (Vincent, Bharadwaj, & Challagalla, 2004). Within the field of tourism, firms that are successful at innovating have been shown to receive numerous beneficial organizational outcomes. Evidence has shown that hotels that generate innovations achieve a greater level of competitive advantage in addition to increasing subsequent consumer preference (Victorino, Verma, Plaschka, & Dev, 2005). The introduction of technology service innovations has resulted in cost-savings (Buhalis, 1999), which frequently take the form of a rapid pay-off (Siguaw, Enz, & Namasivayam, 2000). Finally, within accommodations, professionals rate marketing, promotional and product innovations as being particularly important and impactful to their businesses (Blake, Sinclair, & Soria, 2006).

But innovation no longer needs to be effectively attempted alone, as external partners can be beneficial (Chesbrough, 2003). How are industry upstarts, lacking the resources and capital required to fund a massive in-house resource and development (R&D) lab, outpacing their long-established, market-share possessing rivals? Chesbrough (2003, p.1) details a new direction in innovation, which he deems to be the era of open innovation. Summarizing his review of the state of innovation, Chesbrough observes that, "Companies are increasingly rethinking the fundamental ways in which they generate ideas and bring them to market—harnessing external ideas while leveraging their in-house R&D outside their current operations". Traditionally large companies conducted closed innovation, conducting internal R&D by hiring the best and brightest, and vigorously protecting the intellectual property (IP). Thanks though to the mobility of knowledge workers and their ability to collaborate on a massive scale across great distances (see Web 2.0), it is increasingly difficult to maintain this closed innovation model.

Open innovation (which encompasses crowdsourcing) represents an opportunity for companies to invigorate the innovation process, de-regulating it from merely an internal R&D role, and expanding it to include all of the company's stakeholders: from employees, to partners, to customers, and to the general public. Why expand the innovation process to incorporate all of these disparate parties? The benefits of open innovation include: an increase in the number of innovative ideas, a decrease in the innovation process time, a decrease in the cost of innovation, and a reduction in the time it takes to bring the product or service to market (Sloane, 2011).

3   Obstacles to Innovation in Lodging

Traditionally, hotels were owned and operated by individuals or companies that intended to manage the property for the life of the asset. However, during the 1980s the industry experienced massive building booms, which accelerated the evolution from individual to institutional ownership (Rushmore, O'Neill, & Rushmore, 2012). Until the early 1990s, investments in hotels made little economic sense as many hotels struggled to simply break even. However, as more institutional investors started to buy hotel assets the industry had to start confirming to market yields (Raleigh, 2012). In 2012 alone, private equity funds, the largest net buyers, utilized approximately $7 billion in capital for hotel investments. In combination with Real Estate Investment Trusts (REITs), private equity buyers comprised almost 70 % of the total acquisition volume in the Americas (LaSalle, 2013). This change in hotel ownership structures and capitalization has limited the ability of operators to invest in innovations due to the differing strategic goals of owners.

Institutional ownership generally consists of real estate investment trusts, private equity funds, or publicly traded firms that purchase these assets at a discount, focus on creating operational efficiencies and selling the hotel for a profit within the period of maximum recapture of depreciation, 5–7 years. According to the Hotel Investor Gauge financial returns to investors are promised at an average internal rate of return of 18.5 % over a 5.7 year hold period. Since full service hotels typically average 34.1 % Gross Operating Profit (GOP), and 49.9 % GOP for limited service before debt service or shareholder distributions (STR Analytics, 2013), there is little or no money left after distributions to invest in any disciplined innovation practices, when investors are expecting a strong overall return, after debt service (Raleigh, 2012). In addition, since the typical hotel operates through a partnership of three stakeholders, consisting of the brand, the management firm, the owners, identifying who is responsible for initiating innovative practices and ideas becomes problematic since each stakeholder has its own objectives.

Institutional ownership generally focus on creating operational efficiencies, maximizing returns to investors, growing the asset appreciation, and selling the hotel for a profit within the period of maximum recapture of depreciation (Boettger, 2009). Without any longer term incentives to pursue breakthrough innovation, management firm employees can't be expected to lead major innovation in the industry. The Brand, which in many cases is also a publicly traded company, is motivated to differentiate its product though innovation, but often lacks the resources to invest in research and development of new product ideas. Even when Brands do innovate, their competitive advantage only delivers a short term advantage as product and service enhancements are quickly duplicated by competitors. Hence, while each party has a vested interest in the profitability of the hotel, individual objects differ (maximizing revenue vs. profit, short term vs. long term returns; customer satisfaction vs. labor costs).

Complicating the matter further each partner may (and frequently does) oversee operations at different hotels representing different brands or ownership groups in buildings or on land owned by different entities. For example, in 2012, Virginia based Interstate Hotels & Resorts, operated 354 hotels with 61,984 rooms in over nine countries under 40 different brands. Other major third-party operators included Pillar Hotels and Resorts and White Lodging Services (Hotelmanagement.net, 2012). These operators manage various brands for different owners, and enjoy the benefit of having access to each brands operating procedures and practices. Therefore, new innovations in service or product are quickly shared across the industry. For example, when Westin introduced its Heavenly Bed product in 1999 (Starwood, 2009) it was only a matter of time before other Starwood brands as well as Marriott and Hilton introduced bedding products of their own. Initially, Westin increased its average daily rate by almost twenty dollars per night, but lost its innovative advantage when other brands quickly duplicated this amenity (Fareed, 2005). The responsibility for innovation has been the burden of the Brands, as they are the drivers for product differentiation. For example, it was Barry Sternlicht that created the W Hotel brand in 1998, while serving as Chairman of Starwood Hotels & Resorts Worldwide (Higley, 2013). Hyatt and Hilton both introduced the self-check in kiosk in 2006 and Marriott piloted web based check in services (Higgins, 2006).

The short-term investment in hotels by institutional ownership, and goal conflicts between stakeholders all take their toll on the ability of firms to effectively invest in innovation in the lodging industry. Even when stakeholders do pursue innovation within the industry, it is typically a more traditional approach such as corporate R&D, competitor imitation and outsourcing to a single firm. These existing innovation techniques coupled with limited funding and scope for innovation have resulted in an industry that is becoming homogenous. New techniques, such as crowdsourcing, can help industry stakeholders bypass innovation impediments, potentially imparting innovations and a competitive advantage gain to those that do.

4   Overcoming the Obstacles

4.1   Why Not Outsourcing?

Crowdsourcing, which represents an open call to a large networked group of individuals, is a unique form of outsourcing. Why though should firms consider conducting crowdsourcing instead of tried and true techniques such as outsourcing? Multinational corporations throughout the 1990s and 2000s, guided by the tenants of strategic management, such as focusing on sustainable competitive advantages, pursued opportunities to outsource non-core aspects of their business. Companies sought to divest themselves of operations, and their associated facilities, that weren't contributing to the bottom line, or were unrelated to the central focus on the company (Gonzales, Dorwin, Gupta, Kalyan, & Schimler, 2004; Porter, 2008).

In order to understand why we might crowdsource, we must first understand why we might outsource.

To act strategically a company must align its resources and operations not only to the current state of the external environment (within the business group, the wider industry, and the overall economy), but optimally to the future state of the external environment. Realigning a company's operations is not an easy task. It is even more difficult when a company attempts to reorganize itself in order to capitalize on a disruptive innovation (Christensen, 1997; Danneels, 2004, 2011). It is expected that a hotel chain like Marriott or Hilton will be able to adjust overtime (through renovations and new builds) to an incremental innovation such as an enclosed pool area, or curved shower rods, but can a company survive a disruptive innovation such as the shift from horse and buggy to automobiles or typewriters to computers? One factor that is crucial in reorienting (and surviving) in an ever-changing environment is a company's ability to manage its resources (Barney, 1991; Barney & Arikan, 2001). Company's often lack a rigorous understanding of their own resources and capabilities (Schreyogg & Kliesch-Eberl, 2007). This is especially troubling since a company that doesn't understand its resources in its present state, will undoubtedly have difficulties in understanding how these same resources can be used in a changed environment. Ultimately the better a company understands its resources, and its ability to manipulate and redeploy them, the more adaptable that company will be. The more adaptable a company is, the more likely it will be able to capitalize on the future state of the market (Hansen & Wernerfelt, 1989).

One way in which a company can ensure it is more adaptable is to outsource those functions of the business that aren't contributing to its competitive advantage. Simply put, a competitive advantage is a company's ability to outperform all of its competitors in one or more of its value-chain activities, where a value-chain consists of those activities that are performed in order to deliver a product or service (Porter, 1985, 2008). Those aspects of the business that are less profitable, can be outsourced to external partners, who are able to provide the product or service faster, better and/or cheaper than the focal company could. Reduced costs, higher quality deliverables, access to new technology and increased organizational flexibility are all outcomes anticipated by firms that decide to outsource (McFarlan & Nolan, 1995). Outsourcing has been shown to have a positive indirect effect on the profitability of firms. Specifically, firm strategy has been found to moderate the relationship between outsourcing intensity and financial and innovation performance (Gilley & Rasheed, 2000).

If outsourcing can be an effective solution to the challenge of focusing on competitive advantage and simultaneously making the company more adaptable, then why consider crowdsourcing? The concept of outsourcing can be effective if an activity is not contributing to a competitive advantage. Under these circumstances it is appropriate to consider if an external partner exists that can provide the product or service to the company. Crowdsourcing doesn't seek to supplant this model, merely improve upon it. Many large companies have found themselves in the role of a disappointed outsourcer. Common risks encountered in outsourcing an activity to a supplier include: encountering cost overruns, disputes and litigations, project delays, and a diminished or variable quality of the product or services provided (Aubert, Dussault, Patry, & Rivard, 1999; Bahli & Rivard, 2003). These risks represent an inherent weakness in the outsourcing process.

If outsourcing is a preferred solution, but has inherent risks, how can we seek to mitigate the potential pitfalls of engaging in outsourcing? Crowdsourcing is the act of outsourcing, not just to one party, but instead to a networked group of individuals, each invited to help solve the firm's problems, and each motivated to participate in the work effort for a multitude of motivations. Crowdsourcing takes advantage of intrinsic participant motivations, the diversity of the crowd, Web 2.0 technology and an engaged community in order to overcome the challenges of outsourcing (Richard, 2013).

4.2 What Are the Benefits of Crowdsourcing?

The term crowdsourcing originated in an article written by Jeff Howe in the June, 2006 issue of Wired Magazine. Howe defined the phenomenon as:

> Simply defined, crowdsourcing represents the act of a company or institution taking a function once performed by employees and outsourcing it to an undefined (and generally large) network of people in the form of an open call. This can take the form of peer-production (when the job is performed collaboratively), but is also often undertaken by sole individuals. The crucial prerequisite is the use of the open call format and the large network of potential laborer (2006, p. 5).

In other words, a company is making the decision to outsource a problem, but instead of engaging in the traditional outsourcing process (an RFP to a limited number of established suppliers), the company has decided to make the request open to the wider community of interested parties.

Crowdsourcing has established itself as an effective method for outsourcing based on a confluence of several, only recently developed, facilitating factors. Crowdsourcing relies on the ability of a company to tap into an online community of individuals that are both capable and willing to spend their (mostly discretionary) time in order to develop solutions to the company's problems (Richard, 2013). This "crowd" is fuelled in part by a surplus of underemployed and educated talent that are seeking out opportunities to utilize their accumulated talent and skills in their discretionary time (Benkler, 2006). With the proliferation of the internet, the World Wide Web and consumer technology to access it, there has been a growing commitment to online communities, where individuals with discretionary time and a common interest congregate (Howe, 2008). This has produced a critical mass of participants willing to invest a nominal amount of their discretionary time in crowdsourced efforts (Heylighen, 2007).

In 2009, Fischer surveyed 100 top marketing executives on the subject of crowdsourcing in order to determine their familiarity with the concept and its potential applications. At the time over 70 % of respondents acknowledged familiarity with the term. Fischer reported amongst others two significant findings,

> (1) Senior executives rated crowdsourcing and consumer collaboration groups as effective as internal R&D staff for developing ideas for new product/services; (2) one-half of the executives believed crowdsourcing would produce cost efficiencies ranging from 10 % to 30 % over either traditional in-house approaches or external professional services. Fully 90 % of the executives indicated that crowdsourcing is attractive based on these findings (2009, p. 2).

Crowdsourcing represents a potentially lower cost, faster method for obtaining solutions to an organizations problems as opposed to more traditional methods of outsourcing (Lakhani, Garvin, & Lonstein, 2010). Crowdsourcing relies on mass-collaboration to generate, organize and deliver a vast repository of knowledge to the organization in the form of a practical solution. The problem can require the participants to work together or against each other to develop a specific solution, or by merely contributing produce an immense amount of information that collectively becomes the solution. Social media sites are examples of this form of crowdsourcing, in which the users themselves use the collaboration platform to generate the product itself. Kazman and Chen (2009: 1) note that "the importance of this form of production is undeniable; as of May 2009 five of the 10 most popular Web sites—Myspace.com, YouTube.com, Facebook.com, Wikipedia.com and Blogger.com—were produced this way, according to Alexia.com; with the exception of Wikipedia, all are for-profit enterprises."

Crowdsourcing allows firms the ability to substantially reduce the amount of time it takes to bring new products or services to the market. Unlike traditional outsourcing arrangements, in crowdsourcing, it is the crowd that is being managed, not individuals, and in certain situations the crowd has been shown to be more efficient and provide better solutions than traditional service providers (Dawson & Bynghall, 2011). While this might sound more complex, the crowd is in fact managed primarily by an online collaboration platform. The greater the number of individuals within the crowd working to solve the firm's problem, the greater the variation will be in ideas and solutions generated. This increased variation in ideas is a result of the uniqueness in background and experiences of each one of the participants contributing solutions (Kozinets, Hemetsberger, & Schau, 2008). This phenomenon, in which diversity trumps ability, is explained by Howe (2008) in the field of crowdsourcing, by referencing Page's work (2007) in the area of collective intelligence. Page seeks to better understand why a random collection of problems solvers can outperform a group of higher ability individuals. The proposition? That those groups made up of individuals from the highest echelons of society are in actuality a relatively homogenous group, and that it is the inherent lack of diversity in this group that impedes their efforts to generate the most valuable solutions to problems. Is their average level of solutions higher than that of the random group of individuals? Yes. But remember, it's not the likelihood of meeting the threshold of average that is important, it's who can create the best possible solution that is crucial.

4.3   Why Crowdsourcing for the Lodging Industry?

Why is crowdsourcing the appropriate innovation tool for the lodging industry? Perhaps most importantly it is a low-cost solution relative to more traditional forms of outsourcing. Cost can't be the only justification though, solutions have to be a good fit for the problems that exist within the lodging industry and have the potential to deliver effective, implementable results. Afuah and Tucci (2012) suggest that crowdsourcing is a better mechanism for solving problems than other available alternatives. They propose that some problems lend themselves to crowdsourced solutions, problems that: (1) are easy to delineate, (2) require knowledge not available to the firm, (3) can attract a large, motivated, and knowledgeable crowd, and (4) have solutions that are easily implementable.

Does the lodging industry align with these criteria? The crowd the industry has the potential to attract and motivate is in the tens of millions, including business and leisure travellers across all demographics, representing individuals who possess extensive experience and understanding of the product and services hotels provide. The solutions themselves don't require a specific skill-set or in-depth understanding of the industry; the contributions of someone who has never stayed in a hotel could be as valuable as a seasoned business traveller. Finally the structure of the industry lends itself to simple but powerful solutions. Brands have the ability to implement a product or service innovation across the entire chain within a matter of months, assuming it has buy-in from the other stakeholders.

Marriott, Hyatt and Starwood are just a few examples of firms who have recently begun to go down the path of co-creating solutions by partnering with the crowd. By setting up innovation labs and engaging in mass focus groups via social media, hotel brands are beginning to realize and actualize the potential that exists in seeking out innovations by asking your potential or existing customers to contribute to the process.

5   Enabling Innovation

If investment in innovation, and an acceptance of new innovation techniques are necessities that the lodging industry cannot afford to overlook as the external environment and consumer trends continue to change, then what remains to be done? If firms are to consider an innovation solution such as crowdsourcing, they must have a proper understanding of it, and how to take advantage of it. Firms within the lodging industry would optimally: (1) possess an understanding of the steps that must be taken internally, in order to redeploy their limited resources to best take advantage of crowdsourcing as an innovation technique, and (2) assess which problems they have that have the potential to be solved using crowdsourcing.

In order for crowdsourcing to be properly utilized by the lodging industry, companies within the industry benefit from the realignment of their operations, procedures and culture to better facilitate its adoption and spread. Putting aside the historically recent shift to a service dominated economy, and the advent of ubiquitous computing and Web 2.0 driven content sharing, many firms are still firmly oriented towards a goods dominated system. Traditionally, in a goods dominated system, firms "treated customers as isolated entities—recipients of value—neglecting the customer's own resources and networks for dynamic collaboration value co-creation." (Kazman & Chen, 2009, p. 77) Firms must now think of their customers, and the crowd, as opportunities to co-produce their products and services. Customers, and the greater crowd, collectively represent the opportunity to overcome the limitations of firm-centric value creation.

With the advent of ubiquitous computing, open-source technology, and mass-collaboration, firms now have the ability to tap into what Tapscott and Williams (2006) refer to as "wikinomics." In order to take advantage of this brave new world of collaboration and co-production though, a firm must first take structural steps to facilitate its usage. Tapscott and Williams advocate for the removal of: hierarchical structures, the reliance on internal employees, the protection of all intellectual property, and the focus on shareholders. While these are noble goals—admittedly they are easier said than done. The lodging industry still operates within the bounds of capitalism, is fueled primarily by private equity and operates with three stakeholders. Ignoring the focus on shareholders, which might have been possible even 10 years ago, is now a thing of the past. Additionally, while each stakeholder has the ability within its area to reorient itself into a move horizontal employee structure, change cannot occur as a whole unless all three stakeholders are in agreement. While these limitations are realities, the lodging industry does have room for growth within the areas of reliance on internal employees and the protection of intellectual property.

The challenges of outsourcing work efforts and intellectual property to the crowd have been noted by several researchers in the field of crowdsourcing and open innovation (Lakhani et al., 2010). It is possible though to overcome these obstacles through the pursuit of pilot studies, the utilization of internal champions, and a top management team driven effort to modify the firm's policies to be more crowdsourcing friendly. With champions within the firm identifying problems, and the success of solving small problems, firms can become comfortable with this newer form of innovation (Ford, Richard, & Ciuchta, 2015).

6 Crowdsourcing Solutions Framework

In order to provide recommendations to all of the stakeholders involved, who understandably might have a limited understanding of the inner workings of crowdsourcing, a framework has been constructed that provides example solutions to potential industry challenges based on the stakeholder and the type of solution the crowd can provide.

The first horizontal axis represents the stakeholders in the lodging industry: the owners, the brand and the management firm. The brand is the identity of the hotel, it is responsible for the image, product design, and marketing. The goal of the brand is to drive customers into the hotel to increase revenue. The management firm is the operational core of the hotel, responsible for its employees and processes. The goal of the management firm is to deliver the brand promise as cost effectively as possible. It is motivated to be a good steward of the owner's investment through a fixed percentage of the revenue. The owner provides the funding for the hotel, taking actions in order to maximize its return on investment. As each stakeholder has a unique area of responsibility and goals, it is understandable that each would benefit from crowdsourced solutions in their own way.

The vertical axis represents ways in which the crowd can be called upon in order to provide innovative solutions to lodging industry problems. The authors have chosen to utilize the categories developed by Brabham (2012), *Organization* represents the crowd's ability to collect together and organize information. *Optimization* is the ability of the crowd to be presented with a problem, the solutions to which possess an empirically measurable improvement over the existing state. *Ideation* is the crowd's ability to generate new ideas and concepts, typically matters of taste or preference. Lastly, *Analysis* refers to using the crowd to solve problems that are beyond the organization's current computational abilities.

Alongside the types of problems listed in Table 1 are examples of how crowds might be used to identify innovative solutions to typical lodging problem areas. For example hotel owners could task the crowd with an organization type challenge by asking them to gather information related to existing terms and conditions in addition to law suits and their outcomes. A management firm might decide to conduct an optimization challenge by asking the crowd to develop a more efficient Housekeeping Cart, one that requires less space, or has a greater carrying capacity

Table 1 Crowdsourcing framework in the lodging industry (with examples)

Solution type	Brand	Management firm	Ownership
Organization: Finding and collecting information into a common location and format	Amenity Preferences Wallpaper Color Bedding	Employee benefits Laundry chemicals Accounting software	Financing terms Franchise fees Brand availability
Optimization: Solving empirical problems	Wireless Internet Business Center Layout Room Ergonomics	Housekeeping cart Car pool program Energy savings	Location selection Meeting room design CapEx budgeting
Ideation: Creating and selecting creative ideas	Loyalty Program New Logo Design Kids Programs	Employee menu Staff recognition Cost savings program	Management terms Recreation amenities Spa equipment/design
Analysis: Analyzing large amounts of information	Comment Cards	Employee surveys	Expense statistics

at its current size. A brand might task the crowd with developing an ideation solution; requesting that the crowd generate new benefits and rewards for the brand loyalty program.

7 Conclusion

Crowdsourcing, as an innovation technique, can be beneficial to hotels as they seek to adapt to new trends in the industry. New trends will require new marketing tactics, product offerings, procedures, training and financing. These transitional efforts won't come cheap or easy, and will require a renewed investment in innovation in the industry. It is in this spirit that the authors recommend that the industry consider and explore new innovation techniques—especially ones that are less costly, time consuming, and resource intensive. The authors have outlined below some industry report supported emerging trends, noting how they could be addressed through the pursuit of crowdsourcing solutions.

Guests are seeking out an international presence with a local feel. Crowdsourcing can assist firms that are expanding internationally that need to ensure they are properly catering to the local culture. Tapping into local online communities can allow firms to design competitions that seek to determine what local preferences are, and how best they can be replicated, efficiently, within the hotel. Emerging markets have a lower GDP than developed nations, which allows for the possibility of motivating the crowd through primarily monetary means. Firms seeking cheap labor to complete a distributed task have benefited from crowdsourcing platforms such as Amazon Mechanical Turk. Over one third of Amazon's crowd is made up of participants from developing nations (Ross, Irani, Silberman, Zaldivar, & Tomlinson, 2010).

Guests are seeking out authenticity and personalization. How can hotels optimize their interactions with guests to make them both more authentic and appealing to the individual? Recommendations from the crowd can be sorted and ranked by the crowd, and the hotel can make the determination of which to pursue based on the costs involved. Threadless, a website that allows the crowd to submit and vote on t-shirt designs, operates in a similar manner (Brabham, 2010). By better understanding guest, their needs and wants, hotels can better tailor their offerings to appeal to guest's desire for a more unique, personalized experience.

Guest care about sustainability. How can hotels become more sustainable in the future? The crowd can be tapped to generate ideas for operational practices and product offerings which are: more efficient, reduce consumption, and are more environmentally friendly. The crowd can also be asked to optimize existing processes and procedures. Recently NASA partnered with TopCoder, a crowdsourcing platform with an informational technology and programming crowd, in order to develop a more efficient emergency kit for the International Space Station (McKeown, 2012). What do space saving measures in space have to do with innovation in the lodging industry? This same challenge can be presented to the crowd, but instead of an emergency kit on a space station, it could be the house-keeping cart. A more efficient cart would be able to carry more improving efficiency, reducing waste, in addition to being beneficial to the housekeepers themselves.

Recognizing the inherent value in crowdsourcing as an innovation technique, hotel brands have already begun to incorporate open innovation practices into their research and development efforts. These initial forays into the world of co-creation have already borne fruit. By inviting the guest into the product develop process in addition to soliciting ideas on how to re-imagine the entire hotel experience hotel brands have shown an interest in better methods for engaging their guests, co-creating solutions with their guests, and opening up the innovation process itself to the worldwide crowd (Trejos, 2013). Where the lodging industry leads, the rest of the tourism industry very well could follow. Once the benefits of crowdsourcing are made apparent, and industry practices for crowdsourcing management are formalized, it is expected that crowdsourcing with its ability to deliver robust results faster and cheaper than alternative innovation methods will spread rapidly throughout the tourism industry.

References

Afuah, A., & Tucci, C. (2012). Crowdsourcing as a solution to distant search. *Academy of Management Review, 37*(3), 355–375.

Aubert, B., Dussault, S., Patry, M., & Rivard, S. (1999). *Managing the risk of it sourcing.* Paper presented at the proceedings of the 32nd Hawaii international conference of system sciences (HICSS), January 5–8, Hawaii.

Bahli, B., & Rivard, S. (2003). The information technology outsourcing risk: A transaction cost and agency theory-based perspective. *Journal of Information Technology, 18*, 211–221.

Bardi, J. A. (2006). *Hotel front office management* (4th ed.). New York: Wiley.

Barnes, B. (2014). *But it doesn't look like a Marriott: Marriott international aims to draw a younger crowd.* Retrieved on April 15, 2014 from http://www.nytimes.com/2014/01/05/business/marriott-international-aims-to-draw-a-younger-crowd.html?_r=0

Barney, J. (1991). Firm resources and sustained competitive advantage. *Journal of Management, 17*(1), 99–120.

Barney, J., & Arikan, A. M. (2001). The resource-based view: Origins and implications. In M. A. Hitt, R. E. Freeman, & J. S. Harrison (Eds.), *The Blackwell handbook of strategic management* (pp. 124–188). Oxford, UK: Blackwell.

Barney, J. B., & Hesterly, W. S. (2009). *Strategic management and competitive advantage.* Upper Saddle River, NJ: Pearson Education.

Benkler, Y. (2006). *The wealth of networks: How social production transforms markets and freedom.* New Haven, CT: Yale University Press.

Blake, A., Sinclair, M. T., & Soria, J. A. C. (2006). Tourism productivity. Evidence from the United Kingdom. *Annals of Tourism Research, 33*(4), 1099–1120.

Boettger, J. C. (2009). The asset management cycle and the development of the asset management plan. In G. Denton, L. E. Raleigh, & A. J. Singh (Eds.), *Hotel asset management: Principles & practices* (2nd ed., p. 402). Lansing, MI: American Hotel & Lodging Educational Institute.

Brabham, D. C. (2010). Moving the crowd at Threadless: Motivations for participation in a crowdsourcing application. *Information, Communication & Society, 13*(8), 1122–1145.

Brabham, D. C. (2012). Crowdsourcing: A model for leveraging online communities. In A. Delwiche & J. Henderson (Eds.), *The Routledge handbook of participatory cultures* (pp. 120–129). New York: Routledge.

Buhalis, D. (1999). Information technology for small and medium-sized tourism enterprises: Adaption and benefits. *Journal of Information Technology & Tourism, 2*(2), 79–95.

Chesbrough, H. W. (2003). The era of open innovation. *MIT Sloan Management Review, 44*(3), 35–41.

Christensen, C. (1997). *The innovator's dilemma: When new technologies cause great firms to fail.* Boston, MA: Harvard Business Review Press.

Danneels, E. (2004). Disruptive technology reconsidered: A critique and research agenda. *Journal of Product Innovation Management, 21*, 246–258.

Danneels, E. (2011). Trying to become a different type of company: Dynamic capability at Smith Corona. *Journal of Strategic Management, 32*, 1–31.

Dawson, R., & Bynghall, S. (2011). *Getting results from crowds: The definitive guide to using crowdsourcing to grow your business.* San Francisco, CA: Advanced Human Technologies Inc.

Fareed, J. S. (2005). *Bed, borrow or steal, hotel interactive.* Retrieved on August 15, 2013 from: http://www.ishc.com/uploadedFiles/PublicSite/Resources/Library/Articles/BorroworSteal.pdf

Fisher, S. (2009). *Crowdsourcing: Innovate or die.* Retrieved January 15, 2012 from: Marketing Executives Networking Group website. http://www.mengonline.com/docs/DOC-1896

Ford, R. C., Richard, B., & Ciuchta, M. P. (2015). Crowdsourcing: A new way of employing non-employees? *Business Horizons, 58*, 377–388.

Getz, D., & Carlsen, J. (2005). Family business in tourism. State of the art. *Annals of Tourism Research, 32*(1), 237–258.

Gilley, K., & Rasheed, A. (2000). Making more by doing less: An analysis of outsourcing and its effects on firm performance. *Journal of Management, 26*(4), 763–790.

Gonzales, A., Dorwin, D., Gupta, D., Kalyan, K., & Schimler, S. (2004). *Outsourcing: Past, present and future* (Unpublished paper).

Hansen, G. S., & Wernerfelt, B. (1989). Determinants of firm performance: The relative importance of economic and organizational factors. *Strategic Management Journal, 10*, 399–411.

Heylighen, F. (2007). Why is open access development so successful? Stigmergic organization and the economies of information. In B. Lutterbeck, M. Bärwolff, & R. A. Gehring (Eds.), *Open source Jahrbuch* (pp. 165–180). Berlin: Lehmanns Media.

Higgins, M. (2006). *Go directly to your room key! Pass the desk!* Retrieved on September 1, 2013 from http://travel2.nytimes.com/2006/08/20/travel/20prachotel.html

Higley, J. (2013). *W put 'lifestyle' on map 15 years ago.* Hotel News Now. Retrieved on September 1, 2013 from: http://hotelnewsnow.com/Article/10376/W-put-lifestyle-on-map-15-years-ago

Hjalager, A. M. (2010). A review of innovation research in tourism. *Tourism Management, 31*(1), 1–12.

Hotel Management Survey. (2012). *2012 top third-party management companies.* Hotel Management.net. Retrieved on September 1, 2013 from: http://www.hotelmanagement.net/hospitality-world-network-research/interstate-tops-2012-top-third-party-management-companies-list

Howe, J. (2006). The rise of crowdsourcing. *Wired Magazine, 14*(6), 1–4.

Howe, J. (2008). *Crowdsourcing: Why the power of the crowd is driving the future of business.* New York: Crown Business.

IBIS. (2013). *Global hotels & resorts: Market research report.* Retrieved on 09/01/2013 from http://www.ibisworld.com/industry/global/global-hotels-resorts.html

Kazman, R., & Chen, H. (2009). The metropolis model: A new logic for development of crowdsourced systems. *Communications of the ACM, 52*(7), 76–84.

Kozinets, R., Hemetsberger, A., & Schau, H. J. (2008). The wisdom of consumer crowds: Collective innovation in the age of networked marketing. *Journal of Macromarketing, 28*(4), 339–354.

Lakhani, K., Garvin, D., & Lonstein, E. (2010) *Topcoder(a): Developing software through crowdsourcing.* Harvard Business School General Management Unit Case (pp. 610–632).

LaSalle. (2013). *Americas hotel transaction volume to eclipse 2012 at $18.5 billion in 2013.* Retrieved on 09/01/2013 from: http://www.us.am.joneslanglasalle.com/UnitedStates/EN-US/ Pages/Newsitem.aspx?ItemID=26888

Martínez-Ros, E., & Orfila-Sintes, F. (2009). Innovation activity in the hotel industry. *Technovation, 29*(9), 632–641.

McFarlan, F. W., & Nolan, R. L. (1995). How to manage an it outsourcing alliance. *Sloan Management Review, 36*(2), 9–23.

McKeown, J. (2012). *TopCoder announces experimental crowdsourcing competition to benefit human space flight.* Retrieved on 09/01/2013 from: http://www.prnewswire.com/news-releases/ topcoder-announces-experimental-crowdsourcing-competition-to-benefit-human-space-flight-65162092.html

Page, S. (2007). *The difference: How the power of diversity creates better groups, firms, schools, and societies.* Princeton, NJ: Princeton University Press.

Porter, M. E. (1985). *Competitive advantage.* New York, NY: Free Press.

Porter, M. E. (2008). *Competitive advantage: Creating and sustaining superior performance.* SimonandSchuster.com

Raleigh, L. E. (2012). Hotel investments 101. In L. E. Raleigh & R. J. Roginsky (Eds.), *Hotel investments: Issues & perspectives* (5th ed., p. 381). Lansing, MI: American Hotel & Lodging Educational Institute.

Richard, B. (2013). Cheap solutions: Managing a co-producing crowd of strangers to solve your problems. In B. Ran (Ed.), *Contemporary perspectives on technical innovation, management and policy* (pp. 261–287). Charlotte, NC: Information Age.

Ross, J., Irani, L., Silberman, M., Zaldivar, A., & Tomlinson, B. (2010). Who are the crowdworkers?: Shifting demographics in mechanical turk. In *CHI'10 extended abstracts on human factors in computing systems,* ACM, pp. 2863–2872.

Rushmore, S., O'Neill, J. W., & Rushmore, S., Jr. (2012). *Hotel market analysis and valuation: International issues and software applications* (p. 408). Chicago, IL: Appraisal Institute.

Schreyogg, G., & Kliesch-Eberl, M. (2007). How dynamic can organizational capabilities be? Towards a dual-process model of capability dynamization. *Strategic Management Journal, 28* (9), 913–933.

Siguaw, J. A., Enz, C. A., & Namasivayam, K. (2000). Adoption of information technology in U.S. hotels: Strategically driven objectives. *Journal of Travel Research, 39,* 192–201.

Sloane, P. (2011). The brave new world of open innovation. *Strategic Direction, 27*(5), 3–4.

Starwood. (2009). *Ten years later Westin hotels is still the best in bed.* Retrieved on August 15, 2013 from: http://development.starwoodhotels.com/news/8/32-ten_years_later_westin_ hotels_is_still_the_best_in_bed

STR Analytics. (2013). *Host Almanac 2013: U.S. hotel operating statistics for the year 2012.* Boulder, CO: Smith Travel Research.

Tapscott, D., & Williams, A. (2006). *Wikinomics: How mass collaboration changes everything.* New York, NY: Penguin.

Trejos, N. (2013). *Guests help design the hotel of the future.* Retrieved on April 15, 2014 from http:// www.usatoday.com/story/travel/hotels/2013/11/14/hotel-guests-millennials-design-marriott-holiday-inn/3538573/

UNWTO. (2011). *UNWTO annual report 2011.* Retrieved on September 01, 2013 from http:// www2.unwto.org/en/publication/unwto-annual-report-2011.

Victorino, L., Verma, R., Plaschka, F., & Dev, C. (2005). Service innovation and customer choices in the hospitality industry. *Managing Service Quality, 15*(6), 555–576.

Vincent, L. H., Bharadwaj, S. G., & Challagalla, G. N. (2004). *Does innovation mediate firm performance?: A meta-analysis of determinants and consequences of organizational innovation,* Unpublished manuscript.

Vivion, M. (2014). *A collaborative concept coins Cotel, a new term for crowdsourced business hotel.* Retrieved on April 15, 2014 from http://www.tnooz.com/article/collaborative-concept-coins-Cotel-new-term-for-crowdsourced-hotel/#sthash.RD68QOmL.dpuf

Improving Hotel Industry Processes Through Crowdsourcing Techniques

Jose Luis Galdon-Salvador, Fernando J. Garrigos-Simon, and Ignacio Gil-Pechuan

1 Introduction

Businesses have to reinvent their strategies continuously in order to adapt to increasingly complex and dynamic market realities. In the hospitality industry, it is particularly difficult for companies to set themselves apart from their competitors and to offer better and cheaper products. Nowadays, hotels find it more difficult than before to remain competitive and consumers have unprecedented access to information and networks, which has increased competition in the sector. At the same time, new technologies have created new production models and ways of innovation in which customer participation has become the new value companies need to aspire to (Garrigos-Simon, Lapiedra-Alcamí, & Ribera, 2012). In this vein, the implementation of new techniques and especially the participation of people, have to be considered a vital part of the industry's processes in order to improve and transform the value chain.

Tourism has a very close relationship with new information and communication technologies. It is believed that thorough knowledge of a wide range of quality techniques for spreading information online can improve the business management of tourism managers (Buhalis, 1998). However, tourism companies cannot focus solely on marketing. They must be open to new innovation which can improve all areas of their activities. In order to meet this challenge, our study aims to explore how the participation of customers and other stakeholders in crowdsourcing techniques in different organisational areas can help hotels to be more competitive. Messerli (2011)) suggests that experience in the tourism industry has shown that the role of both direct and indirect dialogue is especially relevant. In this context, the use of new techniques to involve stakeholders in the different phases of the

J.L. Galdon-Salvador (✉) • F.J. Garrigos-Simon • I. Gil-Pechuan
Universitat Politècnica de València, Valencia, Spain
e-mail: jlgaldon12@gmail.com; fgarrigos@doe.upv.es; igil@doe.upv.es

© Springer-Verlag Berlin Heidelberg 2016
R. Egger et al. (eds.), *Open Tourism*, Tourism on the Verge,
DOI 10.1007/978-3-642-54089-9_7

development, creation and selling of tourism products is critical not only to be competitive, but also to survive.

Crowdsourcing techniques centre on this. They are conceived as a combination of traditional outsourcing alongside the participation of a broad range of stakeholders and other people in a particular process. In this chapter, we analyse how the new environment is changing, how it is essential to look at the value chain of organisations in this shifting environment and how we can use crowdsourcing techniques to transform and improve the different sections of the new value chain of organisations.

This chapter attempts to define and explore the importance of crowdsourcing activities in the value chain processes of companies. It begins with an in-depth study of the relevant literature about the transformation of the value chain in tourism and the concept of crowdsourcing. Following this, the paper focuses on describing the main uses of crowdsourcing and also provides several examples of its use in hotels. The chapter ends with the conclusions and limitations of the study.

2   Theoretical Background

2.1   The Transformation of the Value Chain in Tourism

The relevance of supply chain management in general and the value chain of firms in particular, is constant in literature. The concept of the value chain, which was introduced by Porter (1985), suggests that a firm can divide its structure into different activities according to the behaviour of costs and the potential sources of differentiation.

In general, a tourism supply chain can be defined as "a network of tourism organisations engaged in different activities ranging from the supply of different components of tourism products/services, such as flights and accommodation to the distribution and marketing of the final tourism product at a specific tourism destination and involves a wide range of participants in both the private and public sectors" (Zhang, Song, & Huang, 2009, p. 347). However, due the broad definition of the tourism supply chain, in this paper we only aim to focus on the hotel value chain and more specifically, the activities that come under the hotel business umbrella.

Although studies of tourism value chains, tourism supply chains and tourism industry chains are not particularly common in literature (Yilmaz & Bititci, 2006; Zhang et al., 2009), there are some examples of Porter's value chain concept being applied or adapted to the tourism industry (Poon, 1993; Bieger, 1998). In this regard and based on the concept of the tourism industry's "flexible specialisation", Poon (1993) examined tourism industry processes to establish a strategy to make tourism organisations more competitive. More recently, Bauer, Boksberger, Herget, Hierl, and Orsolini (2008) adapted Porter's value chain for e-tourism based on the following five primary activities: infrastructure, technology development, marketing and sales, operations and service. In general, literature stresses that the tourism value chain begins when the customer makes an order (Yilmaz & Bititci, 2006). The creation and transmission of value to tourists is then one of the most relevant factors for organisations and even a source of competitive advantage, especially in the new context characterised by globalised competition and by increasingly informed customers who are more and more demanding (Flagestad & Hope, 2001). Hence, organisations have to respond to these demands if they want to be competitive or, in some cases, simply survive.

To cater for these demands, the use of new innovations and new technological toolkits are obviously essential. Gratzer, Winiwarter, and Werther (2002) pointed out that new technologies in general and the internet in particular, redefine the entire distribution system in the tourism industry, bringing with it increased efficiency, reduced costs and improved customer service.

New innovations are promoting the use of networking and authors such as Kalpic and Bernus (2006) stress that this networking drives firms to work faster, managing more interdependencies and operating in global markets. In this respect, a change in the concept of a firm's value chain is crucial, especially in cases where both the product and supply chain are digitalised (sectors such as telecommunications, banking, entertainment, music, advertising, public sector, etc.) (Peppard & Rylander, 2006).

The behaviour of users changes constantly and is being transformed. The customer is shifting from being a passive client into a hyperactive one who wants to participate in all the production processes (Shiffman, 2008). Therefore, the development of social networks is changing the actual model of production, forcing companies to create links with the market and interact and cooperate with customers and other stakeholders in all the production processes.

Consequently, without the participation of users, we could not interpret the new business framework, as argued by Garrigos, Gil, and Narangajavana (2011). This fact has also been pointed out by Fuchs, Hofkirchner, Schafranek et al. (2010), who noted that users are a very important part in the production of content, in terms of the value added by their tastes, emotions, feedback, etc.

The participation of users in general, made up of many kinds of stakeholders, can be made effective through the use of crowdsourcing techniques, which can be applied to improve almost every part of the value chain of tourism firms in general and hotel enterprises in particular.

2.2 The Use of Crowdsourcing

In general terms, crowdsourcing is the online participative process that enables a task to be carried out to solve a problem (Estellés-Arolas & González-Ladrón-de-Guevara, 2012). Nowadays, crowdsourcing is one of the most innovative developments being used by organisations.

The expression crowdsourcing was coined by Jeff Howe in June 2006. "Crowdsourcing represents the act of a company or institution taking a function once performed by employees and outsourcing it to an undefined (and generally large) network of people in the form of an open call". Crowdsourcing, which also takes the form of "massive outsourcing" or "voluntary outsourcing", is defined in this study as the act of taking a job or task usually performed by an employee of the firm or a contractor (Howe, 2009) and outsourcing it through an open call to a large group of people or a community (crowd or mass) through the internet.

Several authors have defined the term as the outsourcing of tasks to the general internet public (Kleemann, Voß, & Rieder, 2008), which describes a new web-based business strategy (Brabham, 2008), or a new innovation business model through the internet (Ling, 2010). Crowdsourcing can be described as a form of user integration in internal processes of value creation (Kleemann et al., 2008). However and apart from clients or users who can be deemed essential to crowdsourcing, the process can also add all types of stakeholders who are not employees of the firm (Garrigos-Simon et al., 2012), amateurs, or the general public (Estellés-Arolas & González-Ladrón-de-Guevara, 2012). The crowd can help to improve production processes, execute any of the firm's issues, obtain the solution to problems and generate open innovations (ibid). The expansion of social networks has enabled the model to flourish, alongside the development of very diverse types of remuneration and motivation mechanisms for participants in the process (Geiger, Seedorf, Schulze et al., 2011).

Brabham (2008) states that, "crowdsourcing is not only a Web 2.0 buzzword, but is instead a strategic model with the intention of attracting a crowd of individuals capable of providing more and better solutions then traditional forms of business can".

Crowdsourcing allows organisations to capture and analyse large amounts of interesting data, making it possible for people to invent and develop new technologies, finance processes and develop products (crowdfunding), fix the problems of scientific researchers, execute a design task or routine, develop products and processes through the generation or exploitation of creative ideas (Estellés-Arolas & González-Ladrón-de-Guevara, 2012), produce memorable commercials, or rate and recommend products, processes, services, etc.

Poetz and Schreier (2012) highlight the importance of outsourcing the stage of idea generation to a potentially large and unknown population through an open call. In this context, crowdsourcing can be viewed as a general-purpose problem-solving method (Doan, Ramakrishnan, & Halevy, 2011) that can rapidly help organisations in all the processes of a product or service life-cycle (Porta et al., 2008). However, crowdsourcing can be widely applied not only to idea generation or specific problem-solving, but also as a new source of innovation at almost every step of the value chain.

In these processes, the participation of customers and all types of stakeholders or members of the public who are interested in generating new ideas or developing tasks becomes enormously important to the organisation.

3 Empirical Applications

As mentioned above, the main purpose of this study is to assess the transformation of the tourism value chain through the implementation of new models of collaborative participation such as crowdsourcing techniques.

To address the activities that make up an organisation's value, a difference needs to be made between a business's primary activities and its support activities. Primary activities are the activities involved in creation, customer sales, distribution and after-sales service. These activities include internal logistics, operations, external logistics, marketing and sales and customer service. Support activities are responsible for sustaining primary activities, providing purchased inputs, technology, human resources and various functions across the enterprise (infrastructure). As we have previously noted, in the case of e-tourism, recent research (e.g. Bauer et al., 2008) has focused on the activities that are included in Porter's value chain, in the following five activities: infrastructure, technology development, marketing and sales, operations and service.

This section follows a similar approach of the tourism value chain to the one developed by Bauer et al. (2008), in focusing on the use of crowdsourcing in the diverse phases of the tourism value chain.

3.1 Marketing, Sales and Service

According to Li and Petrick (2008), in the future tourism marketing environment, tourists should be considered as value co-creators. Thus, the participation of tourists, as well as other stakeholders, in the creation of value is essential, therefore making crowdsourcing a fundamental tool for organisations' general purposes. More specifically, outsourcing through an open call on the internet can be tied to operational activities, such as marketing (e.g. Starbucks Idea) (Rieder & Voß, 2010). In this vein, extensive crowdsourcing has been utilised to identify a new tourism brand for a country (Messerli, 2011) and this can be extended to diverse kinds of destinations and tourism organisations. An excellent example of this was carried out by the Tourism Authority of Thailand. The government launched an open call asking anybody who had visited the country to submit their "Amazing moments" (http://www.MostAmazingShow.com). The Tourism Authority of Thailand hopes to increase the number of visitors to the country through this innovative idea which shows the attractions of Thailand through the different photographs submitted.

One of the most recent examples of hospitality innovation using this technique is the Hesperia Hotels chain's "Suite H" project. In this programme, centred on the slogan "putting ideas into practice", clients can share their innovative ideas with hotel managers. After a close study, the best ideas are implemented and the owners of the ideas rewarded. Over the last year, 397 ideas have been received as part of this programme, 94 of which have been marked as "possible" whilst 29 are at the development stage.

Crowdsourcing includes advice that customers give to other customers by writing product reviews or uploading information to virtual travel agencies, different networks, specific sites such as ctrips.com, gazetters.com, IGOUGO, TripAdvisor and Wayn.com (Buhalis, Leung, & Law, 2011; Sigala, 2009) or the web sites of hotel companies such as Marriot (Au, Law, & Buhalis, 2010) and Sheraton (Sigala & Marinidis, 2009). It can also help organisations to identify any observable changes in market supply or consumer demand, complementing traditional market research (Kleemann et al., 2008). Moreover, crowdsourcing is useful in improving customer service; for instance, some technology companies are using different crowdsourcing techniques in the UK and Spain to address specific user problems and answer and provide solutions to their demands. This encourages other users to participate in the process.

In addition, we should point out that crowdsourcing is essential to satisfy the individual demands of specific tourist segments, such as college tourists (Zhen, 2010), thus making its use in the marketing arena fundamental. Another of the best-known examples of crowdsourcing in the hospitality industry is the Starbuck's "MyStarbucksIdea" platform (Sigala, 2012b), where customers can share feedback and ideas and make suggestions about existing or new products (Müller, 2011). According to Sigala (2012a), three categories of new services were defined by Starbucks in this initiative to facilitate the online organisation and search for submitted ideas. Each idea was sub-divided into other sub-groups of ideas, such as product ideas (e.g. coffee, tea, food and merchandising, etc.); experience ideas (e.g. ordering, payment, atmosphere, etc.) and involvement ideas (building community, social responsibility, etc.). Another important example is the case of Sheraton. According to Sigala and Marinidis (2009), technological innovations, such as the web map services offered on Sheraton's website, promote the participation of customers, allowing them to search, contribute and read user-generated content about Sheraton properties. Sigala and Marinidis (2009) argue that this is important because Sheraton can take advantage of this user-generated content for new service development (staff can use this feedback for market research and identify opportunities to provide new services); business process improvement (user-generated content allows operational problems identified by guests to be addressed) and CRM (e.g. user-generated content and social networking amongst guests enables the creation of a community of loyal guests that stay at Sheraton properties and increases the opportunities to communicate with them, identifying valuable customers for future personalised targeting and many other CRM practices). If we extend customer participation to other stakeholders through open calls, these benefits will certainly increase.

3.2   Operations

Outsourcing through open calls on the internet, or crowdsourcing, have been used to produce user-generated content for social media websites (e.g. Facebook) (Rieder & Voß, 2010). Crowdsourcing is essential to improve production processes in tourism generally and by extension, in the hospitality sector, especially in a context where networking in the production process is critical.

Crowdsourcing has been used as a mechanism to develop tourism destinations or cities, such as Seattle and Vancouver, as reported by Merchant (2011) and the city of Ghent, which was analysed by these authors. In addition, it offers endless opportunities to contribute to the tourism disaster management process, which is essential for tourism destinations and organisations, as, for example, it complements geospatial analysis with Geographic Information Systems (Faulkner, 2001). Crowdsourcing applications and techniques are also very useful to collect data and offer planning and guides for trips. Hence, augmented reality, mobile platforms, websites and crowdsourcing systems may be enriched by uploading local information that is not provided by classic network members (Leo, 2010). The content and information generated by users of Web 2.0 technologies are having a tremendous impact not only on the decision-making behaviour of internet users, but also on the e-business model that a tourism business needs to develop and to adapt (Sigala, 2009).

This is essential for travel companies and also hotel companies when developing their products and adapting them to the different types of tourists. A closer look at this issue reveals several crowdsourcing applications that provide insight into the problem-solving model that can be generalised and applied to both mundane and highly complex tasks (Brabham, 2008). Particularly, we think that crowdsourcing techniques are useful in improving the development of products and processes. According to Zhang et al. (2009), as product development is not an easy task but rather a complex process, it requires efforts from different players in the supply chain. Hence, the possibilities of crowdsourcing processes in these tasks are crucial.

Of further importance is the management of inventories. According to Zhang et al. (2009), inventory management problems, such as overbooking and revenue/ yield management, have been broadly discussed in tourism literature. These authors argue that crowdsourcing processes can help to create mechanisms, such as algorithms and technological applications, to improve these problems, as well as creating innovative formulas and recommendations for hotels to answer these questions.

In addition to the "MyStarbucksIdea", which is obviously not limited to the area of marketing, as it includes the improvement of operation processes that could be applied to hotels, we think that the participation of users and other stakeholders and the information that they can provide through crowdsourcing processes, as well as their participation in social networks, is important in designing and adapting all kinds of hotel services to cater for customer needs. Finally, we have to stress the importance of crowdsourcing to improve not only operations themselves, but also the strategic use of these operations. For instance, Harpur and Brown (2012), in their analysis of tourism organisations, highlighted that firms which take into account the strategic aspects of their operations can improve the profitability of their company. The financial benefits of outsourcing, therefore, have led to studies into how tourist operations can effectively outsource (Lam & Han, 2005). However, Espino-Rodriguez (2004), who analysed the trend in outsourcing hotel operations and explained the importance of this phenomenon, underlined the relevance of strategic reasons for outsourcing. According to this author, the main reasons centre on improving quality and service, making operations more flexible and concentrating on core operations, compared to the traditional focus on outsourcing for tactical reasons based on cost reductions. Hence, crowdsourcing can enhance the specialisation of hotels in their core competences and ensure the use of external innovations to improve tasks. It is important to highlight the risks of outsourcing to a diverse group of people. In order to maximise process quality, the organisation must have people who regulate quality inputs and manage and select the inputs of the crowd, etc.

To sum up, people can create and submit ideas for products, processes, or the design of all kinds of destinations and tourism organisations, such as hotels and their operations and production processes, in particular.

3.3   Technology Development

This consists of a range of activities that can be broadly grouped into efforts to improve products and processes. New forms of organisation, communication, relationships and innovation management establish new business models. Understanding and anticipating enables organisations and their leaders to prepare for new approaches to innovation and creation.

If we focus on innovation, crowdsourcing is a tool of crucial importance. Much has been written on the importance of innovation as a strategy for achieving competitive advantage (Ottenbacher & Gnoth, 2005), the potential of creating a culture of continuous innovation and innovation as a method to erect barriers to imitation by competitors (Harrington, 2004). We must emphasise that a simple query on the internet should not be confused with crowdsourcing. We talk about crowdsourcing when the company has done previous work to focus on a problem and they manage their ideas as well as possible (Benkler, 2006). In many cases, companies face challenges in their production processes and try to solve them through innovation and new ideas. In these cases, the company can enlist the help of the crowd who not only provide benefits of cost, time and information, but also, more importantly, knowledge. As Brabham (2009) highlights, the processes of a company centre on airing the problem online, choosing the best solution of those proposed, rewarding the winner and mass producing the concept for its own benefit. One of the most interesting examples is the company, Innocentive. This platform allows companies with a problem that cannot be fixed internally (or they do not have the necessary resources to do so) to share it with the crowd to receive proposals for a solution. The company describes the problem as precisely as possible and offers a reward for the best solution received. In this case, after the best solution to the problem has been chosen, the company rewards the winner and carries out this project. There are other platforms like Wilogo that not only offer the solution but are also responsible for the industrialisation and development of the project.

In this sense, one of the current projects on the Innocentive platform is of particular interest to the hospitality field. It is well known that one of the critical problems of hotels is laundry (in terms of costs, energy consumption, etc.). In this case, one of the projects centres on the search for high efficiency washers to improve performance and decrease water and energy consumption. The platform www.solucioneo.com facilitates and enables the application of crowdsourcing in organisations, accelerates innovation to increase competitiveness, opens organisations to external talent, shortens the time within which organisations can find a solution and reduces the risks of innovation. At the same time, it allows organisations to access new ideas that otherwise would not have been possible due to lack of time, knowledge and/or lack of technological assets.

One of a hotel's greatest expenses is its energy costs. A potential challenge could be to present the energy consumption of a hotel and offer a reward for the best energy-saving solution received. This idea has been put into practice in the campaign "Ride a Bike, Help Power the Hotel, & Get a Free Meal in Copenhagen". This project is being carried out by one of the "greenest hotels", the Crowne Plaza Copenhagen Towers. The idea consists of riding a bike to generate electricity for the hotel. People who generate 10 watt hours or more of electricity are rewarded with a free meal, costing about $45.

3.4 Company Infrastructure

This part of the value chain consists of several activities, such as finance, accounting, quality management, public relations and legal and general management. The infrastructure usually supports the entire chain and not only individual activities. The infrastructure of the company is a powerful source of competitive advantage, as it supports the primary activities in decision-making, including good management information systems, sound financial strategy and managing legal operations.

One of the most innovative cases is the company, Wiseri. Their business model centres on trying to differentiate themselves from traditional employment portals by using crowdsourcing. Their experts, known as "wisors", are network users, who have experience in different professional areas and voluntarily assess the applications corresponding to their field. They receive a number of prizes as a reward for their application assessment work. These types of platforms are of great help to human resource departments in companies because they receive a selection of CVs which have been properly evaluated by experts.

In the field of finance, we must highlight the crowdfunding phenomenon, which is a type of crowdsourcing often used by companies. The main idea of crowdfunding is to obtain external finance from a large audience (the "crowd"), where each member provides a very small amount, instead of big investments from small groups.

Kickstarter, the North American company, is probably the best known organisation in this area and presents itself as the largest crowdfunding platform for creative projects in the world. The creators of each project publish the details of their project and establish a funding goal and a deadline. The projects are then evaluated by Kickstarter. Meanwhile, members of the crowd donate money in exchange for a "reward" (mainly the product or the experience in question). The advantage for the patrons is that they only make payments when the project reaches its funding goal and begins the production stage. Kickstarter charges a commission fee of about 5 % of the total project funding obtained (only for projects that reach their goal). As of the end of 2013, Kickstarter had launched 73,065 successful projects (including the successful Pebble Watch and Elevation iPhone Dock). It has also contributed to many projects that have reached their goals in various fields such as technology, design and fashion. The amount of money obtained in all the projects so far has totalled over than $377 million.

Power4projects.com is the first crowdfunding and investment platform for the tourism and leisure industry. The platform enables a wide audience, such as private and professional investors, private equity and venture capital companies, to pinpoint opportunities to invest in projects and companies in the tourism and leisure industry. The platform provides a marketplace for public crowdfunding, crowd investing and for all types of investments.

Another platform with a large number of crowdfunding-based projects is www.lanzanos.com. The variety of projects found on the site includes entrepreneurs looking for funding to set up hotels of all kinds, from bed and breakfast establishments to luxury hotels. In the hospitality sector, this type of technique can be used either to obtain the funding needed for a project in a hotel which is already open, or to finance a new hotel project.

4 Conclusion

Nowadays, new models of organisation, communication, relationships and talent management are breaking the barriers of time and space and establishing new patterns of doing business in tourism. Understanding and anticipation enables organisations and their leaders to prepare for and produce new approaches to promoting innovation and creation and to improving production, marketing and finance. However, change does not only consist of getting to know and understanding this new framework, it requires a change in attitude and, above all, a change of perspective and a new way of thinking aimed at obtaining greater value for firms based on crowd participation. In this new arena, the collaboration of the crowd is considered a part of all of the processes in the hospitality sector.

This paper has shown the importance of crowdsourcing and how it can transform the value chain of tourism organisations in general and hotel firms, in particular. After a detailed study of the transformation of the value chain through the development of new technologies and a review of the concept and the definition of crowdsourcing, our study provides examples of crowdsourcing techniques that can be used to improve the productivity of organisations and especially those in the tourism sector. The work analyses the main activities of organisations, focusing on the most relevant ones introduced by Bauer et al. (2008), namely, infrastructure, technology development, marketing and sales, operations and service.

The existing literature on the crowdsourcing concept is relatively limited. Accordingly, this research adds a novel contribution to crowdsourcing literature and evaluates it and its impact as a source of the transformation of the tourism value chain. Beyond its contribution to literature, the results of this paper also show that crowdsourcing techniques are of tremendous interest to organisations as a step towards making hotel business models successful, via the techniques that encourage crowd participation (Geiger et al., 2011).

We are aware that this is an exploratory study and that these transformations need further consideration. Therefore, future research should test the theoretical topics examined on an empirical basis. However, the paper creates a new frame of analysis, considering certain empirical applications of crowdsourcing techniques and opening new areas of research. This work, finally, is of practical importance for practitioners and executives of tourist firms.

References

Au, N., Law, R., & Buhalis, D. (2010). The impact of culture on eComplaints: Evidence from Chinese consumers in hospitality organisations. In U. Gretzel, R. Law, & M. Fuchs (Eds.), *Information and communication technologies in tourism* (pp. 285–296). New York: Springer.

Bauer, L., Boksberger, P., Herget, J., Hierl, S., & Orsolini, N. (2008). The virtual dimension in tourism: Criteria catalogue for the assessment of eTourism applications. In *Information and communication technologies in tourism* (pp. 521–532). New York: Springer.

Benkler, Y. (2006). *The wealth of networks: How social production transforms markets and freedom*. New Haven/London: Yale University Press.

Bieger, T. (1998). Reengineering destination marketing organizations - The case of Switzerland. *Revue de Tourisme, 53*(3), 4–17.

Brabham, D. C. (2008). Crowdsourcing as a model for problem solving. An introduction and cases, Convergence. *The International Journal of Research into New Media Technologies, 14*(1), 75–90.

Brabham, D. C. (2009). Crowdsourcing the public participation process for planning projects. *Planning Theory, 8*(3), 242–262.

Buhalis, D. (1998). Strategic use of information technologies in the tourism industry. *Tourism Management, 19*(5), 409–421.

Buhalis, D., Leung, D., & Law, R. (2011). eTourism: Critical information and technologies. In Y. Wang & A. Pizam (Eds.), *Destination marketing and management: Theories and applications* (pp. 205–224). Walling: CAB International.

Doan, A., Ramakrishnan, R., & Halevy, A. Y. (2011). Crowdsourcing systems on the World-Wide Web. *Communications of the ACM, 54*(4), 86–96.

Espino-Rodriguez, T. F. (2004). The tendency to outsource hotel operations: Strategic reasons and relationship to activity performance and size. *Tourism Review, 59*(2), 17–25.

Estellés-Arolas, E., & González-Ladrón-de-Guevara, F. (2012). Towards an integrated crowdsourcing definition. *Journal of Information Science, 38*(2), 189–200.

Faulkner, B. (2001). Towards a framework for tourism disaster management. *Tourism Management, 22*, 135–147.

Flagestad, A., & Hope, C. A. (2001). Strategic success in winter sports destinations: A sustainable value creation perspective. *Tourism Management, 22*, 445–461.

Fuchs, C., Hofkirchner, W., Schafranek, M., et al. (2010). Theoretical foundations of the Web: Cognition, communication, and co-operation. Towards an understanding of Web 1.0, 2.0, 3.0. *Future Internet, 2*, 41–59.

Garrigos, F., Gil, I., & Narangajavana, Y. (2011). The impact of social networks in the competitiveness of the firms. In A. B. Beckford & J. P. Larsen (Eds.), *Competitiveness: Psychology, production, impact and global trends*. Hauppauge: Nova Science.

Garrigos-Simon, F. J., Lapiedra-Alcamí, R., & Ribera, T. B. (2012). Social networks and Web 3.0: Their impact on the management and marketing of organizations. *Management Decision, 50* (10), 1880–1890.

Geiger, D., Seedorf, S., Schulze, T., et al. (2011). *Managing the crowd: Towards a Taxonomy of crowdsourcing processes* (Proceedings of the seventeenth Americas conference on information systems, August, 4th–7th, pp. 1–11). Michigan: Detroit.

Gratzer, M., Winiwarter, W., & Werther, H. (2002). State of the art in eTourism. In *Proceedings of the 3rd SouthEastem European conference on e-Commerce*, Nicosia.

Harpur, P., Brown, K., et al. (2012). Contracting and asset management: Establishing an asset specificity framework for determining the optimal management of tourism infrastructure. In J. Mathew (Ed.), *Engineering asset management and infrastructure sustainability* (pp. 329–336). London: Springer.

Harrington, R. J. (2004). The environment, involvement, and performance: Implications for the strategic process of food service firms. *International Journal of Hospitality Management, 23* (4), 317–341.

Howe, J. (2009). *Crowdsourcing: Why the power of the crowd is driving the future of business*. New York: Crown Business.

Kalpic, B., & Bernus, P. (2006). Business process modeling through the knowledge management perspective. *Journal of Knowledge Management, 10*(3), 40–56.

Kleemann, F., Voß, G. G., & Rieder, K. (2008). Un(der)paid innovators: The commercial utilization of consumer work through crowdsourcing. *Technology & Innovation Studies, 4* (1), 5–26.

Lam, T., & Han, M. X. (2005). A study of outsourcing strategy: A case involving the hotel industry in Shanghai, China. *International Journal of Hospitality Management, 24*(1), 41–56.

Leo, H. (2010). Trends in service innovation enhanced by mobile services in the field of tourism in rural and mountain areas. *Aosta Seminar* (pp. 1–19), November 21–23, 2010.

Li, X., & Petrick, J. F. (2008). Tourism marketing in an era of paradigm shift. *Journal of Travel Research, 46*(3), 235–244.

Ling, P. (2010). An empirical study of social capital in participation in online crowdsourcing. *Computer, 7*(9), 1–4.

Merchant, P. (2011). *Workplace diversity in hospitality & tourism*. http://smallbusiness.chron. com/

Messerli, H. R. (2011). Transformation through tourism: Harnessing tourism as a development tool for improved livelihoods tourism planning and development. *Tourism Planning & Development, 8*(3), 335–337.

Müller. (2011). *Social media marketing. A critical and evaluative account on the emergence and principles of social media marketing and its true potential to enhance the marketing initiatives of hotels and other organisations.* Scholarly Essay, 2011. Retrieved October, 22nd from http://www.grin.com/en/e-book/200590/social-media-marketing

Ottenbacher, M., & Gnoth, J. (2005). How to develop successful hospitality innovation. *Cornell Hotel and Restaurant Administration Quarterly, 46*(2), 205–222.

Peppard, J., & Rylander, A. (2006). From value chain to value network: Insights for mobile operators. *European Management Journal, 24*(2–3), 128–141.

Poetz, M. K., & Schreier, M. (2012). The value of crowdsourcing: Can users really compete with professionals in generating new product ideas? *Journal of Product Innovation Management, 29*, 245–256.

Poon, A. (1993). *Tourism, technology and competitive strategies.* Oxford: CAB International.

Porta, M., House, B., Buckley, L., et al. (2008). Value 2.0: Eight new rules for creating and capturing value form innovative technologies. *Strategy & Leadership, 36*(4), 10–18.

Porter, M. E. (1985). *Competitive advantage.* New York: The Free Press.

Rieder, K., & Voß, G. G. (2010). The working customer - An emerging new type of consume. *Psychology of Everyday Activity, 3*(2), 2–10.

Shiffman, D. (2008). *The age of engage.* Ladera Ranch, CA: Hunt Street Press.

Sigala, M. (2009). *WEB 2.0 in the tourism industry: A new tourism generation and new eBusiness models.* Retrieved October 22, 2011, from http://www.traveldailynews.com/pages/show_page/20554

Sigala, M. (2012a). Web 2.0 and customer involvement in new service development: A framework, cases and implications in tourism. In M. Sigala, E. Christou, & U. Gretzel (Eds.), *Web 2.0 in travel, tourism and hospitality: Theory, practice and cases* (pp. 25–38). Surrey: Ashgate.

Sigala, M. (2012b). Social networks and customer involvement in new service development (NSD). The case of www.mystarbucksidea.com. *International Journal of Contemporary Hospitality Management, 24*(7), 966–990.

Sigala, M., & Marinidis, D. (2009). *Exploring the transformation of tourism firms' operations and business models through the use of web map services.* Paper presented at the European and Mediterranean conference on information systems 2009 (EMCIS 2009), Founded and Organised by the Information Systems Evaluation and Integration Group, Brunel University, Izmir, July 13–14.

Yilmaz, Y., & Bititci, U. S. (2006). Performance measurement in tourism: A value chain model. *International Journal of Contemporary Hospitality Management, 18*(4), 341–349.

Zhang, X., Song, H., & Huang, G. Q. (2009). Tourism supply chain management: A new research agenda. *Tourism Management, 30*(3), 345–358.

Zhen, L. (2010). Studies on the attitudes and behaviors of Chinese college students to E-tourism. In *International conference on internet technology and applications, 2010* (pp. 20–22) August, 2010.

Motivation for Open Innovation and Crowdsourcing: Why Does the Crowd Engage in Virtual Ideas Communities?

Ulrich Bretschneider and Jan Marco Leimeister

1 Introduction

Virtual idea communities (VIC) are a new phenomenon in business. These communities, in which distributed groups of individual customers focus on voluntarily sharing and elaborating innovation ideas, are used by firms to integrate customers into ideation for new product development rooted in Chesbrough's Open Innovation paradigm or according to the more general Crowdsourcing principle (Chesbrough, 2003; Afuah & Tucci, 2012). Based on this paradigm, firms transcend their boundaries in order to engage other resources in developing ideas for innovation (Chesbrough, 2003). In this context, customers are seen as a key resource as they often have high product expertise as well as experiences and creativity potential gained by regular product usage (Hestad & Keitsch, 2009). Öberg (2010) describes customers as initiator, as co-producer and as inspiration for business development.

The idea that firms benefit from customer-based, collaborative ideation is not new per se. Since the 1980s, small groups of customers have been brought together in face to face settings to support new product development. Von Hippel's "Lead-User-Approach" and focus groups are examples of such customer integration (Fern, 1982; von Hippel, 1986). By implementing VICs firms move customer-based, collaborative ideation onto the Internet. Many well-known companies, including DELL, Starbucks, Google, SAP, Intel, and BMW, have established such Internet-

U. Bretschneider (✉)
University of Kassel, Kassel, Germany
e-mail: bretschneider@uni-kassel.de

J.M. Leimeister
University of Kassel, Kassel, Germany

University of St. Gallen, St. Gallen, Switzerland
e-mail: janmarco.leimeister@unisg.ch

© Springer-Verlag Berlin Heidelberg 2016
R. Egger et al. (eds.), *Open Tourism*, Tourism on the Verge,
DOI 10.1007/978-3-642-54089-9_8

based ideation forums (Di Gangi & Wasko, 2009). In VICs customers can post their ideas, vote for as well as comment on other customers' ideas and help improve ideas in a collaborative manner, similar to what is currently achieved in lead-user-workshops and focus groups. Firms organize VICs from initial community building to continuous community management. This allows them to control the community throughout, from moderation of the ideation to non-restrictive use of its idea outcome. VICs are supported by Web-based Idea Platforms (WBIP), IT- and Internet-mediated idea management systems, which meet all ideation requirements according to Kipp et al. (2013), i.e., functionalities for idea uploading, storage, commenting, elaboration, and visualization. To sum it up, VICs enable a paradigm shift from real world ideation to virtual ideation with customers.

By shifting customer ideation onto the Internet, firms profit from organizational benefits. First, inviting customers into VICs is less complex than organizing face to face workshops. Once the virtual idea community is established, firms can constantly get back to the customer knowledge base. Furthermore, VIC's WBIP help firms to evaluate and select the most promising customer ideas (Sandström & Bjork, 2010). Second, compared to lead user workshops and focus groups, VICs can help firms attain access to a much broader customer base, respectively a customers' knowledge base (Leimeister, Huber, Bretschneider, & Krcmar, 2009). This raises the likelihood of identifying a number of promising ideas for product development considerably.

To date there is little known about motivations for participating in VICs. Thus, this paper aims at empirically identifying customer motives for participating in VICs. The argument is organized as follows: In the next section, possible motives from open source motivation research have been identified with the help of a literature review. With an online survey, the identified motives then have been queried amongst customers participating in SAPiens, the VIC of the ERP software producer SAP (here the terms "SAP customer" and "SAP user" are used synonymously, since in general customers of a software are also users of this software. In case of SAP, the ones who "buy" the software are typically not the ones who use this software, but in order to ease this circumstance, both terms are used synonymously). The empirical data are analysed with the help of factor analyses. Thereafter, a set of six empirically tested motives are identified.

2   Literature Review

Human motivation has been discussed prominently in the field of open source community research. Various motives are examined that make open source software programmers participate in open source software projects. As open source software communities are basically comparable to VIC it is worth to check if motives examined in the open source domain could be extracted to our case. So there was conducted a literature review. The most relevant empirical studies out of the field of open source research that deal with programmers' motives for

Table 1 Adapted motives

Motive	References
Fun	Contextualized from Hars and Ou (2002), Hertel et al. (2003), Lakhani and Wolf (2005), Shah (2005)
Intellectual stimulation	Contextualized from Lakhani and Wolf (2005)
Recognition	Contextualized from Ghosh, Glott, Kreiger, and Robles (2002), Hars and Ou (2002), Hertel, Niedner and Herrmann (2003), Lakhani and Wolf (2005), Shah (2005)
Self marketing	Contextualized from Hars and Ou (2002), Hertel et al. (2003)
Product improvement	Contextualized from Ghosh et al. (2002), Hertel et al. (2003), Shah (2005)
Need	Contextualized from Ghosh et al. (2002), Hars and Ou (2002), Lakhani and Wolf (2005), Shah (2005)
Learning	Contextualized from Ghosh et al. (2002), Hars and Ou (2002), Hertel et al. (2003), Lakhani and Wolf (2005)
Contact to peers	Contextualized from Ghosh et al. (2002), Hertel et al. (2003)

Source: Own depiction

participation in open source communities were examined. It was focused on its examined motivation factors and analyzed which of them are appropriable for the use of our own survey. Based on the insights of this research eight motives, which are briefly described as follows (see also Table 1), were applied.

The first motive is **fun**. Fun is a prominent motive studied in several open source motivation studies, e.g., Hars and Ou (2002), Lakhani and Wolf (2005), Osterloh, Rota, and Kuster (2002). In open source context, the fun motive is described as having fun or enjoying one-self when programming. Applied to ideas communities the fun motive is manifested in having fun in developing ideas.

The second motive is **intellectual stimulation**. Raymond describes programmers who are motivated by this factor for engaging in open source communities as people "...who enjoys the intellectual challenge of creatively overcoming or circumventing limitations" (1996). In their study Lakhani and Wolf (2005) found out that the top single reason to contribute to open source projects is based on intellectual stimulation. Applied to ideas communities developing ideas for participants is intellectually stimulating.

One motive out of the class of external motives is the so called **recognition** (Hars & Ou, 2002; Hertel et al., 2003). Recognition contains expected reactions of significant others, such as other programmers. Motivation to contribute to an open source community should be higher the more positive the expected reactions of significant others are, weighted by the perceived importance of these significant others. This relation is formally expressed as a multiplicative function. Applied to ideas communities participants expect positive reactions from other participants as well as the organizer. These reactions by thirds may be caused by the submitted ideas displayed on the Internet platform.

Furthermore, people may consider participating in ideas communities as an effective way to demonstrate their capabilities and skills shown through their submitted ideas. Their achievements in ideas communities can be used to demonstrate competence to the organizer of the ideas community or others. Reactions by thirds may be caused on the basis of submitted ideas. Participating in ideas community, therefore, can be a good channel for self-advertisement for those seeking new job opportunities. This phenomenon is mainly discussed in the field of researching motivations of open source programmers as **self-marketing** motive (Hars & Ou, 2002; Hertel et al., 2003).

Insights from open source motivation research reveal that many open source programmers participate in open source projects because of their willing to improve functionality of the software or failures in the lines of code (Hars & Ou, 2002). This could be also relevant for participants of ideas communities. By submitting an idea, participants may accentuate the necessity for improving the functionality or a defect of the underlying product. So, **product improvement** is a motivational factor worth to be include to our survey.

Furthermore, in the open source software research the **need** motive is discussed. As several studies, e.g., Gosh et al. (2002) reveal that programmers engage in open source communities because they has a personal need or just detect a need for a certain kind of software. They appeal to an existing community or even form a new open software community in order to implement their need. Applied to the SAPiens VIC customers may motivate to submit an idea because they detect a certain personal need which they phrase into an idea. So, the need motive seems to be worth included in our study.

Another motive is **learning**. Learning is also discussed in the field of open source motivation research. Hars and Ou (2002) found out that some open source programmers are motivated for participating in open source projects by the prospect of learning experiences. So, customers may also participate in ideas communities to expand their personal skills, capabilities, and knowledge. This motivation factor can be adopted for the present study as well.

Different open source motivation studies found that open source software programmers also seek for **contacts to peers** in order to make new friends or socialize with others (Hertel et al., 2003). When applied to ideas communities it is expected that customer also explain and predict this motive to contribute to ideas communities.

3   Research Setting and Measure

This research focuses on the "SAPiens" VIC. SAPiens (www.sapiens.info) is a VIC initiated and run by the ERP software producer SAP. SAPiens was launched in summer 2009 and targeted users of SAP software. Our research seeks to explore the motives that encourage customers of SAP software to participate in SAPiens community. Since perceived motivation-related issues can best be expressed by customers participating in the SAPiens community themselves, a standardized questionnaire survey have been conducted. For this survey, each of in the literature review identified motives are included. They can be categorized as commonly known motives as summarized in Table 1.

There were 21 items formulated in order to measure the 8 motives. Using a rating scale ranging from 1 (strongly disagree) to 5 (strongly agree), customers were asked to rate the degree to which extent each motive motivated him or her participate. The questionnaire was structured, tested and consequently adapted to the needs of the target audience.

The questionnaire was pre-tested by ten experts pursuing doctoral and Master's degrees in information technology and business administration. The objectives of the pre-test were to ensure that none of the items was ambiguous and to confirm that the items adequately captured the domain of interest. Expert opinions' indicated that the content of the items was valid.

The online survey has been run in November 2011. The questionnaire was implemented using the online-survey service "2aks". Participants of the SAPiens community who submitted at least one idea ($N = 149$)—which indicated that they had actively participated—were provided with a personalized link to the online survey by e-mail. The survey was administered over a period of 4 weeks. A total of 87 customers provided full answers to the questionnaire representing a 58.39 % response rate. Of the 87 customers 70.11 % were men ($n = 61$) and 60.92 % ($n = 53$) were between 20 and 30 years old. Concerning the occupation of the customers, 55.17 % ($n = 48$) were students who were overrepresented in the sample. The rest were either SAP consultants or persons in charge that worked with SAP applications once a day or at least a few times a week.

The high number of students is not unusual, as the community managers of the SAPiens community recruit many different kinds of SAP users, including students of higher education. However, students are only allowed to take part in the SAPiens community if they can verify degrees from so called "TERP 10" courses, i.e., advanced SAP training courses for students of higher education that train students in handling SAP software and that are certified and supported by SAP. Because of this, one could be certain of students' SAP expertise.

4 Survey Results

As can be seen from Table 2, construct validity of the 8 motives and related 21 items has been tested based on an exploratory factor analysis. The items have been analyzed with the help of the statistical software program SPSS 17.0. In order to check whether the data were appropriate for factor analysis, the Measures of Sampling Adequacy (MSA) have been pre-analyzed for the whole data structure as well as for individual items. The items PV2 and IH1 showed MSA values that were lower than 0.5. According to Cureton et al.'s recommendation, who deemed that items achieve sampling adequacy if values are equal to or exceed the criterion of 0.5

Table 2 Rotated component matrix

Items	Components					
I attended the SAPiens community because...	*1*	*2*	*3*	*4*	*5*	*6*
Fun						
... I have fun in working out ideas and creative solutions. *(S1)*	0.065	<u>0.660</u>	0.268	0.065	0.117	−0.039
... I perceive composing creative ideas as a kind of self-realization. *(S2)*	0.043	<u>0.630</u>	0.026	0.209	0.325	0.176
... I take much pleasure in being creative. *(S3)*	0.255	<u>0.785</u>	0.203	0.107	0.118	0.030
Intellectual stimulation						
... I'm stimulated by generating creative ideas. *(IH1)*	*Excluded as item did not achieve critical MSA value*					
... I'm intellectually challenged by developing creative ideas. *(IH2)*	0.190	<u>0.898</u>	0.065	−0.023	0.082	0.135
Recognition						
... I hoped that other customers in SAPiens would appreciate my idea(s). *(ANER1)*	0.423	0.236	0.048	<u>0.610</u>	0.087	0.120
... I hoped that other customers participating in SAPiens would honor my idea(s). *(ANER2)*	0.110	0.452	0.407	0.418	0.096	0.006
... I hoped that SAP would value my idea(s). *(ANER3)*	0.415	0.089	0.131	<u>0.710</u>	0.191	0.284
... I hoped that SAP would appreciate my idea(s). *(ANER4)*	0.046	0.094	0.210	<u>0.832</u>	0.253	0.071
Self-marketing						
... I hoped to show my skills and abilities through my idea(s) to potential employers. *(SM1)*	<u>0.624</u>	0.263	−0.080	0.229	0.400	−0.040
... I hoped to convince SAP of my skills and abilities through my idea(s). *(SM2)*	<u>0.762</u>	0.214	−0.121	0.337	0.160	0.216
... I hoped to demonstrate my skills and abilities through my idea(s). *(SM3)*	<u>0.853</u>	0.003	0.125	0.003	0.164	0.126
Product improvement						
... I want to give a helping hand in improving existing SAP software. *(PV1)*	0.042	0.069	−0.023	0.164	<u>0.644</u>	0.183
... I detected a software bug and I wanted to help fix it. *(PV2)*	*Excluded as item did not achieve critical MSA value*					
Need						
... my idea mirrors a need that is not covered by existing SAP software applications, yet. *(BEDA1)*	0.086	0.205	0.312	0.360	<u>0.670</u>	−0.065

(continued)

Table 2 (continued)

Items	Components					
I attended the SAPiens community because...	*1*	*2*	*3*	*4*	*5*	*6*
...I wish to tell SAP about my certain needs that are not covered by existing SAP applications, yet. *(BEDA2)*	0.141	0.120	0.444	−0.124	0.590	−0.100
...I detected a need for a certain SAP software application and put it into an idea. *(BEDA3)*	0.129	0.364	0.024	0.194	0.578	0.110
Learning						
...I hoped to get learning experiences through the feedback concerning my idea(s). *(L1)*	0.413	0.138	0.426	−0.011	−0.102	0.677
...I hoped to learn from discussions with other customers participating in the SAPiens community. *(L2)*	0.244	0.158	0.041	0.202	0.131	0.785
Contact to peers						
...I hoped to get in contact with other SAP software users in order to talk with them about my idea(s). *(KZG1)*	0.285	0.107	0,644	0.124	−0.099	0.231
...I hoped to get in contact with other SAP software users in order to share experiences and information. *(KZG2)*	0.314	0.348	0.482	0.222	−0293	0.057
Cronbach's Alpha	0.857	0.860	0.772	0.852	0.779	0.804

Source: Own depiction

(Cureton & D'Agostino, 1983), and thus these items were excluded within three iterations. After the sixth iteration all remaining items were above 0.6, and exploratory factor analysis was applicable. The global MSA value has also been pre-checked after the third iteration in order to ensure applicability of explorative factor analysis. With a MSA of 0.729 the stringent 0.5-criteria of Cureton was also met.

The factor analysis resulted in six factors with Eigenvalues higher than 1 (varimax rotation). All six factors explained a total of 66.321 % variance. The first factor explained 14.149 % variance, which was mostly determined by all items representing the expected motive self-marketing. Thus, this factor is called "self-marketing" (component 1 in Table 2). The second factor, mostly determined by all "fun" items, explained 13.887 % variance. The item IH2 also loaded on this factor. According to Raymond (1996) intellectual stimulation can be interpreted as a form of fun. In his empirical study, Raymond found a participant of an Open Source community to be person who "...enjoys the intellectual challenge of creatively overcoming or circumventing limitations..." when writing open source software program (Raymond, 1996). Following this argumentation, this item in factor 2 has been accepted and this factor has been called "fun" (component 2 in Table 2).

The item KZG1 loaded on another factor, which explained 11.066 % variance. This factor (component 3 in Table 2) has been accepted as a single item and has been called "contact to peers". On the fourth factor loading, three items directly explained "recognition" (component 4 in Table 2) (10.040 % variance). The fifth factor, representing a 9.989 % expression of variance, has been called "product innovation and enhancement" (component 5 in Table 2), as all need items, as well as one of two product improvement items, load on it. Is has been accepted that the need and the wish to improve a product can be interpreted as similar aspects. Finally, the sixth factor which explained additional 7.190 % variance was mostly determined by the supposed learning items. This supposed learning (component 6 in Table 2) appeared to be an independent motive. The items ANER2 and KZG2 were excluded, as their values were <0.55, and according to Hair et al.'s recommendation, who deemed that items achieve acceptable factor loadings if values are equal to or exceed the criterion of 0.55 (Hair, Anderson, Tatham, & Black, 1998). After this complex explanatory factor analysis, the results support the contention that our data set has adequate construct validity.

The reliability of the resulting factors was checked using Cronbach's alpha. A Cronbach's alpha of 0.7 or higher (Nunnally, 1978) was used as an acceptable value for internal consistency of the measure. Since the Cronbach's alphas of the four factors range from 0.772 to 0.860 (see Table 2), these values support the contention that all factors had adequate reliability. As examination of validity as well as reliability of an underlying data set by directly applying explanatory factor analysis respectively Cronbach's alpha does not meet modern requirements (Bogazzi, Yi, & Phillips, 1991), according to Straub, Boudreau, and Gefen's (2004) recommendation, the revised data set, based on its six remaining factors and the corresponding 17 items, has been tested by applying confirmatory factor analysis and using Amos 18.0. The Goodness of Fit Index (GFI) was 0.951 and the Adjusted Goodness of Fit Index (AGFI) was 0.933. These indices were well over the under threshold of 0.9, indicating an adequate fit (Browne & Cudeck, 1993). In order to check reliability, all Individual Item Reliabilities, which exceeded the minimum threshold of 0.4 (Homburg & Giering, 1996), have been tested. Hence, good reliability is confirmed (see Table 3).

Further, all factors showed good values for Composite Reliabilities as well as for Average Variance Explained (AVE), and thus convergent validity can be assumed (see Table 3). Values of 0.6 regarding the Composite Reliability and 0.5 for the AVE can be seen as minimum values for indicating a good measurement quality (Bagozzi & Yi, 1988). The discriminant validity of the factors was checked by using the Fornell-Larcker criteria, which claims that one factor's AVE should be higher than its squared correlation with every other factor (Fornell & Larcker, 1981). Tables 3 and 4 depict that discriminant validity can be assumed for the six factors. In sum, our data set was successfully validated using both exploratory and confirmatory factor analysis.

Table 3 Values for individual item reliability, composite reliability, and AVE

Factor	Item	Individual item reliability (≥ 0.4)	Composite reliability (≥ 0.6)	AVE (≥ 0.5)
Self-marketing	MO_SM_1	0.557	0.860	0.608
	MO_SM_2	0.800		
	MO_SM_3	0.564		
	MO_KZG_1	0.503		
Fun	MO_S_1	0.433	0.871	0.639
	MO_S_2	0.577		
	MO_S_3	0.828		
	MO_IH_2	0.647		
Contact to peers	MO_KZG_1	0.490	0.778	0.552
Recognition	MO_ANER_1	0.677	0.860	0.676
	MO_ANER_3	0.927		
	MO_ANER_4	0.424		
Product Improvement and Enhancement	MO_BEDA_1	0.725	0.781	0.574
	MO_BEDA_2	0.427		
	MO_BEDA_3	0.647		
	MO_PV_1	0.418		
Learning	MO_L_1	0.725	0.698	0.536
	MO_L_2	0.626		

Source: Own depiction

Table 4 Squared multiple correlations

	Self-marketing	Fun	Contact to peers	Recognition	Prod Imp + Enh	Learning
Self-marketing		0.00289	0.0729	0.2401	0.0729	0.2704
Fun	0.0289		0.0324	0.0225	0.00289	0.0324
Contact to peers	0.0729	0.0324		0.0729	0.1156	0.1444
Recognition	0.2401	0.0225	0.0729		0.1089	0.2116
Prod Innov + Enh	0.0729	0.00289	0.1156	0.1089		0.0441
Learning	0.2704	0.0324	0.1444	0.2116	0.0441	

Source: Own depiction

5   Conclusion

The purpose of our empirical study was to explore customers' motives for engaging in VICs. Overall, the results suggest that there are six motives that explain why customers participate in VICs. The first motivation is that customers may consider participating in virtual communities as an effective way to demonstrate their capabilities and skills shown through their ideas. Their achievements in VIC can be used to demonstrate competence to the firm or other participants. Thus, participating can be a good channel for self-advertisement; thus, this motive has been called **self-marketing-motive.** Second, evidence has been found for the fact that customers participating in VIC have fun in developing ideas. By doing so, customers are able to satisfy their creative urge and product-related curiosity or customers simply find developing ideas to be **fun.** Third, it has been found that customers also seek for **contacts to peers** in VICs in order to make new friends or socialize with others.

A fourth motive is the **recognition-motive.** As discovered, customers engage in VIC because they hope to receive positive reactions to their submitted ideas displayed on the VIC's Internet platform. They expect positive reactions from other participants as well as from the firm. Idea submitters feel proud when other customers or firms acknowledge their ideas openly in the community. Next, there is the **product innovation and enhancement-motive**. Some customers feel that by participating in VIC, they can influence the firm to incorporate new product features to existing products or even develop completely new products that they find highly valuable in their own context. Their participation thus arises from their individual needs. Further, some customers hope to accentuate the necessity of improving the functionality or a defect of the underlying product. Last of all, there is the **learning-motive**. It has been found, that very often customers engage in a firm's VIC to gain knowledge from participants in VIC. Such customer involvement enhances customers' knowledge about the product, as well as about the underlying technologies.

However, a limitation of this study involves the sample of our motivation survey. Our sample size was relatively small. Despite the fact that the size was certainly adequate for applying factor analyses, our results would have been more meaningful with a higher sample size. For this reason, our results might impose some limitations concerning the generalizability. Future research should test and validate our approach by collecting more data sets.

Our results contribute to the body of knowledge on Online Innovation Communities (OIC). OIC is a generic term for communities aiming to facilitate open and user driven innovation in some way (Ståhlbröst & Bergvall-Kåreborn, 2011). Many different forms of OIC are available on the Internet. The above discussed Open Source Communities represent one form of OIC. Another example for OIC is a so-called user innovation communities where users join a network with the aim to create content collaboratively (Ståhlbröst & Bergvall-Kåreborn, 2011). This phenomenon can be seen in, for example, Google Maps, YouTube and Wikipedia, where users jointly produce content for others to view and use (Ståhlbröst & Bergvall-Kåreborn, 2011). Innovation intermediary communities are further examples of OIC. In these communities, users are invited to be involved in all phases of the innovation process on a voluntary basis and these OICs have the role to act as mediators between different stakeholders such as users and companies (Antikainen, Mäkipää, & Ahonen, 2010; Muhdi & Boutellier, 2011; Ståhlbröst & Bergvall-Kåreborn, 2011).

There are studies that explore why users participate in these OIC. However, while scholars such as Jeppesen and Frederiksen (2006), Hars and Ou (2002), Ståhlbröst and Bergvall-Kåreborn (2011) provide empirically validated insight on user motivation in open source communities, innovation intermediary communities and user innovation communities, little is known about user motivation in VIC. Our results firstly provide insights on this with the help of empirically validated data. Therefore, this research contributes not only by deepening the knowledge base of OIC in general, but primarily by expanding the body of knowledge to the relatively new phenomenon of VIC.

Against this backdrop, our study has also major practical implications for companies in the tourism industry. More and more companies from the tourism industry are beginning to implement VICs because they realized that they can take advantage of the collective intelligence of tourists. The key knowledge that tourism companies can access here are the tourists' local knowledge and knowledge of destinations already visited. This crowd knowledge is an important source for generating ideas for new services and products taking in consideration the needs of tourists. Companies from the tourism industry may draw on our insights to systematically design and implement VICs. We found evidence for motives that sufficiently explain why the crowd engage in ideation activities on VICs in general. Knowing these motives is a valuable insight for managers of tourism related VICs in particular, since they can draw on our insights to systematically design and implement customized incentive structure that would attract tourists to participate in VICs from the tourism industry.

References

Afuah, A. N., & Tucci, C. (2012). Crowdsourcing as a solution to distant search. *Academy of Management Review, 37*, 355–375.

Antikainen, M., Mäkipää, M., & Ahonen, M. (2010). Motivating and supporting collaboration in open innovation. *European Journal of Innovation Management, 13*, 100–119.

Bagozzi, R. P., & Yi, Y. (1988). On the evaluation of structural equation models. *Journal of the Academy of Marketing Sciences, 16*, 74–94.

Bogazzi, R., Yi, Y., & Phillips, L. (1991). Assessing construct validity in organizational research. *Administrative Science Quarterly, 36*, 421–458.

Browne, M. W., & Cudeck, R. (1993). Alternative ways of assessing model fit. In K. A. Bollen & J. S. Long (Eds.), *Testing structural equation models*. Newbury Park: Sage.

Chesbrough, H. (2003). The era of open innovation. *Sloan Management Review, 44*, 35–41.

Cureton, E. E., & D'Agostino, R. B. (1983). *Factor analysis: An applied approach*. Hillsdale, NJ: Erlbaum Associates.

Di Gangi, P. M., & Wasko, M. (2009). Steal my idea! Organizational adoption of user innovations from a user innovation community: A case study of dell IdeaStorm. *Decision Support Systems, 48*, 303–312.

Fern, E. F. (1982). The use of focus groups for idea generation: The effects of group size, acquaintanceship, and moderator on response quantity and quality. *Journal of Marketing Research, 19*, 1–13.

Fornell, C., & Larcker, D. F. (1981). Evaluating structural equation models with unobservable variables and measurement error. *Journal of Marketing Research, 18*, 39–50.

Ghosh, R. A., Glott, R., Kreiger, B., & Robles, G. (2002). *The free/libre and open source software developers survey and study-FLOSS*. International Institute of Infonomics, University of Maastricht.

Hair, J. F., Anderson, R. E., Tatham, R. L., & Black, W. C. (1998). *Multivariate data analysis* (5th ed.). Upper Saddle River, NJ: Prentice-Hall.

Hars, A., & Ou, S. (2002). Working for free? Motivations for participating in open-source projects. *International Journal of Electronic Commerce, 6*, 25–39.

Hertel, G., Niedner, S., & Herrmann, S. (2003). Motivation of software developers in open source projects: An internet-based survey of contributors to the Linux kernel. *Research Policy, 32*, 1159–1177.

Hestad, M., & Keitsch, M. (2009). Not always a victim! On seeing users as active consumers. *International Journal of Product Development, 9*, 396–405.

Homburg, C., & Giering, A. (1996). Konzeptionalisierung und Operationalisierung komplexer Konstrukte: Ein Leitfaden für die Marketingforschung. *Marketing Zeitschrift für Forschung und Praxis, 18*, 5–24.

Jeppesen, L., & Frederiksen, L. (2006). Why do users contribute to firm-hosted user communities? The case of computer-controlled music instruments. *Organizational Science, 17*, 45–63.

Kipp, P., Wieck, E., Bretschneider, U., & Leimeister, J. M. (2013). 12 years of GENEX framework: What did practice learn from science in terms of web-based ideation? In *11th international conference on Wirtschaftsinformatik (WI2013)* (pp. 565–576), Leipzig, Germany.

Lakhani, K. R., & Wolf, B. (2005). Why Hackers do what they do. Understanding motivation and effort in free/open source software projects. In J. Feller, B. Fitzgerald, S. Hissam, & K. R. Lakhani (Eds.), *Perspectives on free and open source software*. Cambridge, MA: MIT.

Leimeister, J. M., Huber, M., Bretschneider, U., & Krcmar, H. (2009). Leveraging crowdsourcing: Activation-supporting components for IT-based ideas competitions. *Journal of Management Information Systems, 26*, 197–224.

Muhdi, L., & Boutellier, R. (2011). Motivational factors affecting participation and contribution of members in two different Swiss innovation communities. *International Journal of Innovation Management, 15*, 543.

Nunnally, J. C. (1978). *Psychometric theory* (2nd ed.). New York: McGraw Hill.

Öberg, C. (2010). Customer roles in innovations. *International Journal of Innovation Management, 14*, 989–1011.

Osterloh, M., Rota, S., & Kuster, B. (2002). *Open source software production: Climbing on the shoulders of giants*. MIT Working Paper. Cambridge, MA: MIT.

Raymond, E. S. (1996). *In the new Hacker's dictionary* (3rd ed.). Cambridge, MA: MIT.

Sandström, C., & Bjork, J. (2010). Idea management systems for a changing innovation landscape. *International Journal of Product Development, 11*, 310–324.

Shah, S. K. (2005). *Motivation, governance & the viability of hybrid forms in open source software development*. Working paper, University of Washington.

Ståhlbröst, A., & Bergvall-Kåreborn, B. (2011). Exploring users motivation in innovation communities. *International Journal of Entrepreneurship and Innovation Management, 14*, 298–314.

Straub, D., Boudreau, M. C., & Gefen, D. (2004). Validation guidelines for IS positivist research. *Communication of the ACM, 13*, 380–427.

von Hippel, E. (1986). Lead users: A source of novel product concepts. *Management Science, 32*, 791–805.

The Value of Crowdfunding: The Significance of Community-Financed Projects Beyond the Act of Financing

Christian Papsdorf

1 Introduction

In 1885, Joseph Pulitzer, publisher of the "Brooklyn Sunday Press", asked the general public via his newspaper for donations to finance the construction of the pedestal of the Statue of Liberty. As a reward the contributors' names would be published in the newspaper. Before long 120,000 people had, together, donated the required 105,000 USD (Leimeister, 2010). This example is a very early case of Crowdfunding which gets an entirely new dynamic in the context of Internet communication.

Crowdfunding—preliminary defined as "the use of the Internet to raise money through small contributions from a large number of investors" (Bradford, 2013)—is a relatively recent phenomenon. Less than 10 years ago, the term was coined in 2006, the first companies began looking for venture capital by addressing the crowd of (unknown) Internet users. Since then this field of Internet communication, mainly related to start-ups, has been characterised by huge dynamics. Thousands of intermediating platforms which connect entrepreneurs and donators have been founded. Some of them disappeared fairly immediately, while others are extremely successful. Although only a very small share of the overall external financing is funded by the crowd of Internet users, Crowdfunding somehow revolutionised the long standing alliance between entrepreneurs on the one hand and banks, venture capitalists or business angels on the other hand by adding a new player to the game.

Referring to this, the crucial aim of Crowdfunding is to "harness the power of the crowd to fund small ventures, projects that are unlikely to get funded by traditional means" (Gerber et al., 2012). This understanding of democratised economies certainly is only one way of looking at it. In almost the same manner one could define Crowdfunding as an act of outsourcing business hazards to Internet users.

C. Papsdorf (✉)
Department of Sociology, Chemnitz University of Technology, Chemnitz, Germany
e-mail: christian.papsdorf@soziologie.tu-chemnitz.de

© Springer-Verlag Berlin Heidelberg 2016
R. Egger et al. (eds.), *Open Tourism*, Tourism on the Verge,
DOI 10.1007/978-3-642-54089-9_9

Additionally, these users are meant to buy the products or services afterwards. In a sense, they are, therefore, persuaded to pay twice, a fact which will be discussed in more detail later on. First, a brief insight into a striking example of Crowdfunding will help better understand how it works.

Beyond any doubt *Kickstarter* currently is the most influential Crowdfunding platform. It was founded in 2009 and has successfully funded over 40,000 projects in different areas, such as journalism, film, art, food, mobility, technology or fashion. At this juncture more than 600 million dollars have been donated. A project typically includes the following steps: First, Project Creators introduce their innovation to the Kickstarter Team for a preselection. Secondly, they publicise the innovation online with a video, some pictures and a detailed description including problems. The entrepreneurs to be then have to set a funding goal and a deadline (of up to 60 days). Once the project is launched (for instance a short documentary film about eco-tourism in Uganda or a food tourism conference), web users can pledge as much money as they want. If the funding goal is achieved before the deadline ends the money will be disbursed. If not, the pledgers get their money back. Successful projects often earn way more than the set goals. So-called backers or pledgers (the donating users) do not profit financially, albeit creators often offer rewards (e.g. a t-shirt for a smaller pledge or a watch for bigger ones) to thank their supporters.

Although Crowdfunding is spreading rapidly, only little attention has been paid to this issue. So far scientific studies have mainly focused on specific aspects of Crowdfunding. Agarwal et al. (2011), for instance, showed that Crowdfunding, despite the wide geographic dispersion of Internet communication in general and the location of the investors in particular, distance still plays a role in as much as local investors are more likely to invest at an early stage. In view of this, Ward and Ramachandran (2010) ascertained that peer effects, and not network externalities, influence the investors' decision-making.

Kaltenbeck (2011) and Mollick (2012) also elaborated advantageous and disadvantageous factors (such as recruitment, story telling, social media usage, funding goal) and strategies which influence the success of Crowdfunding projects. Rewards have a positive influence on the amount of loans as well, as Hildebrand et al. (2011) found out. Burtch et al. (2012) examined both the antecedents and consequences of the contribution process and point out that contributions are subject to a crowding out effect. Additionally, Gerber et al. (2012) showed that people are motivated to participate because of social interactions. Moreover, there are different studies related to various fields of Crowdfunding, such as raising money for scientific research (Wheat et al., 2012) or for the recording industry (Kappel, 2009). Furthermore, issues of law seem to play an important role (Hazen, 2012; Pope, 2011).

This chapter attempts to develop a more general perspective on Crowdfunding which is an issue which, to date, only little attention has been paid to, with the exception of Ordanini et al. (2011) who examine how and why consumers turn into Crowdfunding participants. There are two crucial questions to be answered below: First, what is the genuine gain of Crowdfunding for project creators? Secondly, what prevents project supporters from feeling exploited when spending their time and money on start-ups. Therefore, rather than on platforms in the narrow sense, the following arguments will concentrate on entrepreneurs and Internet users. First of all an essential (sociological) definition and conceptualisation of Crowdfunding have to be elaborated. Building on these, the first hypothesis will assume that the act of funding is not the most valuable activity of the web users. Rather, their feedback (often sticky information) is the most interesting (and valuable) part of Crowdfunding. The second hypothesis will highlight the fact that points of critique which are often expressed, e.g. users who do not get a fair deal in various crowd phenomena (Kleemann et al., 2008), are neutralised by focussing on the financial dimension. Ironically, this new transparency does not affect a more equitable role for users. This second hypothesis will be discussed in close relation with Crowdsourcing as an initial trend for outsourcing enterprise functions to the crowd.

2   Conceptualisation of Crowdfunding

Crowdfunding can be seen as a subcategory of Crowdsourcing, which is the oldest trend of outsourcing economy related activities in Web 2.0. This section first has a look at Crowdsourcing. Crowdsourcing can be defined as a strategy of outsourcing activities, which are usually done by paid organisations or paid individuals through an open call to a crowd of unknown Internet users, which provides direct economic advantages to Crowdsourcers, Crowdsourcees or both. This means first and foremost that although Crowdfunding follows the same logic of reorganising labour structures, it primarily refers to another aim, i.e. whereas Crowdsourcing is outsourcing labour, Crowdfunding is about financing. However, both phenomena have in common that users take the place of professionals, a fact which also applies to Crowdlending, Crowddonating and Crowdinvesting. This chapter intends to show that a detailed examination of Crowdfunding illustrates that there are many similarities between Crowdfunding and Crowdsourcing.

Although Crowdfunding is a very young phenomenon, it has been defined in many different ways. As cited in the introduction, Bradford (2013) specifies four characteristics. According to him Crowdfunding is limited to online communication and is focussed on fundraising for any types of projects. Also characteristic for Crowdfunding is the fact that a large number of contributors donate small amounts of money. However, what is meant exactly by "small amounts" remains ambiguous. For a start-up 1000 Dollar will not be particularly helpful. For private contributors, on the other hand, the same amount will be quite a lot of money. Belleflamme et al. (2012a) specify this point. According to them the "small" amounts are provided by individuals, instead of soliciting a small group of sophisticated investors. This implies that existing forms of investing are partially replaced and not complemented by Crowdfunding. Lehner (2013) defines the role of the Internet more precisely, stating that social media, in particular, are not just one way of communication among others as they assume a wide range of functions beyond pure communication. In fact, Crowdfunding is empowered by social media communication as users generate content and support network activities for start-ups. Viral networking and marketing for instance are used to enable the mobilisation of users within a relatively short period of time (Hemer, 2011).

Bradford (2013) shows that Crowdfunding can also be related to non-profit projects. In the majority of cases it is certainly business-related. As Burtch et al. (2012) state, a number of platforms are used to connect users and start-ups. Hence, entrepreneurs usually do not launch a Crowdfunding project on their own website. Secondly, users choose between a variety of projects competing for money. As Kaltenbeck (2011) shows, Crowdfunding was not invented in the 2000s, but is a very old phenomenon. For a long time, aid organisations raised money within the limits of offline communication. Nowadays, web technologies seem to make this process much more efficient, which is probably one reason why entrepreneurs increasingly choose to tap this potential. Said analogy between the old fundraising and the new Crowdfunding leads us to another interesting point: An adequate number of contributors can only be activated in case of a common interest. In the case of Crowdfunding this interest normally is the attempt to bring a really innovative product to market. These aspects of a definition clearly show how strong Crowdfunding and Crowdsourcing are related. Hence, the thesis of this paper seems to be prolific.

Beyond the above mentioned aspects of a definition of Crowdfunding some conceptual points help gain a deeper insight into the phenomenon. A question which needs to be addressed first of all is whether contributors get any kind of reward or not. This really striking point leads us to a differentiation within Crowdfunding. The act of outsourcing questions of financing can be realised by initiating Crowdfunding, Crowddonating, Crowdlending or Crowdinvesting projects. Crowdfunding in this regard is quite similar to Crowddonating, because no rewards, voting rights or the like are guaranteed to the donators. In some cases they get incentives, thankful mentions or a gift coupon for upcoming products or services. Contrary to this form of online gift making, Crowdlending is much more related to the conventional credit system. Crowdlending is a form of peer-to-peer crediting, consequentially the money has to be paid up to the lenders (either without or with interest). Once again, unlike the different models referred to above, Crowdinvesting explicitly grants financial rewards (such as shares of the company or gain sharing) and a voice in the meeting of shareholders or alike (Applehoff et al. 2013). Some authors, like Bradford (2013), prefer deviant categorisations, such as the donation model, the reward model, the pre-purchase model, the lending model and the equity model. In fact, both classifications in categories are based upon the same issues, albeit named differently. When Belleflamme et al. (2012a) compared these forms of Crowdfunding they found out that entrepreneurs prefer conventional Crowdfunding if the initial capital requirement is relatively small, and Crowdinvesting if the required capital is much higher.

Kappel (2009) makes a distinction between ex post facto Crowdfunding and ex ante Crowdfunding. The first type of this differentiation takes place whenever financial support is offered for products which are ready for production, e.g. when an innovative smartphone is already functioning, but needs some money for the production of a first small batch series. Ex ante Crowdfunding refers to projects that only consist of an idea, such as the production of a band's debut album. The participants, therefore, hope to achieve a mutually desired result, but have no guarantee of success. Ex ante Crowdfunding is often used in the entertainment industry by independent filmmakers, artists, writers, and performers to bypass traditional keepers of the purse, while the ex post facto model is usually found in relation to physical products. Furthermore, Belleflamme et al. (2010) show that Crowdfunding projects initiated by non-profit associations are far more likely to achieve their target level of capital than corporations. Hazen (2012)) adds one more dimension of differentiation: the extent to which the initiative is embedded. Initiatives are single and independent when they have no background in an institution or are set up by individuals. Projects can also be initiated by and embedded in private or public organisation with the intention of remaining part of this organisation. And thirdly, projects may begin as independent start-ups, but will be transformed into a firm or organisation after succeeding the founding process.

As stated above, to date no all-embracing definition and conceptualisation has been formulated. In view of the fact that Crowdfunding is both a new and dynamic phenomenon, this is not surprising. The questions analysed so far, however, give an impression of how Crowdfunding can be discussed in terms of social science in general and sociology in detail. This concept of Crowdfunding will underlie the following theoretical framing and hypothesis to be discussed.

3   Theoretical Background

Crowdfunding did not emerge by chance but rather as a consequence of multiple societal and economic developments. Three striking processes within the last decades need to be mentioned in this respect. On the level of theory of society the rise of the network and information society as well as an increase in mediated communication via Internet needs to be stated. As far as the economic perspective is concerned, it is evident that more and more functions and activities are outsourced, initially to subcontractors and other companies, meanwhile to customers and users. The third development ties in with this process. Areas which used to be clearly separated, e.g. production and consumption, have, in the recent past started to merge. Because of this, new roles and social figures have come into being such as the working customer (Voß and Rieder, 2007), the working user (Papsdorf, 2009) or the investing user. In the context of online communication such new hybrids seem to have developed exceptionally easily. Crowdfunding is only one of many Web 2.0 innovations which transform formerly passive consumers into active users. Especially those transformations related to the business world have rightly been criticised because of the fact that the working user does not receive appropriate payment for any work done (Kleemann et al., 2008). This and other drawbacks of Crowdfunding need to be discussed here in order to get a complete picture.

To begin with, the rise of the network and information society and an increase in mediatised communication via the Internet some reflections from a macrosociological perspective are unavoidable. As Bell (1973) already diagnosed, industrial societies are transforming into information societies. This leads to changes not only in economies but in the whole complex of social structures. Crucial for these rearrangements is a new hegemony of theory over practice. Accordingly, scientists displace capitalists as major figures in modern societies. These assumptions are fortified by Castells' (2001) thesis of the network society, which is characterised by a consequent application of knowledge and information as resources and accelerated coupling of technological and societal development. Three processes are at the basis of the network society: The revolution of information technologies (especially the Internet), the restructuring of (global) capitalism in reaction to the crisis in the 1970s and liberalism-oriented social movements made individualised and decentralised utilisation of new technologies possible. As Castells (2005) adds later on, the Internet transforms practices in nearly all fields of economy. This includes the relationship with suppliers and customers, manufacturing processes, relationships to other companies or financing and investing in stocks. This shows that there is a close correlation between considerable societal changes and new forms of communication. By mediating more and more communication via the Internet preconditions, operating modes and consequences of communication in general are being converted. So online communication is necessarily digital, networked, irrespective of time and space, modular, automated, open and distinguished by user participation (Papsdorf, 2012). On the one hand these developments are significantly driven by economics whereas on the other hand they also affect them.

Essential conditions for the emergence of Crowdfunding can also be found in the field of economics. One trend is to increasingly externalise more and more functions. Inasmuch as the act of outsourcing is well-known, here only a new variation of this strategy is to be presented. The Internet in particular enables the outsourcing of functions of organisations, not only to subcontractors, but also to individuals among the crowd of web user. Therefore, not only sections like customer relationship, production or quality management, but equally compartmentalised tasks, like beta testing, mass customisation, innovation or content generation are delegated to the crowd. Although Crowdsourcing actually is (and probably will stay) of little societal importance, hundreds of thousands companies must be considered a success story. Before describing the user's role in detail, a second process related to this needs to be discussed, i.e. the transition from closed to open to user innovation.

Well in the nineteenth century enterprises developed innovations and inventions largely autonomously, also independent of university research. The early innovative entrepreneur, as shown by Schumpeter (1950), was a capitalist, who continually sought to conceal research and development, whereas in open innovation-models, companies seek cooperation with research establishments, start-ups, suppliers, competitors or even customers (Chesbrough, 2003). This state changed rapidly due to the fact that the economic environment of enterprises became more and more capable of innovation. Cooperation and at least a partial opening became essential. Recently, companies have discovered that customers can be a valuable source of ideas and innovations. Hence, user innovation stands for a process of systematic investigation and integration of users' knowledge and creativity with the use of modern information and communication technology. These strategies seem to promise competitive advantages, such as reducing the time between invention and market launch, a reduction of incidental costs (by outsourcing) and raising market acceptance.

These changes which originally began in the offline world and now show a noticeably greater dynamism due to Internet communication, have given rise to entirely new, hybrid roles like working customers, working users or investing, respectively donating users. The working customer has become a well-known phenomenon if we think of, for example, self-service technologies (e.g. in restaurants or at ticket machines) or furniture that has to be assembled at home. With online banking or Crowdsourcing, we have a clear case of the working user. Investing and donating users, on the other hand, represent a brand new phenomenon that certainly affiliates to the logic of the previous hybrids. These developments have recently been challenged. This new wave of capitalistic colonisation (Papsdorf, 2009) has been subjected to considerable criticism. On the one hand, enterprises exploit the leisure time and the privacy of users. On the other hand, users are either underpaid or do not receive any payment at all. Also, apart from a direct remuneration, users are disadvantaged in contrast to companies, as rights of intellectual property, which are relevant in case of idea or design competitions, or bare comments on new business ideas or on innovative products, descend to corresponding companies or intermediate platforms. Consequently, more and more regular jobs are replaced by Crowdworkers.

In summary, Crowdfunding seems to be a logical consequence of societal, economic and technical developments. While the technological potentials of Web 2.0 accomplished the necessary prerequisites, an increasing interconnection of the world and the mediatisation of communication as well as the manifold outsourcing strategies induced a social climate that accentuates cooperation in projects and innovative thinking as undoubted state of the art (Boltanski and Chiapello, 2003). In this context, a number of Web 2.0 projects came up, such as wikis, open source publications, podcasts, social network sites, platforms for pictures and videos, as well as economic projects in the narrow sense, like Crowdworking, Crowdfunding or Cloudworking. As Boltanski and Chiapello (2003) show, these types of projects always have a downside, inasmuch as requirements of individuals are exploited by companies and individuals are being badly paid. The following section will demonstrate how those theoretical issues help paint a clear picture of Crowdfunding.

4   Results

As shown above, Crowdfunding and Crowdsourcing are closely related to each other. However, simply stating that Crowdsourcing is about outsourcing labour and Crowdfunding is about outsourcing financing is an untenable simplification. In fact, the act of financing is only one part of Crowdfunding. In addition, further tasks are performed by users. In this connection, four crucial aspects need to be mentioned: Feedback or rather transfer of knowledge, network building, evaluation of market-ability and the acquisition of first buyers. While the first two functions are directly deduced from Crowdsourcing, the latter two seem to be a Crowdfunding-specific adaption of Crowdsourcing principles. For this reason, it becomes apparent that the aspect of funding is a most welcome occasion to implement more or less conventional Crowdsourcing strategies. These four listed functions will now be analysed in more detail.

The above-mentioned statements about company-based changes clarified that companies had to gradually open up to accumulate sticky information directly from their customers instead of relying on expensive, slow and only partially efficient market research. With the emergence of Web 2.0 it is now possible to get in touch with a huge number of people directly, in an automated and targeted way. Often customers' opinions are desired when new products or services need to be evaluated or existing ones need to be improved. Until now professionals, such as consultants or scientists, undertook such tasks. By integrating user feedback and knowledge in general, users become quasi-experts who should, subsequently, buy the products (partially) developed by themselves. In case of Crowdsourcing these strategies became known to the general public and have been comparatively successful. A closer examination shows that Crowdfunding platforms fulfil those functions as well.

Another closer look at Kickstarter reveals how this works exactly. By way of example, a project named "Plug" (Marcombes, 2013) can be found that intends to collect 67,000 USD to bring a device to market which synchronises data of different computers, smart phones or tablets easily over the Internet. Both software and hardware have been developed by a small team of "creatives and geeks" and are ready for serial production. Apart from the fact that the funding goal has been exceeded by multiple hundreds of thousands USD, the crowd of funders has written a large number of comments. They often encourage the team of developers, compliment ideas, but also critically scrutinise the technical details. Users ask, for example, if the newest standards of data transfer can be integrated or if a power supplier for 100 V can be offered. Similarly, questions referring to potential problems, such as conflicts between same files on different devices are asked. The developer team on its part thanks for the support and tries to answer the questions as well as possible.

What is happening here, is a direct and immediate dialog between developers on the one hand and on the other hand funders who are at the same time customers, consumers, observers and critics. Users in a way become co-developers, as they give really useful and fresh input. Especially those who invested money (even small amounts) tend to act constructively and with regard to developers' restrictions. This form of communication generally is way more cooperative than conflict-ridden. This process has several consequences: The users (and future customers of the product or service) develop an understanding for decisions taken and are able to understand why products are the way they are. Users do not have to accept the product as planned by the developer but can influence the product's features or price instead, even though final decisions rest with the project team. Even without a formal right to vote suggestions and criticism are considered, because money also has to be raised in the future. The users' feedback, moreover, helps avoid the risk of launching a product, users will not like, which often is the case.

The next function beyond financing to be referred to is network building. In the course of a change from closed to open and user innovation it becomes more and more important to be connected with various actors. Especially for start-ups it is not always easy to connect with the right people. Networks are not only essential for user comments and criticism, but platforms of this kind also allow entrepreneurs to meet other professionals. These include for instance distribution partners, suppliers, consultants or marketing strategists. With this in mind, platforms for Crowdfunding can be seen as a meeting point for persons interested in start-ups, innovation or financing. Considering the unbelievable overload of information, "such virtual places" are profoundly important to reduce the complexity. Kickstarter, for instance, submits all projects to a pre-selection, which guarantees a high level of innovation and relevance. It is, therefore, not surprising that nearly half of all projects meet their goal amount. Network activities not only take place within the Crowdfunding platforms, but go far beyond these, as people connect with and, at a later stage, within other social network sites. The following example demonstrates the benefit of this process. Last winter the team of a classical Swiss skiing area raised funds on a Crowdfunding platform called "100-days". 5000 Swiss Franc were required to extend the Arosa snowpark. A new ramp should make the skiing area even more attractive for tourists. To support the funding process the users can embed a banner into their webpages or blogs, Facebooks "I like" button can be clicked and the belonging Twitter Account can be followed. This way, users start promoting and transferring the project based on Kickstarter in both networks. There it becomes visible to friends, family and, what is even more, to professionals. The bigger the network, the more probable it is to find helpful contacts.

Crowdfunding has another function which is of great importance, especially for founders. Entrepeneurs often use Crowdfunding for start-ups. Although prototypes, beta versions and samples already exist, it is hard to predict whether products or services will sell successfully. In the economic sense, products and services are only successful when one can make money with them. This can never be completely assessed in advance. Promising ideas and projects fail as not enough buyers can be found. Conventional market analyses often fail to predict the success of a product or service reliably and only inadequately predict consumer acceptance. This is especially the case for really innovative products which open up new markets. The Crowdfunding process, in contrast, obviously offers a better instrument for predicting future market success. If an idea succeeds in case of Crowdfunding, the appropriate service or product is likely to sell well. Burtch et al. (2012)) even assume that the length of the Crowdfuding process correlates positively with the subsequent sale of the product or service. This is a result of the general "ability to generate attention for entrepreneur's ventures" (Burtch et al. 2012, p. 6) of Crowdfunding. Crowdfunding platforms, in this sense, are like pre-markets or quasi-markets, which have a good predictive power because of their structural similarity to real key markets. Within both, people only spend money (as a donation or as a payment), when they are convinced of the product or business idea in general. Furthermore, people do not receive an equivalent value for their donation, for which reason they consider even more carefully, who will get the money. As Belleflamme et al. (2010) point out, Crowdfunding platforms help inform users about the value of the product: They ensure public attention, are used as a promotion device, or as a way of gaining better knowledge of consumer preferences.

Another look at Kickstarter clearly shows that highly funded projects such as "Bubble Pod", a clockwork turntable that grips smartphones and then rotates them 360° to create easily panoramas of landscapes for touristic and personal use, are very well sold. Of course it is not perfectly clear, if products sell well because of the success in the Crowdfunding process or if the Crowdfunding process was successful because the product is convincing and unique anyway. Nevertheless, the latter is more plausible, also because not all of the former Crowdfunding projects can be identified as such.

Fourthly, Crowdfunding enables entrepreneurs to find the first purchasers for their product or service. This is done by giving users a version of the crowdfunded product as a gift or an incentive in exchange for some form of financial support. The above-mentioned example of the "Bubble Pod"-project shows how this works exactly: The first 249 users pledging 15 GBP, the first 1500 backers pledging 20 GBP get one of the Plug devices for their donation. The first 100 users pledging 35 GBP as well as the 500 first users, who pledged 40 GBP or more, get a Bubble Pod Pro Pack (including a wide angle lens) which will cost 50 GBP in regular sale. This strategy has been highly effective many times: The project not only gets starting capital, valuable feedback by the community, a great network, and the evaluation of marketability, but also several thousands of buyers. Considering the fact that customer acquisition normally is very cost-intensive, these kinds of sales are profitable despite the discount.

Apart from these explicit purchases, there also are implicit purchases. This is the case, when users announce in their comments that they will buy the product as soon as it is available in a certain configuration or for worldwide shipping. Additionally, these comparatively easily acquired first buyers generate more profit as they entail further customers, such as friends, colleagues or family members. Belleflamme et al. (2012b) argues that some of the Crowdfunding models are designed explicitly to obtain the money required for initiating the production by pre-ordering strategies. A clever opportunity, therefore, is to "use some self-selecting device so as to induce well-paying consumers to reveal themselves. In this sense, Crowdfunding can be

contribution	immaterial	financial
benefit		
mutual	networking	find first purchasers
one-way	get feedback evaluate marketability	acquire seed capital

Fig. 1 Five functions of Crowdfunding in two dimensions (*Source*: Author's own graph)

seen as a special form of behaviour-based price discrimination" (Belleflamme et al., 2012b).

Hence, four crucial ideal function types beyond the acquisition of seed capital can be found. They are closely interrelated, influence each other and can be combined in two dimensions (Fig. 1):

This means that on the one hand, as illustrated above, the five functions can be divided up into immaterial and financial contributions to the project. On the other hand a distinction can be made between a system with mutual benefits (user and entrepreneurs both gain) and unilateral advantages (only the initiators of Crowdfunding benefit).

In case only the initiators or entrepreneurs gain (financially) from the process, the question arises why users give away their money to companies or start-ups and why, so far, this phenomenon has neither been challenged nor criticised. Both the mutual gain of networking and of pre-ordering products are only related to a certain part of all pledgers. In fact, the criticism Crowdsourcing received could also be applied to Crowdfunding, inasmuch as both phenomena are structured almost similarly and share nearly the same functions. Considering the criticism on Crowdsourcing in detail, the reason for this purpose becomes obvious. The criticism of Crowdsourcing concerns the instrumentalisation of the Web 2.0 culture of participation by skilful marketing for business objectives as well as the fact that working users are either paid badly or not at all. In case of Crowdsourcing the financial aspect remains controversial.

Within the scope of Crowdfunding this problem is solved in a highly extraordinary way. On the one hand, the question of payment is no longer concealed or downplayed. On the other hand, the answer to this question is reversed, as users are not getting paid for their engagement, but are, in contrast, spending money themselves. Once more: Users support commercial organisations not only by supporting them with their work, but also by donating their money (often without compensation). There is no doubt that several individual reasons exist for user participation, e.g. an intrinsic motivation for learning. But in view of the amount of users and projects it is strange, if not ironical that users not only give their time, but also their money away. In general, Crowdfunding works for the same reasons as Crowdsourcing works: Contribution is highly voluntary and basically privileged organisations present themselves as needy and dependent on user input: Within the scope of Crowdsourcing they can solely develop a new product, slogan or logo with the help of the "Wisdom of crowds" (Surowiecki, 2005), and Crowdfunding implies that founding a company or manufacturing a new product is only feasible with user support. Whereas Crowdsourcing refers to the Web 2.0 culture, Crowdfunding additionally applies to something like a culture of honorary office and donation. How the postulate of voluntariness and neediness is transformed into actual engagement of the Internet user exactly, can only be answered by means of qualitative social research. Here, however, it becomes clear that explicitly pointing out the financial dimension and, thereby, also the criticism regarding the exploitation goes at the expense of the user rather than benefiting the user. This does not at all mean that Crowdfunding projects generally have to be criticised, nor that their initiators are bad people per se. It does mean, however, that Crowdsourcing has, in a way, reached a new level with users not only giving companies their time but also their money. This fact should be borne in mind, when discussing Crowdfunding as the next big thing.

5   Conclusion

As shown above, Crowdfunding arose and became popular on no account by accident. The opposite is actually the case, Crowdfunding is a direct consequence of societal and economical developments. These encompass, in detail, the rise of the network and information society as well as an increase in mediated communication via the Internet and, for the economical domain, the fact that functions and activities are increasingly outsourced, initially to subcontractors and other companies, meanwhile to customers and users. As a result, new roles and social figures such as the working customer, working user or investing user, come into being. The results obtained in the course of this work clarify that Crowdfunding is directly linked to Crowdsourcing, as it entails four nearly similar functions beyond the aspect of financing and answers the criticism. What do these results imply for the individuals and organisations involved?

It becomes clear that Crowdfunding for project initiators is financially interesting in two respects: On the one hand founding capital can actually be acquired, on the other hand first purchasers can be won. Moreover, as the crowd provides feedback and a network, Crowdfunding overall seems to be highly attractive. So far only the positive effects have received attention. However, Crowdfunding also involves costs: A high quality promotional video has to be produced, user and customer service has to be provided, community management can be time-consuming and in case Crowdfunding fails, it effects the exact opposite of the goal. In the latter case, the Crowdfunding campaign becomes an evidence for missing marketability of a service or product and can cause refusal elsewhere. And, last but not least, Crowdfunding platforms are well rewarded for their popularity. Often ten percent of the profit are kept as a fee.

Additionally, the platforms play the role of the "gate-keepers", as they decide which projects will get through the pre-selection. 50 % of all published projects generally reach their goal amount. For this reason, Crowdfunding platforms partly take over the role of banks, venture capitalists or business angels as they assess which projects are promising and which are not. Platforms without pre-selection often have poor attendance and often do not achieve their goal amount. At the moment, Kickstarter is by far the most important platform. More specialised platforms, i.e. for science, the non-profit sector or arts, will considerably gain in importance.

For technology and innovation enthusiasts Crowdfunding will remain a highly fascinating field. Despite the far-reaching transparency it must be underlined that users significantly support companies or other organisations with their work and money across time and space at a global level. In capitalist societies such as the US or the countries of the European Union, it is not surprising that users work for companies with their private resources and in their leisure time, but it would certainly not be necessary.

It is difficult to give a forecast regarding the future development, because Crowdfunding is a relatively recent and dynamic phenomenon. However, it can be assumed that the euphoric initial phase will be replaced by a quieter phase of consolidation. For this phase it is reasonable to assume that the emphasis of Crowdfunding will generally shift towards Crowdinvesting, whereby users will be able to get their share of any commercial success. Another view on Crowdsourcing leads to the question which functions enterprises will outsource next. Apart from the active feedback of the users, the passive, unreflected behaviour of the same will presumably become of interest. Within the scope of big data the purchasing, communication or motional behaviour, for instance, can be transferred to organisations in real-time via smart devices. Provided that respective organisations are able to convince users to collaborate and to eliminate their concerns about the protection of personal data (if existing), purchasing intentions, private networks, cash flows, spatial preferences, the circadian rhythm and even physical conditions can be exploited directly.

Acknowledgements The author wishes to thank Marijke Roelandt-Toschev for translation and proof-reading.

References

Agarwal, A., Catalini, C., & Goldfarb, A. (2011). *The geography of crowdfunding*. NBER working papers 16820, National Bureau of Economic Research (pp. 1–61).

Applehoff, D., da Costa, D., & Brettel, M. (2013). Crowdfunding und -investing in Start-up- und Seedingphasen junger Unternehmen. In F. Piller & D. Hilgers (Eds.), *Praxishandbuch Technologietransfer* (Innovative Methoden zum Transfer wissenschaftlicher Ergebnisse in die industrielle Anwendung, pp. 91–111). Düsseldorf: Symposion.

Bell, D. (1973). *The coming of post-industrial society: A venture in social forecasting*. New York: Basic Books.

Belleflamme, P., Lambert, T., & Schwienbacher, A. (2010). *Crowdfunding: An industrial organization perspective*. In: SSRN eLibrary, Online: http://economix.fr/pdf/workshops/2010_dbm/Belleflamme_al.pdf

Belleflamme, P., Lambert, T., & Schwienbacher, A. (2012a). Crowdfunding: Tapping the right crowd. *Venture Capital: An International Journal of Entrepreneurial Finance, 15*(4), 313–333.

Belleflamme, P., Lambert, T., & Schwienbacher, A. (2012b). Crowdfunding: Tapping the right crowd. *Journal of Business Venturing, 29*(5), 585–609.

Boltanski, L., & Chiapello, É. (2003). *Der neue Geist des Kapitalismus*. Konstanz: UVK.

Bradford, S. C. (2013). Crowdfunding and the federal securities laws. *Columbia Business Law Review, 1*(1), 1–30.

Burtch, G., Ghose, A., & Wattal, S. (2012). An empirical examination of the antecedents and consequences of contribution patterns in crowd-funded markets. *Information Systems Research, 24*(3), 499–519.

Castells, M. (2001). *Das Informationszeitalter. Wirtschaft, Gesellschaft und Kultur: Die Netzwerkgesellschaft*. Opladen: Leske+Budrich.

Castells, M. (2005). *Die Internet-Galaxie: Internet, Wirtschaft und Gesellschaft*. Wiesbaden: VS, Verl. für Sozialwiss.

Chesbrough, H. W. (2003). *Open innovation: The new imperative for creating and profiting from technology*. Boston, MA: Harvard Business Review Press.

Gerber, E. M., Hui, J. S., & Kuo, P. (2012). *Crowdfunding: Why people are motivated to post and fund projects on crowdfunding platforms*. Online: http://www.juliehui.org/wp-content/uploads/2013/04/CSCW_Crowdfunding_Final.pdf

Hazen, T. L. (2012). *Crowdfunding or fraudfunding? Social networks and the securities laws – Why the specially tailored exemption must be conditioned on meaningful disclosure*. Online: http://papers.ssrn.com/sol3/papers.cfm?abstract_id=1954040##

Hemer, J. (2011). *A snapshot on crowdfunding*. Fraunhofer ISI working paper, Karlsruhe.

Hildebrand, T., Puri, M., & Rocholl, J. (2011). *Skin in the game: Incentives in crowdfunding*. Berlin: ESTM.

Kaltenbeck, J. (2011). *Crowdfunding und Social Payments im Anwendungskontext von Open Educational Resources*. Berlin: epubli.

Kappel, T. (2009). Ex ante crowdfunding and the recording industry: A model for the U.S. *Loyola of Los Angeles Entertainment Law Review, 29*(3), 376–385.

Kleemann, F., Voß, G. G., & Rieder, K. (2008). Un(der)paid innovators: The commercial utilization of consumer work through crowdsourcing. *Science, Technology and Innovation Studies, 4*(1), 5–26.

Lehner, O. M. (2013). Crowdfunding social ventures: A model and research agenda. *Routledge Venture Capital Journal, 15*(3), 289–311. Forthcoming.

Leimeister, J. M. (2010). Crowdsourcing: Crowdfunding, crowdvoting, crowdcreation. *ZfCM Controlling & Management, 56*(6), 388–392.

Marcombes, S. (2013). *Lima: The brain of your devices*. Online: http://www.kickstarter.com/projects/cloud-guys/plug-the-brain-of-your-devices

Mollick, E. (2012). The dynamics of crowdfunding: Determinants of success and failure. *Journal of Business Venturing, 29*(1), 1–16.

Ordanini, A., Miceli, L., & Pizzetti, M. (2011). Crowd-funding: Transforming customers into investors through innovative service platforms. *Journal of Service Management, 22*(4), 443–470.

Papsdorf, C. (2009). *Wie Surfen zu Arbeit wird. Crowdsourcing im Web 2.0.* Frankfurt a. M./New York: Campus.

Papsdorf, C. (2012). Die Beteiligung an Web 2.0-Phänomenen aus Perspektive des Mediatisierungsansatzes. In T. Beyreuther, K. Duske, C. Eismann, S. Hornung, & F. Kleemann (Eds.), *consumers@work. Zum neuen Verhältnis von Unternehmen und Usern im Web 2.0* (pp. 193–205). Frankfurt a.M./New York: Campus.

Pope, N. D. (2011). Crowdfunding microstartups: It's time for the securities and exchange commission to approve a small offering exemption. *Journal of Business Law, 13*(4), 101–129.

Schumpeter, J. A. (1950). *Kapitalismus, Sozialismus und Demokratie.* Bern: Francke.

Surowiecki, J. (2005). *Wisdom of crowds.* London: Anchor.

Voß, G. G., & Rieder, K. (2007). *Der arbeitende Kunde. Wenn Konsumenten zu unbezahlten Mitarbeitern werden.* Frankfurt a.M./New York: Campus.

Ward, C., & Ramachandran, V. (2010). *Crowdfunding the next hit: Microfunding online experience goods.* Working paper.

Wheat, R. E., Wang, Y., Byrnes, J. E., & Ranganathan, J. (2012). Raising money for scientific research through crowdfunding. *Trends in Ecology & Evolution, 28*(1), 71–72.

Open Innovation in the Tourism Experience Sector: The Role of Practice Based Knowledge Explored

Hindertje Hoarau

1 Introduction

> Our ideas for improvements and new products come from tourists and travel agents who are looking for certain types of products. People asked about fishing with a real Icelandic fisherman, so we now offer a sea-angling tour. Many people also told us they wanted to see puffins, but they thought a three-hour whale watching tour was too long. So we started thinking about what we could do for those wanting a shorter trip to only see puffins, and we developed the puffins-exclusive tour.

These are the words of a manager working for a whale-watching company in Iceland describing how innovation processes in experience-based tourism can be implemented. Being open to input from people outside of an organisation (such as tourists or travel agents) can set innovation processes in motion. But what does 'openness' mean for innovation processes in tourism experience firms?

The purpose of this chapter is to provide an explorative and conceptual discussion of the concept of openness within a tourism experience context. Tourism innovation is generally acknowledged to be the result of complex processes (Sørensen, 2004) rather than the 'simple' outcome of entrepreneurs' personal creativity (Schumpeter, 1934). A key component of innovation is therefore the sharing of explicit and tacit knowledge (Nonaka & Takeuchi, 1995; Weidenfeld, Williams, & Butler, 2010). Nonaka and Takeuchi have argued that firms actively seek to manage knowledge flows and applications, which involves identifying knowledge resources, absorbing tacit and explicit knowledge and redistributing such knowledge within or between organisations. These knowledge flows contribute to and facilitate blurred boundaries between firms (Weidenfeld et al., 2010), thereby opening up their innovation processes. Within this line of thinking, Chesbrough (2011; Chesbrough, Vanhaverbeke, & West, 2006) has argued for

H. Hoarau (✉)
Bodø Graduate School of Business at University of Nordland, Bodø, Norway
e-mail: hhh@uin.no

© Springer-Verlag Berlin Heidelberg 2016
R. Egger et al. (eds.), *Open Tourism*, Tourism on the Verge,
DOI 10.1007/978-3-642-54089-9_10

the 'open-innovation paradigm' in which firms intentionally use internal and external knowledge sources in their innovation processes. Instead of having all knowledge in house, such as research and development (R&D) departments, firms can establish networks with other actors to access and develop knowledge. However, R&D plays a less prominent role in the tourism experience sector than in other economic sectors due to the size and type of tourism firms' products (services and experiences). According to R&D studies, innovation capacity is closely and positively correlated with the size of an enterprise (Rogers, 2003); moreover, studies in many countries demonstrate that the tourism-experience sector is dominated by micro and small enterprises, most of which are owned and operated by a single person or family (Hjalager, 2002). Furthermore, little mutual trust exists among tourism enterprises, which often consider one another to be competitors, not colleagues (Hjalager, 2002). In addition to lack of R&D and trust, tourism-experience firms do not seem to design innovation processes and establish networks for innovation intentionally; rather, the innovation strategy of tourism firms is regarded more as 'innovating by doing'. In these processes, the roles of customers and suppliers are crucial for innovation because of adjustments to customers' changing demands and the offering of new materials and technology by suppliers (Hall, Hall, & Williams, 2008). Hjalager (2002) has argued that due to the structural and behavioural features of the tourism industry, the transfer of knowledge has to be considered in a broader context than the traditional R&D and research-based knowledge channels. Hence, to understand open-innovation processes in tourism, how knowledge is shared and with whom, in this sector, must be taken into account. This chapter continues with discussing innovation in experience tourism and exploring the underlying epistemological assumptions about knowledge and innovation. Subsequently, innovation theories that address openness will be discussed. An integrated, practice-based model is proposed for understanding the relational and co-creational aspects of knowledge and innovation processes in the tourism experience context. The framework will be further illustrated with an example of nature-based tourism.

2   Innovation in Experience-Tourism

Tourism has always been subject to changes, reflecting shifts in tastes and preferences, technologies and political-economic conditions, which result in innovation. Innovation in tourism has been defined as the generation, acceptance and implementation of new ideas, processes, products or services (Hall et al., 2008). Innovations in tourism include minor and major adaptations of products and services, rarely involving entirely new products and/or new markets but rather differentiation, product line extensions via brand policies or changes in the cost (price)/quality ratio of the products (Weidenfeld et al., 2010). Innovation is generally characterised by changes that differ from business-as-usual or that represent a certain degree of discontinuance of previous practices for the innovating firm (Hjalager, 2002).

Hjalager (2010) cites five categories in which tourism innovation can take place: 1) product innovations in which products (services and experiences) are reshaped or reinvented; 2) process innovations, which are "backstage initiatives aimed at escalating efficiency, productivity and flow" (p.2); 3) managerial innovations, which are internal shifts within an organisation; 4) marketing innovations; and 5) institutional innovations, which are new "structure or legal framework[s] that efficiently redirect or enhance the business" (p. 3) within an entire field. Innovation in the tourism sector follows patterns that are, to some degree, different than those in the manufacturing sector (Sundbo, Orfila-Sintes, & Sorensen, 2007). One of the main observations of such differences is that most service innovations are not technological, but rather consist of a behavioural change (Sundbo, 1997). Tourism innovation has many features in common with innovation in the service sector as a whole (Hall et al., 2008), but differences also exist, especially in those sub-sectors of tourism in which the core business is to offer experiences.

Experience is a mental phenomenon, which means that it does not concern physical needs (as goods do) or solving material or intellectual problems (as services do) (Sundbo & Sørensen, 2013). Experience offers great value to people who demand it and who are willing to pay a high price for experience-stimulating business activities (Sundbo & Sørensen, 2013). Commercial experiences have always been at the heart of entertainment and tourism businesses such as amusement parks, theme restaurants and nature-based attractions. Pine and Gilmore (1999) have defined 'experiences' as occurring when a company intentionally uses services as the stage, and goods as props, to engage individual customers in a way that creates a memorable event (Pine & Gilmore, 1999). Since Pine and Gilmore's well-known contribution, many authors have embraced the concept of the experience economy. The emerging tradition, or paradigm, of experience economy studies examines the formal economic activities related to experiences and how they can be managed and developed (Sundbo & Sørensen, 2013). A shift has occurred from the company to the customer in understanding who is responsible for creating experiences. The company is only able to make a value-proposition, while the actual value is co-created with all stakeholders involved in the experience (Boswijk & Olthof, 2012). Co-creating a valuable and memorable experience makes the tourism industry heavily reliant on information exchanges, whether in terms of information provided to tourists or the information accumulated by tourism companies about tourists. When creating experiences, understanding tourists' preferences and tastes becomes increasingly important. The people who work most closely with tourists are the employees involved in the experience. This circumstance renders most tourism sub-sectors labour intensive, and the quality of the labour input shapes the tourism experience (Hall et al., 2008).

Innovation within experience firms has become a specialised field within innovation research because the nature of delivering experiences to tourists has consequences for how the tourism experience sector innovates (Fuglsang, Sundbo, & Sorensen, 2011; Sundbo, 2009; Sundbo & Sørensen, 2013). Stamboulis and Skayannis (2003) have argued that the distinction of experience as a separate, valuable commodity offers new perspectives for analysis and strategy. These authors argue that experience involves the creation of a myth or narrative and is therefore a knowledge-intensive process. Knowledge must be created and utilised in the production process with respect to the generation of the theme, the technologies involved and the customer's anticipated interests and tastes. The task of tourism experience firms is then to inform and steer the innovation process that leads to the creation of new experience themes.

3   Epistemological Assumptions

Knowledge plays a key role in organisations' innovation and performance (Cavusgil, Calantone, & Zhao, 2003), and Nonaka and Takeuchi (1995) go as far as to say that innovation is, in fact, knowledge creation. The question 'what is knowledge' is therefore an important starting point in discussing innovation. The answer depends on one's epistemological assumptions and whether such assumptions are rooted in an objectivist or practice-based perspective (Hislop, 2009). The objectivist perspective conceptualises knowledge as a codifiable object/entity and is therefore referred to as the 'epistemology of possession' (Cook & Brown, 1999) because knowledge is regarded as an entity possessed by people or groups. The objectivist perspective has been widely challenged by proponents of the practice-based perspective, which emphasises that knowledge is embedded within and is inseparable from work activities or practices (Newell, Robertson, Scarbrough, & Swan, 2009).

Both perspectives distinguish between explicit and tacit knowledge. Within the objectivist epistemological framework, tacit and explicit knowledge are regarded as distinctive with their own characteristics. Tacit knowledge is understood as subjective, personal, context specific and difficult to share, while explicit knowledge is objective, impersonal, codifiable and easy to share (Hislop, 2009). The practice-based perspective rejects the idea that tacit and explicit knowledge are independent of one another and suggests that they represent two aspects of knowledge and are inseparable and mutually constituted (Hislop, 2009: p.36).

Tacit knowledge is considered to be important for innovation. Nonaka and Takeuchi (1995) discuss why Japanese companies are so successful in innovating and renewing themselves. These authors conclude that the role of tacit knowledge is these companies' key to success. Once the importance of tacit knowledge is realised, one begins to conceptualise innovation differently. The essence of innovation, then, is to recreate the world according to a particular ideal or vision (Nonaka & Takeuchi, 1995) rather than simply compiling diverse bits of data and information. Hence, organisational knowledge creation is a process of mobilising individual tacit knowledge and making this knowledge accessible for the innovator to expand its innovation possibilities (Sundbo & Fuglsang, 2002). This understanding inherently assumes relationships and systems between individuals and organisations as the context of knowledge sharing.

Hjalager (2002) has identified four different channels, or systems, for knowledge sharing: trade, technological, infrastructural and regulation. The trade system consists of a number of trade associations, employers' organisations and unions. The technological system refers to knowledge that is embodied in technology and is carried over, in this tangible form, into tourism firms. The infrastructural system refers to the "free goods" that tourism firms rely on, such as natural resources, cultural attractions, townscapes, and traffic systems, among other assets. Knowledge regarding these infrastructural elements also reaches the tourism firms when they utilise and interact with such elements. Hjalager (2002) argues that it is important to acknowledge that the transfer of knowledge in tourism takes place through these filters. The systems, or filters, are composed of individual stakeholders, and connectedness as a source of knowledge and ideas is well documented in the tourism innovation literature. For example, customers, employees, conferences, management, public sources and newspapers are all considered to be sources of new ideas and knowledge (Hall et al., 2008). Fuglsang et al. (2011) have examined these sources of ideas and knowledge for innovations in tourism. In their research, they identify management and employees as the most important source of ideas and knowledge for innovation. Their results indicate that there is a very strong bottom-up approach to innovation from employees, customers and market sources (Fuglsang et al., 2011). What these stakeholders have in common is that they are closely involved in producing the experience product. In addition to the filters mentioned by Hjalager (2002), it is possible to identify a fifth filter, namely the product- or experience-system. This system refers to the stakeholders who are involved in the co-creation of the tourism experience product, such as customers and employees. Tacit and explicit knowledge is shared during the co-creation of the experience and is absorbed by the tourism firm. This knowledge is embedded in the practices undertaken by organisational staff and tourists; hence, the knowledge these actors possess is localised and specific and is shaped by the particular demands of their contexts (Hislop, 2009). The epistemological assumptions about knowledge that form the foundation of this chapter are therefore routed in a practice-based perspective.

Practice includes both physical and cognitive elements, which are inseparable. Knowledge use and development are therefore regarded as a fundamental aspect of activity (Hislop, 2009: pp. 33). Thus, knowledge needs a context in order to be created—a shared social, physical and mental space for the interpretation of information, interaction and emerging relationships that serves as a foundation of knowledge creation (Sundbo, 1998). Communities of practice form such a context and are regarded as critical to the sharing of knowledge within and across organisations. Hence, understanding networked practices can provide insight into innovation processes, as practices help foster an environment in which knowledge is created and shared and can be used to improve effectiveness, efficiency and innovation (Swan, 2002). Whereas systems and networks refer to the existence of relationships between stakeholders, practices refer to the activities stakeholders are engaged in together. In a way, practice is a qualitative aspect of relationships that refers to what is being shared between stakeholders. For example, practices such as experience tours, in which tourists, employees and other stakeholders are interacting, play an essential role in knowledge sharing for innovation. According to Gherardi (2000), thinking of learning through participation in practice enables us to focus on the fact that, in everyday practices, learning takes place in the flow of experience, with or without our awareness of it. Innovation can then be regarded as a benefit of these processes of learning, sharing and integrating knowledge. For firms, it becomes strategically important to participate in these shared learning processes, as knowledge that is relevant for innovation is typically distributed across a wide range of sources both inside and outside the organisation. From this perspective, flows of knowledge are seen as inextricably linked to social relations developed through shared practices. These practices highlight the ways in which partners in the innovation process learn, adapt and re-evaluate their roles and commitments, as a response to prior experiences of working together.

A practice-based perspective could provide important additional insights into the nature and role of objects in innovation (Swan, Bresnen, Newell, & Robertson, 2007) because knowing, learning and innovation are understood as courses of action that are materially mediated and situated within a field of human and non-human 'actants' (Gherardi, 2006). Knowing and innovating have become material activities, which means that sociality is related not only to human beings, but also to symbolic, cultural and natural artifacts (Corradi, Gherardi, & Verzelloni, 2010). Like humans, these non-humans can be mediators. These entities do not determine collective action and do not act like stakeholders, but they do participate in the action and ensure its continuity (Paget, Dimanche, & Mounet, 2010). The concept of practice thus adopts a renewed conception of materiality as a form of distributed agency that has an intimate relationship with humans (Gherardi, 2009). Central to the practice perspective is acknowledgement of the social, historical and structural contexts in which knowledge is manufactured as well as the collective and provisional nature of knowledge (Corradi et al., 2010). Practice is always the product of specific historical conditions resulting from previous practice that are transformed into present practice (Gherardi, 2000). In nature-based tourism systems, this context is composed of humans and non-humans, such as artefacts, concepts or nature, and these actors play a special role in sharing knowledge, learning and innovation. Performing a practice, like creating a nature tourism experience, requires understanding this socio-technical context and how to align humans and non-humans to reach the goal of the practice.

4   Exploring Openness in Tourism Innovation

Thus far, innovation in tourism and the different epistemological approaches to knowledge have been discussed. In this section, innovation theories that address openness and connectedness between stakeholders and their assumptions about knowledge will be explored. Swan has argued that literature from different theoretical perspectives, such as marketing, industrial ecology, and tourism studies, has highlighted the positive role of networks in relation to innovation, arguing that innovation is more likely to occur between collaborating groups and organisations (Swan, 2005). Networked innovation is defined as 'innovation that occurs through relationships that are negotiated in an ongoing communicative process'. It is at the intersections of individuals and organisations, through the operation of local and global networks, that distributed knowledge can be brought together and integrated into new products, processes and services (Swan, 2005).

This understanding of the innovation-process has led to the development of theories and concepts that focus on, and try to understand, interrelatedness. The idea of innovation systems, for example, is that single stakeholders do not innovate in isolation; they are part of networks. The literature on innovation systems is primarily oriented towards incremental change, building on existing competencies, and moving along a technical trajectory according to a techno-economic paradigm (Nooteboom, 2001). Asheim and Isaksen (2002) argue that integrating global knowledge and networks into local innovative processes is of crucial importance. Networking becomes a capability that companies can develop to enhance their competitive advantage. In addition to learning about and adapting to change, connecting to sources of knowledge, values and ideas outside the company can be a way to differentiate from other businesses through the unique character of those relationships. Hence, knowledge is understood as a resource or commodity that can easily be transmitted between different networks and stakeholders. Knowledge is viewed as an important resource in distinguishing a firm from its competitors, which is important because innovation strategies look increasingly similar and commoditised; thus, increasingly more firms try to improve their innovation performance through intensifying collaboration and learning across industry networks and partnerships, thereby expanding their innovation (Chesbrough et al., 2006).

The idea that innovating firms need to open up to outside relationships has received, among others, the label of 'open innovation' (OI) (Chesbrough et al., 2006), which has recently been extended to services (Chesbrough, 2011). Openness generally refers to ways of sharing with others and inviting their participation. OI is the use of purposive inflows and outflows of knowledge to accelerate internal innovation and expand the markets for external use of innovation (Chesbrough, 2011; Chesbrough et al., 2006). OI suggests that valuable ideas can come from inside or outside the company and can reach the market from inside or outside the company as well (Chesbrough et al., 2006). A benefit from OI for value creation comes from the participation of many more individuals and firms in the market. OI combines internal and external ideas into new products, architectures, and systems through a network of stakeholders (Chesbrough, 2011; Chesbrough et al., 2006).

In the marketing literature, the concept of open-innovation can be linked to the evolution from a resource- to a service-dominant logic (Vargo & Lusch, 2008). In a resource-dominant logic, value creation is perceived to take place in a value chain that has been identified by Porter (1985) as a tool to both conceptualise and innovate businesses. The value chain is a product-focused approach to thinking about a business in which competitive advantages come from having better, differentiated or the lowest cost products. The resource-dominant logic in general and value-chain in particular have framed the way practitioners think about their business (Chesbrough, 2011). However, Normann and Ramirez (1993) argue that the value-added notion is "outdated", as it is grounded in the assumptions and models of an industrial economy. Chesbrough et al. (2006) have developed this notion further by arguing for a new business model: 'open service innovation'. In an open innovation setting, firms intentionally use internal and external sources of knowledge to turn new ideas into commercial products and services (Chesbrough et al., 2006). In the open-service paradigm, Porter's value chain is still the point of departure, but co-creation and relationships are incorporated into the chain by allowing processes and outputs interact with customers, external sources of ideas, technologies and services. In Chesbrough's open service value chain, there are still inputs, processes and outputs, but these components are no longer interacting exclusively with internal support functions. Instead, they also interact with external sources of ideas, technologies and services, which lead to open innovation. It seems that both the open-innovation and open-service innovation approaches view knowledge from an objectivist epistemology. Knowledge is regarded as an entity or object that people possess and that can be easily transmitted between different communities. The assumption about knowledge is that it is possible to develop a type of knowledge and understanding that are free from individual subjectivity (Hislop, 2009). In addition, knowledge is considered to be derived from an intellectual process that can be important in different organisations. Thus, innovation approaches based on the resource- and knowledge-based view of the firm fundamentally view knowledge from an objectivist perspective and focus mainly on how knowledge of stakeholders is absorbed in the firm and utilised for innovation.

Service-dominant logic brings the idea of openness in innovation processes closer to a practice-based perspective on knowledge because one of the foundational premises of the service dominant logic is that the customer acts as co-creator. Value is defined by and co-created with the consumer rather than embedded in output. Prahalad (2004) understands co-creation as the joint creation of value by the company and the customer by allowing the customer to co-construct the service experience to suit his or her context. This process involves joint problem definition and solving, which requires continuous dialogue. The role of the company is to create an experience environment in which consumers can have an active dialogue and co-construct personalised experiences; the product might be the same, but the customers can construct different experiences. These types of high-quality interactions that enable an individual customer to co-create unique service experiences with the company are the key to unlocking new sources of competitive advantage (Prahalad, 2004). Chesbrough (2011) also argues that co-creation with customers can create more meaningful experiences for customers, who will then get more of what they really want. Hence, the role of customers in an open innovation process is that of co-creator of service experiences. The larger role for co-creation in the open-innovation literature slowly shifts the understanding of knowledge away from a purely objectivist perspective. Knowledge is increasingly regarded as personalised and individual, contributing different value for different customers.

One example of a relational, open approach to innovation that understands knowledge more as practice-based is the strategic-reflexivity approach, which describes innovation as pull-oriented towards market possibilities and other stakeholders (Sundbo, 1998). From this attitude towards driving forces of innovation follows that the strategic reflexivity approach understands innovation as a social process where stakeholders manipulate and perform strategies and roles. Hence, this approach addresses both the networked nature of knowledge and the interpretations of stakeholders in order 'to do' something with new knowledge. The concept of reflexivity stems from temporary sociology (Malerba, 2006) and attempts to understand the phenomenon in which people in our modern society follow their own trajectory in a world that is full of possibilities and dangers. Therefore, individuals inevitably reflect upon their own situations and try to determine what decisions to make. Sundbo and Fuglsang (2006) argue that innovation is a way to develop solutions to (socially constructed) problems of firms and individuals and to reduce risks. To survive in the modern world, firms need to be able to make interpretations and choices, recruit personnel who are engaged in critical dialogue, establish reflexive roles and change the relationship to the environment to become more complementary and flexible (Malerba, 2006). Thus, by strategically reflecting upon the firm's internal and external environment, people acquire new ideas and knowledge for change and innovation. This process is illustrated by Hoarau et al. in the handbook of research on innovation in tourism industries (Alsos et al., 2014) where they discuss how local network relations and actors' attitudes influence innovative behaviour in adaptation to environmental change. However, acquiring knowledge is one thing, but absorbing it into the organization, so it can be applied in innovation processes, is yet another. Although knowledge is the engine that drives innovation, tourism firms can have problems and challenges when trying to absorb external knowledge for innovation. The main challenge is to access and absorb tacit knowledge as this type of knowledge is personal and sticky and therefore difficult to acquire and assimilate into the existing knowledge pool of organizations. However, knowledge is also difficult to imitate and is therefore important for developing original and competitive innovations (Hoarau, 2014). See Hoarau (2014) for a further discussion on how tourism managers can overcome these challenges and develop abilities to absorb knowledge for innovation.

The strategic reflexive approach to innovation is quite similar to what Ordanini and Parasuraman (2011) have proposed as innovation viewed through a service dominant lens. They have derived three relevant drivers for service innovation based on the premise of the service dominant logic: collaborative competences, dynamic capability of customer orientation and knowledge interfaces (Ordanini & Parasuraman, 2011). Collaborative competences are based on the idea that the customer always plays an active role in service offerings by integrating his or her own set of resources and competences into any service activity (Ordanini & Parasuraman, 2011). To be able to reflect on the environment, tourism companies need to collaborate actively with their customers. Insight into market possibilities comes from this collaboration with customers. Ordanini and Parasuraman (2011) argue that effective new service development depends on the continuous renewal,

Table 1 Tourism-innovation approaches

Innovation approach	Epistemological assumptions about knowledge	Innovation process	Role of innovator
Innovation systems	Objectivist perspective	Occurs through relationships that are negotiated in an ongoing communicative process	Stakeholders do not innovate in isolation; they are part of networks
Open-innovation	Objectivist perspective	Purposive inflows and out-flows of knowledge to accelerate internal innovation and expand the markets for external use of innovation	Letting processes and outputs interact with customers, external sources of ideas, technologies and services Cooperation as capability
Strategic reflexivity	Practice-based perspective	Pull oriented towards market possibilities and other environmental stakeholders.	Interpretation, reflexivity, sense-making
Innovation through service dominant lens	Practice-based perspective	Depends on the continuous renewal, creation, integration, and transformation of information and knowledge.	Co-creation, collaborative competences, dynamic capability of customer orientation and knowledge interfaces

creation, integration, and transformation of information and knowledge. Knowledge is understood as being embodied in people (customers) and as socially constructed and culturally embedded, thereby moving more towards a practice-based perspective.

Table 1 summarises the different approaches to innovation and includes the understanding of knowledge in these different approaches.

5 Discussion: Practice-Based Open Innovation in Tourism

The starting point for understanding innovation processes in experience tourism is the tourism system, or community of practice, in which stakeholders such as tourists, guides, other employees, wildlife, by-standers and artefacts co-create value and knowledge. The tourism system is organised around an attraction or experience and includes all stakeholders involved, including the natural and cultural environment and objects that are part of the experience.

The next step is to examine what practices are happening within the tourism experience system and what role the different stakeholders play in these practices. Different knowledge communities meet during activities, which offer possibilities for knowledge sharing. Knowledge sharing is different when the activity is, for example, a tour or a meeting with government officials. However, tourism innovators share and co-create knowledge, learn and reflect upon what they learn, in all practices they are involved in (Hoarau & Kline, 2014). The practice-based nature of knowledge/knowing assumes that knowledge develops through practice: people's knowledge develops as they perform activities and gain experience (Hislop, 2009). This phenomenon could explain why tourism employees play such an important role in the innovation processes of tourism firms. The more experience employees have, the more knowledge they have about the practices and the stakeholders involved. Stakeholders who are engaged in creating the experience should be understood as mediums for sharing knowledge and values that can be brought back in the firm so it can be incorporated in innovation processes. This task is not easy because much of the knowledge involved in providing or consuming experiences is tacit and gained from experience (Hoarau, 2014). Customers can express their explicit needs (and, to some extent, their tacit needs as well) by talking about them or writing them down. However, tacit needs are expressed through interaction and practice, and this type of knowledge needs to be shared and co-created with the provider to become accessible for the firm. When customers share their tacit needs, a company acquires a unique insight that can help with marketplace differentiation. Given that explicit knowledge is generally considered to be easier for competitors to imitate, tacit knowledge is increasingly regarded as a key to competitiveness (Weidenfeld et al., 2010). Managing knowledge co-creation effectively, therefore, requires developing ways to share tacit knowledge between stakeholders, tourism employees and innovators.

By strategically reflecting upon and interpreting knowledge, ideas for improvements and innovations are developed (Hoarau & Kline, 2014). These ideas are unique because people and their experiences are unique. The practice perspective argues that all knowledge is socially constructed in nature, which makes it subjective and open to interpretation. Thus, knowledge is never completely neutral and unbiased, and to some extent inseparable from the values of those who produce it (Hislop, 2009; p. 40). The meaning people attach to language/events is shaped by the values and assumptions of the social and cultural context in which they live and work. According to Hislop (2009), pre-existing values and assumptions influence the process of knowledge construction/knowledge interpretation in deciding what is considered to be 'relevant'. Tourism employees and tourists themselves often have different cultural and social backgrounds, which can make absorbing knowledge in innovation processes more complicated. Personal values are a strong compass for understanding the world, and tourism innovators form attitudes towards people and events in their environment based on their values, knowledge and interpretations (Hoarau et al., in Alsos et al., 2014). This phenomenon renders personal ethics a key determinant of business behaviour, especially with regards to ethical/environmental issues. Reflection that is based on values and their relationship to learning and practice has been a research focus and a recurring theme in organisation and management learning (Keevers & Treleaven, 2011). Reflection has also been identified as an important theme by some tourism researchers. For example, Ateljevic and Doorne (2000) and Thomas, Shaw, and Page (2011) do not view tourism actors as rational, problem-solving machines but as influenced by values in their business practices and decision-making processes.

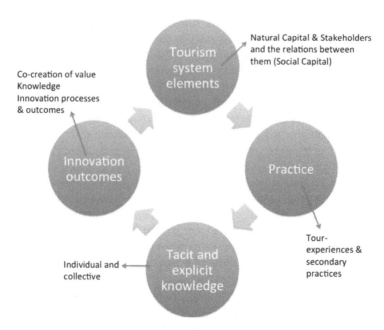

Fig. 1 Framework for open-experience innovation

Insight into innovative behaviour and outcomes is also essential in understanding the choices tourism firms have made and the paths they have chosen. Even more important are the impacts these changes have on the overall tourism system. Innovating means changing the configurations of objects, stakeholders and people, which sets new learning processes in motion. Therefore, open-innovation in the tourism experience sector should be understood as a circular process.

Figure 1 shows the different elements of a practice-based approach to open innovation in experience tourism that have been discussed in this chapter.

The framework will be further illustrated with an example from whale-watching, as a form of nature-based experience tourism.

5.1   The Example of Whale Watching

Whale watching has become a booming worldwide industry that attracts approximately 10 million people a year who spend more than 1.25 billion US dollars (Einarsson, 2009). The number of whale watchers is increasing by 12 % a year, which is more than three times that of the overall tourism industry (Einarsson, 2009). There are 495 communities in 87 countries and territories that now offer whale-watching tours. Due to entrepreneurship and growth in this sector, innovation is important to stay competitive, attract tourists and develop unique paths of innovation and improvement.

The tourism system of whale watching can be understood as having a core and outer layers. The core is organised around the whale-watching experience. Around the core are stakeholders such as the municipalities, tourism offices, competitors and other tourism companies that play a facilitating role in creating the experience. Whale-watching companies are often involved in global research networks, and NGOs and certifying agencies form an outer layer of stakeholders in the system. During the core experience-practice, different stakeholders are involved in various value-creation processes. For example, the employees of the tour company, tourists, scientific researchers and non-human elements such as wildlife, landscape, weather, and boats are all present in the tour practice. Because these components are part of the practice, they influence the outcome of the value created during that particular tour.

All stakeholders who are present during this practice bring their tacit and explicit knowledge into use in order to create value. The guides have knowledge about the whales and other wildlife; the captains use their knowledge of the sea, weather and wildlife in order to find the whales; and the tourists apply their previous experiences, expectations and knowledge about tours into the practice. In some types of wildlife tourism, such as whale-watching, naturalists or scientists are often involved in the tour practice as well. These experts bring their knowledge about their study objects (whales and other cetaceans) into practice (Hoarau & Kline, 2014).

By interacting and co-creating value, this combined knowledge contributes to the quality of the tour experience. People and non-human stakeholders involved in this practice are able to learn and absorb knowledge observed during this practice. This type of learning and knowledge sharing always takes place in two-directions; they learn from each other. For example, the guides learn about the preferences and behaviour of tourists and from the researchers on board. Tourists learn from the guides and researchers with whom they are interacting. The wildlife learns from the practice by becoming accustomed to whale-watching boats. Whales and dolphins, in particular, like other intelligent mammals, are able to learn from the experience. In addition, knowledge is embedded in the technology used during the tour. The type of boat and other equipment used influence the way tourists and employees learn and experience. To translate knowledge into innovation, tourism employees need to reflect strategically and critically upon the knowledge learned in practice. This phenomenon is an important element in the absorptive capacity of tourism firms. Innovation processes and outcomes change the configuration of the tourism system. New stakeholders might become involved, new technology and artefacts might be introduced, or new ways of creating the experience might be adopted. For example, investing in a new boat leads to the development of different types of tours. A whale-watching company that buys a sailboat creates different experiences than a company that buys a fast Zodiac. These companies invest and innovate in different directions based on what is important to them. This behaviour affects the co-creation and knowledge sharing processes again, thereby setting in motion new innovation processes.

6 Conclusion

This chapter has suggested, described and briefly illustrated a framework for open-experience innovation. The main underlying assumptions are that tourism is a phenomenon in which different stakeholders are connected in tourism systems with ever-changing values and that interactions with other cultures in practice drive all involved stakeholders towards continuous knowledge sharing, learning and innovation. In addition, innovation in tourism is an adaptive process in which interaction, sense making and reflection play central roles.

This chapter has explored what openness means for tourism experience innovation and has developed the framework based on a practice-based perspective. The 'open experience innovation' framework understands innovation in tourism in a circular manner. The framework goes beyond previous research and has potential positive implications for understanding innovation in the tourism experience sector, as the practice-based approach seems especially suitable for the tourism experience sector. Due to the connectedness of stakeholders in tourism systems and the engagement of these stakeholders in practices, they continuously co-create and re-invent their world. Consequently, innovation processes are steered towards new themes of experience, which allows tourism firms to differentiate and compete in a global tourism experience market. Innovation in tourism should therefore be understood as a 'perpetual mobile' powered by the connections, practices, knowledge and values of the stakeholders involved. The framework for open innovation in the tourism experience economy can be used by practitioners and academics to guide innovation processes or research.

Acknowledgement This chapter is written as part of the research project Northern InSights (http://www.opplevelserinord.no/), which is partly financed by The Research Council of Norway.

References

Asheim, B., & Isaksen, A. (2002). Regional innovation systems: the integration of local "sticky" and global "ubiquitous" knowledge. *Journal of Technology Transfer, 27*, 77–86.

Ateljevic, I., & Doorne, S. (2000). 'Staying within the fence': Lifestyle entrepreneurship in tourism. *Journal of Sustainable Tourism, 8*(5), 378–392.

Boswijk, A., & Olthof, S. (2012). *Economy of experiences*. Amsterdam: European Centre for the Experience Economy.

Cavusgil, S. T., Calantone, R. J., & Zhao, Y. (2003). Tacit knowledge transfer and firm innovation capability. *Journal of Business Industrial Marketing, 18*(1), 6–21.

Chesbrough, H. (2011). *Open services innovation*. San Francisco: Jossey-Bass.

Chesbrough, H., Vanhaverbeke, W., & West, J. (2006). *Open innovation: Researching a new paradigm*. Oxford: Oxford University Press.

Cook, S., & Brown, J. (1999). Bridging epistemologies: The generative dance between organizational knowledge and organizational knowing. *Organization Science, 10*(4), 381–400.

Corradi, G., Gherardi, S., & Verzelloni, L. (2010). Through the practice lens: Where is the bandwagon of practice-based studies heading? [Proceedings Paper]. *Management Learning, 41*(3), 265–283.

Einarsson, N. (2009). From good to eat to good to watch: Whale watching, adaptation and change in Icelandic fishing communities. *Polar Research, 28*(1), 129–138.

Fuglsang, L., Sundbo, J., & Sorensen, F. (2011). Dynamics of experience service innovation: Innovation as a guided activity - results from a Danish survey. *Service Industries Journal, 31* (5), 661–677.

Gherardi, S. (2000). Practice-based theorizing on learning and knowing in organizations. *Organization, 7*(2), 211–223.

Gherardi, S. (2006). *Organizational knowledge: The texture of workplace learning*. Malden, MA: Blackwell.

Gherardi, S. (2009). Knowing and learning in practice-based studies: An introduction. *The Learning Organization, 16*(5), 352–359.

Hall, C., Hall, M., & Williams, A. (2008). *Tourism and innovation*. London: Routledge.

Hislop, D. (2009). *Knowledge management in organizations. A critical introduction*. Oxford: Oxford University Press.

Hjalager, A. M. (2002). Repairing innovation defectiveness in tourism. *Tourism Management, 23* (5), 465–474.

Hjalager, A.-M. (2010). A review of innovation research in tourism. *Tourism Management, 31*(1), 1–12.

Hoarau, H. (2014). *Knowledge acquisition and assimilation in tourism-innovation processes* (pp. 1–17). In: Scandinavian Journal of Hospitality and Tourism.

Hoarau, H., & Kline, C. (2014). Science and industry: Sharing knowledge for innovation. *Annals of Tourism Research* (Accepted for Publication).

Hoarau, H., Wigger, K., & Bystrowska, M. (2014). Innovation and climate change: The role of networked relations and the attitudes of tourism actors on Svalbard. In G. A. Alsos, D. Eide, & E. L. Madsen (Eds.), *Handbook of research on innovation in tourism industries* (pp. 303–324). Cheltenham: Edgar Elgar.

Keevers, L., & Treleaven, L. (2011). Organizing practices of reflection: A practice-based study. *Management Learning, 42*(5), 505–520.

Malerba, F. (2006). Innovation and the evolution of industries. *Journal of Evolutionary Economics, 16*(1), 3–23.

Newell, S., Robertson, M., Scarbrough, H., & Swan, J. (2009). *Managing knowledge work and innovation*. Hampshire: Palgrave Macmillan.

Nonaka, I., & Takeuchi, H. (1995). *The knowledge-creating company: How Japanese companies create the dynamics of innovation*. New York: Oxford University Press.

Nooteboom, B. (2001). *Learning and governance in inter-firm relations*. SSRN eLibrary.

Normann, R., & Ramirez, R. (1993). From value chain to value constellation - Designing interactive strategy. *Harvard Business Review, 71*(4), 65–77.

Ordanini, A., & Parasuraman, A. (2011). Service innovation viewed through a service-dominant logic lens: A conceptual framework and empirical analysis. *Journal of Service Research, 14* (1), 3–23.

Paget, E., Dimanche, F., & Mounet, J.-P. (2010). A tourism innovation case: An actor-network approach. *Annals of Tourism Research, 37*(3), 828–847.

Pine, B. J., & Gilmore, J. H. (1999). *The experience economy: Work is theatre & every business a stage*. Boston, MA: Harvard Business School Press.

Porter, M. E. (1985). *Competitive advantage: creating and sustaining superior performance*. New York: Free Press.

Prahalad, C. K. (2004). *The future of competition: Co-creating unique value with customers*. Boston, MA: Harvard Business School Press.

Rogers, E. M. (2003). *Diffusion of innovations*. New York: Free Press.

Schumpeter, J. A. (1934) [2008]. *The theory of economic development: An inquiry into profits, capital, credit, interest and the business cycle* (R. Opie, Trans., German). New Brunswick, NJ: Transaction Publishers.

Sørensen, F. (2004). *Tourism experience innovation networks: Tourism experience innovations and the role of geographically organised production and information innovation networks.* PhD, Roskilde University, Roskilde.

Stamboulis, Y., & Skayannis, P. (2003). Innovation strategies and technology for experience-based tourism. *Tourism Management, 24*(1), 35–43.

Sundbo, J. (1997). Management of innovation in services. *Service Industries Journal, 17*(3), 432–455.

Sundbo, J. (1998). *The theory of innovation: Entrepreneurs, technology and strategy.* Cheltenham: Edward Elgar.

Sundbo, J. (2009). Innovation in the experience economy: A taxonomy of innovation organisations. *Service Industries Journal, 29*(4), 431–455.

Sundbo, J., & Fuglsang, L. (2002). *Innovation as strategic reflexivity.* London: Routledge.

Sundbo, J., Orfila-Sintes, F., & Sorensen, F. (2007). The innovative behaviour of tourism firms-Comparative studies of Denmark and Spain. *Research Policy, 36*(1), 88–106.

Sundbo, J., & Sørensen, F. (2013). Introduction to the experience economy. In J. Sundbo & F. Sørensen (Eds.), *Handbook of experience economy.* Cheltenham: Edward Elgar.

Swan, J. (2002). The construction of 'communities of practice' in the management of innovation. *Management Learning, 33*(4), 477–496.

Swan, J. (2005). The politics of networked innovation. *Human Relations, 58*(7), 913–943.

Swan, J., Bresnen, M., Newell, S., & Robertson, M. (2007). The object of knowledge: The role of objects in biomedical innovation. *Human Relations, 60*(12), 1809–1837.

Thomas, R., Shaw, G., & Page, S. J. (2011). Understanding small firms in tourism: A perspective on research trends and challenges. *Tourism Management, 32*(5), 963–976.

Vargo, S., & Lusch, R. (2008). Service-dominant logic: Continuing the evolution. *Journal of the Academy of Marketing Science, 36*(1), 1–10.

Weidenfeld, A., Williams, A. M., & Butler, R. W. (2010). Knowledge transfer and innovation among attractions. *Annals of Tourism Research, 37*(3), 604–626.

Open Innovation: A Chance
for the Innovation Management of Tourism
Destinations?

Birgit Pikkemaat and Mike Peters

1   Introduction

According to Huizingh (2011, p. 2) 'open innovation has become one of the hottest topics in innovation management'. Open innovation implies that a single firm cannot innovate in isolation, but it has to engage with different types of partners to acquire ideas and resources from the external environment to stay competitive (Chesbrough, 2003; Dahlander & Gann, 2010). So far open innovation has mainly been analysed in manufacturing industries and only a few studies have investigated it for smaller organizations (Lee, Park, Yoon, & Park, 2010; van de Vrande, de Jong, Vanhaverbeke, & de Rochemont, 2009; Zeng, Xie, & Tam, 2010). One of these studies confirms that 'future research should broaden the scope by studying open innovation in broader samples, also capturing small enterprises and firms in services industries' (van de Vrande et al., 2009, p. 436).

Since the beginning of the new millennium a number of research initiatives have been investigating innovation management patterns, particularly in the accommodation sector (Martínez-Ros & Orfila-Sintes, 2009; Orfila-Sintes & Mattsson, 2009; Ottenbacher, 2007; Pikkemaat, 2008; Pikkemaat & Peters, 2005; Sundbo, Orfila-Sintes, & Flemming, 2006; Volo, 2004). Little research was carried out to analyse innovation management processes and triggers at the destination level (Paget, Dimanche, & Mounet, 2010; Pechlaner, Fischer, & Priglinger, 2006; Weiermair & Pikkemaat, 2005). Although destinations consist of various stakeholders interested in innovation processes, a discussion of open innovation mechanisms within

B. Pikkemaat (✉)
Institut für innovativen Tourismus, Innsbruck, Austria
e-mail: b.pikkemaat@i-fit.at

M. Peters
KMU und Tourismus, Institut für strategisches Management, Marketing und Tourismus, Universität Innsbruck, Innsbruck, Austria
e-mail: mike.peters@uibk.ac.at

© Springer-Verlag Berlin Heidelberg 2016   153
R. Egger et al. (eds.), *Open Tourism*, Tourism on the Verge,
DOI 10.1007/978-3-642-54089-9_11

tourism destinations is scarce (Hjalager, 2010). Recently Hjalager and Nordin (2011) focussed on the aspect of user-driven innovation in a conceptual way.

When evaluating open innovation at a destination level several aspects have to be considered, such as the nature of the tourism product, different structures and leaderships of destination management organizations (DMOs), and a variety of entrepreneurial processes and collaboration within the destination. The aim of the present pilot study is, therefore, to investigate the opportunities and threats of open innovation management of tourism destinations. Consequently, the research examines whether open innovation is an appropriate tool to improve the innovation management process for tourism destinations. Furthermore, the research paper will derive challenges for destination management organization in order to use open innovation management.

First of all, a literature review is presented to critically discuss the concept of open innovation at a destination level. In more detail, the paper undertakes a review of the relevant literature regarding: (i) innovation management at a destination level, (ii) the concept of open innovation and (iii) the challenges of open innovation for destination management. Research questions conclude this part of the paper before an empirical study is presented. In this study 37 interviews with managers of tourism businesses, such as managers of DMOs as well as its chairmen and supervisory board, hotel and cable car entrepreneurs were conducted in Tyrol, Austria. The qualitative data gathered describes the variety of innovation management aspects in destinations, e.g. stimuli and sources for ideas, the innovation management process, and types of cooperation in the destination, internal and external networking and entrepreneurs' involvement. The average duration of the interviews was approximately 40 min. Interviews were transcribed and analysed with MAXQDA, qualitative content analysis software.

The data will be analysed and discussed with regard to the former literature review and the derived research questions. Managerial implications focus on DMOs and target the development of open innovation management processes within tourism destinations. Limitations of the study will briefly be reflected before the paper concludes with recommendations for further research.

2 Three Pillars of Innovation for Tourism Destinations

Innovation can be interpreted as a tool entrepreneurs use to exploit changes as opportunities (Drucker, 1985). In the literature a large number of definitions exist, each having different foci: innovation is a creation of something new; it is diffusion and learning; or it might be change, a process or an event. Innovation can be defined as an entrepreneurial event but also as a context level process seeing innovation as an act capturing institutional frameworks in a geographic region (Ahmed & Shepherd, 2010, p. 5). Referring to entrepreneurship much has been written about the renewed importance of entrepreneurs driving markets and innovation in the 'new economy' (Norton, 2001): primarily innovation means successfully producing and managing processes at the firm level which allow the commercialisation of new ideas or inventions. Urabe (1988, p. 3) outlines the fact that innovation 'consists of the generation of a new idea and its implementation into a new product, process, or service, leading to the dynamic growth of the national economy and the increase of employment as well as to a creation of pure profit for the innovative business enterprise.' Rogers (2003, p. 12) adds 'innovation is an idea, practice, or object that is perceived as new by an individual or other unit of adoption.' The main pillar of innovation is entrepreneurship: the process which is necessary to develop innovations. The entrepreneur has been amply described by the late Josef Schumpeter (1934) as a visionary who is able to envision the new world and who creates new products and processes through creative destruction of old institutions, processes and products. Galbraith (2002, p. 6) put more emphasis on the process when defining innovation as 'the process of applying and developing a new idea to create a new product, process or business.' The entrepreneurial process of implementation and development of an idea that becomes a commercialized product or service is therefore defined as innovation.

Entrepreneurial processes differ from (small) business management processes where the latter start with the growth of a business and, after reaching the maturity phase of growth, end with harvesting the profits. The stages of entrepreneurship on the other hand are characterized by the following phases: 'Innovation'-, a 'triggering Event'- and the 'Implementation' phase often summarized as the *entrepreneurship process* (Bygrave, 1987; Hatten, 1997). An entrepreneurial event such as the foundation of a small business marks the end of the entrepreneurial process in the Schumpeterian sense. At the beginning of the entrepreneurial process an innovative idea typically leads the entrepreneurial mind to think about possible future plans to open up a business. But only a triggering event, such as the loss of a job or the successful gathering of resources to support these ideas will bring an organisation to life (Hatten, 1997). Other triggering effects identified in empirical studies are a certain level of dissatisfaction of the individual (Herron & Sapienza, 1992) or the perception of a current business opportunity (Gynawali & Fogel, 1994). Educational experiences can equally represent the triggering events as push and pull factors toward entrepreneurship.

Finally, the entrepreneurial event (Shapiro & Sokol, 1982) happens and product or services are commercialised and the business organisation is formed. There is still scope for further research in tourism focussing on entrepreneurial processes. A conceptualization of the entrepreneurial process was proposed by Koh (1996) who derived a conceptual model comprising eight stages of entrepreneurial and, later, managerial processes (Fig. 1).

The entrepreneurial process in tourism is conceptualized as eight interacting stages in which each stage is impacted by unfolding environmental events (classified as C = community environmental events and P = personal environmental events). Koh's process model already symbolizes the needs to enable entrepreneurial behaviour within a destination community. Communication and therefore community control in innovation processes are high and a so-called 'closed innovation' is not possible or sustainable at all.

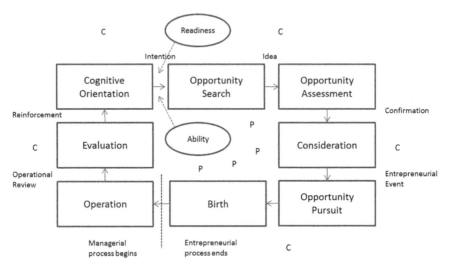

Fig. 1 Conceptual community tourism entrepreneurship model. *Source*: Koh (1996, p. 31)

However, for the purpose of our empirical enquiry below the first entrepreneurial phase, the cognitive orientation of individuals should be analysed in detail, and three psychological indicators can be used to define the cognitive orientation towards tourism entrepreneurship: the attitude towards entrepreneurship; the attitude towards the travel industry; and the knowledge of the tourism industry.

The attitude towards entrepreneurship or the willingness for entrepreneurial independence can be a negative or positive one. In the latter case founding an enterprise may be viewed as a chance to improve one's socio-economic lifestyle. Others may perceive stress, inconvenience or negative pressure when thinking of entrepreneurship in tourism. Certainly, a positive attitude towards entrepreneurship alone is not sufficient to motivate a person to found a tourism business, but the intention to create a business in tourism only occurs when the attitude towards entrepreneurship is positive (Koh, 1996).

Innovative ideas or entrepreneurial attitudes have often already existed for years before a triggering event opens a window of opportunity to found a business. The mind-set or attitude of an individual to become an entrepreneur lays the foundations for future entrepreneurial activities (Airey & Frontistis, 1997). Similar to Koh (1996), Bird (1989) identified individual intentionality as a state of mind, the directing attention, the experience, and the action toward a specific goal. These intentions are again influenced by a variety of personal, sociological, and environmental variables.

The second pillar underlying innovation processes and behaviour in organisations deals with knowledge management and organisational learning. Contingent on the transparency of knowledge and know-how outside and inside the firm (Romhardt, 1997) knowledge management incorporates various phases from the determination of knowledge goals and objectives to the evaluation of alternative

methods of knowledge acquisition, robust internal further development and distribution of knowledge and the utilisation of knowledge through its transformation
into organisational capabilities and competencies (see e.g. von Krogh, 1995;
Nonaka and Takeuchi, 1995). Closely associated with organisational learning and
knowledge management are processes of organisational redesign and reengineering
through new information technologies (Davenport, 1993). Information technologies, social media and open communication have become the main drivers of
innovation within the last decade: customers are becoming part of the innovation
process as demonstrated early in software development (see Fuller & Matzler,
2007; von Hippel, 2001).

A third major pillar of innovation is the organisation: Much of what has been
reported on the creation of the ideal type of organisational climates for innovation
(see e.g. Clark, 1995) refers to organisational processes, structures and incentive
systems utilized in the field of change management. A detailed description can be
found in Galbraith (1977) where top management is viewed as the entrepreneurial
master of change and change agent, creating structures and processes which allow
for the creation of new ideas through innovation enhancing information and
decision making systems, the employment and utilisation of idea generators,
rewards systems to enhance risk taking and supra motivation, for creating the
right composition of R&D work in teams and for creating appropriate
organisational places for the experimentation of new processes and/ or products
and services. Similarly management and organisational efforts are needed to link
the 'innovative organization' within the firm with its routine functions of periodic
production and marketing (Cooper, 1993; Kleinschmidt and Cooper, 1991). Management of change (and for that matter also innovation management) has become
first and foremost an exercise in reducing resistance to change among stakeholders
now involving human resource strategies in the form of new patterns of recruitment
and training and development, redesign of work and the formation and/or
repositioning of skills (see e.g. Jick, 1995). There is general agreement that
innovative organisations differ greatly from non-innovative routine organisations
in terms of structure, processes, reward systems and leadership (Galbraith, 2002;
Peters, 2009). One of the questions to be raised subsequently in the context of
innovation in the tourism industry will have to address these issues of innovation
entrepreneurship and innovation management.

The three pillars of innovation discussed above also play a major role in the
tourism industry and on a company level one might find various forms of innovation
processes as entrepreneurship, knowledge and know-how, and organizational climates and structures differ from each other. However, tourism products are created
as an amalgam of different single-firm products and service and various tourism
destination stakeholders contribute to the customers' overall holiday satisfaction.
The tourism value chain is a compilation of many company offers which have to be
aligned, coordinated and managed as one holistic product bundle. Therefore the
three pillars of innovation are different in the case of tourism destinations.

Entrepreneurship still plays a major role in creating and pursuing innovations.
However, entrepreneurs must be able to cooperate and they can hardly grow

without cooperation or the creation of networks in the regions. Therefore entrepreneurs must be able to balance their individual opportunity seeking behaviour with cooperative regional and/or tourism development goals.

Knowledge and know-how use and creation as the second pillar of innovation is of utmost importance on both company and destination level. As destinations are geographical, restricted competitive product and service bundles, collective know-how must also be generated to enable competitive advantages.

Finally, organisational structures or, in the destination context, governance structures have to be developed in order to allow entrepreneurial processes and thus innovation to happen at the company-level and to coordinate a process of destination innovation, e.g. for the creation of destination events.

DMOs play a much more important role in both stimulating innovation processes amongst stakeholders in the destination and structuring and supporting the innovation process itself. Although the DMOs external marketing function is dominant, internal marketing measures become more important as they are a prerequisite for further joint tourism development initiatives.

3 The Management of Open Innovation

Innovation processes can be very diverse and sometimes they can be labelled closed or open innovations. Closed innovation refers to the fact that the company generates novel products or services under total control, while open innovation allows company external stakeholders to influence the innovation process (Chesbrough, 2003). Closed innovation an hardly be sustainable because an exchange and communication with the environment is denied and internal competencies and market-relevant knowledge can hardly be further developed (Chesbrough, 2004). Open innovation is different as it is 'about bridging internal and external resources throughout the entire innovation process to make innovation happen.' (Lindegaard, 2010, p. 19). Open innovation therefore has a strong networking imperative (Enkel, Gassmann, & Chesbrough, 2009). It is defined as using 'purposive inflows and outflows of knowledge to accelerate internal innovation and to expand the markets for external use of innovation, respectively.' (Chesbrough et al., 2006, p. 1). It becomes obvious that entrepreneurs need to be cooperative and managers of knowledge across company boundaries.

Innovation process management has gone through various phases: from a linear technology-push innovation process (from the 1950s) to the linear market-pull innovation process (mid-1960s) and the third generation was characterized by a combination of push-pull innovation (early 1970s). More interactive-parallel processing innovation processes were needed in the 1980s when competition intensified and product-life cycles got shorter. The integration of information technology as another milestone cumulated in today's open innovation process (Ahmed & Shepherd, 2010). The latter is a network approach, which can evolve to 'an ecosystem (or network of opportunities) made up of a series of nodes (small start-ups, inventors, brokers), which are held together by mutual self-interest, trust and open communications.' (Ahmed & Shepherd, 2010, p. 174).

Open innovation can only be undertaken given: the ability to manage stakeholders; the willingness to accept that not all experts are part of their own business; the willingness to support knowledge creation in the company; as well as the understanding that failures can be interpreted as opportunities (Lindegaard, 2010, p. 22). Another important prerequisite for open innovation is the understanding that communication within the company's stakeholders is important, and that open innovation hinders raising intellectual properties (Lindegaard, 2010, p. 23; De Vrande, de Jong, Vanhaverbeke, & de Rochemont, 2008). Such a network innovation culture certainly influences innovation processes, such as for instance all the phases in the stage-gate® innovation model. Idea development, screening and all the following decision phases follow the network innovation approach and therefore are based on communication patterns between company stakeholders (Peters, 2009). Major stakeholders in the network are customers who are motivated to assist and contribute in the development process (Lakhani & von Hippel, 2003), inventors such as universities and research labs, venture capital firms, channel partners, trade associations and others.

In tourism destinations we find a destination based network with a variety of geographically concentrated stakeholders producing the holiday-product as well as destination external stakeholders, such as tour operators, potential customers, inventors or venture capital firms. However, the destination network is very complex as we find strong links (and sometimes overlaps) between policy players, entrepreneurs, pressure groups and customers. It can therefore be assumed that open innovation displays specific and hitherto unobserved characteristics. The empirical investigation attempts to shed more light upon the innovation processes in the tourism destination and it explores barriers and motivators of open innovation within the tourism destination. With the help of qualitative interviews we will be able to explore the pillars of innovation processes in destinations and open innovation elements within the tourism destinations innovation process.

4   Empirical Study

4.1   Case Description and Procedure

The research was carried out in the alpine region of Tyrol. Tyrol is one of the most tourism-intensive destinations. The tourism intensity index (as measured by overnight per inhabitant) was 62 in 2012 compared to Austria's index of 16. Overall, more than 23,000 hospitality firms hosted more than 44.3 millions overnight stays in 2012 (Statistik Austria, 2013). As in other peripheral areas of Austria, most hospitality firms are micro sized, having fewer than 10 employees. We find great differences with regard to size, finance and leadership between large urban hotel chains and small, family-owned and family-run hotels in peripheral areas (Pikkemaat & Peters, 2005). The latter dominates rural tourism in Austria, in particular in Tyrol. This dominance of small and micro sized family hotels lead to an increased demand for communication and cooperation within the destination to foster destination development through strategy and long-term oriented management. Leadership for the whole destination is often taken over by a few but strong 'tourism families': Powerful and strong hotel entrepreneurs influence destination development especially when holding core tourism businesses such as cable car companies or tourism attractions. As a result these leading tourism entrepreneurs are often not interested in cooperative measures as they cannot see any advantage for their already well-established business Therefore, innovation processes are often micro processes, dominated by a few strong players and neglecting innovative inputs of other destination value chain components (Raich & Zehrer, 2013).

The explicit goal of the study was to answer the question as to which determinants drive innovation processes in tourism destinations. For this purpose an interview guideline was developed covering questions about the very different needs for innovation, the triggers and stimuli for innovation processes, success factors for innovation, entrepreneurial factors as well as cooperation and networking factors.

The interviews were conducted in Tyrolean destinations in November and December 2008 and the average length of the interviews was 40 min, with the longest lasting more than an hour. In sum 37 tourism experts were interviewed covering 23 of 36 Tyrolean destinations, including the 12 most successful destinations as well as 11 less successful tourism destinations in terms of tourist arrivals. Destinations chosen for the sample (listed here in increasing number of overnight stays) were Ötztal with more than 3.2 millions of overnight stays in 2007, Paznaun-Ischgl, Innsbruck, Mayrhofen, Erste Ferienregion Zillertal, Seefeld, Serfaus-Fiss-Ladis, Stubai, Wilder Kaiser, Kitzbüheler Alpen—Brixental, Achensee and St. Anton am Arlberg, Tiroler Zugspitz Arena, Pitztal, Kitzbühel, Alpbach, Kaiserwinkl, Wildschönau, Lechtal, Reutte, Mieminger Plateau und Fernpass-Seen, Imst-Gurgltal und finally Hall-Wattens with about 278,000 overnight stays (Land Tirol, 2007).

Various stakeholders in the destinations were selected for interviews: 12 CEOs of DMOs, 6 chairmen of DMOs who also run tourism enterprises, 8 owners or managers of cable car companies, 5 also running other tourism enterprises, and 11 tourism entrepreneurs. Thirty three respondents were male while only four were female. They are between 45 and 60 years of age and the majority have been employed in tourism for more than 15 years.

As validity is seen as the most important quality criterion of qualitative research—because the other two quality criteria (objectivity and reliability) have to be modified in qualitative research—the study focussed on meeting these criteria. Validity describes two aspects: first, if interviews are authentic and honest; and second, if the transcription reflects the statements of the interviewees. Moreover, validity is fulfilled when the interesting research questions are gathered (Bortz & Döring, 2002, pp. 326).

The language used during the interviews was German. Hence, citations used for the analysis are translated from participants' statements. Interviews were transcribed and analysed with qualitative content analysis software, maxqda version 2007. maxqda's advantage is a more systematic and objective analysis of the data. Following the transcription, each author analyzed the empirical material and formed thematic blocs in interpreting the interview transcripts (Rubin & Rubin, 1995). Categories were defined and text material had to be allocated to the categories. Correlations between single excerpts and interferences of codes were determined by complex text retrieval. Using this analysis tool, contexts and thought patterns of single interviews could be identified.

4.2   Results

First, empirical results with respect to the three pillars of innovation will be discussed. Second, the question whether open innovation is an adequate tool for destination management will be answered.

The majority of interviewees perceive Tyrol as an innovative tourism destination where many innovative tourism attractions and destination values have been developed during the last two decades. Analysing the success factors of innovation management in destinations, the study highlights the importance of cooperation and communication as main success factors for innovation management in destinations. *'The one and only possibility to develop new products and increase innovation is cooperation.'* (DMO, I8) Cooperation is seen as a tool to develop the destination: *'Cooperation—we need more cooperation as these are crucial for destination development. (...) The younger ones are much more cooperative.'* (Hotel, DMO, I29) Furthermore, entrepreneurship as a main stimulator of innovation was a strong focus of discussion with the interviewees.

Overall, results show that some ideas which evolved in the tourism destinations are more efficiently developed in smaller circles of entrepreneurs. The interviewees pointed out that it is not possible to develop and manage all products or themes on the destination level. For example, it seems difficult to vote in a plenary meeting of the DMO which tourism markets should be focussed on in the future. What is needed is a small group of leading, networking entrepreneurs who are interested in the development and success of the tourism destination. 'In the past, if we wanted to realize a project, it was always the same: two or three leading entrepreneurs took the (financial) responsibility and developed something new and successful. The more people involved in the very first phase, the less the project is realized, because then everybody is talking but nobody is working and taking responsibility.' (Cable Car, I16)

As success factors for entrepreneurship, the following were mentioned to be most important: entrepreneurs should share their experiences and act in networks; and they should be characterized by courage, fantasy and creativity as well as the willingness to take risks. For the implementation of innovations, motivated employees and a strong will to realize the innovation project are essential: '*Inno-vation comes from employees, we need motivation strategies.*' (Cable Car, I16) '*Where there's a will, there's a way.*' (Hotel, I34).

Many interviewees perceive low professionalism regarding innovation process management in the tourism industry. They demand further education for both entrepreneurs and employees, in particular with regard to project and innovation management: '*There is a strong potential for innovations in Tyrol. But good ideas need to be supported and nurtured, implementation often fails because of a lack of know-how and professionalism.*' (DMO, I9) '*There is a need for education and training, for entrepreneurs but also for employees. Job expansion, that is important because it educates and high staffing costs can be reduced.*' (Cable Car, Hotel, I35) '*It needs focussed support, project development and coaching. We are not able to manage it in the destination*' (Congress, I2) '*DMOs should send one of their employees to a one-year training focussing on innovation management. Tailored education and training programmes, not for cable car companies but for all the other tourism-related industries*' (Cable Car, I16).

A few tourism experts are convinced that the younger, more tourism educated third generation of tourism entrepreneurs is much more cooperative than the older generation. Another interesting aspect is added from a younger hotelier in the sample: '*We need more local circles with trainers who strongly discuss innovation with business owners on a regional level. We need to re-invent the gastro-meetings*' [Wirtestammtische] (Hotel, DMO, I26). He asks for more informal communication between the entrepreneurs/hoteliers within the destination and adds that in the past the 'old' tourism generation organized a lot of successful destination development projects within a group of regulars. Besides regular tourism round tables, the establishment of communication platforms in general is seen as an important aspect for increasing cooperation in destinations, such as excursions or meetings. '*We need more excursions, but to successful destinations. If you show successful projects, the easier it is to convince others. The results of excursions are often a better communication because you have to get together and talk about other things; that is a very positive result.*' (Cable Car, I25) '*We need a platform which can bundle all the stakeholders' interests in a destination and we need a professional coach.*' (DMO, I9) '*Best practice presentations of those who made it (...)*

Others stress the fact that impulses and leadership from outside the destination are essential: '*Many here have great ideas but dare not mention them. It needs a mentor (...). Workshops for joint development of ideas and projects, small groups and working collectively—that is important*'. (DMO, I23) In general, all agree that cooperation depends on the ready willingness of the involved or uninvolved cooperation partners.

Managers of DMOs in their daily business depend highly on an efficient cooperation with tourism entrepreneurs in the destination. According to some hoteliers, cooperation between hoteliers is often difficult as they don't trust each other.

Furthermore experts are of the opinion that the willingness to cooperate can be stimulated by government-funded aid. Respondents have no idea how to convince entrepreneurs not interested in cooperation of the need for co-operation, as they will not change their opinion as a result of government-funded cooperation. The only way to further intensify cooperation and gain new partners lies in the success of cooperation projects in the destination: '*One has to reach the critical mass with new ideas. That's how tourism and value develop.*' (Hotel, DMO DMO, I6) *We need to talk much more in our destination. (. . .) you can only motivate when showing where it will lead to.*' (Cable Car, I32)

Knowledge and know-how are seen as the main pillars for the development of professional strategies, both at the entrepreneurial and the destination level. Experts often lack this professionalism as they are engaged in their daily operational business: '*Hoteliers should work at the strategy and the development of the hotel, but not in the hotel itself*' (Hotel, I13). As mentioned before, many tourism entrepreneurs of the first and second generation have no tourism management or management education at all and lack of know-how to efficiently plan and implement innovative projects. As for employees, the majority believe that it makes no sense to train them in innovation, as hotels are micro-sized and staff turnover is tremendously high. One interviewee explicitly asks for more know-how from universities: '*Especially regional planning projects need detailed studies which are very cost-intensive. We should cooperate with universities, not only with consulting firms.*' (Congress, I2).

Regarding organisational and governance aspects, bureaucratic barriers are often mentioned: '*The government should offer competent consultancy and offer non-bureaucratic subsidies. Sometimes good feelings are more important than structural processes. However bureaucratic barriers need to be avoided.*' (Hotel, DMO, I29) Besides bureaucracy financial, problems of destination developments arise: '*The problem is—many enterprises have to close down. We need to find external international investors to invest in these businesses. Therefore we need tax incentives or we have to reduce infrastructural development costs to attract lead businesses.*' (Hotel, DMO, I33). '*It makes no sense to keep dead businesses alive with subsidies. These businesses have to contribute something.*' (DMO, I37) Furthermore, the interviewees are aware of the fact that less tourism in many tourism valleys of Tyrol implicates fewer infrastructure investments, creates less value and accordingly boosts emigration. From the tourism experts' point of view, tourism policy often neglects this fact and prevents new tourism projects due to bureaucratic barriers.

Regarding open innovation, the first question in the interview was about the main drivers of innovation: where ideas come from and the possible sources of innovation. Results confirm that a lot of ideas exist but again know-how gaps in development and implementation often prevent successful new projects: '*There are many ideas in the destination, but it needs a stimulus—external or internal*' (Hotel, DMO, I17) '*Ideas lie on the roads. One just has to pick them up.*' (Hotel, I5). '*We don't lack ideas; we have more than enough ideas. What we often need is the further advancement of good ideas: someone who takes responsibility for the project development.*' (Hotel, DMO, I 33)

A few respondents comment on the lack curiosity and willingness to implement new ideas in the tourism industry. Since the tourism industry in Tyrol has been developing well in the last few decades, entrepreneurs are saturated and risk-averse. *'Many entrepreneurs don't search for new ideas, they aren't curious anymore. We should learn from the industry—they are still curious'* (Travel Agency, I12)

Respondents agree about the importance of carefully observing the market, both within the destination as well as global trends all over the world. In particular, travelling to new and very different (best practice) destinations is mentioned as an important source for getting new insights into markets and developing new ideas. *'Going to workshops, looking at new markets, we need to get out, together'* (Cable Car, I21) Experts of leading destinations with large ski areas (Ischgl, Serfaus, Pitztal, Stubai) focus on active and strategic market analysis as triggers of innovation while respondents of the smaller destinations, often without any ski resorts, refer to meetings and talks with other tourism colleagues as triggers of innovation.

In more detail, the following triggers of innovation were discussed by the tourism stakeholders: observing worldwide trends, travelling, taking time off and having a holiday and experiencing other tourism best practices, curiosity, observing and analysing the needs and wants of guests, talking to international guests, global competition, destination leadership, imitation of products, reading specialist literature, visiting exhibitions and trade fairs, meetings and networking with other tourism experts, looking at leading companies and finally making more use of their employees. Some of the respondents perceive employees as a major source of information, others cannot imagine receiving stimuli from them. The latter argue that turnover in the sector is very high and therefore it does not make sense to qualify and train employees in terms of innovation management, and moreover they are absent from their workplace during their training days. *'Employees have to be trained how to provide service, how to interact with guests. This on the job training has to take place within the tourism businesses and not outside.'* (Hotel, I1)

Summarizing the above, the results explicitly underline a high innovation potential in Tyrol and three large areas of support arise: entrepreneurship, knowledge and know-how, in particular about project development and cooperation and communication. According to the study, open innovation is limited to travelling to new markets and destinations, cooperation and networking and, for a very few, talking to guests. It is neither sufficiently focussed on employees and guests, nor managed strategically.

4.3 Discussion

The study shows that in the alpine tourism industry, with its micro sized and family owned and managed hotels, innovation is usually driven by cooperation and entrepreneurship. Therefore, cooperation should be better facilitated by government as well as knowledge (in particular project and innovation management of new ideas) and know-how initiatives (platforms, workshops, expert excursions, etc.). Respondents are less aware of managing open innovation with respect to employees and guests. Only a very few see contacts and conversations with guests as a source of innovation. Employees in micro-sized businesses lack the support of entrepreneurs in terms of delivering new ideas and innovation. According to the literature (Fuller & Matzler, 2007) and open innovation activities in other industries (e.g. the car industry), a huge source of innovation with high potential is still not being used in tourism. More knowledge and know-how for tourism entrepreneurs, in particular about including employees and customers in open innovation management, seems to be of the utmost importance. Qualification measures on a destination level can be offered for both tourism entrepreneurs, and employees (or managers) to create the awareness of innovation management. Windows of opportunities can only be seen when opportunity recognition is enhanced: learning to search in the best places (e.g. focusing on changes in the environment); learning to search in the best ways (e.g. seeking emerging patterns); the exposure to a broad range of business experience and knowledge; and the exposure to a broad range of business opportunities are enablers of opportunity recognition (Baron & Shane, 2008). DMOs can provide support for active search, prior knowledge and networking, but also for the awareness or alertness of its destination stakeholders to recognize potentially valuable opportunities (Volkmann, Tokarski, & Grünhagen, 2010, p. 85).

Open innovation and open research and development (R&D) go hand in hand. However, the tourism destination is an amalgam of very different companies with different R&D imperatives. In a regular market, once the firms accept the notion of interorganizational innovation collaboration, every entrepreneur 'who does not participate will cope with serious competitive disadvantages.' (Enkel et al., 2009). In the tourism destination, some owner managers or entrepreneurs can still be free riders and profit from the collaboration of others in the network. The interviewees pointed out that micro-firms are hardly embedded in the innovation networks of their destinations. Therefore, destination governance structures could focus on a greater inclusion of small business sub-networks or associations.

Open innovation demands flexible destination networks which allow both the development of innovations based on the destinations core resources and external stimuli. The latter can be created by an increase in market research activities including market trends dissemination amongst destination stakeholders. Furthermore, it might be an advantage to consider the inclusion of destination external stakeholders (such as international experts from different industries) in the boards within the destination (Beritelli, Strobl, & Peters, 2013). Closed communities guarantee trust and locally accepted governance, but by increasing destination connections with external directors on their boards, the destination can gain additional knowledge and know-how (Beritelli et al., 2013; Strobl & Peters, 2013).

The interviewees underline that all three of the pillars of innovation discussed above are of high relevance for managing innovation at the destination level. Entrepreneurship, knowledge and know-how as well as governance structures strongly determine cooperation and destination's innovation management and its openness to its stakeholders. However, the interviews also highlight that open innovation calls for a deeper analysis of collaborative entrepreneurship processes with special emphasis on the early stages of entrepreneurship. Stimulation of open innovation in the destination needs constant information and network management. On the one hand, strategic tourism development is based on a careful analysis of destination resources; on the other hand monitoring of market chances is based on the analysis of external information (about market chances, consumer preferences etc.). Both areas can become the DMOs' clear future strategic focus.

5 Conclusion

Once more it becomes evident that innovation management needs a more professional and strategic approach to tourism, both on the destination level as well as on the single business level. Innovation management in destinations is closely linked to networking and cooperation, which is sometimes difficult as businesses and entrepreneurs have to balance their interests between competition and cooperation within and beyond destinations. For the future development of innovation management in tourism, the innovation process has to be more open: in particular, customers' and guests' opinions should be treated as valuable sources for improving products and services. DMOs can play a mediating role when external stimuli need to be transferred into the destination (see Fig. 2, external circle). Furthermore, DMOs can foster collaborative innovation networks and support them by providing innovation project structure and a framework for innovation processes (see Fig. 2,

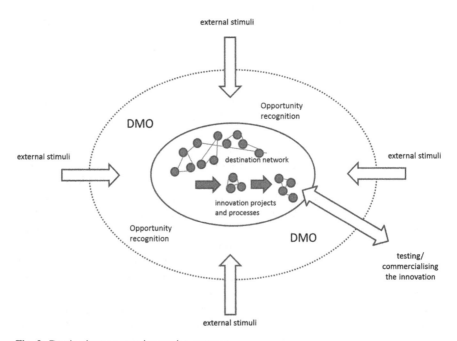

Fig. 2 Destinations as open innovation systems

inner circle). Finally, measuring the fit of innovations with the overall destination value chain and the assessment of market reactions can be functional tasks of a modern open innovation-oriented DMO.

With regard to the limitations of the study, the choice of respondents has to be mentioned: Interviews were only conducted with successful key players in selected destinations in Tyrol, which is the most successful (in terms of overnights) winter destination in the world. Furthermore, interviews may have been influenced by actual developments in the destination.

Further research in this area is required. First, more empirical research into tourists' instead of entrepreneurs' perception and evaluation of innovation in tourism is needed: How do tourists perceive innovation? Do they require innovation? Are they satisfied with new products and innovation in the destinations? Which tourist segments demand which innovation? Second, the disciplines have to be extended and interdisciplinary research should be carried out, e.g. psychologists can deliver fruitful insights into entrepreneurs' characteristics and lifestyles.

References

Ahmed, A. K., & Shepherd, C. D. (2010). *Innovation Management*. Pearson: Harlow.

Airey, D., & Frontistis, A. (1997). Attitudes to carriers in tourism: An Anglo-Greek comparison. *Tourism Management, 18*(3), 149–158.

Baron, R. A., & Shane, S. (2008). *Entrepreneurship: A process perspective*. Mason: Thomson.

Beritelli, P., Strobl, A., & Peters, M. (2013). Interlocking directorships against community closure: A trade-off for development in tourist destinations. *Tourism Review, 68*(1), 21–33.

Bird, B. J. (1989). *Entrepreneurial behaviour*. Glenview, IL: Scott, Foresman and Company.

Bortz, J., & Döring, N. (2002). *Forschungsmethoden und Evaluation für Human- und Sozialwissenschaftler*. Berlin: Springer.

Bygrave, W. (1987). The entrepreneurial paradigm (I): A philosophical look at its research methodologies. *Entrepreneurship: Theory and Practice, 14*(Fall), 7–25.

Chesbrough, H. (2003). *Open innovation: The new imperative for creating and profiting from technology*. Boston, MA: Harvard Business School Press.

Chesbrough, H. (2004). Managing open innovation. *Research Technology Management, 47*(1), 23–26.

Chesbrough, H., Vanhaverbeke, W., & West, J. (2006). *Open innovation: Researching a new paradigm*. Oxford: Oxford University Press.

Clark, J. (1995). *Managing innovation, change, people, technology and strategy*. London: Sage.

Cooper, R. G. (1993). *Winning at new products*. Reading, MA: Addison Wesley.

Dahlander, L., & Gann, D. M. (2010). How open is innovation? *Research Policy, 39*(6), 699–709.

Davenport, T. H. (1993). *Process innovation. Reengineering work through information technology*. Boston, MA: Harvard Business School Press.

De Vrande, V., de Jong, J. P. J., Vanhaverbeke, W., & de Rochemont, M. (2008). Open innovation in SMEs: Trends, motives and management challenges. *Technovation, 29*(6–7), 423–437.

Drucker, P. F. (1985). The discipline of innovation. *Harvard Business Review, 63*(3), 67–72.

Enkel, E., Gassmann, O., & Chesbrough, H. (2009). Open R&D and open innovation: Exploring the phenomenon. *R&D Management, 39*(4), 311–316.

Fuller, J., & Matzler, K. (2007). Virtual product experience and customer participation – A chance for customer-centred, really new products. *Technovation, 27*(6–7), 378–387.

Galbraith, J. R. (1977). Organization design: An information processing view. *Organizational Effectiveness Center and School, 21*, 21–26.

Galbraith, J. R. (2002). Designing the innovating organization. *Organizational dynamics, 10*(3), 5–25 (Winter 1982).

Gynawali, D. R., & Fogel, D. S. (1994). Environments for entrepreneurship development: Key dimensions and research implications. *Entrepreneurship: Theory and practice, 18*(4), 43–62.

Hatten, T. (1997). *Small business: Entrepreneurship and beyond*. London: Prentice Hall.

Herron, L., & Sapienza, H. J. (1992). The entrepreneur and the initiation of the new venture launch activities. *Entrepreneurship: Theory and practice, 17*(1), 49–55.

Hjalager, A.-M. (2010). A review of innovation research in tourism. *Tourism Management, 31*(1), 1–12.

Hjalager, A.-M., & Nordin, S. (2011). User-driven innovation in tourism – A review of methodologies. *Journal of Quality Assurance in Hospitality & Tourism, 12*(3), 289–315.

Huizingh, E. K. R. E. (2011). Open innovation: State of the art and future perspectives. *Technovation, 31*(1), 2–9.

Jick, T. (1995). *Managing change*. Burr Ridge, IL: Irwin.

Kleinschmidt, E., & Cooper, R. G. (1991). The impact of product innovativeness on performance. *Journal of Product Innovation Management, 8*(4), 240–251.

Koh, Y. (1996). The tourism entrepreneurial process: A conceptualization and implications for research and development. *Revue de Tourisme-The Tourist Review-Zeitschrift für Fremdenverkehr, 51*(4), 24–41.

Lakhani, K. R., & von Hippel, E. (2003). How open source software works: "Free" user-to-user assistance. *Research Policy, 32*, 923–943.

Land Tirol. (2007). *Nächtigungen der Tourismusverbände*. Innsbruck.

Lee, S., Park, G., Yoon, B., & Park, J. (2010). Open innovation in SMEs – An intermediated network model. *Research Policy, 39*(2), 290–300.

Lindegaard, S. (2010). *The open innovation revolution*. Hoboken, NJ: Wiley.

Martínez-Ros, E., & Orfila-Sintes, F. (2009). Innovation activity in the hotel industry. *Technovation, 29*(9), 632–641.

Nonaka, I., & Takeuchi, H. (1995). *The knowledge-creating company*. New York/Oxford: Oxford University Press.

Norton, R. D. (2001). *Creating the new economy: The entrepreneur and the U.S. resurgence*. Cheletenham: Edward Elgar.

Orfila-Sintes, F., & Mattsson, J. (2009). Innovation behavior in the hotel industry. *Omega -The International Journal of Management Science, 37*(2), 380–394.

Ottenbacher, M. (2007). Innovation management in the hospitality industry: Different strategies for achieving success. *Journal of Hospitality & Tourism Research, 31*(4), 431–454.

Paget, E., Dimanche, F., & Mounet, J.-P. (2010). A tourism innovation case: An actor-network approach. *Annals of Tourism Research, 37*(3), 828–847.

Pechlaner, H., Fischer, E., & Priglinger, P. (2006). Die Entwicklung von Innovationen in Destinationen – die Rolle der Tourismusorganisation. In B. Pikkemaat, M. Peters, & K. Weiermair (Eds.), *Innovationen im Tourismus* (pp. 109–117). Berlin: Erich Schmidt Verlag.

Peters, M. (2009). Strategische Produktentwicklung und Unternehmertum. In H. Pechlaner & E. Fischer (Eds.), *Strategische Produktentwicklung im Standortmanagement: Wettbewerbsvorteile für den Tourismus* (pp. 31–45). Berlin: Erich Schmidt.

Pikkemaat, B. (2008). Innovation in small and medium-sized tourism enterprises in Tyrol, Austria. *Entrepreneurship and Innovation, 9*(3), 1–11.

Pikkemaat, B., & Peters, M. (2005). Towards the measurement of innovation – A pilot study in the small and medium sized hotel industry. *Journal of Quality Assurance in Hospitality and Tourism, 6*(3/4), 89–112.

Raich, F., & Zehrer, A. (2013). Einfluss der Besonderheiten und Ausprägungen touristischer Netzwerke auf die Produktentwicklung. *Zeitschrift für Tourismuswissenschaft, 5*(1), 5–21.

Rogers, E. M. (2003). *Diffusion of innovations*. New York: Free Press.

Romhardt, K. (1997). Interne und externe Wissenstransparenz als Ausgangspunkt für organisatorische Innovation. In F. Heidelore & T. Radel (Eds.), *Organisation and innovation* (pp. 15–18). München/Mering: Hampys.

Rubin, H. J., & Rubin, I. S. (1995). *Qualitative interviewing: The art of hearing data*. Thousand Oaks: Sage.

Schumpeter, J. A. (1934). *The theory of economic development*. Cambridge: Harvard University Press.

Shapiro, A., & Sokol, L. (1982). The social dimension of entrepreneurship. In J. A. Kent, D. L. Sexton, & K. H. Vesper (Eds.), *Encyclopedia of entrepreneurship* (pp. 72–88). Englewood Cliffs, NJ: Prentice Hall.

Statistik Austria. (2013). Retrieved October 2, 2013, from http://www.statistik.at/web_de/statistiken/tourismus/index.html

Strobl, A., & Peters, M. (2013). Entrepreneurial reputation in destination networks. *Annals of Tourism Research, 40*(1), 59–82.

Sundbo, J., Orfila-Sintes, F., & Flemming, S. (2006). The innovative behaviour of tourism firms – Comparative studies of Denmark and Spain. *Research Policy, 36*(1), 88–106.

Urabe, K. (1988). Innovation and the Japanese management system. In K. Urabe, J. Child, & T. Kagono (Eds.), *Innovation and management: international comparisons* (pp. 3–26). Berlin: Walter de Gruyter & Co.

van de Vrande, V., de Jong, J. P. J., Vanhaverbeke, W., & de Rochemont, M. (2009). Open innovation in SMEs: Trends, motives and management challenges. *Technovation, 29*(6/7), 423–437.

Volkmann, C. K., Tokarski, K. O., & Grünhagen, M. (2010). *Entrepreneurship in an European perspective*. Wiesbaden: Gabler.

Volo, S. (2004). Foundation for an innovation indicator for tourism: An application to SME. In P. Keller & T. Bieger (Eds.), *The future of small and medium sized enterprises in tourism* (Vol. 46). St. Gallen: AIEST.

von Hippel, E. (2001). PERSPECTIVE: User toolkits for innovation. *Journal of Product Innovation Management, 18*(4), 247–257.

von Krogh, G., & Venzin, M. (1995). Anhaltende Wettbewerbsvorteile durch Wissensmanagement. *Die Unternehmung, 53*(6), 417–436.

Weiermair, K., & Pikkemaat, B. (2005). Can destinations create value through innovation? In P. Keller & T. Bieger (Eds.), *Innovation in tourism – Creating customer value* (pp. 213–228). St. Gallen: AIEST.

Zeng, S. X., Xie, X. M., & Tam, C. M. (2010). Relationship between cooperation networks and innovation performance of SMEs. *Technovation, 30*(3), 181–194.

Managing Open Innovation in Small and Medium-Sized Enterprises (SMEs)

Sabine Brunswicker

1 Introduction

Over the past years, open innovation has been adopted by firms from different sectors and countries and receives increasing attention in the scholarly discussion. The research field is mushrooming and has started to expand to new levels and areas (Chesbrough & Brunswicker, 2014). One of those areas is the SME sector (Brunswicker & van de Vrande, 2014). The expansion of research on open innovation in the SME sector is a logical step as open innovation assumes that innovation has become a more level playing field, in which large firms have moved away from keeping full control over all innovation activities (Chesbrough, 2006). In addition, prior work on SMEs and innovation has already pointed out the importance of organizational boundary spanning activities for innovation in SMEs in order to overcome their liability, smallness, and scarce resources (Baum, Calabrese, & Silverman, 2000; Edwards, Delbridge, & Munday, 2005; Lee, Park, Yoon, & Park, 2010). Very recent empirical studies clearly suggest that SMEs purposively open up to external sources of knowledge, and engage in different kinds of open innovation practices ranging from external knowledge sourcing among customers, suppliers or universities to technology licensing (Brunswicker & Vanhaverbeke, 2015; Parida, Westerberg, & Frishammar, 2012; van de Vrande, de Jong, Vanhaverbeke, & de Rochemont, 2009; Wynarchyzk, Piperopoulos, & Mcadam, 2013). They also suggest that open innovation in SMEs is quite particular for reasons such as limited access to complementary resources in order to commercialize ideas and also less developed managerial capabilities for innovation (Lee

S. Brunswicker (✉)
Research Center for Open Digital Innovation, Purdue University, West Lafayette 47907, IN, USA

ESADE Business School, Barcelona, Spain
e-mail: sbrunswi@purdue.edu

© Springer-Verlag Berlin Heidelberg 2016
R. Egger et al. (eds.), *Open Tourism*, Tourism on the Verge,
DOI 10.1007/978-3-642-54089-9_12

et al., 2010; Parida et al., 2012; Robertson, Casali, & Jacobson, 2012). Thus, findings on how to manage open innovation in large firms cannot be directly transferred to the context of SMEs, and further research is needed to advance our understanding on managing open innovation in SMEs, in particular in the services sector.

There is evidence that open innovation equips SMEs with the ability to improve their financial innovation performance (Brunswicker & Vanhaverbeke, 2015; Laursen & Salter, 2006; Parida et al., 2012). In light of this potential performance effect and the economic relevance of SMEs, there is also a practical motivation to better understand how to implement and manage open innovation in SMEs. In Europe, for example, more than 60 % of private sector jobs are in the SME sector and more than 90 % of all businesses are SMEs (Acs & Audretsch, 1987; European Commission, 2003; OECD, 2009). The tourism sector, one of the world's largest sectors, supporting 266 million jobs and generating 9.5 % of global GDP, is dominated by SMEs. Ninety-nine percent of the businesses in the tourism sector in Europe and US are Classified as SMEs (OECD, 2014; WTTC, 2014). SMEs in the tourism and hospitality industry do not necessarily engage in R&D intensive technology development but innovate their service processes or realize a new business model (Nieves & Segarra-Ciprés, 2014). While innovation in services share similarities with their counterparts in manufacturing, internal managerial capabilities for innovation and transformation are of high importance in services and occur in more incremental innovations (Nijssen, Hillebrand, Vermeulen, & Kemp, 2006; Thomas & Wood, 2014; Vanhaverbeke, 2012). In light of performance potential of open innovation in SMEs and the particular nature of innovation in tourism firms, this chapter aims to explicate the concept of open innovation in SMEs with a particular focus on services and tourism SMEs and to answer the following research question: How can we conceptualize open innovation in tourism SMEs and what are organizational capabilities for managing open innovation within them? To answer this question this paper takes an organizational boundary spanning perspective and makes the assumption that open innovation is a distributed innovation process in which SMEs *purposively* manage inflows and outflows of knowledge across their organizational boundaries in order to create and capture value (Brunswicker & van de Vrande, 2014; Chesbrough & Bogers, 2014).

2 The Particular Nature of Open Innovation in SMEs in Tourism

As the term suggests, small and medium-sized enterprises (SMEs) are characterized by their "smallness", which is usually measured with an upper ceiling for number of full-time employees, yearly turnover, and/or annual balance sheet total.[1] It is widely

---

[1] Referring to the official definition of SMEs laid down in the European Commission Recommendations 2003/361/EC, they employ less than 250 employees. In addition to the headcount ceiling,

recognized that SMEs make a significant contribution to our economies and that SMEs, compared to large firms, also have the capacity for innovation (Acs & Audretsch, 1988). However, prior studies suggest that innovation processes and models in SMEs are quite different compared to large firms (Edwards et al., 2005): They are usually flexible, fast decision makers and quicker in reacting to changing market demands (Vossen, 1998). At the same time, they face limitations in terms of material, human, and resource factors (Acs & Audretsch, 1987). Moreover, they generally have less formalized R&D and innovation procedures. Due to the liability of smallness, SMEs cannot cover all innovation activities required to successfully realize an innovation. Thus, innovation in SMEs regularly has an external and boundary-spanning component. Indeed, there has been a long tradition of research on the role of external relationships and networks in SMEs (Birley, 1985; Edwards et al., 2005; Macpherson & Holt, 2007). Innovation research in the hospitality and tourism sector also points out that interorganizational networks are essential for the competitiveness of SMEs in this sector (Hjalager, 2010; Thomas & Wood, 2014; Valentina & Passiante, 2009).

One major finding of prior work is that strategic alliances and partnerships with large firms enable SMEs to innovate, in particular if they are young. Dyadic partnerships and multi-actor alliances help them to get access to critical resources, to extend their competencies, and also to build legitimacy and reputation. SMEs that are involved in multiple ties that relate to different external larger partners are also more innovative than those that use only one type of tie (Baum et al., 2000). With the increased trend towards 'customer-oriented' and integrated service offerings in the tourism sector, business partners are essential to better align multiple offerings (Aldebert, Dang, & Longhi, 2011). Further, existing literature on SMEs anchored in the theoretical lens of social capital and social network ties emphasizes the preference of entrepreneurs for informal and social contacts that may provide opportunities and at the same time shape the development of a firm (Macpherson & Holt, 2007). In fact, SMEs that belong to formal *and* informal networks are more innovative than others. One factor driving this positive association is the presence of a large variety and diversity of personal relationships with members of the business networks in which the SME is embedded in; personal networks support the diffusion of innovation within networks of SMEs (Ceci & Iubatti, 2012). Despite these benefits, social and personal relationships are often strongly embedded in the economic actions of SMEs and are therefore not purposively "utilized" for open innovation. For example, SMEs regularly lack the capability to *proactively* articulate their needs for external knowledge (Bessant, 1999). Even though they could build upon strong external relationships and interpersonal networks to engage in open innovation, SMEs often don't have the internal capabilities required to do so (Bougrain & Haudeville, 2002). Further, organisational and social relationships

---

an enterprise "officially" qualifies as SME if it meets either the turnover ceiling of less than 50 million euros or the annual balance sheet ceiling 43 million euros but not necessarily both (European Commission, 2003).

can act as a barrier to innovation as such ties may close opportunities (Macpherson & Holt, 2007). SMEs even run the risk of becoming too dependent upon their relationships.

Overall, literature indicates that inter-organizational linkages and networks are important drivers of innovation in SMEs. However, existing studies reveal a paradox: Even though SMEs regularly have strong inter-organizational ties, they struggle with making the best use of these ties. Studying open innovation in SMEs should provide insights into how SMEs can use network relationships and social capital by *purposively managing* inflows and outflows of knowledge. If SMEs become proficient in applying and managing open innovation, they can use their relationships in a positive manner rather than becoming dependent upon them. As the locus of innovation regularly resides at the network level, open innovation in SMEs naturally is quite specific and different from large firms; it postulates researchers to explore the unique challenges in leveraging and managing open innovation in SMEs.

Besides network dependency, the *type* of innovation is also shaping the particular nature of open innovation in tourism SMEs. In general, the term SME is regularly associated with high-tech start-ups, new small firms, and entrepreneurial firms. However, SMEs subsume more than just young technology entrepreneurs and science-based ventures from high-tech sectors (de Jong & Marsili, 2006; Gans & Stern, 2002). It also includes established SMEs that are at a later organisational lifecycle stage, as well SMEs that innovate in low-tech sectors or services (Koberg, Uhlenbruck, & Sarason, 1996; Santamaría, Nieto, & Barge-Gil, 2009). Small service firms, such as those in the tourism sector, are exposed to the distinct nature and very particular challenges of services innovation (Aldebert et al., 2011; Mina, Bascavusoglu-Moreau, & Hughes, 2014; Thomas & Wood, 2014). In tourism services the customer takes a central role in the value creation process. Value is not transferred in a transactional manner but co-created in a service exchange process between the firm and the customer. The inseparability of production and consumption makes services distinct from manufactured products, and puts the customer in a central role in the service production process. The *interaction* between the organization and the customers shapes the perceived service quality, experience, and efficiency of resource allocation (Schneider, Ehrhart, Mayer, Saltz, & Niles-Jolly, 2005), and the customer holds an active role in the service production process and the way value is created and perceived. This has significant implications on services innovation in tourism, which imply new roles of the customer in the service co-creation process or completely novel service systems in which multiple actors co-create service value in a very interactive manner (Sampson, 2010; Vargo & Akaka, 2009). In service sectors like tourism, innovations may not just emerge from novel interactions with the customer but from novel alignments and exchange relationships of a variety of actors that co-create value both for and with customers (Aldebert et al., 2011). The highly interactive and intangible nature of services value creation suggests that the open innovation concept is particularly important for them. Indeed, existing studies highlight that tourism firms are naturally more dependent upon external knowledge sources for innovation than manufacturing firms (Leiponen, 2005; Love, Roper, & Hewitt-Dundas, 2010; Nieves & Segarra-Ciprés, 2014). However, little is known about how these services SMEs may *purposively* manage external and internal knowledge flows that span their organizational boundaries, which modes of open innovation are best suited for them, and what internal organizational capacities are need to benefit from openness. The following chapter will briefly map out relevant open innovation modes in tourism SMEs by drawing upon recent theoretical contributions on open innovation and empirical studies on openness in SMEs.

3 Modes of Open Innovation in SMES

There are multiple ways in which SMEs may engage in open innovation, ranging from traditional modes like consortia to emerging and often digitally enabled practices like innovation crowdsourcing, in which SMEs engage with a large number of external strangers to solve innovation problems (Afuah & Tucci, 2012; Sigala & Christou, 2014). Open innovation is often broadly categorized in two different modes, namely *inbound* and *outbound* open innovation. In inbound open innovation, external knowledge flows inside the organization, whereas in outbound open innovation, internal knowledge travels across the firm's organizational boundaries to find new paths to market and commercialization channels (Dahlander & Gann, 2010).

3.1 Inbound Modes of Open Innovation

Inbound open innovation can be further subdivided into two modes of open innovation, namely *sourcing* and *acquiring*. Sourcing refers to how firms make use of external sources of knowledge without an immediate compensation to the sources for the knowledge that flows over the organization's boundaries. Acquiring implies an immediate financial compensation. Existing literature on open innovation clearly suggest that inbound open innovation is more widely adopted in the SME sector than outbound open innovation. Sourcing is the preferred mode of inbound open innovation because it requires fewer or less financial resources than transaction-oriented modes like acquisitions or external licensing (van de Vrande et al., 2009). This preference for free inflows of knowledge is in line with the general trend of open innovation adoption. In one recent study on large firms, results show that open innovators are "net takers" and focus on free inflows of knowledge rather than free outflows (Chesbrough & Brunswicker, 2014). Due to the liability of smallness and lack of resources, sourcing is a particularly important mode of inbound open innovation in SMEs. A broad *sourcing* strategy offers SMEs significant innovation performance benefits. In their influential study, Laursen and Salter (2006) found that greater search breadth, measured as the number of sources that firms use to access external innovation-related knowledge, has a positive effect on innovation performance. When exploring sourcing strategies in more detail, we learned that SMEs differ in how they combine different types of sources of external knowledge (Brunswicker & Vanhaverbeke, 2015). Some open up only along the value chain while others heavily draw upon universities and research organizations to access precompetitive and technological know-how. In addition, others make heavy use of network partnerships, which are characterized by mutual trust and access to complementary resources.

A recent empirical typology of external sourcing strategies in SMEs based on a firm-level dataset of more than 1,400 SMEs in Europe clearly suggests that it matters how SMEs combine different sources of knowledge (Brunswicker & Vanhaverbeke, 2015). It identified five different sourcing types: (1) *Minimal searchers*, (2) *supply-chain searchers*, (3) *technology-oriented searchers*, (4) *application-oriented searchers*, and (5) *full-scope searchers*. *Minimal searchers* do not actively interact with external sources to combine internal and external innovation potentials. They are not willing to open up their innovation-related processes and activities. *Supply-chain searchers* rely on traditional supply-chain linkages. Interactions do not relate to universities and research organizations, and thus, they do not purposively manage inflows of technological knowledge of high novelty. *Technology-oriented searchers* actively interact with universities, research organizations, and intellectual property rights (IPR) experts. They also take the challenge to manage inflows of knowledge of high technological and market risk. Trusted relationships rather than market-based interactions, characterize the sourcing strategies of technology-oriented searchers. *Application-oriented searchers* regularly interact with value chain actors (such as customers and suppliers), and rank particularly high on ties with indirect customers. They consider customers as value generators rather then value receivers, and purposively manage downstream knowledge flows. *Full-scope searchers* open up broadly and engage with a diverse set of sources. They show a very strong focus on managing inflows of pre-commercial knowledge and insights of new inventions while at the same time actively learning about novel business opportunities from direct and indirect customers. Trusted and complementary partnerships also play a very important role for them.

While SMEs may benefit from the breadth of the full-scope sourcing strategy and the purposive management of a large number of external sources, an application-oriented sourcing strategy in which they are particularly focused on downstream actors such as direct and indirect customers also offers significant innovation benefits (Brunswicker & Vanhaverbeke, 2015). Thus, application-oriented search is an alternative smart move and equips SMEs with the opportunity to propel their innovation performance without investing in interactions with all types of external sources. Application-oriented sourcing is particularly relevant for SMEs in the tourism sector. If they purposively interact with direct and indirect customers, they learn about emerging needs, opportunities for improving service satisfaction, new means to increase service experience, and gain insights about potentially greater service efficiency.

Overall, existing literature stresses the critical role of sourcing innovation-related knowledge outside of organizational boundaries. However, SMEs can also move beyond interactions with dedicated agents, that is, organizations they already know or that they purposively pick to access new knowledge (Afuah & Tucci, 2012). They may also make use of extra-organizational open innovation crowds and innovation crowdsourcing, in which they engage and interact with a large number of unknown outsiders to solve innovation problems. Today, it is mostly large open innovation giants like P&G, or fast moving consumer companies that engage with the customer and user crowd to develop novel product ideas. Evidence on the adoption of crowdsourcing in SMEs, and in particular in tourism SMEs, is rare. While literature on e-commerce and a case example on e-tourism highlights how loosely coordinated crowds of users can contribute to the evaluation and diffusion of a digital service, there is little work on how small tourism firms make use of the user crowds for developing new service products, service processes, or even business models (Sigala & Christou, 2014). A few recent case studies in other industries like the Ocean Optics case, a 25-year-old US-based photonics technology SME with about 200 employees and more than 50 million dollars in sales, provide insights that crowdsourcing may offer SMEs a novel generative mechanism for creating novel product ideas (Brunswicker & van de Vrande, 2014). The diversity of the crowd provides the potential for outlier ideas and truly novel perspectives towards the problem to be solved. In the Ocean Optics case, crowdsourcing increased their innovation capacity by at least four times within the first year, made a positive impact on the firm's brand value, and drove the firm's strategic change. However, particular design elements of the crowdsourcing were instrumental for the positive results. For example, crowdsourcing was not designed in a sense of unidirectional inflows, but was handled in an interactive way with deep engagement and collaboration within the crowd and also with the SME's internal employees. In addition, they also collaborated with some of their strategic customers to co-invest in the crowdsourcing activity. While this case highlights that crowdsourcing may also be a viable option for SMEs, there is not sufficient insight into the suitable design strategies for crowdsourcing and innovation contests to be implemented by tourism SMEs. Since SMEs they cannot build upon an established brand value, as large firms and established brands can, unique incentive mechanisms, co-branding, and the involvement of regional public agencies may positively shape the participation in crowdsourcing may positively shape the participation and utilization of crowdsourcing by tourism SMEs.

3.2   Outbound Modes of Open Innovation

Recent studies on open innovation in SMEs suggest that outbound open innovation in which internal innovation-related knowledge flows from inside across the organizational boundaries to be used by other organizations and individuals receives little attention in SMEs (van de Vrande et al., 2009). These findings are in line with the overall adoption trend of open innovation both in large and small firms: Inbound open innovation is dominating outbound open innovation (Brunswicker & van de Vrande, 2014; Chesbrough & Brunswicker, 2014). *Outbound open innovation* subsumes two sub-modes: revealing and selling. In essence, outbound open innovation requires innovators to give up exclusivity to innovation-related knowledge. When SMEs *reveal* internal knowledge, legal-exclusion rights are either ineffective, or are purposively waived by the firm (Henkel, 2006; Henkel, Schöberl, & Alexy, 2014). Revealing also implies that SMEs freely reveal internal knowledge without an immediate compensation for their internal innovation-related knowledge (Dahlander & Gann, 2010).

Gruber und Henkel (2006) showed that free revealing might enable SMEs to overcome their disadvantages in innovation, namely their liability of newness, liability of smallness, and market entry barriers. Their study on open source software (OSS) SMEs, who participate in and freely reveal knowledge in development communities, suggests that free revealing enables them to overcome the *liability of newness*. Through active participation in the OSS community, they quickly build visibility and reputation. In addition, they can address their *liability of smallness* and lack of resources as the OSS community provides access to voluntary contributions and 'free' development resources, which they would usually build inside the organization. In addition, OSS may also *reduce the market entry barriers* that large incumbent firms have erected through intensive R&D investments. We argue that free revealing is not just restricted to OSS as the principles of OSS can be found in other sectors such as e-commerce, healthcare, and e-science (Levine & Prietula, 2014). Free revealing may offer very specific benefits to SMEs, as it may reduce entry barriers and sunk costs (Brunswicker & van de Vrande, 2014). Unfortunately, the existing literature on open innovation in SMEs remains relatively silent about the role of free revealing in SMEs. In addition, it does not explore whether and how SMEs selectively reveal knowledge when interacting with external partners while keeping some of their innovation-related knowledge secret in order to secure economic benefits from their innovation efforts (Henkel, 2006; Henkel et al., 2014).

In contrast, SMEs may also maintain some legal exclusivity over innovation-related knowledge and *sell* this knowledge on the market. Indeed, many technology-driven and venture-capital backed entrepreneurial firms successfully out-license know-how and technologies as an alternative to developing a product and selling it on the market (Gans & Stern, 2002). Out-licensing or other pecuniary outbound modes like patent selling can provide SMEs with the opportunity to exploit a proprietary technology outside the core business without having to invest in vertical integration and building (or acquiring) complementary assets (Bianchi, Campodall'Orto, Frattini, & Vercesi, 2010; Teece, 1986). While such a strategy has been identified as a common outbound open innovation strategy in large firms, it is also a viable option for SMEs, particularly for those that engage in technological innovations and operate in environments with strong intellectual property rights regimes (Alexy, Criscuolo, & Salter, 2009; Alexy, Henkel, & Wallin, 2013). Formal intellectual property rights (IPRs), such as patents and trademarks, play a critical role for successfully entering the market for ideas (Arora, Fosuri, &

Gambardella, 2001; Arora & Gambardella, 2010). For example, if knowledge is protected by means of a patent, the transfer of the underlying knowledge becomes much easier as patents help to define the intellectual property rights explicitly (Alexy et al., 2009; Leiponen & Byma, 2009). In addition, IPRs may also serve as a signalling device, demonstrating technological capability. Particularly for small, start-up firms, having a patent is almost a prerequisite to receive any kind of VC funding or for larger firms to be willing to cooperate (Gans & Stern, 2003). However, using formal IPRs is not a viable option for all types of SMEs. Prior studies on SMEs suggest that a large proportion of SMEs finds patents less efficient than informal mechanism for protecting know-how and establishing some form of exclusivity. Examples of such mechanisms are speed and secrecy (Kitching & Blackburn, 1998). Obtaining a patent and maintaining it is usually a complex and costly process, which makes patents less attractive to SMEs (Penin, 2005). In services, formal IP protection is even more difficult, if not impossible. Even though services product innovation may be tangible and thus, can potentially be protected via patents, critical innovation-related knowledge of the service process may not be patentable. As the copyright system for protecting intangible assets is much weaker than the patent system, services SMEs face difficulties in engaging in the market for ideas in which they could trade ideas in a transactional manner (Miles, Andersen, Boden, & Howells, 2000). At the same time, digital technologies are becoming increasingly important in the tourism services as well. This trend may increase the opportunity for tourism SMEs to establish formal IP protection through patents or copyrights.

To conclude, both free (and selective) revealing and selling are relevant outbound modes of open innovation in SMEs in the services sector. However, there is no one-size-fits all for engaging in outbound open innovation in SMEs. A range of external as well as internal contingency factors may affect the adoption and the effect of different outbound strategies. For example, the technological environment and the speed therein, or the strength of the appropriability scheme of the sector shape the adoption and the effect of a particular strategy. Future research on outbound modes of open innovation in SMEs will hopefully provide further insights to increase our understanding of open innovation in tourism SMEs.

3.3   Interactive and Networked Modes of Open Innovation

Interactive and networked modes of open innovation are a particular characteristic of open innovation in SMEs. This mode conceptualizes open innovation as an interactive rather than a linear and unidirectional process of knowledge flows across organizational boundaries (West & Bogers, 2014). It is a hybrid innovation process containing multiple feedback loops across multiple boundaries at different stages of the innovation process, and in multiple directions. Case studies on open innovation in SMEs illustrate the nature of this mode. For example, CAS, an SME market-leader in the field of customer relationship management (CRM) software for

SMEs in Germany, has adopted a very interactive mode of open innovation. In a regular exchange with strategic business partners and customers through joint innovation road mapping, they identify market needs and strategic business areas in an interactive manner. Information systems and collaboration technologies support this process. Equipped with a deeper understanding of the market needs, they interact with research partners and universities to identify potential technological solutions. Business partners and customers are not excluded from the identification of such technological solutions; they also participate in the prioritization of these technological solutions. The open innovation model at CAS is characterized by multiple feedback loops and interactions with both downstream and upstream partners. Such interactions take place at various phases of the innovation process and span different knowledge domains. CAS facilitates the interaction of customers, business partners that develop 'vertical' solutions for the cloud-based CMR solution, as well as upstream suppliers and research partners. Thus, it considers itself as a "platform player", around which an innovation network forms (Brunswicker, 2013). When they jointly explore novel value propositions with their partners, they may also need to adapt their own business model to capture some value from it. Thus, open innovation is strategic in nature, and implies that SMEs do not just organize the 'creative crowd' in the front-end of open innovation, but also focus on the early consideration and interaction with downstream partners and other actors that hold critical complementary resources and assets in order to realize and implement the novel value proposition.

The strategic role of business networks in SMEs implies that open innovation in SMEs is directly linked to the business strategy and the firm's overall strategic objectives. While large firms can implement open innovation without changing their business strategy, the shift towards open innovation in SMEs regularly goes hand in hand with a strategic change and the adaption of the SME's business model (Vanhaverbeke, 2012). Value creation and interactive mechanisms are very critical when services firms engage in open innovation. As highlighted above, services value is co-created rather than transferred and thus the identification and development of novel services requires intensive interactions with co-creation partners and customers in order to explore novel services ideas and implement them. Thus, for SMEs in the tourism sector it is particularly critical to deeply engage in co-creation relationships with downstream partners and realize novel customer exchange mechanisms which increase service quality, service experience or service efficiency (Vargo & Lusch, 2007). Customer and user communities not only act as a source of novel ideas but they also hold a critical role in creating and diffusing the novel services through 'social influence' and community-driven diffusion mechanisms. User communities can enable SMEs to build their brand, and also diffuse this brand (Füller, Schroll, & Hippel, 2013).

Overall, interactive mechanisms and extra-organizational value network relationships with individual actors or even extra-organizational communities are a critical mode of open innovation in SMEs, and require deeper consideration in future research in the tourism sector.

4   The Internal Antecedents of Open Innovation in SMEs in Tourism

Open innovation poses new managerial challenges. Both scholars and practitioners agree that open innovation requires internal capabilities and has an internal component (Laursen & Salter, 2006; Spithoven, Clarysse, & Knockaert, 2010; West & Bogers, 2014). On the one hand, there are internal organizational practices, systems and routines for managing open innovation and related knowledge flows in SMEs. On the other hand, the transition from closed towards open innovation implies some kind of organizational change, which usually spans different phases (Chiaroni, Chiesa, & Frattini, 2011; Teece, 2007). It is also important to understand how SMEs can manage the transition from closed towards open innovation, which is quite different from the transition observed in large firms. As discussed previously open innovation in SMEs is regularly linked directly to the business model, and thus implies a strategy change and the adaption of the SME's business model (Vanhaverbeke, 2012). This is particularly true for SMEs in the tourism sector. Thus, the change process in the SME regularly relates to a change in the business model.

4.1   Internal Organizational Practices for Open Innovation

The first perspective links back to the seminal work of Cohen und Levinthal (1990) on absorptive capacity. Firms require the ability to absorb external knowledge in order to benefit from it (Cohen & Levinthal, 1990). Absorptive capacity is a pre-requisite for inbound open innovation and is built through formal R&D. In line with this argument, a range of studies on inbound open innovation, and especially on sourcing of external knowledge, indicate that openness has an internal component and requires internal R&D (Dahlander & Gann, 2010). In tourism SMEs, R&D is usually not a formal process and absorptive capacity cannot be inferred from a measure like R&D expenditures (Thomas & Wood, 2014). Given their limited resources, SMEs may also call upon third parties to support them in building absorptive capacity (Spithoven et al., 2010).

Even though absorptive capacity is important for open innovation, it concentrates on using external knowledge internally only and neglects other important organizational capabilities which are required in open innovation; neither does it address all dimensions of managing knowledge flows in open innovation, nor does it acknowledge the distributed character of knowledge in open innovation. For example, absorptive capacity does not capture the specifics of outbound open innovation. It also does not address the question of how to apply innovative knowledge and means to turn it into successful outcomes (Bianchi et al., 2010). Recent theoretical contributions propose additional capacities (groups of capabilities) for managing different knowledge processes in open innovation, which complement the construct of absorptive capacity (Robertson et al., 2012). While there are new knowledge capacities required for managing the acquisition and retention of knowledge at the intrafirm and interfirm level, open innovation also implies new capacities for applying knowledge, and turning external and internal knowledge into successful outcomes. Examples of such knowledge capacities for managing open innovation are accessive, adaptive, and integrative capacities (Robertson et al., 2012).

Further, these knowledge capacities do not function "automatically" and therefore firms need some sort of a higher order capacity to guide these capacities. Thus, innovation management capacities represents relevant facilitators for open innovation in SMEs; however, they are regularly lacking in SMEs (Brunswicker & Vanhaverbeke, 2015; Robertson et al., 2012). Literature on innovation in tourism highlights that SMEs are particularly limited in their ability to manage innovation internally (Thomas & Wood, 2014). As innovation is organizationally pervasive, the required innovation management capacity relates to different managerial levels. They include strategic as well as operational components for effective and efficient attainment of organizational innovation goals (Brunswicker & Vanhaverbeke, 2015). In a recent empirical quantitative study based on more than 1,400 SMEs, results show that a particular mix of four internal organizational practices facilitates SMEs in benefiting from open innovation. These organizational practices related to different stages of the innovation process: (1) *Long-term investment processes*, (2) *innovation strategy processes*, (3) *innovation development processes, and* (4) *innovation project control. Long-term investment processes* enable SMEs to build sufficient internal knowledge in order to sense external knowledge. An *innovation strategy* supports the identification of future business opportunities and the exploration of new technologies, solution principles or market functions. *Innovation development processes* subsume formal processes and systems that provide structure for moving an idea from its inception to commercialization, and *innovation project control* describes the coordination mechanism to effectively and efficiently manage individual innovation projects through process and output control. For SMEs to benefit from a full scope sourcing strategy, they require *all four* practices and routines. Jointly they mediate and channel external knowledge inside the firm. Innovation strategy processes are particularly important. In contrast, application-oriented sourcing does not demand such a sufficient managerial capability. It is sufficiently supported by an operational capacity for managing the development process, and effective and efficient innovation project control (Brunswicker & Vanhaverbeke, 2015).

While internal organizational practices provide the foundational building blocks for successful open innovation, SMEs need to build upon them and establish very targeted practices for the open innovation mode they have chosen and realized. As interactive mechanisms and network relationships are an important mode of open innovation in tourism SMEs, literature suggests that they need to establish "coordination" and "governance" capabilities in order to align their value network. In some cases, they need to successfully act as a hub (Brunswicker, 2013; Gardet & Fraiha, 2012). To do so, different coordination practices may constitute their success in governing an interactive and networked mode of open innovation.

Examples of such practices are a diligent mix of informal, semiformal, or formal *communication* practices. In addition, they need to decide upon the proper allocation of *decision rights* and intellectual property rights (IPR) among the innovation partner network, as these rights align incentives and also direct innovation activities (Gardet & Fraiha, 2012). The governance mode may also change over time, as with increasing trust, tourism SMEs may also increase their ability to negotiate a stronger position in the network and maintain higher control over the interactive innovation process.

4.2 Managing the Change from Closed Towards Open Innovation

The second perspective of managing open innovation in SMEs is about the transition from closed towards open innovation over time. As highlighted in prominent case studies on large firms, such as the case study on Procter and Gamble, this transition implies significant organizational change and transformation (Dodgson, Gann, & Salter, 2006; Huston & Sakkab, 2006). Regularly, a first open innovation project triggers a more fundamental and strategic change (Chiaroni et al., 2011; Gassmann, Ellen, & Chesbrough, 2010). Chiaroni et al. (2011) describe the change process from closed towards open innovation, highlighting the important role of the top management in enabling the change and the need for a champion promoting the change along different managerial levels. Further, they show that in large firms the starting point of the transition is a change at the organisational structure level. The establishment of a new independent open innovation unit (or role) represents an important trigger for change and sends signals to other organisational units (Chiaroni et al., 2011). In SMEs there might be different triggers. For example, in a small tourism firm, units that develop integrated solutions for the customer might trigger a change for greater opportunities. Such units might take the role of an internal promoter of open innovation through a pilot project and the purposive design and management of a promoter network for open innovation (Fichter, 2009).

5   Conclusion

SMEs are of high economic relevance in the tourism sector. As open innovation offers a range of benefits for innovation, tourism SMEs can reap such benefits by engaging in the appropriate open innovation mode. This paper presents a conceptualization of open innovation in SMEs that subsumes open innovation modes and internal organizational practices for them. It highlights that there are different modes available for tourism SMEs: (1) inbound, (2) outbound, and (3) networked modes of open innovation. The latter one, the interactive and networked mode, is particularly important for open innovation in tourism SMEs, and requires deeper consideration in future management practice and research. At the same time, this chapter highlights that managing open innovation in tourism SMEs is quite specific in nature and requires a well-developed internal capacity. SMEs in the tourism sector need to establish internal managerial capabilities in order to benefit from open innovation. To mange the transition from closed towards open innovation, new functions inside the organization might be required. However, for new practices to flourish, they require foundational organizational practices and routines for innovation that span strategic and operational practices and routines. They provide the foundations for specific open innovation practices and tools, such as internal open innovation roles and promoters.

Today, there is only marginal insight into the specific nature of open innovation in SMEs in the tourism sector and there are manifold research questions to be explored. In particular, research into new *inbound* open innovation practices like crowdsourcing and the role of digital technologies within them is needed. In addition, a deeper examination of advantages and disadvantages of *outbound* open innovation like selling and revealing is encouraged. At this stage it is too early to draw any conclusions related to potential outcomes of such research. There are great opportunities for exploring the specifics of open innovation in the tourism SMEs. Thus, future research should build upon this conceptual paper that provides a framework for potential research. Both theoretical and empirical research is encouraged. Overall, research on open innovation in tourism SMEs will benefit open innovation scholars as well as researchers that have specialized on the tourism sector. In addition, it will also provide fruitful insights for scholars from adjacent areas like entrepreneurship and innovation studies.

References

Acs, Z. J., & Audretsch, D. B. (1987). Innovation in large and small firms. *Economics Letters, 23,* 109–112.

Acs, Z. J., & Audretsch, D. B. (1988). Innovation and firm size in manufacturing. *Technovation, 7,* 197–210.

Afuah, A., & Tucci, C. L. (2012). Crowdsourcing as a solution to distant search. *Academy of Management Review, 37,* 355–375.

Aldebert, B., Dang, R. J., & Longhi, C. (2011). Innovation in the tourism industry: The case of tourism@. *Tourism Management, 32,* 1204–1213.

Alexy, O., Criscuolo, P., & Salter, A. (2009). Does IP strategy have to cripple open innovation? *MIT Sloan Management Review, 51,* 71–77.

Alexy, O., Henkel, J., & Wallin, M. W. (2013). From closed to open: Job role changes, individual predispositions, and the adoption of commercial open source software development. *Research Policy, 42,* 1325–1340.

Arora, A., Fosuri, A., & Gambardella, A. (2001). Markets for technology and their implications for corporate strategy. *Industrial and Corporate Change, 10,* 419–451.

Arora, A., & Gambardella, A. (2010). Ideas for rent: An overview of markets for technology. *Industrial and Corporate Change, 19,* 775–803.

Baum, J. A. C., Calabrese, T., & Silverman, B. S. (2000). Don't go it alone: Alliance network composition and startups performance in Canadian biotechnology. *Strategic Management Journal, 21*, 267–294.

Bessant, J. (1999). The rise and fall of 'Supernet': A case study of technology transfer policy for smaller firms. *Research Policy, 28*, 601–614.

Bianchi, M., Campodall'Orto, S., Frattini, F., & Vercesi, P. (2010). Enabling open innovation in small- and medium-sized enterprises: How to find alternative applications for your technologies. *R&D Management, 40*, 414–431.

Birley, S. (1985). The role of networks in the entrepreneurial process. *Journal of Business Venturing, 1*, 107–117.

Bougrain, F., & Haudeville, B. (2002). Innovation, collaboration and SMEs internal research capacities. *Research Policy, 31*, 735–747.

Brunswicker, S. E. F. (2013). Managing open innovation in SMEs: A good practice example of a German software firm. *International Journal of Industrial Engineering and Management, 4*, 33–41.

Brunswicker, S., & van de Vrande, V. (2014). Exploring open innovation in small and medium-sized firms. In H. Chesbrough, V. Wim, & J. West (Eds.), *Frontiers in open innovation*. London: Oxford University Press.

Brunswicker, S., & Vanhaverbeke, W. (2015). Open innovation in small and medium-sized enterprises (SMEs): External knowledge sourcing strategies and internal organizational facilitators. *Journal of Small Business Management, 53*(4), 1241–1263.

Ceci, F., & Iubatti, D. (2012). Personal relationships and innovation diffusion in SME networks: A content analysis approach. *Research Policy, 41*, 565–579.

Chesbrough, H. (2006). New puzzles and new findings. In H. Chesbrough, W. Vanhaverbeke, & J. West (Eds.), *Open innovation: Researching a new paradigm*. Oxford: Oxford University Press.

Chesbrough, H., & Bogers, M. (2014). Explicating open innovation: Clarifying an emerging paradigm for understanding innovation. In H. Chesbrough, V. Wim, & J. West (Eds.), *Frontiers in open innovation*. London: Oxford University Press.

Chesbrough, H., & Brunswicker, S. (2014). A fad or a phenomenon? The adoption of open innovation practices in large firms. *Research-Technology Management, 57*, 16–25.

Chiaroni, D., Chiesa, V., & Frattini, F. (2011). The open innovation journey: How firms dynamically implement the emerging innovation management paradigm. *Technovation, 31*, 34–43.

Cohen, W. M., & Levinthal, D. A. (1990). Absorptive capacity: A new perspective on learning and innovation. *Administrative Science Quarterly, 35*, 128–152.

Dahlander, L., & Gann, D. M. (2010). How open is innovation? *Research Policy, 39*, 699–709.

de Jong, J. P. J., & Marsili, O. (2006). The fruit flies of innovations: A taxonomy of innovative small firms. *Research Policy, 35*, 213–229.

Dodgson, M., Gann, D., & Salter, A. (2006). The role of technology in the shift towards open innovation: The case of Procter & Gamble. *R&D Management, 36*, 333–346.

Edwards, T., Delbridge, R., & Munday, M. (2005). Understanding innovation in small and medium-sized enterprises: A process manifest. *Technovation, 25*, 1119–1127.

European Commission. (2003). *The new SME definition: User guide and model declaration*. Brussels: European Commission.

Füller, J., Schroll, R., & von Hippel, E. (2013). User generated brands and their contribution to the diffusion of user innovations. *Research Policy, 42*, 1197–1209.

Fichter, K. (2009). Innovation communities: The role of networks of promoters in Open Innovation. *R&D Management, 39*(4), 357–371.

Gans, J. S., & Stern, S. (2002). The product market and the market for "ideas". Commercialization strategies for technology entrepreneurs. In: Melbourne Business School and Intellectual Property Research Institute of Australia (Ed.), *Working Paper ed.* Melbourne.

Gans, J. S., & Stern, S. (2003). The product market and the market for "ideas": Commercialization strategies for technology entrepreneurs. *Research Policy, 32*, 333–350.

Gardet, E., & Fraiha, S. (2012). Coordination modes established by the hub firm of an innovation network: The case of an SME bearer. *Journal of Small Business Management, 50*, 216–238.

Gassmann, O., Ellen, E., & Chesbrough, H. (2010). The future of open innovation. *R&D Management, 40*, 213–221.

Gruber, M., & Henkel, J. (2006). New ventures based on open innovation – An empirical analysis of start-up firms in embedded Linux. *International Journal of Technology Management, 33*, 356–372.

Henkel, J. (2006). Selective revealing in open innovation processes: The case of embedded Linux. *Research Policy, 35*, 953–969.

Henkel, J., Schöberl, S., & Alexy, O. (2014). The emergence of openness: How and why firms adopt selective revealing in open innovation. *Research Policy, 43*, 879–890.

Hjalager, A.-M. (2010). A review of innovation research in tourism. *Tourism Management, 31*, 1–12.

Huston, L., & Sakkab, N. (2006). Inside Procter & Gamble's new model for innovation: Connect and develop. *Harvard Business Review, 84*, 58–66.

Kitching, J., & Blackburn, R. (1998). Intellectual property management in the small and medium enterprise (SME). *Journal of Small Business and Enterprise Development, 5*, 327–335.

Koberg, C. S., Uhlenbruck, N., & Sarason, Y. (1996). Facilitators of organizational innovation: The role of life-cycle stage. *Journal of Business Venturing, 11*, 133–149.

Laursen, K., & Salter, A. (2006). Open for innovation: The role of openness in explaining innovation performance among U.K. manufacturing firms. *Strategic Management Journal, 27*, 131–150.

Lee, S., Park, G., Yoon, B., & Park, J. (2010). Open innovation in SMEs—An intermediated network model. *Research Policy, 39*, 290–300.

Leiponen, A. (2005). Organization of knowledge and innovation: The case of Finnish business services. *Industry and Innovation, 12*, 185–203.

Leiponen, A., & Byma, J. (2009). If you cannot block, you better run: Small firms, cooperative innovation, and appropriation strategies. *Research Policy, 38*, 1478–1488.

Levine, S. S., & Prietula, M. J. (2014). Open collaboration for innovation: Principles and performance. *Organization Science, 25*(5), 1414–1433.

Love, J. H., Roper, S., & Hewitt-Dundas, N. (2010). Service innovation, embeddedness and business performance: Evidence from Northern Ireland. *Regional Studies, 44*, 983–1004.

Macpherson, A., & Holt, R. (2007). Knowledge, learning and small firm growth: A systematic review of the evidence. *Research Policy, 36*, 172–192.

Miles, I., Andersen, B., Boden, M., & Howells, J. (2000). Service production and intellectual property. *International Journal of Technology Management, 20*, 95–115.

Mina, A., Bascavusoglu-Moreau, E., & Hughes, A. (2014). Open service innovation and the firm's search for external knowledge. *Research Policy, 43*, 853–866.

Nieves, J., & Segarra-Ciprés, M. (2014). Management innovation in the hotel industry. *Tourism Management, 46*, 51–58.

Nijssen, E. J., Hillebrand, B., Vermeulen, P. A. M., & Kemp, R. G. M. (2006). Exploring product and service innovation similarities and differences. *International Journal of Research in Marketing, 23*, 241–251.

OECD. (2009). *The impact of the global crisis on SME and entrepreneurship financing and policy response*. Paris: OECD Publication.

OECD. (2014). *OECD tourism trends and policies 2014*. Paris: OECD.

Parida, V., Westerberg, M., & Frishammar, J. (2012). Inbound open innovation activities in high-tech SMEs: The impact on innovation performance. *Journal of Small Business Management, 50*, 283–309.

Penin, J. (2005). Patents versus ex post rewards: A new look. *Research Policy, 34*, 641–656.

Robertson, P. L., Casali, G. L., & Jacobson, D. (2012). Managing open incremental process innovation: Absorptive capacity and distributed learning. *Research Policy, 41*, 822–832.

Sampson, S. (2010). The unified service theory. In P. P. Maglio, C. A. Kieliszewski, & J. C. Spohrer (Eds.), *Handbook of service science*. New York: Springer.

Santamaría, L., Nieto, M. J., & Barge-Gil, A. (2009). Beyond formal R&D: Taking advantage of other sources of innovation in low- and medium-technology industries. *Research Policy, 38*, 507–517.

Schneider, B., Ehrhart, M. G., Mayer, D. M., Saltz, J. L., & Niles-Jolly, K. (2005). Understanding organization-customer links in service settings. *Academy of Management Journal, 48*, 1017–1032.

Sigala, M., & Christou, E. (2014). Social computing in travel, tourism and hospitality. *Computers in Human Behavior, 30*, 771–772.

Spithoven, A., Clarysse, B., & Knockaert, M. (2010). Building absorptive capacity to organise inbound open innovation in traditional industries. *Technovation, 30*, 130–141.

Teece, D. J. (1986). Profiting from technological innovation: Implications for integration, collaboration, licensing and public policy. *Research Policy, 15*, 285–305.

Teece, D. J. (2007). Explicating dynamic capabilities: The nature and microfoundations of (sustainable) enterprise performance. *Strategic Management Journal, 28*, 1319–1350.

Thomas, R., & Wood, E. (2014). Innovation in tourism: Re-conceptualising and measuring the absorptive capacity of the hotel sector. *Tourism Management, 45*, 39–48.

Valentina, N., & Passiante, G. (2009). Impacts of absorptive capacity on value creation. *Anatolia, 20*, 269–287.

van de Vrande, V., de Jong, J. P. J., Vanhaverbeke, W., & de Rochemont, M. (2009). Open innovation in SMEs: Trends, motives and management challenges. *Technovation, 29*, 423–437.

Vanhaverbeke, W. (2012). *Open innovation in SMEs: How can small companies and start-ups benefit from open innovation strategies?* Leuven, Brussels: Flanders District of Creativity.

Vargo, S. L., & Akaka, M. A. (2009). Service-dominant logic as a foundation for service science: Clarifications. *Service Science, 1*, 32–41.

Vargo, S. L., & Lusch, R. F. (2007). Service-dominant logic: Continuing the evolution. *Journal of the Academy of Marketing Science, 36*, 1–10.

Vossen, R. W. (1998). Relative strengths and weaknesses of small firms in innovation. *International Small Business Journal, 16*, 88–94.

West, J., & Bogers, M. (2014). Leveraging external sources of innovation: A review of research on open innovation. *Journal of Product Innovation Management, 31*(4), 814–831.

WTTC. (2014). *Mission of the World Travel & Tourism Council*. Accessed September 23, 2014, from http://www.wttc.org/mission/

Wynarchyzk, P., Piperopoulos, P., & Mcadam, M. (2013). Open innovation in small and medium-sized enterprises. *International Small Business Journal, 31*, 1–16.

Part II
Case Studies: Information Level

Netnography: The Mint Journey

Michael Bartl and Nayeli Tusche

Learning Objectives

- Realize what Netnography is all about.
- Understand why Netnography is considered an Open-Innovation initiative.
- Undergo the process of a Netnography project along an international practical business case.
- Analyze the advantages and limitations of Netnography.
- Illustrate the potential of Netnography across the tourism industry.

1 Introduction

There is no doubt that the Internet has changed the manner in which we communicate and interact, thus the way we share and get information. As a result, consumers are increasingly turning to computer-mediated communication for information on which to base their decisions regarding products or brands, but also destinations, hotels or restaurants (Kozinets, 2002). For example, Tripadvisor had, as of June 2014, according to its website, more than "150 million reviews and opinions from travelers around the world". But also networking sites such as Facebook allow members to form and join travel-related groups and debates. In general, while a growing number of tourism consumers are joining online discussion sites to post messages about their travel experiences around the world, the number of message boards which are dedicated to travel activities is rising (Mkono, 2012). Examples of such platforms include Tripadvisor.com, Igougo.com, Virtualtourist.com, Travbuddy.com, etc. Consumers rely on such cyber-places,

M. Bartl (✉) • N. Tusche
HYVE AG, Munich, Germany
e-mail: michael.bartl@hyve.net; nayeli.tusche@hyve.net

© Springer-Verlag Berlin Heidelberg 2016
R. Egger et al. (eds.), *Open Tourism*, Tourism on the Verge,
DOI 10.1007/978-3-642-54089-9_13

i.e. newsgroups, chat rooms, blogs, forums, review platforms and social networking sites to share ideas, experiences, build relationships and keep in contact to fellow consumers who do not only share the same interests, but who are perceived as objective information sources (Kozinets, 2002). They are sometimes called "virtual communities" (Rheingold, 1993), implying that "virtual" might be less "real" than physical communities (Jones, 1995), yet "these social groups have a 'real' existence for their participants, and thus have consequential effects on many aspects of behavior, including consumer behavior" (Kozinets, 1998). For this reason many researchers prefer the term "online community" to refer to such internet-based forums.

An endless number of topics, problems, products, brands, services and places are discussed in online communities, whose importance and impact is being increasingly recognized by companies, marketers and researchers. On the one hand, the dialogue in online communities reveals that one goal of consumers in joining such discussions is attempting to inform and influence fellow consumers about products, brands or services (Kozinets, 1999; Muniz & O'Quinn, 2001). On the other hand, one principal objective of market research is to identify and understand needs, wishes, experiences, motivations, attitudes, perceptions and decision-making influences of consumers towards products, brands and services. As a result, this ever growing number of consumer-driven online conversations in cyber-space, sometimes called Social Media Revolution, creates an infinite and valuable source of consumer knowledge and ideas (Bartl, Füller, Mühlbacher, & Ernst, 2012; Füller, Bartl, Ernst, & Mühlbacher, 2006; Sawhney, Verona, & Prandelli, 2005). However, without a systematic procedure to identify, collect and analyze large volumes of consumer conversations on the Internet, researchers are confronted with information overload. In this case study on the perception of mint around the world, we introduce Netnography as one powerful, innovative and systematic approach aiming to use the rich dialogue of the online community landscape for market research, marketing and new product or service development.

2 Theoretical Background of Netnography

Marketing professor Robert Kozinets introduced Netnography in 1998. The word "Netnography" is a linguistic blend of two words: "Internet" and "Ethnography". It is also known as multimedia cyber-anthropology, virtual ethnography and webnography. As defined by Kozinets, Netnography is a qualitative, interpretive research methodology that uses Internet-optimized ethnographic research techniques to study the social context in online communities. Thus, unlike ethnography, Netnography focuses only on social groups represented in the Internet in forums, blogs, chat rooms, consumer portals and user generated content platforms. Such cyber-spaces do not only provide rich data (Füller, Jawecki, & Mühlbacher, 2007; Kozinets, 1999, 2002; Lagner & Beckman, 2005; Luthje, Herstatt, & von Hippel, 2005; Muñiz & Schau, 2005; Nelson & Otnes, 2005), but due to the anonymity given in such forums, members feel free to discuss in an open, liberating way and to

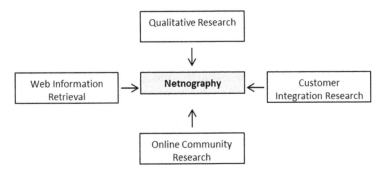

Fig. 1 Theoretical touch points of netnography

express their real thoughts in their natural language (Dholakia & Zhang, 2004; Kozinets, 2009). In addition, in contrast to ethnography, Netnography is in most cases unobtrusive and data is collected by observation only (Bartl, 2007). Hence, Netnography is an empathic way of understanding the consumer's world through the analysis of the online community dialogue.

As a complex research method Netnography spans several scientific fields. The four theoretical aspects of Netnography, as illustrated in Fig. 1, include: (1) qualitative research, (2) online community research, (3) web information retrieval and (4) customer integration research.

Netnography is classified as a **qualitative research** method, as it focuses on understanding the social context in online communities. When applied to the field of market and consumer research, its goal is to understand wishes, perceptions, attitudes, opinions and rituals of consumers in online communities. Research data for Netnography consists of online dialogue between community members. Such communication is mostly in text form and is freely available in the Internet. As a result, this data type defines "content analysis" as an adequate qualitative research methodology that can be applied in Netnography.

Netnography is clearly an **online community research** method (Kozinets, 1998, 2002), which has mainly been used in the field of online market research. To understand the significance of online community research for marketing, it is important to understand its value proposition for producers. As large pools of information and product know-how, virtual consumer communities represent an important innovation source (Bartl, Hueck, & Ruppert, 2009; Bartl, Jawecki, Stönner, & Gastes, 2011; Bilgram, Bartl, & Biel, 2011; Bilgram, Füller, Bartl, Biel, & Miertsch, 2013). Not only do they allow producers to establish dialogue and breed loyalty, but they facilitate direct and low-cost access to consumers and lead users (Belz & Baumbach, 2010). By monitoring online communities, businesses can quickly recognize trends, improve risk management, identify lead users and target groups and react to new market conditions faster.

Web information retrieval is an essential part of Netnography, as it provides the software tools to find, extract and prepare the research data (Bartl, 2007). It focuses on finding, extracting and preparing information from the Internet with state of the art software tools. In this context, it is important to point out basic similarities and differences between Netnography and Web Monitoring. Both methods are based on web information retrieval and content analysis, yet, the level of automatization, quantity of input data and quality of the results differ. Web Monitoring is a highly automatized and continuous process. Based on predefined topics, a Web Monitoring software constantly tracks and analyses online content in search for keywords to discover patterns, trends, valences, etc. Automatic web information retrieval and natural language processing are key underlying technologies of Web Monitoring. Although automatic web information retrieval offers access to large quantities of data, current development of natural language processing algorithms limits the quality of results. On the other hand, Netnography is a one-time passive methodology. Small amounts of data are processed manually but with a higher degree of quality.

Yet, can Netnography be considered a Customer Integration Method or an Open Innovation Initiative? The answer is clearly yes, Netnography can be classified as a customer integration method (Bartl et al., 2009, 2012; Piller, Vossen, & Ihl, 2012) as it establishes an active, creative and social collaboration process between producers and customers regarding new product development (Piller et al., 2012). In this context, Netnography can be classified as a "passive" co-creation method, because it mainly "listens into" the consumer dialogue. Yet, "listening into" the customer domain is one of the central modes of sharing knowledge with customers in the innovation process (Piller, Ihl, & Vossen, 2010). As a consequence, Netnography has the potential to provide the researcher or company with useful consumer insights based on data collected from the Internet, as in online communities (Kozinets, 2002) for example, which are valuable during the early stages of the innovation process (Sawhney et al., 2005). This also reflects the main idea of open innovation, to be open for information coming from outside the company (Chesbrough, 2003).

3   The Process of Netnography: The Example of "The Mint Journey"

To provide a deeper understanding of the Netnography process, the method is presented with a case study on the topic "The Mint Journey" conducted for a global supplier of fragrances, flavorings, cosmetic active ingredients, raw materials as well as functional ingredients. The company has two divisions: (1) Flavor and Nutrition and (2) Scent and Care. The division Flavor and Nutrition develops, produces and sells flavors and functional ingredients that are used in snacks, sweets, desserts, dairy products, ice cream, beverages and nutritional supplements around the world. In addition, this division has identified several core taste competences. Core competences describe specific strengths of the company, thus areas in which this company differentiates from the other global competitors and has the ability to

Fig. 2 Netnography process

deliver added value and a clear competitive advantage over their customers. It encompasses a combination of knowledge, skills and ways of working, utilized together to improve performance and deliver the required customer benefit. One of these core competencies is mint, an area where this global company is constantly seeking to (1) sustain or build a customer-perceived leadership position and (2) have a clear vision, positioning ambition, growth and profit targets. However, the company has identified needs regarding their consumer understanding of "mint". In order to sustain or build a perceived leadership position they wanted to better understand how the consumer feels about mint in general and in regards to typical mint products, such as chewing gum. For this reason, the flavor supplier decided to implement an international Netnography project seeking to gain fresh and inspiring consumer insights. However, how is mint linked to travelling and the tourism industry? The answer is simple: mint is a flavor which appears to be present in the journey of tourists from the very first moment, starting with a mint candy in the airplane to fight boredom, nausea or to avoid bad breath sitting so close to a neighbor, to a delicious exotic dish, a refreshing cocktail on the beach, or a chewing gum before kissing the holiday fling. This strong connection between tourism and mint made travelling forums and blogs an excellent source for the purpose of this project.

The mint-project covered Russian, French, Italian, English, American, German and Brazilian online communities. By applying clearly defined steps, as illustrated in Fig. 2, it is possible to select, extract, analyze and aggregate consumer statements in a systematic way in order to explore deep consumer insights and transfer them into customer-oriented product and marketing solutions.

3.1 Definition of the Research Field

Every Netnography project starts with the definition of the research questions and the research field. This includes the systematization of topics, trends, markets, brands and products of major interest, for example, by elaborating a multi-layered mind map. In this case, the overall goal of the company was to understand the:

- **Acceptance** of mint products
- **Associations** of consumers with mint products
- **Motivations** to consume mint in its different forms
- **Emotions** elicited through the consumption of mint
- **Moments** of mint consumption

- **Benefits** of consuming mint
- **Barriers** to consuming mint
- **Consumer typologies** when it comes to the consumption of mint

With the ultimate goal of identifying deep consumer insights and mint-topics that are of crucial relevance to consumers, instead of focusing on one single research question or product, the Netnography adopted a very broad approach and included various product categories (e.g. oral care, beverages, food, chewing gum and sweet confectionary) in the analysis.

3.2 Community Identification and Selection

The second step of Netnography consists in identifying online communities and other Internet sources relevant for the research, such as discussion forums, blogs, consumer portals and other user generated content platforms. The starting document for the search is the mind map containing research questions, topics and keywords from Step 1. With the help of online search engines, different search queries with keywords are implemented, resulting in a large number of results, thus web pages or platforms, whose relevance needs to be evaluated by the researcher. In order to do so, the researcher utilizes a set of **qualitative and quantitative criteria**. Qualitative criteria include topic focus, data quality, demographics, language type, interaction type and profile editing. Quantitative criteria include benchmarks such as number of messages, frequency of usage, member activity and data quantity or interaction level. The result of the selection process is generally a pool of 3–20 online sources per country, representing the main bulk of data for the following in-depth analysis. For the Mint project, a total of **781 potential online communities and blogs** dealing directly or indirectly with mint were reduced to **a total number of 102**, representing the most suitable resources for the goals of the project in the seven countries. These final communities have diverse thematic backgrounds such as beauty and care (www.beautyjunkies.de), diet (e.g. www.lowcarbfriends. com), parenting (e.g. www.cafemom.com), health (e.g. http://www. forumhealthcare.org), gardening (e.g. www.ths.gardenweb.com), questions and answers (e.g. answers.yahoo.com), food (www.egullet.org), beverages (www. bevnet.com), reviews (www.ciao.com), as well as communities focusing on women, men or teens as user groups. More interesting is the fact that many online communities and blogs focus solely on sweet confectionary and chewing gum. Examples include www.suessigkeiten-blog.de, www.candy.org, www.gumalert. com, www.candyaddict.com or www.zomgcandy.com. GumAlert is a review-blog written by two very chewing-gum-involved sisters. For them, gum is one of life's greatest little pleasures. They started GumAlert in April 2009 with the ultimate goal of getting free gum from gum companies, which actually happened sooner than they expected. The blog includes an impressive collection of honest and truthful chewing gum reviews. As a consequence, a vast expertise on mint can be found here. Similarly, travelling forums such as www.lonelyplanet.com or www. tripadvisor.com were crucial for the present project. Community members on such travelling forums and blogs do not only share their experiences and what they found special during their journey, but their posts reveal tremendous involvement with food and beverage consumption, during a very intensive time full of new impressions and constant encounters with new products, which ultimately represent new ideas and inspiration for companies. In addition, they share their experience with common products (e.g. chewing gum or tea) in different parts of the world, make product-relevant comparisons and even discuss whether these products would be successful in their own country as well.

3.3   Community Observation and Data Collection

In the third step the researcher immerses herself into the selected communities and observes them with the aim of understanding their social context. This is a critical aspect of a Netnography project. According to Kozinets, just as in ethnographic studies, a researcher won't be able to extract consumer insights successfully, without a considerable understanding of the culture, discourse and interactions of a specific community and its social context. Therefore, observation includes extensive search, reading and selection of discussions and messages, which deliver answers to the research questions. Note that this approach represents an unobtrusive strategy to study the behavior of the consumer in the natural context of the community and is therefore free from bias, which may arise through the involvement of the researcher, resulting in an unwanted experimental research setting. Although qualitative data analysis software helps to file data, organize data and facilitate interpretation, to the authors' knowledge no software tools or semantic algorithms exist yet, which can reliably identify and qualitatively interpret statements relevant for the research questions stated. Therefore, the data retrieval itself is carried out manually. In the case of the Mint Netnography a total of **3388 consumer posts** were incorporated into the analysis.

Once selected data have been downloaded, the qualitative context analysis follows. In this phase the researcher analyzes data, in order to discover patterns and relationships, similarities and differences within and across the collected online consumer statements. Although software-supported, qualitative content analysis still requires a lot of manual work. The researcher tags the different information chunks of all the selected consumer posts with the help of a coding system. This system is built by the researcher combining an inductive (evolutionary) as well as a deductive (predefined) approach. At the same time, the researcher records her own observations, thoughts, peculiarities and distinctive features. During the Mint Netnography, a total of **387 codes were utilized for the detailed analysis** of the 3388 selected consumer posts.

3.4   Data Analysis and Aggregation of Consumer Insights

After the content analysis has been concluded, a crucial step follows: The interpretation with regards to research questions and the aggregation into consumer insights. The consumer insights developed in this study are presented in point 4.

Netnography usually does not end with the generation of consumer insights. A major challenge is to transfer them into marketable solutions or at least initial ideas. Consumer insights can enable both incremental and radical innovations. The uniqueness and success of derived solutions depends on the alignment between the consumer insights and solution features. As with any creative process, the translation of insights into solutions does not necessarily follow a predefined process. Hence, in the final step of the research, netnographers are encouraged to collaborate closely with product developers and marketing teams to create deliverables.

3.5   Exemplary Minty Findings

The Mint Netnography delivered global consumer insights, thus deep consumer understandings, which were relevant for all analyzed countries, as well as regional ones, referring to specific aspects which were only relevant for a specific country. Such insights reflect the global mobility of consumers today. For example, the Netnography showed that a Mojito is a very popular way to consume mint in Germany. A Mojito induces vacation feelings in community members, accompanied by images of summer, the sun and the beach. As a result, community members feel relaxed and are put in a good mood every time they have a Mojito (e.g. as a beverage, but also as a flavor in tobacco). A similar effect was observed in the consumption of the trendy beverage called Hugo. This drink, made of elderflowers, mint, lime and Prosecco, is originally from South Tyrol. The study showed that Hugo was already replacing the popular aperitif Aperol Spritz and was becoming more and more popular throughout Germany.

Interestingly, the Russian consumer online dialogue revealed that the flavor of mint in the form of candies or chewing gum was and still is a popular and traditional remedy against nausea and sickness, especially in the context of travelling. In addition, it represents an alternative to modern drugs against travel-sickness and ears popping on flights. Therefore, it seems that in Russia mint chewing gum, and especially mint candy, is ideal companions for travelers who suffer from travelling nausea. Currently, airlines' "take-off" sweets are frequently citrus flavored; however, community members' statements revealed the significant potential of mint "take-off" confectionary:

> Oh, I am experienced in this. First of all, yes, mint candies often help; they were even handed out in the airplanes; I remember this, although it was in the year 2005. No wonder that they are called "take-off" bonbons. (Jenser)

On the other hand, the analysis landscape revealed *la delicatezza italiana e la lé gèreté française* as well. In contrast to English community members, the French and Italians appreciate delicate, polite, pleasant and natural mint flavors or scents. These consumers do love mint, but according to them, it should not be too strong, too present, aggressive or synthetic. They welcome delicate flavors in toothpaste, chewing gum and candy, and encourage a gentle touch of mint in perfumes, diverse beauty and care products, and food (e.g. pasta, muffins, mousse or meat).

Moreover, our analysis revealed that community members from different countries consider mint in its various forms (e.g. flavour and scent) and products (e.g. toothpaste, chewing gum, shower gel, mouthwash) to be the ideal day-starter. In mint they see an energy-boosting motor, which helps them confront and "kickstart" the day in the morning. But what do consumers exactly mean by "kickstart"?

> The most important thing for me by doing this is that I really have a very fresh, in this case also minty taste in my mouth—it feels good and helps to remove any potential remaining sleepiness in the morning. (dik1609)

> The essential oil of mint is an oil of middle fugacity. It refreshes cools and revitalizes. The aroma of mint essential oil can tone up the body, relieve stress and recharge it with energy. The smell of peppermint helps to cheer up, buck up and continue working. (Vikki V)

Such invigorating, revitalizing or rejuvenating effects of mint play a major role on summer vacations. According to community members, during hot days, mint creams relieve fatigue in their legs and fill them with vitality. Mint shower gels are nearly as refreshing as an ice bath and help consumers feel more dynamic, especially after a long night of partying. Mint lemonade, mint water and mint liquor chase the heat away and act as perfect thirst quenchers; even the mint essential oil is more refreshing than an ice-cream when sprayed together with water.

4 Key Challenges for the Future

Along the case study conducted for the flavor supplier, Netnography is shown to be a successful tool for gathering unfiltered and unbiased deep consumer insights on a variety of topics on a global level, as well as on a country specific level. To create customer and brand related concepts the flavor company is seeking relevant consumer insights and trends, in order to deliver the relevant flavor solution as a key to market success. According to the company, consumer insights from the Mint Netnography are more than relevant to its customers and add value to brand related classical qualitative consumer research methodologies. Hereby, the main advantage of Netnography is definitely the quality of the results, while the disadvantage may be the small data sample and the very intensive and time-consuming manual work. The opposite is true for quantitative Web Monitoring approaches that enable automatization, high processing speed and the large amount of data included in the research. Yet, the lack of richness in the results is undeniable.

Nowadays market research institutes and IT companies offer web monitoring services, crawling the Internet in search of relevant content to analyze it quantitatively and analyze it via frequency counting and natural language processing algorithms. However, the problem lies in the generated results of such automated tools. The underlying original statements, thus the "voice of the customer", either disappear or are not aggregated in a proper manner to facilitate managers' decision making in the field of innovation. In fact, there is no software or machine possessing the same intelligence and experience as well-trained researchers, who are capable of learning the language of the selected communities, read between the lines, understand ironic or sarcastic posts or automatically identify, select and analyze relevant statements. For this reason, today Netnography combines qualitative research with advantages of quantitative methodologies by replacing previously manually performed activities through automatized IT solutions. However, the Netnography approach will always rely for the most part on the capabilities of the researcher. Therefore, Netnography does not aim to fully automatize the process in the future, but rather maintain and emphasize the qualitative and exploratory nature of the method.

Moreover, there is little doubt that online has become the "new black" in market research. Only the possibility to have direct access to data, without having to participate and to travel, makes standard offline data collection methods, such as ethnography or face-to-face interviews, dispensable or at least inconvenient for many researchers. On this account, Netnography could play a valuable role in enhancing our understanding of rapidly changing tourist markets and the growth of new markets (Wu & Pearce, 2013). Still, many consumer insights managers ask themselves: How real is virtual and might virtual be the "new real" or why listen to online conversations? The answer is simple: online enables conversations that were not possible before (Levine, 2001) and provides researchers with access to people who were otherwise difficult to reach. In addition, the anonymous nature of most online interactions might open up netizens and their expressions more, in the absence of an obtrusive researcher, allowing for an empathic and unbiased understanding of the consumer and her needs. In addition, Netnography allows for (1) multi-faceted insights and supplementary perspectives based on a large group of different individuals rather than a few dominant opinion leaders (e.g. focus groups), (2) reflected and detailed postings due to the asynchrony of online interaction and the "natural" research environment, (3) multiple extensive forms of self-expression through social media features and (4) practicality of getting or deepening additional information spontaneously or ad hoc. However, netnographic research has its shortcomings as well. Often the researcher won't be able to verify or even identify important information such as age, place of residence or income, which may be determining aspects when it comes to travelling. In addition, some platforms might be manipulated or managed by corporations in a manner that enables a desired business image, so that negative customer reviews, for instance, are deleted by website administrators (Mkono, 2012). In such cases, the experience of the researcher with online dialogues and social media landscapes will be decisive in the interpretation of the data.

5   Key Conclusions and Learning Outcomes for the Tourism Industry

- Netnography can be classified as a passive customer integration method, as it establishes an active, creative and social collaboration process between companies and customers regarding new product/service development.
- "Online ethnography" provides researchers with access to conversations that were not possible before and to target-groups who were otherwise difficult to reach.
- Netnography allows for multi-faceted insights and supplementary perspectives based on a large group of different individuals.
- Reflected and detailed postings due to the asynchrony of online interaction and the "natural" research environment are Netnography's key tools.
- The Netnography approach will always rely for the most part on the capabilities and experience of the researcher.
- Even if growth in the emergence of automated, mostly quantitated web information retrieval technologies can be observed, Netnography will emphasize its qualitative and exploratory nature.
- Analogous to other sectors, enormous quantities of data pertaining to consumer experiences, perceptions, problems and intentions to travel in relation to tourism can be retrieved and analyzed systematically with the aid of Netnography.
- Netnography may play a valuable role in enhancing the understanding of a rapidly growing and changing tourist market.
- It can be expected that more tourism researchers will adopt online-based fieldwork as the number of online postings relating to travelling experiences continues to grow.
- "The Mint Journey" project shows that travelling forums and blogs may be a very valuable source of consumer dialogue on a variety of consumer goods. Netizens of these online communities share what they take on their trip (e.g. electronic goods, music, books, clothes or food), their intense time with these objects and their experience with foreign products in different countries.

Acknowledgements The present work benefited from the input of Dr. Anne Grünhagen, who provided very valuable comments and ideas to the writing but especially to the undertaking of the project summarized here. Moreover, the authors wish to thank Prof. Dr. Jutta Roosen, Head of the Department of Marketing and Consumer Research at the Technical University of Munich, for her valuable support in the preparation of the present paper.

References

Bartl, M. (2007). Netnography – Einblicke in die Welt der Kunden, Planung und Analyse. *Planung & Analyse, 5*, 83–87.

Bartl, M., Füller, J., Mühlbacher, H., & Ernst, A. (2012). Manager's perspective on virtual customer integration for new product development. *Journal of Product Innovation Management, 29*, 1031–1046.

Bartl, M., Hueck, S., & Ruppert, S. (2009). Netnography research – community insights in the cosmetics industry. In *ESOMAR consumer insights conference*, Dubai.

Bartl, M., Jawecki, G., Stönner, J. H., & Gastes, D. (2011). Review of a decade of netnography research. In *ESOMAR live conference papers*, Miami.

Belz, F. M., & Baumbach, W. (2010). Netnography as a method of lead user identification. *Creativity and Innovation Management, 19*, 304–313.

Bilgram, V., Bartl, M., & Biel, S. (2011). Getting closer to the consumer – How Nivea co-creates new products. *Marketing Review St Gallen, 1*, 34–40.

Bilgram, V., Füller, J., Bartl, M., Biel, S., & Miertsch, H. (2013). Eine Allianz gegen Flecken. *Harvard Business Manager, 3*, 63–68.

Chesbrough, H. (2003). The era of open innovation. *MIT Sloan Management Review, 44*, 35–41.

Dholakia, N., & Zhang, D. (2004). Online qualitative research in the age of E-commerce – Data sources and approaches. *Qualitative Market, Media and Opinion Research, 5*, 1–9.

Füller, J., Bartl, M., Ernst, H., & Mühlbacher, H. (2006). Community based innovation – How to integrate members of virtual communities into new product development. *Electronic Commerce Research Journal, 6*, 57–73.

Füller, J., Jawecki, G., & Mühlbacher, H. (2007). Innovation creation by online basketball communities. *Journal of Business Research, 60*, 60–71.

Jones, S. G. (1995). Understanding community in the information age. In S. G. Jones (Ed.), *Cybersociety: Computer-mediated communication and community* (pp. 10–35). Thousand Oaks, CA: Sage.

Kozinets, R. (1998). On netnography – Initial reflections on consumer research investigations of cyberculture. *Advances in Consumer Research, 25*, 366–371.

Kozinets, R. (1999). E-tribalized marketing? – The strategic implications of virtual communities of consumption. *European Management Journal, 17*, 252–264.

Kozinets, R. (2002). The field behind the screen – Using netnography for marketing research in online communications. *Journal of Marketing Research, 39*, 61–72.

Kozinets, R. (2009). *Netnography: Doing ethnographic research online*. Thousand Oaks, CA: Sage.

Lagner, R., & Beckman, S. C. (2005). Sensitive research topics – Netnography revisited. *Qualitative Market Research: An International Journal, 8*, 189–203.

Levine, R. (2001). *The Cluetrain Manifesto: The end of business as usual*. Cambridge: Perseus.

Luthje, C., Herstatt, C., & von Hippel, E. (2005). User-innovators and "local" information – The case of mountain biking. *Research Policy, 34*, 951–965.

Mkono, M. (2012). Netnographic tourist research: The internet as a virtual fieldwork site. *Tourism Analysis, 17*, 553–555.

Muniz, A. M., & O'Quinn, T. (2001). Brand community. *Journal of Consumer Research, 27*, 412–432.

Muñiz, A. M. J., & Schau, H. J. (2005). Religiosity in the abandoned apple Newton brand community. *Journal of Consumer Research, 31*, 737–747.

Nelson, M. R., & Otnes, C. C. (2005). Exploring cross cultural ambivalence – A netnography of intercultural wedding message boards. *Journal of Business Research, 58*, 89–95.

Piller, F., Ihl, C., & Vossen, A. (2010). A typology of customer co-creation in the innovation process, SSRN eLibrary.

Piller, F., Vossen, A., & Ihl, C. (2012). From social media to social product development – The impact of social media on co-creation of innovation. *Die Unternehmung, 65*, 7–27.

Rheingold, H. (Ed.). (1993). *The virtual community – Homesteading on the electronic frontier*. Reading, MA: Addison-Wesley.

Sawhney, M., Verona, G., & Prandelli, E. (2005). Collaborating to create – The internet as a platform for customer engagement in product innovation. *Journal of Interactive Marketing, 19*, 4–17.

Wu, M.-Y., & Pearce, P. L. (2013). Appraising netnography: Towards insights about new markets in the digital tourist era. *Current Issues in Tourism, 17*(5), 463–474.

Prospects of Technology-Enhanced Social Media Analysis for Open Innovation in the Leisure Industries

Markus Lassnig, Mark Markus, Robert Eckhoff, and Kathrin Parson

Learning Objectives

- Appreciate the relevance of online communities for open innovation.
- Understand different approaches for the analysis of social media for innovation purposes.
- Demonstrate how the concept of "Innovation Signals" has been applied in the leisure industry.
- Identify the challenges of an interdisciplinary concept of social media analysis.

1 Introduction

The growth, significance and future potential of social media are considerable. While many companies already use the social web for public relations and marketing purposes, according to current market studies, there is a huge untapped potential for utilising social media for strategic innovation purposes (cf. CFO Innovation Asia, 2010; Eich, 2009; HBR, 2010). According to a survey made by the Harvard Business Review Analytic Services (2010), many organisations seem more focused on "making noise" in social media than in understanding and participating in the ongoing conversations about them and their services/products. Half of the companies that use social media regard the stronger awareness of the organisation and its products and services as the major benefit. On the other hand, an in-depth analysis and understanding of social media content and its transformation into business

M. Lassnig (✉) • M. Markus • R. Eckhoff • K. Parson, M.A.
Salzburg Research Forschungsgesellschaft mbH, Salzburg, Austria
e-mail: Markus.Lassnig@salzburgresearch.at; Mark.Markus@salzburgresearch.at;
Robert.Eckhoff@salzburgresearch.at; Kathrin.Parson@salzburgresearch.at

© Springer-Verlag Berlin Heidelberg 2016
R. Egger et al. (eds.), *Open Tourism*, Tourism on the Verge,
DOI 10.1007/978-3-642-54089-9_14

opportunities, innovation chances and novel products and services are still at their infancy.

The following chapters will deal with the questions what does it mean to use social media for open innovation activities and how can this be done? Companies in tourism and leisure as well as in other industries search for ways to unlock the strategic innovation potential of social media. For this purpose, they can pursue different strategies—a technology-focused and a social-scientifically driven one— each of which is associated with particular strengths and weaknesses. This article will explain both strategies and introduce a new, complementary concept to combine the two strategies and discuss emerging challenges.

2   The Relevance of Online Communities in the Early Phase of Innovation

Successful product and service innovation is no more a purely product or process-driven technical question that can be solved by companies internally. Nonetheless, surveys confirm that enterprises tend to be enamoured into their products and technologies neglecting the importance of environmental factors for the success of innovations. In fact, an insufficient analysis of markets and customers very often constitutes the main reason for failed innovations (Cooper, 2002; Franke, 2008).

An example from the ski industry will illustrate that: For many years, all the big producing companies of skis so strongly concentrated on the optimisation of their existing products in their daily business and this lead to a severe constraint in the detection of chances for innovations that derived out of new developments in their business environment and markets. In the beginning, most companies missed the development of twin-tip skis, where—different to classical Alpine skis—the anterior end as well as the back end of the skis are bent up. At the same time, the demand for such an alternative form of skis had become apparent in diverse online communities, where the "evangelists" of a new skiing culture described in detail how they bent up the back end of their skis by themselves in order to be able to ski rearwards and perform tricks on the piste. An analysis of online communities, e.g. by means of web monitoring, might have detected this special demand and associated opportunities for innovations in time.

Successful innovation management is increasingly a question of bringing products and services in line with environmental developments. This is especially true since the complexity of markets and products is rising and values and desires in demands are changing sustainably. Here, the analysis of the social web can help. Innovation signals like e.g. consumer opinions and desires, latent demands, changed values, ideas for products and critique in services very early emerge in online communities. Systematic social media monitoring allows companies to detect openly communicated as well as latent customer demands, to identify influential opinion leaders and to better assess emerging trends and market developments. In this way, the progress of trends can be better tracked and relevant data for the assessment of issues and ideas can be collected in order to be able to make respective strategic and operative decisions at an early stage. This gives enterprises the opportunity to expand their market position by developing products and services closer to customer needs and react to important developments earlier than their competitors (Grothe & Maisch, 2010).

3 Approaches for the Analysis of Social Media for Innovation Purposes

3.1 Two Common Analytical Approaches

Social web analysis currently takes place mainly along two different streams: (1) the partially or fully automated, technical approach (social media mining and monitoring) and (2) the manual, socio-scientific approach (content analysis, e.g. netnography).

The automated approach is used to browse unstructured online texts by means of computer linguistics (natural language processing). Vast amounts of unstructured information are analysed automatically via the use of algorithms, semantic processing, statistics and grammatical rules. A substantial drawback of the quantitative, computer linguistics based approach, however, is the lack of in-depth insight. In the context of usually more complex innovation projects it is often described as not being precise enough and failing to accommodate for the structure and the problems of the text (Kilzer, 2012).

The socio-scientific approach applies the method of content analysis. The netnography method—a modified form of ethnography developed by Kozinets and used for analysing online communities—has achieved wide popularity (Kozinets, 2002). The study focus of it are not the individuals themselves but their interaction in the context of the internet. And herein lies the greatest advantage of this method for innovation research: the possibility to obtain the necessary in-depth analysis which can later be translated into product and service innovations. The method however is not very efficient as the researchers need to screen, code and interpret (with the help of software assisted procedures) all posts in online communities themselves. The consequence is an enormous amount of time required for the process as well as a strong focus on a specific field of study and a limited number of posts and sources.

3.2 A Complementary Approach for the Analysis of Social Media for Innovation Purposes

Our concept called "Innovation Signals" makes the next step in the exploitation of user-generated content for strategic innovation purposes by combining quantitative

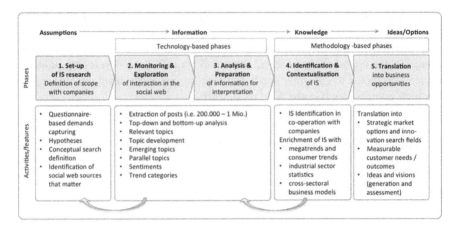

Fig. 1 Innovation signals research process—how does it work?

and qualitative methods. The Innovation Signals (IS) research approach does not rely on technology alone (phases 2 and 3 in Fig. 1), but unfolds in the development of social media mining technology in unique combination with interpretative methodology development (phases 4 and 5). While there are many social media mining technology providers on the market focusing on detection and monitoring, there are currently no approaches focusing on contextualisation and translation of information into business opportunities. The goal is to automatically detect innovation signals in the social web and to associate the information with relevant industry statistics and trends. The results are then interpreted through the raster of innovation theory and are finally translated into business opportunities and ideas. The subsequent diagram depicts the different phases and the overall structure of the Innovation Signals research process that will be described in more detail below.

Phase 1—The set-up of Innovation Signals research mimics the traditional research design of empirical social science. The main goal is to formulate research hypotheses and define conceptual search terms, which contain between 20 and 50 English and German keywords. Then, 40–50 publicly accessible social web sources (forums, communities, blogs, newsgroups) are identified and quickly assessed, according to a catalogue of criteria (e.g. quality of contents, length of contributions, intensity of contribution etc.).

Phase 2 and 3—Detection and monitoring of information and opinions in the social web: This social media mining-based technology provides automatic detection of relevant keywords and topics of interest in sources selected before. It first extracts a large amount of user posts (e.g. 100,000 posts) and then the tool—accessible via a web front-end—automatically detects emerging keywords, topics and sentiments from compiled discussions and user's publicly available opinions. The Innovation Signals technology provides answers to the questions in the context of product development and trend detection such as: How do users talk about existing products? What are critical issues? What issues are discussed very intensively? What are emerging topics? How do topics change over time? The technology enables experts to analyse and interpret detected innovation signals in an easy and intuitive way and also to save the most important posts for additional manual analysis and coding.

Phase 4—Identification and contextualisation of innovation signals: The automated analysis of textual content enables an efficient information processing, but the machine-processed information still remains ambiguous. In order to enable effective research, the interactions in the social web must be structured additionally and analysed with social scientific methodology. This means to associate user generated content with relevant statistics, trends and theories to amplify the meaning of the information and to understand the consumers' conversations better and in a broader context.

Phase 5—Translation into business opportunities: This phase of the research process utilises user generated content (in close co-operation with customers/companies) as an additional information source for strategic decision making with regard to the kind of innovation (product, process, business models, strategic innovation fields) to be pursued in order to determine the focus of the product innovation and market strategies and/or to detect new markets and new ideas.

4 Application in the Ski Industry

The business of producing skis is characterised by an intense cut-throat competition and an extremely high pressure to innovate. For this reason, one of the leading ski manufacturers decided to investigate customer needs more accurately and source them from online communities as a base for developing new marketable ideas. Internally, the company had limited experience with the use of social media in innovation management. The ski manufacturer commissioned Salzburg Research, a research institute specializing in innovation management and social web analysis, to support their early innovation phase. Part of the mission was to identify possible areas of innovation and new customer needs using the social web.

In a kick-off workshop with the company, we identified the relevant search fields, i.e. the areas in which to look for innovative customer needs and solutions. The challenge here was to find a good balance between defining the search fields and the consequent search concepts in a way sufficiently focused to avoid fuzzy results and providing a definition broad enough to include important yet silent innovation signals. We selected 24 specific ski forums derived from the objectives of the ski manufacturer, from which we extracted a total of 170,000 posts.

In analysing these sources, we used both a top-down approach, searching for pre-defined keywords and a bottom-up approach, identifying new topics that are frequently discussed by users in the communities. In the targeted ski forums, the most frequent posts were related to skiing equipment, followed by discussions on driving technique, safety, etc. Emerging topics included new trends such as the increased use of photo and video while skiing or discussions about special needs of older skiers. Accordingly, we found a large number of posts that dealt with joint-

Fig. 2 Frequencies of important key words associated with the megatrend ecology

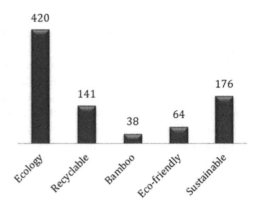

gentle driving style, joint-friendly ski or special characteristics that should be considered when designing ski for skiers above 50 years. In total, we selected over 300 authentic user posts that provided valuable ideas and information to specific product improvements and other innovations. We translated these posts into 61 customer need statements (Ulwick, 2005), which we reviewed and prioritised in a customer survey. Among the top ten customer needs were joint-friendly skis, eco-friendly ski manufacturing, more grip on ice, simple handling, etc.

For each identified customer need and the related topics, we created trend analyses, which visualised the customer needs underlying the megatrend and their development over time (see Fig. 3). We defined e.g. the megatrend ecology in conjunction with ski-specific keywords (see Fig. 2) and calculated the strength of the trend towards ecology from the sum of the frequencies of these ski-related keywords.

While the trend strength provides a rough estimate of the "buzz" on the internet, i.e. the intensity of the megatrend, concrete posts allow to identify related users' needs. For instance, an exemplary user post on eco-friendly ski wax may read as follows: "I was placing an off-season order on REI.com and saw that they had a ski wax brand I'd never heard of called Ethica. Instead of using petroleum base, Teflon, or the like, they use vegetable-based glycerides and natural polymers and subscribe to the Twelve Principles of green Chemistry...". Hence, we found eco-friendly ski wax or an environmentally sound manufacturing process of skis are increasingly often discussed in online communities. Both represent a growing customer need related to the ecology megatrend that we depicted quantitatively using our trend analysis (Fig. 3). Thus, in skiing the importance of ecology seems to have increased, especially since 2006. Today, after a peak in 2010 it is slightly decreasing but still on a relatively high level.

Another example of the contextualisation of the results is the sentiment analysis, i.e. the analysis of the affective tone of the posts. For this purpose we use word lists that assign sentiment values to common words in a certain language, which acts as foundation for the sentiment values of a post. This analysis provides e.g. a

Fig. 3 Analysis of the megatrend ecology in the ski industry. The high volatility of the online activities are due to the seasonality of winter sports (the highest value of the specified period is defined as 100 %)

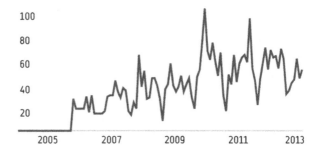

comparison, representing the number of positive and negative sentiments associated with various ski manufacturers. In addition, customer associations with a brand, for example with words such as 'fun' or 'performance' can be compared. As a result, the company gains a much broader view over potential innovation fields that are prioritised and put into the context of larger societal trends.

In the current case, this helped the ski producer to identify future strategic innovation projects and reduce the error rate of their innovations (for a definition of innovation error rate see Christensen, 1997).

5 Key Challenges for the Future

The presented complementary approach of Innovation Signals is characterized by both a significant depth of information compared to the solely IT-based approaches as well as a much higher level of efficiency with respect to the manual socio-scientific methods such as content analysis and netnography. It provides the necessary information quality required for innovation purposes on the one hand and enables a continuous, automated monitoring and analysis of the social web on the other hand. Indeed, this is very important, since a permanent screening of innovation signals from the social web represents a prerequisite to systematic and continuous innovation management.

In this way, the concept of Innovation Signals unites the strengths of both the socio-scientific and the IT-based approaches. Crossing interdisciplinary boundaries and establishing a common language between technological development and socio-scientific research have been great challenges in the technical and sociological conceptualisation and implementation of Innovation Signals. The challenge in this process combining different disciplines is to overcome disciplinary boundaries and jargons and understand the assumptions in each scientific discipline, valuing different outcomes as well as discussing research problems from different perspectives.

Applying Innovation Signals in the ski industry has revealed further room for improvement. It has become evident that the complementary approach still needs to be revised and refined both on the sociological as well as on the technological side.

On the technical side some parts of the sentiment analysis need to be improved and enhancements in the front- as well as in the back-end (e.g. accelerating the process of extracting posts from forums and other online communities) need to be pursued. On the sociological side some methodological components (e.g. the content-analysis based coding) need to be more systematised and standardised. Translating some of these socio-scientific methodological challenges into technical solutions will again require further interdisciplinary co-ordination work and synchronisation. Successful synchronisation between social and computer scientists will remain a key challenge for the future.

Further challenges are based on the practical experiences and applications of Innovation Signals in the business and market environment.

A new product progresses through a sequence of various stages beginning with development, introduction into the market and then turning to growth, maturity and decline. Regarding the different stages of the product lifecycle, Innovation Signals is located between the development and market introduction phases. As Innovation Signals has already been successfully applied in the ski industry we have gained a deeper understanding of customers' needs. A further challenge for the future is to revise and adjust certain methodological components of Innovation Signals to better fulfil the customer's expectations and to deliver more added value. Companies applying Innovation Signals do not only want to receive objective data, which are analysed and visualised. The data need to be contextualised, interpreted and ideally connected with the companies' strategic goals. Therefore a key challenge for the future will be to focus on better integrating Innovation Signals into a comprehensive innovation strategy consulting process.

In addition, it will be essential to develop adequate marketing strategies and differentiate the initial Innovation Signals product into a basic and a premium product version, which places an even stronger emphasis on the attainable information quality and hence the socio-scientific aspect of Innovation Signals.

6   Key Conclusions and Learning Outcomes for the Tourism and Leisure Industries

- Across different sectors of the economy, there is a huge potential for utilising social media for innovation purposes. This is especially true for the tourism and leisure industries, where social media can provide a vast amount of relevant information.
- There are different approaches for the analysis of social media for innovation purposes: A primarily technical approach (social media mining and monitoring), a manual, socio-scientific approach (e.g. netnography) and a complementary approach as presented in the concept of "Innovation Signals": This approach unites the strengths of both the IT-based and the socio-scientific approaches. It provides the necessary information quality required for strategic innovation

activities on the one hand and enables a continuous, automated monitoring and analysis of the social web on the other hand. In fact, it represents best practice in interdisciplinary cooperation and synchronisation.

- Future challenges lie in further refining and revising technological and sociological aspects of Innovation Signals: (i) technological: further improvement of the sentiment-analysis, enhancements in back- and front-end functionalities and (ii) sociological: systemising the coding process. Furthermore, it is highly important to integrate Innovation Signals into a comprehensive innovation strategy consulting process to generate more added value to innovation activities of companies.

References

CFO Innovation Asia. (2010). *Social media's potential to impact bottom line largely untapped.* http://www.cfoinnovation.com/content/social-medias-potential-impact-bottom-line-largely-untapped

Christensen, C. M. (1997). *The innovator's Dilemma. When new technologies cause great firms to fail.* Harvard: Collins Business Essentials.

Cooper, R. G. (2002). *Top oder Flop in der Produktentwicklung. Erfolgsstrategien: Von der Idee zum Launch.* Weinheim: Wiley.

Eich, D. (2009). *Rapid innovation: The potential to utilize social media and user generated content to create strategic competitive advantage, differentiation and elite brand experiences.* http://www.brainreactions.com/rapid-innovation-the-potential-to-utilize-social-media-and-user-generated-content-to-create-strategic-competitive-advantage-differentiation-and-elite-brand-experiences.html

Franke, N. (2008). User Innovation – Anforderungen und Chancen für Unternehmen. In *Handout of the innovations symposium 08*, 29th October 2008. Salzburg University of Applied Sciences.

Grothe, M., & Maisch, B. (2010). Potenziale des online-trend-monitorings. In P. Brauckmann (Ed.), *Web-monitoring. Gewinnung und Analyse von Daten über das Kommunikationsverhalten im Internet* (pp. 131–156). Konstanz: UVK Verlagsgesellschaft.

HBR, Harvard Business Review Analytic Services. (2010). *The new conversation: Taking social media from talk to action.* http://www.sas.com/resources/whitepaper/wp_23348.pdf

Kilzer, F.-J. (2012). Social-media-analyse. In P. Wippermann & J. Krüger (Eds.), *Werte-index 2012* (pp. 136–137). Hamburg: New Business Verlag.

Kozinets, R. V. (2002). The field behind the screen: Using netnography for marketing research in online communities. *Journal of Marketing Research, 39*, 61–72.

Ulwick, A. (2005). *What customers want: Using outcome driven innovation to create breakthrough products and services.* New York: McGraw Hill.

Review Platforms in Destinations and Hospitality

Barbara Gligorijevic

Learning Objectives

- To analyse four social media platforms with a specific focus on the travel, tourism and hospitality industries: TripAdvisor, IgoUgo, Zagat and Thorn Tree—Lonely Planet, identify their *modi operandi* and unique selling propositions.
- To understand issues related to marketing practices and how companies could harness the power of user-generated content (UGC), also known as electronic 'word-of-mouth' (eWOM), to enhance their brand equity.
- To gain insights about marketing communication opportunities that social media provides: for travellers and patrons to become informed, create content and provide information—assisting others in making informed decisions, hence creating an environment within which user-generated content and marketing-generated content (MGC) are complementary.
- To identify methods how companies in the tourism sector can successfully incorporate social media, as part of the promotional mix for their products and services.

1   Introduction to User Created Reviews

In the tourism and hospitality industries, new ways have emerged as to how and where consumers look for recommendations and product reviews. Travellers have become increasingly independent from third party service providers and more self-reliant in organising their trips and leisure time (Buhalis & Law, 2008; Jacobsen &

B. Gligorijevic (✉)
Queensland University of Technology, Brisbane, QLD, Australia
e-mail: barbara.gligorijevic@qut.edu.au

© Springer-Verlag Berlin Heidelberg 2016
R. Egger et al. (eds.), *Open Tourism*, Tourism on the Verge,
DOI 10.1007/978-3-642-54089-9_15

245

Munar, 2012). Beyond the advancements of ICT and the strong migration of consumers to online booking and reviewing websites, the most recent wave of change was driven by the increasing popularity of social networking websites (Buhalis, 1998; Dellarocas, 2003; Grissemann & Stokburger-Sauer, 2012; Kang & Schuett, 2013; Li, Li, & Hudson, 2013) demonstrating the true meaning of social media—in this case, online collaboration and travel-experience-sharing among consumers.

The inclusion of social media into the promotional mix has significantly changed how companies communicate with their customers, but, more importantly, how customers publicly express their opinions, level of satisfaction or review the quality of delivered services (Leung, Law, van Hoof, & Buhalis, 2013; Li et al., 2013; Mangold & Faulds, 2009). This marketing tool has become such an important part of promotional activities that is difficult to imagine an enterprise that is not utilising online user-created reviews, forums, blogs, social networking or micro-blogging platforms as part of its marketing strategy. This is even more so in industries such as tourism and hospitality, where quality of service is measured by personal experience and relies heavily on electronic word-of-mouth recommendations (Au, Law, & Buhalis, 2010; Cooper & Hall, 2008; Dellarocas, 2003; Hennig-Thurau, Gwinner, Walsh, & Gremler, 2004; Jiang, Gretzel, & Law, 2010; Papathanassis & Knolle, 2011; Steffes & Burgees, 2009).

Post-trip evaluations and travellers' reviews, in the form of user-generated content (UGC), have created a parallel, and rather effective, assessment system in comparison to the more traditional classifications, such as hotels' or restaurants' star ratings in travel guidebooks. The latter have been known to be disputed for their accuracy and devaluation of content (Gligorijevic & Bruns, 2010; Norum, 2008; Smith, Menon, & Sivakumar, 2005). The use of social media to organise tourist trips is found to be greatly beneficial for travellers; preparing them for their adventures by providing "better knowledge of destination, cost savings, belonging to groups with similar interests, and fun using the tools" (Para-López, Bulchand-Gidumal, Gutierrez-Taño, & Díaz-Armas, 2011). This type of evaluation of products and services is an insightful and simple way for travellers and patrons to understand what to expect when arriving at an establishment for the first time. When written by non-professionals that have a first-hand experience of a destination with a service provider or local business, reviews disseminated via online word-of-mouth recommendations have proven to be more effective in assisting first time visitors, customers or patrons in making informed decisions (Gligorijevic & Bruns, 2010). The specifics of this type of electronic word-of-mouth marketing suggest that interpersonal influence is achieved on a large scale and is a cost-effective marketing tool in tourism and hospitality (Dwyer, 2007; Litvin, Goldsmith, & Pan, 2008).

Electronic word-of-mouth communication, or an informal exchange of information among peers about products and services, "in which the sources are considerate [sic] independent of commercial influence" (Litvin et al., 2008), is found to be a widely available, influential, descriptive, useful, personalised and trustworthy type of online content. As such, it is a great supplement to marketing-generated content

(MGC), which is often perceived to be biased, and as favouring certain products and brands (Brown, Broderick, & Lee, 2007; Dellarocas, 2003; Hennig-Thurau & Walsh, 2003; Jumin, Park, & Ingoo, 2011; Park, Lee, & Han, 2007). In that context, the term 'electronic word-of-mouth' is used here to describe any type of online content, including but not limited to; reviews, ratings, recommendations, information, suggestions, advice and any other type of assistance offered and generated by fellow travellers and patrons featuring their personal experiences and opinions, yet not under the control or influence of companies or brand owners.

The practice of electronic word-of-mouth exchange, or the posting and reading of user-created travel reviews, ratings and recommendations, and its impact on travel operators' brand equity will be explored in more detail throughout this case study. In this book the three stages of crowdsourcing practices are defined as informing, creating and providing. This particular case study focuses on the fundamental aspect of user-generated content—informing. In every information search, the 'informing' part is the crucial stage of the process (during which information is collected and analysed) because it provides the data on which purchasing decisions are based. Accordingly, this case study is focused on websites that provide information generated by users, but are utilised by businesses to inform the general public and potential customers, and to promote their products and services.

To best describe why reviewing platforms have proven to be not only opinion boards (electronic message boards), but useful travel and hospitality experience advisories that facilitate the exchange of electronic word-of-mouth information, four websites will be reviewed. They each have different business models. Some of these websites are commercial entities that harvest UGC to obtain visits and bookings, others have adopted more of a personalised approach, offering specific travel experiences and unique advertising environments for travel operators. This case study depicts how various companies, some successfully and some less effectively, have combined social media technologies and consumer-created online reviews, and utilised them as a unique selling proposition for the company that owns the reviewing platform.

2   Reviewing Platforms

Customer reviews of travel and tourism have proven to be one of the most successful crowdsourcing practices across service industries (Jacobsen & Munar, 2012; Sotiriadis & van Zyl, 2013). However, harnessing and managing eWOM in an effective way across social media platforms may be a difficult task for many businesses (Blackshaw & Nazzaro, 2006; Hudson & Thal, 2013). While the websites of travel and hospitality operators have endorsed customer feedback as a standard feature, in some cases, these appear to be merely part of the customer care service. As such, they have failed to provide adequate settings for consumers to actively post their opinions or recommend their products to other travellers. By contrast, travel and hospitality reviewing platforms such as TripAdvisor, Yelp and

IgoUgo, which offer collaboration and a sense of 'community' for consumers, also represent yet untapped specialised market niches for businesses offering a customer base of prospective buyers. As well as offering their services and promoting businesses, reviewing platforms have become imminent information sites for those searching for information, seeking advice and/or helping others (Gligorijevic & Luck, 2012).

User-generated content, in the form of personalised travel and hospitality experiences, has a significance and importance for people conducting online searches relating to particular destinations (Munar, 2012). According to Xiang and Gretzel (2010), social media websites featuring eWOM information appear on the first few pages of search results and represent a considerable part of search engine listings in online tourism-related search queries. As such, they are "quite substantial in terms of the size of their sites, the up-to-date nature and relevance of their contents, and the level of connectivity with other sites on the Internet, considering the specific ranking algorithms used by Google" (ibid). Furthermore, user-created travel reviews are more prominent, in comparison to marketing-generated content (Yoo & Gretzel, 2009). Xiang and Gretzel's (2010) results show that three major categories of social media content dominate search engine listings: virtual communities (websites such as IgoUgo and Thorn Tree—Lonely Planet), consumer review sites (for example, TripAdvisor and Zagat), and personal blogs and blog aggregators (for instance, Blogspot).

In a study about the use of social media for organising vacations, Para-López et al. (2011) confirmed that users gain greatly from utilising this approach to arrange trips, whereas obtaining better knowledge of destinations, understanding how to make cost savings, developing a sense of belonging to groups with similar interests, as well as attaining hedonistic benefits—being interestingly engaged throughout the process. In that sense, compared to marketing-generated content (MGC) that rarely allows interaction with or between consumers, using social media to become informed when planning and preparing for travelling introduces yet another dimension to the consumption of UGC—entertainment. This is becoming a significant aspect of generating online traffic, as attractiveness of content on websites suggests that more traffic will possibly result in higher sales. The effects of UGC on travel and hospitality online brands will be discussed in the next section.

3 Adoption of Social Media and Implications

Social media offers an array of different opportunities for companies to connect with their customers (Parise, Guinan, & Weinberg, 2008). User-generated content, co-created and disseminated via social media platforms, represents a crucial part of companies' external communication with their customer base. These are valuable touch points in the marketing communication strategy since co-creation results in higher level of engagement with a brand or a service provider. Various social media forms and formats are emerging and constantly evolving and, although it is difficult to categorise them, the definition proposed by Kaplan and Haenlein is blogs, social networking sites, virtual social worlds, collaborative projects, content communities and virtual game worlds (2010). Sotiriadis and van Zyl, (2013) extend this categorisation, appropriating it for the tourism industry to blogs and micro-blogs (Blogger, Twitter, Travel Blog), social networking sites (Facebook, LinkedIn), collaborative projects (Wikipedia), content community sites (YouTube, Flickr) and websites designed for feedback (online forums and websites with product reviews).

In this study, travel and tourism websites, such as IgoUgo and ThornTree, are described as online forums with a strong sense of community, where the exchange of personal travel experiences take place. The websites TripAdvisor and Zagat thrive on user-generated content in the form of reviews and ratings, and represent a commercial variant with a strong portfolio of marketing products offered to the holiday, leisure and hospitality industries. The third category of websites, such as Booking and Hotels, are those that feature reviews and ratings, but do not foster communities attached to the core of their businesses. As such they will not be part of this case study.

3.1 TripAdvisor

Since 2000, TripAdvisor has assisted travellers to gather travel and accommodation information, helping them to plan and take trips. It is one of the most visited travel-related websites, currently being rated in online worldwide traffic as the 192nd (Alexa.com, 2013). In China, the company is operating under the brand name 'Daodao'. TripAdvisor is visited by more than 260 million unique online visitors every month, leaving over 100 million reviews about 2.7 million businesses in the accommodation, hospitality and attractions industries (TripAdvisor, 2013). The unique selling proposition of this brand is over 150 million contributions from website's visitors, creating the largest database of user-generated content in the travel and hospitality industries (ibid). Co-creation and engagement with the content (reviewing and rating) are the key drivers for popularity of this brand, and repeatedly bring visitors to their webpages.

In 2011, its then mother company, Expedia Inc., decided to spin-off their 'TripAdvisor' travel advisory business and its many travel brands. Since the creation of the spin-off, TripAdvisor has acquired several start-up trip planning and travel-related content websites, as well as a photo sharing service. Some of these brands were incorporated into the core of the TripAdvisor business, while some were liquidated (Vivion, 2013). The company has not only successfully obtained promising start-ups and, with them innovated their services, but it is aggressively expanding its brand's domain across a wide spectrum of social media websites. This further suggests that new entrants to the online travel and holiday industry will face strong rivalry from TripAdvisor.

The TripAdvisor business model relies on the aggregation of UGC that attracts a high number of visitors to its website, with significant revenue from advertising and listing fees for other businesses. The website is a market leader, operating in 30 countries, with the largest repository of travel reviews for over 400,000 destinations. The site offers restaurant reviews, creating rankings based on the UGC of its contributors, while catering for the hospitality industry and its clientele. Reviewers are awarded badges, showing their level of contribution and number of posted reviews. Reviewed establishments are allowed to respond to their reviews and the issues addressed in them are publicly visible to everyone. Naturally, not all reviews are from satisfied customers, in which case the feature allows both parties to state their case and this assists companies to service their clients beyond the check-out point.

Besides reviews, the TripAdvisor website offers an online forum that provides traveller support by destination experts—dedicated volunteers who not only contribute by posting content, but also assist members with their inquiries about designated destinations. Destination experts, being either local residents or frequent visitors, provide travel-related advice, recommendations and up-to-date information. Travel guides, catalogue-style, free tourist guides, currently obtainable for 49 cities, although based on UGC posted by the site's visitors, are a feature that caters for more traditional tourists. Apparently TripAdvisor is working hard to appeal to all kinds of travellers by offering family, business and luxury travelling styles and diversified travel themes (such as adventure, beaches, skiing, spa, shopping, family fun, history and culture, romance, and casinos). The brand is evidently determined to gain a market share in all market niches.

In order to spread its influence beyond the online travel industry, one of the major strategic moves by TripAdvisor was tapping into the social networking activities of its members through partnership with Facebook, thereby allowing TripAdvisor users to display their travelling destinations and to see locations visited by their friends. The functions of Social Graph, where Facebook users are able to incorporate friends and their recommendations into their online searching experiences, became, in its true meaning, a personalised recommendation system that relies on word-of-mouth among people who are already displaying high levels of trust among dispersed social ties (Jumin et al., 2011; Ugander, Karrer, Backstrom, & Marlow, 2011).

TripAdvisor offers free access to content and free hosting of posted user-created reviews, which, consequently, generate the traffic necessary for its commercial services of online advertising, bookings and reservations. This has created an ecosystem where travellers and businesses coexist and are being offered divergent types of services. It is a perfect combination of highly demanded user-generated content, which is considered to be unbiased, and highly exposed marketing-generated content with accurately targeted, potential customers. The brand is vigorously appropriating smaller websites, extending its brand portfolio and establishing TripAdvisor as the most diversified brand among online reviewing platforms. It has become a market leader.

3.2   IgoUgo

IgoUgo, owned by the Sabre Holdings Corporation, started its operation in 2000 as an online travel community offering the firsthand experiences of genuine travellers as online travel journals. At the beginning, the website functioned as price comparison and direct booking service, later developing a strong sense of community among its users and becoming the premium recommendation website and library of personal travel stories. Booking features are still a very significant part of its business (Sharkey, 2008), as well as traditional online advertising. Community spirit and dedicated members have nurtured the spirit of co-creation on this website for years, and were the main force that kept its travel blog active. In November 2013 it was announced that IgoUgo will no longer accept new posts. The brand that resonated with enthusiasm and loyalty will no longer exist, as the company shifted its focus on Travelocity as the key brand in their portfolio of travel websites.

The IgoUgo website also caters for those who are not planning to travel, but are eager readers about exotic destinations, via its forums, blogs, travel journals and archives. Articles of good quality are awarded badges and labels, such as the "Best of IgoUgo", "Cheer" and "Flag", or points, emphasising authors' status within the community, their level of contribution and their importance in providing stimulating travel stories for increased readership or visits to the website. There are over 8000 reviewed destinations, classified by geographical regions, and 330,000 travel photos contributed by community members. IgoUgo encourages visitors to the website to create personalised profiles describing their travelling styles, favourite destination and to share their experiences, while fostering the community spirit. There is a strong emphasis on travel personalities and travelling styles, aiming at those with non-traditional travel experiences to contribute (Gligorijevic & Bruns, 2010).

The integration of social networking sites was focused on Twitter, Facebook, Pinterest and Google+, offering current and future members a taste of IgoUgo's content. Other social sharing functions offered are via Digg, StumbleUpon, Baidu, LinkedIn, Del.icio.us and Hyves. The IgoUgo Twitter account is dominated by the community manager's postings, with a lower number of followers than TripAdvisor. Postings on its Facebook page are closely monitored by IgoUgo staff, who readily respond to inquiries. IgoUgo 'pins' (a form of place mark) on Pinterest are diversified and cover a wide array of themes. There is a noticeable presence of IgoUgo content on all of the abovementioned social media spaces, however, there is a strong sense that the majority of content postings and interactions between members are still happening on the IgoUgo website and within its forums. Offering various links across social networking websites and embracing social media functionality appeared to be the right direction for this company that once strived to become a true Web 2.0 and social media travel advisory. Nevertheless, the executive decision to close its travel blog by the end of 2013, and to shift the focus on the booking brand Travelocity, left many of their contributors feeling nostalgic. The IgoUgo brand, that once gathered the community of passionate travellers and fostered the spirit of co-creation, left an unattended market niche in reviews of travel destinations and local attractions.

3.3 Zagat

Zagat was established in 1979 as a restaurant guidebook for food connoisseurs. The idea behind the Zagat survey was to generate restaurant recommendations from patrons, which were later edited and published as summaries (Sharkey, 2008), contrary to publishing practices of that time to print and circulate restaurant reviews that were written by professional food critics. In 2008, Zagat was sold to Google, and its content was integrated and offered as part of search engine listings. Google, a company known for its search engine, advertising technologies and free email, was, for a while, negotiating to purchase Yelp, another market leader that provides UGC for the hospitality industry. However, Google decided to focus on Zagat and its comprehensive database of customer reviews, adding value to its search listings (Barth, 2011). Zagat's competitive advantage was a large database of reviews co-created by peers, connoisseurs and patrons of fine dining establishments across the United States (US) and major international capitals. Their contributions and insights into hospitality industry were the unique selling proposition of this brand for many years, increasing its value and importance among other professionally created reviewing restaurant guides.

By appropriating Zagat's surveys, as one of the 56 acquisitions completed in 2011, Google achieved a competitive advantage by obtaining its content and expertise. Zagat, a trade name that offered a long-standing reputation of trusted reviews, brought to Google more than its community of users and a comprehensive database of reviews; it enhanced the value of Google's 'Places' business listing pages (Hof, 2011). However, it was evident that the Zagat company did not have a clearly formed strategy and direction for future development.

Zagat, a latecomer to online space, embraced digital applications as part of their 'growth strategy'. The Zagat survey extended the brand's reach beyond printed and digital restaurant guides in 2010 with Zagat Golf, an iPhone application available free, that featured over 1000 rated and reviewed United States golf courses. In addition, branded merchandise, such as t-shirts, clothing, apparel for chefs, selected wines and leather-bound guidebook editions, allowed the company to diversify its target audience, creating high visibility and brand awareness in the premium segment of the hospitality industry.

For years, Zagat's name resonated with a strong reputation in the hospitality industry, offering edited user-created content and relying on paid membership. However, the brand's low market penetration, focus on the US market, inadequate international positioning and low digital presence were obstacles that needed a sharp change of strategy within an environment where customers were, and still are, using their smart phone to obtain free information online. The change of management combined with Google's online dominance, have given this brand a fresh start and a new digital appeal, while offering their content for free. Recently, Google have announced a new reviewing interface and that its evaluating process will be significantly simplified, abandoning Zagat's standard 30 point scale (Gaskell, 2012). The reviewing process starts with the verification of a reviewer on Google + and, once bundled with Google 'Wallet', it will be fully integrated into the Google 'Local' reviewing system. As such, it will provide a reliable source of restaurant reviews from identified and socially networked patrons. The questions are whether Zagat's brand is strong enough to survive this integration and will the brand be able to face challengers such as Yelp?

3.4 Thorn Tree: Lonely Planet's Online Travel Community

Established in 1972 as Lonely Planet Publications, the company became famous for its paperback guidebooks for ardent travellers, at first in Australia and the United Kingdom and, subsequently, globally. In 2011, the company and its brand, Lonely Planet, with a publishing portfolio of over 500 titles, was acquired by BBC Worldwide. Without a clear strategy and faced with declining sales of hard copies and a diminishing market share, BBC Worldwide decided to sell the company to NC2 Media, with significant losses in Lonely Planet's market value (BBC, 2013; Neill, 2011; Robins, 2010). Thorn Tree, an online forum that gathered travel enthusiasts and featured their co-created content, was a flagship of the Lonely Planet brand among other travel and tourism websites.

Thorn Tree (TT), an online travel forum, was initiated in 1996 as part of the Lonely Planet brand and, today, has over one million members (private correspondence with a Thorn Tree moderator, circa March 2010). Members are encouraged to ask questions, offer advice and even to help others to plan their trips. There is a significant difference between the Lonely Planet publications, written by professional travel writers, and the Thorn Tree content, which thrives on UGC created by travellers. Thorn Tree, already an established online community, has managed to become a brand on its own among travellers, offering information about destinations by regions, travel-related themes, forums, bookings, insurance and Lonely Planet guidebooks.

Thorn Tree has a friendly community of active travellers offering advice, but also some less experienced people who visit the site to read about exotic destinations and unorthodox travel experiences. The forums provide an extensive knowledge base for those who are looking for information beyond travel catalogues. In the TT forums, the journey begins at the 'Departure Lounge' by selecting a destination. It continues in 'The Lobby', with various recommendations and wisdom from experienced travellers about assorted travelling styles, and ends up at the 'Sell, Swap and Meet Up' section, where more than just advice is offered or exchanged. The discussions display a good dose of humour and helpfulness among the participants. This small, but closely woven, community is not active under the same name in other social networking platforms where Lonely Planet brand is emphasised and endorsed.

The shopping section of the TT forums, with guidebooks, resembles an advertisement from an old-fashioned bookshop. Although the company offers electronic books and mobile applications, there is a strong sense that it is still clinging to its old publishing glory. Sadly, the company seemed to have underestimated the strength of the Thorn Tree brand, especially among the dedicated members of its online community, who greatly contributed by posting user-generated content. There is a little evidence of any plans for a stronger online presence of the Thorn Tree brand in social media space in the future, suggesting that the marketing strategy of BBC Worldwide was mainly focused on further developing the Lonely Planet brand.

Under the new management, it was announced that Lonely Planet's digital assets would be the focus of their future development (Clampet, 2013). This news was followed by restructuring of the book production department, which is responsible for editing and layouts of the physical guidebooks, indicating that an urgent shift in strategy was needed. However, it is not clearly stated whether the two brands, Lonely Planet, known as the traditional publisher of guidebooks, and Thorn Tree, the online travel forum, will be merged.

It is evident that UGC and social media have greatly assisted Lonely Planet to bridge the gap between traditional and online publishing. TT's forums and community spirit have kept the brand active in social media space before it embraced Facebook, Flickr, Instagram, Pinterest and Twitter as part of their brand awareness strategy. It is difficult to predict the future of the Thorn Tree brand or its online forums. Due to its feeble connection to the mother enterprise Lonely Planet, it is unlikely that it will continue to exist as it is. At the same time, a well-established community of travellers, still active within the TT forums, continue to be a valuable source of UGC for Lonely Planet.

4 Key Conclusions and Learning Outcomes for the Tourism Industry

The travel and tourism industries have been strongly impacted by accessibility to information, ICT and the adoption of social media applications (Buhalis & Law, 2008; Hays, Page, & Buhalis, 2013; van Zyl, 2009; Xiang & Gretzel, 2010). Marketing modus operandi in travel and hospitality has significantly changed from traditional advertising and delivery of information through face-to-face communication with agencies and local operators, moving online to reviewing platforms for delivering bundled information packages, combining UGC and MGC and, consequently, bookings. Social media platforms not only provided travel operators with a more affordable alternative to traditional advertising, but allowed social interactions and exchange of word-of-mouth information. This process assisted in boosting customers' interest in travel destinations, tourism operators and hospitality establishments.

The four presented reviewing platforms differ significantly. TripAdvisor represents the largest collection of UGC, destinations and visitors, and is an absolute market leader. This website caters for travellers and travel operators, offering a well-tailored and complementary set of services to both target markets. IgoUgo, a substantially smaller database of destinations used to offer a more comprehensive and personalised approach to travel, managed to create a brand of its own, attracting a specific type of traveller but was eventually winded down. The brand was well known among those who looked beyond commercial tourism offerings. Zagat, a leader in restaurant guidebooks and a somewhat traditional brand, was given a second life via Google's bundled information offerings. It remains to be seen whether the brand will be able to face any challenges imposed by new leadership and if it is strong enough to survive its conversion to social media. Thorn Tree, the oldest online travel forum with a small, but strong, online community that continually contributes UGC, is facing new challenges. Not only does the brand have a low digital presence across social networking sites, it seems that the community is left without support from its parent company, Lonely Planet.

The brands presented in this case study showcase the utilisation of UGC to appeal to a wide range of travellers and patrons, and to attract them to their websites. Once there, the visits are expected to be converted to sales. However, managing user-generated content, its creation, validation, editing, hosting and archiving, is not an easy task; neither is nurturing of online communities. Due to the rapidly changing social media landscape, it is difficult to predict the future of these reviewing platforms as some of them have already or will cease to exist Nevertheless, it is safe to say that some of them will survive, while others may transform or completely disappear. Even with changes, user-created reviews, ratings and recommendations will remain one of the strongest selling propositions for travel destinations, as well as reviewing websites. In this section we have discussed and learned that:

- Reviewing platforms for travel destinations changed the marketing approach and practices in travel, tourism and hospitality industries from traditional advertising to electronic word-of-mouth marketing.
- Social networking sites have enhanced the presence and increased the marketing communication touch points of travel and hospitality brands, these reviewing platforms harness the co-creation process as their unique selling proposition.
- Reviewing platforms provide expertise, support and know-how from experienced travellers to those who are seeking advice and relevant information when planning trips. As such, they provide access to specific market niches of different types of travellers for marketers and advertisers.
- User-generated content, in the form of reviews, ratings and recommendations, is attracting millions of eyeballs to reviewing platforms; providing online traffic and a steady advertising revenue stream for these websites.

Acknowledgements This case study partly draws on research delivered in a report written by Gligorijevic, B. and Bruns, A. in 2010 and published by Smart Services CRC under the research project, New Media Services titled "Ratings and Recommendations Websites in the Travel and Tourism Industry". This research was carried out as part of the activities of, and funded by, Smart Services CRC through the Australian Government's CRC programme (Department of Innovation, Industry, Science and Research).

References

Alexa.com. (2013). Alexa traffic ranking – TripAdvisor.com. *Alexa Traffic Ranks*. Available from: http://www.alexa.com/siteinfo/tripadvisor.com

Au, N., Law, R., & Buhalis, D. (2010). The impact of culture on ecomplaints: Evidence from Chinese consumers in hospitality organisations. In U. Gretzel, R. Law, & M. Fuchs (Eds.), *Information and communication technologies in tourism 2010* (pp. 285–296). New York: Springer.

Barth, C. (2011). Google paid $151 million to get Zagat, Ditch Yelp. *Forbes*. Available from: http://www.forbes.com/sites/chrisbarth/2011/10/27/google-paid-151-million-to-get-zagat-ditch-yelp/

BBC. (2013). BBC worldwide sells lonely planet business at £80m loss. *BBC News*. Available from: http://www.bbc.co.uk/news/entertainment-arts-21841479

Blackshaw, P., & Nazzaro, M. (2006). *Consumer – generated media 101: Word-of-mouth in the age of the web-fortified consumer*. New York: Nielsen BuzzMetrics.

Brown, R., Broderick, A., & Lee, N. (2007). Word of mouth communication within online communities: Conceptualizing the online social network. *Journal of Interactive Marketing, 21*(3), 2–20.

Buhalis, D. (1998). Strategic use of information technologies in the tourism industry. *Tourism Management, 19*(5), 409–421.

Buhalis, D., & Law, R. (2008). Progress in information technology and tourism management: 20 years on and 10 years after the Internet – The state of eTourism research. *Tourism Management, 29*(4), 609–623.

Clampet, J. (2013). Lonely planet's new boss on the future of the travel brand. *Skift Travel*. Available from: http://skift.com/2013/03/19/interview-lonely-planets-new-boss-on-why-he-wanted-lonely-planet/

Cooper, C., & Hall, M. (2008). *Contemporary tourism: An international approach*. Amsterdam: Elsevier.

Dellarocas, C. (2003). The digitization of word of mouth: Promise and challenges of online feedback mechanisms. *Management Science, 49*(10), 1407–1424.

Dwyer, P. (2007). Measuring the value of electronic word of mouth and its impact in consumer communities. *Journal of Interactive Marketing, 21*(2), 63–79.

Gaskell, A. (2012). Is Google going cold on Zagat? *Technorati*. Available from: http://technorati.com/social-media/article/is-google-going-cold-on-zagat/

Gligorijevic, B., & Bruns, A. (2010). *Ratings and recommendations websites in the travel and tourism industry*. Sydney: New Media Services, Smart Services CRC.

Gligorijevic, B., & Luck, E. (2012). Engaging social customers – Influencing new marketing strategies for social media information sources. In V. Khachidze et al. (Eds.), *Contemporary research on e-Business technology and strategy: iCETS 2012, CCIS 332* (pp. 25–40). Berlin: Springer.

Grissemann, U. S., & Stokburger-Sauer, N. E. (2012). Customer co-creation of travel services: The role of company support and customer satisfaction with the co-creation performance. *Tourism Management, 33*(6), 1483–1492.

Hays, S., Page, S. J., & Buhalis, D. (2013). Social media as a destination marketing tool: Its use by national tourism organisations. *Current Issues in Tourism, 16*(3), 211–239.

Hennig-Thurau, T., Gwinner, K., Walsh, G., & Gremler, D. (2004). Electronic word-of-mouth via consumer-opinion platforms: What motivates consumers to articulate themselves on the internet? *Journal of Interactive Marketing, 18*(1), 38–52.

Hennig-Thurau, T., & Walsh, G. (2003). Electronic word of mouth: Motives for and consequences of reading customer articulations on the Internet. *International Journal of Electronic Commerce, 8*(2), 51–74.

Hof, R. (2011). What Google gets from Zagat: Location, location, location. *Forbes*. Available from: http://www.forbes.com/sites/roberthof/2011/09/08/what-google-gets-from-buying-zagat/

Hudson, S., & Thal, K. (2013). The impact of social media on the consumer decision process: Implications for tourism marketing. *Journal of Travel and Tourism Marketing, 30*, 156–160.

Jacobsen, J. K. S., & Munar, A. M. (2012). Tourism information search and destination choice in a digital age. *Tourism Management Perspectives, 1*, 39–47.

Jiang, J., Gretzel, U., & Law, R. (2010). Negative experiences always lead to dissatisfaction? Testing attribution theory in the context of online travel reviews. In U. Gretzel, R. Law, & M. Fuchs (Eds.), *Information and communication technologies in tourism 2010* (pp. 297–308). New York: Springer.

Jumin, L., Park, D. H., & Ingoo, H. (2011). The different effects of online consumer reviews on consumers' purchasing intentions depending on trust in online shopping malls. *Internet Research, 21*(2), 187–206.

Kang, M., & Schuett, M. A. (2013). Determinants of sharing travel experiences in social media. *Journal of Travel and Tourism Marketing, 30*, 93–107.

Kaplan, A., & Haenlein, M. (2010). Users of the world, unite! The challenges and opportunities of social media. *Business Horizons, 53*, 59–68.

Leung, D., Law, R., van Hoof, H., & Buhalis, D. (2013). Social media in tourism and hospitality: A literature review. *Journals of Travel and Tourism Marketing, 39*, 3–22.

Li, X., Li, X., & Hudson, S. (2013). The application of generational theory to tourism consumer behavior: An American perspective. *Tourism Management, 37*, 147–164.

Litvin, S. W., Goldsmith, R. E., & Pan, B. (2008). Electronic word-of-mouth in hospitality and tourism management. *Tourism Management, 20*, 458–468.

Mangold, W. D., & Faulds, D. J. (2009). Social media: The new hybrid element of the promotion mix. *Business Horizons, 52*, 357–365.

Munar, A. M. (2012). Social media strategies and destination management. *Scandinavian Journal of Hospitality and Tourism, 12*(2), 101–120.

Neill, G. (2011). BBC wipes £33.8 m off lonely planet value. *The Bookseller*. Available from: http://www.thebookseller.com/news/bbc-wipes-%C2%A3338m-lonely-planet-value.html

Norum, R. (2008). The less-than-lonely planet. *Guardian, Travel Blog*. Available from: http://www.guardian.co.uk/travel/blog/2008/apr/14/thelessthanlonelyplanet

Papathanassis, A., & Knolle, F. (2011). Exploring the adoption and processing of online holiday reviews: A grounded theory approach. *Tourism Management, 32*, 215–224.

Para-López, E., Bulchand-Gidumal, J., Gutierrez-Taño, D., & Díaz-Armas, R. (2011). Intentions to use social media in organizing and taking vacation trips. *Computers in Human Behaviour, 27*, 640–654.

Parise, S., Guinan, P., & Weinberg, D. (2008). The secrets of marketing in a Web 2.0. *The Wall Street Journal, Business section*. Available from: http://online.wsj.com/article/SB122884677205091919.html

Park, D. H., Lee, J., & Han, I. (2007). The effect of on-line consumer reviews on consumer purchasing intention: The moderating role of involvement. *International Journal of Electronic Commerce, 11*(4), 125–148.

Robins, T. (2010). The end of the guidebook? *Financial Times*. Available from: http://www.ft.com/cms/s/2/3e422f40-a0ed-11df-badd-00144feabdc0.html#axzz2gEvGveXf

Sharkey, J. (2008). Online reviews of hotels and restaurants flourish. *The New York Times*. Available from: http://travel.nytimes.com/2008/01/22/business/media/22reviews.html?_r=0

Smith, D., Menon, S., & Sivakumar, K. (2005). Online peer and editorial recommendations, trust, and choice in virtual markets. *Journal of Interactive Marketing, 19*(3), 15–37.

Sotiriadis, M. D., & van Zyl, A. C. (2013). Electronic word-of-mouth and online reviews in tourism services: The use of Twitter by tourists. *Electronic Commerce Research, 13*(1), 103–124.

Steffes, E., & Burgees, L. (2009). Social ties and online word of mouth. *Internet Research, 19*(1), 42–59.

TripAdvisor. (2013). *About TripAdvisor*. Available from: http://www.tripadvisor.com/PressCenter-c6-About_Us.html

Ugander, J., Karrer, B., Backstrom, L., & Marlow, C. (2011). *The anatomy of Facebook social graph*. Cornell University Library. arXiv:111.4503[cs.SI].

van Zyl, A. S. (2009). The impact of Social Networking 2.0 on organisations. *The Electronic Library, 27*(6), 906–918.

Vivion, N. (2013). TripAdvisor shutters Wanderfly. *Tnooz*. Available from: http://www.tnooz.com/article/tripadvisor-shutters-wanderfly/

Xiang, Z., & Gretzel, U. (2010). Role of social media in online travel information search. *Tourism Management, 31*, 179–188.

Yoo, K. H., & Gretzel, U. (2009). Comparison of deceptive and truthful travel reviews. In W. Höpken, U. Gretzel, & R. Law (Eds.), *Information and communication technologies in tourism 2009* (pp. 37–48). Wien: Springer.

Review Platforms in Hospitality

Alexander Fritsch and Holger Sigmund

Learning Objectives

- Understand the role of hotel reviews in the booking decision process.
- Identify the influence of hotel reviews and ratings for the purchase decision.
- Get an overview of relevant Internet platforms in hospitality and explore their business models.
- Discover the role of Google and social media platforms when it comes to hotel reviews.
- Discuss current trends and upcoming challenges in relation to online guest feedback.

1 Introduction

The Internet has become the main source of information when it comes to booking decisions. Therefore, online research has surpassed personal recommendations, guides or tourist agencies in their significance (Eurobarometer, 2011). German users spend on average an unbelievable amount of 9 h for holiday research on the Internet in the course of which they typically visit an average of 13 different websites before making their decision. A good quarter of users invests between 12 and 25 h for research, visiting up to 50 different websites (FUR, 2011). According to Google, it takes an average of 55 searches until someone actually buys a travel service (Friedlander, 2011). With the rise of Web 2.0 and Social Media, the importance of User Generated Content (UGC) has risen dramatically (Kaplan & Haenlein, 2010). Regarding the hospitality industry, online reviews and

A. Fritsch (✉) • H. Sigmund
Tourismuspartner, Bregenz, Austria
e-mail: info@tourismuspartner.co.at

© Springer-Verlag Berlin Heidelberg 2016
R. Egger et al. (eds.), *Open Tourism*, Tourism on the Verge,
DOI 10.1007/978-3-642-54089-9_16

ratings have gained enormous influence on the performance and success of a hotel. A 1 % increase in a hotel's online reputation score not only allows a 0.89 % increase in price, but also triggers an occupancy increase of up to 0.54 % (Anderson, 2012).

2   The Role of Reviews in the Booking Decision Process

Reviews are involved in the booking decision by the vast majority of guests. With slight variations, depending on the country and target group, hotel reviews play a very significant role within the hotel booking decision-making process. In a study in the U.S., half of the surveyed travelers even indicated that they would not book a hotel without reading any reviews about it (TripAdvisor, 2012a). Looking at the moment of the booking decision—meaning the point in time of the decision for or against choosing a particular hotel—an even clearer picture emerges. In a study The Modul University Vienna has investigated the relative importance of different factors during the booking decision (Dickinger, 2008). The result: personal recommendations and reviews have the relatively highest influence on the booking decision. In an investigation on behalf of the association "Internet Reisevertrieb e.V. (VIR)", more than a thousand Internet users were asked how much they are influenced by reviews when choosing an accommodation. Only 4 % reported being influenced "a little". The rest (96 %) admitted to being "very" or at least "somewhat" influenced (VIR, 2011). A third of users changes their booking decision after visiting social media pages, such as hotel review portals (World Travel Market's Industry Report, 2012).

"For many guests the evaluation platforms are a channel to take revenge on the hotel owner, because if something goes wrong and a guest is perceived by the hotel not as a customer, but as a nuisance, one still has the channel of public appeal" (Gatterer & Rützler, 2012). Even recognized tourism consultants share this negative concern with many hotel owners. But the hard numbers prove them wrong: for TripAdvisor, the amount of positive ratings is over 80 % and the average rating is about four out of five points (TripAdvisor, 2011). Most of the users who have submitted reviews on TripAdvisor declared as the main reason to "help" other users and/or the hotel. More than 90 % of the 7000 respondents agreed to this statement (Gretzel, Yoo, & Purifoy, 2007). Incidentally, reasons like "taking revenge" were relatively unimportant (10 % agreed with this reason). Other reasons for negative reviews were "to advise others against bad service", "retribution" or even "to vent one's anger" (Gretzel et al., 2007).

Reviews are generally read in order to assure one's purchasing decision. Unlike consumer goods, tourism products are non-material services (Bieger, 2008). A trip includes a variety of services (accommodation, food, transportation, recreation, etc.). Consistency and quality are determined by several factors and are therefore harder to control and to represent. Consumers crave guidance in wading through the abundance of destinations and hotels. They trust the majority opinion ("social proof"). About 80 % of travelers ignore extreme reviews and primarily form their opinions based on a general analysis of the various feedbacks, as well as from the pictures and descriptions of the hotel (TripAdvisor, 2012a). Information from review portals are used differently depending on the point of progress in the research (Schmeißer, 2008). Anyone just starting to look for suitable accommodation—who is right at the beginning of his decision—uses reviews purely for "general informational purposes". This means that a user looks for "anchors" such as recommendation rates, seals of approval, or overall scores to make an initial choice. Only in the more advanced decision-making process does the user notice the contents more selectively. When a pre-selection is made, he is then more interested in the details. In this phase, individual reviews are read and compared with each other.

More and more destinations and tour operators integrate reviews online, as well as in brochures and catalogues. They use the sales advantage of well-rated, "popular" hotels. The focus for agencies and online booking portals is on increasing the number of bookings. Also, tourist organizations can actively influence the quality of the local offer.

3   Hotel Review Portals at a Glance

Worldwide, there are more than 100 online portals that collect hotel reviews. In addition to the classic hotel review sites such as TripAdvisor, HolidayCheck, Zoover, TopHotels & Co., there are also numerous other online booking portals which integrate reviews on their sites.

For many years, the main focus of online booking platforms was on the price. The ranking was based on the principle of rating the hotels according to the best price. This often had the consequence that hotels tried to maneuver their way to the top ranking through a clever online price representation strategy (e.g. reducing the basic price by a small margin below their competition). In contrast, nowadays, the online hotel shopper can confidently focus on quality, rather than on price only. Many portals arrange their hotel listings according to their "popularity" and reviews. As a result, the high emphasis on the price in the industry is gradually declining in favor of the quality standards of the guests. This makes perfect sense because "popular" offers apparently sell much better than "cheap" offers.

3.1   Relevant Online Travel Portals with Reviews[1] (Table 1)

Table 1 Relevant online travel portals with reviews

Portal	Particularly relevant markets	Business model[a]	Rating system	Hotel comment possible?
TripAdvisor	International	Metasearch	1–5 points	Yes
Trivago	International	Metasearch	Summarizes the ratings and reviews of various portals	No
Priceline	North America, international	Online travel agency	1–10 points	Yes
Booking	International	Online travel agency	1–10 points	Yes
Expedia	International	Online travel agency	1–5 points, recommendation	Yes
Venere	Italy, International	Online travel agency	1–10 points	Yes
Hotels.com	International	Online travel agency	1–5 points	Yes
HolidayCheck	German-speaking countries	Online travel agency	1–6 'suns', recommendation	Yes
HRS	International, German-speaking countries	Online travel agency	1–10 points, recommendation	Yes
Zoover	Benelux	Click-out	1–10 points	Yes
Yelp	International	Advertising	1–5 stars	Yes
TopHotels	Russia	Click-out	1–5 points	Yes
Orbitz	United States	Online travel agency	1–5 points	No
ebookers	Europe	Online travel agency	1–5 points	No
Ratestogo	Europe, international	Online travel agency	1–5 points	No

Source: Fritsch and Sigmund (2013)
[a]Often a combination of different business models

---

[1] As of February 2014, own selection.

3.1.1   TripAdvisor

TripAdvisor is the most visited holiday and travel portal in the world. With more than 150 million reviews, TripAdvisor has also the highest number of guest feedback (TripAdvisor, 2013). In 2013, TripAdvisor started the so-called "Metasearch" as its primary model to make business: Users can compare prices of hotels and are then forwarded to the respective online booking portals. Hotels have the opportunity to register for free at the "Management Center" and are able to manage any entries on TripAdvisor in order to respond to reviews, and to make use of various free marketing tools.

3.1.2   Trivago

Trivago is a company lately acquired by Expedia Inc., which specializes in "Metasearch" of hotels. According to its own statement, Trivago operates the world's largest hotel price comparison website. In 31 different country portals, the reviews of other portals (e.g. HolidayCheck, Booking.com, Venere, Zoover, and others) are integrated into Trivago's website, which are converted to an evaluation index of 100 points.

3.1.3   Priceline and Booking.com

Both portals are part of the U.S. Priceline Group. Like most other online booking portals, Priceline and Booking.com integrate their own rating system in their portals. Over 400,000 hotels are bookable through the Priceline Group. Booking.com is the worldwide market leader among hotel booking platforms and has collected more than 25 million hotel reviews. Each day, over 600,000 room nights are reserved on Booking.com. Online bookers are automatically prompted by e-mail after their stay to leave a hotel review.

3.1.4   Expedia, Venere and Hotels.com

Expedia.com was launched in 1996 by software giant Microsoft. Since 1999, Expedia is an independent NASDAQ-listed company. Amongst others, Expedia owns the brands Hotels.com, Venere.com and Egencia, the last being a purely business travel booking company. Expedia.com is also a tour operator and not only a hotel booking agency. Hotels.com and Venere.com are purely online booking portals for accommodations, therefore acting as an agent, similar to Booking.com. All Expedia portals include hotel ratings, with no single uniform system being used.

Each platform has, however, integrated its own rating system. Some of the platforms also use TripAdvisor reviews.

3.1.5 HolidayCheck

HolidayCheck is a company based in Switzerland, which is a member of the German 'Tomorrow Focus' Group (Hubert Burda Media). Each month, up to 25 million people visit the online portals. HolidayCheck is particularly relevant if a hotel's guest structure includes tourists from German-speaking countries. Since the acquisition of Zoover (Netherlands) by its parent company in the summer of 2012, both companies together have become the self-reported market leaders for hotel reviews in Europe. HolidayCheck is operated as a classic travel agency with about 100 booking partners (tour operators, online travel agencies).

3.1.6 HRS

In the German-speaking world, HRS can claim to be at the top of the online booking sites for hotels and is the market leader among business travelers. The company was founded back in 1972, long before the Internet boom. According to HRS, currently about 250,000 hotels are featured on their website worldwide, and another 210,000 hotels are offered on their subsidiary, Hotel.de. The business model follows that of a classic online travel agency. The review options are extensive. A hotel is rated in several areas and categories, and the average rating is shown as well. At HRS, the hotel owners can respond with a comment on the reviews, while this feature is not offered at Hotel.de.

3.1.7 Zoover

Zoover is the most important online portal for hotel reviews of the Benelux countries. Zoover currently operates 24 different country portals. Profits are made through the "click-out" model. At Zoover it is also possible for hotel owners to create their own login in order to be able to influence their own representation, as well as to respond to guests' reviews.

3.1.8 Yelp

Yelp is one of the world's largest online portals for reviews of local businesses. On Yelp, mainly restaurants, but also hotels and other services are evaluated. Yelp acquired the German review portal Qype in late 2012 and subsequently integrated Qype-content into its own database. Hotel owners can join for free and add their own presentation with photos, text, downloads, and contact information. In addition, they can reply to reviews publicly or privately.

3.1.9   TopHotels

TopHotels is one of the main hotel review portals in Russia. Like on other portals, TopHotels offers a "click-out" model for booking a hotel, where the user is first directed to a separate comparison portal, Turpoisk.ru. A special feature of TopHotels is an advanced comment function, similar to a forum or a blog. This means that multiple comments by hotel owners and other guests can be posted.

3.1.10   Orbitz, Ebookers, Ratestogo

Orbitz Worldwide is part of the GDS provider Travelport (Galileo and Worldspan). In a manner of speaking, Orbitz.com is the U.S. American counterpart to Opodo, since it was also founded by the leading airlines and then was sold. Europe relies on the Orbitz brand Ebookers.com. Another well-known brand is Ratestogo, which is specialized in last-minute hotel deals. The portals use a 5-point rating and recommendation system, but none currently offer a comment function for hotel owners.

Hotels should closely monitor and optimize their listing on review and booking portals. All portals constantly offer new opportunities and implement design changes. Generally speaking, the more a hotel is featured in online portals with full details and attractive photos, the more visible and thus findable it will be to potential new guests. Hospitality businesses can influence the channels which provide them with online bookings by controlling where guest feedback is posted. They should encourage reviews in those portals that are strategically important for them—for example, because they cover relevant target markets or collaborate with key booking partners.

3.2   *Google and Reviews*

Search engines play a major role in holiday research. With a global market share of about 85 % for all search engines, Google is a de facto monopoly (Netmarketshare, 2012). Travel is one of the most important advertising sectors on Google. Google has increasingly "localized" its search results. This means that for a large number of search results, the location, as well as the type of company, plays a crucial role. When a user in Google searches for 'Hotel London' for example, companies from 'Google+ Local' results are displayed. These 'Google+ Local' results are supplemented by a separate Google rating and review system. Reviews can only be created by Google users. Comments can be posted on those reviews by the hotel management. This is done through the 'Google+ Local' account of the administrator for the hotel.

3.3 Social Networking Portals

Social networking sites like Facebook or Google+ are playing an increasingly important role for hotel reviews. The boundaries between these services and traditional hotel review portals are becoming blurred more and more.

Facebook is the largest social network site in the world. Although now a certain "Facebook Fatigue" is observable (Gernert, 2012), the network can highly affect the online reputation of companies. Opinions about hotels can be formulated and exchanged on Facebook, for example in form of star ratings, text reviews or general comments/posts on the Facebook pages of the hotel or those of individual users. In the moment, feedback via Facebook does not impact the average grades or the ranking in traditional review portals typically used for travel planning like TripAdvisor.

Google+ is a social network of the search-engine-giant, which is in direct competition with Facebook. This network offers similar opportunities as Facebook and is getting increasingly linked to the search functionality of Google. Google+ and Google's own rating system are increasingly becoming more connected to each other.

Hotel reviews are increasingly interlinked with the possibilities and options of social networks. Thus, a TripAdvisor account can be linked to somebody's own Facebook profile. As a result, the hotel reviews and activities of friends connected via Facebook are displayed prominently. Optionally, any personal review can be shared automatically with Facebook friends. Meanwhile, every fourth review on TripAdvisor is written by a Facebook connected user (TripAdvisor, 2012b).

An end of this development is not foreseeable. One thing seems certain: hotel reviews are becoming increasingly combined with personal recommendations; and social networks are a great way to do this.

4 Key Challenges for the Future

The acceptance of reviews and how they are dealt with still vary considerably from destination to destination. In some countries, dealing actively with guest feedback is considered one of the key challenges in the hotel industry. On the other hand, there are regions in which businesses are only beginning to understand its importance. One thing is clear, however: the significance of this issue for the hotel sector is rising considerably.

Today, as many as 20 % of Google searches regarding holiday topics are executed via mobile devices (Buchholz, 2011). But searching for a suitable accommodation is not the only thing increasingly done via mobile devices; submitting a review is, too—perhaps even during the stay. This will present an entirely new challenge to hoteliers: How do they react properly to the criticism of a guest who is still in the hotel?

Opinions and assessments are all the more relevant, the more they conform to the preferences of the user. Who knows these better than the user himself and his peers? Linking up with social networks such as Facebook or Google+ adds an interpersonal dimension to the reviews. Thus, reviews of the "peer group" are presented to the user in a more prominent fashion, for instance through a direct integration into search results.

Is the #1 hotel on TripAdvisor also my first choice? These days, ratings and especially rankings tend to be based on the general opinion, on mainstream taste. Finding the right accommodation which suits individual needs is still often a rather tedious task, despite all the reviews. In the future, intelligent search systems could facilitate this search by "learning" about personal preferences. Another option are portals that make a pre-selection for different user groups—the way it was done before there were online reviews. Hence, hotel co-operations such as "The Leading Hotels of the World" and specialized tour operators will remain popular. Only one thing is changing: Nowadays, guests actively participate in quality control.

How successful can a manufacturer hope to be whose product is rated "deficient" by test magazines? Most probably the product will quickly disappear from the market—unless it changes significantly for the better. A similar trend is emerging in all those tourism regions where pioneering hotels are actively and successfully working with reviews. The pressure on other businesses is rising. Consequently, good quality hotels will thrive while those with deficits will have it significantly tougher than before.

5 Key Conclusions and Learning Outcomes for the Tourism Industry

- Online hotel reviews strongly influence the booking decision and therefore have direct impact on a hotel's distribution strategy and longterm success.
- Hotel review platforms like TripAdvisor are among the most used Internet offers when it comes to travel research and booking.
- What will Google do? The biggest search engine progressively integrates its own review and rating system for travel products. Google's strategy could heavily influence online travel in future.
- Bad quality travel products cannot sell anymore—because of the transparency online reviews bring to the hospitality industry. This is a chance for good quality products and a thread for products with deficiencies. Without "social proof", the best marketing effort do not bring the desired results anymore.

References

Anderson, C. (2012). The impact of social media on lodging performance. *Cornell Hospitality Report, 15*, 4–11.

Bieger, T. (2008). *Management von destination.* München: Oldenbourg.

Buchholz, N. (2011). Search engine update. In *Presentation from Google Travel UK at World Travel Market 2011.*

Dickinger, A. (2008). *Customer reviews as drivers of hotel online booking.* Accessed July 7, 2010, from www.modul.ac.at/blog/2008-08-customer-reviewsas-drivers-of-hotel-online-booking

Eurobarometer. (2011). *Survey on the attitudes of Europeans towards tourism* (Analytical Report, Wave 3). Accessed September 11, 2012, from http://ec.europa.eu/public_opinion/flash/fl_328_en.pdf

Friedlander, R. J. (2011). *Best practices in hotel reputation management.* Accessed July 17, 2012, from www.sabrehospitality.com/blog/2011-06-15/best-practices-in-hotel-reputation-management

Fritsch, A., & Sigmund, H. (2013). *Managing hotel reviews* (pp. 8–18). Stuttgart: Matthaes.

FUR. (2011). *Die 41. Reiseanalyse RA 2011.* Accessed September 4, 2012, from www.fur.de/index.php?id=zentrale_ergebnisse

Gatterer, H., & Rützler, H. (2012). *Hotel der Zukunft* (p. 78). Stuttgart: Matthaes.

Gernert, J. (2012). Wie wird facebook wieder cool? *Die Zeit, 38*, 23.

Gretzel, U., Yoo, K. H., & Purifoy, M. (2007). *Online travel review study: Role and impact of online travel reviews.* College Station, TX: Texas A & M University, Laboratory for Intelligent Systems in Tourism.

Kaplan, A., & Haenlein, M. (2010). Users of the world, unite! The challenges and opportunities of social media. *Business Horizons, 53*(1), 59–68.

Netmarketshare. (2012). *Desktop search engine market share.* Accessed August 3, 2012, from www.netmarketshare.com/search-engine-market-share.aspx?qprid=4

Schmeißer, D. R. (2008). Kundenbewertungen in der eTouristik – Segen oder Fluch? Psychologie der Reiseentscheidung im Social Web. In D. Amersdorffer et al. (Eds.), *Social web im tourismus.* Berlin: Springer.

TripAdvisor. (2011). *TripAdvisor seminar presentation.* Accessed September 17, 2012, from http://de.slideshare.net/eTourismAfrica/trip-advisor-seminar

TripAdvisor. (2012a). *Wie Reisende Bewertungen interpretieren: Die Fakten.* Accessed May 5, 2012, from http://tripadvisor4bizde.wordpresP.com/2012/03/01/wie-reisende-bewertungen-interpretieren-die-fakten

TripAdvisor. (2012b). *TripAdvisor reveals travelers' social sharing habits.* Accessed September 26, 2012, from http://hotelmarketing.com/index.php/content/article/tripadvisor_reveals_travelers_social_sharing_habits

TripAdvisor. (2013). *TripAdvisor now offers 150 million reviews and opinions with 50 million pieces of content posted in the past year.* Accessed February 28, 2014, from http://www.tripadvisor.com/PressCenter-i6611-c1-Press_Releases.html

VIR, & IUBH. (2011). *Studie zur Bedeutung & Glaubwürdigkeit at Bewertungen auf Internetportalen.* Ergebnispräsentation einer Online-Befragung von 1.039 Nutzern.

World Travel Market's Industry Report. (2012). Accessed February 28, 2014, from http://www.wtmlondon.com/RXUK/RXUK_WTMLondon/2015/documents/WTM-Industry-Report-2014.pdf

Exploring TripAdvisor

Kyung-Hyan Yoo, Marianna Sigala, and Ulrike Gretzel

Learning Objectives

- Understand the key features of TripAdvisor and its value added services for travellers and businesses.
- Analyse TripAdvisor's business model and identify possible areas in which open innovation could be realised.
- Explore how TripAdvisor represents, influences, and shapes the Open Innovation in Tourism (OIT) phenomenon.
- Identify key challenges for the future.
- Gain insights from a case analysis and provide recommendations for TripAdvisor as well as the tourism industry.

1 Introduction

The second generation of Web-based services (Web 2.0) allows online users to form and participate in social communities to (co-)create and distribute Web content (Gillin, 2007). A growing number of Web users participate in such content

K.-H. Yoo (✉)
William Paterson University, Wayne, NJ, USA
e-mail: yook2@wpunj.edu

M. Sigala
University of South Australia, Adelaide, Australia
e-mail: marianna.sigala@unisa.edu.au

U. Gretzel
University of Queensland, St Lucia, QLD, Australia
e-mail: u.gretzel@business.uq.edu.au

© Springer-Verlag Berlin Heidelberg 2016
R. Egger et al. (eds.), *Open Tourism*, Tourism on the Verge,
DOI 10.1007/978-3-642-54089-9_17

sharing and related online social activities (Sigala, Christou, & Gretzel, 2012). Brenner and Smith (2013), as part of the Pew Research Center, reported that 72 % of online U.S. adults use social networking sites today and more than a third of American consumers rate products/services (37 %) or post comments/reviews about products/services (32 %) online (Pew Internet & American Life Project, 2013). Among various user-generated content topics, tourism-related contents are often the most popular issues shared and consumed by users (Miguens, Baggio, & Costa, 2008). Importantly, social media use has increasingly been integrated into all phases of the tourism experience. The findings of PhoCusWright (2013) show that over eight in ten U.S. online travellers are active on social networks and more than half of them even access social sites while travelling to post about their trips.

The content created by travellers is perceived as highly trustworthy (Dickinger, 2011), credible and relevant (O'Connor, 2010), and up-to-date and engaging (Gretzel & Yoo, 2008); thus, trip planners often take consumer-generated travel reviews into account during their decision-making process as the intangibility of tourism experiences makes pre-purchase trial impossible and therefore increases the need for accounts of first-person experience reports (Gretzel & Yoo, 2008; Mazzarol, Sweeney, & Soutar, 2007; Sweeney, Soutar, & Mazzarol, 2008; Zeithaml, 1981). As such, user-generated content plays an important role in influencing destination awareness and selection as well as destination brand and image creation (Munar, 2011; Tussyadiah & Fesenmaier, 2009). While there are various websites that provide traveller-generated content, TripAdvisor is the world's largest travel content community (TripAdvisor.com, 2013a) and the most popular travel information site (O'Connor, 2010), empowering users to write, search, and share travel reviews. According to a presentation by TripAdvisor at the Social Media in Tourism Australia Symposium (TripAdvisor.com, 2013b), most social media traffic to travel websites comes from four sources: Facebook, TripAdvisor, Twitter, and Pinterest. Among them, TripAdvisor drives the most consumers, who spend more time on the site and view more pages (PhoCusWright, 2012).

In light of this situation, this case study explores TripAdvisor to understand its role in social media within the tourism landscape and specifically in relation to the "Open Innovation in Tourism (OIT)" phenomenon by analysing its key features, services, and business model approach. From this case analysis, key challenges and insights will be drawn and discussed.

2 Main Features and Value Added Services

TripAdvisor was founded in February 2000 and was a subsidiary of online travel services provider Expedia until late 2011, when it was spun off in a public offering (Hoover's Company Records, 2013). In the past decade, the company has grown rapidly and has expanded its reach to 34 countries and 21 languages (TripAdvisor.

com, 2013a). In addition, it manages and operates over 20 other travel media brand websites including virtualtourist.com, cruisecritic.com, seatguru.com, and onetime. com (TripAdvisor.com, 2013a). The TripAdvisor platform provides more than 125 million travel reviews and opinions covering over 3 million tourism businesses. It attracts over 260 million unique monthly visitors and more than 80 new contributions are posted every minute (TripAdvisor.com, 2013a).

As the world's largest travel site, TripAdvisor offers various services targeting both consumers and businesses and continuously adds new services and features to meet the evolving needs of travellers and tourism providers. These various services offered by TripAdvisor make it difficult to categorise it as a specific business. The Standard Industrial Classification (SIC) system categorises TripAdvisor as a part of the "Data processing and preparation" industry while the North American Industry Classification System (NAICS) puts the company into the "Travel Agencies" industry. Indeed, TripAdvisor can be considered a type of travel intermediary as it mediates between tourism demand and supply and facilitates transactions. On the one hand, it gives travellers a platform to search and share reviews of various travel businesses and destinations (Hoover's Company Records, 2013; O'Connor, 2010; TripAdvisor.com, 2013c) and allows them to directly compare offers. On the other hand, it enables tourism suppliers to better understand their travellers (e.g. profile, preferences), promote their businesses, and monitor their competitors (e.g. services, offers, and limitations). However, TripAdvisor is also an infomediary, specialising in the so called 'Big Data' field and focussing on linking and serving the needs of both tourism demand and supply by providing a technological platform through which content can be created, analysed and distributed to meet the needs of travellers and tourism firms.

TripAdvisor's corporate communications (2013a, b, c) and previous literature (e.g. O'Connor, 2010) discuss its key features. These features and the associated values delivered are summarised in Tables 1 and 2. Figure 1 further illustrates how some of these features are implemented on the TripAdvisor website.

3 Business Model: Actors, Resources, and Value Co-creation

The development and continuous expansion of TripAdvisor's business model is based on its corporate mission, namely to *"Help travellers around the world plan and have the perfect trip"*. To achieve this, TripAdvisor's strategy is built around the collection, analysis, exchange, and exploitation of travel information among tourism stakeholders. The core competitive asset of the company is its technological infrastructure and platform connecting tourism demand and supply and whose functionality empowers TripAdvisor to enable value co-creation in innovative ways. Specifically, the platform enables travellers to upload and share travel reviews as well as interact and engage in discussions with other travellers in

Table 1 TripAdvisor's key features/services and value added for consumers

Consumer—demand side	
Key features/services	Description and value added
Travel reviews and ratings	*Reputable crowd sourcing*: Travellers can view reviews and ratings generated by other travellers and see reviewer profiles enhanced by photos, badges, and the number of helpful votes received from other travellers. This comprehensive reputation management system helps users in determining the helpfulness of reviews and/or reviewers. It also increases the intrinsic (i.e. self-esteem) and extrinsic (i.e. get a better score than others) motivation of users to contribute reliable reviews.
Profile	*Customisation*: Users can edit their profiles, so they can search and view travel reviews and suggestions according to their travel preferences and profile *Status*: Users can display their expertise and obtain recognition for their contributions.
Reviews at a glance	*Content aggregation*: It allows travellers to see a summary of other travellers' ratings, types of travellers, and the latest reviews.
Trending now	*Social influence*: Travellers can see the latest reviews and contents added for a destination.
Candid traveller photos/videos	*"Behind-the-scenes" information*: Travellers can post photos and videos along with a review.
Forums	*Social interaction/Collaboration*: Members can ask for advice and share their opinions.
Saves	*Customisation*: Travellers can personalise their trip planning by saving travel reviews to personal "My Trips" folders.
Maps	*Mash-up information*: Dynamic maps visualise travel-related information (e.g. hotel price and availability) in one place.
Destination guides	*Crowd sourcing*: Travellers can view the online destination travel guidebooks created by other travellers. *Collaboration*: Travellers edit and contribute to the destination travel guidebooks using a Wiki function.
Hotel selection tool and popularity index	*Information filtering*: Travellers can sort a destination's most popular hotels by different sorting criteria (e.g. price, traveller rating, or luxury) and see the rank of a specific hotel compared to other hotels at the destination.
Trip watch/newsletter	*Customisation*: Travellers can receive customised e-mail alerts on specific hotels, attractions, and destinations.
GreenLeaders program	*Decision support*: Travellers can identify environmentally-friendly options.

(continued)

Table 1 (continued)

Consumer—demand side	
Key features/services	Description and value added
Metasearch	*Decision support*: Prices for different airlines/ booking platforms are displayed simultaneously to allow for price comparisons.
Vacation rental calculator	*Decision support*: Travellers can compare their accommodation options with vacation rental homes and calculate the costs and savings.
Flights with fees estimator and alerts	*Decision support*: Travellers can estimate entire costs of a flight including ticket price, fees for checked luggage, and in-flight food service and entertainment. If subscribed to alerts, they will be notified when prices drop.
Facebook integration: Use of Facebook's social graph	*Information filtering*: Travellers can view reviews contributed by Facebook friends, who they know and trust more than strangers. *Interaction and networking*: Travellers can find and interact with people they know (friends) and strangers (e.g. users wishing to visit Paris can find people who have previously visited the city). *Crowd sourcing/Status*: Users promote their profiles within their Facebook network to build social status. This creates incentives to add more content for the benefit of others: 35 % of new reviews are from Facebook-connected users (TripAdvisor.com, 2013b).
Apps	*Location-based/offline services*: Apps provide travellers with location-specific content when on the go and with offline city guides.
Gamification: Apps for massive multiple user social games or opinion polls	*Social networking*: Travellers can create their travel profile (i.e. where they have been, where they wish to go, and favourite destinations/providers) to display their expertise and information needs to others. Travellers can also use it to find others wishing to travel to the same place and co-organise a trip. *Entertainment*: It adds a fun element to search and content creation.

order to obtain trip-planning support (i.e. explore, dream, plan, and share travel experiences) (Sigala, 2010). The platform also has the capability to collect, analyse and provide this user-generated content to tourism suppliers in such a way that they can exploit it for: advertising/promotion; brand-awareness building; identifying and understanding potential target markets to more effectively develop and implement marketing campaigns; and improving their tourism offers. Moreover, the market intelligence (i.e. information about travellers and competitors) that is available through the TripAdvisor platform helps tourism firms improve the effectiveness of their service development process (Sigala, 2012). Travellers benefit from the business exploitation of these information resources, as firms can later serve them with more

Table 2 TripAdvisor's key features/services and value added for businesses

Business—supply side	
API	*Content generation*: TripAdvisor makes the following information available on partners' websites through its API: traveller photos, detailed reviews and rating data for accommodations, attractions, restaurants, and destinations.
Registered business	*Brand awareness, lead generation and monitoring*: Businesses can register on TripAdvisor. This is an additional entry point for customers to learn and write/read reviews for businesses and is a tool for monitoring customer feedback.
Business response	*Customer service*: Opportunity to respond to traveller reviews to optimise customer relationships or manage specific complaints.
Business listings	*Promotion*: Hotels and accommodations can post their special offers and announcements in the hotel listings pages and access visitor analytics.
Metasearch	*Lead generation*: Hotel price metasearch results appear on hotel listing pages. This can generate cost-per-click leads for travel agencies and providers.
Related hotels recommendation	*Search marketing*: TripAdvisor recommends hotels based on travellers' search criteria.
Display Ad/sponsorship	*Brand building and promotion:* Brand awareness and promotion opportunity for travel-related businesses.
TripAdvisor widgets	*Sales generation*: Widgets allow tourism firms to add TripAdvisor content to their own website. Some widgets display the latest reviews and awards of the tourism firms, while others promote the best of the local area, link to the firm's TripAdvisor page, or encourage customers to review the firm.
Review Express	*Content generation and performance measurement*: The Review Express Dashboard provides business owners with performance data on their email campaigns and reviews generated from Review Express. It gives business owners the option to send bulk emails to their past guests asking them to write a review about their experience.
Rave Review widget	*Brand image and sales generation*: A marketing tool that allows hotel, restaurant, and attraction owners to display a five-star TripAdvisor review on their own websites. The product is available to establishments that have received outstanding reviews and are in good standing on the site.
GreenLeaders program	*Brand image and sales generation*: The TripAdvisor GreenLeaders Program helps hotels and B&Bs that have adopted environmentally-friendly practices get the recognition they deserve.
TripAdvisor Connect	*Sales generation*: TripAdvisor Connect offers different levels of capability/functionality: • TripAdvisor Connect—Providers can bid for metasearch traffic • TripAdvisor Connect Plus—Providers can bid for metasearch traffic and automate review collection efforts using TripAdvisor's Review Express service • TripAdvisor Connect Premium—Providers can bid for traffic, automate review collection, and track the results of their activity to measure their return on investment.

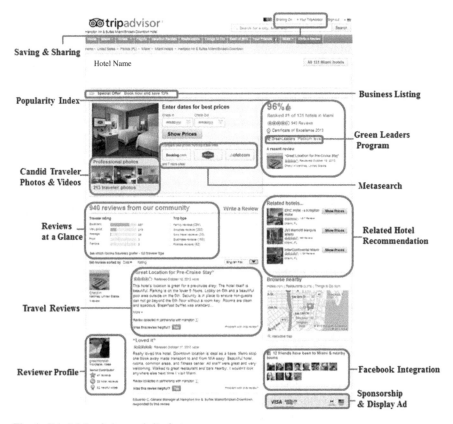

Fig. 1 TripAdvisor's key website features

appealing and personalised offerings. Furthermore, the TripAdvisor content and opportunities for interaction enable travellers to 'plan their perfect trip'. Overall, TripAdvisor positions itself as a one-stop trip-planning online venue for travellers and a valuable platform in supporting critical business functions for tourism providers, travel intermediaries, and destinations.

Hence, the core of TripAdvisor's business model and strategy is the development, continuous enhancement, and maintenance of the platform and its contents through features that further facilitate and encourage value creation for travellers and firms. TripAdvisor provides and operates this platform that enables resource exchanges and co-creation amongst stakeholders while of course also generating revenue for itself through advertising and promotion services (Table 3).

For TripAdvisor's business and revenue model to work, the company has to solve problems associated with network externalities (the availability of travel reviews and information attracts travellers to the platform, more travel information resources attract more tourism suppliers, more tourism suppliers will pay TripAdvisor if more travellers go to the platform and contribute content, and travellers will not visit the platform unless there is an availability of a huge amount

Table 3 TripAdvisor's revenue model: major sources

Click-based Ad	Represented 74 % of total revenue (+21 % compared to the second quarter of 2012)
Display-based Ad	Thirteen percent of total revenue (+18 % compared to the second quarter of 2012)
Subscriptions, etc.	Thirteen percent of total revenue (+68 % compared to the second quarter of 2012)
Business listings	Special offers, announcements, mobile upgrades, etc.

Source: TripAdvisor Financial Results document (second quarter 2013 financial results) and Investor Presentation

of travel information). This requires continuous innovation. Thus, to increase the invaluable base (i.e. consumer-generated online travel information) that attracts traffic from travellers and in turn persuades businesses to also use and invest in the platform, TripAdvisor has recently developed gamification applications to motivate and inspire travellers to contribute content and interact with others in order to exchange travel resources (Table 1). Gamification is the application of game-play mechanisms to non-game contexts with the purpose of increasing customer loyalty, commitment, and participation in co-creation applications (Sigala, 2015). The fun-ware design of TripAdvisor's gamification applications uses various behavioural, feedback, and progression game elements and mechanics (e.g. Xu, 2011) to increase travellers' engagement with the platform. For example, users are motivated to upload information about cities, destinations, suppliers, and attractions that they have visited as well as contribute travel reviews, because this information appears in their user profile as a scorecard and on a leader board, which in turn represents their level of expertise (i.e. international traveller or not, visited famous places or not). This leader board creates a kind of competition/game among users that motivates them to continually upload as much information as possible to increase their self-esteem and social status online. This leader board also motivates interaction and exchanges among users, as it enables travellers to find others with similar travel profiles (e.g. who have been in specific places, so they can e-mail them to get more personalised tips). Traveller profiles also feature a scorecard showing their evaluation score as contributors of reviews, which is based on the score that others are giving them for the reviews that they have written. This game approach motivates travellers to write not only many travel reviews but also good quality reviews. At the same time, the information added to the travellers' profiles allows businesses to derive market intelligence and better target promotional campaigns.

From a co-creation perspective (Storbacka, Frow, Nenonen, & Payne, 2012), TripAdvisor's business model can be summarised as follows:

- Customer value creation: The value proposition of the firm in terms of how it helps the customer to co-create value. TripAdvisor facilitates the generation of content by travellers and increases the value of this content by linking it to information and services provided by businesses/destinations.

- Earnings logic: How the actors generate value for themselves and others (mutual betterment). TripAdvisor generates revenue by offering businesses opportunities to derive market intelligence, provide customer service, manage their online reputation, and implement targeted advertising campaigns.
- Resources and capabilities of the actors: What resources and capabilities the actors possess and how they exchange them for co-creating value. TripAdvisor provides the technical platform through which value is co-created.

The major actors supporting TripAdvisor's business model are: The travellers, the tourism suppliers, and other (tourism) partners (e.g. intermediaries, destinations, travel websites, and Facebook). Table 4 explains in depth the three elements of TripAdvisor's business model by giving some examples of resources being exchanged amongst actors (top right in boxes), as well as examples of value (economic, social, and/or emotional value) that actors create when exchanging these resources (bottom left in boxes). Resources that actors may possess and exchange can relate to the following types: tangible or intangible resources (e.g. tools, software, and information); human resources (e.g. skills, knowledge, and virtual communities); and relational ones (e.g. relations to partners and suppliers, and network membership). To be sustainable in the long term, relations between the actors should lead to win-win situations, e.g. actors should give but also get resources and there should be a fair, transparent, and equal distribution of value creation amongst actors.

Figure 2 provides another visualisation of the resource exchanges amongst the actors comprising TripAdvisor's co-creation ecosystem. Its star shape clearly demonstrates TripAdvisor's central role and its technological platform for facilitating resource exchanges. It also illustrates the possible opportunities to continuously add new types and additional actors to the ecosystem.

Given the rapid technological advances, increasing global competition, and the fast-changing consumer demands and trends, it becomes evident that the long-term sustainability and competitiveness of the TripAdvisor business model heavily depends on its ability to continuously update and enrich its value added services and functionality. As no one firm can nowadays solely rely on internal capacities and resources to create innovation and value, the competitiveness of TripAdvisor significantly relies on its ability to maintain and evolve its ecosystem whereby existing and/or new actors join the network in order to provide, exchange, and combine new and existing resources that will ensure the continuous co-creation of value. Hence, TripAdvisor should continuously search and identify potential actors who may possess valuable resources that can be mixed with its own resources and/or the resources of other actors within the ecosystem in order to generate new value. Areas of service development and resources on which TripAdvisor has been focusing during recent years to expand and enrich its ecosystem and value added generation capabilities are the following: Social media capabilities, mobile services, internationalisation of services, and travel content resources. Table 5 provides some of the most interesting additions of partners to the TripAdvisor ecosystem by also identifying their value added services. Other recently added

Table 4 Relations between the actors of the TripAdvisor co-creation ecosystem: Resource exchanges and value co-creation amongst actor dyads

Resources provided by / Value delivered to	TripAdvisor	Tourism firms[a]	Travellers	Facebook	Other websites
	Exchange of resources				
TripAdvisor	*Value creation* –	*Content, promotional offers, and demand for advertising* Development of travel content (e.g. city guides) and offers (e.g. special offers), generation of revenue	*Content, profile, and website usage* Content can be leveraged for business purposes	*User profiles, social networks, and platform for extended user interactions* Access to potential users, support in motivating content creation, website traffic	*Added functionality (e.g. booking and availability search tools/price comparison tools) and access to new specialised content (e.g. airport information)* Expansion of value offering
Tourism Firms	*Access to customers, website traffic, and effective marketing and brand-building tools whose impact/value can be easily measured* Target marketing, performance measurement, and campaign management	–	*Feedback and requests* Market intelligence	*Platform for promotion and market intelligence* Target marketing and greater reach	*Membership database and content provision for various devices and/or countries* Target marketing and provision of more distribution channels for generating sales
Travellers	*Development of a loyal traveller community and trip-planning support tools* Search and access to travel information, access to traveller	*Information, promotional offers, and customer service* Provision of special offers, responses to complaints, and new/better services	–	*Networking tools, consolidated profiles across platforms, personalised information, and content search and sharing tools* Socially validated	*Booking tools, additional information, content provision for various devices and/or countries, and networking tools* One-stop trip planning

				nformation and opportunity for identity construction	
	network for getting advice and starting discussions, and access to tourism firms for complaints/appraisals				
Facebook	*Access to and use of travellers' profiles and content contributions* Expansion of the influence and promotion of FB in other platforms, becoming a standard for social networking, and the enrichment of FB content with travel specialised content	*Content and promotional offers, and demand for FB ads* Enrichment of FB with travel specialised content and offers, and revenue	*Rich content* Enrichment of FB with travellers experiences/ content that can be exploited for advertising purposes	–	*Content and platform integration* Expansion of the influence and promotion of FB in other platforms, becoming a standard for social networking, and enrichment of FB content with travel specialised content
Other websites	*Access to member database and website traffic* Promotion to a new membership database and a new channel for revenue generation and advertising	*Content and promotional offers* Identification of new tourism firms for generating revenue	*Content and website usage* Expansion of their target market and market intelligence	*Social network data* Market intelligence	–

[a]Tourism firms may be hotels, restaurants, attractions, etc.

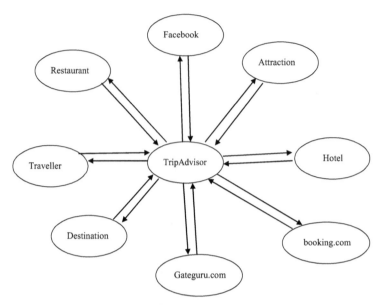

Fig. 2 TripAdvisor's co-creation ecosystem: an open system enabling the plug and play of new actors

partners not listed in Table 5 include Tingo (money back hotels), Booking Buddy (cheap flights), Smarter Travel (travel guides), SniqueAway (hotel deals), Airfarewatchdog (airfare deals and trends), and FlipKey (vacation rentals).

4   Open Innovation Approach

Open innovation is based on the assumption that an organisation cannot just rely on its own resources but has to engage with partners in order to innovate (Dahlander & Gann, 2010; Sigala & Chalkiti, 2014). West and Gallagher (2006) define it as systematic encouragement and exploration of a range of internal and external sources for innovation. While in the context of Web 2.0 open innovation is often focused specifically on obtaining customer input in the innovation process (Baglieri & Consoli, 2009; Sigala, 2012), Dahlander and Gann (2010) identify four different kinds of open innovation based on whether the resources are used internally or externally and whether direct monetary compensation is involved; there are two forms of inbound innovation (acquiring and sourcing) and two kinds of outbound innovation (selling and revealing).

TripAdvisor does not build its innovation approach based on customer input but rather acquires technology and innovative services from other companies or acquires entire companies in order to be able to integrate their tools into its platform. It also engages in selling/licensing as well as revealing by releasing its

Table 5 Expansion and enrichment of the TripAdvisor co-creation ecosystem

Actor	Value co-creation	Facts
Facebook (collaboration with social graph)	'Wisdom of friends' services, gamification value and benefits, generation of Web traffic, enhanced awareness, and increase in TripAdvisor user numbers and engagement (contributions and interactions)	• TripAdvisor averaged nearly 38 million monthly Facebook visitors to its website and Facebook app during a quarter, and it remains the #1 travel app on Facebook. • Facebook app: Cities I've Visited, an interactive map that allows travellers to pin where they've been and where they're going next and share it with their friends. More than 20 million people have added more than 1.5 billion cities to their TripAdvisor Cities I've Visited maps, and it has consistently been Facebook's #1 travel application since its launch in June 2007. • TripAdvisor grew marketable members more than 80 % year-over-year to 53 million, according to company logs. • 35 % of the new reviews are from Facebook-connected users. • More than 1 billion open graph actions.
EveryTrail (purchased by TripAdvisor)	Allows TripAdvisor customers to access walking tours, city guides, and hiking trails from their smartphones	Mobile downloads rose dramatically from two million in 2010 to 13 million in 2011, while monthly unique visitors via smartphones and tablets skyrocketed to 16 million in 2011 from a mere four million in 2010 due to TripAdvisor's launch of 20 free Mobile City Guides for Android and iOS.
Where I've been (purchased by TripAdvisor)	Allows users to pinpoint their travels on an interactive map	More than two billion travel 'pins' collected by TripAdvisor.
Holiday lettings (purchased by TripAdvisor)	Generate users/sales and business, and expand and enrich travel content.	Sales in the U.S. dropped from 61 % of 2010 sales to 55 % in 2011; TripAdvisor made up for it in the U.K. and in other countries.

(continued)

Table 5 (continued)

Actor	Value co-creation	Facts
		TripAdvisor nowadays also features information search and travel reviews for vacation homes.
International acquisitions: Virtualtourist.com, holidaywatchdog.com, and travel booking comparison site onetime.com	Generation and internationalisation of traveller and business users, and travel content enrichment	Accounting for 24 % of sales in 2010, countries outside the U.S. and U.K. saw revenue rise to 29 % in 2011.
Acquisitions for content enrichment: Jetsetter, CruiseWise, Niumba, GateGuru, and SeatGuru	Travel content enrichment (airport maps, stores, tips, weather and flight status; seat maps; and flight search) Content provision in mobile platforms	• SeatGuru mobile app downloads doubled year-over-year. • Including downloads of Jetsetter and GateGuru, TripAdvisor reached 50 million cumulative downloads and the average unique monthly visitors via smartphone and tablet devices grew over 200 % year-over-year to approximately 79 million for the quarter ending on June 30, 2013, according to company logs.
Third-party social networking applications	TripAdvisor has extended its brand exposure to millions of people through applications on popular third-party social networking sites	• TravelPod's Traveler IQ Challenge, which determines a traveller's knowledge of geography with a timed test, has been played by more than 2.5 million people since June 2007. • Local Picks, a Facebook app that provides dining recommendations from locals and friends to discover and choose the best places to eat.

Source: TripAdvisor website

API to selected TripAdvisor partners and making a variety of tools available to tourism firms that can play a critical role in designing new value added services. What is remarkable is the extent to which TripAdvisor engages in these activities. The approach has allowed TripAdvisor to significantly build on its original techno-logical innovation and expand its influence within the tourism industry.

5 Key Challenges for the Future

Most of TripAdvisor's activities/offerings are proprietary. To enable actors to participate in its ecosystem and exchange resources, TripAdvisor should adopt and maintain an open technology infrastructure whereby potential partners can 'plug and play' and seamlessly integrate their own platform to exchange resources with others (e.g. the integration of the API of the social graph of Facebook with the TripAdvisor platform or the integration of the availability and booking search engines of various travel websites with TripAdvisor to create the TripAdvisor connect functionality). Thus, the adoption of open source software and/or industry standards are equally important in supporting open innovation, as is the nurturing of an open organisational culture aiming to identify and manage partners and success-ful partnerships with various actors.

TripAdvisor's main value proposition is access to contents provided by travel-lers. Its success therefore depends drastically on travellers' ability and willingness to use the platform. Competition is increasing from other social media platforms and TripAdvisor will have to make sure that consumers continue to believe in the value of the TripAdvisor community. Encouraging high-quality content generation is a major issue within this context, with TripAdvisor struggling to detect deceptive reviews (Yoo & Gretzel, 2009). Another challenge is to identify and continuously engage so-called lead users (Baglieri & Consoli, 2009), e.g. such as the currently featured Destination Experts (Hochmeister, Gretzel, & Werthner, 2013).

Another issue could be the reliance on revenue from click-based advertising and a large portion of revenue coming from one market, namely the United States (TripAdvisor.com, 2013c). Greater diversification and geographical spread of rev-enue sources seems to be critical.

Most importantly, the way consumers plan trips is changing, with much greater focus being placed on at-destination decision making, transactions with non-traditional tourism players (e.g. through AirBnB), and reliance on mobile technology to obtain decision support. TripAdvisor will have to closely watch these developments in order to identify new partners that can move the TripAdvisor co-creation ecosystem into the next era of trip planning.

6 Key Conclusions and Learning Outcomes for the Tourism Industry

- TripAdvisor's success is inherently built on continuously adding value to its services through the expansion of its co-creation ecosystem.
- TripAdvisor's role as a focal firm in the ecosystem depends on the willingness of consumers to provide content and use the platform for trip planning.
- TripAdvisor's outbound innovation focus is critical to stimulate innovation within the tourism industry and auxiliary industries.
- TripAdvisor's innovation approach is not as open as it could be.
- TripAdvisor's ecosystem reflects the networked nature of tourism and therefore provides important insights for the tourism industry in terms of how innovative service provision can be structured to serve both customer and business partner needs.
- Technological innovations are key drivers for structural changes in the tourism industry.
- Web 2.0 supports new models for collaboration and network building that have yet to be fully explored by many players in the tourism industry.
- Understanding the different ways in which open innovation can be structured is critical for tourism industry players in order to identify innovation opportunities.

References

Baglieri, D., & Consoli, R. (2009). Collaborative innovation in tourism: Managing virtual communities. *The TQM Journal, 21*(4), 353–364.

Brenner, J., & Smith, A. (2013). *72 % of online adults are social networking site users.* Accessed August 13, 2013, from http://www.pewinternet.org/~/media//Files/Reports/2013/PIP_Social_networking_sites_update.pdf

Dahlander, L., & Gann, D. M. (2010). How open is innovation? *Research Policy, 39*, 699–709.

Dickinger, A. (2011). The trustworthiness of online channels for experience-and goal-directed search tasks. *Journal of Travel Research, 50*(4), 378–391.

Gillin, P. (2007). *The new influencers: A marketer's guide to new social media.* Fresno, CA: Quill Driver Books.

Gretzel, U., & Yoo, K.-H. (2008). Use and impact of online travel reviews. In P. O'Connor, W. Höpken, & U. Gretzel (Eds.), *Information and communication technologies in tourism 2008* (pp. 35–46). Vienna, Austria: Springer.

Hochmeister, M., Gretzel, U., & Werthner, H. (2013). Destination expertise in online travel communities. In L. Cantoni & Z. Xiang (Eds.), *Information and communication technologies in tourism 2013* (pp. 219–230). Berlin: Springer.

Hoover's Company Records. (2013). *Hoover's company records-in-depth records about TripAdvisor, Inc.* Accessed August 13, from LexisNexis database.

Mazzarol, T., Sweeney, J., & Soutar, G. (2007). Conceptualizing word-of-mouth activity, triggers and conditions: An exploratory study. *European Journal of Marketing, 41*, 1475–1494.

Miguens, J., Baggio, R., & Costa, C. (2008). Social media and tourism destinations: TripAdvisor case study. In *The Proceedings of IASK ART2008 (Advances in Tourism Research 2008),* Aveiro, Portugal, May 26–28. Accessed August 5, 2013, from http://www.iby.it/turismo/papers/baggio-aveiro2.pdf

Munar, A. M. (2011). Tourist-created content: Rethinking destination branding. *International Journal of Culture, Tourism and Hospitality Research, 5*(3), 291–305.

O'Connor, P. (2010). Managing a hotel's image on TripAdvisor. *Journal of Hospitality Marketing & Management, 19,* 754–772.

Pew Internet & American Life Project. (2013). *Trend data (adults): What internet users do online.* Accessed November 2, 2013, from http://www.pewinternet.org/Static-Pages/Trend-Data-(Adults)/Online-Activites-Total.aspx

PhoCusWright. (2012). *Benchmarking the impact of social media on tourism websites.* Accessed October 30, 2013, from http://connect.phocuswright.com/2012/11/benchmarking-the-impact-of-social-media-on-tourism-websites/

PhoCusWright. (2013). *How U.S. travelers use social media.* Accessed August 5, 2013, from http://www.phocuswright.com/research_updates/how-us-travelers-use-social-media-infographic

Sigala, M. (2010). Measuring customer value in online collaborative trip planning processes. *Marketing Intelligence and Planning, 28*(4), 418–443.

Sigala, M. (2012). Exploiting web 2.0 for new service development: Findings and implications from the Greek tourism industry. *International Journal of Tourism Research, 14,* 551–566.

Sigala, M. (2015). The application and impact of gamification on trip planning and experiences: The case of TripAdvisor's funware. *Electronic Markets: The International Journal of Networked Markets, 25*(3), 189–209.

Sigala, M., & Chalkiti, K. (2014). Investigating the exploitation of web 2.0 for knowledge management in the Greek tourism industry: An utilisation-importance analysis. *Computers in Human Behavior, 30,* 800–812.

Sigala, M., Christou, E., & Gretzel, U. (2012). Web 2.0 in travel, tourism and hospitality: Theory, practice and cases. Aldershot: Ashgate Publishers.

Storbacka, K., Frow, P., Nenonen, S., & Payne, A. (2012). Designing business models for value co-creation. In S. L. Vargo & R. F. Lusch (Eds.), *Special issue – Toward a better understanding of the role of value in markets and marketing, review of marketing research* (Vol. 9, pp. 51–78). Bingley: Emerald Group Publishing Limited.

Sweeney, J., Soutar, G., & Mazzarol, T. (2008). Factors influencing word of mouth effectiveness: Receiver perspectives. *European Journal of Marketing, 42,* 344–364.

TripAdvisor.com. (2013a). *TripAdvisor fact sheet.* Accessed August 12, 2013, from http://www.tripadvisor.com/PressCenter-c4-Fact_Sheet.html.

TripAdvisor.com. (2013b). TripAdvisor – DMO best practices. In *Presentation at the social media in tourism Australia symposium,* July 17–18, 2013, Wollongong, Australia. Accessed August 15, 2013, from https://www.dropbox.com/sh/gy4x9mtmlst26kk/W7L0ooVwYX

TripAdvisor.com. (2013c). *Investor presentation.* Accessed August 13, 2013, from http://ir.tripadvisor.com/events.cfm

Tussyadiah, I. P., & Fesenmaier, D. R. (2009). Mediating tourist experiences: Access to places via shared videos. *Annals of Tourism Research, 36*(1), 24–40.

West, J., & Gallagher, S. (2006). Challenges of open innovation: The paradox of firm investment in open-source software. *R&D Management, 36*(3), 319–331.

Xu, Y. (2011). *Literature review on web application gamification and analytics* (CSDL Technical report, 11–05).

Yoo, K.-H., & Gretzel, U. (2009). Comparison of deceptive and truthful travel reviews. In W. Höpken, U. Gretzel, & R. Law (Eds.), *Information and communication technologies in tourism 2009* (pp. 37–48). Vienna, Austria: Springer.

Zeithaml, V. A. (1981). How consumer evaluation processes differ between gods and services. In J. H. Donnelly & W. R. George (Eds.), *Marketing of services* (pp. 186–190). Chicago, IL: America Marketing Association.

Opening Up Government: Citizen Innovation and New Modes of Collaboration

Stefan Etzelstorfer, Thomas Gegenhuber, and Dennis Hilgers

Learning Objectives

- Understand what the concept of open government (transparency, participation, collaboration) means for municipalities.
- Explore how the city of Linz and its administration realized different open government principles on a local level.
- Analyse how the city successfully managed to implement the interactive mapping and reporting platform "*Schau auf Linz*" ("Look after Linz").
- See what positive spillovers were created by this platform for the municipality's attractiveness to tourists.

1 Introduction

On November 19, 1863, Abraham Lincoln outlined governing goals in his Gettysburg Address: a "government of the people, by the people, for the people." Until now, "by the people" has primarily manifested through democratic elections, but new technology platforms and models of open government allow for a richer manifestation of Lincoln's vision. U.S. President Barack Obama's Open Government Directive demonstrated how technology platforms can be used to involve citizens in the political process. The Open Government Directive's principles are transparency, participation, and collaboration (Orszag, 2009). The directive gener-

S. Etzelstorfer • T. Gegenhuber (✉) • D. Hilgers
Johannes Kepler University Linz, Linz, Austria
e-mail: stefan.etzelstorfer@gmail.com; thomas.gegenhuber@jku.at; dennis.hilgers@jku.at

© Springer-Verlag Berlin Heidelberg 2016   257
R. Egger et al. (eds.), *Open Tourism*, Tourism on the Verge,
DOI 10.1007/978-3-642-54089-9_18

ated numerous projects at the federal level (for a review, see Wise, Paton, & Gegenhuber, 2012), and bolstered the popularity of open government at all levels.[1]

Open government is essentially the application of user- and open-innovation principles in the public sector (Chesbrough, 2006; von Hippel, 2005). The core idea is systematically integrating citizens and other stakeholders in policy and the public value creation process (Hilgers, 2012; Lathrop & Ruma, 2010; Noveck, 2009; Tapscott & Williams, 2006; Wise et al., 2012). The open government paradigm emphasizes the active role of citizens as co-producers whose expert knowledge in certain areas can contribute to better outcomes. This integration blurs classic boundaries of the political-administrative system. Web-based communications and relatively low-cost access to devices such as PCs make the scalability and magnitude of integrating citizens into the public value creation process possible (Baldwin & von Hippel, 2011; Hilgers, 2012; Lakhani, Lifshitz-Assaf, & Tushman, 2012; Picot, Reichwald, & Wigand, 2003; Reichwald & Piller, 2009). Hilgers (2012) proposes an open government framework encompassing three major areas for implementing open government: citizen ideation and innovation (e.g. contests), collaborative service delivery (e.g. the interactive mapping and reporting citizen-sourcing application *"SeeClickFix"*), and collaborative democracy (e.g. New Zealand calls upon citizens to review proposed parliamentary bills via a wiki-based tool).

Globally, federal governments including those of the United Kingdom, the Republic of Ireland, Japan, and Austria have become involved in open government, but there has also been significant momentum at the local and state/provincial levels. For instance, "open cities", a project the European Union co-funds, aims to implement open innovation instruments in seven major European cities: Amsterdam, Barcelona, Berlin, Bologna, Helsinki, Paris, and Rome (www.opencities.net). Smaller cities also embrace open government principles. Essen, a city in the central German Ruhr area, harnessed citizens' ideas for reducing noise pollution. Freiburg is one of many German cities to employ a participatory budget, one crafted with major input from citizens (Wise et al., 2012).

In this article, we emphasize the application of open government at the local level. We maintain that the local level provides significant opportunities since the propensity for experimentation is greater, investments are lower, issues are less complex, and constituent stakeholders are far closer to and more invested in the activities of government. Local governments play a key role in the policy process. Large-scale changes to policy, funding, and political affiliation are ultimately felt on the local level, where citizens can discern differences in service delivery and quality of life. Although all systems of local government differ, "what they do have

---

[1] One should note that recent political debates in the U.S., such as over the NSA scandal, reveal a discrepancy between the rhetoric of transparency and key policy issues in which the U.S. government acts opaquely. This variance raises two questions: first, to what extent are open government practices decoupled from the core activities of government? Second, where does the transparency imperative conflict with other policy goals? The answers to these questions, however, lie beyond the scope of this paper.

in common is that there is no order of government between them and the communities they serve. This is also their strength and democratic claim; they are the government closest to the people" (Steytler & Kincaid, 2009).

There is still little open government literature that considers the local level. Notable exceptions are Dobusch, Forsterleitner, and Hiesmair (2011), who crafted a manual for digital policies in a local context, or Alfano (2011). The latter conducted a case analysis on the Venice local government's implementation of online services including an interactive online mapping and reporting platform for urban maintenance problems. Alfano (2011) shows how these services influence the structure of government. Our article addresses several gaps in the literature. Regarding open government in general, we maintain that open data is more than just an instrument to achieve transparency. Since open data is a key element in many local initiatives, we argue for adding it to Hilgers (2012) open government framework. Next, the current literature provides little insight regarding the conditions for viability of an open government initiative such as a citizen-sourcing platform for mapping and reporting urban maintenance problems. Further, we know little about the challenges and barriers that exist for open government initiatives. Given that organizations are historically contingent, we ask what role the local context and prior policies play in implementing open government policies. Finally, there is hardly any literature about the spillover of open government to other local task areas. While there is a discussion on open source principles' applicability for providing better tourist information systems (Watson, Akselsen, Monod, & Pitt, 2004), there is virtually no literature on how local open government initiatives may create positive spillovers for city tourism. City tourism is a sector that suffered less than other sectors (e.g. automobile industry) in the recent economic crisis and is a driver of growth for many nations (Roland Berger, 2012). More importantly, city tourism is a crucial source of economic stimulation for local communities.

Against the backdrop of this book's goal, we show how open government positively effects the tourism sector. The City of Linz, Austria, case serves as an illustration of our arguments. The remainder of this contribution is structured as follows: first, we provide an overview of the City of Linz with a focus on digital policies. Second, we discuss the extent to which the open government framework captures Linz's open government policies. We show that the City of Linz case provides a rationale to extend Hilgers (2012) open government framework by adding "open data and open commons" as a new area. Third, we review how Linz implemented the application "*Schau auf Linz*" ("Look after Linz"), an interactive mapping and reporting platform for urban maintenance needs. Describing how the platforms works, we draw upon a contingency approach (Afuah & Tucci, 2012; Lakhani et al., 2012) to examine whether structure, design, and process of "*Schau auf Linz*" fulfils the literature's proposed requirements. The case demonstrates the limits of this approach and provides preliminary insight into how to overcome barriers for implementation by leveraging existing policies. Additionally, we examine transparency's influence on the political-administrative process. Finally, we outline open government's effect on the tourism sector, revealing the insight that a well maintained and citizen-centric service infrastructure may have a positive influence on local attractiveness to tourists.

2 The City of Linz: Laboratory for Digital Policies

2.1 From "ARS Electronica" to Open Commons Region

The provincial capital of Upper Austria, Linz has a population of approximately 190,000. A significant driver for Linz's economy is the steel producer Voestalpine Corporation, which provides thousands of jobs to the region. For this reason, Linz qualifies as an industrial, blue-collar city. Linz has been open to both cultural and technological change as important drivers of growth and quality of life.

In 1979, Linz created the "ARS Electronica", which provided a forum for experimenting with digital culture. The initiative is part avant-garde festival, competition, on-going showcase for excellence in digital art, and part media art lab offering artistic expertise for R&D projects. The ARS electronica festival attracts an international audience and the "Prix ARS Electronica", started in 1987, is the so-called "Oscar of computer art." Past winners of the Prix include Wikipedia (2004) for digital communities, Creative Commons (2004), Linux (1999) for net vision, and the Pixar movie "Toy Story" (1996) for computer animation (see www.aec.at/prix). In recent years, the local government was able to transfer the innovation potential of the ARS electronica into local politics (Dobusch & Forsterleitner, 2007). The festival is important for the tourism sector, since it not only contributes to local value creation, but also is one of the few events promoting Linz to an international audience.

The first "digital policy" project in Linz was the "hotspot initiative". The government of Linz has taken on a mandate to provide infrastructure services at affordable prices, and web access is no different. In collaboration with a local internet provider (in which the government owns shares) Linz offers free Wi-Fi in approximately 120 public squares, libraries, and community or youth centres (see www.linz.at/hotspot_Portal). The next goal of the city government was to extend the free Wi-Fi to public transportation. People spend a lot of time commuting via mass transit, and can use that time to check email, use web applications, and engage in productive or simply enjoyable activities. Not everyone has the same access to all-inclusive data plans, especially citizens in lower income brackets. Also, tourists benefit from the free Wi-Fi access, since they can avoid wasting money on roaming fees or the need to search for a free Wi-Fi spot. The Linz city council approved a motion to provide free accessible Wi-Fi on streetcars and in the most frequented bus shelters. The city-owned public transport authority (LINZ AG) equipped one streetcar as a prototype in January 2010. The prototype was successful; by the end of 2013, the LINZ AG is scheduled to equip all trams with free Wi-Fi access.

The public space server was another City of Linz project. Dobusch and Forsterleitner (2007) assert that "public space was and is the responsibility of the government. Everyone has the right of free speech and free assembly and government has to ensure that these rights are maintained. There is no reason why this should be different in the virtual space." In September 2009, the public space server launched, granting 1GB of free web space to all Linz residents over age 14

Dobusch and Forsterleitner (2010). The service includes access to an email address, web space with SQL-Databases, and numerous pre-configured web applications including Joomla, Typo3, blogging software, and a media wiki. Complementing and supporting the web space, the city-owned centre for continuing education offers free advice and courses (see http://pssinfo.public1.linz.at).

Additional projects include the creative commons subsidy model for supporting artists, an interdisciplinary master's program in web science at Johannes Kepler University (JKU), and a creative commons licence making published content available. The rationale for the last policy is that information that the government creates and funds with taxpayer money should be free and publicly available. The City has chosen to use the "Attribution-Non Commercial-No Derivation 3.0" licence, which means that while people can freely access and share the work, they must attribute content to the City of Linz, they may not use content to create derivate works, and may not use it for commercial purposes.

By using creative commons licences, Linz made the first steps towards open data. The next phase was to develop a sustainable process for integrating the web into local public policy initiatives. The City's IT department, in collaboration with Gustav Pomberger, computer science professor at the Johannes Kepler University, conducted the study "Open Commons Region of Linz" (Pomberger & Kempinger, 2010). The report summarizes the role of local government in establishing an open commons region. In the past, public funds for economic development have largely focused on capital infrastructure, such as roads and institutions. In a knowledge economy, it makes sense to invest in intellectual property, shared data, and ideas as well. The foundations of an Open Commons Region are the tangible and intangible freely-accessible public goods of a society, which include open source software, open data, open street maps, open educational resources, and freely-accessible creative works in the areas of film, music, and photography (Dobusch & Forsterleitner, 2010; Gegenhuber & Forsterleitner, 2011). The goal is not to build a repository for government information, but rather a platform that supports a vibrant public-private ecosystem. As the CTO of Linz Gerald Kempinger notes, "[w]e welcome every initiative—from citizens, community groups, and enterprises" (Glechner, 2010).

In this context, the role of government is to create a framework for public knowledge, draft appropriate legislation, build awareness, and support budding initiatives that citizens and private enterprises establish. Towards these ends, the City of Linz developed a framework for the first open commons region in Austria. The framework encompasses numerous building blocks; for simplicity's sake, we present only four in detail:

- *Open data*: the Open Commons region is the foundation of a vibrant public-private ecosystem and new business models combining public incentives and stimulus with private sector innovation and value creation. The open data platform www.data.linz.gv.at provides governmental and administrative data. The "Apps4Linz Contest", launched in spring 2012, called upon citizens to submit ideas for apps based on provided data sets (see also Sect. 2.2).

- *Conference*: the goal is both to showcase local communities, corporations, and institutions; and to broaden the base of insights with international experts. Linz hosted two conferences in August 2012 and May 2013.
- *Education*: the expansion of educational offerings in the field of open commons is a key policy goal. Some of the first prototypes were the open courseware platform and interdisciplinary master's program in web science at Johannes Kepler University.
- *Collaboration*: the public-private ecosystem will only flourish through collaborative initiatives amongst all sectors. By providing solid geo-data, for instance, the *OpenStreetMap.org* community is a possible partner for government collaboration.

The open commons region's success depends on numerous players' activities. Certainly, the effort to create this region is complex. For that reason, the City of Linz founded an agency to coordinate activities, provide advice, support educational offerings, publish reports, and organise the annual open commons conference, among other events. Part of the agency's mandate is a specific open commons clearing department to coordinate infrastructure and deal with legal questions pertaining to licensing and intellectual property rights. The Open Commons agency also supported a recent city initiative implementing the interactive mapping and reporting application "*Schau auf Linz*" ("Look after Linz"). The idea is based on the example of the British "*FixMyStreet*", or the American equivalent "*SeeClickFix*". City council member and Vice Mayor of Linz Christian Forsterleitner successfully introduced a motion in the City Council to create an application that provides such an online service where citizens can file complaints and report urban maintenance needs. If concerned citizens see damage (e.g. potholes), they can click on a map (via a webpage or mobile phone app), describe the damage, and the City's public works department will fix the problem. The process is transparent: everyone can see which issues are reported and how long it will take to resolve them. The administration has the opportunity to comment publicly on any reported issues, e.g. providing a justification as to why they have not fixed a problem (Gegenhuber & Forsterleitner, 2011).

2.2 Applying the Open Government Framework to the City of Linz

To what extent do the City of Linz initiatives fall under the heading of open government? To answer this question we match the City of Linz initiatives with Hilgers and Ihl's (2010) open government framework. Figure 1 summarizes the framework.

Regarding "citizen ideation and innovation", the open commons region launched an app contest ("Apps4Linz") to popularise the open government data platform. The contest allowed the City of Linz to tap into outside individuals'

Citizensourcing Framework for Open Government

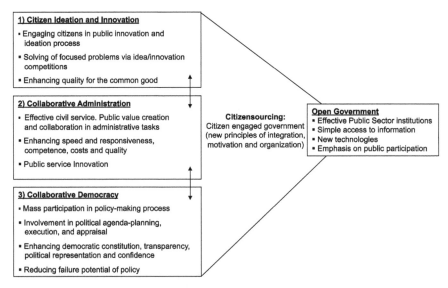

Fig. 1 Open Government framework. *Source*: Hilgers & Ihl (2010, p. 74)

expertise. Like the *appsfordemocracy.org* contest in Washington, D.C., "Apps4Linz" was less costly yet much faster than conducting the same kind of sourcing via traditional procurement processes (Hilgers, 2012). The contest yielded 39 entries. In addition to three main prizes, a special prize (1000 €) went to an application that created value for the tourism sector. The winner in this category was "Linz Finder". Amongst other benefits, this app provides information about interesting venues, helps with finding restaurants, and locates nearby Wi-Fi hotspots.

"*Schau auf Linz*" ("Look after Linz") is a prototypical case for citizen sourcing. The interactive mapping and reporting application enables the integration of citizen participation into the administrative processes. "*Schau auf Linz*" is not only a tool for reporting and fixing problems such as potholes; it is also an instrument for continuous improvement, such as better traffic light control for frequently used junctions (Hilgers, 2012).

The City of Linz has no typical web-based open government projects that fall into the "collaborative democracy" category. A noteworthy project is the recent attempt to integrate citizens into the political process and strategy development was the new cultural development plan. Instead of holding an online discussion, Linz staged numerous workshops from October 2011 through May 2012. Facilitators structured the idea-generation process through their moderation; all workshop results were well-documented online (http://kep.public1.linz.at). The ideas arising from the workshops served as the foundation for the first draft of a strategy paper. In the next step, political committees, the cultural advisory board, and several other

Table 1 Open government initiatives in Linz

Open government area	Projects and initiatives
Citizen ideation and innovation	"*Apps4Linz*" contest "*Linz-Logo*" contest
Collaborative administration (Citizen sourcing)	Interacting mapping and reporting application "*Schau auf Linz*"
Collaborative democracy	New cultural development plan (KEP Neu) http://kep.public1.linz.at
Open data and open commons (creating a vibrant public-private ecosystem)	Open data platform Creative commons licence for city of Linz publications Open commons conference

experts reviewed the paper. After this extensive review process, the City Council finally approved the cultural development plan. One goal of this plan is to further promote the City of Linz as a destination for culture-oriented tourism.

The open government framework does not allow, however, for capturing the open commons and data initiative of the City of Linz. Recall that the underlying principles for open government are transparency, participation, and collaboration. Transparency is a precondition for collaboration and participation. Neither is effective without citizens having access to the required information to fulfil the tasks (Hilgers, 2012). Open government literature documents how transparency enables citizens to monitor and influence political processes (Meijer, Curtin, & Hillebrandt, 2012). The presence of open data and open commons may contribute to transparency, but the focus on open commons and open data creates a vibrant public-private ecosystem that may be decoupled from achieving transparency in the political process. Open data or open commons may enable innovation that creates value within the public sphere; it also allows innovation that creates value solely for the private sector. For this reason, we add open data and/or open commons to the open government framework of Hilgers (2012). Table 1 summarizes the areas of the extended open government framework in which Linz has launched initiatives:

2.3   Case study "Schau auf Linz"

Previous initiatives seemed to pave the way for a cutting-edge digital policies laboratory that shaped the path to the open commons region. So far, literature on open- and user-innovation provides a framework, which explains under which conditions crowdsourcing (and thus also citizen sourcing) is a viable option for a firm (Afuah & Tucci, 2012; Lakhani et al., 2012). This contingency perspective, however, provides little insight into the challenges and barriers organisations may face in the implementation process. As a remedy, we suggest examining local contexts and prior policies to provide insight into why open government initiatives are (or are not) successful.

The municipality of Linz has a long tradition in achieving service orientation that satisfies citizens' needs. For over 10 years, the new City Hall has featured a service office based on a one-stop shopping system. An employee directly handles services such as proof of address, passports issuing, or special registrations (e.g. for dogs, parking permits etc.), without requiring citizens to visit specific departments. Additionally, a specific municipal department, the "tele-service department" handles citizens' concerns via phone. For many issues, the well-trained and -informed personnel can immediately and competently answers citizens' needs. If the tele-service department cannot immediately solve concerns, citizens are connected to relevant offices. In addition, tele-service centre staff answers email inquiries and professionally process requests, suggestions, and complaints; and are responsible for complaint management. Each issue is documented in an electronic file to ensure that citizens receive answers to all of their inquiries.

We suggest that the "Schau auf Linz" case is particularly interesting due to the enduring interaction between the public administration (which receives reports and must respond) and citizens (who file complaints and expect speedy responses). "Schau auf Linz" has an impact on the administration's daily work and core processes. In contrast, the open data platform is static. The administration may face pressure from citizens who request more datasets, but this discussion would probably receive little media attention. We use a case study approach (Eisenhardt, 1989; Yin, 2003) for our exploration, since there is still limited literature on open government implementation at a local level. We deploy the following methods: two expert interviews (Bogner & Menz, 2002; Meuser & Nagel, 2010) with city administration officials, document analysis (Flick, 2011; Lamnek, 2010) of city administration internal documents; as well as platform analysis (e.g. examining citizens' reports, analysing discussions).

The platform functions simply. Essentially, citizens post their questions (complaints, claims, suggestions, etc.) online on the homepage (see Fig. 2) or via mobile application, and identify the location on a virtual map. Once the post is online, other people can endorse the concern, comment, or add further issues. The tele-service department responsible for running "Schau auf Linz" informs users of a case's current status and is responsible for sharing the issues users raise with other departments in the administration. City employees work to resolve the problem and write a post if the problem is resolved, so all citizens can see when the issue is resolved (see Fig. 2 for a summary of how the platform works.)

Four types of complaints are distinguishable: first, there are issues that apply directly to a specific municipal department, including rubbish, broken infrastructure, and traffic. These complaints can usually be resolved quickly, e.g. regarding a garbage pick-up that needs to be made, or snow removal that has yet to take place. (The answer in this case might be, for instance, that there is a fixed plan for snow or garbage removal, referencing the overall situation as part of the response: "[t]here are 1,600 kilometres [of] road network to clean in Linz, please understand that it takes some time to clean all roads".) Experts in the different municipal departments

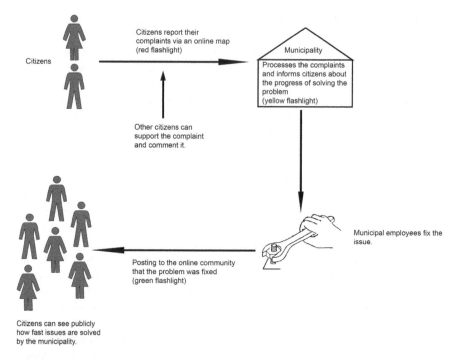

Fig. 2 Design of the platform

must deal with others individually (e.g. a no-parking sign), and generally take more time to solve them. Second, there are issues that deal with complaints belonging to companies under the municipality's purview, e.g. public transport or accommodation. Since the government owns the majority of shares, they generally treat these complaints as though the concerns belong under the authority of a specific department, e.g. LINZ AG as a publically-owned urban infrastructure company. Third, there are issues that apply to companies (public or private) where no municipal authority is in force at all. For instance, a broken elevator at a railway station in Linz belongs to the Austrian Federal Railways (ÖBB), so the company receives notice that a complaint was made. Fourth, some issues deal with complaints concerning private property within the urban area, where the City normally has no influence (e.g. rubbish on a private estate).

Hilgers (2012) notes that one of the most important preconditions and fundamental principles for collaboration and participation is transparency, which enables and encourages citizens to influence political-administrative processes (Meijer et al., 2012). Two instruments should foster the transparency of the platform: first, a communication tool for citizens, adequate to lay bare the problem-solving process. At any time people should be able to access information regarding the progress of their complaints or issues. Achieving these goals, a so-called "flashlight system" ensures that users can follow the status of their complaints. "*Schau auf Linz*" uses four colours (red, yellow, green and white). Once an issue is online and visible to all, it turns red. Once the complaint enters the problem-solving process, the system creates an electronic file and sets the flashlight to yellow. It then forwards the problem to the relevant department, which sets a time limit within which to provide an answer or a settlement. Once an issue is resolved, the flashlight turns green. Although the application has only been in use since the beginning of 2013, one of the experts noted that adjustments have already been made regarding the traffic light system. Some questions turned green too quickly, without the issue being fully resolved. For example, a user asked for a no-parking sign immediately before an intersection to prevent cars from parking at the corner and blocking the view required to proceed safely through the intersection. But because the Austrian Road Traffic Act (StVO) already prescribes a parking ban 5 m from any intersection, there was no possibility of local authority action. Consequently, another colour (white) was introduced by the tele-service department to denote issues that cannot be properly resolved.

Second, the simple fact that users can directly post their issues without preliminary screening of their contents has already engendered a better understanding of the municipality's actions and decisions. The public can discuss different needs and points of view. For example, Linz decided to end a program in public spaces and parks that provides free garbage bags for dog waste disposal. One person complained on "*Schau auf Linz*" that the disposal bags were unavailable at the park, creating a lot of attention within the community and sparking numerous additional postings. The City responded with the reason why they stopped providing free disposal bags, and noted that the savings would go towards future preservation of parks and playgrounds. Dog owners showed a lack of support, but other citizens welcomed the reallocation of funds. Citizens thus attained a better understanding of the rationale driving the administration's decisions.

Lakhani et al. (2012) suggest that if a problem is modular and the knowledge required to solve the problem is widely distributed, crowdsourcing can be a viable option for the firm. Afuah and Tucci (2012) posit that several factors influence the likelihood that a firm will outsource the problem in the form of an open call to the crowd: The problem characteristics (ease of delineation, transmission, and modularizability), characteristics of knowledge required for the solution, crowd characteristics, solution evaluation requirements, and information technology's pervasiveness and cost. "*Schau auf Linz*" beneficially fulfils most of these criteria. Regarding problem characteristics, citizens use a well-structured interface to report problems and make suggestions in previously-defined areas. The textual information citizens provided, enriched with pictures and GPS information, simplifies the transmission of problem descriptions. Regarding effective distance for problem solving, it is reasonable to assume that the city administration would have sufficient knowledge to fix most problems. However, (a) it would be too costly to continuously monitor the entire city for issues requiring resolution, and (b) citizens have tacit knowledge of the existence of some problems through their daily experience. Consequently, it is reasonable for the city administration to aim to leverage citizens' reporting practices. Knowledge needed to report issues is widely-distributed (that is, all citizens can identify and report problems), and there are many users who are able to report issues via online app or smartphone. Interest (in having a problem fixed) and identity (contributing to the social good) also motivate citizens (Kohler, Füller, & Hutter, 2013; Wise et al., 2012). There is a high level of IT pervasiveness and low cost information technology. Regarding solution evaluation requirements, "*Schau auf Linz*" does not do very well. Despite a high number of reported issues, not all of them useful, each report requires an individual answer. One of the experts highlighted how the platform is an alternative means of raising complaints and does not replace former channels. Since the platform's installation in January 2013, the total number of complaints has risen significantly. In the last few years, for example, figures rose between 1300 and 1500 complaints from January to June. In the first half of 2013, however, there have already been more than 3000 complaints. From the beginning on, the challenge was thus how to deal with those who constantly complain about everything and do not give any actionable information? Regarding this problem, two aspects deserve more detailed examination:

First, we see that different communities use "*Schau auf Linz*" for specific concerns, but at the same time our preliminary analysis suggests self-regulation effects on the platform. Regarding the former, some issues seem to be raised by multiple parties simultaneously, e.g. the demand for a car-free main square in Linz. Within 24 h, more than 60 complaints about the same cars parked on the main square were articulated on the application. Regarding the latter, users do not only lodge complaints and inquiries, they also comment on and evaluate entries of others. As a result, citizens provide unwritten rules of behaviour for themselves. They evaluate whether entries are appropriate, leaving positive or negative comments. A positive side-effect for the municipality is that other users can sanction a violation of unwritten practices of platform use in a direct tone that the municipality itself could never adopt, and mostly fulfil the task of determining whether complaints are "not important" or "unnecessary". The norms and practices of the community have a self-regulating effect. Especially during the implementation process of "*Schau auf Linz*", some departments feared that primarily grumblers would use the platform. This concern has to some extent become reality, however, we suggest that self-regulation through public sanctioning may reduce useless complaints in the long term, an effect that official rules or measures of the city authority could never achieve.

Second, we contend that prior policies and context within the administration mitigated the challenge for evaluating numerous ideas. The view of public administration has evolved rapidly over the past few decades. The introduction of new paradigms led away from the classic Weberian bureaucratic structure to instruments based on the model of new public management. Also, the City of Linz shifted towards the new public management paradigm. This change did not happen by pushing aside the whole idea of the Weberian model, but took place continuously or evolutionarily, so that only "minor changes accumulate[d] over time" (Walgenbach & Meyer, 2008) and new initiatives grew from established instruments (Meyer, Seiwald, Polzer, & Höllerer, 2012). Thus, according to Lepsius (1997), institutional change within the municipality is an ongoing process. The aforementioned service office for citizens' and the tele-service department for complaints' establishment was driven by the new public management spirit. A key success factor for "*Schau auf Linz*" is pre-existing and well-functioning complaint management in the tele-service department. Politt and Bouckaert (2011) state that administrative systems are generally rather static and difficult to change. Underlining this observation, they take the hypothetical example of a benefit-claiming system where people come to a physical office, fill out a form, and receive appropriate payment from counter staff if the claim is in order. Introducing new computer technology would allow faster, more efficient, and less staff-intensive handling of the procedure. Forgetting to properly train staff in new computer technology, may mean that the new process results in complications precluding predicted benefits. Thus, the platform "*Schau auf Linz*" must be a supplement to existing tools rather than a substitute. In other words, the implementation of the "software" (i.e. the platform) only made sense because the essential and necessary "hardware" (i.e. adequate resources in the city administration) was already in place.

Nevertheless, this new way of communicating "at eye level" is a completely new experience for some experts. Departments and officials who had so far had less direct contact with citizens have more difficulties adapting to this new way of communicating. In fact, this is in line with Weber's theory of official jurisdictional areas, specialization and hierarchy. The principle of specialization in particular refers to competence and expertise, i.e. officials have to be qualified and specially trained for their assignments (Alfano, 2011). As Weber (1978) states, "bureaucratization offers [...] the optimum possibility for carrying through the principle of specializing administrative functions according to purely objective considerations. Individual performances are allocated to functionaries who have specialized training and who by constant practice increase their expertise". On the contrary, by using the platform "*Schau auf Linz*," every citizen is able—at least in theory—to offer advice to experts and develop and deliver new ideas in equal partnership with professionals. Some officials may fear that their expertise is undermined through using this platform. The necessary transformation of the civil servant's role may lead to tensions within the organization and is one of the key challenges for the long-term success of "*Schau auf Linz*". (See Table 2 for a summary of the key characteristics of the platform).

2.4   From Open Government to Open Tourism

Although not initially intended, open government initiatives can have positive spillover in the tourism sector. Platforms such as "*Schau auf Linz*" ("Look after Linz") help repair broken infrastructure or clear waste faster and more effectively, thereby contributing to tourists' perception that Linz is a clean city. The City of Linz recognized the potential of new technologies and the accompanying opportunities early on. Projects like free Wi-Fi in more than 100 public places grew to include public transportation. In addition, "Apps4Linz" resulted in numerous apps

Table 2 Key facts and figures of the platform "Schau auf Linz"

Platform "Schau auf Linz" ("Look after Linz")
General information
• Interactive mapping and reporting platform for urban maintenance needs—http://schau.auf. linz.at
• Country: Austria, Province: Upper Austria, City: Linz (capital city. 190,000 inhabitants)
• 2013: more than 4000 complaints; about 1100 registered users (even though not required)
Characteristics of the platform
• Low-level access to keep platform as simple as possible (no registration required), use via webpage or mobile application
• Platform integrated in professional complaint management located in a specific municipal department ("tele-service centre")
• Each issue is documented in an electronic file within the tele-service-department
• "Flashlight system" allows citizens to follow the status of a complaint
• No preliminary screening of contents: citizens publicly discuss different views—better understanding of decisions of municipality, highly-satisfied citizens
• Platform is a supplement, not a substitute (total number of complaints has already risen significantly in 2013)
Similar projects
• "SeeClickFix": http://de.seeclickfix.com
• "FixMyStreet": http://www.fixmystreet.com
• "Maerker-Brandenburg": http://maerker.brandenburg.de

that are also useful for tourists (beyond the aforementioned application "Linz Finder"):

• *"Linz pflückt"* ("Linz picks"): the application shows more than 2000 public fruit trees in the city. Supplementary information like maturity and fruit category comes from the City of Linz nursery and contains information on species, genus, tree height, etc. The fruit from the trees is freely available public domain, which any person may pick and eat. At the moment, the program is also available as an app for Android devices. Those without Androids can use the mobile version on the website.

• *"Lilli"*: the application shows the current departure times of buses and trams of the public transportation (LINZ AG). It also maps the distance from door to door.

• *"Spin City"*: the application would utilize information continuously fed from other cyclists to ease cycling in Linz and provide a memorably positive experience.

Although these apps are useful for tourists, the municipal tourism agency has yet to promote them. Additionally, most applications are only available in German. Despite this promising development, the City of Linz should mobilize additional resources to leverage the full potential of open government for the tourism sector.

For instance, the City of Linz could launch open government initiatives more directly linked to the tourism sector, thereby producing more visible effects. For instance, the "open cities" project, a collaboration of various metropolitan city governments, launched the first "Open Data App Challenge" in March 2012. The organizers sought the best open data applications to solve citizens' everyday urban problems. In May 2013, three initiatives to specifically harness ideas from citizens to improve cities' tourist services launched (www.opencities.net):

- *"Open Data HackAtHome"*: the goal is to bring together open data and sensor networks to help cities find new ways to manage big challenges and benefits of tourism today.
- *"Urban Lab"*: making public space available for the development of innovative projects that address unmet needs. It must still be tested on the street, and has yet to launch on the market. For this project, the City of Barcelona has already tested intelligent urban waste management, noise monitoring systems and parking management solutions.
- *"Crowdsourcing"*: an open call to collect ideas for improving tourist services in cities. The initiative approaches ideas including public services, spatial planning, and mobile applications, and focuses on improving city tourist services.

We conclude that using the "power of the crowd" not only contributes to a better government, but also improves tourist services in cities.

3 Key Conclusions and Learning Outcomes for the Tourism Industry

- The open innovation paradigm shows that the innovation process of product and service development is becoming more open, emphasizing the importance of external knowledge, and involving a broad range of external actors. Increasing entrepreneurial success of open innovation in companies raises the question whether these principles are transferable to reinventing public sector organisations. A next step beyond e-government (which constitutes the technological and cultural basis), this contribution presents the first Austrian example of how collaboration with citizens for public administrations can offer new means of service delivery and increasing public life value.
- The case presented, *"Schau auf Linz"*, enables an efficient feedback mechanism for the citizens and fast, efficient access to local service administrations. It is a nimble website where everybody can report problems with the local environment. The complaint then goes to the relevant local authority who can fix it. *"Schau auf Linz"* is a model for mapping data and a platform the municipally provided to foster interactions and dialogue with the citizenry. This mechanism allows public units to address the knowledge and creativity of its citizens by conducting these kinds of open calls on idea-, innovation-, or complain-platforms. So open government constitutes the formal discipline and practice of leveraging discoveries and expertise of others as input for the administrative and political process through formal and informal relationships. Informal

relationships (e.g. broad open calls for spotting broken public infrastructure) constitute the "innovativeness" of the open government paradigm.

- This development may have tremendous impact on the tourism capacity of a region as well. The City of Linz is a best practice example of a transformation process from an industrial steel- and coal-producing city to a modern service industry venue and a tourism and vacation hotspot that attracts tourists from all over the world—especially with its cultural offerings and liveable urban scenery. Only an efficient and well-managed public administration is able to offer a competitive, attractive, and sustainable local community and a city worth living in. To adopt new instruments of open innovation and open government makes sense and new forms of collaboration with the diverse stakeholders of public sector units may lead to innovative regions fit for the future. The case presented, "Schau *auf Linz*", is a cheap and smooth-running example of how to clean up a city and fluently react to citizens' demands. Practices like this one will strengthen the reputation and appearance of a whole region, and hopefully encourage many tourists to stop in Linz.

Acknowledgements We are grateful to the City of Linz for collaborating with us in this research enterprise. Thomas Gegenhuber thanks the Austrian Academy of Sciences for funding his work.

References

Afuah, A., & Tucci, C. L. (2012). Crowdsourcing as a solution for distant search. *Academy of Management Review, 37*(3), 355–375.

Alfano, G. (2011). Adapting bureaucracy to the internet. The case of Venice local government. *Information Polity, 16*(1), 5–22.

Baldwin, C., & von Hippel, E. (2011). Modeling a paradigm shift: From producer innovation to user and open collaborative innovation. *Organization Science, 22*(6), 1399–1417.

Bogner, A., & Menz, W. (2002). Das theoriegenerierende Experteninterview: Erkenntnisinteresse, Wissensformen, Interaktion. In A. Bogner, B. Littig, & W. Menz (Eds.), *Das Experteninterview. Theorie, Methode, Anwendung.* Wiesbaden: VS Verlag für Sozialwissenschaften.

Chesbrough, H. W. (2006). Open innovation: A new paradigm for industrial organization. In H. W. Chesbrough, W. Vanhaverbeke, & J. West (Eds.), *Open innovation* (pp. 1–12). Oxford: Oxford University Press.

Dobusch, L., & Forsterleitner, C. (2007). *Freie Netze. Freies Wissen: Ein Beitrag zum Kulturhauptstadtjahr Linz 2009.* Wien: echomedia.

Dobusch, L., & Forsterleitner, C. (2010). *Knowledge space Linz: Free knowledge as a task for local government.* Available at: http://www.dobusch.net/pub/uni/Dobusch-Forsterleitner (2010)Integrata-Sammelband.pdf (German).

Dobusch, L., Forsterleitner, C., & Hiesmair, M. (2011). *Freiheit vor Ort. Handbuch kommunale Netzpolitik.* München: Open Source Press.

Eisenhardt, M. (1989). Building theories from case study research. *Academy of Management Review, 14*(4), 532–550.

Flick, U. (2011). *Qualitative Sozialforschung. Eine Einführung* (4th ed.). Reinbek: Rowohlt Taschenbuch Verlag.

Gegenhuber, T., & Forsterleitner, C. (2011). Lasst die Daten frei! Open Government als kommunale Herausforderung und Chance. In L. Dobusch, C. Forsterleitner, & M. Hiesmair (Eds.), *Freiheit vor Ort. Handbuch kommunale Netzpolitik*. München: Open Source Press.

Glechner, C. (2010). *Linz sees open commons future*. Available at: http://futurezone.orf.at/stories/1657554 (German text) (dl. August 24, 2010).

Hilgers, D. (2012). Open Government: Theoretische Bezüge und konzeptionelle Grundlagen einer neuen Entwicklung in Staat und öffentlichen Verwaltungen. *Zeitschrift für Betriebswirtschaft, 82*, 631–660.

Hilgers, D., & Ihl, C. (2010). Citizensourcing – Applying the concept of open innovation to the public sector. *International Journal of Public Participation (IJP2), 4*(1), 67–88.

Kohler, T., Füller, J., & Hutter, K. (2013). Crowdsourcing social innovation, submitted to the EMAC 2013 Conference, Istanbul.

Lakhani, K. R., Lifshitz-Assaf, H., & Tushman, M. L. (2012). *Open innovation and organizational boundaries: The impact of task decomposition and knowledge distribution on the locus of innovation* (Working Paper, Boston).

Lamnek, S. (2010). *Qualitative Sozialforschung*. Weinheim: Beltz Verlag.

Lathrop, D., & Ruma, L. (2010). *Open government: Transparency, collaboration and participation in practice*. Sebastopol: O'Reilly Media Inc.

Lepsius, M. R. (1997). Institutionalisierung und Deinstitutionalisierung von Rationalitätskriterien. In G. Göhler (Ed.), *Institutionenwandel (Leviathan Sonderheft 16)* (pp. 57–69). Opladen: Westdeutscher Verlag.

Meijer, A. J., Curtin, D., & Hillebrandt, M. (2012). Open government: Connecting vision and voice. *International Review of Administrative Sciences, 78*(1), 10–29.

Meuser, M., & Nagel, U. (2010). Experteninterviews – wissenssoziologische Voraussetzungen und methodische Durchführung. In B. Friebertshäuser, A. Langer, & A. Prengel (Eds.), *Handbuch Qualitative Forschungsmethoden in der Erziehungswissenschaft* (3rd ed., pp. 457–471). Weinheim: Juventa.

Meyer, R., Seiwald, J., Polzer, T., & Höllerer, A. (2012). Manifestationen von Verwaltungsparadigmen im österreichischen Haushaltsrecht. In D. Hilgers, R. Schauer, & N. Thom (Eds.), *Public Management im Paradigmenwechsel. Staat und Verwaltung im Spannungsfeld von New Public Management, Open Government und bürokratischer Restauration* (pp. 89–103). Linz: Trauner Verlag.

Noveck, B. S. (2009). *Wiki government: How technology can make government better, democracy stronger, and citizens more powerful*. Washington, DC: Brookings Institution Press.

Orszag, P. R. (2009). *Open government directive. Memorandum for the heads of executive deparments and agencies*. Washington, DC.

Picot, A., Reichwald, R., & Wigand, R. (2003). *Die grenzenlose Unternehmung* (5th ed.). Wiesbaden: Gabler.

Politt, C., & Bouckaert, G. (2011). *Public management reform. A comparative analysis – New public management, governance, and the Neo-Weberian State*. Oxford: Oxford University Press.

Pomberger, G., & Kempinger, G. (2010). *Studie Open-Commons-Region Linz*. Fakten, Perspektiven, Maßnahmen (German). Available at: http://www.linz.at/images/ko-Studie_Open_Commons_Region_Linz.pdf

Reichwald, R., & Piller, F. T. (2009). *Interaktive Wertschöpfung: Open Innovation, Individualisierung und neue Formen der Arbeitsteilung* (2nd ed.). Wiesbaden: Gabler.

Roland Berger. (2012). *European capital city tourism report – Analysis and findings*.

Steytler, N., & Kincaid, J. (2009). *Local government and metropolitan regions in federal systems*. Montreal: McGill-Queen's University Press.

Tapscott, D., & Williams, A. D. (2006). *Wikinomics: How mass collaboration changes everything*. Toronto: Penguin Group (Canada).

von Hippel, E. (2005). *Democratizing innovation*. Cambridge, MA: The MIT Press.

Walgenbach, P., & Meyer, R. (2008). *Neoinstitutionalistische Organisationstheorie*. Stuttgart: Kohlhammer.

Watson, R., Akselsen, S., Monod, E., & Pitt, L. (2004). The open tourism consortium. *European Management Journal, 22*(3), 315–326.

Weber, M. (1978). Economy and society. In G. Roth, & C. Wittich (Eds.). Berkeley: University of California Press.

Wise, S., Paton, R. A., & Gegenhuber, T. (2012). Value co-creation through collective intelligence in the public sector: A review of US and European initiatives. *VINE: The Journal of Information and Knowledge Management Systems, 42*(2), 251–276.

Yin, R. K. (2003). *Case study research. Design and methods. Applied social research methods series*. Thousand Oaks: Sage.

Part III
Case Studies: Creation Level

Crowdsourcing in the Tourism Industry: From Idea Generation Towards Merchandizing User-Generated Souvenirs

Johann Füller, Katja Hutter, and Giordano Koch

Learning Objectives

- Appreciate the relevance of crowdsourcing in the tourism context.
- Understand the combination of offline as well as online crowdsourcing activities.
- Demonstrate how a sustainable multi contest crowdsourcing platform especially designed for small and medium sized enterprises (SME) has been applied in the tourism industry.
- Identify the challenges to develop a sustainable open innovation process, which is attractive for SMEs.

J. Füller (✉)
University of Innsbruck, Innsbruck, Austria

HYVE AG, Munich, Germany
e-mail: johann.fueller@uibk.ac.at

K. Hutter
University of Innsbruck, Innsbruck, Austria

NASA Tournament Lab, Harvard University, Cambridge, MA, USA
e-mail: katja.hutter@uibk.ac.at

G. Koch
University of Hamburg, Hamburg, Germany

HYVE Innovation Community GmbH, Munich, Germany
e-mail: giordano.koch@hyve.de

© Springer-Verlag Berlin Heidelberg 2016
R. Egger et al. (eds.), *Open Tourism*, Tourism on the Verge,
DOI 10.1007/978-3-642-54089-9_19

1 Introduction

In times of wikis and social networks concepts like crowdsourcing (Howe, 2008), co-creation (Winsor, 2005), user innovation (Von Hippel, 2005), virtual customer integration (Dahan & Hauser, 2002), and open innovation (Chesbrough, 2003) became quite popular, describing the promising, active role consumers may play in the previously firm-dominated world of product development and production. Researchers as well as consultants claim to virtually engage consumers in co-creation activities such as the generation, design, refinement, and testing of new concepts and products (Chesbrough, 2003; Dahan & Hauser, 2002; Prahalad & Ramaswamy, 2003) in order to generate new ideas for future products and services that appropriately meet consumers' wants and needs.

Idea contest platforms, as one form of co-creation and crowdsourcing platforms, are en vogue among companies. Besides the benefits of gaining many innovative solutions for a posed problem, the application of idea and design contests enables companies to engage consumers as one of their most relevant groups of stake-holders and offers outcomes such as first user centered needs, innovative ideas, positive word of mouth (Kozintes, Wilner, Wojnicki, & de Valck, 2010), and collective commitment towards new offerings (Nambisan & Baron, 2007). Further they are supposed to have a favorable impact on participants' loyalty intentions towards the hosting firm. The basic argument is that the ongoing involvement and interaction over several weeks with a company and its products as well as the personal engagement that occurs while developing new ideas for the respective company leads to stronger and deeper relationships between the company and its users, and thus results in an increase in loyalty intentions (Nambisan & Baron, 2007) (Table 1).

In light of the aforementioned organizational use of idea contest platforms, one of the huge advantages for small and medium-sized enterprises (SMEs) observed to date, pertains to the privileged organizational proximity to the customer in the form of personal contact; the integration of such customers in different stages of the value creation process, as well as the exploitation of their needs and requirements as source for inventions and creativity. Moreover, the closeness and proximity to the

Table 1 Crowdsourcing and its impact on innovation and marketing

Innovation...
• The generation of creative ideas for new product and services
• The identification of trends due to the immediate feedback from other participants
• The determination of lead user for further innovation studies
Marketing...
• The presentation of the hosting firm/brand as innovative and customer-oriented
• The intense interaction with various stakeholder groups
• The emergence of new and the increase of current customer-relationships
• The strengthening of the brand due to viral marketing

Source: Belz & Peattie (2009)

customer as well as a greater flexibility enabled SMEs to stay competitive in increasingly globalized markets. Notably, the organizational leverage of the internet and Web 2.0 technologies by large firms provides such firms likewise with the opportunity to exploit the advantages of customer proximity in contrast to SME's which typically tend to struggle for economic survival. Despite this development studies show for instance that less than 10 % of Austrian SMEs systematically use cooperation or collaborations with external partners to support their innovation activities (OECD, 2008). According to the European Commission, SMEs are nowadays the driving forces for competitiveness, employment, and innovativeness in the European Union (European Commission, 2005). Previous research has shown that innovation increases the chances of an SME's economic survival by 22 % (Chefis & Marsili, 2006). Based on these figures a political as well as scientific interest in supporting innovation in SMEs becomes obvious (Edwards, Delbridge, & Munday, 2005; Jones & Tilley, 2003).

Generally, research on output orientated crowdsourcing activities within the context of the tourism industry is scarce. Much research rather focuses on the use of social media channels and thus appears to be marketing driven. Since the tourism industry is typically characterized by a few global players mostly positioned as holistic tour operators, the social media research has focused strongly on those players and the impact of user stories, experiences, and evaluations on their business. However it seems that, the tourism industry is particularly characterized to a greater extent by many small and medium-sized companies. This ensures that the country or even region-specific flair is considered as very important for the overall tourism industry. As described above, the former advantages of being faster, more dynamic, creative, and thus profiting from the customer proximity has recently been challenged by social media affinity of the global players. Consequently, crowdsourcing may also provide within the tourism industry a valuable approach for SMEs to reclaim their customer focused advantages, by relying on the creativity and innovativeness of tourists and integrating them into their own product as well as service development.

The rapid growth of the crowdsourcing market has led to the continuous emergence of new use cases. The following case will show how external designers, enthused consumers, tourists as well as locals may be integrated in an idea and design contest for SMEs offering souvenirs from the local tourism region in South Tyrol, Italy.

2   The Case: Open Innovation Südtirol (OIS)

The "Open Innovation Südtirol" (OIS) (www.openinnovation-suedtirol.it) platform was established in 2012 by the South Tyrol national association for craftsmen.[1] The online community-based platform was especially designed for SMEs to improve

---

[1] LVH—Landesverband der Handwerker.

Fig. 1 Innovation process supported by the OIS platform

the innovative capacity and the commercial success of the SME in the following four innovation phases (see Fig. 1).

In the first phase the online innovation contest platform aimed at integrating external ideas, solutions, product and technologies that will be the major focus of the case study. The South Tyrol national association for craftsmen partnered with HYVE, an innovation agency based in Munich with an in-depth experience of running crowdsourcing and open innovation projects. The team developed an online contest that was hosted on its proprietary platform, IdeaNet, which could be adapted to a corporation's design and identity standards. The non-virtual OIS laboratory based at the TIS innovation park supported SMEs during phase two, three and four especially for concept elaboration, rapid prototyping, computer simulations and also offered workshops to discuss the market launch and the distribution of regional products and services.

The core element of the platform is the innovation contest platform where regional SMEs could run their own innovation challenge by utilizing external knowledge and collaboration partners. Currently, seven different contests have been conducted on the OIS platform for distinctive regional SMEs operating in various industries. Table 2 provides an overview of the contest subject, the hosting organization, duration, and also shows contribution statistics.

The contests differed in terms of industry and problem description and were run between 5 and 12 weeks depending on the complexity and the extent of the contest challenge. Each contest showed its own menu including a starting page explaining the contest overview, the challenge description, timeline, statistics, latest submission and new registered members. Additionally, there was a contest information page providing a in depth contest description and an introduction of the jury team; a pool of submissions—presenting all idea submission; and a pool of participants—listing all members who were contributing on the contest platform.

Registered participants could submit their own designs or evaluate the designs of others using a rating of 1–5 and could comment on a defined criteria (e.g., functionality, degree of innovativeness, feasibility, market attractiveness). Participants could also provide feedback using a commenting tool and post messages.

A contest jury, which consisted of the company's CEO and four experts depending on the topic of the contest selected three winning designs and communicated the winners to the community. Besides the announcement of the winners, the jury session was also presented with photos of the contest platform.

After the accomplishment of the seventh contest the OIS platform was accessed by more than 486,658 visitors. Even though the platform was solely provided in the South Tyrolean native languages German and Italian, visitors from 107 different

Table 2 Innovation contest run by the OIS platform

#	Contest subject	Duration (weeks)	Statistics	Prize (total)
1	Design: Souvenirs made of wood sponsored by Hofer Heinrich KG	8	346 participants 298 ideas 1672 evaluations 691 comments	3000 €
2	Packaging and branding: Concepts for MoCem sponsored by Moling Alberto GmbH	12	88 participants 54 ideas 440 evaluations 253 comments	3000 €
3	Architecture: The timber house of the future sponsored by Holzmar—Othmar Castlunger	7	170 participants 327 ideas 606 evaluations 339 comments	3000 €
4	Design: Wood instead of plastics sponsored by *Tischlerei Lunger OHG*	6.5	80 participants 81 ideas 163 evaluations 57 comments	Non-monetary rewards
5	Grocery: The reinvention of bacon sponsored by Luis Moser GmbH	7	73 participants 93 ideas 131 evaluations 53 comments	1750 €

(continued)

Table 2 (continued)

#	Contest subject	Duration (weeks)	Statistics	Prize (total)
6	Design: The revolutionary children's bed sponsored by Complojer	7	93 participants 83 ideas 107 evaluations 154 comments	3000 €
7	Packaging and branding: Egg seeks new packaging sponsored by Buchhütterhof	5	56 participants 60 ideas 136 evaluations 71 comments	800 € + Non-monetary rewards

nations were registered. Nevertheless, majority of the visitors originated from Italy followed by Germany and Austria. Moreover, registered members came from 33 nations. 73.4 % of the OIS users originated from Italy, 14.4 % from Germany, and 7.5 % from Austria (all other nations amounted to a portion of 4.7 %).

The 1721 OIS profiles consist of 1618 private user profiles and 103 company profiles which represents a proportion 5.9 %. The OIS community contributed 1721 comments on the ideas and thus facilitated an assurance and improvement of the idea quality since the idea submitters have the opportunity to adapt their ideas and to implement the received feedback.

To assess the quality and innovativeness of the ideas, the community itself was asked to rate the submitted innovations. In total the ideas received on average about six votes from the community measured with a five point scale.

An analysis of the platform profiles revealed a nearly balanced distribution of female and male platform participants. Female and male participants differed slightly regarding their innovation output: 59.5 % of the ideas were submitted by men and 40.5 % by women respectively.

The difference was even greater, considering other activity variables of the two groups (excluding the administrator activities): 67.8 % of all comments were submitted by men and 32.2 % by female participants. Besides, 63.6 % of the idea evaluations were provided by male and 36.4 % by female innovators.

Linking our discussion to the above introduced table of already conducted contests the following two chapters will focus on two selected contests in more detail.

2.1 Souvenirs Made of Wood

The wooden souvenir contest ran from June to August 2012 and asked for new design concepts around souvenirs made out of wood. The hosting organization—carpenter Hofer—was particularly interested in which kind of souvenirs would visitors take along or could be used as a gift (see Fig. 2). He aimed at finding a souvenir, which would be characterized as high-quality, design-driven, modern but at the same time traditional and somehow linked to South Tyrolean sense of life. All contributions had to have a regional association and had to be related to South Tyrol. Local wood had to serve as the major component, moreover natural and sustainable materials could be combined.

By applying a mainly online focused activation and recruiting strategy, potential participants were invited to register on the OIS platform, familiarize themselves with the problem context, explore the given information, questions, and supporting materials, and actively taking part by evaluating or commenting on already existing user generated content, or uploading their own contributions. Due to the close communication structure with the project team and especially the active role of Mr. Hofer, we were able to adapt communication, motivation, and activation activities on a daily basis, during the live phase. This concluded in providing additional information and clarification regarding certain topic descriptions or intense activation and recruiting activities identifying topic relevant experts and inviting them to the platform.

Within the contest period of 8 weeks, 346 members registered. Two hundred and ninety-eight ideas were submitted ranging from home appliances, jewelry and accessories, lifestyle products and toys. Besides pictures, blueprints and detailed descriptions, the contest participants provided 1672 evaluations (1–5 point scale) and feedback through 691 qualitative comments. Considering the fact that this campaign was the start campaign of the OIS project, the emerged statistics may be used as an indicator for the huge potential of crowdsourcing in touristic problem setting.

At the end of the design contest a jury comprising of four experts evaluated the submitted designs and the three top-scoring designs received prizes of 1500 €, 1000 €,

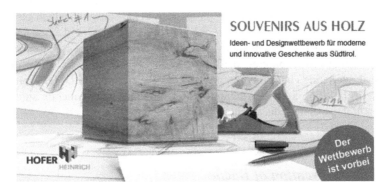

Fig. 2 Wood Souvenir Contest—Hosted by Carpeter Hofer

Fig. 3 Selected designs from the Wood Souvenir Contest

Fig. 4 The "Wooden Wrapper Covering a South Tyrolean Wine Bottle" on the market

and 500 €, respectively. The hosting organization—Carpentry Hofer—selected various designs for commercialization. Referring to Fig. 3 carpentry Hofer produced and afterwards launched the first and second winner. The first winner was a wooden set of desk utensils designed in the style of a well-known South Tyrolean church and the second winner was a premium wooden wrapper covering a South Tyrolean wine bottle, which not only could it be very easily produced, but also communicated all relevant aspects of quality, sustainability as well as South Tyrolean tradition.

Applying a fast rapid prototyping approach, Mr. Hofer was able to identify the most promising way to produce the second place idea, the wooden wrapper covering a South Tyrolean wine bottle and launched it afterwards to the market (Fig. 4.)

This initial OIS campaign showed that on the one hand small SMEs may profit from crowdsourcing activities. In this specific case, carpentry Hofer was able to launch a new product range focusing on wooden made souvenir, which gave him the possibility to diversify his product portfolio and enable to build a new business unit. On the other hand, the case showed the innovation and marketing potential of industry related crowdsourcing platforms. Without investing much money into traditional marketing channels (e.g. print, radio, TV etc.) the initial OIS campaign was able to build up a vivid community and simultaneously generate significant attention in the social media world.

2.2 The Reinvention of Bacon

A second campaign was run by Luis Moser—specialized on high-quality bacon, sausage and cold meat products which were commercialized in various retails

Fig. 5 Contest platform—bacon served differently and three winning designs

Fig. 6 First product on the market

stores within South Tyrol. His aim was to extend the portfolio with new innovative products especially addressing tourist and visitors. The new products had to be served in bars, ski lodges, motorway service areas or other location besides the retail stores. In addition, the initiator was trying to find innovative packaging ideas and designs for his products. Consequently, this campaign asked the community the following questions: How should the products be offered, should it be combined with other groceries? How does a pleasant packaging look appealing to customers at various points of sales?

The contest ran from April to June 2013 and was accompanied by a professional recruiting and community management strategy. Besides it was executed in cooperation with German and Italian speaking blogs, communities and forums. In the end, 73 active members on the platform submitted 93 ideas, which ranged from new innovative products to non-existing packaging concepts. Furthermore, the contest participants contributed 131 evaluations and 53 qualitative comments on the platform. Similar to the first campaign, a jury comprising of six experts evaluated the idea submissions and awarded the first prize with 1000 €, the second prize with 500 €, and the third prize with 250 € (see Fig. 5).

Shortly after the end of the contest Luis Moser successfully launched a new product to the market, which was also inspired by users, and tourists' suggestion on the crowdsourcing platform (see Fig. 6).

3 Key Conclusions

Summarizing the potential benefits of the OIS crowdsourcing platform we found that the project was able to facilitate several objectives for all involved parties at the same time. The following paragraphs will focus on three perspectives including SMEs, users, tourists as well as public institutions.

3.1 SMEs' Perspective

- **Innovation focus**: While browsing through the idea pool on the OIS platform, the potential of collective as well as collaborative development of creative ideas and innovative concepts by utilizing external parties and external knowledge was evident. From discussions with the contests' hosts we realized that the ideas, additionally uploaded documents and especially the feedback and emerged discussions provided valuable insights about consumer needs and wishes. Due to a sophisticated evaluation system we also expected that we would prospectively find a decrease of the risks of flop-rates, due to the early involvement of most valued stakeholders and honest feedback. However, the project also showed that crowdsourcing should not only focus on the virtual part, but should find a balanced mixture of online and offline components. Due to the direct connection to the consulting services and the OIS laboratory, the craftsmen had the possibility to further develop new ideas discussed on the platform in a real setting in collaboration with selected users/tourists and experts. Focusing on the innovation perspective, the analyzed project revealed that crowdsourcing provides a rich source for the touristic industry, especially for SMEs.
- **Marketing focus**: As a second sub-perspective we will now concentrate on the marketing potential of crowdsourcing activities in the touristic industry. The reported numbers of visitors, registered members as well as shared ideas may serve as an indicator for the marketing potential. The analysis showed that, the craftsmen were able to find new customers or invited already existing contacts and thus deepened their relationship. Taking into account that the first contest aimed at developing a totally new environment, we may also state that the OIS project was able exploit new customer as well as product markets. Especially for SMEs OIS definitely increased the markets' research capacity and breadth, while reducing cost and time to market launch. Although we had a strong product focus on the platform, the campaign offered valuable customer insights, resolved service gaps, and discovered new revenue opportunities. Saying that the project resulted in increased customer loyalty is maybe too early, but we can see already that a continuous possibility of collaboration and regular conversation develops a positive impact on the steadily growing community.
- **Network focus**: Last but not least, SMEs where able to register as their own company profiles on the platform including the possibility to show their

competence as well as portfolio and thus enabling the emergence and maintenance of networks among SMEs and a transfer of knowledge since companies could collaborate, exchange information, and present themselves.

3.2 Users' or Tourists' Perspective

From a user' respectively tourists' perspective we may conclude four important insights and learnings.

- First of all, users or tourists may contribute as creative, need driven, and with user experience equipped innovators. While an active platform contribution implicates also rewarding experiences from social interactions with other like-minded community members and platform experts, this community driven "innovation experience" can be described as a very important driver for crowdsourcing activities in a touristic setting.
- Second, we saw that a crowdsourcing platform has the potential to attract not only the locals but also foreigners. In our specific case tourism plays an important role since many creative people coming from Germany, Austria or other European countries are familiar with South Tyrol as a tourist region and are positively attached. Consequently, we could interpret the OIS platform also as a campaign aiming on increasing the intensity as well as quality of the relationship, engagement and finally loyalty between the tourist and the vacation region.
- Third, users or tourists can be engaged to become multipliers or finally even real ambassadors of the region, their SMEs and products or services. By relying on concepts like word of mouth, virtual snow ball effects and networks logics we know that a crowd of creative, motivated and engaged people have the ability to significantly support marketing activities of a company or in our case a vacation region.
- Fourth, users or tourists play the classical role of being a consumer, buying the newly developed products and take it home as a souvenir or present for their family and friends.

3.3 Public Institutions' Perspective

From a public institutions' perspective such a crowdsourcing platform also offers a number of positive side effects and learnings.

- From our perspective, the systematically linked network of locals, creative tourists, SMEs as well as the related challenges including a variety of ideas and engage participant in lively discussions to form a vivid and highly creative platform for the region.

- Such a crowdsourcing platform has the potential to support local SMEs to become more innovative, simultaneously enabling engaged people to positively spread the word about the respective region, its culture, products and unique economy and thereby generate additional revenues within the local economy.

Linking the aforementioned dimensions and key learnings together, we see great potential for crowdsourcing activities in a touristic setting relying on the collaboration among relevant stakeholder within a creative and innovate setting.

4 Learning Outcomes for the Tourism Industry

- The case study relies on of a sustainable multi contest crowdsourcing platform especially designed for small and medium sized enterprises (SME). The cases demonstrate how external designers, enthused consumers or interested tourists regardless of their geographic location may be integrated in an "idea and design contest" for small enterprises offering souvenirs from the local tourism region.
- The project faced the challenge to develop a lean open innovation process, which is attractive for SMEs. Further, the open innovation process was not only designed to be generative for ideas and solution, but also support SME during the product realisation and diffusion phase (e.g. market launch).
- The following issues were successfully addressed in order to solve the above introduced challenges:
  - Combination of online and offline activities: we developed a crowdsourcing platform process, which was accompanied by several offline services such as a product development laboratory, creative workshops, launch activities, or conferences. All channels where centrally coordinated and supportive to each other.
  - Supportive offerings to guide SMEs through the open innovation process: since craftsmen or small SMEs have typically no previous experience with open innovation activities, we developed a set of additional service offerings such as workshops, trainings, presentations, which contributed to educate SMEs in applying open innovation tools successfully.
  - Fast prototyping: In order to demonstrate the potential efficiency and effectiveness gains as well as the agile innovation process, we enabled the SMEs to use a fast prototyping process. This allowed first product exhibitions in workshops, or meetings after a few weeks.
  - Active integration of the community throughout the innovation and product development process: as explained above, the Open Innovation Südtirol platform served not only for innovation purposes. However, we used similar mechanisms to develop marketing concepts, ask for prize sensitivity or support the market launch of the developed products.
  - Integrated stakeholder management: Generally, open innovation programs benefit from a well-steered stakeholder network. This seems especially

important with regard to a locally integrated and sustainable open innovation program. Consequently, we developed a stakeholder management, which were able to integrate the media, universities, the local economy and governmental institutions as well as citizens and tourists. This "multi-channel" triggered various kickbacks and supported in recruiting and activating community members, motivate SMEs to participate as well as finally launch and sell the products to the market.

- The presented case shows that a locally integrated Open Innovation program may develop the power to link the local economy (focus on SMEs) with citizens and especially tourists and generate additional value for all involved stakeholder potentially.

References

Belz, F. M., & Peattie, K. (2009). *Sustainability marketing: A global perspective*. Chichester: Wiley.

Chefis, E., & Marsili, O. (2006). Survivor: The role of innovation in firms' survival. *Research Policy, 35*(5), 626–641.

Chesbrough, H. W. (2003). *Open innovation: The new imperative for creating and profiting from technology*. Boston, MA: Harvard Business Press.

Dahan, E., & Hauser, J. (2002). The virtual customer. *Journal of Product Innovation Management, 19*, 332–353.

Edwards, T., Delbridge, R., & Munday, M. (2005). Understanding innovation in small and medium-sized enterprises: A process manifest. *Technovation, 25*, 1119–1127.

European Commission. (2005). *The new SME definition – User guide and model declaration*. Luxembourg: Enterprise and Industry Publication.

Howe, J. (2008). *Crowdsourcing – How the power of the crowd is driving the future of business*. London: Random House Business Books.

Jones, O., & Tilley, F. (2003). *Competitive advantage in SMEs: Organising for innovation and change*. Hoboken, NJ: Wiley.

Kozintes, R. V., Wilner, S., Wojnicki, A., & de Valck, K. (2010). Networks Of narrativity: Understanding word-of-mouth marketing in online communities. *Journal of Marketing, 74*, 71–89.

Nambisan, S., & Baron, R. A. (2007). Interactions in virtual customer environments: Implications for product support and customer relationship management. *Journal of Interactive Marketing, 21*, 42–62.

OECD. (2008). *Open innovation in global networks*. Paris: Organization for Economic Cooperation and Development.

Prahalad, C. K., & Ramaswamy, V. (2003). The new frontier of experience innovation. *MIT Sloan Management Review, 44*, 12–18.

Von Hippel, E. (2005). *Democratizing innovation*. Boston, MA: The MIT Press.

Winsor, J. (2005). SPARK: Be more innovative through co-creation. Agate Publishing.

Collecting Tour Plans from Potential Visitors: A Web-Based Interactive Tour-Planner and a Strategic Use of Its Log Data

Yohei Kurata

Learning Objectives

- To help novice tourists from the difficulty of tour planning with the aid of computer-aided tour planning service.
- To overcome the usability problems of previous tour recommenders.
- To discuss the applicability of its user log data to marketing analysis.
- To seek the possibility of user involvement in the creation of destination data.

1   Introduction

It is often a hard task for novice tourists to design their own tour plan, especially when they are visiting a foreign city on a tight schedule. To relieve them from such difficulty, researchers have developed several systems that generate custom-made tour plans, taking the user's preference into account (e.g., Garcia, Arbelaitz, Linaza, Vansteenwegen, & Souffriau, 2010; Goy & Magro, 2004; Lee, Kang, & Park, 2007). These systems, however, tended to exclude the user's participation in the process of planning (Seifert, 2008)—they typically aim at generating an optimal tour plan under given constraints in a single or few steps. We, therefore, developed a computer-aided tour planning system, called *CT-Planner*, which emphasizes the collaboration between the system and its users (Kurata, 2010). CT-Planner stands for Collaborative Tour Planner, and also City Tour Planner as it mainly targets city-scale day trips. Here we introduce its latest version, *CT-Planner 4.3* (http://ctplanner.jp), and explain its relation to crowdsourcing.

Y. Kurata (✉)
Tokyo Metropolitan University, Hachioji, Japan
e-mail: ykurata@tmu.ac.jp

© Springer-Verlag Berlin Heidelberg 2016   291
R. Egger et al. (eds.), *Open Tourism*, Tourism on the Verge,
DOI 10.1007/978-3-642-54089-9_20

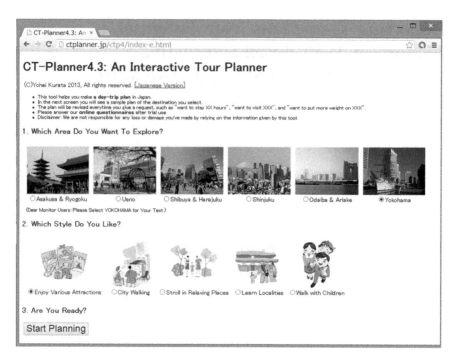

Fig. 1 Initial screen of CT-planner 4.3

Our system has two goals. The apparent goal is to provide tour planning service to novice tourists via the Web. With CT-Planner, people can consult on their plan from anywhere at any time, as much as they want, without worrying about asking human advisors in unfamiliar foreign languages. CT-Planner may be useful not only for detailed planning, but also for selecting destinations. Concrete image of tour plans, which are customized for individual users, will help the users to grow their expectation for the destinations that CT-Planner supports and lead the users to an actual visit in future. Another goal of our system, although it is not explicitly advertised, is to collect log data from a large number of users. With CT-Planner's user log, we can analyse, for instance, which POIs attract users' attention and what kind of tour plans are welcomed by specific groups of users. The result will be highly useful for marketing analysis. It helps destination management offices to examine their promotion strategies, as well as travel agencies to design their package tours (Hara et al., 2012).

2 CT-Planner: An Interactive Tour Planner

Figure 1 shows the initial screen of CT-Planner 4.3. Here you are asked to select a destination and your favourite travel style. Currently CT-Planner supports six destinations in and around Tokyo, and lists five travel styles, namely *Enjoy Various*

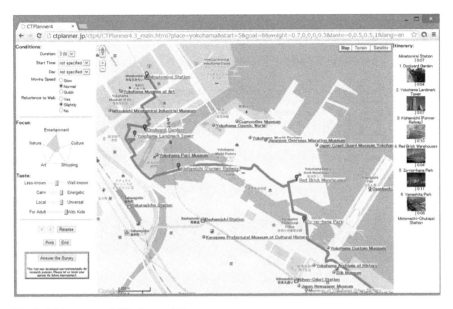

Fig. 2 Main screen of CT-planner 4.3

Attractions, *City Walking*, *Stroll in Relaxing Places*, *Learn Localities*, and *Walk with Children*. We adopted these five travel styles based on the result of our GPS-based activity survey on foreign tourists visiting Tokyo (Aratani, Shimada, Ota, & Hara, 2012).

When you click the *Start Planning* button in Fig. 1, you will see the main screen like Fig. 2. It shows the route of an initial plan on the map, together with its itinerary on the right end. We use Google Maps API to generate the map and, accordingly, you can zoom/scroll the map and even see the corresponding satellite image to check the detail of the route. The left side of the screen shows your tour conditions and user profile. When you modify your conditions or profile, the plan is updated instantly. The conditions consist of five items: *tour duration*, *start time*, *day of the week*, *walking speed*, and *reluctance to walk*. If you set the *start time* to 5:00 p.m., for instance, your plan will skip most museums because they are usually closed on evening. Similarly, if you set the *reluctance to walk* to *yes*, your plan will become shorter in the sense of total walking distance. The user profile consists of *focus* and *taste* parts, which are represented by a five-axial radar chart and a set of four sliders, respectively. If you put more weight on *culture* by clicking the radar chart, for instance, your tour plan will visit more museums. Similarly, if you move the top slider to the right end, your plan will visit popular places more likely. The initial value of the profile is determined based on your initial choice of travel styles, in order to relieve you from a time-consuming process of profile setting.

If you click the name of a POI on the map or the itinerary, a small info-window appears at its location (Fig. 3). This info-window shows the POI's name, estimated value for you (one- to five-stars), short description, expected staying time (which

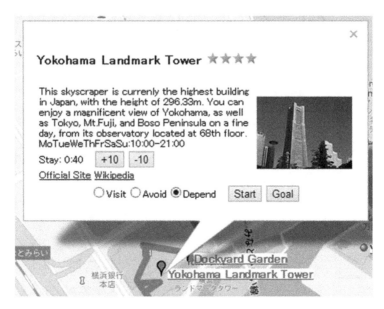

Fig. 3 An example of a POI's info-window

you can adjust), hyperlinks to the POI's official website and corresponding Wikipedia page (if available), and several buttons. If you click the *Visit* button, the system keeps generating tour plans which visit this POI as long as possible. Conversely, once you click the *Avoid* button, the system no longer shows the plans that visit this POI. You can also set the POI as the start or goal location of your tour.

Our system expects an iterative cycle of the following interactions:

1. The user examines the sample plan and POIs shown one the map,
2. The user gives an additional piece of his/her request, and
3. The system revises the plan accordingly.

This cycle is repeated until the user gets satisfied with the outcome. The merit of this design is that the users are not forced to specify their request at the beginning of tour planning (Kurata, 2010). Typically, a certain part of request pops up on the users' mind after they start tour planning. Another merit of our interface design is that the users can specify which POIs they want to visit or not, but they are not forced to do that. In other words, they can directly request the system to include some POIs in the plan and to exclude some from the plan, and at the same time they can leave the selection of other unfamiliar POIs to the system, giving their conditions and profile for reference.

After the planning, you can print out your plan and bring it to the destination. Interestingly, some of our test users, who visit the destination after making their plan, did not exactly follow their plan. Some of them mentioned that they were able to change their schedule flexibly because they had learnt the presence of some interesting POIs from their experience of computer-aided tour planning. This indicates an unexpected secondary role of CT-Planner as an educational tool for novice tourists (Kurata, Hara, Murayama, & Shimada, 2013).

3 Marketing Analyses Making Use of CT-Planner's Log Data

CT-Planner's web server records all operations and plans generated by its users. It also records the users' IP address with which we can identify their accessing location. If a large number of people use CT-Planner from various places, its user log will serve as precious data for marketing analysis. It is very costly for a destination to conduct a marketing survey that targets potential tourists, especially when the survey needs to be conducted internationally. With CT-Planner's log data, however, we will be able to know the demands of potential tourists on our destination without cost. In addition, as long as CT-Planner is used by many people, it will be able to keep monitoring the trends of their demands.

We are currently planning the following series of analyses using CT-Planner's user log:

- Statistical analyses for summarizing tour plans made by all or a specific group of users, which derive (for instance):

  - The average length of tour durations,
  - Viewing rate of each POI (i.e., how much percentage of users have opened its info-window),
  - Selecting rate of each POI (i.e., how much percentage of users have made the tour plans that visit it), and
  - Clusters of POIs (i.e., which POIs are often listed together in user-generated tour plans), as well as the hierarchy among them.

- Statistical analyses for comparing the above statistical indexes between two groups (e.g., European and Asian users) and identifying significant differences.
- Data-mining analyses for discovering a small number of unique tour plans among a large number of tour plans.

The use of CT-Planner' log data for marketing analysis is viewed as a sort of crowdsourcing, in the sense that we ask crowds to make tour plans and to evaluate our destinations indirectly. A unique point of this crowdsourcing is that the reward for the participants is not money or score, but an experience of unique service which drastically reduces the cost of tour planning tasks.

4 User Participation in the Creation of Destination Data

We made an Excel-based data editor, with which people can easily make a destination data (i.e., tourist facilities, transportation hubs, and their network) for CT-Planner. This editor asks its user to input in a table the basic data of each POI, including its location (latitude and longitude). Then, its macro program automatically derives the routes between every pair of POIs making use of Google Directions API. Last two years we tested this editor with six undergraduate students. All of them successfully made unique destination data. Through the collaboration with them, we learnt that the involvement of volunteer users in data creation is effective not only for expanding the destinations that CT-Planner supports, but also for enriching the diversity of our service. We are, therefore, seeking the possibility of another crowdsourcing for CT-Planner—asking crowds to create destination data for our CT-Planner. Some people have a strong passion to guide their hometown or favourite places. Once they find that CT-Planner is an effective platform for approaching potential tourists, they will gladly join the collaborative creation of destination data for CT-Planner. In addition, the link to existing resources of tourist destination data will accelerate this collaboration.

5 Key Conclusions and Learning Outcomes for the Tourism Industry

- With web-based tour planning service, people can consult on their tour plans casually from anywhere at any time.
- CT-Planner's interactive approach looks highly user-friendly, because its users are allowed to specify his request piece by piece and not forced to evaluate unfamiliar POIs.
- The user log of web-based tour planning service will serve as a promising crowd data, as it enables us to analyse and monitor the demands of potential tourists without cost.
- CT-Planner considers two types of crowdsourcing: implicit crowdsourcing through daily service for marketing analysis and explicit crowdsourcing for the enrichment of its destination data.

Acknowledgements This work is supported by JST RISTEX's research program on Needs-oriented Service Science, Management and Engineering (project title: "Architecting service with customer participation based on the analysis of customer experience and design processes: sophisticating tour design processes as a case study").

References

Aratani, K., Shimada, S., Ota, J., & Hara, T. (2012). Classification of inbound tourist activities using GPS log data toward service innovation. In *12th Japan-Korea Design Engineering Workshop* (pp. 28–31).

Garcia, A., Arbelaitz, O., Linaza, M., Vansteenwegen, P., & Souffriau, W. (2010). Personalized tourist route generation. In F. Daniel & F. M. Facca (Eds.), *Current trends in Web Engineering. Lecture Notes in Computer Science* (Vol. 6385, pp. 486–497). Berlin: Springer.

Goy, A., & Magro, D. (2004). STAR: A smart tourist agenda recommender. In *Configuration Workshop at ECAI* (pp. 8/1–8/7).

Hara, T., Shimada, S., Yabe, N., Kurata, Y., Aoyama, K., & Hompo, Y. (2012). Value co-creation in tourism: Incorporating non-expert's design into expert's design activities. In L. Freund & J. Spohrer (Eds.), *1st International Conference on Human Side of Service Engineering*.

Kurata, Y. (2010). Interactive assistance for tour planning. In C. Hölscher, T. F. Shipley, M. Olivetti Belardinelli, J. Bateman, & N. S. Newcombe (Eds.), *Spatial Cognition VII. Lecture Notes in Artificial Intelligence* (Vol. 6222, pp. 289–302). Berlin: Springer.

Kurata, Y., Hara, T., Murayama, K., & Shimada, S. (2013). A user test of a tour planning support tool CT-planner 4 monitored by international students. In *10th Conference of Society for Tourism Informatics* (pp. 56–57) (in Japanese).

Lee, J., Kang, E., & Park, G. (2007). Design and implementation of a tour planning system for telematics users. In O. Gervasi & M. L. Gavrilova (Eds.), *Computational Science and Its Applications – ICCSA 2007, Lecture Notes in Computer Science* (Vol. 4707, pp. 179–189).

Seifert, I. (2008). Collaborative assistance with spatio-temporal planning problems. In T. Barkowsky, M. Knauff, G. Ligozat, & D. Montello (Eds.), *Spatial Cognition V. Lecture Notes in Computer Science* (Vol. 4387, pp. 90–106). Berlin: Springer.

CrowdCity: Crowdsourcing an Online Smart City Magazine

Paul Blazek

Learning Objectives

- Communicate the added value that you offer for active user participation.
- Install an easy contribution process to rise the number of authors.
- Trigger viral growth by using social media sharing functionalities.
- Focus on ideas as content rather than just on documentations.

1   Introduction

Cities play a crucial part in the tourism industry. They are not only the economic and administrative centers of countries (Sassen, 2001) and shape the image of how countries are perceived by tourists but they become increasingly the target destinations of travellers. With their travel infrastructure like airports they fescilitate a growing number of touristic activities.

The growing interest and exposure in city tourism correlates with a rising number of short term trips. Tourists discover the fascination of exploring culture, sights, entertainment, shopping etc. activities accumulated in one place.

The changes in personal expectations recorded in the age of individuality lead to a change in the way how the "consumption of the city travel experience" takes place.

A growing number of tourists is starting to look for the "real experience", collecting authentic impressions and being eager to understand the rhythm, the heartbeat of a city and its inhabitants (Florida, 2005).

P. Blazek (✉)
cyLEDGE Media, Vienna, Austria
e-mail: p.blazek@cyledge.com

© Springer-Verlag Berlin Heidelberg 2016   299
R. Egger et al. (eds.), *Open Tourism*, Tourism on the Verge,
DOI 10.1007/978-3-642-54089-9_21

Participative formats consequently grow integrating visitors into activities with locals. Inhabitants offer walking tours or theme-driven adventures and workshops. Alternatives to classic hotel options like the homestay internet service Airbnb can round up the stay with a personal touch and local insight.

This sharing of authentic experiences and amenities goes along with an increasing interest to communicate own views on visited destinations, for both sides: visitors and expats or locals who already live in the cities.

For this purpose the internet offers a wide range of publishing possibilities starting from own blogs, social network tools like Facebook, micro blogging tools like Twitter, to platforms that allow different degrees of content participation. Castells speaks of a communication realm that is fuelled by this rise of a new form of societal communication that he calls *mass self-communication*, reaching from own media channels to the use of social media tools (Castells, 2010).

In the latter category there are popular web platforms like TripAdvisor and Yelp focussing on collecting user content and feedback on physical entities associated with a travelling experience. We also find online magazines that completely open up the content creation to the crowd. All these models of gaining thematic substance are driven by means of crowdsourcing. Richard Florida has reflected widely on how the creative class influences the development of cities and how they shape the appearance of urban reality. He believes that "creativity has emerged as the single most important source of economic growth" (Florida, 2004). Henry Chesbrough sees that co-creation enables value creation as an important process in open innovation thinking (Chesbrough, 2011).

Our project CrowdCity.com is meant to be an extension to this field bringing to life the term *Crowd City*, which describes the participation scenario of people that use information and communication technologies to share their knowledge and ideas in order to inspire others in their use of urban environments (Blazek, 2012).

2 Main Product Offering

The initial point for launching CrowdCity.com in 2012 was the fact that Vienna has been ranked on the very top in several studies that investigated the Smart City status quo of cities worldwide. In addition to economic factors, these studies suddenly highlighted criteria like livelihood, possibilities for citizens to be creative as well as involvement of citizens in urban planning processes. Embracing the challenge of being a Smart City, Vienna is changing the experience that it offers to visitors and citizens: in addition to historical patterns, modern urban development is paving a path for creativity, innovation and fascinating modern life stories.

CrowdCity was born to create a new kind of creativity-enhancing, co-creational conversation about urban development that is considered as "smart" in a broader sense than the common definition of the term Smart City. In fact definitions of a Smart City vary widely. It has become a very popular term to describe the use of new technology applications such as RFID and the "Internet of Things" to provide more efficient infrastructures and services. But there are also definitions that lay

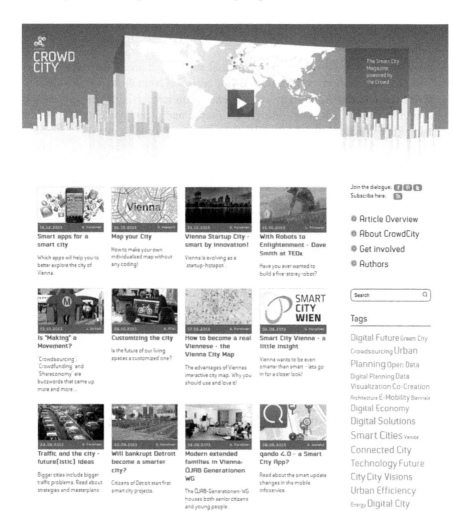

Fig. 1 Screenshot CrowdCity. *Source*: www.crowdcity.com

more emphasis on scenarios of intelligent, integrated work closely linked to the concept of Living Labs and user-generated services.

The idea of CrowdCity is to make it a place for contributions of citizens and visitors (Fig. 1), not limiting it to stories about Vienna alone but opening it up for worldwide relevance. What is citizen's perception of a so called Smart City? What is being considered as a smart project, a smart building or even a smart way of living and travelling in cities? The goal is to increase the understanding of Smart Cities and to encourage ideas and different views, bringing together the crowd: opinion leaders, urban advocates, journalists, bloggers and "everyday people". On CrowdCity citizens from across the globe can submit their content to be edited and published for free.

3   How to Get the Crowd Involved

On the website www.CrowdCity.com potential authors get access by registering an account. The registration requires minimal information from the applicants: Name, username, email address and city of residence. After receiving their registration confirmation authors can start editing their profile and create content. All articles submitted are checked by a CrowdCity editor to comply with quality guidelines before being released on the website. Questions from authors are answered by email or phone.

The main communication channel is the website www.CrowdCity.com itself. To get in touch with the potential content creating crowd, a digital appearance in social media channels was achieved by creating Facebook, Twitter and Pinterest accounts:

- www.facebook.com/CrowdCity
- www.twitter.com/CrowdCity
- www.pinterest.com/CrowdCity

Prior to the launch of the website Twitter was used to establish a first group of followers. The idea was to gain a critical mass of interested readers and to attract potential authors. CrowdCity went online with four initial articles. Promotional activities comprised a press release including a teaser video and a Facebook campaign.

4   Status Quo, Business Model and Crowdsourcing Approach

4.1   Status Quo

Looking at the contributions that have been submitted within one year from launch on, the outcome is:

- The number of registered authors is 13. This amount stays below expectations and is subject of improvement.
- The numbers of articles written per registered author is also below expectations. Only one author wrote 27 articles, but 80 % of all authors didn't publish more than three articles.
- Main topics are mobility, environment, tourism, culture and creativity.
- Articles covering touristic issues are mainly related to the city of Vienna or Austria.
- Readers have few possibilities to interact with the created content. They can share an article via different social media applications, but can't rate or comment the articles directly on CrowdCity.com. Instead they are offered to comment on the CrowCity Facebook page.

- CrowdCity wants to deliver quality content and therefore has chosen a curated content approach, which doesn't allow authors to publish their articles directly. According to feedback that was gathered from authors and potential authors, this approach leads to a submitting barrier.

4.2 Business Model

CrowdCity started as a non-commercial project. Nevertheless it is necessary to cover operational costs and the need for a business model is indispensable. As a first approach online ads and promotional content are considered for 2014.

- Online ads
  CrowdCity offers ad space for companies with products or services that target the smart city and tourism market.
- Promotional content
  Another issue consists of establishing CrowdCity as a distribution site for companies or institutions who are involved in smart city and tourism issues. To avoid the publication of obvious promotional advertisements strict guidelines have to be issued. CrowdCity will only accept content with genuine information.

4.3 Crowd Sourcing Approach and Ongoing Improvements

A set of adjustments are planed to be implemented to support the content creation process and attract more authors:

- Interaction on topics
  Creating a space for collaborative writing on CrowdCity should trigger broader interaction and discussion on innovative urban concepts for better living and traveling. Primarily the main focus is to collect ideas and ongoing innovation in the urban context rather than publishing "documentations". This approach will also attract companies or city representatives who want to communicate city related innovations and projects and look for more interaction with the crowd.
- Extended registration options
  Interaction on topics takes place when the involved parties (including companies and city representatives) get the possibility to post subjects and issues they want to be informed about. Different registration modes are offered to new users depending on the role they want to play in the process: inspirational input, writing or research work. The new set-up also includes the option to comment articles directly on CrowdCity.

- Mapping functionality

    The user interface of CrowdCity gets an additional visualisation feature for submitted content. Each article referring to a specific place is pinned on a digital world map reflecting hot spots of location-based user-generated CrowdCity contributions.

5 Key Challenges for the Future

The key challenges for the future are to establish CrowdCity as an open and collaborative "space for reading and writing" and get more users involved. Future content focuses on the following activities:

- Use of the mapping functionality for gamification concepts to lure potential contributors.
- Communicating the relevance of Smart City issues as an added value for citizens and tourists.
- Identification of other online-magazines, social networking sites and online forums with similar target groups to post and teaser submitted CrowdCity articles and establish content cooperations.

Another issue is to implement a submission process that allows authors to directly publish their content. Quality control happens while articles are already online and not prior to submission. This would further reduce the submitting barrier for potential authors. The risk of poor content is surely reduced taking into account the implementation of multiple registration roles and the commenting features that will have a quality monitoring effect. Nevertheless a CrowdCity editor still is needed to screen the content and assure quality guidelines on a regularly basis.

6 Key Conclusions and Learning Outcomes for the Tourism Industry

- Consider relevance of urban developments and local innovation in contrast to classical information from city guides.
- Build a content engagement strategy for your website. Establish syndication connections and plan for some targeted promotion to ensure that each piece of content gets noticed by key influencers.
- Get local advertisers on your website. Get involved with sites, companies and local niche markets that offer new services or information for their citizens (e.g. pop-up events, hotspots published on local sites, insider tips, new mobile apps).
- Provide authentic stories about new local trends and technical innovations that are of importance for city tourists.

References

Blazek, P. (2012). Hong Kongs digitale Positionierung. Die Bedeutung von Informations- und Kommunikationstechnologie-Innovationen für die wirtschaftsräumliche Entwicklung. *Göttinger Geographische Abhandlungen*, Heft 119, Göttingen.

Castells, M. (2010). *The rise of the network society* (2nd ed.). New York: Blackwell.

Chesbrough, H. (2011). *Open service innovation: Rethinking your business to grow and compete in a new era*. San Francisco: Jossey-Bass.

Florida, R. (2004). *The rise of the creative class*. New York: Basic Books.

Florida, R. (2005). *Cities and the creative class*. New York: Routledge.

Sassen, S. (2001). *The global city. New York, London, Tokyo* (2nd ed.). Princeton, NJ: Princeton University Press.

References

How Quebec City Crowdsources Locals to Promote Its Destination

Frederic Gonzalo

Learning Objectives

- Understand the mechanics of a recent social campaign tapping into local wisdom.
- Explain the context, challenges and goals set forth by this campaign.
- Demonstrate how goals were achieved and surpassed.
- Highlight learning outcomes and how campaign can scale in time.

1 Introduction

Quebec City is a beautiful fortified city, with less than one million residents, combining its French heritage and culture with cobblestone streets, quaint boutiques and fabulous dining options. It is, however, a small city when compared with the average North-American metropolis or even with other big Canadian cities, including Toronto or nearby Montreal, which is only a 2½ h drive away. So competing on advertising money alone is hardly an option when seeking to attract international or domestic travellers to the city.

Quebec City Tourism is a membership-based organization, representing over 1000 members in Quebec City and surrounding areas. Its total budget for 2012 was $22 million, including a $12.8 million marketing budget. Here are a few highlights of its most recent tourism performance (Fig. 1).

Quebec City Tourism has never been a trailblazer in its web marketing approach, using a more traditional approach in mainstream media, offline and online, with

F. Gonzalo (✉)
Gonzo Marketing, Quebec City, Quebec, Canada
e-mail: Frederic@gonzomarketing.biz

© Springer-Verlag Berlin Heidelberg 2016   307
R. Egger et al. (eds.), *Open Tourism*, Tourism on the Verge,
DOI 10.1007/978-3-642-54089-9_22

- Nearly 4.5 million tourists per year (2010), including over 1.0 million from 75 countries outside Canada
- $1.34 billion in annual tourism spending (2010)
- 23,600 regular full-time tourism-related jobs in 2010
- Approximately 550 hotel establishments with a total capacity of nearly 16,800 rooms.
- 4th destination in Canada, after Toronto, Montréal, and Vancouver (number of visitors)

Fig. 1 Quebec City Tourism statistics. *Source*: Quebec City Tourism annual report 2012

web banners and other classic paid media tactics, i.e. AdWords, remarketing, etc. It was rather late to jump on-board the social media bandwagon, with a slow start late in 2011 on platforms such as Facebook and Twitter, and developing a mobile application earlier in 2012. So it is with this in mind that, earlier in 2013, they worked to build a campaign meant to generate buzz and online traffic, along with the clear intent to tap into local wisdom for the summer season: *l'effet Québec*! (Loosely translated: the Quebec effect!)

2 Open Innovation Approach

Together with their ad agency Cossette, Quebec City Tourism sought to generate some buzz about the destination. On a new microsite www.effetquebec.com, locals but also anyone who's been to Quebec City were invited to share their secrets, hidden gems or favourite spot, activity or restaurant in the city. It was an innovative way to embrace collaborative platforms, by way of a simple and user-friendly site (Fig. 2).

Two types of content were available for participation. On one hand, you could simply vote in different rankings, according to the following categories:

- **Safe bets**: restaurants or spots where you're sure things will be delicious, no matter what time of day or season.
- **Culinary discoveries**: where the chef goes the extra mile and dining is truly an experience of itself.
- **Fast food**: where one can have quality food, quick and on the cheap, and with that little extra in the ambiance.
- **Family fun**: activities and things to do that are great for families of all ages.
- **The Great Outdoors**: the best spots near Quebec City or even within the city to indulge with rivers, mountains and all the fresh air one could want.
- **Shop 'til you drop**: where to go to find those fancy items or hard-to-find antiques.
- **Unique to Quebec City**: things to do or see, places we like to go... those experiences that make the city what it is, in particular for locals.
- **Have a drink**: where to go to have a beer, a martini or a local specialty drink and where locals like to hang around.

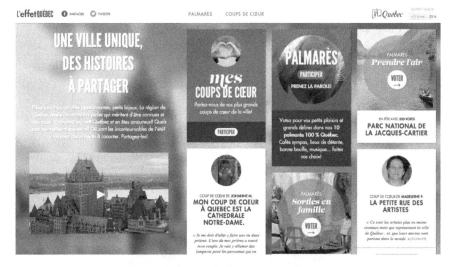

Fig. 2 Effet Quebec website, summer of 2013. *Source*: www.effetquebec.com

- **Big events**: Quebec City boasts is fair share of big annual events, among which its fames Winter Carnival. But what other events are not as famous but just as much fun?
- **Culture mecca**: which are the favourite spots, museums, art galleries or historical sites that locals like to go to?

On the other hand, you could simply manually enter your *coup de coeur*, or little secret, about a favourite place, attraction, event or restaurant. This, in turn, became content people could vote on if the entry fit into one of the above 10 categories.

Votes and content shared on the microsite could also be tied with either a Twitter or Facebook account, ensuring the contest greater reach and virality and thus more potential sharing through people's networks.

To ensure participation from the beginning, minimal content had already been pre-loaded on the site by a group of test users (local citizens), and a 6-weeks long contest was launched with aspirational weekly prizes to be won. Thus from May 6th to June 17th 2013, the contest brought an overwhelming amount of traffic to the site, exceeding expectations by a landslide.

3 Outcomes

Preliminary results after 6 weeks into the campaign were as follows:

- Over 7200 new emails gathered with permission for future communication
- 40,000 visits to the site, of which 30,000 were unique visitors

Fig. 3 Partners such as Aquarium du Quebec embracing the campaign. *Source*: Screenshot: Aquarium du Quebec, Facebook page, June 2013

- Average user spent 3:19 min on the site, meaning it had stickiness and great content
- Over 37,000 votes entered on the various rankings
- More than 1800 coups de coeur, or little secrets, shared by locals
- More than 13,000 suggested places or attractions for future vote

What Quebec City Tourism did not expect but were delighted to see is how some of their members embraced the competition and the possibility to be ranked among the Top 10 best Family fun activities, or among the Top 10 Unique experiences in the city. For example, the Aquarium du Quebec posted on their Facebook page, inviting their fans to go and vote in order for it to remain on top in one of the ranking. The Train of Massif de Charlevoix did likewise, sending out a dedicated newsletter to its 25,000 email database inviting people to vote, even tying a promotional offer to the effort (Fig. 3).

4   Key Challenges for the Future

Moving forward, there are a few challenges that will need to be addressed in order to scale such a campaign in time. Here are the three most important ones:

Maintaining Interest Throughout the Year The microsite is getting more traffic than expected in the middle of summer, and once the 6-weeks contest is over, mostly because Quebec City Tourism members embraced the campaign and are pushing their clientele to vote. In coming months, it will be fairly easy to reignite locals with sharing different places or activities in the Fall or during Winter, which are very distinctive seasons in this province. But what will happen when Year 2 comes around?

Investing Marketing Dollars to Promote Social A collaborative approach such as this one holds great potential but very often will remain a hit amongst a niche audience of savvy social media users, influencers and bloggers. In order to scale to a broader population, some traditional initiatives may be required, reaching out to everyday people who won't have contributed to the first edition of the campaign: radio ads and sponsorships, newspaper, live events, etc.

Tapping into Travellers' Insights Last but not least, it will be interesting to see if Quebec City Tourism opens up this initiative to travellers to the city. Even if they keep the whole approach in French-only, knowing that 91 % of all tourism in the province of Quebec is actually domestic (thus, mostly French-speaking), this could also provide scalability in time, mixing it up with locals' knowledge and what visitors may or may not agree with!

5 Key Conclusions and Learning Outcomes for the Tourism Industry

- **Social media goes hand in hand with other campaigns**: the folks of Quebec City Tourism had the foresight to build in this campaign with other, more traditional tactics that were to take place during the summertime. For example, in their traditional newspaper ads in nearby cities such as Montreal, instead of placing a marketing slogan or other tagline, ads featured *coups de coeur* from locals, taken from the effetquebec.com site, with a picture of that local making its testimonial.

  But the simple fact one could share a vote or content input via a Facebook or Twitter is what made the viral component such as success. Another learning aspect is that this social campaign was not fully integrated with other ongoing marketing tactics outside the province of Quebec, as it was in French only. It remained an effort targeting locals above all, missing out on a more global audience.

- **Tapping into local wisdom is like tapping into a goldmine**: As can be seen with the statistics shared above, locals were very generous in their participation and since this was a first-time experiment, it marks a clear signal for future campaigns: when tapping into local pride to share insiders' information, people love to show they are "in the know". Stories shared were sad, romantic, funny and most often personal. Since authenticity is what more and more people seek nowadays, in particular for an upcoming destination or trip, the content generated from this campaign is perfectly aligned with this concept and allows connecting with how locals live their city.

- **Are rewards and contests really necessary?** Not really, it appears. There are very few people who emailed or sent a message on Facebook to ask who the winners were or when the draw would take place, because quite honestly most people shared content or voted just because there was a common sense of it being "a fun thing to do". If anything, putting in a contest component drew some confusion, as some people thought—and still do, perhaps—that the microsite as well was only there for a 6-weeks period. So while the contest drew some attention to this initiative, it did not play a defining role in its success.
- **Social proof is stronger than advertisement**: Preliminary feedback post-campaign showed that customers who saw the ads with locals' testimonials thought they were more impactful than standard advertisement. This tends to corroborate findings showing that only 14 % of consumers trust traditional advertisement anymore (4).

In conclusion, the Effet Québec was a great hit for Quebec City Tourism, its members and locals who participated. But more importantly, it becomes a tremendous resource for content campaign moving forward, allowing potential visitors to get a better understanding of things to see, eat or do while in Quebec City during an upcoming trip. This initiative was set to continue during the Winter 2014 season, and preliminary results have been encouraging, promising for a Phase during Summer 2014!

References

Quebec City Tourism (QTC). (2012). Performance report. Accessed May 10, 2014, from http://www.quebecregion.com/en/about-quebec-city-tourism/documents/

QTC website. Accessed August 9, 2013, from www.effetquebec.com

Aquarium du Quebec Facebook page. Accessed June 6, 2013, from https://www.facebook.com/aquariumduquebec

Involvement of Tourist Visitors to the UNESCO World Heritage Site of Goa, India

Mihir Ignatius Nayak and Kurt Luger

Learning Objectives

- Realize the need for greater involvement of tourists in the heritage discourse.
- Understand how social media is empowering and encouraging tourists to take part in the construction of heritage and what effects this has on the Heritage Site.
- Analyze how the participatory nature of social media is resulting in new socially created meanings of heritage.
- Identify the key intercultural challenges with regards to tourist involvement that UNESCO World Heritage Sites such as Goa face in the future.

1 Introduction

The aim of this chapter is to discuss the importance of tourist involvement at UNESCO World Heritage Sites. Till now, heritage has been a mostly top-down affair with tourists confined to the mere role of spectators at World Heritage Sites. Tourist visitors possessed little opportunity to add their own interpretations of the heritage site to the public discourse. However, in order to create a wider discourse of heritage in the public sphere, it is essential that tourist visitors to World Heritage Sites such as Goa are involved in the selection, interpretation and communication of heritage.

M.I. Nayak, M.A. (✉) • K. Luger, Ph.D.
University of Salzburg, Salzburg, Austria
e-mail: Mihir.Nayak@stud.sbg.ac.at; kurt.luger@sbg.ac.at

© Springer-Verlag Berlin Heidelberg 2016
R. Egger et al. (eds.), *Open Tourism*, Tourism on the Verge,
DOI 10.1007/978-3-642-54089-9_23

2   The UNESCO World Heritage Site of Goa, India

The "Churches and Convents of Goa", as the UNESCO World Heritage Site of Goa, India is officially known, has been a UNESCO World Heritage Site since November 1986 (UNESCO, 1986). In its recommendation report, ICOMOS (1982, p. 3) stated that

> the churches and convents of Goa are an outstanding example of an architectural ensemble which illustrates the work of missionaries in Asia.

The highlight of the UNESCO World Heritage Site of Goa, India is the Basilica of Bom Jesus and the tomb of St Francis Xavier that is placed within:

> At the Church of Bom Jesus, Goa conserves Saint Francis-Xavier's tomb. Beyond its fine artistic quality (commissioned in 1665 by the Grand Duke Ferdinand II of Tuscany, it was executed in Florence and includes admirable bronze work by Giovanni Battista Foggini), the tomb of the apostle of India and Japan symbolizes an event of universal significance the influence of the Catholic religion in the Asian world in the modern period (ICOMOS, 1982).

While the rest of India was colonized by the British and this reflects in its built heritage, Goa is a former Portuguese colony and the Portuguese colonial influence is clearly visible in its *"gleaming whitewashed churches with Portuguese-style facades" and "crumbling forts [that] guard rocky capes and estuary entrances"* (Menon, 1993).

However, not everyone sees the UNESCO World Heritage Site of Goa, India in such a positive light. While the Portuguese and other European tourists marvel at the outstanding architecture of the monuments of Goa, they remain unaware that the same monuments also represent a symbol of Portuguese colonial oppression to the Indian visitors.

3   The Need for Tourist Involvement

Although heritage selection in the past was mostly top-down with the Government holding most of the control, experts now believe that a more open, participatory approach is needed.

> Heritage results from a selection process, often government-initiated and supported by official regulation…[but] It is time, too, to recognise more fully that heritage protection does not depend alone on top-down interventions by governments or the expert actions of heritage industry professionals (Logan & Smith, 2012).

Instead, tourist visitors to the UNESCO World Heritage Site of Goa, India must also be involved in the selection, interpretation and communication of heritage.

Although Tunbridge and Ashworth (1996) warn that heritage interpretation at the heritage site might be dissonant, a conflict filled past need not and should not be avoided. Instead of limiting them to a nostalgic viewpoint, tourists might be interested in a constructive yet critical discussion of the more difficult aspects of the destination's history (Rodrian, 2011).

> Interpretation at World Heritage Sites "should place less emphasis on coherent narratives where the rough edges of real inter-communal relations are smoothed over and should encourage a more dynamic and perhaps unfinished, even messier, version of historical events....the World Heritage Site should be a scene of dialogue rather than conflict, where attempts to continue to include and resolve differences rather than to police or exclude those who challenge official narratives Hitchcock (2005).

Thus, instead of presenting tourists with only the positive aspects of the UNESCO World Heritage Site of Goa, these tourist visitors might also be interested in taking part in a critical discussion on the more dissonant aspects of its history such as the Portuguese Inquisition, forced conversion of Hindus and ill treatment of the local population by the Portuguese. Further research is needed into how these tourist visitors to the UNESCO World Heritage Site of Goa can become more involved in the heritage discourse.

In a recent UNESCO study "Benchmarking World Heritage and Tourism", conducted by Swiss and Austrian researchers in collaboration with the respective country offices of UNESCO, a comparative, indicator-based quality assessment of World Heritage regions and of how tourism is managed at World Heritage sites was conducted with Involvement and Support being one of the criteria measured. In related ongoing doctoral thesis by the author, the aim is to add to the results of the UNESCO study "Benchmarking World Heritage and Tourism" by conducting empirical research into how tourists can be involved in the process of heritage selection and interpretation at the UNESCO World Heritage Site of Goa, India (Fig. 1).

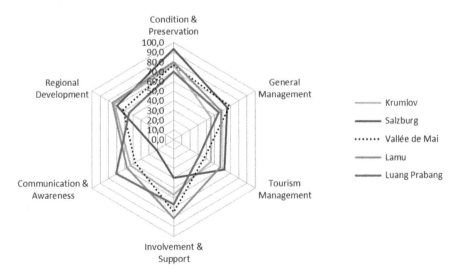

Fig. 1 Criteria for evaluation of UNESCO World Heritage Sites. *Source*: Internal Report Benchmarking World Heritage and Tourism, 2011

4   The Tourist Involvement Approach

Participatory culture is said to be a culture where "*not every member must contribute, but all must believe that they are free to contribute when ready and that what they contribute will be appropriately valued*" (Jenkins, Puroshotma, Clinton, Weigel, & Robinson, 2006).

With the advent of social media, a 'culture of participation' has now been introduced into the heritage field. Social media enables the tourist visitor to play a more active role in the selection and communication of heritage as well as empowering and encouraging tourists to play an active role in the construction of heritage at the World Heritage Site and its related dialogue. The participatory culture of social media has thus had a very deep effect on the very nature of the World Heritage Site.

According to Leonhard (2009 cited in Munro & Richards, 2011), a 'culture of information' (usually top–down) has been replaced with a 'culture of communication' (both bottom up as well as horizontal). These communications are increasingly happening using social media tools such as reviews on TripAdvisor, photographs on Flickr, retweets on Twitter or comments on Facebook. Tourists, who are currently deciding which heritage destination to visit or what heritage attractions to see at a particular destination, base their decisions on content generated via social media. As a result, conversations that take place on social media ultimately end up shaping the cultural heritage at a UNESCO World Heritage Site.

Despite the growing importance of social media in the heritage field, however, few World Heritage Sites have social media strategies and fewer still have social media strategies that include tourist visitors as important stakeholders. The UNESCO World Heritage Site of Goa still lacks a comprehensive social media strategy and fails to include tourist visitors in its social media strategy. "*These voices are often not represented, yet they could add significant value to the role of social media in facilitating the creation of true forms of shared heritage*" (Ciolfi, 2012). However, Chan (2008) sees the situation changing with the advent of new social media strategies that are being created with the goal of promoting tourist involvement in social media. Anderson (2009) warns that for a social media strategy to be effective, it is important to listen to and let the tourist visitors decide the topics and areas that are of interest to him or her. "*[It is all] about deciding when to listen, when to take part and when to stimulate and cultivate conversations*" (Munro & Richards, 2011).

Not only has social media encouraged a 'participatory culture' in the field of heritage communication, it has also been very effective in the co-creation of heritage, with museums and other heritage sites utilising social media tools and platforms to "*enrich and sometimes [even] create exhibits*" (Ciolfi, 2012). The author cites the examples of the Metropolitan Museum of Art, the Smithsonian Institution and the Victoria and Albert Museum where such co-creation of exhibits has taken place. Unfortunately, little attention is paid to this important aspect of social media.

Cultural heritage is not only created in museums and heritage sites but the creation of cultural heritage is increasingly taking place online, say Russo, Watkins, Kelly, and Chan (2010). Fairclough (2012) posits that social media has affected both the access to as well as the nature of cultural heritage. Social media allows tourists from across the globe to 'see into', as it were, each other's cultural heritage, thus ending up in a dual sharing of cultural heritage on a global as well as an intercultural scale. Social media empowers the tourist visitor co-create and share their own versions of cultural heritage online. *"The walls of a museum [or heritage site] are potentially dissolved by social media"* (ibid, p. xvi) and as a result, the entire process of heritage selection, interpretation and dialogue is moving online.

Mobile is an area that is gaining greater importance within the field of social media. Giaccardi (2012) highlights the fact that new mobile technologies and multi-communication devices such as smartphones allow tourists to access social media on the move, thus allowing heritage tourists to participate in the heritage discourse online, irrespective of whether they are currently at the World Heritage Site or not. By giving tourists access to heritage wherever they are in the world, social media brings cultural heritage into the daily discourse, instead of limiting it to something that can only be accessed when at the World Heritage Site itself.

Giaccardi (2012) predicts that the participatory nature of social media will result in new socially created heritage concepts with individual tourists now having the ability to attribute their own values and meaning to the World Heritage Site. Tourists interpret heritage based on the frame of reference that they experience in their own daily lives such that interactions with the past result in the creating of a more personal vision of the future (Lowenthal, 2005).

5   Key Challenges for the Future

World Heritage Sites face many key challenges in the future, with regards to the involvement of tourists and their cultural backgrounds.

Tourists at UNESCO World Heritage Sites such as Goa come from a heterogeneous mix of cultures and backgrounds and to be able to encourage their involvement in the heritage sphere in the future, the World Heritage Site *"needs to allow spaces for these groups of stakeholders to provide a contribution in order to make the heterogeneity of communities surrounding heritage a feature not a hindrance"* (Ciolfi, 2012). Every single tourist community visiting the World Heritage Site must be encouraged to actively interact and participate in the selection, interpretation and communication of the cultural heritage at the site. According to Rodrian (2011), this critical discourse between the heritage site and its history needs to take place with the participation of different cultures and their own perspectives. Only then will the resulting cultural heritage be commonly owned by all the tourist cultures visiting the World Heritage Site.

UNESCO World Heritage Sites have the unique potential to transform themselves into spaces of intercultural dialogue where cultural differences can be sorted out and a common cultural heritage created (Maddern, 2005). Both Maddern (ibid) and Hitchcock (2005) suggest that World Heritage Sites should aim to include the different ethnic and cultural perspectives and ideologies of their tourist visitors and promote themselves as transcultural spaces. After all, UNESCO World Heritage Sites, as the name itself suggests, are part of the heritage of the world and thus enjoy a universal relevance for all mankind, including the different tourist nationalities that choose to visit the World Heritage Site. Hitchcock (2002) suggests that World Heritage Sites be turned into spheres of transcultural exchange involving the tourist visitors where the mutual exchange and intermingling of different cultural influences of the tourist visitors will result in the creation of a common heritage. This concept of UNESCO World Heritage Sites becoming meeting points of transcultural exchange can help combat negative notions of heritage sites being 'empty meeting grounds' (MacCannell, 1992).

Transcultural participation and dialogue at UNESCO World Heritage Sites can only take place when tourists from different cultures commonly create and share meaning, despite the fact that they have different perspectives and come from different backgrounds (Sadri and Flammia, 2011 cited in Saretzki & May, 2012). Harms (2012) says that the most essential requirement for effective transcultural participation and dialogue is the realization that one's own culture is not the only truth and neither is it the only means of seeing and interpreting heritage. Without such an attitude of respect and open mindedness, effective tourist participation and transcultural dialogue will never be possible at UNESCO World Heritage Sites such as Goa. UNESCO strongly agrees that all cultures have equal value, status and dignity (Albert, 2002) and it is vital that tourists both recognise and respect this.

> Effective intercultural dialogue entails promoting dialogue between individuals in all the complexities of their multiple identities and ensuring the necessary conditions of equality among them...the latter involves recognition, by all parties, of the dignity and value of all cultures involved (UNESCO, 2009).

The main aim of the UNESCO World Heritage Convention is to "*promote and foster international understanding based on mutual cultural respect...the dialogue between cultures...must fundamentally seen as a dialogue between equal partners who have equal rights*" (Huefner, 2002). By stating unequivocally that all cultures enjoy the same dignity and value and deeming different cultural communities to be seen as equal partners with equal rights, UNESCO is openly rejecting any kind of cultural hierarchy with regards to heritage.

> ...an open attitude towards exchange with other cultures, a willingness to get to know them and learn to understand them, respect for the diversity of cultures and for human rights...Only through respect for cultural diversity, through tolerance, dialogue and cooperation, will it be possible to create a climate of trust and understanding which will contribute to...international peace and security (ibid).

As intercultural tensions rise in different parts of the world, destinations with UNESCO World Heritage Sites such as Goa will be called upon to play a role in defusing these tensions in the future. As both Franquesa and Morell (2011) and Bandarin (2002) state, tourist involvement in heritage sites can serve as an instrument of peace and reconciliation. Involvement in heritage sites provides a unique opportunity to solve the intercultural tensions that exist in world heritage regions. Learning to communicate with other tourists on the basis of equal respect can help jointly resolve conflicts that may arise in the region.

> ...a lot of our heritage is uncomfortable to one person or the other, for one reason or another. World Heritage learning is another opportunity for dealing with conflict, for searching common ground. Coming to terms with uncomfortable heritage dimensions can be a beautiful learning challenge (Merkel, 2002).

6   Key Conclusions and Learning Outcomes for the Tourism Industry

- Although heritage selection in the past was a top down affair, with the control resting largely in the hands of the state, many experts are now calling for a more open, participatory approach including greater involvement of tourists.
- Social media enables the tourist visitor to play a more active role in the selection and communication of heritage, empowering and encouraging tourists to take part in the construction of heritage at the destination, thus having a profound effect on the World Heritage Site.
- Not only has social media encouraged a 'participatory culture' in the field of heritage communication, it has also been extremely effective in the co-creation of heritage.
- Cultural heritage is not just being created in museums and heritage sites but increasingly taking place online. Social media empowers the tourist visitor co-create and share their own versions of cultural heritage online. The participatory nature of social media results in new socially created meanings of heritage with individuals being able to attribute their own values and meaning to the heritage product.
- Tourists at UNESCO World Heritage Sites such as Goa come from a heterogeneous mix of cultures and backgrounds and in order to facilitate their involvement in the heritage discourse, UNESCO World Heritage Sites in particular have the potential to become spaces of intercultural dialogue where cultural differences can be worked out and a common cultural heritage can be created.

References

Albert, M. (2002). UNESCO conventions – Historical contexts and references. In UNESCO Deutsche-Kommission e.V. (Ed.), *Nature and culture* (pp. 19–26). Cottbus: Deutsche UNESCO-Kommission e.V.

Anderson, E. R. (2009). Next generation campaign management: How campaign management will evolve to enable interactive marketing. *Journal of Direct, Data and Digital Marketing Practice, 10*(3), 272–282.

Bandarin, F. (2002). Preface of the Director of UNESCO World Heritage Centre, Paris. In UNESCO Deutsche-Kommission e.V. (Ed.), *Nature and culture* (p. 15). Cottbus: Deutsche UNESCO-Kommission e.V.

Chan, S. (2008). Towards new metrics of success. In J. Trant & D. Bearman (Eds.), *Museums and the web 2008: Selected papers from an international conference* (pp. 13–22). Toronto: Archives and Museum Informatics.

Ciolfi, L. (2012). Participation and the creation of shared heritage. In E. Giaccardi (Ed.), *Heritage and social media: Understanding heritage in a participatory culture* (pp. 69–86). Oxon: Routledge.

Fairclough, G. (2012). Others: A prologue. In E. Giaccardi (Ed.), *Heritage and social media: Understanding heritage in a participatory culture* (pp. 14–17). Oxon: Routledge.

Franquesa, J. B., & Morell, M. (2011). Transversal indicators and qualitative observatories of heritage tourism. In G. Richards & W. Munsters (Eds.), *Cultural tourism research methods* (pp. 169–179). Oxford: CABI.

Giaccardi, E. (2012). Introduction: Reframing heritage in a participatory culture. In E. Giaccardi (Ed.), *Heritage and social media: Understanding heritage in a participatory culture* (pp. 1–10). Oxon: Routledge.

Harms, K. (2012). Emotionsarbeit im interkulturellen Kontext. *Zeitschrift fuer Tourismuswissenschaft, 4*(2), 197–208.

Hitchcock, M. (2002). Souvenirs, cultural heritage and development. In Ministry of Culture and Information of Vietnam, Walloon Brussels Region, Asia-Europe Foundation, Laboratory of Anthropology of Communication (University of Liege, Belgium) (Eds.), *Cultural Heritage, Man and Tourism. Report of the Asia-Europe Seminar Hanoi (Vietnam) 5–7 October 2001* (pp. 71–80). Liege: CRD

Hitchcock, M. (2005). Afterword. In D. Harrison & M. Hitchcock (Eds.), *The politics of world heritage: Negotiating tourism and conservation* (pp. 181–186). Clevedon: Channel View.

Huefner, K. (2002). The World Heritage Convention 30 years down the line: what shape should it take in the future. In UNESCO Deutsche-Kommission e.V. (Ed.), *Nature and culture* (pp. 141–146). Cottbus: Deutsche UNESCO-Kommission e.V.

ICOMOS. (1982). *Advisory body recommendation.* Accessed February 9, 2013, from http://whc.unesco.org/en/list/234/documents/

Jenkins, H., Puroshotma, R., Clinton, K., Weigel, M., & Robinson, A. J. (2006). *Confronting the challenges of participatory culture: Media education for the 21st century.* Chicago, IL: The MacArthur Foundation. Accessed December 8, 2012, from http://www.newmeidaliteracies.org/files/working/NMLWhitePaper.pdf

Logan, W. S., & Smith, L. J. (2012). Series general co-editors foreword. In L. Smith & N. Akagawa (Eds.), *Intangible heritage* (pp. 12–13). Oxford: Routledge.

Lowenthal, D. (2005). Stewarding the future. *CRM: The Journal of Heritage Stewardship, 2*(2), 6–25.

MacCannell, D. (1992). *Empty meeting grounds.* London: Routledge.

Maddern, J. (2005). Huddled masses yearning to buy postcards: The politics of producing heritage at the statue of Liberty-Ellis Island national museum. In D. Harrison & M. Hitchcock (Eds.), *The politics of world heritage: Negotiating tourism and conservation* (pp. 23–34). Clevedon: Channel View.

Menon, K. (1993). *Case study on the effects of tourism on culture and the environment: India – Jaisalmer, Khajuraho and Goa.* Bangkok: UNESCO Principal Regional Office for Asia and the Pacific.

Merkel, C. M. (2002). Going learning places: World heritage and life-long-learning. In UNESCO Deutsche-Kommission e.V. (Ed.), *Nature and culture* (pp. 147–152). Cottbus: Deutsche UNESCO-Kommission e.V.

Munro, J., & Richards, B. (2011). The digital challenge. In N. Morgan, A. Pritchard, & R. Pride (Eds.), *Destination brands: Managing place reputation* (pp. 141–154). Oxford: Butterworth Heinemann.

Rodrian, P. (2011). Heritage als Konstruktion touristicher Mediatoren. *Zeitschrift fuer Tourismuswissenschaften, 3*(1), 25–41.

Russo, A., Watkins, J., Kelly, L., & Chan, S. (2010). Participatory communication with social media. *Curator: The Museum Journal, 51*(1), 21–31.

Saretzki, A., & May, C. (2012). Welterbetourismus – ein interkulturelles Medium? *Zeitschrift fuer Tourismuswissenschaft, 4*(2), 151–166.

Tunbridge, J., & Ashworth, G. (1996). *Dissonant heritage: The management of the past as a resource in conflict*. Chichester: Wiley.

UNESCO. (1986). *World heritage committee tenth session: Report of the Rapporteur*. Accessed February 9, 2013, from http://whc.unesco.org/en/list/234/documents/

UNESCO. (2009). *Investing in cultural diversity and intercultural dialogue*. Paris: UNESCO.

The InnoWellen Case Study: The Use of Web-Based Idea Competitions as a Tool of Stakeholder Participation in the Leisure Industry

Benjamin Kreitmeir

Learning Objectives

- Investigate in what way web-based idea competitions can be used to initiate and support active stakeholder participation in destinations.
- Explore how to apply web-based idea competitions to innovations relevant to destinations.
- Demonstrate how a web-based idea competition can be initiated among stakeholders of a destination.
- Evaluate advantages and constraints of a web-based idea competition as a stakeholder participation tool.
- Observe how web-based idea competitions can be improved and give examples for further research needs on the topic.

1 Introduction

The InnoWellen case study is about stakeholder participation in the innovation process of tourism destinations and its challenges. Open Innovation is a new and promising concept in innovation management. It includes, amongst other criteria, the participation of stakeholders in innovative processes. Until now, Open Innovation has mainly been discussed in the context of businesses rather than managing destinations.

The aim of this case study is, therefore, to examine how active participation in the form of crowdsourcing as an instrument of Open Innovation can be initiated and promoted for innovations relevant for destinations. An additional aim is to gain primary insights into the use of crowdsourcing in destinations.

B. Kreitmeir (✉)
Management Center Innsbruck, Innsbruck, Austria
e-mail: b.kreitmeir@gmail.com

© Springer-Verlag Berlin Heidelberg 2016
R. Egger et al. (eds.), *Open Tourism*, Tourism on the Verge,
DOI 10.1007/978-3-642-54089-9_24

To achieve this, the web-based idea competition 'InnoWellen.de' was created using the crowdsourcing web-platform 'unserAller'. Here, the public were asked to contribute new ideas on how to make the local swimming pool of the destination Oberammergau more attractive for visitors. The results of the activities on the website were subsequently analyzed.

The findings of this study show that crowdsourcing can be used successfully to initiate public participation in innovations of destinations. The results of this study also show that participation can easily be controlled through the contents of the tasks given. Yet, there is evidence that people who are more strongly affected by a project, *e.g.* locals, feel the need to participate in a more comprehensive way rather than just sticking to a specific task.

It also showed that crowdsourcing is especially effective to catch the various existing interests and identifications of new stakeholders of a destination. The significance of the relevant communication channels also became apparent when using Open Innovation and crowdsourcing to activate participation. Lastly, on the basis of this case study recommendations could be deduced to optimize similar crowdsourcing projects.

2 Participation and Cooperation as a Base for Innovation in the Leisure Industry

The initiation of innovation in destinations is to be viewed against the backdrop of conflict between competition and cooperation. On the one hand, *competition* motivates businesses to innovate. On the other, *cooperation* is an essential foundation for innovation where business sectors are fragmented and for small businesses in tourist destinations. Innovations in destinations happen through the cooperation of participants by pooling and combining their knowledge, technologies, abilities, experience and competence in various ways. In order to make the most of the innovative potential, the destination has to establish learning processes that span across the different branches of existing businesses (Tschurtschenthaler, Peters, & Pikkemaat, 2005).

A prerequisite for innovation in tourism is a joint market-orientated development and implementation of innovation through complementary services that are willing to share innovative solutions (Pikkemaat, Peters, Weiermair, & Auer, 2006). This is precisely the idea behind Open Innovation as Lindegaard states: "*Everyone involved in an open innovation process focuses on problems, needs and issues and works them out together*" (Lindegaard, 2010). The intention of Open Innovation is the participation of many individuals and businesses in a collective process of innovation. This can lead to the development and growth of a common 'Business Eco-system' (Chesbrough, 2011).

Small and middle-sized businesses can use their resources more efficiently and in a more versatile way through Open Innovation. For example, they could broaden their product range through external ideas and with that achieve economies of scope (Chesbrough, 2011).

The customer's participation in the innovation process has the advantage that the customer's creative potential and needs are directly part of the product development. This in turn reduces the financial risk of the new product (Tschurtschenthaler et al., 2005). The guest plays an essential part as an external factor in tourism products. Therefore, the opportunity to integrate the customer from the start into the development of new products presents itself especially in tourism (Pikkemaat et al., 2006).

3 The InnoWellen Case: An Open Call for Cooperative Innovation

The InnoWellen case study investigates the way web-based idea competitions can be used as a tool of Open Innovation and crowdsourcing, and to initiate and support active stakeholder participation in the leisure industry. Typical stakeholders of a destination are the residents, local business owners, local and government bodies and the tourists. However, this list could be continued depending on how detailed the segmentation criteria are set.

3.1 The Implementation of the Web-Based Idea Competition 'InnoWellen'

The tourist destination Oberammergau is an idyllic town in Southern Bavaria, surrounded by Alpine mountains. It has a population of about 5200 inhabitants with an average age of 45. Oberammergau is renowned for its art and craft traditions. It is particularly well-known for its wood-carving and the world-famous passion play, which is performed every 10-years with great enthusiasm by around 2200 Oberammergau locals.

The council of Oberammergau operates the 39-year-old public swimming pool 'Wellenberg'. In recent times, the subject "Swimming pool Wellenberg" regularly appeared in the local media. In short, the precarious financial situation of the Wellenberg has been well-known for several years. Currently it operates with a yearly deficit of 700,000 € (figures from 2011). The pool is seen as dated and in need of renovation. Accordingly, the costs have spiralled out of control over the last number of years. Additionally, customer numbers have dropped every year. Some new pools that pose serious competition have also opened in the region.

In order to resolve the problems at Wellenberg, various strategies were discussed. An external consulting firm executed a feasibility study and an economic audit. When finally the closure of the Wellenberg was favoured by the council, a citizens' initiative in favour of keeping the pool was formed, which led to a local referendum whether the pool should be kept open or closed down. With a 52 % turnout and a clear majority of 78 %, The Oberammergau citizens decided in favour of keeping the Wellenberg pool open and with that the council were obliged to run it.

Recently the council of Oberammergau announced the introduction of measures to reduce running costs, and the commitment to invest 3.5 million euros to renovate the pool and make it more attractive. The necessity for innovation, due to pressure from competitors, and the obvious high interest of the Oberammergau citizens, was the reason to choose this depicted case for a joint project of innovation.

3.2 Preparing and Initiating the Web-Based Idea Competition

In order to prepare the initiation of the idea competition, the purpose of the project was formulated in consultation with the Mayor of the city as thus:

> The aim of InnoWellen is to generate innovative ideas in order to make the public swimming pool more attractive, in cooperation with an undefined crowd, who most likely take part through self-selection and therefore can be seen as stakeholders of the infrastructure project.

Since the Mayor was convinced of the great value of citizen contribution and finding out more about the tourists' needs, the investigator tried to get the cooperation of further key members of the community, such as the tourism director and local council at an early stage in the process. Unfortunately the council could not be convinced of the advantages of opening the innovation process to the public. Even though this reaction was to be expected, it also was quite surprising if one takes into account the positive attitude of the Mayor towards the project, and that the low degree of 'openness' was made clear by the initiator from the beginning, meaning, the decisive power would remain completely with the council.

Considering these circumstances the investigator decided to launch the InnoWellen project as a bottom-up initiative, which means that the driving forces had to come from the public and not from the official bodies.

In order to communicate the purpose of the project to the public, further steps had to be accomplished in preparation. Transparent conditions of participation and a precise crowdsourcing task were formulated. Furthermore an animated video was published on YouTube and www.InnoWellen.de explaining the purpose and rules.

Conditions of Participation:

- *All submitted ideas will be published on the projects website after the project closing date and they represent non-committal proposals for the operator (local council) of the swimming pool.*
- *InnoWellen is not a political forum.*

- *In the case of the council of Oberammergau, e.g. the operators, wanting to implement your idea, you are prepared to transfer any intellectual property rights free of charge.*
- *The providers of the three most popular ideas (rated by the crowd) win a voucher.*

Theory tells us that in many crowdsourcing cases the intrinsic outweighs the extrinsic motivation (Frey, Lüthje, & Haag, 2011). However, in this case, there was an additional incentive of 410 €, in total, in vouchers for holiday-apartments, restaurants and Amazon, for the three most popular ideas provided.

In order to activate the 'Crowd' for the innovation project, a carefully formulated task was necessary to avoid misinterpretations. It was important to consider leaving only one suitable aspect of a problem to be solved by the 'Crowd', instead of getting caught up in a whole problem complex. In addition, the right measure had to be found between very *specific* and very *generic* questioning (Gassmann, 2010).

The Crowdsourcing Task:

Imagine you are the operator of a public swimming pool. Which attractions would you fit your pool with to inspire your guests?

The above crowdsourcing task is deliberately generic and not constrained to a specific target group. This is for the purpose of investigating a great variety of interests and possible market positions for the re-designed public pool. The crowd-sourcing task was deliberately kept simple by capturing only one aspect (how to achieve enthusiasm through new attractions) of a much greater problem, which encompasses, for example, financing, production, staffing, sustainability, and much more.

Based on the type of crowdsourcing task, a suitable crowdsourcing platform and community were found with the 'unserAller platform' from the crowdsourcing software company 'innosabi'. The unserAller platform was set up, allowing participants in the first phase of the competition to publish ideas as well as comment on ideas of others and take a final vote on ideas in the second phase.

Last but not least, a PR and media strategy was prepared for the purpose of getting as much of the 'Crowd' activated as possible. However, since the project was a bottom-up initiative there was typically a small budget for public relations. Therefore, the focus of communication measures had been on social media channels. Notwithstanding this, the local newspaper managed to feature the topic twice during the project.

3.3 Outcomes and Evaluation of the InnoWellen Case Study

At the implementation phase after 5-weeks there had been 1074 visitors on the platform, 31 of which were active contributors, either rating, commenting or posting an idea on the InnoWellen project site of the unserAller platform. In total

74 % of the contributors submitted 76 ideas and 58 % rated ideas. However, surprisingly, only two contributors commented on ideas.

Subsequently, a catalogue of the Crowd's contributions during the implementation phase was created, labelled and categorised. Innovativeness, feasibility and affinity were considered, with the aim to present the catalogue of contributions to the Mayor, who promised to hand it over to the management of the public swimming pool.

Most of the contributions of the participants were of an innovative character. This fact shows that stakeholders have precious, innovative potential that can be acquired with crowdsourcing.

However, the meta-aim of the InnoWellen project was to investigate in what way active participation among stakeholders can be triggered and supported with idea competitions in the leisure industry.

The InnoWellen case study, with 31 participants and 76 submitted ideas, is an empirical example of how the public Crowd can participate in the development of touristic infrastructure through idea competitions. It has to be taken into account, however, that ultimately, InnoWellen was a bottom-up initiative with limited commitment of the local council, and limited financial resources and communication channels. Finally, the power of decision-making could not be decentralized, and a promise of implementation of ideas could not be given.

Part of the InnoWellen concept consisted in using crowdsourcing to make the possibilities of participation more efficient. Transaction costs for participation could be reduced through the use of an online platform. It was noticeable, however, that the obligatory registration, and the time it took to find your way on the platform website, can still pose substantial transaction costs. This could eventually prohibit participation. The registration process does on the other hand, prevent the publication of unqualified contributions.

Although 76 ideas had been submitted to the InnoWellen case study, the expected collaborative idea generation via comment function on the platform, did not occur within the setting of the study. One possible explanation is that the InnoWellen crowdsourcing-task was designed to be more competitive than collaborative.

It lies in the nature of crowdsourcing that whoever is interested in the topic is involved via self-selection. Different to traditional methods, there are no pre-selected specific target groups. In this way, new stakeholders can be found and a great variety of interests can be captured. The fact that the majority of the contributions within the InnoWellen idea competition could hardly be clustered, underline this effect.

This opening however, goes along with a loss of control for existing authorities and initiators. This loss of control can be regulated, but not completely avoided, through a precisely formulated crowdsourcing-task and structure and clearly defining the power of decision transferred to the public. This case study reflects the classical hurdles that are repeatedly mentioned in destination management literature in the context of participation initiatives. Traditional authorities, in this case the local council, could feel challenged through crowdsourcing initiatives, and block a true decentralization of deciding power.

In the case of InnoWellen and crowdsourcing in general, an undefined Crowd *per se* is asked to participate and not just those who are directly affected by a problem. Those directly affected, in this case the inhabitants of the town, tend to want to participate in the whole task and not just in the aspect presented in the crowdsourcing task. This crowdsourcing method is restricted in that different stakeholders cannot participate in different ways. As amongst stakeholders there are some more or less strongly affected, it could be useful to grant different stakeholders varying grades of participation.

3.4 *Résumé of Web-Based Idea Competitions as a Tool for Activating and Supporting Stakeholder Participation in the Leisure Industry*

According to what showed to be the strengths and weaknesses of web-based idea competitions in the InnoWellen project, it can be said that this form of crowd-sourcing is useful, thought it is not by any means a universal participation tool. And, as like with any other participation tool, its implementation has to be evaluated against the respective situation and aim. As Bramwell, has stated, no participation tool on its own can meet the requirements of planning for a tourism project (Bramwell & Sharman, 1999). Therefore, it is advisable for the management of tourist destinations to use crowdsourcing in connection with a balanced variety of tools.

Bearing in mind the cooperative character of tourist destinations, it can be ascertained that innovation has practically always, even before the 'invention' of Open Innovation, been an 'open' process, or should be open, in the opinion of researchers and experts. The InnoWellen case study showed nevertheless, that the Open Innovation idea is not always compatible with what is practiced in local committees. And for them the use of social media mechanisms is still often unknown territory, which is difficult to assess.

4 Implications for the Optimisation of Web-Based Idea Competitions in the Leisure Industry and Further Research Needs

Concerning the rise of digitalisation, particularly in social processes, it seems clear that internet-based participation tools, such as the InnoWellen idea competition, are more and more likely to be used also in the context of the leisure industry, to complement traditional participation tools.

However, the InnoWellen case study showed that a web-based idea competition used as a participation tool has advantages as well as constraints. Therefore, a major optimisation can be seen in combining crowdsourcing and web-based idea competitions with other traditional participation tools, *e.g.*, citizen working groups, workshops, surveys, and so on. Also, further research is needed to investigate which participation tool-mix is adequate in order to balance out strength and weaknesses of crowdsourcing as a participation tool for managing stakeholders in the leisure industry. Subsequently, crowdsourcing software and platforms should then support the application of a method mix and provide interfaces for other participation tools. In this way crowdsourcing software can be tailored to the needs of managing the leisure industry stakeholders.

Moreover, new participative innovation tools like web-based idea competitions can change little, if respective authorities and decision makers are not willing to share their power. For this reason key individuals need to find out more about how this resistance can be overcome when implementing crowdsourcing in the leisure industry.

5 Key Conclusions and Learning Outcomes of the InnoWellen Case Study

- Active participation among expected but also new stakeholders can be triggered and supported with a web-based idea competition in the context of a leisure industry infrastructure innovation.
- Crowdsourcing and, in particular, web-based idea competitions used as a participation tool in the leisure industry cannot meet all requirements of managing stakeholders and therefore should be implemented within a participation tool-mix.
- It is important not to oversee the relevance of clear communication and the need of resources in order to reach the potential participants.
- Be prepared for resistance from existing authorities and decision makers as this is part of the game, while introducing participative innovation tools.
- If one aims for a joint innovation as a result, a web-based idea competition can be a good starting point. However, the ideas must be taken further to be implemented as sustainable solutions.

References

Bramwell, B., & Sharman, A. (1999). Collaboration in local tourism policymaking. *Annals of Tourism, 26*(2), 392–415.

Chesbrough, H. W. (2011). *Open services. Rethinking your business to grow and compete in a new era.* San Francisco: Jossey-Bass.

Frey, K., Lüthje, C., & Haag, S. (2011). Whom should firms attract to open innovation platforms? The role of knowledge diversity and motivation. *Long Range Planning, 44*(5–6), 397–420.

Gassmann, O. (2010). *Crowdsourcing. Innovationsmanagement mit Schwarmintelligenz.* München: Hanser.

Lindegaard, S. (2010). *The open innovation revolution. Essentials, roadblocks, and leadership skills.* Hoboken, NJ: Wiley.

Pikkemaat, B., Peters, M., Weiermair, K., & Auer, M. (2006). *Innovationen im Tourismus.* Berlin: Enrich Schmidt.

Tschurtschenthaler, P., Peters, M., & Pikkemaat, B. (2005). *Erfolg durch Innovation. Perspektiven für den Tourismus- und Dienstleistungssektor. Festschrift für Klaus Weiermaier zum 65. Geburtstag.* Wiesbaden: Deutscher Universitäts-Verlag.

Potential of Open Innovation Models in the Tourism Sector: Three Case Studies

Marut Doctor, Marc Schnyder, and Sandra Bürcher

Learning Objectives

- Acquire in-depth knowledge on the implementation of the open innovation approach with crowdsourcing as a tool in the tourism industry.
- Moderate and analyse the virtual innovation processes in tourism.
- Scrutinize of the strengths and weaknesses of open innovation models used in the tourism sector.
- Identify success factors and obstacles that arise when implementing open innovation projects in Swiss tourism enterprises.

1 Introduction

1.1 Problem Statement

Small and medium size businesses (SMEs) operating with the tourism sector rarely have their own research and development department or an explicit research and development budget. Thus open innovation processes are worth considering as an opportunity to generate, develop and implement new product and service ideas with relatively low financial and human costs (Laursen & Salter, 2006).

M. Doctor (✉) • M. Schnyder
Institute of Tourism, University of Applied Sciences Western Switzerland, Delémont, Switzerland
e-mail: marut.doctor@hevs.ch; marc.schnyder@hevs.ch

S. Bürcher
Institute of Geography, University of Berne, Bern, Switzerland
e-mail: sandra.buercher@giub.unibe.ch

© Springer-Verlag Berlin Heidelberg 2016   333
R. Egger et al. (eds.), *Open Tourism*, Tourism on the Verge,
DOI 10.1007/978-3-642-54089-9_25

Three examples of open innovation processes which are accompanied from beginning to end, will be explored within three tourism case studies. Their aim of is to provide a deeper knowledge of the implementation of the open innovation approach within the tourism industry.

1.2 Selection of the Participating Firms in the Tourism Sector

Due to the economic slowdown in Europe tourism firms were reluctant to participate in the proposed innovation projects. In particular, the financial crisis affected tourism SME's, as they typically have limited budgets in comparison to other economic sectors. Among approximately 100 Swiss tourism firms (mostly SME's and a few large companies) asked to participate, only the following three companies agreed to participate in the study i.e. Graubünden Tourism in Chur (abbreviated as GR Tourism), SBB Real estate (abbreviated as SBB) in Berne and the Canton Valais Rescue Organization (abbreviated as OCVS) in Sierre.

1.3 Use of Crowdsourcing

Until recently innovation generally only took place in special divisions inside firms. The collection of new ideas was therefore closed innovation, as not open to the public (Chesbrough, 2003). As this was the case for the three firms which took part in our study, we initiated an open innovation process using crowdsourcing as an open innovation tool (Hammon, 2013). The open innovation approach was applied based on work by Reichwald and Piller (2006), Reichwald, Meyer, Engelmann, and Walcher (2007), Thomke (2003) and Von Hippel (2005).

As a first step each participating firm had to formulate a specific question related to a problem to be solved, using the open innovation platform http://www.atizo.com (a virtual brainstorming platform with thousands of creative thinkers). Then, over 6–8 weeks, the website http://www.atizo.com served as a platform to find an answer for this question. During this period, the company could collect ideas from innovators, i.e. from a broad public. For potential innovators, enrolling on the platform www.atizo.com was free. All innovators could see and comment on the ideas of the other innovators. The authors of the best ideas received a prize. The evaluation of incoming ideas was carried out independently by each participating company.

The participating tourism firms had to pay the discounted price of 4800 CHF (instead of 8800 CHF for firms in other fields than tourism) for the use of the platform www.atizo.com. So Atizo granted in this case a special discount of 4000 CHF for the participating tourism firms. The payment of a prize for the best ideas was recommended by Atizo, but was optional for the participating companies.

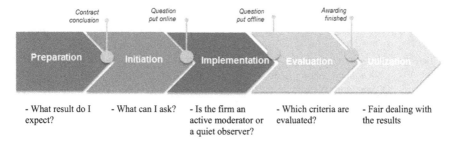

Fig. 1 The five steps of the Crowdsourcing process with an example of key questions. *Source*: Final CTI-Report (2010)

Finally, the offered premiums of the three participating tourism firms were between 1000 and 3000 CHF.

Our case study crowdsourcing projects follow a 5-step process (Fig. 1).

2 Open Innovation Approach

2.1 Data Collection

To create knowledge around the problem related questions input onto the atizo platform, on the basis of descriptive analysis, three qualitative interviews with experts of the participating firms were performed. Thus experts were directly confronted with the crowdsourcing approach and the general action question. The methodology of the qualitative empirical procedure was taken from Lamnek (2005) for the interview concepts and from Bähring et al. (2008) for the guidelines for the qualitative questions to the experts. For most of the experts, the concept of the research problem was clear after a short introduction and an explanatory phase. In the next interview step, questions on the specific topic could follow directly. In order to ensure complete data collection, as well as a code of practice, interviews were recorded and transcribed.

Three expert interviews were performed at three stages per firm: before the implementation of the crowdsourcing projects (just before step 3 of the crowdsourcing process, Fig. 1), in the middle (middle of step 3) and after the evaluation (after phase 4). So, in all, nine interviews took place. Generally, the questions asked during the interviews were mainly open. In the case of ambiguous answers, more specific questions followed, in order to have the most exact information possible.

Table 1 gives an overview for GR Tourism, SBB and OCVS on the problem questions, the duration of the crowdsourcing projects (from the publication of the question on the web until its removal), the number of ideas and the prizes for the best innovators.

In addition to the general question each enterprise formulated a more detailed problem characterization for innovators, in order to describe better their

Table 1 Participating firms and action questions in the frame of the Crowdsourcing projects

Enterprise	Problem question	Begin	End	Number of ideas	Prize in CHF
GR tourism	What do you expect from a Community-Website for the holiday region Graubünden (contents, functions, design and marketing)?	06/05/09	05/07/09	365	2000
SBB	How can the SBB increase the attractiveness of big railway stations?	12/04/09	28/05/09	490	3000
OCVS	How to raise awareness of the winter sports fans concerning accidents risks on and beside ski runs?	01/09/09	18/10/09	341	1000

Table 2 Detailed action question for the SBB and one of the best replies (ideas)

Detailed questions	Example of ideas
The SBB seeks especially ideas to improve the following aspects: • How can the user friendliness of the big railway stations be improved with specific services? • How can orientation possibilities, room availability and the free moving space be better promoted? • How can travelers better find their way through the information flow? • How can waiting and stay in the big railway stations become more interesting? • How can disturbance sources be avoided in the future? This search for ideas doesn't deal with: • Changing the timetable • Changing the supply of SBB trains	**Separate passenger flows**: Separation of the passenger flows for each direction marking the walking direction and a fast lane for travelers in a hurry **Orientation**: Several lights show the way to the train and specify the localization of a dynamic product service (for example where precisely on the platform is the restaurant car) **Use of a mobile phone**: as a personal output system for navigation in railway stations for rail and station supplies **Well-being**: Creation of rooms for relaxing and entertainment **Green oasis**: Creation of a green oasis (in- and outside with plants, it may be combined with water and limits of entry)

expectations. As an illustration for this, Table 2 shows the detailed question for the SBB and one of the best replies (ideas) to this question.

2.2 Results

In the frame of this study, a comparative results analysis of the third expert interview answers of the three enterprises was performed. This interview deals among other things with the comparison of the project expectations of the tourism actors with the project reality. Thanks to these main results it was possible to identify on the one hand the strengths and the weaknesses of the use of crowdsourcing and on the other hand the use of open innovation processes in tourism firms. The interview consists mainly of the following four parts:

- General questions
- Statistical data on the project
- Questions on resources and technology acceptance
- Questions at the end of the project

2.2.1   General Questions

Support, Customer Service All the interviewed firms are, on the whole, happy with the technical support by Atizo for the chosen open innovation platform www. atizo.com. This was however not the case for the content and methodological support. Generally, tourism firms are significantly smaller than firms in other economic sectors (for example, in the financial, pharmaceutical and energy industries). This means that tourism firms have also comparatively smaller budgets at their disposal. They can therefore not afford to spend more money for an external crowdsourcing consultant or an external innovation process moderator, in contrast to banks, insurances and energy providers.

Number of Ideas All the interviewed firms were very positively surprised by the great number of ideas on the open innovation platform as well as the great number of innovators. The number of generated ideas was greater than expected for all of the three enterprises (341 for the OCVS, 365 for GR Tourism and 490 for the SBB).

Quality of Ideas The interviewed firms were rather disappointed with the quality of the ideas (this concerns especially OCVS and GR Tourism). They noticed that many innovators read only the general question (in Table 1), without considering the detailed question (in Table 2). OCVS and GR Tourism also found that ideas remained generally on a superficial level. In addition, OCVS regrets that the innovators hardly consider the remarks of the other innovators, i.e. hardly react to the other ideas and comments. A reason could be that the innovators think that a comment such as "your idea is unrealistic" is too subjective and are convinced that their idea is good. Some of them also just put quickly ideas on the platform in order to increase their chance to be awarded.

2.2.2   Project Statistical Data

Prize and Award Criteria On one hand, SBB awarded cash prizes for 12 ideas and distributed a free daily train passes for 40 other ideas. The prize value (see Table 1) was therefore divided into 12. On the other hand, GR Tourism and the OCVS distributed awards for four ideas only. The criteria for giving awards to the best ideas varied among the three firms. The main criteria were: does the idea answer the question, the innovation magnitude, the potential pace of

Table 3 Enterprises' evaluations of the ideas regarding the feasibility (the sum doesn't have to be 100 %)

Firm	Idea already known (%)	Idea already implemented (also by competitors) (%)	Unrealistic idea (%)	New idea, but can currently not be implemented (%)	New and implemented idea	Number of ideas awarded
SBB	60	20	15	30	5 %	12 (+40 daily pass)
GR Tourism	65	0	10	20	<5 %	4
OCVS	80	0	15	5	(No data)	4

implementation of an idea, the success potential, the originality, the low costs, the feasibility, if it concerns a broad public and if the innovator considers the other innovators' remarks. The companies' evaluations of the ideas were independent of the evaluations of the innovator community and were generally not influenced by them.

Evaluation of the Ideas in Figures Table 3 shows the satisfaction of the three firms related to the selected criteria. For example, the table shows that 40 % of the ideas were already known by the SBB, and even 80 % by the OCVS. In contrast to the two others, the SBB carried out already 20 % of the proposed ideas shortly after the end of the project. The rate of new ideas was on the whole 35 % for the SBB, i.e. the highest rate of new ideas from the three firms (30 % new, but currently not realizable and 5 % new but realizable ideas). This rate was significantly lower for the OCVS, with only 5 %. As already mentioned, the SBB had the highest prize level.

2.2.3 Questions on the Resources and the Technology Acceptance of Crowdsourcing

Crowdsourcing Project Benefit All the firms share the same opinion with regard to crowdsourcing projects being especially useful to collect ideas and to carry out brainstorming. The SBB finds that a proportion of 5 % of very good and realizable new ideas is sufficient. The evaluation of all these ideas involves a lot of work for the firms. It would therefore be desirable to have suitable filters in order to save time for the evaluation of the ideas (see learning outcomes section).

Sense of Crowdsourcing Project Implementation As it is often the case for tourism businesses, none of the project partners have a research and development (R&D) division. This project therefore makes sense for product development. On the one hand, the SBB is ready to use this method several times a year. On the other hand, OCVS finds that this kind of idea collection is only useful when problems concern young people (they were generally over represented among the innovators).

Platform Technology Every firm considered the platform as user friendly. Problems which occurred in this project (but dependent on the enterprise):

- Rather improvement propositions than new ideas
- Some innovators considered only their own needs
- Not representative of the population (youth over represented)
- Use of the platform for marketing goals

2.2.4 Questions at the End of the Project

Development of the Quality of the Ideas It is difficult to show a clear trend regarding the particular time in the project when the quality of ideas improved or deteriorated.

Innovator Community Structure This aspect was satisfactory only for the SBB and GR Tourism. The OCVS would have liked a better representation of the different age classes and a better geographical distribution. In addition, the French-speaking participants were clearly underrepresented, although this firm is located in the French-speaking part of Switzerland, unlike the two others. Ideally, the innovator community should represent a broad public.

General Appreciation Within the Enterprise Assessments differed from firm to firm. As already seen in the evaluation of the ideas in Table 3, the SBB was the most satisfied, followed by GR Tourism. Both enterprises would carry out again crowdsourcing projects, but with the prerequisite that the problem question is well formulated. On the other hand, the OCVS would not perform a crowdsourcing project in the domain of prevention. However, the OCVS doesn't exclude such a project in other innovative domains.

This experience was a pleasant surprise for the SBB and they had expected that only 5 % of the ideas would be operational. It has however to be considered that the SBB is neither a pure tourism nor a small or medium size company.

On one hand, the GR Tourism project leader communicated details of the crowdsourcing project in a limited way within the company. On the other hand, GR Tourism was the only enterprise which received positive reactions from three or four other firms regarding project participation.

The OCVS was rather disappointed with the knowledge gained through the implementation of crowdsourcing. This firm considered that many innovators put ideas on the platform mainly to win a prize without necessarily considering what already exists.

3 Key Conclusions and Learning Outcomes for the Tourism Industry

On the whole, there are big differences in the general appreciation of the different crowdsourcing projects. For the SBB, the expectations were fulfilled and they would be ready to carry out a new crowdsourcing project. The appreciation of GR Tourism is quite similar, although they were disappointed with the quality of the ideas. On the other hand, the OCVS would not carry out a similar project concerning prevention. However, the OCVS would think about doing a similar project in another sector using an open innovation platform. The OCVS was especially disappointed by the fact that many innovators put their idea on the platform only to win a prize.

However there are also similarities among the three participating firms. Firstly, each of them is happy with the quantity of ideas but less with their quality. The ideas collected on the platform are therefore rather useful especially for brainstorming aims. Secondly, the opinion of all the participating enterprises is that the key to success lies in a very precise question formulation, i.e. at the starting phase of the crowdsourcing process.

The learning outcomes of the open innovation use for the tourism industry can be summarized in five points:

- To improve the quality of the ideas, the key to success for all the firms is a very well formulated question. It is therefore worthwhile spending time formulating the problem question.
- One should technically force the innovators to read the detailed question, before they put an idea on the platform and technically filter the ideas which remain superficial and which don't reply to the question. This would substantially simplify the evaluation work.
- As the size and the available resources of enterprises in tourism are generally small, client support from the platform operator should increase, without obliging these enterprises to pay an additional contribution for an external consultant.
- Experts in the field of the problem question should support the platform, in order to stimulate reactions between the innovators. If the experts find an innovator's idea bad, that innovator should withdraw his idea. This would reduce the enterprise evaluation time.
- One should also be careful that the innovator sample represents well the population concerned by the question.

References

Bähring, K., Hauff, S., Sossdorf, M., & Thommes, K. (2008). Methodische Grundlagen und Besonderheiten der qualitativen Befragung von Experten in Unternehmen: Ein Leitfaden. *Die Unternehmung – Swiss Journal of Business Research and Practice, 62*(1), 89–111.

Chesbrough, H. W. (2003). *Open innovation – The new imperative for creating and profiting from technology*. Boston: Harvard Business School Publishing Corporation.

Final CTI-Report (authors not named). (2010). *Open Innovation: KTI-Projekt* (Nr. 9150.1 PFES-ES), Abschlussbericht. Bern, Sierre, St. Gallen, Zürich.

Hammon, L. (2013). *Crowdsourcing – Eine Analyse der Antriebskräfte innerhalb der Crowd*. Hamburg: Verlag Dr. Kovac.

Lamnek, S. (2005). *Qualitative Sozialforschung*. Basel: Lehrbuch, Beltz Verlag.

Laursen, K., & Salter, A. (2006). Open for innovation: The role of openness in explaining innovation performance among U.K. manufacturing firms. *Strategic Management Journal, 27*, 131–150.

Reichwald, R., Meyer, A., Engelmann, M., & Walcher, D. (2007). *Der Kunde als Innovationspartner, Konsumenten integrieren, Flop-Raten reduzieren, Angebote verbessern*. Wiesbaden: Gabler Verlag.

Reichwald, R., & Piller, F. (2006). *Interaktive Wertschöpfung – Open Innovation, Individualisierung und neue Formen der Arbeitsteilung*. Wiesbaden: Gabler Verlag.

Thomke, S. (2003). *Experimentation matters: unlocking new potentials of new technologies for innovation*. Boston: Harvard Business School Press.

Von Hippel, E. (2005). *Democratizing innovation*. Cambridge: MIT Press.

Crowdsourcing as a Tool to Help Generate Innovation in Small and Medium-Sized Hotels

Jennifer Menzel

Learning Objectives

- Analyse the concept of crowdsourcing in its ability to support small hotel businesses.
- Identify potential crowdsourcing tools to be applied to small hotel businesses.
- Understand how crowdsourcing can help hotel businesses in the innovation process.

1 Introduction

The ability to innovate is crucial for survival in highly competitive markets such as the hotel industry. For small and medium sized enterprises (SMEs) in particular, this ability is a key success factor in the continuous offer of innovative services, with the objective of prevailing over leading hotel concerns. However, due to their size, SMEs are confronted with certain weaknesses that inhibit the creation of innovation, such as restraints of time, finances, know-how and qualified personnel (Pikkemaat & Holzapfel, 2007).

Recent technological developments and the shift towards active consumerism have brought about the concept of 'crowdsourcing' (Howe, 2008). Crowdsourcing describes the act of a company outsourcing certain operational or creative tasks, usually performed by the company itself, to an undefined crowd outside the company over the internet, thus providing them with external resources in order to produce innovative goods and services collectively (Howe, 2007).

J. Menzel, M.A. (✉)
Managament Center Innsbruck (MCI), Innsbruck, Australia
e-mail: jennifer.menzel@web.de

© Springer-Verlag Berlin Heidelberg 2016   343
R. Egger et al. (eds.), *Open Tourism*, Tourism on the Verge,
DOI 10.1007/978-3-642-54089-9_26

Many successful implementations by well-known companies such as Threadless (www.threadless.com), Starbucks (www.mystarbucksidea.com), and Tchibo (www.tchibo-ideas.de) demonstrate the potential of crowdsourcing to contribute value through cost advantages, problem solving, innovation and consequently profit maximization.

Considering the supposed benefits of crowdsourcing and the competitive situation in the hotel market, it is observable that the adaptation of the concept as a tool for innovation has not been explored in context with the hotel industry.

In order to understand to what extent crowdsourcing can contribute to the creation of innovation in small and medium sized hotels a case study has been conducted, whereby the implementation of three different crowdsourcing tools is applied in a small hotel. The object of the case study is Hotel Harzer Hof; a small hotel in Scharzfeld, Germany close to the touristic Harz Mountain area. The applied instruments, chosen based on a detailed analysis of crowdsourcing initiatives in other industries, comprise an external suggestion system, an idea contest, as well as the inclusion of a virtual community for the creation of innovation. In the following section the case object and its characteristics will be introduced before the concept of crowdsourcing and its potential to contribute to the creation of innovation are analysed in Sect. 3. In Sect. 4 the initiatives conducted within the case study and its findings will be demonstrated. In the last two sections key challenges for the future, key conclusion of the case study and learning outcomes will be presented.

2 Main Product Offering and Value Added

Hotel Harzer Hof is situated in Scharzfeld, a village with 1900 inhabitants in the rural district Osterode am Harz, close to the Harz Mountains. As a hotel with 39 beds, 6 employees and less than two million in total revenue, it counts as a small enterprise (Henschel, 2005). The third-generation family business has 17 guest rooms, three apartments, a wedding suite, an à-la-carte-restaurant, a bowling alley, a theatre, a beer garden and a banquet hall for up to 120 people.

The hotel has an average occupancy rate of 18.2 % and an average length of stay of 1.8 days, which is significantly below the region's average of the region (34.4 %; 4 days, though including rehabilitation centres, apartments and pensions) (Landesbetrieb für Statistik und Landesbetrieb für Statistik und Kommunikationstechnologie Niedersachsen, 2010).

The hotel is managed by a married couple. Routine daily tasks dominate the schedule for managing the hotel. The extent to which strategic planning can be undertaken is restricted by a lack of time and knowledge of procedures. Management is structured to a certain extent (such as weekly staff allocation and ware purchase), but decisions (e.g. marketing and arrangements) predominantly depend on intuitive feelings or prior experiences with customers.

Organization is flexible and communication with staff is carried out on a personal level within the daily collaboration. The hotel team consists of six employees (four full-time, two apprentices) plus a temporary staff of seven people. The high number of temporary staff accounts for a lack of trained, qualified personnel.

With regards to the fiscal situation, the Harzer Hof shows a typical financial weakness in that the enterprise boasts little proprietary capital. This leads to restricted credit-status, meaning that profits need to be reinvested, before being realized.

Innovation activities focus mainly on customer retention and acquisition, and typically comprise small improvements to existing offers, such as a new menu, different booking packages, or the arrangement of various events. Ideas are implemented intuitively following the principle of trial and error.

The managing hoteliers are aware that constant innovation is necessary to maintain a competitive advantage. However, they feel hindered by a lack of time and financial resources. Furthermore, they claim that the necessary engagement of temporary staff in the generation and implementation of new ideas is distinctly lacking. The crowdsourcing initiative is designed to deliver additional, external resources to expand the base for idea generation, which should result in greater potential for promising ideas, both for improvements and problem solving.

3 Business Model and Need for Innovation

3.1 Contribution of Crowdsourcing to Innovation

Considering the hotel industry, one can find clear strengths and weaknesses concerning the capability of innovation. Strengths, like little formalized organizational structure, short communication lines, high flexibility, strong customer focus and quick adaptability all foster innovation, whereas a lack of know-how, capital, time and in particular staff, hinder it (Minder, 2001; Pikkemaat & Holzapfel, 2007; Wagner & Kreuter, 1998).

Crowdsourcing offers new possibilities for enterprises to economically harness the collective wisdom and creative talent of geographically dispersed people for the creation and optimization of business products and processes, and consequent maximization of their value (Brabham, 2008; Lakhani & Jeppesen, 2007; Piller, 2006; Prahalad & Ramaswamy, 2004). This value creation consists of innovative problem solving with the goal of either differentiation, or cost reduction. The interaction of the participating crowd is based on their own initiative and by choice (Reichwald & Piller, 2006).

Knowing this raises the possibility that hotel businesses, too, could use crowdsourcing to gain additional external resources and knowledge in order to expand existing innovative capacities and harness these with modest financial and time input. Furthermore, the broad base of potential customers (due to the high travel intensity), the customer-oriented and flexible organisation, and the direct interaction with the customer hypothesise the applicability of crowdsourcing tools in small hotel businesses (Menzel, 2011).

3.2 A Derivation of Crowdsourcing Tools

Crowdsourcing had already been taking place as a form of economic production long before the term was coined. Today, crowdsourcing initiatives are conducted in different countries, industries and areas of business, with the help of various tools, implemented within a range of time frames, and with varying intensities. This underlines that crowdsourcing is a complex and versatile concept. Menzel (2011) analysed best-practise examples to structure existing implementations of the concept in order to derive applicable instruments (see Fig. 1).

As seen in Fig. 1, crowdsourcing can either be the foundation of a business or it can be integrated into an existing business model. The former typically denotes platforms that use crowdsourcing for the creation of services/goods, intermediaries of crowdsourcing initiatives or businesses that offer crowdsourcing platforms for use by others. The latter consists of individual crowdsourcing initiatives conducted alongside the existing business model. These initiatives can be creative or operative in nature, and can be implemented temporarily or continuously. The degree of integration of the user also differs; the user can be asked to evaluate or filter already existing services/goods, create content, or share knowledge. The actual implementation can be conducted through open idea contests, the integration of an idea platform in the homepage of the enterprise or the usage of virtual communities. Depending on the objective, available resources and operating conditions, the implementation can be conducted autonomously or with the help of crowdsourcing platforms or other intermediaries (e.g. agencies; service providers).

Recently, models have evolved which enable initiatives to be conducted with restricted resources, which has greatly increased the potential of crowdsourcing as a tool for small and medium sized hotel businesses. Among these are e.g. building a community via social networks; software-as-a-service provider for integrating a corporate idea platform; and crowdsourcing platforms for the posting of idea contests (Menzel, 2011).

4 Open Innovation Approach

4.1 Conduction of Crowdsourcing Initiative

Overall this case study shall clarify whether the use of crowdsourcing can be beneficial for the innovation capacity of small hotels with little resources. In greater detail, it shall be examined, which crowdsourcing tools can be integrated in SME-hotels and to what extent these impact upon the typical weaknesses of the generation of innovation. A set of three crowdsourcing tools is implemented over a period of 6 weeks for the case hotel. With regards to the identified lack of resources of SMEs, the following instruments have been chosen based on their low requirements in terms of time and financial resources:

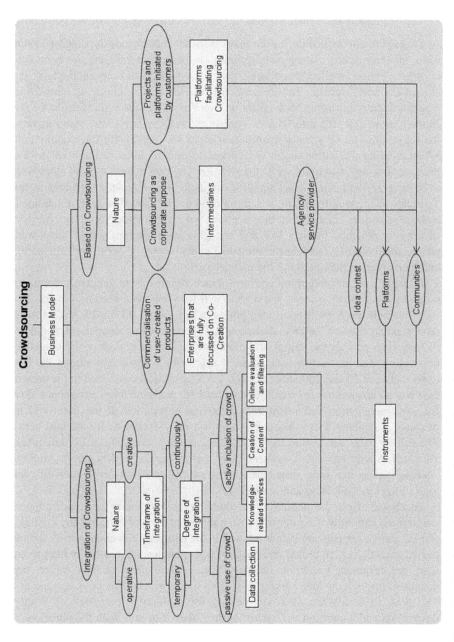

Fig. 1 Conception of the integration of crowdsourcing. *Source*: Menzel (2010, p. 57)

- The integration of an external suggestion system on the hotel website using *UserVoice*.
- An open idea contest with the help of the crowdsourcing platform *Bonspin*.
- The evaluation of a generated idea through the corporate *Facebook* community.

UserVoice allows visitors of the hotel website to continuously suggest or rate ideas for innovation on their own initiative. In order to participate, users need to click on a button labelled "Feedback", which is visible at all times on the left hand side of the hotel website. The integration is carried out by adding an html-Code, generated after registering for an offer of UserVoice, into the hotel website's code. In the present case, the free "Basic"-version offered by UserVoice, with functions for suggesting, rating and commenting on ideas was chosen for the examination. When clicking the button, users were asked to provide ideas to improve service, product offerings, and usability of the website. The best three out of 30 ideas were to be rewarded with a free hotel night for two including a three-course-dinner menu. To create awareness, the forum was introduced in the "News"-section of the hotel-website as well as via a post on the Facebook page of the Hotel. With the objective of keeping potential barriers low and engaging participation, simple ideas were posted anonymously, rated, and commented in the beginning of the implementation and then again in the middle of the enquiry period.

Bonspin is a crowdsourcing platform which enables users to submit, comment on and further develop ideas, but also to call for ideas on a specific project. The incentive scheme is built upon idea points, which cost 1.00 € excl. VAT for the requester and is worth 0.60 € to participants. When setting up an open call for ideas, the requester sets up the length of the contest (1, 2, 4 or 8 weeks), the objective, description, and amount of idea points that are being distributed among the best ideas (between 20 and 1000 idea points). The idea contest conducted in the present case was an anonymous open call running for 1 week asking for extraordinary ideas for guest acquisition and retention. A detailed description of the hotel and its premises was given. Fifty idea points were set up as incentive for the best ideas. The call for ideas was sent to the Bonspin community consisting of 1799 members via email. A reminder email was sent 2 days before the end of the contest. After the contest, idea points were distributed based on the hoteliers' evaluation of each idea's novelty, usefulness and feasibility.

Facebook offers the possibility of building up and interacting with an own corporate community. In order to do so, a representative of the company creates a free-of-charge fan page. People interested in the company can connect with the fan page and read, like, comment on and share posts, photos and videos. In the present case, the corporate Facebook fan page was used to have an idea, which was generated through the idea contest, evaluated by the hotels' Facebook community. The post, in which the idea was put up for evaluation, consisted of a short description and a question as to whether they liked it or not. With the objective of engaging additional interaction, the community was also asked to further elaborate on the idea. Fans were able to interact by clicking the "Like"-button or commenting on the post.

To find out to what extent these tools can support the innovation generation of SME hotel businesses, each instrument was evaluated based on the participation and performance of users, the financial input needed, and the time invested in implementation and supervision.

4.2 Findings

The integration of UserVoice promised product improvement through customer suggestions in idea generation and idea evaluation. Results show that during the enquiry period of 5 weeks no ideas had been generated or commented. This could be for several reasons. The crowdsourcing initiative was only accessible to homepage visitors, which greatly limited the potential reach. Hotels with a higher amount of website visitors have a greater reach and therefore might yield different results. Also, homepage visitors are more likely to be new guests, who supposedly do not know the product offering as well as recurring guests, and therefore cannot yet evaluate potential improvements. Furthermore, users might not have seen the "Feedback"-button or the English term "Feedback" might not have been understandable to the website users, who are mainly German speakers. However, the free of charge module, and the easy integration and use of the instrument allow hotels to experiment with this tool at low-risk and allows for an individual evaluation of the benefits.

The idea contest through the crowdsourcing platform Bonspin proved to be a fruitful opportunity to integrate users in the innovation process. Nine people contributed approximately 65 ideas in 1 week, of which nine have been classified as potential innovations for the Hotel Harzer Hof. Through growth in knowledge and personnel resources, the solution space has been expanded and at the same time the innovation capacity of the small business has been extended. The application took up little financial (60 €) and time resources (less than 5 h) and was technically easy to implement. Therefore, no risk was involved and the implementation was compatible with the day-to-day business.

The inclusion of the corporate Facebook-community in the process of idea acceptance brought about satisfactory results. The participation in the idea evaluation on the Facebook wall of Harzer Hof was above average compared to prior postings. For a valid estimation of market acceptance the participation was notably low. However, this tool represents a valuable opportunity to densify ideas through user suggestions and to get timely feedback on future innovation activities. Furthermore, the community supports the promotion of the newly published ideas by interacting with the Facebook fan page, as friends of fans are automatically informed about their activities. Due to the little input of resources (no cost, 2 h/per month) and the user-friendliness of the tool, a continuous application is operable.

In summary, the tools of the integrated idea platform, the open idea contest and idea evaluation through the community can be considered as possible implementations of a small and medium-sized hotel. All three tools are easy to integrate and use, requiring little time and finances. The yield and the effects on the weaknesses in the generation of innovation turn out to be different amongst the tools.

The integration of UserVoice was possible with few resources, but was not productive in expanding personal or knowledge resources, at least in the way it was implemented.

The open idea contest is well-suited to fully outsourcing the idea generation phase, as additional manpower and a gain in knowledge were achieved with little input of resources.

The third tool, using the Facebook community for idea acceptance, proved to be partially suited. It not only allows a first evaluation of newly generated ideas, but also enables a consolidation of ideas through additional propositions. However, it is not recommended to fully outsource the idea acceptance as the size and interaction of fans required for a reliable market acceptance is restricted.

5 Key Challenges for the Future

The concept of crowdsourcing is still evolving and together with fast technological development, it will be a challenge to monitor this dynamic phenomenon and harness its potential to its fullest. One can assume that more effective and efficient methods for the use of external resources will evolve, especially with respect to internet-based tools. This opens up new possibilities for small and medium-sized hotels to learn about new approaches and ideas for sustainable business development, stemming from external resources. However, ideas alone will not lead to innovation. It is the hotelier's responsibility to put the gained ideas into practice and turn them into economic value. As Confucius said: "The essence of knowledge is, once having it, to apply it".

6 Key Conclusions and Learning Outcomes for the Tourism Industry

- Crowdsourcing tools can be constructively used in the hotel industry.
- Possible crowdsourcing tools comprise idea contests, crowdsourcing platforms and virtual communities.
- The fruitfulness of crowdsourcing is directly associated with the tool chosen for its implementation.
- Crowdsourcing expands innovation capacity through external creative potential, knowledge and manpower.
- Crowdsourcing initiatives can be implemented in a time and cost-friendly manner, corresponding well with the limited available resources and high risk-aversion.

- The concept is still evolving and requires observation for future potential to be grasped.

References

Brabham, D. (2008). Crowdsourcing as a model for problem solving. *Convergence: The International Journal of Research into New Media Technologies, 14*(1), 75–90.

Henschel, K. (2005). *Hotelmanagement*. München [u.a.]: Oldenbourg.

Howe, J. (2007). http://crowdsourcing.typepad.com/. Last visited: March, 30, 2014.

Howe, J. (2008). *Crowdsourcing: How the power of the crowd is driving the future of business* (pp. 23–127). New York: Crown Business.

Lakhani, K. R., & Jeppesen, L. B. (2007). Getting unusual suspects to solve R&D puzzles. *Harvard Business Review, 85*(5), 30–32.

Landesbetrieb für Statistik und Kommunikationstechnologie Niedersachsen. (2010). Beherbergung im Reiseverkehr in Niedersachsen 2009. In G. Hurth, *AW: Aktuelle Statistik der Beherbergungsbetriebe*. E-Mail: Gabriele.Hurth@LSKN.Niedersachsen.de, 22.07.2010

Menzel, J. (2011). *Crowdsourcing: Neue Methode der Innovationsgenerierng in kleinen und mittleren Hotelbetrieben* (pp. 47–58). Saarbrücken: Verlag Dr. Müller.

Minder, S. (2001). *Wissensmanagement in KMU: Beitrag zur Ideengenerierung im Innovationsprozess* (pp. 79–84). St. Gallen: KMU Verlag HSG.

Pikkemaat, B., & Holzapfel, E. M. (2007). Innovationsverhalten touristischer Unternehmer: Triebkräfte und Hemmnisse. In R. Egger & T. Herdin (Eds.), *Tourismus:Herausforderung: Zukunft* (pp. 241–258). Wien: LIT.

Piller, F. T. (2006). *Mass Customization: Ein wettbewerbsstrategisches Konzept im Informationszeitalter* (p. 89). Wiesbaden: Gabler.

Prahalad, C. K., & Ramaswamy, V. (2004). *The future of competition: Co-creating unique value with customers* (p. 140). Boston: Harvard Business School Press.

Reichwald, R., & Piller, F. T. (2006). *Interaktive Wertschöpfung: Open Innovation, Individualisierung und neue Formen der Arbeitsteilung* (p. 44). Wiesbaden: Gabler.

Wagner, M., & Kreuter, A. (1998). Erfolgsfaktoren innovativer Unternehmen. *IO Management, 10*, 34–41.

Co-creation in Club Tourism

Katsutoshi Murakami

Learning Objectives

- To understand the shift in trends of customer demand and how tourist agencies are able to offer satisfactory customer experience by leveraging co-creation.
- To demonstrate ways of developing new products and increasing customer loyalty while saving cost at the same time by customer engagement.
- To present that there is an opportunity in tapping into senior citizens' willingness to be involved in society.

1 Introduction

Tourist agencies usually offer customers standardized products and services as other industries tend to do so in Japan. They have seen their own business was to arrange transportation, accommodation and sightseeing for customers at offices or online. These products were usually package tours offering a pre-fixed schedule including sightseeing spots, hotel reservations and transportation which may only differ slightly.

However, customer demands have changed from simply sightseeing to gaining new experiences such as interacting with local residents, learning new culture and taking part in local events. They also want flexibility of the choices of destination, schedule and prices to choose from, and are seeking friends to travel with to share their travel experience.

K. Murakami (✉)
Nomura Research Institute, Ltd., Tokyo, Japan
e-mail: k2-murakami@nri.co.jp

As a consequence, package tour sales have declined over the years and industry growth has stalled. Sales volumes of tourist agencies have slid by 19 % from 7.75 trillion yen in 2002 to 6.29 trillion yen in 2011. The number of Class 1 travel operators that is able to plan domestic and international package tours was 855 in 2002 but fell to 738 in 2011 (Japan Tourism Agency, 2013).

2 Co-creating with Customers in Club Tourism

Company-centric, conventional travel agencies are trying to survive by economy of scale. These companies used to consider the ability to procure huge volumes of airline tickets and hotel rooms that contributed to profitability as key factor of success. This has changed with the spread of internet where airlines and hotel chains can now sell directly to customers online. While many companies are struggling, one tourist agency is flourishing by innovation of product, service and business process. The key was focusing attention on senior citizens, their experience and co-creation.

Club Tourism is a subsidiary of a second largest tourist agency in Japan, KNT-Club Tourism Holdings Co., Ltd. and attracts about five million customers as members to their community dubbed "the club" (Takahashi, 2008). The main target customers are senior citizens. What is unique about this initiative is that the company offers new experiences in their tours through customer engagement. Not only is this central to their business but is also how they differentiate from their competitors. Through this engagement with community members, Club Tourism is able to better understand how senior citizens may think or behave, and use this information to improve product, service and business process.

What Club Tourism sells is the experience of travelling. Customers are buying the experience of precious interactions with local people they meet and the exposure to new culture or hobbies.

Club Tourism was established as a direct marketing division in 1986. They conducted direct marketing using call centers and sent direct mails to customers. Although direct marketing allowed the company to save cost and offer lower priced tours, it was difficult to differentiate their tours to customers not used to direct marketing, as tours were usually sold at outlet retail stores then. So the company launched theme-oriented tours in order to overcome this difficulty in attracting customers to purchase their tours. Some example activities were climbing famous Japanese mountains, painting, photography, dancing, and participating in local festivals.

3   Enhancing Value by Customer Engagement

3.1   Co-creating New Products and Services Through Club Activities

Uniqueness of Club Tourism tours are the tour guides who support the trip on site and play an important role by creating an opportunity for direct communication between customers and Club Tourism employees.

The guides help develop new tours by directly asking customers what kind of trip they wish for next, while travelling together, instead of conducting marketing surveys and analyzing customer needs that competitors usually carry out on a separate occasion.

Under this model, company-customer engagements take place through club activities. The guide is a friend whom they can easily speak to and a tour planner, but they are responsible for taking care of each club. Guides listen to customer opinions and preferences and then incorporate them into future plans.

Customers are involved in planning new events which may or may not be directly related to tours and may even start up a new club as a part of club activities.

Club member customers become close to guides as they are, in a way, friends who they have worked together as a group. This allows the community to voice their opinions more easily. Although Japanese consumers, notably senior citizens, hesitate to express their opinion as their own unlike Western consumers, this system enables them to speak freely and even complain as a group.

Club Tourism learned that direct interaction with customers is an effective way to develop popular new tours and has turned this insight into knowledge the organization can leverage on.

3.2   Travel Friends Circle

Club Tourism also found out through direct interactions with customers that senior citizens in particular are looking for other people to travel with.

Although the company had assumed customers already had people to travel with such as their family and friends, it turned out that many of the senior citizens did not because of the loss of their partners and the fact that there are nuclear families increasing in Japan.

As such, in 1991, Club Tourism experimentally formed a group called the "Circle of friends to travel with" as one of its clubs. In this circle, customers made new friends with common hobbies or interests though travelling together, and this experimentation was very successful. This success was evidence that customers will happily pay for the experience as travelling together with friends by joining the tour. There seemed to be value in doing something with your friends not the tour per se. This was contrary to commonly held views underlying ordinary tours offered by other tourist agencies.

Club Tourism has been increasingly creating new clubs since then and the total number of clubs amounts to approximately 200. They have become one of the main divisions driving both top and bottom line growth by a dramatic increase of customers through the introduction of clubs. Furthermore, they have drawn much attention from competitors given the present difficulty the industry faces. Several examples are presented that offers unique experiences to Club Tourism customers.

3.3   Examples of the Clubs

3.3.1   Club RaRa

The regular club of the "Circle of friends to travel with" is "Club RaRa." The object of the club is not simply travelling, but making friends through the tours. The main club members are senior citizens from their 50s to the 70s who are feeling alone, or housewives whose husbands are busy and whose children have grown up. They join because they could travel alone. Package tours and hotel rooms are usually available only from two persons. Travelling alone incurs extra charges. This shows how companies assume customers travel together with partners. However, there are in fact many customers who wish to travel alone, but are unable to under the present product offering.

Club RaRa tours are tailored for customers who could only participate alone. At first the participants hesitate to communicate with others, but eventually open up as most of the other participants are also joining by themselves and realize that they probably share the same feelings. Club RaRa provides opportunities to introduce themselves and plans dinners among participants who are mostly similar in age.

Many make friends through this club and increase their loyalty for Club Tourism and repeatedly participate in other tours. Thanks to Club RaRa, the company was able to reduce the cost of gaining new customers who never purchase tours as they have no one to travel with.

3.3.2   Mountain Climbing Club: Climbing 100 Famous Japanese Mountains

This club is for mountain climbers and hikers. Club Tourism learned that senior citizens who used to climb mountains alone when they were young, are looking for climbing partners, for safety and fun after they have become older. Based on this learning, Club Tourism has set up this club and provides opportunities to meet people who share their interests.

The mountain climbing tours involves climbing a series of 100 mountains. This tour consists of 100 independent tours. Although customers may choose to quit or skip some tours, most participants continue to climb to meet their friends whom they met in this club. Club Tourism celebrates the final trip by issuing an original certificate.

Club Tourism is now preparing another club to climb the 200 famous Japanese mountains targeting those who have completed climbing 100 mountains. This shows that community based human networking and events that take place in succession are successful at securing customers. Ordinary tours only generate one-time revenue, pushing travel agencies to promote higher priced tours in order to increase sales. On the other hand, these club tours will promise long-lasting revenue and Club Tourism does not necessarily have to promote expensive tours for the customers. The mountains are located both near and far away from Tokyo and some become a full-day or an overnight trip using trains or airlines if necessary. Such participants naturally purchase both lower and higher priced tours.

3.3.3   History Club

This club is for history lovers. Club Tourism's uniqueness is that it focuses attention on what takes place prior to and after the trip. Before and after the tour, club members gather and study in detail the history associated with the destination at Club Tourism classrooms.

An example is a tour which visits historical ruins and monuments related to famous samurai warriors around the sixteenth century. All participants study the details of a samurai lifestyle, and common ways to battle in those days before the tour. Afterwards, they share their findings and photos and discuss the topics that most people are interested in researching next. The following destination would be decided based on customer opinion and mutual agreement.

Club Tourism has a variety of club tour line-ups with a specific focus on interests and hobbies of customers and plans gatherings in advance and after the tours such as dancing, singing and painting events. After learning the topic, they put their knowledge in practice at the destination. For example, hula dance club members learn how to dance and practice before the tour and perform the dance at a dinner party several months afterwards. Dancing in Hawaii becomes a motivation to learn and a goal to achieve. After the tour, event participants share their experiences with other club members, and begin setting the next goal such as participating in a hula dance contest around the world.

Club Tourism intends to improve customer experience through setting up these events. These are usually free of charge. This positive cycle of new tour development changes the traditional methods of demand forecasting and reduces company risks associated with product development and promotion costs.

4 Co-creating Business Process with Customers

4.1 Customer Involvement in Business Process

Club Tourism not only co-creates values with customers by developing new tours, but also does so by the participation of customers in the business process. Many customers become Club Tourism employees who support their business at a low wage or even for free.

Club Tourism publishes a variety of member magazines every month and delegates the distribution of those magazines to Club Tourism customer who are also employees called "Eco Staff". They are very loyal to Club Tourism and happy to work at an inexpensive rate. The wage could range from approximately 4000 to 20,000 yen per month depending on the amount of deliveries made.

More than 10,000 Eco staff distributes magazines to many families in Japan. They visit each Club Tourism customer homes and deliver the magazines by hand. They deliver to homes located within their neighbourhood by bicycle or on foot at their own pace. Eco staff does not regard this as a difficult task and usually see it as a good exercise to improve their health.

Moreover, most of them are retired senior citizens and are motivated by meeting people through these delivery jobs. They are keen to participate in society and are willing to communicate with others. This is the reason why most staffs are satisfied with this role despite the small financial compensation.

4.2 Customer as Tour Guides

Another example is cooperation by a friendly "Fellow staff". They are amateur tour guides, around 40–65 years old, who are also Club Tourism's customers. The company recruits personnel who are not looking to make money for a living but is looking for a sense of purpose and fulfilment in life. They earn lower salaries than usual other Club Tourism professional tour guides.

For instance, half a day town walking tour that costs 10,000 yen per person requires lower operation cost so Club Tourism assigns fellow friendly staff to attend these less expensive tours.

They perform sufficiently in such tours as it does not require extensive professional knowledge and skill as a tour guide. Their job includes counting the number of participants and touring together with the group. The course is set in a particular region where the staffs are very familiar about, because they are local residents or used to work in that neighbourhood.

As mentioned earlier, Club Tourism provides classroom lessons before and after the tour. To offer this event for free, Club Tourism recruits instructors from customers who used to be school teachers.

This example shows that when the firm considers its own business from a customer perspective, what was previously considered as a boundary expands dramatically and the customers become involved in the business process voluntarily. By focusing on the kinds of value senior citizens hold, companies could effectively win customers and cut costs successively. Club Tourism was able to increase customer loyalty and improving business efficiency at the same time.

5 Key Challenges for the Future

5.1 New Interactive Platform Using IT

Club Tourism's next challenge is to establish an infrastructure of human networking via information technology. Club Tourism considers that the most important networking means is face to face human interactions, but also considers that IT could support and enhance networking experience of customers.

Club Tourism provides a variety of interaction modes which includes both customer-to-company and customer-to-customer interactions. Friendly staffs could be seen as human channels, as they communicate with customers not only face to face during tours and events, but also make calls to individual customers after the event. Club Tourism's outlets are called "Salons" with a more comfortable atmosphere than the usual travel agency outlets. As other channels, Club Tourism incorporates call centres, monthly newsletters, Eco staff, a Web site and own social networking services.

The main customers of Club Tourism are senior citizens and they are reluctant to use new technology. Despite the fact that the human channel is relatively expensive compared with the IT channels, deploying new IT solutions such as SNS, smart phone solutions, apps will not solve this situation. The company has to find and develop new platforms that offer customer interaction using new technology.

5.2 Strengthening of Partner Networks

Another challenge is expanding the networks with partners and managing the quality of partners. Travel agencies have conventionally had close relations with tour operators such as hotels and tourist facilities. Despite this, Club Tourism needs to make new relationships with unconventional partners related to tour themes and events. For example, in case of the hula dance club, hula dance instructors and dance event promoters are necessary in order to satisfy club member needs. These kinds of personnel were not necessary when Club Tourism only provided the Hawaii package tour, but this is now an essential part of club activities and experiences of customers.

Of course, the existing partner networks will be a valuable resource to tap into for the travel agencies intending to enhance customer experience. However, once the firm focuses on customer experiences, they need to expand their existing partner networks.

In addition, in order to sustain the value and branding of the total experience, the company has to improve service quality offered by partner companies. Club Tourism inspects quality and supervises partner companies such as hotels based on customer feedback. Such quality management system of partner companies has become more important. It is necessary to improve quality management of services as Club Tourism is unaware of the quality measurements which are applicable for unconventional partners.

6 Key Conclusions and Learning Outcomes for the Tourism Industry

Co-creation with the customer community was a key factor of success. This is continuously innovating Club Tourism business model, driving sales and lowering operating costs. Club Tourism transformed the notion of travel from where to visit to what to do there. As a viable business model, group tours with common interests and activities are able to leverage existing capabilities and business infrastructures. Customers increase their loyalty and engagement with the clubs through activities before and after the tours. The following points are the key takeaways from Club Tourism's case;

- Focusing on co-creation by customer experience

  At Club Tourism, there are about 200 specific themed-clubs. New events and tours are planned monthly based on co-created, customer requests. The next destination is agreed on by club members. Club Tourism assists and facilitates club member interaction, booking and ticketing. The role of Club Tourism is to support customers not only visit where they wish to go, but also in doing what they wish to do.
- Avoiding price competition

  Tours are reasonably priced, and the events are more or less free. Customers perceive the tour prices as cheaper, because they see the tour as a part of total experience that they are able to enjoy with other club members. Club Tourism does not necessarily need to make tours cheap, because the competitors cannot provide such total experiences as Club Tourism does.
- Involving customers into business process

  Customers are involved in the planning, execution of clubs and events, and even more in the business process. Particularly, "Eco staff" and "Fellow friendly staff" are semi-professional employees recruited from customers. This contribution reduces operation cost and also enriches company-customer interactions. It also allows the company to adopt a customer-centric product development.

Co-Creation with customers at Club Tourism is what gives them the competitive advantage.

- This business model introduces a completely different paradigm. This is necessary for companies still holding on to conventional ways of business in order to weather the difficulties facing the tourism industry.

References

Japan Tourism Agency. (2013). Ministry of land, infrastructure, transport and tourism. *White Paper on Tourism in Japan.*

Takahashi, H. (2008). Risou no ryokougyou, Kurabu Tsuurizumu no himitsu [Ideal tourism: Secret of club tourism]. *The Mainichi Newspapers.*

Gamification: Best Practices in Research and Tourism

Dorothée Stadler and Volker Bilgram

Learning Objectives

- Gaining insights into the concept of gamification.
- Learning from gamification best practices in open innovation.
- Understanding how gamification can change the tourism industry.
- Challenging the common definition of gamification.

1   Introduction

Recently, gamification has become a major buzzword in a variety of fields, fueled by successful applications such as Nike + FuelBand or Foursquare, which use game mechanics in their own ecosystem in order to engage users more deeply and create satisfying experiences for their users. Nike + FuelBand is a device that measures all kinds of activities. It presents each workout session's data and lets users compete with one another and reach workout goals. Foursquare, a popular social-networking app, allows its users to "check into" places they visit, awarding them with points for various actions in order to win certain activity related "badges" and gain virtual ownership over places. For instance, users may become the "mayor" of a restaurant or other points of interest when they are the most frequent visitors to the specific location. Gartner (2011) and Deterding, Dixon, Khaled, and Nacke (2011) describe gamification as the application of game elements in non-game contexts based on the following five game elements:

- Compelling narrative
- Clear rules and goals

D. Stadler (✉) • V. Bilgram
HYVE Innovation Research GmbH, Munich, Germany
e-mail: Dorothee.stadler@hyve.de; Volker.bilgram@hyve.de

© Springer-Verlag Berlin Heidelberg 2016   363
R. Egger et al. (eds.), *Open Tourism*, Tourism on the Verge,
DOI 10.1007/978-3-642-54089-9_28

- Reasonable and well-balanced challenges
- Quick and open feedback
- Presence of social interaction and relationships

Gamification has already found its way into a wide range of industries and is an increasingly popular strategy in many different disciplines within companies such as market research, ideation, R&D, or marketing. In particular, the trend towards open and distributed innovation systems has given rise to "gamified" mechanisms. In open innovation environments, research has revealed that a crucial driver of participation is intrinsic motives such as an enjoyable experience or interacting with like-minded peers (Füller, 2010). In order to foster compelling experiences and spur participation and activity rates of external actors in open innovation systems, gamification offers a variety of opportunities. In this chapter, we provide some insights into the concept of gamification in two specific contexts which have recently profited from open innovation principles: the market research industry and the tourism industry.

The market research industry pins its hopes on "gamified" elements which may spur consumer engagement and thus increase willingness to participate. Traditional market research methods are not necessarily considered an appealing way to interact with a company nowadays. In fact, companies are increasingly facing the problem of decreasing participation rates and a certain level of market research fatigue. Thus, "gamified" market research might offer a way out of this dilemma by activating and involving the crowd in a more democratic voting.

In the travel and tourism sector, "gamified" approaches have been argued to be a major trend in the coming years grabbing a sizable share of social media expenditure (Meloni & Gruener, 2012; WTM, 2011). Employing gamification, travel companies seek to encourage users to share experiences and personal photos to increase brand awareness and user loyalty.

In the following, real world examples taken from new market research and the tourism industry are introduced to give an idea of how the theoretical concepts are translated into these specific domains.

2 Gamification in New Market Research

A key task in open innovation processes is the selection of the best ideas and designs generated by the crowd (King & Lakhani, 2013). Recently, a novel innovation research method, which involves users in an enjoyable activity, has been applied: the "matching game" (Füller et al., 2010; Hacker & von Ahn, 2009). The matching game is a selection approach applied to identify consumers' preferences regarding various alternatives, and is a good example of research with embedded gamification elements.

In a matching game, two randomly selected participants play against each other. In each round they have to decide between two alternative designs or concepts.

Fig. 1 Example of a matching game—Smart project. *Source*: http://www.smart-design-contest.
com/matching-game

Their decision is not based on their individual preference, but on what each individual thinks the other player favours. Whenever both players select the same concept or design they get a "match" and earn reward points. With the help of such a consumer selection process the most promising design or concept can be identified using game-based mechanisms. In two real world examples, Haller, Hutter, Füller, and Möslein (2012) found that matching games could be a promising approach to select the best designs and increase participants' intention of future participation in crowd votings. Figure 1 shows an example on how the matching game was presented to the participants in such a study.

3 Gamification Applied in the Tourism Industry

3.1 My Indonesian Moments

The tourism industry is one of the leading industries in terms of opening up to consumers and co-creating value with them. This is especially visible on review sites such as Tripadvisor and Holidaycheck. These platforms have empowered consumers to evaluate and share their experiences and thus have brought about a radical shift of power towards consumers. However, more recently, open innovation approaches in tourism have been extended to the ideation of new products and services.

The JARING IDE initiative is an open innovation contest platform (Boudreau & Lakhani, 2013; Terwiesch & Xu, 2008) built to co-create innovative ideas for Indonesia in the field of tourism and development.

Since 2012, a strong and active community has been built to support the Indonesian tourism industry by conducting several contests over the following years. The second contest was about sharing individual experiences in the country Indonesia. Community members were called to submit images of their favourite moments or a story of their individual experience in Indonesia. The best submission was rewarded with being part of the ITB, a leading travel trade show in Berlin. At this very popular trade fair the winning pictures and stories were embedded in the official presentation of Indonesia. What is more, the favourite images and stories could win trips to Indonesia. The main goal of this contest was to create awareness of Indonesia as a tourism destination with a high level of user engagement and stickiness.

On this platform, shown in Fig. 2, the five core principals of gamification based on Gartner (2011) were applied to create awareness of the tourism industry in Indonesia.

The first characteristic of gamification is a **compelling narrative.** By creating an interesting and appealing story line in which tasks are embedded, users are more likely to be willing to participate in a study than if they were simply asked to complete those tasks in a traditional fashion. Here, the narrative is a time-boxed contest with prizes to win. In this contest the participants were taken into the world

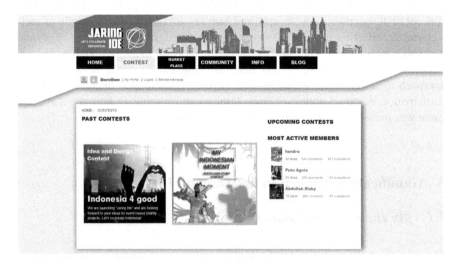

Fig. 2 JARING IDE platform. *Source*: www.jaring-ide.com

of Indonesia. By supporting the platform with appealing pictures and a prominent name "My Indonesian Moment", users can immerse themselves in the task and create their own stories around Indonesia.

When applying game-mechanics, **clear rules and goals** need to be communicated. They are the core elements of any game. Before starting a game the rules need to be known by all players. The JARING IDE platform transparently communicates the rules of participation in a separate section. All important information on the submission and evaluation process, jury decision and prizes were announced to the members before the start of the contest during the sign-up process.

Furthermore "gamified" tasks need **reasonable and well-balanced challenges** that are demanding but do not overstrain and thus demotivate participants. For "My Indonesian Moment", the main challenge was to select appropriate images that were fascinating and described the participant's relation to Indonesia in a unique way. The contest rules clearly defined the challenge by listing the evaluation criteria which would be applied by the jury. Thus, participants were aware that creativity, uniqueness, professionalism and content would be most relevant within the evaluation.

The fourth characteristic of gamification is **providing quick and open feedback**. In contests, this is typically implemented by commenting and voting functionalities on the contest's website as well as by awarding points or prizes to particularly active members. Both community members and the contest jury can evaluate and discuss submissions to intensify feedback during the contest.

The fifth and last principle of gamification is the **presence of social interaction and relationships** between players. Games are seldom played alone and typically require some sort of social interaction. In the case of "My Indonesian Moment", the possibility to comment on other players' ideas provides this social interaction. In addition, social media channels like Facebook were used to spread information about the contest via word-of-mouth and to link participants' contributions to their own networks outside the contest network.

This contest was the second project within an ongoing digital initiative for the Indonesian tourism industry to co-create and innovate with creative consumers and customers for a future Indonesia. Almost 18,000 visitors and 1992 submitted ideas with over 9313 ratings by 860 active members show the success of this initiative.

3.2 Discover Hong Kong City Walks

Another example highlighting how gamification can be applied to services in the tourism industry is the "Discover Hong Kong City Walks" mobile application. The app essentially "gamifies" city tours (see Fig. 3) and can be seen as an alternative to regular city guides. Initiated by the Hong Kong tourism board, this mobile app offers tourists the most interesting walking tours in the city structured around different topics such as "cosmopolitan flavours", "adventure in architecture", "travel through time" or "experience living culture". Each city tour consists of

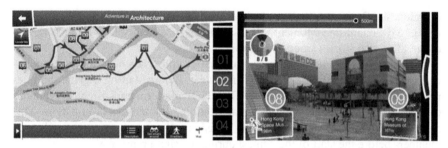

Fig. 3 Discover Hong Kong City Walks (Mobile application). *Source*: https://play.google.com/
store/apps/details?id=com.cherrypicks.HKTB&hl=en

several interesting sightseeing points. Whenever tourists complete 50 % or above of
a walk, participants receive a "stamp" of a tour. These stamps can be shared on
Facebook. The app regularly provides feedback by reminding users to explore
sights, communicating the progress of the tour or warning if the user strays off
track. This mobile application has been available since 2011 on Android and iOS
devices. According to Google play, between 50,000 and 100,000 users have
downloaded the Android app so far (No data on iOS downloads available).

4   Towards a Broader Definition of Gamification

The definition of gamification presented above is grounded in game design theory
and is generally rather strict about what characterizes a game or "gamified"
application. However, not all "gamified" approaches necessarily comprise all
gamification principles. Hence, we suggest rethinking the concept of gamification.
Huotari and Hamari (2012) offer an alternative definition of gamification in the
context of service marketing, allowing for a more versatile use of the term. The
main idea behind Huotari and Hamari's definition is that it is not the design patterns
that make a game appealing to users but the "joyful experience". Furthermore, what
is a game or gameful experience is subjective by nature. Huotari and Hamari's
therefore characterize gamification as a "process of enhancing a service with
affordances for gameful experiences in order to support users' overall value creation", where the term "affordances" captures the fact that the creator of a game
cannot control how users perceive it.

This definition is particularly interesting in the context of tourism, as tourism is
in its core a service industry. Services often not only share the feature that the
moment of value creation coincides with the moment of value provision by a
company, but need to be co-created, i.e. the user contributes to the value delivered.
According to Vargo and Lusch (2004), the customer is always a co-creator of value.
In the services marketing literature, those separate parts of value creation are often
called value-in-exchange, i.e. the value provided by a firm, and value-in-use, i.e. the
value extracted by the customer, respectively (Grönroos & Voima, 2013). Service

providers can create affordances for joyful experiences giving users the possibility to increase their side of value production. For example, gamification may facilitate consumers' part in value co-creation by making the act of extracting value from a company's offering more playful and encouraging Hence, "gamified" approaches may turn the act of co-creating value itself more appealing. Offering users a "gamified" and interactive tour guide which enables them to share their experiences with their friends, for instance, creates additional value-in-use. Users may not only experience the travel destination using the app, but actually derive pleasure from having shared experiences with their friends. Additionally, individuals using the "gamified" app may curate the content to reflect personal values and express themselves. The created value not only emanates from self-expression and sharing, but especially from the feedback and emotions users receive. Therefore, gamification may enrich the service and turn a city tour into a live "slideshow" with friends and family back home. Gamification is a tool to allow for higher user engagement and thus increased value of the service to the user, which in turn would translate into business goals such as the differentiation of products and services.

5 Key Challenges for the Future

Businesses in all kinds of industries have discovered gamification as a key strategy to improve processes. Examples from a wide variety of contexts reveal multiple purposes gamification may serve. Being a relatively novel phenomenon, there is no universally accepted concept of "gamification" yet. While a majority of researchers describe constituting principles and conditions (ex-ante) conducive to gamification, describing gamification from an ex-post perspective might add a valuable dimension. Therefore, in line with Huotari and Hamari, we suggest extending research to the ends instead of the means only. Subjective outcomes of game-based mechanisms such as task enjoyment or a state of flow may serve as indicators for the presence of gamification. Thus, this purpose-centered addition to the concept emphasizes the affordance for gameful experiences taking subjectivity into account. If done right, gamification can help users co-create and enhance the value of services methods and therefore provide benefits to various steps in the value creation chain.

6 Key Conclusions and Learning Outcomes for the Tourism Industry

- Apply gamification with a clear goal in mind and never for the sake of itself.
- Think outside the box of scores and "afford" gameful experiences.
- Use gamification in all stages of your value creation chain: from idea-generation to actual provisioning of a service or product.

References

Boudreau, K. J., & Lakhani, K. R. (2013). Using the crowd as an innovation partner. *Harvard Business Review, 91*, 61–69.

Deterding, S., Dixon, D., Khaled, R., & Nacke, L. (2011). From games design elements to gamefulness: defining "gamification". In: *Proceedings of the 15th International Academic Mindtrek Conference*, Tampere, Finland.

Füller, J. (2010). Virtual co-creation of new products and its impact on consumers' product and brand relationships. In L. Toombs (Ed.), *Academy of management annual meeting: Dare to care*. Montréal: Academy of Management.

Füller, J., Möslein, K. M., Hutter, K., & Haller, J. B. A. (2010). Evaluation games – How to make the crowd your jury. In *Service Science – Neue Perspektiven für die Informatik. Lecture Notes in Informatics (LNI) – Proceedings, Series of the Gesellschaft für Informatik* (Vol. P-175) Long Version: CD only, Leipzig.

Gartner. (2011). *Gartner says by 2015, more than 50 percent of organizations that manage innovation processes will gamify those processes*, 2011. Available from: Gartner Newsroom. Retrieved April 4, 2014, from http://www.gartner.com/it/page.jsp?id=1629214

Google Play. (2014). Retrieved April 4, 2014, from https://play.google.com/store/apps/details?id=com.cherrypicks.HKTB&hl=de

Grönroos, C., & Voima, P. (2013). Critical service logic: Making sense of value creation and co-creation. *Journal of the Academy of Marketing Science, 41*(2), 133–150.

Hacker, S., & von Ahn, L. (2009). Matchin: Eliciting user preferences with an online game. In *Proceedings of the SIGCHI Conference on Human Factors in Computing Systems* (pp. 1207–1216). Boston, MA: ACM.

Haller, J., Hutter, K., Füller, J., & Möslein, K. (2012). Play or vote: Matching games as new approach for design evaluation in innovation. In M. M. Cruz-Cunha (Eds.), *Handbook of research on serious games as educational, business and research tools* (Vol. 1, pp. 520–538).

Huotari, K., & Hamari, J. (2012). Defining gamification – A service marketing perspective. In *Proceedings of the 16th International Academic MindTrek Conference*, Tampere, Finland, October 3–5, 2012.

King, A., & Lakhani, K. R. (2013). Using open innovation to identify the best ideas. *MIT Sloan Management Review, 55*(1), 41–48.

Meloni, W., & Gruener, W. (2012). Gamification 2012, market update, consumer and enterprise market trends. *Gaming Business Review*, M2 Research.

My Indonesian Moment. (2012). Retrieved April 4, 2014, from https://www.jaring-ide.com/contests.php

Smart Design Contest. (2010). Retrieved April 4, 2014, from http://www.smart-design-contest.com/matching-game

Terwiesch, C., & Xu, Y. (2008). Innovation contests, open innovation, and multiagent problem solving. *Management Science, 54*(9), 1529–1543.

Vargo, S. L., & Lusch, R. F. (2004). Evolving to a new dominant logic for marketing. *Journal of Marketing, 68*, 1–17.

WTM. (2011). Technology: Gamification of travel. In *WTM Global Trends Report 2011*. Retrieved April 4, 2014, from http://www.wtmlondon.com/files/onsite_global_trends_v3_lo.pdf

Open Service Prototyping

Christiane Rau, Julia Jonas, and Fiona Schweitzer

Learning Objectives

- Demonstrate how open service prototyping is applied in tourism.
- Identify the challenges of co-creating service prototypes.
- Explore how customers can be integrated in developing innovative services.
- Explain the issues related to the use of different types of prototypes.

1   Introduction

Prototyping originally derived from technical disciplines (Kochan, 1997). It has a long standing tradition as a method to increase new product development efficiency by enabling iterative trail-and-error approaches. Especially with the trend towards open innovation, prototyping has been identified as a method to enable the early integration of relevant stakeholders in the innovation process (Doll, 2008; Schrage, 1999). Prototyping, broadly defined as the visualization of an idea (Reichwald, Möslein, Kölling, & Neyer, 2008), is used to support all stages of the innovation process from idea generation (see e.g. Lim, Stolterman, & Tenenberg, 2008) to final testing (see e.g. Burger, Kim, & Meiren, 2009). As such, prototyping supports the design of customer-centric, innovative product and service offerings right from the very beginning of and throughout the innovation process (Blomkvist & Holmlid, 2011).

C. Rau (✉) • F. Schweitzer
University of Applied Sciences Upper Austria, Wels, Austria
e-mail: christiane.rau@fh-wels.at; fiona.schweitzer@fh-wels.at

J. Jonas
University of Erlangen-Nuremberg, Nuremberg, Germany
e-mail: julia.jonas@wiso.uni-erlangen.de

© Springer-Verlag Berlin Heidelberg 2016
R. Egger et al. (eds.), *Open Tourism*, Tourism on the Verge,
DOI 10.1007/978-3-642-54089-9_29

While being used mainly in new product development, prototyping provides several benefits when it comes to new service development, e.g. decrease of project risk and failure (Drews, 2009) or a higher quality of services (Holmlid & Evenson, 2007). Nevertheless, prototyping for services is different from prototyping products due to the characteristics that distinguish services from products, i.e. intangibility, heterogeneity, inseparability, perishability (Parasuraman, Zeithaml, & Berry, 1985). Several challenges arise from these unique characteristics of services. Hence, prototyping as a method is being transferred to open service development taking into account the special requirements of services. In this chapter, we provide a classification of available tools to prototype services.

Following the service-dominant logic, customers are regarded as co-creators of value in the service delivery process (Vargo & Lusch, 2004). From this perspective, it is only a short step to see that customers can be part of the value co-creation already in the innovation process of a service. As Bessant and Maher (2009) stress, the co-creation of innovation with consumers can be a source for sustainable competitive advantage.

We propose open service prototyping as a method to enable the collaborative design of service innovations together with customers. In this chapter, we will in particular address two questions: How can prototyping help to make intangible services tangible to enable customers to provide feedback and to co-design services towards competitive, innovative service offerings? Which prototyping tools can be used to support the open service design process?

To answer these questions, we outline three different types of prototyping tools and provide three case studies to illustrate their use in the tourism industry.

2 Methods for Open Service Prototyping

To support open service innovation service prototypes have to enable the development of a shared mental model among service developers and potential customers. Due to the intangibility of services, this is difficult. For Vermeulen and van der Aa (2005) services' intangibility is the major challenge new service development. To overcome this challenge service prototypes need to support service designers as well as customers as potential co-designed to build a shared mental model of the service idea. Referring to service prototyping as a form of visual representation, Möller (2007) recognized that communication with stakeholders improved, as abstract discussion about a concept is replaced by communication about the concrete prototype. Prototypes can be considered boundary objects, which means that they have different meanings for different social groups, but the general context—the essential message—can be commonly understood (Star & Griesemer, 1989). Thereby, mutual understanding as the basis for interactive co-designing is enabled. As such, prototyping is a tool to align different mental models between service designers and customers and, hence, foster cooperative design (Neyer, Doll, & Moeslein, 2008). Depending on the need for feedback, prototypes can focus on elements of the service, i.e. the service environment, or the interaction between service providers and customers, or simulate both simultaneously. Furthermore prototypes can stimulate customers to engage in an active dialogue. Thus, to provide feedback should be as easy as possible.

In general, we distinguish three types of prototypes to enable open service innovation: (1) real world prototypes, (2) IT-supported prototypes, and (3) virtual reality prototypes.

2.1 Real World Prototypes

It is argued that services are intangible. Real world prototypes provide a material-ized, a tangible representation of a service. As such, they support a dialogue with potential customers. Real world prototypes exist in the form of abstract models (such as e.g. LEGO® or paper prototypes) or concrete models (such as e.g. role-plays). Neyer et al. (2008) find that real world prototypes installed in public help to stimulate potential customers to provide feedback on service ideas. The aim of the prototype is not to provide a realistic visualization but to enhance communication among customers and service designers. Communication can unfold around a real object or a situation experienced on the spot (e.g. if a role-play approach is chosen).

The following case of napcabs illustrates how various real world prototypes supported the development of sleeping cabins for travellers at international airports. napcabs is an entrepreneurial spin-off, founded by students of Munich's Technical University (TU Munich). The company offers cabins, requiring only 4 m^2, as private spaces for travellers to relax at international airports. Being installed in high-security transit zones in airport terminals, they provide travellers with a place to rest and recover. The spin-off is supported by sponsors such as the Munich Airport or OSRAM.

In the development of their service idea, the entrepreneurs relied on diverse forms of prototyping tools to refine their idea. Naturally, the team started with visualizing roughly broad ideas through sketches. With the evolving concept they built downsized paper models of the sleeping cabins, LEGO® prototypes and real-dimension models.

In the development phase the team used LEGO® to interactively design their service concept. To understand requirements and possibilities when offering a service in the highly restricted high-security transit zones in an airport terminal, they built and simulated the service process. The napcabs team used LEGO® to optimize the cabins' placement inside the airport environment. Trying out several options deepened the understanding of requirements and possibilities. The CEO of napcabs stressed in particular the prototypes' importance for integrating potential customers in the design process: The customers' feedback quality has significantly improved by the prototyping tool in use. The prototype supported the formation of a shared understanding between the entrepreneurial team and its potential customers, a prerequisite for a valid feedback process. Especially, when an innovative service is proposed, customers might have difficulties to imagine the future service and thus provide valid feedback. Napcaps' CEO states:

> [...] Sleeping cabins. This word alone calls up very different associations in different people. Some people imagine these things from Japan, these very tiny things, others imagine medical cabins, used for irradiation... it was immensely important to be able to show customers and others stakeholders how this could look like...the way we imagined it to look like.

At napcabs' prototyping tools have been extensively used to try different scenarios and design concepts. Especially the importance of letting-go prototypes to create something new has been stressed. A lot of prototypes had to be destroyed to build up new versions. It is proposed that working with a prototype enables a team to force themselves to build a new prototype from scratch and to find a consensus when required. The process of destroying a previous idea together might psychologically enable the team to finish a certain version of the idea and to start over with a new version of the concept jointly. While the heart of the idea—to offer travellers a quiet, cosy place to relax—stayed the same, the way to realize it changed and evolved over time.

The environment, in which a service is executed, influences whether the customer perceives the service to be positive or negative on a subconscious level. To plan the facility merely theoretically without trying out its effects on the people inside is likely to fail. The necessity to put oneself in the customer's shoes, when designing facilities has been stressed in the case of napcabs. Thus finally, the nabcap's entrepreneur team recognized that they had to go inside the cabs to really experience whether it feels crowded there or whether enough space is available to sojourn comfortably. So they built up models of several facility prototypes in original size. Due to extensive facility prototyping, at the end, they iterated towards a situation in which the customer feels comfortable, even if the space is extremely limited. Having built several different prototypes, LEGO® prototypes, but also real size facility prototypes, the CEO concluded:

> Two days ago, I have been in the final version of the cabin and I am really proud. You are not afraid, it does not feel narrow; it feels totally cosy and protected. You know...you want your island, you want to feel protected. There have been various steps from the idea to drawing to different prototypes. Finally, we had 3D prototypes to see how it can be design really stylish and ...you see...step by step it came into being...

After winning several competitions with their business concept, the official launch of the cabs has been on the 21th of July, 2008 at the Munich Airport (see Fig. 1).

Fig. 1 Napcabs at the
Munich Airport

2.2   IT-Supported Prototyping

While the previously presented approached relies solely on tangible real world
prototypes, the approach of IT-supported prototyping is combining real world
prototypes with IT. Specific aspects of a service, such as particular objects in-use
(e.g. an information terminal) as well as entire service concepts can be prototyped.
A prominent example of the later type of prototype can be seen in the so-called
ServLab, developed by the Fraunhofer IAO in Stuttgart. Basically, the ServLab
integrates a three-dimensional projection of the "servicescape" and a role-play
approach (Ganz, 2006; Myritz, 2009; Reichwald et al., 2008). The space in front
of the projection space is used as stage for professional actors who simulate service
processes. The stage is surrounded by an area where the audience is able to watch
the service process. The people in the audience are equipped with a ted system with
which they can express their opinion during the simulation. Afterwards a dialogue
is initiated by a moderator who guides the process from an operator's panel (see
e.g. Myritz, 2009; Segelström & Holmlid, 2009). As Meiren and Burger mentioned:
"The service is presented in the ServLab in the same format as it is intended to be
delivered afterwards. This allows a discussion of new concepts with customers,
employees and management without requiring abstract process models or complex
storyboards." (Meiren & Burger, 2008: 7). The following case examines the
development of an innovative check-in concept by Accor S.A. relying on
IT-supported prototyping.

Accor S.A. is a French hotel group representing diverse brands, such as All
Seasons, Ibis, Mercure, Novotel, and Pullmann, operating in more than 91 countries.
To develop an innovative check-in concept, the following case from Accor examines prototyping in the hotellery sector by making use of the ServLab format. First,
the initial idea for an automated check-in counter was tested with real world
prototypes at in five different pilot hotels of the Pullman brand. Here, the check-
in counter of the hotel lobby has been removed, automated counters have been
installed, front-line staff has been trained and guests of the Pullman hotel have been

confronted with the automated counters. While this approach allowed receiving feedback immediately, the downside of this approach is that customers might negatively experience such a "beta version" of a service. As it is known from service research, already single negative service experiences heavily influence customers' perception of a brand. "I always thought, it is like an open-heart operation", an Accor Manager reflects. Thus, his interest on prototyping services inside the ServLab grew. At ServLab, the service environment as well as the interactions can be simulated with specialists and guests before being installed in test hotels. If necessary, the concept can be stopped in an early phase without creating extensive sunk costs or destroying customers' loyalty. The major advantage is that customers do not directly connect a prototype to the brand. Given this, also extremely innovative service concepts can be simulated, learning from mistakes and iterative improvements are enabled, without endangering the service brand. Moreover, initial flaws can be removed before going live with customers.

For the Ibis brand, the idea of the automated check-in counter was revisited. The idea was to offer two different check-in alternatives, a quick check-in and a comfort check-in. Parameters like manpower should stay the same and the appealing of an economy brand should be maintained. To address the challenge, the use of a machine for self-service was simulated as well as a check-in done by receptionists using a mobile device. It has been probed to completely remove the check-in counter of the hotel lobby. The aim was to evaluate whether the customer is already prepared to cope with the innovative concept. Inside the ServLab, the spatial conditions were projected onto the walls and actors simulated the service process (see Fig. 2). In the audience, potential guests were asked to express their opinions with remotes while the service is simulated and taped. The feedback, given more in detail at the end, will focus on the before seen demonstration. Opinions can be underpinned by the video-taped sequences. The prototype, the simulation, is used as a communication platform. Due to the visualization, it could be recognized quickly, that the customer loses orientation inside the lobby and reacts with insecurity and discomfort to the spatial situation.

Fig. 2 Simulation in the ServLab

What could be learned in different iterations in the ServLab was the foundation to simulate the service with front-line, operations, and HR staff as well as brand's Regional Directors. Thereby it was figured out than a different arrangement of check-in machines in the lobby is needed and the limitations of the comfort check-in concept were understood better. If a large number of guests for Comfort Check-in would be expected, the concept reaches its limits soon. After the simulation the comfort check-in concept has been rejected. The manager stated:

> That means we figured out that one idea did not work out and how another idea could work out...which is quite good.

Even if the refined service concept was finally not implemented due to budget constraints, the prototyping approach was successful. The possibility to simulate wild ideas that could not been tried in real-world settings with sophisticated customers, was appreciated by the involved managers.

2.3 Virtual Reality Prototypes

Virtual realities are computer-based environments. Virtual worlds are inhabited by its users who interact via avatars or digital representations of themselves. Depended on the virtual word, users can be able to move, chat, and interact. Hence, virtual realities provide the possibility to simulate a service settings as well as service processes with its inherent interactions. The service can be introduced and avatar-based feedback can be input for iterative circles of refinement (Kohler, Matzler, & Füller, 2008). Virtual realities can also provide the possibilities to actively integrate users in the development process. For instance, they can create objects used in the service process and share them with others (Kohler, Fueller, Matzler, & Stieger, 2011).

Second Life (SL) is the most known virtual world. The world is created by its residents and provides room and tools for business, education, non-profits to establish residences (www.lindenlab.com). SL is not goal-directed, the gaming experience does not have a certain target and no mission is provided (Bonsu & Darmody, 2008). Avatars mainly are motivated to hang around in SL by the provided experience of the virtual environment, the possibility to contribute creatively and the possibility for social interaction (Jung and Kirchgeorg, 2007). Second Life delivers a fast and cheap means to prototype services and gain fast and cheap feedback from international users (Schüller, Doll, & Szugat, 2008).

The hotel chain Starwood introduced a virtual aloft hotel in second life to test-market the hotel's concept, its design and to tap users for ideas (Jana, 2006). Starwood Hotels operates, manages, and franchises brands such as Le Méridien, Sheraton, and St. Regis. It is one of the leading international hotel chains with around 1000 associates in nearly 100 countries (Starwood, 2012). aloft is a self-service hotel in the portfolio, advertising with the slogan "Style at a Steel".

Starwood's aloft hotels have integrated avatars in their service development by asking them to provide feedback. The interviewee of avatay explained:

> You can image an avatar which walks through the rooms. You can click on this avatar and your camera is following him. Thereby you can see how he is moving, which objects he clicks on, means what he touches and ...there it gets a little more complicated, you can detect in which area he is located. Thereby you can see, if he is drawn to special locations and how long the avatars stay there. Of course you can immediately conduct interviews, means you can start talking to them using the chat function provide commentary field in which they can post their opinions or distinct feedback.

In addition, a blog has been installed to discuss issues concerning hotel's design. In general, chats, blogs or commenting functions can be used to relate to the users. Moreover, especially useful for facilities design projects, avatars can be tracked. It can be observed where avatars stand still, how long they do so, or what they observe most interested. In the case of Accor, based on the feedback generated in SL, several changes to the overall design of aloft have been made. Schiller (2007) stated that the feedback has been included on the one hand in the virtual world, but more importantly, also in the real aloft hotels.

2.4   Discussion

Service prototyping on one hand and the integration of co-creating customers or further stakeholders on the other hand are proven to be highly beneficial for the quality, the speed-to-market, and the success of a new service offering. All presented approaches for service prototyping are valuable ways to develop, try and test services together with team members, customers or an unknown crowd.

Real world prototypes are easily implementable without too high costs and bring the advantage of true interactivity and ease of use. The playful way to represent service processes is easy to understand for everybody. This way it is possible to include stakeholders without professional knowledge or stakeholders without a "common language" from various disciplines at once. Real life prototypes are implementable throughout the steps of the innovation process, but they only allow the integration of either invited or locally approachable participants. It is possible and advisable to co-create service concepts in e.g. LEGO® prototypes together with customers or suppliers in workshops, where information can be kept confidential. Still this prototyping approach requires a priori definition of participants, invitations, scheduling, and presence of the prototyping team.

Another way of real life prototypes presented, is the acting out of beta offerings in the real service environment. When having access to the real service scape, high fidelity prototypes can be implemented and services in a final development stage can be tested as beta versions under real conditions with real people. Especially for the start-up in our case, it was highly profitable for the development team to go where the service delivery should happen in the end. Still, image and brand issues with existing customers have to be foreseen for pilot tests that, in their nature, include the possibility of failure and mistakes.

IT-supported prototyping can increase the perceived tangibility of service prototypes and force a detailed observation of the service process. High quality feedback can be achieved and even facets of a service offering can be adjusted. Still, the IT-supported concept as presented at ServLab is a workshop-based approach that demands a selection and invitation of participants.

The virtual prototyping approach could overcome this barrier of "presence" to integrate also distant customers and other stakeholders in the service innovation process. In a virtual reality such as Second Life, either invited or even interested unknown people from the crowd out there can experience a rather nature-like service environment whenever they want from their home computer without travelling. Of course, the realistic presentation of a service scape and concept demands high effort and resources for scenery composition and programming from the service provider's side and an affinity for virtual worlds from the user's side. Next to owning an account, the ability to work with computers in general and to use a tool like Second Life and its functions of moving, chatting, etc. which are crucial for collaboration, cannot be presumed from potential co-creators. In its early stage, Second Life gave great expectations for the implementation in service prototyping, especially due to the very interactive and naturalistic atmosphere. Though, the hype and users have gone and its implementation for open service prototyping has become doubted.

3   Key Conclusions and Learning Outcomes for the Tourism Industry

- Prototyping proves to be highly beneficial for enabling open service innovation in the tourism industry.
- Prototypes support customers to articulate their latent needs and thus provide vital input for new service development.
- Prototyping service innovation—and in particular radical service innovation— can be useful to identify barriers to customer acceptance early in development without threating the service brand.
- Prototyping is not limited to real world simulations any more. Recent advances in IT opened up new possibility to enhance service development. The given cases show the potential benefits IT-enabled prototypes as well as virtual prototypes can provide for companies in the tourism industries that strive to integrating their customers.

Acknowledgements   The cases have been developed based on extensive interview data. We are grateful to Camilla Walcher (napcabs), Thomas Burger (Fraunhofer IAO), Thomas Kohler (University of Innsbruck) and Cisco Agostinos (Accor Group). Thank you for sharing your insights and challenges with us.

References

Bessant, J., & Maher, L. (2009). Developing radical service innovations in healthcare—The role of design methods. *International Journal of Innovation Management, 13*(4), 555–568.

Blomkvist, J., & Holmlid, S. (2011). Existing conceptualisation of prototyping and prototypes. In *Nordic Design Research Conference* (pp. 53–65). Helsinki, Finland: School of Art and Design.

Bonsu, S. K., & Darmody, A. (2008). Co-creating second life: Market consumer cooperation in contemporary economy. *Journal of Macromarketing, 28*(4), 355–366.

Burger, T., Kim, K., & Meiren, T. (2009). Visualizing and testing service concepts. In R. Alt (Ed.), *First International Symposium on Services Science, ISSS 2009. Proceedings*, March 23–25, 2009, Leipzig, Germany. Berlin: Logos Verlag.

Doll, B. (2008). Mit Prototypen ein Gründerteam entwickeln: Ergebnisse einer empirischen Untersuchung. *Wirtschaftspsychologie aktuell, 4*, 35–38.

Drews, C. (2009). Unleashing the full potential of design thinking as a business method. *Design Management Review, 20*(3), 38–44.

Ganz, W. (2006). Germany: Service engineering. *Communications of the ACM, 49*(7), 79.

Holmlid, S., & Evenson, S. (2007). Prototyping and enacting services: Lessons learned from human-centered methods. In *Proceedings from the 10th Quality in Services Conference, QUIS*, June 14–17, 2007. Orlando: University of Central Florida, Rosen College of Hospitality Management.

Jana, R. (2006) Starwood hotels explore second life first. *BloombergBusinessweek. Innovation & Design*, August 22, 2006. Retrieved March 24, 2014, from, http://www.businessweek.com/stories/2006-08-22/starwood-hotels-explore-second-life-first

Jung, K., & Kirchgeorg, M. (2007). *User behavior in second life: An empirical analysis and its implications for marketing practice*. HHL-Arbeitspapier Nr. 80. Leipzig Graduate School of Management.

Kochan, A. (1997). Rapid prototyping trends. *Rapid Prototyping Journal, 3*(4), 150–152.

Kohler, T., Fueller, J., Matzler, K., & Stieger, D. (2011). Co-creation in virtual worlds: The design of the user experience. *MIS Quarterly, 35*(3), 773–788.

Kohler, T., Matzler, K., & Füller, J. (2008). Avatar-based innovation: Using virtual worlds for real-world innovation. *Technovation, 29*(6), 395–407.

Lim, Y. K., Stolterman, E., & Tenenberg, J. (2008). The anatomy of prototypes: Prototypes as filters, prototypes as manifestations of design ideas. *ACM Transactions on Computer-Human Interaction (TOCHI), 15*(2), 1–7.

Meiren, T., & Burger, T., (2008). ServLab. Visualising and simulating new services. In W. Ganz, F. Kicherer, A. Schletz, (Eds.), *European association for research on services – RESER – New horizons for the role and production of services. RESER 2008. Conference proceedings*, September 25–26, 2008, Stuttgart, Germany (p. 10). Stuttgart: Fraunhofer IRB Verlag.

Möller, M. (2007). *Innovationsexperimente. Kundenintegrierendes Vorgehensmodell zur Entwicklung mobiler Dienste bei diskontinuierlichen Innovationen*. Wiesbaden: Deutscher Universitäts-Verlag/GWV Fachverlage GmbH.

Myritz, R. (2009). Dienstleistungen aus dem Labor – Neue Ideen für den Mittelstand entwickeln. Karlsruhe: itb – Institut für Technik der Betriebsführung im Deutschen Handwerksinstitut e.V.

Neyer, A.-K., Doll, B., & Moeslein, K. M. (2008). Service Innovation: Der Beitrag des Prototyping als Instrument der Innovationskommunikation. *Zeitschrift Führung und Organisation, 77*(4), 208–214.

Parasuraman, A., Zeithaml, V. A., & Berry, L. L. (1985). A conceptual model of service quality and its implications for future research. *Journal of Marketing, 49*(4), 41–50.

Reichwald, R., Möslein, K. M., Kölling, M., & Neyer, A.-K. (2008). *Services made in Germany*. Leipzig: CLIC – Center for Leading Innovation & Cooperation.

Schiller, M. (2007). Virtual aloft re-opening on Tuesday, 8 May. *Aloft in second life: A developers report*. Retrieved January 10, 2008, from www.virtualaloft.com

Schrage, M. (1999). *Serious play*. Boston: Harvard Business School Press.

Schüller, C., Doll, B., & Szugat, M. (2008). Ein Experimentarium für Innovationen: Nutzen und Grenzen virtueller Prototoypen in Second Life. Retrieved 2013-08-03, from, www. unternehmertum.de/publication/view/57416/Nutzen+und+Grenzen+virtueller+Prototypen+in +Second+Life

Segelström, F., & Holmlid, S. (2009). Visualization as tools for research: Service designers on visualizations. *Paper presented at the Nordic Research Conference, NorDes*, August 30, 2009–September 1, 2009, Oslo, Norway.

Star, S. L., & Griesemer, J. R. (1989). Institutional ecology, translations' and boundary objects: Amateurs and professionals in Berkeley's Museum of Vertebrate Zoology, 1907–39. *Social studies of science, 19*(3), 387–420.

Starwood. (2012). *A better way to experience the world: Starwood hotels & resorts worldwide, inc. 2013 proxy statement & 2012 annual report*. Retrieved 2013-08-12, from, http://development. starwoodhotels.com/writable/resources/2012_hot_annual_report.pdf

Vargo, S. L., & Lusch, R. F. (2004). Evolving to a new dominant logic for marketing. *Journal of Marketing, 68*(1), 1–17.

Vermeulen, P., & van der Aa, W. (2005). Organizing innovation in services. In J. Tidd & F. M. Hull (Eds.), *Service innovation: Organisational responses to technological opportunities & Market Imperatives* (pp. 35–53). London: Imperial College Press.

Flinkster: The Carsharing Platform of Deutsche Bahn AG

Petra Ringeisen and Robert Goecke

Learning Objectives

- Get an insight of how Deutsche Bahn opened its carsharing IT-platform used for Flinkster to third party carsharing service providers such as car rental companies, automotive companies and a multitude of regional and international carsharing organisations.
- Analyse a multi-tenant platform concept, which enables Flinkster to offer a German-wide carsharing service in more than 140 cities and gives its customers access to carsharing offers in other European countries.
- Learn how the open carsharing platform supports open innovation in the field of intermodal mobility in tourism.

1 Introduction

Carsharing is one of the most prominent examples of collaborative consumption: Consumers use cars cooperatively either by using a commercial carsharing service providing a pool of cars which may be reserved and used ad hoc for a usage based fee or by sharing their own cars with other users, who also pay for each usage in a peer-to-peer carsharing network. In any case there must be a coordinating instance, which operates an IT-platform for the localization and reservation of the shareable

P. Ringeisen
DB Rent GmbH, Frankfurt, Germany
e-mail: petra.ringeisen@deutschebahn.com

R. Goecke (✉)
Faculty of Tourism, Munich University of Applied Sciences, Munich, Germany
e-mail: robert.goecke@hm.edu

© Springer-Verlag Berlin Heidelberg 2016
R. Egger et al. (eds.), *Open Tourism*, Tourism on the Verge,
DOI 10.1007/978-3-642-54089-9_30

cars as well as the billing and settlement between car users and car provider(s). To be attractive for the users every carsharing service needs to achieve both a critical mass of users and a critical mass of cars. Without a critical mass of cars, carsharing is not attractive for users because of the limited opportunities to find an available car nearby when it is needed. On the other hand, without a critical mass of users and demand a car fleet will remain idle and will waste capital as well as parking space. The same economies of critical mass are relevant for the development and provisioning of a carsharing IT-platform with typically high fixed costs. It makes sense to share such an IT-platform itself between different carsharing providers, so that the necessary IT-investment can be amortized faster. If the coordinating IT platform is shared between different carsharing providers, it also becomes easy to give customers of one carsharing provider access to the car pools of cooperating carsharing providers and vice versa. Sharing a common IT-platform and opening the proprietary fleets of different carsharing providers to cross usage is a new form of B2B-co-creation started by DB Rent GmbH, which even supports intermodal tourist mobility.

DB Rent GmbH was founded in 2001 by the German railway company Deutsche Bahn AG to develop and offer rental mobility solutions complementary to the classic rail services as well as fleet management and full service leasing. DB Rent was a pioneer in establishing the mobile-phone driven "Call a Bike" bicycle sharing services in major German cities like Munich, Frankfurt or Berlin and introduced the "Flinkster" carsharing service in 2009, which now is available in more than 140 German cities. One reason, why Flinkster could expand so rapidly into so many cities was the opening of its Flinkster carsharing IT-platform to third party providers.

2   The Flinkster IT-Platform for Open Carsharing

Flinkster is based on the own-developed Flinkster IT-platform. It offers services for customer registration, supports Web-/App-/Phone based car search and booking for users, enables card based car access with mobile car computers for driver guidance and car monitoring as well as billing and settlement processes for three types of carsharing (for carsharing types and their history see also Schwieger, 2012; Peterle, 2012):

Station based carsharing: The customer picks up the car at a Flinkster station typically next to a central railway station. This type of carsharing supports especially intermodal connectivity between rail and car mobility and on demand mobility in inner cities. After usage the car is returned to the Flinkster station by the customer.

Parking area based carsharing: The city is divided into different city quarters with a public parking lot. Flinkster cars need to be returned at the same city quarter where they have been picked up. Munich actually is covered by around

Driver Registration

Register once with driver licence and personal identity card at next Flinkster sales office. Select payment method and get Flinkster customer card / access key and a special driver licence seal.

Car Reservation

Via Internet, Smartphone-App or Hotline find nearest available Flinkster car or any Flinkster car station in cities with Flinkster service. Choose and book a car from many different car types and brands.

Open Car and Drive

Flinkster cars can be recognized by their unique color design. Approach Flinkster customer card to the card reader behind the windscreen of the car. The car key can be found within the glovebox inside the car or a key tresor with customer card access.

Refilling the car at gas stations is free of charge and public parking is either reduced or free of charge depending on the city.

Return the Car

Depending on the carsharing type return the car to the Flinkster station or the specific parking lot in your city quarter. With one way sharing park the car at any public parking lot in the city. Repose the car key into the glovebox or key tresor and lock the car with your Flinkster card.

Fig. 1 Flinkster carsharing process from a user perspective. *Source*: Deutsche Bahn (2014)

50 areas. Parking area based carsharing is very useful for citizens and tourists whose carsharing trips start and stop next to their home or hotel. Even the combination with public transport services like bus or metro is supported.

One-way carsharing: Users can pick up and return Flinkster cars at every public parking space or parking lot in a city. This type of carsharing enables users to use cars in the most flexible way. But cars tend to be always at different places and users need some luck to find an available car next to them. One-way carsharing is offered with the partner Citroën Multicity in Berlin.

The registration and usage process of the Flinkster carsharing service is illustrated from the perspective of an end user in Fig. 1.

3 Business Models of the Flinkster Open Carsharing Platform

To provide rail users and other customers with complementary carsharing mobility services in as many cities as possible, DB Rent decided to open its Flinkster carsharing IT-Platform to third party service providers. In addition to classic franchising partnerships of DB Rent with local sales and carsharing operators the Flinkster IT-platform itself can also be "shared" with independent partners in two new ways:

- **Application and fulfillment service providing:** Third party carsharing providers without own IT-Systems may use the multi-tenant capabilities of a "white label" version of the Flinkster IT platform to implement their own carsharing processes and manage their own customers. In this case DB Rent acts as an application service provider and offers also additional customer support services as a general carsharing fulfillment service provider.
- **Carsharing intermediation and broker services**: Third party carsharing providers might decide to offer their services to Flinkster customers and vice versa. Flinkster carsharing can be offered to customers of third party carsharing providers. In this case both partners act as carsharing intermediaries or carsharing brokers. Their customers get access to carsharing in many cities where the other partner is not present (cross usage). Rail travellers benefit from this arrangement because they gain access to carsharing at more destinations. Regional carsharing providers gain national reach for their customers.

Also combinations of both business models are possible and all services can be transparently billed and settled with the end customers as well as with the corresponding third parties involved. Typical partners who use the Flinkster platform are regional carsharing providers in smaller cities or established rental car companies who want to introduce own branded carsharing offerings. Even well-known car manufacturers use the open Flinkster IT-platform in their car dealer networks to provide carsharing services for customers with a preference for their specific car models and fleets. It was even possible to open the Flinkster IT-platform to third party carsharing providers in the Netherlands, Austria and Italy.

4 Flinkster's Open Innovation Approach

The possibility to use a proven open carsharing platform with standardized interfaces helps inventors of innovative mobility solutions to implement new forms of carsharing without the need to invest heavily into a new development of the underlying complex IT and process management infrastructures. While DB Rent is able to gain additional returns from its early infrastructure investments and know how, smaller and regional carsharing operators can start new businesses with lower market entry barriers because they don't have to reinvent all the basic platform features. By the intermediation of customers for cross usage of the partner's carsharing network all participating partners have fewer problems to reach a critical mass of customers for their services. Recent carsharing innovations implemented by DB Rent and its partners on the Flinkster IT-platform are:

- **Corporate carsharing** especially optimized for employees of companies and other organizations intending to reduce their company car fleets. Here it is important to support multi-tenant third party fleet management functions and processes.
- **E-carsharing** with fleets of electric cars which have to meet special challenges because special battery recharging processes with innovative electric charging station networks have to be supported by the carsharing platform.

New partners such as private companies and big public organizations needed to be connected step-by-step with the Flinkster carsharing platform to implement the new process variants for these specialized carsharing offerings.

Figure 2 gives an impression of the international partnership network (status: February 2014) of Flinkster. The carsharing platform has become the heart of an international business eco system for carsharing mobility solutions with continuous growth following a platform leadership strategy (on business-eco-systems and platform leadership see Moore, 1997; Gawer & Cusumano, 2002).

Especially the innovation field of e-carsharing, where DB Rent operates also its own e-Flinkster fleet in Berlin, Hamburg, Frankfurt, Stuttgart, Düsseldorf, Saarbrücken and Magdeburg is complex: Many regions in Germany and Europe have implemented ambitious local electro-mobility research projects with hetero-geneous networks of local partners e.g. public transport services, city owned electricity suppliers, tourism organisations, university researchers, hotels, parking space providers, traffic control systems, car insurance and telematics system pro-viders etc. to evaluate new forms of eco-efficient individual mobility. The Flinkster carsharing platform connects different partners in some of those projects, which is another way to support the underlying open innovation processes and so the Flinkster eco-system becomes also an open innovation platform for green mobility solutions.

An innovation field of new public research interest for example is social media based peer-to-peer carsharing. In this form of collaborative consumption customers offer their own private cars on sharing platforms like Autonetzer, Nachbarschaftsauto or tamyca either to limited user groups or to the public for a fee. The sharing economy will bring many new ideas in those fields which require flexible open platforms for fast tests and reliable implementations. Future open innovation platforms will lower the transaction costs for sharing innovations and foster the sharing economy.

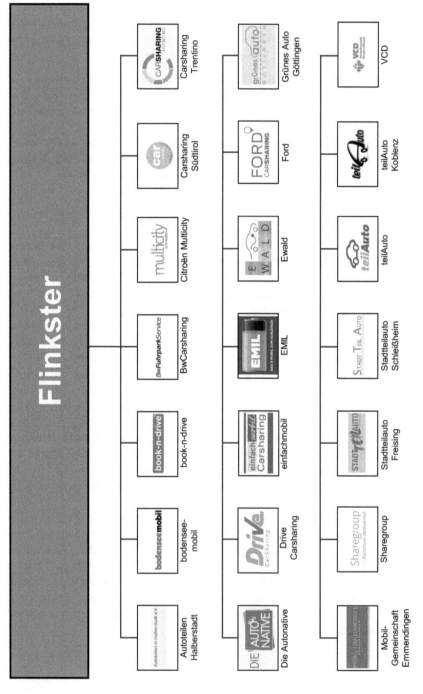

Fig. 2 Flinkster carsharing business eco-system. *Source*: Deutsche Bahn (2014)

5   Key Challenges for the Future

A key objective for DB Rent as a Deutsche Bahn company is to promote innovative ways of intermodal connectivity between the innovative individual transportation models like car and bike sharing with regional, national and international public transport services. Tourists as well as local residents in any destination or city will use green public transport and individual mobility solutions only if they are always easy to combine and open for one another.

Two technologies are key enablers for seamless intermodal mobility throughout the whole travel chain:

- **Customer Card Systems**: Customer cards like BahnCard or other smart tags may be augmented with various technologies like RFID, chips, barcodes, etc. to use them as configurable access key or user licence for different transportation services and vehicles.
- **Smartphone Mobility Apps**: To plan and combine intermodal transport-services in a user friendly way, special apps for smartphones and mobile pads have to provide simple orientation and guidance for the traveller. Where can I find the next available car or bike? When and where can I change to the bus or the train? How long and how expensive are alternative intermodal routes from location A to B? Can I reach location C with an electric car that has a given battery load? These are all questions a mobility app must answer together with advanced booking and billing services.

With BahnCard 25 mobil plus, Deutsche Bahn Long-Distance started a pilot project in December 2012 in cooperation with DB Rent, VBB and VDV, a national provider of a standardized ticketing, billing and settlement platform used by many regional public transport cooperations in Germany.

Figure 3 shows how a single card gives card holders comfortable access to four mobility services—the BahnCard 25 mobil plus can be used for long distance and public transport as well as car and bike sharing. Such an intermodal approach requires the integration of Flinkster IT-platform with the Rail-IT-platforms of Deutsche Bahn AG (Kurz & Beuttler, 2010) and the open public transport VDV ticketing core application. The cross usage of cars of different carsharing providers also requires further standardization of the procedures and technologies how users get access to the car. On the other hand, the design and comfortable handling of all the other in-car on-board services and functionality as well as the fleet structure and pricing will remain competitive differentiators even between cooperating carsharing competitors.

The interconnection of open IT-platforms of transportation and sharing service providers with existing destination card systems of regional tourism organisations offers huge new potentials to bundle intermodal transportation systems with touristic ferry, cable car services, etc. New dimensions of intermodal mobility for tourists and residents will be developed in urban areas as well as in regional and rural tourism regions. This was one of the key results of a workshop of an EU

long-distance transport discount

Flinkster customer card & access key

public transport e-ticket – loadable as separate option

Call a Bike rental at service terminals

Fig. 3 Integration of intermodal rail and public transport services with car and bike sharing with BahnCard 25 mobil plus. *Source*: Ringeisen (2013)

Interreg funded innovation project in April 2013 in Munich with 20 innovation managers of Austrian and Bavarian tourism destinations. There, the Flinkster platform with its cooperation concept was presented and various mobility problems and solution scenarios for rural tourism areas were discussed in another open innovation process.

6   Key Conclusions and Learning Outcomes for the Tourism Industry

From this case study about the Flinkster carsharing platform approach of Deutsche Bahn AG the following implications can be drawn for future open tourism initiatives:

- Innovative mobility solutions for collaborative consumption are enabled and rely heavily upon IT platforms which give customers access to those services always and everywhere and which support all underlying business processes of the service providers.
- The opening of those mission critical IT-platforms to third party service providers in other cities or with complementary service offerings promotes the diffusion of carsharing services and generates additional usage and revenue streams for the platform provider.
- B2B co-creation might help cooperating innovators to reach critical geographical reach and critical masses of resources and customers faster.
- Open inter-connectable IT-platforms are key drivers for innovative forms of cooperation and service bundling to combine different public and individual transportation services into eco-efficient intermodal travel chains.

- Many future open tourism innovations will rely on open IT-platforms where service providers and customers can participate in collaborative innovation processes.

References

Deutsche Bahn AG. (2014). *Flinkster*. Accessed February 2014, from http://www.flinkster.de

Gawer, A., & Cusumano, M. A. (2002). *Platform leadership*. Boston, MA: Harvard Business School Press.

Kurz, E., & Beuttler, J. (2010). Informationsmanagement bei der Deutschen Bahn. In A. Schulz, U. Weithöhner, & R. Goecke (Eds.), *Informationsmanagement im Tourismus* (pp. 97–117). München: Oldenbourg Verlag.

Moore, J. F. (1997). *The death of competition: Leadership and strategy in the age of business ecosystems*. New York: Harper Collins.

Peterle, J. (2012). *A study of the innovation adoption process of car sharing in Germany*. Saarbrücken: Südwestdeutscher Verlag für Hochschulschriften.

Ringeisen, P. (2013). Vernetzung für nachhaltige intermodale Mobilität – Carsharing im urbanen Raum. In *Presentation for the Workshop "Innovation by Networking" of the Innovation Academy for Destination Managers of Fachhochschule Salzburg and Hochschule*. Munich, April 12, 2013

Schwieger, B. (2012). *Second generation car-sharing: Developing a new mobility services target groups and service characteristics*. Saarbrücken: Südwestdeutscher Verlag für Hochschulschriften.

Case Study INNOTOUR: Providing Open Innovation in Tourism Education, Research and Business Development

Janne J. Liburd and Anne-Mette Hjalager

Learning Objectives

On completion of this case study, the reader should be able to:

- Examine INNOTOUR as a provider of open innovation.
- Understand how web 2.0 can facilitate open tourism education, research and business development.
- Critically reflect upon challenges and hindrances related to open tourism innovation.
- Understand the meaning of *copyleft*.

1 Introduction

This case study reports on the collaborative opportunities, experimental and critical experiences gleaned from the development of the web 2.0 platform called INNOTOUR. Web 2.0 refers to the principles and practices of facilitating information sharing and social interaction by users generating, altering, and uploading web-based content (O'Reilly, 2005) whereas the first generation Internet limits users to the passive viewing and download of largely copyrighted information (Liburd, 2012).

Providing control of distribution, reproduction, adaptation, and translation of digital and broadcast rights, copyright is widely accepted for protecting the rights of the original creator. By contrast, the underpinning philosophy of web 2.0 involves working jointly with others and sharing property to collaboratively produce new services, information, or knowledge. The reciprocal relations are replicated in the

J.J. Liburd (✉) • A.-M. Hjalager
University of Southern Denmark, Kolding, Denmark
e-mail: liburd@sdu.dk; hjalager@sam.sdu.dk

© Springer-Verlag Berlin Heidelberg 2016
R. Egger et al. (eds.), *Open Tourism*, Tourism on the Verge,
DOI 10.1007/978-3-642-54089-9_31

copyleft movement. A play on the word copyright, *copyleft* describes the licensing practice of removing or modifying copyright restrictions to legally distribute copies and adapted versions of the work of others, while requiring that the same freedoms be preserved in future versions (Liburd, 2012; Liburd & Hjalager, 2012).

Knowledge is a commodity of significant value, and an object for intellectual property rights protection. Already in 2010, Liburd and Hjalager argued that knowledge produced in, and disseminated through universities was under increasing pressure. The traditional knowledge paradigm is challenged by the enhanced distributive capacity of web 2.0 practices, including bottom-up, interactive and open collaboration in online content generation (Benkler, 2006; Brown & Adler, 2008; Liburd, 2012). Increasingly, socially constructions of knowledge complement and replace old practices of hoarding and accumulation whereby the traditional manifestations of immaterial property rights are gradually undermined. The soundness of the *copyleft* movement exposes a need to embed new principles in broader political vision for the future. This is underlined by organisations like the OECD (2007) and the Swedish Research Council (2009) advocating that publicly funded research results should be made accessible by 'giving knowledge for free', as it is phrased by OECD. They are searching for new economic models, pragmatically realizing that good intensions and ethical standards will not suffice and neither will small fragments of educators, no matter how enthusiastic. Indeed, recent experience demonstrates that sharing and collaboration are not in contrast to economic objectives, and that economic exchange and business opportunities enter into new formats (Liburd & Hjalager, 2010).

Across the many web 2.0 tools and sites, there is a reciprocal dedication to content development and open innovation. Harnessing the collective wisdom of tourism educators, students, and the tourism industry may open for collaborative content generation, creativity and innovation in the tourism industry. As noticed by Huber and Hutchings (2008) open learning has an advantage in terms of space for experimentation, which is further explored in the following in the case of the INNOTOUR platform.

2   INNOTOUR: An Open Innovation Platform

The University of Southern Denmark (hereinafter SDU) in 2009 launched an experimental web 2.0 platform for tourism education, research, and business innovation, www.INNOTOUR.com. INNOTOUR strives to be an online hub for students, teachers, researchers, and businesses with an interest in tourism innovation. INNOTOUR is described as "an experimental meeting place for academics, students and enterprises with an interest in tourism and innovation, and who are seeking to enhance their knowledge, products and skills" (www.INNOTOUR.com).

INNOTOUR facilitates open innovation through collaboration in tourism education, research, and business development. INNOTOUR is envisaged in international teaching and research contexts and is available both as a tool and to provide

Table 1 The INNOTOUR objectives

• To improve the quality and efficiency of tourism training through use of a broad spectrum of technological tools and teaching methods
• To involve students and partner companies in the development and spread of advanced educational resources
• To strengthen international cooperation and share knowledge on innovation in tourism, and to market INNOTOUR as a hub for knowledge creation
• To assist commercial enterprise and society in tourism-related innovation processes by establishing relationships and open dialogue to communicate experiences
• To promote a creative culture, which tolerates experimentation and error, and thereby encourages students and researchers to go beyond conventional knowledge in the effort to create something newTo play an important and internationally recognised role in tourism research
• To build mutually beneficial relationships with partners in the developing world
• To provide a testing ground for the efforts of SDU to develop new teaching and learning methods, and cooperation practices
• To build bridges between academic skills and campuses

Source: Liburd (2013, p. 128)

collaboration between universities, with industry, with society, and beyond. The key objectives of INNOTOUR are summarised in Table 1.

The INNOTOUR platform is dedicated to five main user groups, illustrated to the left in the screen shot in Fig. 1.

Most of the resources are openly available, but contributors to INNOTOUR must register to comment and upload content. The five user groups share resources to a great extent, in accordance with the philosophy of INNOTOUR of reciprocity and collaboration. The top bar of the front page lists a range of open resources, which deserves further attention before addressing select elements from the specific user areas. The open resources include the 'Innovation cases', 'Innovation tools', and 'Commercial corner', which deserve initial attention.

2.1 Innovation Cases

Tourism innovation, creativity and business are the principal subject areas of INNOTOUR's Innovation cases. Continuous innovations in industry and destinations are crucial to economic growth, and innovations are important parameters in the experiences and potential return visits of tourists (Dwyer & Edwards, 2010; Hjalager, 2010a). The innovation cases describe actual innovations in the tourism industry and at tourism destinations. They represent different ways of working with innovation and include examples of product, process, marketing, and logistical innovations. The innovation cases are a central feature of INNOTOUR. Each case is equipped with photos and links to the companies, or organisations involved. Videos are embedded if available. It is important to note that the cases are not

Fig. 1 INNOTOUR front page (www.INNOTOUR.com)

marketing material, but have the character of best innovation practice, or an innovation process, or innovation experiences from a professional environment.

Innovation cases can be applied as a tool for teachers to set a context or provoke discussion in teaching and learning. Students can be asked to prepare an innovation case and upload it onto INNOTOUR by use of the detailed instructions and template provided. Feasibly, upload of an innovation case may be part of a larger project, where the students work with other academic products and presentations.

2.2   Innovation Tools

This section is primarily of interest for tourism businesses and students. The **INNOWHEEL** is uniquely developed for INNOTOUR. It is a creativity tool which helps users to move beyond conventional thinking. The user is challenged to think creatively about possible innovations in relation to product, target group, distribution channel, and customer needs in hitherto unseen combinations. User-driven innovation has been the subject of much discussion in Denmark, as elsewhere. INNOTOUR aims to summarise available methods and to provide students and businesses with both practical advice, links to cases, and theory, in order to generate curiosity and entrepreneurial activity.

Other creativity tools are introduced, such as the interactive *Innovation ability tests*, which are aimed for use by companies, but may also be of relevance to students in project assignments. The *Risk assessment test* of INNOTOUR is grounded in theory and research in business and social economics and it can be applied in the classroom as well as in connection with problem solving. The *Dilemma games* are a tool particularly relevant in educational contexts. The objective is to contemplate difficult issues and discuss possible options. *Academic resources* comprise references to important innovation literature in tourism and serves as a supplement to library services. It is possible to search by keywords, author, etc., and any geographic site referred to in the articles will appear on Google Maps.

2.3 Commercial Corner

Innovative suppliers are invited to present their products and ideas. They can explain to the tourism industry how supplies in combination with the unique character of the tourism business can result in new products and services. This is a place for tourism enterprises to keep updated with the newest supplies. Innovation in tourism relies on the creativity of the tourism businesses, and the suppliers to the tourism industry are particularly important for the continued development and sustainability of the tourism industry (Hjalager, 2010b).

Next, the main resources of the five sites dedicated to different user groups will be outlined, the first of which is for **Students**. The area designated to tourism students contains a number of menu items with varying pedagogical intent and potential application, among which are the **TEFI Courses**. This area hosts online lecturers, student assignments, and shared curricula dedicated to exploring values-based education, feasibly introduced as part of blended learning.

Student blogs are used by students to express themselves with regards to actual academic topics and to respond to the opinions and interpretations of other students. A blog discussion can be used as a prelude to classroom discussions, so that students are ready for critical reflections when they meet in class (Liburd & Christensen, 2013, pp. 101). Offering opportunities for networking outside of the immediate study environment, students may use blogs for networking with tourism students across cultural and national borders. It is possible to pose subject related questions to other students and to open new topics for discussion.

INNOTOUR introduces **Student wikis** as a tool for online communities and project groups, where several students can contribute, revise, and further develop a document in a joint, iterative and interactive process. This allows for greater depth of learning and a more intensive process than, for example, traditional lectures (Liburd & Christensen, 2013, pp. 101). The **Student forum** serves as a discussion forum where the topics can be raised by teachers and tutors.

2.4   Academics

Designed as a resource for those who undertake research in tourism innovation, business development, destination development, sustainability, etc., the site is dedicated to tourism academics. A number of resources have been opened but are yet to be populated with information and debate. One of these is **the Copyleft forum** which raises copyright challenges and dilemmas for researchers using web 2.0 technologies for knowledge dissemination.

INNOTOUR lists six *Creative Commons* license options for contributors. These range from restrictions on redistribution without modification, via non-commercial distribution, copy, display, and derivative works based upon it, but for non-commercial purposes only, to attribution where others may copy, distribute, display, remix, and edit the copyrighted work, and derivative works based upon it, if credited as requested by the original author (http://www.innotour.com/about-innotour/creative-commons).

2.5   Enterprises

Aiming to expose innovative tourism businesses while not serving as a marketing platform, INNOTOUR provides enterprises with the opportunity to enhance their visibility by contributing with innovation experiences. Links are provided to the **Innovation tools, Commercial corner,** and **Innovation cases**. The national tourism organisation in Denmark has a **VisitDenmark Forum** for collaboration with tourism students. Here, ideas for networking activities, internships, and applied dissertations are exchanged. In addition to the site for tourism academics, INNOTOUR for tourism enterprises is the least visited area of INNOTOUR to date, which will be critically addressed below.

2.6   Teachers and Tutors

A fourth site is dedicated to educators who teach tourism innovation, business development, creativity, experience design, sustainability, marketing, etc. There is also a special section dedicated to teachers and tutors, which amongst others is inspired and shaped by project partners. Designed to make the lives of tourism teachers more interesting through collaboration in various forms, including a **Teacher's wiki**, guidance on course work integration, **Shared teaching resources**, and **Teachers and tutors forum**.

2.7 BEST EN Lecture Series

The fifth site is the BEST EN Sustainability Series, representing the latest addition to INNOTOUR. Here, the **BEST EN Modules** are part of a larger movement of universities adopting *Open Educational Resources* as a tool to promote learning in society at large. Each of the modules links to individual tutorials of thematic relevance to sustainable tourism development. The tutorials are comprised of a video, slides, literature suggestions, case studies and student assignments. A blogging function allows for student feedback and commentary.

3 Key Challenges for the Future

INNOTOUR opens up for new ways of teaching, learning, and collaboration in academia, with the tourism industry and relevant organisations. It stipulates fairly radical changes in the aims and epistemologies of tourism education and research, and opposition and critique should be anticipated. The web 2.0 approaches to openness and the democratisation of knowledge has been criticised on the basis that academic standards are undermined by amateurs (e.g. Carr, 2010; Keen, 2007). Pointing to the challenges and inherent tensions in web 2.0 education, Dohn argues that

> Web 2.0 activities have distributive peer responsibility and no designated experts to control the quality of interaction and production whereas in education, of course, the right and duty of assessment is ultimately the teacher's. (Dohn, 2009, pp. 359)

In many ways, the web 2.0 philosophy of reciprocity and openness runs against traditional, academic practices. These are sustained by copyright regulation, hierarchical power structures, and individual meriting, among others, to which the limited interest by researchers to date may also be attributed. This intrinsic lack of coherence is complemented by practical issues of time constraints, neo-liberal university governance (Ayikoru, Tribe, & Airey, 2009), limited technological understanding and lacking awareness of web 2.0, and of INNOTOUR in particular, which further impede on open research collaboration. The question about how and who are to assess the quality of tourism research in a reliable way to ensure accuracy, consistency, and trustworthiness in open collaborative environments has been addressed elsewhere (e.g. Liburd, 2012). Suffice here to note that it may pose a hindrance for engagement in INNOTOUR for tourism researchers. Similar contentions may be found among tourism enterprises and their lack of attention to open innovation and web 2.0 collaboration. The development of new forms and norms to evaluate open access contributions while maintaining standards of quality and good scientific practice, are in dire need of critical inquiry.

The set of technological options provided by web 2.0 and INNOTOUR also calls for ethical considerations of innovation and creativity. There is ample historical evidence of innovations having led to ethically disastrous outcomes. This requires self and group monitoring in communication, problem solving, and mutual respect among the users who engage in online collaboration. Referred to as netiquette, it may be necessary for users to discuss and agree on a code of good, ethical, online behaviour, including forms of cooperation, tone, communication, knowledge sharing, respect, and deadlines. Mindful of the global, digital divide, INNOTOUR encourages respect for self and others through open interaction, communication, and equitable access.

These emerging practices coincide with calls for open innovation (Chesbrough, 2003) and democratic innovation (von Hippel, 2005). Chesbrough and von Hippel state that innovation resources are not restricted, and should not be controlled by local, cultural practices or closed networks. Conscious of the global digital divide, knowledge may be easily acquired and shared in an open access research environment, and based on *copyleft* licensing, which includes

> original scientific research results, raw data and metadata, source materials, digital representations of pictorial and graphical materials and scholarly multimedia material (Berlin Declaration, 2003).

Web 2.0 makes it increasingly possible to broadly draw on innovation competencies and to rely on the participation and feedback of users from different cultures. In line with the Berlin Declaration (2003) on open access, Chesbrough and von Hippel provide numerous examples of how secrecy and control in isolated research and development structures are not beneficial for innovation processes in rapidly changing environments. Often cited examples are open source high-tech innovations, e.g. the GNU/Linux computer operating system, Apache software, the Dobson telescope. Users collaborate to create solutions for specific problems, innovations, or improvements of existing codes and products, which are deposited in at least one online repository with unrestricted distribution and long-time archiving. The ideas of open innovation and collaboration are only gradually emerging in tourism, for example through INNOTOUR's BEST EN Modules and international cases of innovation for sustainable tourism (Liburd et al., 2013; Benckendorff & Lund-Durlacher, 2013), which also have the potential to develop as valuable resources for the tourism industry.

4   Key Conclusions and Learning Outcomes for the Tourism Industry

Social networks and the web 2.0 movement can be seen as primary providers for collaboration and knowledge exchange (Racherla & Hu, 2010). This case study has reported on the tools, functionalities, and collaborative resources of the INNOTOUR platform.

Aiming to serve as a knowledge hub for students, academics, enterprises, and teachers with an interest in tourism innovation, the philosophy of INNOTOUR is open, experimental, and reciprocal. Users share properties and generate the content where resources are shared to a large degree, although students, academics, enterprises, and teachers have access to different materials through dedicated sub-sites.

While the idea of collaboration is usually perceived as a positive, the direct and individual pay-offs are not clear-cut, nor are reflections about aims, what is good for self and for others, necessarily part of deeper considerations (McWilliam, Green, Hunt, Bridgstock, & Young, 2000). These structural, social, and individual factors that influence open collaboration should be subject to further analysis.

In 2008, Airey argued that there is an obvious need to search for new possibilities to assist the tourism industry to not only overcome barriers towards innovation but to facilitate much wider capacity building through education. Interactive communication and collaboration are at the core of web 2.0, which may be used to support more seamless knowledge development processes, reciprocal knowledge transfer and exchanges to enhance innovation and learning in the tourism industry.

In short, the three key learning outcomes for the tourism industry can be identified as follows: Access to knowledge is a key parameter in competition. Open collaboration may enhance industry competitiveness, and *copyleft* retains opportunities for copyright protection and adaptation of non-commercial purposes.

References

Airey, D. W. (2008). *Tourism education: Life begins at 40*. Paper. School of Management, University of Surrey. Online. Accessed February 20, 2010, from http://epubs.surrey.ac.uk/cgi/viewcontent.cgi?article=1039&context=tourism

Ayikoru, M., Tribe, J., & Airey, D. (2009). Reading tourism education: Neoliberalism unveiled. *Annals of Tourism Research, 36*(2), 191–221.

Benckendorff, P., & Lund-Durlacher, D. (Eds.). (2013). *International cases in sustainable travel & tourism*. Oxford: Goodfellow Publishers Ltd.

Benkler, Y. (2006). *The wealth of networks. How social production transforms markets and freedom*. New Haven: Yale University Press.

Berlin Declaration on Open Access to Knowledge in the Sciences and Humanities. (2003). Accessed July 4, 2011, from http://oa.mpg.de/files/2010/04/berlin_declaration.pdf

Brown, J. S., & Adler, R. P. (2008). Minds on fire: Open education, the long tail, and learning 2.0. *Educause Review 43*(1), 16–32. Accessed May 16, 2010, from http://www.educause.edu/EDUCAUSE+Review/EDUCAUSEReviewMagazineVolume43/MindsonFireOpenEducationtheLon/162420

Carr, N. (2010). *The shallows. How the internet is changing the way we read, think and remember*. London: Atlantic Books.

Chesbrough, H. (2003). *Open innovation. The new imperative for creating and profiting from technology*. Boston: Harvard Business School Press.

Dohn, N. B. (2009). Web 2.0: Inherent tensions and evident challenges for education. *International Journal of Computer-Supported Collaborative Learning 4*(3). Accessed May 2, 2009, from http://www.citeulike.org/journal/springerlink-120055

Dwyer, L., & Edwards, D. (2010). Sustainable tourism planning. In J. J. Liburd & D. Edwards (Eds.), *Understanding the sustainable development of tourism* (pp. 19–44). Oxford: Goodfellow Publishers.

Hjalager, A.-M. (2010a). A review of innovation research in tourism. *Tourism Management, 31*(1), 1–12.

Hjalager, A.-M. (2010b). Supplier-driven innovations for sustainable tourism. In J. J. Liburd & D. Edwards (Eds.), *Understanding the sustainable development of tourism* (pp. 148–162). Oxford: Goodfellow Publishers.

Huber, M. T., & Hutchings, P. (2008). What is next for open knowledge? In T. Iiyoshi & M. S. V. Kumar (Eds.), *Opening up education: The collective advancement of education through open technology, open content, open knowledge* (pp. 417–428). Cambridge, MA: MIT Press. Accessed October 2, 2009, from http://mitpress.mit.edu/opening_up_education/

Keen, A. (2007). *The cult of the Amaterur. How today's internet is killing our culture.* New York: Double Day Broadway Publishing Group.

Liburd, J. J. (2012). Tourism research 2.0. *Annals of Tourism Research, 39*(2), 883–907.

Liburd, J. J. (2013). *Towards the Collaborative University. Lessons from tourism education and research.* Professorial Dissertation. Print & Sign: University of Southern Denmark.

Liburd, J. J., & Christensen, I.-M. F. (2013). Using web 2.0 in higher tourism education. *Journal of Hospitality, Leisure, Sport & Tourism Education, 12*, 99–108.

Liburd, J. J., & Hjalager, A.-M. (2010). Changing approaches to education, innovation and research – Student experiences. *Tourism Journal of Hospitality and Tourism Management, 17*, 12–20.

Liburd, J. J., & Hjalager, A. M. (2012). From copyright to copyleft. Towards tourism education 2.0. In I. Ateljevic, N. Morgan, & A. Pritchard (Eds.), *The critical turn in tourism studies: Creating an academy of hope* (pp. 96–109). Oxon: Routledge.

Liburd, J. J., Carlsen, J., & Edwards, D. (Eds.). (2013). *Networks for innovation in sustainable tourism. Case studies and cross case analysis.* Melbourne: Tilde University Press.

McWilliam, E., Green, A., Hunt, N., Bridgstock, M., & Young, B. (2000). Inviting conversations? Dialogic difficulties in the corporate university. *Higher Education Research & Development, 19*(2), 237–253.

O'Reilly, T. (2005). *What is web 2.0? Design patterns and business models for the next generation software.* Accessed July 20, 2011, from http://oreilly.com/web2/archive/what-is-web-20.html

OECD. (2007). *Giving knowledge for free: The emergence of open educational resources.* Paris: OECD.

Racherla, P., & Hu, C. (2010). A social network perspective of tourism research collaborations. *Annals of Tourism Research, 37*(1), 1012–1034.

Swedish Research Council. (2009). *Remit.* Accessed May 29, 2010, from http://www.vr.se/inenglish/aboutus/remit.4.44482f6612355bb5ee780001601.html

von Hippel, E. (2005). *Democratizing innovation.* Cambridge, MA: MIT Press.

Part IV
Case Studies: Provision Level

The Crowdfunding Ecosystem: Benefits and Examples of Crowdfunding Initiatives

Reinhard Willfort, Conny Weber, and Oliver Gajda

Learning Objectives

- Understand crowdfunding as democratic tool to boost innovation
- Appreciate the concept of the crowdfunding ecosystem
- Demonstrate how an open innovation and a crowdfunding platform work
- Explore how to get more than ideas and financial support from emotionally and personally motivated "co-thinkers"

1 Introduction

According to the Framework for European Crowdfunding (De Buysere, Gajda, Kleverlaan, & Marom, 2012) one of the most promising tools to help enable economic growth, job creation, and innovation is crowdfunding, as it is a highly democratic tool and means of funding new ideas, small business and job creation across Europe. While examining the topics of open innovation and crowdsourcing in the course of this book from a holistic point of view and analysing them considering their suitability to the tourism industry, crowdfunding will be discussed in this chapter with regards to its practical applicability in tourism.

R. Willfort (✉)
ISN – Innovation Service Network GmbH, Graz, Austria
e-mail: reinhard.willfort@innovation.at

C. Weber
ISN – Innovation Service Network GmbH, Graz, Austria
e-mail: conny.weber@innovation.at

O. Gajda
European Crowdfunding Network, Hamburg, Germany
e-mail: oliver.gajda@gmail.com

© Springer-Verlag Berlin Heidelberg 2016
R. Egger et al. (eds.), *Open Tourism*, Tourism on the Verge,
DOI 10.1007/978-3-642-54089-9_32

The need for innovation in the tourism industry is obvious, as the lifetime of new products is steadily getting shorter and increased competition forces companies to surprise customers and guests with new offers. Innovation management aims to systematically implement innovation in organisations (Schumpeter, 1911). More specifically, innovation management focuses on how to derive profitable products and services from creative outputs within an organisation (Cooper, 1987). Innovation management has significantly changed, especially towards approaches for supporting the innovation process and gathering ideas from outside the organisation. In the advent of Web 2.0 these approaches have become increasingly computer-based while enabling access to large user communities. This phenomenon is summarised under the term open innovation (Chesbrough, 2003) and goes one step further by including external resources, i.e. stakeholders, end-users or communities in the innovation process. According to Chesbrough (2003) open innovation means that valuable ideas can come from inside or outside the company and can go to market from inside or outside the company as well. Even more precisely is the term of crowdsourcing, which describes an organization leveraging the power of crowds for generating and assessing new ideas as well as the development and marketing of new products and services.

Crowdfunding is a special form of crowdsourcing. The idea of crowdfunding is to collect many small amounts from a community in order to support and realise a certain project, and thus to provide a new dimension of venture capital financing. Similar to crowdsourcing all stakeholders interested in a project idea can support the realisation of the project with their funds. The recognition for the funders rises from a "thank you" up to a price or other rewards.

In a nutshell, crowdfunding is when "co-thinking" micro investors provide small amounts for big ideas. Combined with the intelligent use of "crowd-technologies", crowdfunding shapes new ways of entrepreneurship. The difference to traditional ways of financing such as credits or individual investors is mainly that a larger group of investors raises smaller amounts to realise a project. By spreading the investments across different projects the risk of an individual investor is lower and investors can build up a portfolio with different crowdfunding allocations. The necessity of alternative ways of financing is obvious due to the hard restrictions of many banks caused by the ailing financial system.

A new stage of crowdfunding has reached with the phenomenon of equity-based crowdfunding, in short called crowdinvesting. This form of crowdfunding is very interesting for the tourism industry as it delivers financial returns on investments. While crowdfunding is frequently used for financing smaller projects in the cultural and arts scene, crowdinvesting provides additionally an equity financing for innovation projects of small and medium sized enterprises (SMEs) or start-ups.

2   Recent Development of Crowdfunding Initiatives

In the meanwhile several crowfunding platforms exist and first projects, also some related to the tourism industry, have been successfully funded. Approximately 800 different crowdfunding initiatives exist globally and the raised funds exceeded USD 5.1 billion in 2013 (Massolution, 2013). Since 2012, the "European Crowdfunding Network" (http://europecrowdfunding.org), joined by relevant crowdfunding experts, aims at establishing the development of crowdfunding on a common European level. The ECN brings together crowdfunding platforms and stakeholders across Europe in building a professional and transparent industry.

Probably the best known platform is "Kickstarter" in the US, where crowdfunding activities are already granted legally, in order to activate private investments and to create new jobs by supporting start-ups with private investments. Crowdfunding in general is just a logical consequence of the current financial and market developments. With saving accounts offering 1.7 % interest at best, inflation at more than 2 % and entrepreneurs having a very hard time getting venture capital to finance innovative ideas, a new market with new players and offerings is opening up. Effectively, crowdfunding has a disruptive impact on financing projects, start-ups or even communities and regions, by allowing value creation on many levels, not only regarding financial aspects. In addition to gathering venture capital, companies also get access to a valuable network with the right people from their respective industry. Investors get an opportunity to support sensible projects with a reasonable investment and to be closely involved in implementation without having to be entrepreneurs themselves. Every micro-investor has the chance to build a portfolio of different equity holdings and thus to reduce the individual risk they are exposed to in this way. Crowdfunding has the potential to successfully write a storyboard for a new kind of innovation ecosystem, with direct and transparent funding.

From an international point of view, platforms such as Kickstarter, Indiegogo and Startnext have enabled crowdfunding to pick up speed in recent years. The global market is currently estimated at USD 500 billion (Massolution, 2013). But as elsewhere, not all that glitters here is gold. There are also those who warn against succumbing blindly to the hype surrounding crowdfunding. A major challenge that must be addressed before crowdfunding and crowd investing can establish well is a balance between demand and offer. For example, in Austria there are currently many requests for projects but not enough crowdfunding investors to cover the demand. After committing more and more of their money to alternative investment vehicles in the past years and then watching these investments tank, many investors have become much more cautious again. However, crowdfunding has the potential to bring the financial system a little closer back to the original intent and trust of banking.

Another hurdle to overcome when writing the storyboard for a new culture of innovation, is accepting the risk of failing projects. At this moment, entrepreneurs whose projects fail quickly become subject of ridicule, which understandably limits the motivation for a new start. This is differently in the USA, where investors make their decisions by taking into account the experiences made by an entrepreneur before.

3 A Concept for a Crowdfunding Ecosystem

The crowdfunding ecosystem (Fig. 1) presented in this chapter describes a theoretical framework covering a new defined innovation process for crowdfunding projects, and is highly applicable to the tourism industry. A traditional innovation process starts with the (creative) finding of ideas, validating these ideas, realising an idea i.e. a new product or service, and finally to market the idea. Basically, the concept of the crowdfunding ecosystem also follows this process; however, it includes the "wisdom of crowds" (Surowiecki, 2005) in all phases.

In the crowdcreativity phase an organisation, entrepreneur or any other individual can start an open idea contest for gathering ideas from the crowd on a certain challenge. In a next step, these ideas are validated and assessed by the community. Finally, the crowdcreativity network consisting of a community of "co-thinkers", creatives, entrepreneurs and organisations shape the selected idea to a final concept for a new product, service or start-up. Mostly, the main bottleneck for realising an idea is the lacking support of relevant know how and risk capital. Thus, the second crowdfunding phase aims at supporting the realisation of a good project idea by providing both, know-how and coaching by experienced innovation experts, investors and multipliers, and financial support.

This "Crowdbusiness" Ecosystem has been realised with two platforms in Austria. In the following, these two initiatives, which support the crowdfunding ecosystem, i.e. the process from finding a great idea up to realising a crowdfunding project, are shortly presented. The crowdcreativity phase is covered by the neurovation.net platform, an open innovation and idea management platform. For supporting the crowdfunding phase the 1000×1000.at platform has been developed. In the following both will be described more in detail.

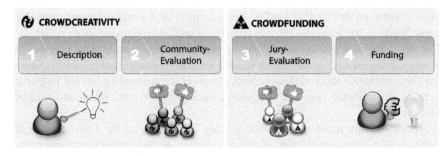

Fig. 1 The crowdfunding ecosystem (*Source*: Author's own elaboration)

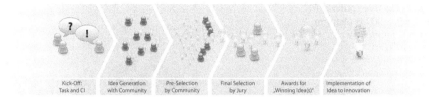

| Kick-Off: | Idea Generation | Pre-Selection | Final Selection | Awards for | Implementation of |
| Task and CI | with Community | by Community | by Jury | „Winning Idea(s)" | Idea to Innovation |

Fig. 2 The crowdcreativity process supported by NEUROVATION.NET (*Source*: Author's own elaboration)

4 An Open Innovation Paltform as Example for Crowdceativity

The open innovation and idea platform Neurovation.net (Willfort, Tochtermann, & Neubauer, 2007) with more than 6000 users is closely linked with the crowdfunding platform 1000×1000.at. Any organisation or individual person can post a challenge and start an open idea finding contest with the community or only with a selected group (Fig. 2). At the same time, anyone who has an idea can submit it here, can contribute to idea contests or start a first market test in form of a community assessment. The aim of this platform is to take advantage of the "wisdom of the crowds" and to receive new ideas, improve existing ones, validate and select ideas, or get feedback on a new product or service.

Ideally, teams are formed that can contribute complementary skills for further implementation. The most promising ideas are chosen by the community and invited to submit further documents, such as a business plan. After this detailed assessment of the concept, a crowdfunding expert jury, e.g. of the 1000×1000.at platform, then examines the idea and selects the most promising projects from the list.

5 An Example of an Austrian Crowdfunding Initiative

After a successful evaluation and elaboration of a project idea by the community and expert jury, this idea can apply for crowdfunding on the 1000×1000.at network. This platform went online in March 2012. Compared to e.g. Germany, in Austria there weren't much activities in the field of crowdfunding due to the limited willingness of accepting risks in financing—which is at least a frequent complaint in the local entrepreneurship scene. Besides the platform Respekt.net, there was essentially no way to finance projects through crowdfunding. The aim of the 1000×1000.at platform is to provide information about new, transparent forms of investments like crowdfunding. The medium-term goal is to increase the network up to 10,000 crowdinvestors.

Fig. 3 The three pillars of
the 1000×1000.at platform
(*Source*: http://www.
1000x1000.at)

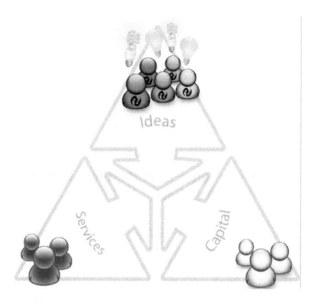

The 1000×1000.at platform is based on three main pillars (Fig. 3): *Ideas* for new projects or companies applying for crowdfunding. *Services*, covering the assessment of a new project, or the support for realising and implementing a mature project idea. And *Capital*, stating the basis for successful crowdfunding coming from interested investors.

Anyone who wants to be an investor on 1000×1000.at must first register on the platform. Depending on the project, people can invest between 250 and 5000 euros in equity based crowdfunding mode. Investors receive participation certificates in accordance to their investment. These certificates allow the participation in the annual profits of their supported company and to receive a proportionate holding in the assets of the company in the event that the company is sold. The maximum financial support a project idea can receive in Austria through e.g. the 1000×1000. at crowdinvesting platform is limited to 250,000 euros since 5th of July 2013.

Business ideas that are not suitable for crowdfunding are proposed to interested partners, usually VIP members of the 1000×1000.at investor network or other partners, and thus also have the chance to get support and further assistance. Business ideas that are already sufficiently developed can go straight to the jury phase. Projects are continuously selected and proposed to all investors for funding. Basically, everyone can invest in every project. However, it is not recommended to invest all capital in only one project. By building a portfolio of different projects the risk can be reduced significantly as it is not likely that all projects may fail.

One of the most important aspects regarding the realisation of crowdfunding are security aspects and transparency. Before a new crowdfunding project starts at 1000×1000.at, the maximum target amount and the fundraising period are defined. The investors then transfer the funds to an escrow account where the capital is hold temporarily. Once the minimum amount specified by the crowdfunding project is reached, the overall investment is considered to have been successful. If the minimum amount is not reached within the specified fundraising period, all provided capital is returned to the participating investors.

The platform itself generates income by collecting a fee for acting as a broker between investors and companies. Anyway, the platform operator only gets earnings for its services when the funding has been arranged successfully. Further services offered by the platform are support services for the realisation of a project by experienced innovation experts. This service takes over a part of the risk and at the same time ensures a high probability of project success.

There are basically four types of crowdfunding: donation-based, reward-based, equity-based, and lending or debt-based. Of course, the different crowdfunding models also correspond to slightly different motivations in funders, though they all are to some degree intrinsic motivations. Donation-based crowdfunding is based on contributions that are intended towards more or less charitable objectives. With reward-based crowfunding investors receive a tangible item or service in return for their funds. Lending-based crowdfunding is comparable to a credit contract, i.e. the credit is being repaid over a period of time. Equity -based crowdfunding allows investors to receive a shareholding contract based on equity-like instruments or revenue sharing in the project/business (Please refer to De Buysere et al., 2012 for more details).

1000×1000.at provides reward based and equity-based crowdfunding. Unlike platforms like Kickstarter and Indiegogo, which are acting only in reward based crowdfunding mode, the equity-based crowdfunding investors receive an entitlement to participate in the profits and asset value of the company. However, the invested funds are venture capital and investors lose in the case a project fails. Currently, equity-based crowdfunding is not legally possible in the USA, where platforms only provide tokens of appreciation or initial prototypes to the donors in the event of success. The typical exit scenario of a major investor is not the primary goal of crowdinvesting. But wealthier investors can help companies and projects at a very early phase with a relatively small amount of capital and can watch the company growing.

6   Key Conclusions and Learning Outcomes for the Tourism Industry

Not only for the tourism industry, the probably most important and interesting aspect of the here presented crowdfunding ecosystem concept, i.e. the combination of open innovation and crowdfunding provides the fan community, consisting of the "co-thinkers" of a project, who are emotional and personally motivated and deal in trustful relationships.

> Crowdfunding can offer unique support for budding and existing entrepreneurs on multiple levels. No other investment form, be it debt or equity, can provide the benefits of pre-sales, market research, word-of-mouth promotion, and crowd wisdom without additional cost. (De Buysere et al., 2012)

Examples of crowdfunding for tourism projects are springing up as we speak, for example, Up Greek Tourism (http://www.upgreektourism.gr/) crowdfunded billboard campaigns for Greece as a vacation destination successfully in London's Piccadilly Circus, New York's Time Square and Washington DC's Verizon Center. Another example on the Indiegogo platform is the "Karma Project", which aims at supporting a Sherpa village in Nepal to create their own sustainable tourism project to raise money for a medical clinic. On the German platform Startnext (http://www.startnext.de) also two tourism related projects have been successfully crowdfunded: A documentary about the opportunities and threats of tourism in Berlin, as well as the book "Alltagstourist" by Eva Jung.

The main benefits that crowdfunding initiatives might deliver for the tourism industry go beyond funding:

- Gathering new ideas from the crowd, i.e. hotels can ask their (potential) guests for the favourite interior design
- The interaction with the crowd validates ideas for products, services or business models in an early stage
- Crowdfunding is a powerful tool for market analysis, because it allows testing whether there is a demand for a new product or service
- Crowdfunding is a perfect marketing instrument as it promotes an idea to early adopters
- Crowdfunding allows lowering the innovation risk as the community and co-thinkers, e.g. investors or other stakeholders, can provide direct feedback and share their experiences and know-how with the entrepreneur
- Open innovation and crowdfunding initiatives are emotional and personally motivated which guarantees success

In a nutshell, the storyboard for a new ecosystem of innovation in the tourism industry has been written and is starting to become reality.

References

Chesbrough, H. W. (2003). *Open innovation. The new imperative for creating and profiting from technology.* Boston, MA: Harvard Business School Press.

Cooper, R. G. (1987). New products: What separates the winners from losers. *Journal of Product Innovation Management, 4*(3), 169–184.

De Buysere, K., Gajda, O., Kleverlaan, R., & Marom, D. (2012). *A framework for european crowdfunding,* 1st ed. Found on August 1, 2013 on http://www.crowdfundingframework.eu

Massolution, C. F. (2013). *The crowdfunding industry report, 2013.*

Schumpeter, J. A. (1911). *The theory of economic development: An inquiry into profits, capital, credit, interest and the business cycle.* Cambridge, MA: Harvard University Press.

Surowiecki, J. (2005). *The wisdom of crowds.* New York: Anchor Books.

Willfort, R., Tochtermann, K., & Neubauer, A. (2007). *Creativity@Work für Wissensarbeit. Kreative Höchstleistungen am Wissensarbeitsplatz auf Basis neuester Erkenntnisse der Gehirnforschung.* Aachen: Shaker Verlag.

Beyond the Offer: Co-creation in Tourism: When Your Guest Becomes Your Partner, Value Emerges

Frank T. Piller and Christian Gülpen

Learning Objectives

- To understand what customer co-creation is
- To understand how the idea of integrating consumers into the value creation process can be applied to the tourism industry
- To understand how this helps to create additional value and brand loyalty

1 Introduction

The tourism industry is a field with fairly tough competition. Over the past decades, most imaginable ways of spending one's holiday have been offered and today's tourist is free to visit almost every part of the world, limited mainly by their budget and potentially hindering political circumstances. Finding the next big idea to satisfy customer's desire for new experiences promises competitive advantage and an edge in securing market shares.

One increasingly popular angle of approach is to include customers into the creation of their own vacation experience and, thereby, the creation of value. This concept called "Customer Co-Creation" is not new. Yet, so far, its potential for a wide variety of tourism-related branches has not even remotely been used to its full extent by most.

Due to its nature, co-creation can be applied to generate new unique selling propositions in almost every branch of tourism industry. Knowing about the power

F.T. Piller • C. Gülpen (✉)
Technology and Innovation Management Group, RWTH Aachen University, Aachen, Germany
e-mail: piller@time.rwth-aachen.de; guelpen@time.rwth-aachen.de

© Springer-Verlag Berlin Heidelberg 2016   413
R. Egger et al. (eds.), *Open Tourism*, Tourism on the Verge,
DOI 10.1007/978-3-642-54089-9_33

of creating an unforgettable experience not only for, but together with their guests and visitors holds a lot of untapped opportunities for most tourism managers.

In this chapter we will take a look at what co-creation with customers is and how it can be applied to tourism-related ventures. To do so we will give a number of examples of already existing cases of (tourism related) customer co-creation and explain why these special activities offered are suited to create additional value for the host. At the very end we also provide a large assortment of related literature for more in-depth reading on the subject of co-creation.

The examples given in this chapter cannot cover every branch and aspect of tourism industry. Doing so would far exceed the scope of this chapter. Rather, they are meant to give inspiring examples to those responsible for innovation in their respective tourism-related venture—from the manager of an international travel agency to the owner of a small restaurant in a holiday area.

2   The Theory: What Is Co-creation with Customers?

The term customer co-creation denotes an open innovation approach where customers actively take part in the design of a new offering. It is an active, creative, and social process between producers (retailers) and customers (users). While customers can become actively involved and take part in many activities along the value chain, the focus of this chapter is on engaging smart customers in the design of new services.

The main objective of a company engaging in co-creation is to enlarge its base of information about needs, applications, and solution technologies that resides in the domain of customers and users creation (Piller & Ihl, 2009; Ramaswamy & Gouillart, 2010). The methods used to achieve this objective include user idea contests (Ebner, Leimeister, Bretschneider, & Krcmar, 2008; Piller & Walcher, 2006; Füller, 2010), consumer opinion platforms (Hennig-Thurau, Gwinner, Walsh, & Gremler, 2004; Sawhney, Verona, & Prandelli, 2005), toolkits for user innovation (von Hippel & Katz, 2002; Franke & Piller, 2004), and communities for customer co-creation (Franke & Shah, 2003; Füller et al., 2008).

Note that there is a large difference between customer co-creation and the lead user concept as introduced by Eric von Hippel (1988). Lead users are intrinsically motivated to innovate, performing the innovation process autonomously and without any interaction with a manufacturer. It then is the task of the interested firm to identify and capture the resulting inventions. Our understanding of customer co-creation, in contrast, is built on a firm-driven strategy that facilitates interaction with its customers and users. Instead of just screening the user base to detect any existing prototypes created by lead users, the firm provides instruments and tools to a broader group of customers and potential customers to actively co-create a solution together (Ramirez, 1999).

Consider these examples of customer-creation in various industries:

- **Fujitsu Computers (FSC)**, a large IT hardware and infrastructure provider, organized an online idea contest for webmasters and IT professionals to get their ideas about how data centers will work in the future, what services will be required by users, and which topics will be of strategic importance. Participants were asked not just to provide needs but conceptual ideas for possible solutions. Participants became members of an innovation community, commenting on the ideas of others, developing ideas further, and providing suggestions for techno- logical realization. Despite a rather low monetary incentive (the best idea was rewarded 5000 Euro) and a high level of required technological expertise, more than 200 active users contributed to the contest—most of them during work time and with permission of their employer.

- **Emporia Telecom**, an Austrian mobile phone manufacturer, demonstrated in a recent co-creation contest that the user base for this kind of engagement is not just young web-savvy people, but also a much larger community of senior citizens. The task they identified was to develop age-specific mobile phones in terms of functionality and design. Using an online platform, users could submit ideas for both functional hardware features and innovative services. Contrarily to the beliefs of many, Emporia learned that senior customers are very willing to engage in an online co-creation project. Overall, more than 6000 users visited the contest site, spending more than 800 h there, and generated more than 200 highly elaborated ideas. Several ideas from the contest made it into prototyping and further development in the company (Leyhausen & Vossen, 2011).

- **Muji** is a Japanese specialty retail chain, selling all kind of consumer commo- dities, furniture, apparel, and food items (Ogawa & Piller, 2006). The company is famous in Europe for its powerful internal design practice; it continuously involves customers in product development. In its Japanese home market, the company receives more than 8000 suggestions for product improvements or new product ideas each month. Suggestions are sent on postcards attached to cata- logues, as e-mails, or via feedback forms on the company's website. On the sales floor, sales associates are encouraged to collect notes on customer behavior and short quotes from sales dialogues. But the most important means of interaction with its customers is its online community, Muji.net, with approximately 410,000 members. For evaluating new concepts and proposals, the company asks the opinion of its product managers, but also hosts a broad evaluation and collaborative decision process, asking its community to vote on the products which should be introduced next. Recent data shows that products that went through the screening of the crowd perform on average three times better than products that were selected by an internal steering committee.

What do these examples have in common? Despite a range of industries, different cultural contexts, and various target age groups, these examples show how firms can create value with large groups of customers and users, moving beyond workshops with selected lead users. We also see very different tasks, ranging from designing household items to creating functional technological concepts.

3 Practical Application: Inspiring Examples

In this part we will showcase a number of concrete examples of co-creation with customers within or closely related to the holiday industry. As said, these examples are meant to demonstrate how the general concept of co-creation can be applied to different sorts of tourism-related ventures. They should spark a thought to come up with new ideas how value can be created by integrating the traveler into one's own commercial offerings.

3.1 How Hotels Raise Brand Loyalty

One if not the most important asset in the travel industry is customer brand loyalty. It is relatively easy to attract new guests to one's own place by using glossy images and flowery descriptions. However, guests will decide whether or not he is going to come back—and whether or not their experiences will motivate him to recommend to their friends. For this reason, the guest's brand experience, which is tightly connected to the guest's product experience, is of outmost importance. Vacations, being the "best time of the year", need to be special in some, ideally in many ways. This realization has sparked a lot of interesting ideas for activities that, by getting travelers involved, increase their product experience and help to create brand loyalty.

One such activity has been offered by the **Viceroy Anguilla Hotel**. Realizing that tourists love to take home not only memorized experiences but also physical pictures of their travel location, the hotel has come up with some special idea: Not to photograph but to actually paint the beauty of the island's landscape. Since this tends to require slightly more skill than just taking a picture with one's camera, a specialist, modernist painter Lynne Bernbaum, guides interested guests through the process of painting a scene from the island.

This activity adds value to everybody involved. It offers the traveler a unique experience and something to take home besides the memories and the newly gained painting skills, namely the picture he painted. It also builds up brand loyalty if the guest enjoyed the experience and now memorizes the hotel at a place where offers beyond the standard are to be expected. Also, at a price of $45/person, these classes probably gain the hotel higher revenue than selling the standard postcard displaying the island's landscape.

Another very important part about any hotel-based holiday is the food you are served. However, eating at a hotel's restaurant has become a standard experience for many travelers by now and this part of the product experience will in most cases mainly depend on the chef's quality.

Given this, getting guests involved into this aspect of their stay sounds like a great opportunity to offer a special experience and, hence, create value.

Two examples of doing exactly this are the Oliverio Restaurant at Avalon Hotel, Beverly Hills, and the Cocoa Lab at Ritz-Carlton Hotel, Charlott. Both do invite their guests to participate in a unique cooking experience, preparing their own Italian pasta or desserts, respectively. These and other food-centered workshops are both a social activity and a learning experience and can easily be offered by many if not most hotel restaurants.

After all these cooking classes including consumption of the self-made food, some health-oriented guests might wish to spend some time in the hotel's gym. In case of the Crown Plaza, Copenhagen, though, this sportive activity might lead to even more eating and hence partially defeat its original purpose: The hotel offers guests free meals for using stationary bikes which have been modified to generate "green" energy that helps to power the hotel. A \$36 meal voucher requires the production of 10 watt-hours on the bike. During the exercise process, progress is being displayed to the guest.

While this offer will most likely not be suffice to significantly reduce the hotel's need for traditionally produced electricity, the idea has merit and offers travelers two extra incentives for sportive activities: free meals and a contribution to save the environment. This, combined with the experience of a non-traditional sports offer in itself can contribute to make the stay memorable and motivate to return.

3.2 The Pride of the Maker: Commodity Production with Consumers

Another approach to create value not only for but with customers is especially interesting for more rural areas. The traditional farm vacations with small children do still have their important place in exploiting these areas for tourism. During these, travelers typically carry out numerous activities to help farmers with the daily operation of their farm, like taking care of animals or cleaning out barns. However, another kind of agrarian tourism has great potential to complement these.

Applying the idea of co-creation on farm-related products, farms and wineries have begun to offer tourists (and locals) the opportunity to not only buy their goods but participate in their actual production. Guests help with the actual farm work or production process and get to take their own good home with them—at a fee.

One prominent example is that of self-produced wine. Wineries like the **Pasadena Neighborhood Winery** or **The Wine Foundry** offer personal involvement into custom wine production. Guests are invited to select the type of wine, help to sort, crush, ferment and press fruit, design packaging and custom labels, bottle and cork the wine and finally take the product home. The Wine Foundry even offers ways to monitor the growth progress of "your" wine by the means of weather updates and images.

The option to visit the winery and get physically involved into the production process adds additional value beyond just receiving individualized bottles of wine. The experience of helping to create the product themselves generates a feeling of pride and affiliation to not only the wine itself but also the winery and its staff, making the process an important part of the "product". Provided, of course, the production experience has been a pleasant and enjoyable one.

A similar experience is being promised by some **coffee farms** like those connected to the **agro ecotourism project** where tourists can visit coffee producing plantations in Nicaragua where they can stay with local families. Travelers are offered an "opportunity to get to know and share the everyday life, inclusive learning to cook typical dishes [. . . and] to participate in various cultural activities (music, theatre, crafts, etc.)." Furthermore, they can participate in the production process of coffee production, including harvesting, seeding and so on.

A comparable yet maybe not as "adventurous" example of creating value through co-creation with tourists is being offered to visitors of the Alps. The **Käseschule Allgäu** introduces their guests to learn how to produce their own cheese from fresh local milk. Besides being able to taste a lot of local cheese types—which is a great marketing opportunity—customers can take their own cheese home after completing of the workshop.

Local cheese producers in Bavaria take things one step further by inviting their guests to live the life of an alpine herdsman for the duration of 5 days, getting an exclusive and intense insight into the profession. This particular offering even receives funding from the State of Bavaria.

4 Key Conclusions and Learning Outcomes for the Tourism Industry

- Above we have presented a number of examples of offers made to tourists (and, partially, locals as well) that involve the guest into the process of value creation. This is being achieved by "outsourcing" parts of the production process to the customers who do either invest their work to create some sort of good that he can take away (self-painted images, self-made wine) or consume right on the spot (self-grilled steak) or into just the experience of the stay (farm vacations, sailing trip). In both cases, travelers are willing to engage in activities (which can sometimes even be considered work → farm vacations) *and* pay an extra to do so.
- This leads to the conclusion that there is a market for what can be called the proactive vacation. Tourists wanting to do more than just relax on poolside or visit some sights desire integration into activities that sometimes require a considerable amount of effort but leaves them with the proud feeling of having produced something themselves, be it a physical good or a special experience.

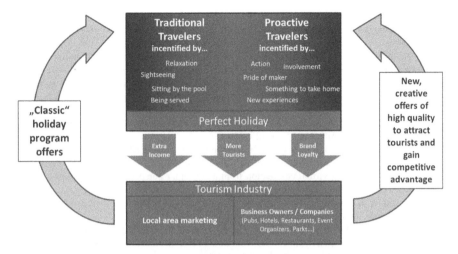

Fig. 1 The proactive vacation model: profiting from co-creating tourists

- Both local area marketing officials and business owners in tourism areas can profit from this realization. Knowing the openness of visitors to be involved into various activities can lay grounds for the creation of various offers that can in turn mean a considerable competitive advantage for both individual tourism businesses (hotels, restaurants...) and a tourism area as a whole.
- However, offering not just any activity *but the right ones* requires both excellent knowledge of the respective target group (including new, potential target groups) and the will to come up with new ideas that have not yet been offered by (a large number of locally close) competitors. Creativity in tapping this market segment can significantly increase the guest's product experience, thereby creating brand loyalty, customer satisfaction and, finally, value (Fig. 1).

References

Bullinger, A. C., Neyer, A. K., Rass, M., & Moeslein, K. M. (2010). Community-based innovation contests: Where competition meets cooperation. *Creativity and Innovation Management, 19*(3), 290–303.

Burkitt, L. (2010). Need to build a community? Learn from Threadless. *Forbes*, January 7, 2010. Online at http://bit.ly/8WYmdH

Diener, K., & Piller, F. T. (2010). *The market for open innovation*. Raleigh, NC: Lulu.

Ebner, W., Leimeister, M., Bretschneider, U., & Krcmar, H. (2008). Leveraging the wisdom of crowds: Designing an IT-supported ideas competition for an ERP software company. In *Proceedings of the 41st annual Hawaii international conference on system sciences (HICSS 2008)*.

Ebner, W., Leimeister, J. M., & Krcmar, H. (2009). Community engineering for innovations: The ideas competition as a method to nurture a virtual community for innovations. *R&D Management, 39*(4), 342–356.

Franke, N., & Piller, F. T. (2003). Key research issues in user interaction with user toolkits in a mass customization system. *International Journal of Technology Management, 26*(5), 578–599.

Franke, N., & Piller, F. T. (2004). Toolkits for user innovation and design: An exploration of user interaction and value creation. *Journal of Product Innovation Management, 21*(6), 401–415.

Franke, N., & Schreier, M. (2010). Why customers value self-designed products: The importance of process effort and enjoyment. *Journal of Product Innovation Management, 27*(7), 1020–1031.

Franke, N., Schreier, M., & Kaiser, U. (2010). The "I designed it myself" effect in mass customization. *Management Science, 56*(1), 125–140.

Franke, N., & Shah, S. (2003). How communities support innovative activities: An exploration of assistance and sharing among end-users. *Research Policy, 32*(1), 157–178.

Füller, J. (2010). Refining virtual co-creation from a consumer perspective. *California Management Review, 52*(2), 98–122.

Füller, J., Matzler, K., & Hoppe, M. (2008). Brand community members as a source of innovation. *Journal of Product Innovation Management, 25*(6), 608–619.

Hennig-Thurau, T., Gwinner, K. P., Walsh, G., & Gremler, D. D. (2004). Electronic word-of-mouth via consumer-opinion platforms: What motivates consumers to articulate themselves on the internet? *Journal of Interactive Marketing, 18*(1), 38–52.

Katz, R., & Allen, T. (1982). Investigating the not invented here (NIH) syndrome. *R&D Management, 12*(1), 7–19.

Leimeister, J. M., Huber, M., Bretschneider, U., & Krcmar, H. (2009). Leveraging crowdsourcing: Activation-supporting components for IT-based ideas competition. *Journal of Management Information Systems, 26*(1), 197–224.

Leyhausen, F., & Vossen, A. (2011). We could have known better – Consumer-oriented marketing in Germany's ageing market. In M. Boppel, S. Boehm, & S. Kunisch (Eds.), *From grey to silver* (pp. 175–184). Berlin: Springer.

O'Hern, M. S., & Rindfleisch, A. (2009). Customer co-creation: A typology and research agenda. In K. M. Naresh (Ed.), *Review of marketing research* (Vol. 6, pp. 84–106). Armonk, NY: Sharpe.

Ogawa, S., & Piller, F. T. (2006). Reducing the risks of new product development. *Sloan Management Review, 47*(Winter), 65–72.

Piller, F. T. (2010). *Ten reasons why I consider Quirky.com as best in crowdsourcing and open innovation.* MC&OI News (Web Blog), October 2010. http://mass-customization.blogs.com/mass_customization_open_i/2010/10/

Piller, F. T., & Ihl, C. (2009). *Open innovation with customers – Foundations, competences and international trends.* Expert study commissioned by the European Union, The German Federal Ministry of Research, and the European Social Fund. Published as part of the project "International Monitoring." Aachen: RWTH ZLW-IMA.

Piller, F. T., & Walcher, D. (2006). Toolkits for idea competitions: A novel method to integrate users in new product development. *R&D Management, 36*(3), 307–318.

Prandelli, E., Sawhney, M. S., & Verona, G. (2008). *Collaborating with customers to innovate: Conceiving and marketing products in the networking age.* New York: Edward Elgar.

Prandelli, E., Verona, G., & Raccagni, D. (2006). Diffusion of web-based product innovation. *California Management Review, 48*(4), 109–136.

Ramaswamy, V., & Gouillart, F. (2010). *The power of co-creation.* New York: Free Press.

Ramirez, R. (1999). Value co-production: Intellectual origins and implications for practice and research. *Strategic Management Journal, 20*(1), 49–65.

Saadi, S. (2010). T-shirts are just the start for Threadless. *Bloomberg Businessweek*, September 20, 2010 (pp. 24–26).

Salvador, F., de Holan, M., & Piller, F. T. (2009). Cracking the code of mass customization. *MIT Sloan Management Review, 50*(3), 71–78.

Sawhney, M., & Prandelli, E. (2000). Communities of creation: Managing distributed innovation in turbulent markets. *California Management Review, 42*(4), 24–54.

Sawhney, M., Verona, G., & Prandelli, E. (2005). Collaborating to create: The internet as a platform for customer engagement in product innovation. *Journal of Interactive Marketing, 19*(4), 4–17.

Thomke, S., & von Hippel, E. (2002). Customers as innovators: A new way to create value. *Harvard Business Review, 80*(4), 74–81.

Toubia, O., & Florès, L. (2007). Adaptive idea screening using consumers. *Marketing Science, 26*(3), 342–360.

von Hippel, E. (1988). *The sources of innovation*. Cambridge, MA: MIT Press.

von Hippel, E. (2005). *Democratizing innovation*. Cambridge, MA: MIT Press.

von Hippel, E., & Katz, R. (2002). Shifting innovation to users via toolkits. *Management Science, 48*(7), 821–833.

Working Customers in the Hotel Industry: And Why They Work

Kerstin Rieder, Marco Schröder, Isabel Herms, and Anita Hausen

Learning Objectives

- Demonstrate the development of a new type of consumer, the working customer
- Identify ways in which working customers contribute to the process of service delivery in hotels
- Reveal the relevance of customers' working conditions
- Explore the role of these working conditions for customer work motivation.

1 Introduction

The following investigation focuses on the trend towards a new type of consumer, the working customer (Voß & Rieder, 2005), namely in the hotel industry. Tasks that were previously carried out by employees are now outsourced more and more to customers. The main aim of the present work is to demonstrate the relevance of the customers' "working conditions" for their willingness to take over the role of the working customer.

K. Rieder (✉)
Aalen University, Aalen, Germany
e-mail: kerstin.rieder@hs-aalen.de

M. Schröder
Augsburg University, Augsburg, Germany

I. Herms
BAD GmbH Gesundheitsvorsorge und Sicherheitstechnik, Petersberg, Germany

A. Hausen
Ulm University, Ulm, Germany

© Springer-Verlag Berlin Heidelberg 2016   423
R. Egger et al. (eds.), *Open Tourism*, Tourism on the Verge,
DOI 10.1007/978-3-642-54089-9_34

The study presented here was part of the research project *Professionalization of Interactive Work* which included the collection and analysis of quantitative and qualitative data in various different fields of service work (Dunkel & Weihrich, 2012, 2013). The project was funded from 2008 to 2012 by the German Federal Ministry of Education and Research and the European Social Fund of the European Union. In this paper, the focus is on the quantitative data on customer "work motivation" in the hotel.

At the hotel, customers are subject to many expectations to take over activities that were previously carried out by employees. They often book their hotel room through the Internet, without the help of a service worker. In some hotels, check-in is done with a credit card and without the support of employees. Breakfast is usually no longer served by employees and instead, there is a buffet where customers serve themselves and at some hotels, customers even have to cook their own breakfast egg. They are also expected to cooperate when it comes to cleaning the rooms. They are, for instance, asked to indicate if towels should be cleaned by laying them on the floor. Finally, guests are often asked to evaluate the hotel in order to help the organization improve the service quality. Thus, customer contributions to the process of service delivery in the hotel industry may be part of the development of innovation processes, for example, if customers suggest new forms of service (open innovation, Chesbrough, 2003; Reichwald & Piller, 2009).

In the following analysis, various forms of customer participation to service creation and service delivery will be considered. Thus, activities which are part, and those which are not part of open innovation processes, will be covered.

2   The Working Customer Thesis

Research on the customer's active role dates back to the 1970s, with precursors as early as in 1930s.[1] Three different lines of research with little reference to each other can be identified. The aim of the working customer thesis was to synthesize the findings of these separate traditions (Voß & Rieder, 2005). The thesis refers to fundamental quantitative and qualitative changes in the relationship between enterprises and customers.

In many sectors, services are being replaced by self-service, often with the aid of self-service technology. Hence, customer contributions to the process of service delivery are changing quantitatively. Examples can be found at restaurant chains (self-service including cleaning up), in financial services (online banking; online brokering) at the railway (vending machines, tickets in the Internet), air traffic

---

[1] Banard published some early assumptions on the management of customers in which he largely puts customers on the same level as employees 1938 and further elaborated on them in a later text (see Barnard, 1940).

(e-ticket; check-in automats), at the hair dresser (self blow-dry) and in many other fields.

Moreover, customers not only serve themselves, they also work for other customers. Accordingly, the customers' contribution to service delivery is changing qualitatively. One example is the online retailer Amazon, where, customers advise other customers, for example by writing book and product reviews. They also evaluate private sellers who use Amazon's platform for their sales. Other examples are providers like Holidaycheck or Tripadvisor, where customers evaluate travel offers. Open innovation (including customers in the development of services or products) is also part of this qualitative change in the relationship between customers and enterprises.

An important driver of these quantitative and qualitative changes are technical innovations like Web 2.0 that allows new forms of collaboration between customers and enterprises (Kleemann, Voß, & Rieder, 2008).

The trend towards the working customer has far-reaching consequences, for customers as well as for enterprises (Voß & Rieder, 2005; Rieder & Voß, 2013). For customers, this means they conduct a completely new form of work in their private lives. This work is to a great extent characterized by the rules and resources of enterprises, thus jeopardizing customer privacy. Moreover, it is a kind of work that is usually unpaid, which entails the risk of working customers being exploited by profit-oriented enterprises. There is also the risk that specific groups of customers are excluded from self-services which require specific and sometimes quite advanced technical competencies (Rieder, Laupper, Dorsemagen, & Krause, 2008).

But for enterprises too, the integration of customers in the process of service delivery bears certain risks. In contrast to employees, customers are not subject to selection processes and do not have to present formal qualifications. There are also usually no customer development processes which would aid adaption to the expectations of enterprises (Gouthier, 2003). Hence, it is unclear to what extent the work of customers is in accordance with the quality standards of the enterprises. Moreover, it is far from certain that customers are motivated to carry out tasks that are given to them, according to the demands of the firm (Rieder & Voß, 2010; Hornung, Kleemann & Voß, 2011). The customer remains "unmanageable" (Gabriel & Lang, 2006).

However, the trend towards the working customer also entails new opportunities and advantages for customers and for enterprises. From the enterprise perspective, outsourcing to customers may offer major benefits: lower costs through reduction of complexity, higher productivity through more effective resource utilization, higher value of offerings through immaterial consumer labor and higher sales through recommendations (Cova & Dalli, 2009; Hornung et al., 2011; Reichwald & Piller, 2009). Moreover, especially co-creation and open innovation can enhance understanding of the needs and preferences of customers, or specific groups of customers, and increase the quality of products and services (Prahahalad & Ramaswamy, 2004; Reichwald & Piller, 2009). Furthermore, with open calls for user or customer contributions, enterprises may also gain substantial publicity, which sometimes seems to be a main reason for issuing such calls (Kleemann et al., 2008). From the perspective of customers, assuming the role of working customer may sometimes ultimately lower the prices of products and services through the input of this free labor. Especially co-design and open innovation can be seen as an opportunity to perform motivating and satisfying tasks, to unfold creativity and receive recognition. Moreover, open innovation may enable participation and the democratization of innovation (von Hippel, 2005; Reichwald & Piller, 2009; Rieder & Voß, 2013).

3 Customers' Working Conditions and Motivation

An important subject of research in the fields of work psychology and sociology is the humane design of working conditions. If customers are also workers, this raises the issue of their working conditions (Rieder, Matuschek, & Anderson, 2002; Schroer & Hertel, 2007). A consideration of customers' working conditions, as an aspect of service quality, seems important for several reasons:

- If it is expected that customers take over parts of the work, it is the enterprise's responsibility to establish appropriate structures. It is therefore necessary to consider that customers do not bring any formal qualifications to their work and form a quite heterogeneous group. Indeed, it is possible that customers use their exit-option if they are not content with working conditions that come with a specific service (Hirschman, 1970). However, for customers, this option is not always easy to implement if they really need the service. This requires a good overview of the features of different services and possible alternatives, and what is more, alternatives are not always available. The railways are a good example, for which in many regions, only one provider serves the market. If working conditions are not designed to suit the needs of all possible customers, there is the danger of some groups being excluded from the use of specific goods and services. In a study on the consequences of the spread of self-service technology for seniors, it was for example, shown that older people took long detours to find a station where tickets were still sold at the counter and not at the automat (Rieder et al., 2008). Others may not even be able to reach such a station at all.
- However, it is also in the interest of enterprises to offer really good working conditions to their customers, because it is likely that this may contribute to customer willingness to work. Studies on customers' or users' "work motivation" come from open-source and open-content projects like Linux or Wikipedia (Kleemann et al., 2008). They show that, although extrinsic motivators play some role (for example, career opportunities, Robles, Scheider, Tretkowski, & Weber, 2001), intrinsic motivation is especially predominant. A study based on the Job Characteristics Model (Hackman & Oldham, 1980) shows, that autonomy, task significance and skill variety are factors which, mediated by intrinsic motivation, are related to engagement in an open-content project (Schroer & Hertel, 2007).

In order to study the working conditions of customers, concepts from work psychology and ergonomics can be transferred to the specific situation of working customers. In this manner, a questionnaire for the analysis of customers' working conditions was developed. The questionnaire builds upon an existing one dealing with working conditions of patients in a hospital (Rieder, 2005) and was adapted to the situation of customers at a hotel. It contains five scales: control, disturbances, information, ambiance and emotional climate.

The first three scales refer to psychological action regulation theory which originally lay the ground for analyzing the working conditions of employees (Ulich, 2011). According to action regulation theory, control (decision latitude) on the one hand and barriers (like informational impediments, interruptions and time pressure) on the other hand, are key aspects of working conditions. There are many studies based on action regulation theory and similar models like the demand-control model or the job-demands-resources model, indicating that control at work has positive implications for worker health, their motivation and personal development. In contrast, barriers (or excessive demands) yield adverse effects for the physical and psychological wellbeing of employees (for example, Leitner & Resch, 2005, for an overview, see Backé, Seidler, Latza, Rossnagel, & Schumann, 2012; Nieuwenhuijsen, Bruinvels, & Frings-Dresen, 2010; Ulich, 2011). The questionnaire analyzes these working conditions as follows:

- *Control*: This scale covers control as regards the content and temporal planning of customers during service consumption and active contribution to service delivery. It examines whether and to what extent customers have the opportunity to realize their own ideas.
- *Disturbances*: This scale covers problems and hindrances during both service consumption and active contribution to service delivery (for example, interruptions or time pressure)
- *Information*: This scale examines whether customers receive all necessary information during service consumption and active contribution to service delivery. Lack of information is seen as a barrier to action regulation.

With reference to the results of studies in the field of paid work as well as results on the motivation of users working in open-source and open-content projects (see above), it is asserted that *control* is positively related to the customer readiness to become working customers. In contrast, it is assumed that disturbances as well as a lack of information impede the customers' action regulation and are negatively related to the customers' work motivation.

As another aspect of customers' working conditions, the ambiance at the enterprise is taken into account. This refers to the examination of the work environment in the field of ergonomics (Schlick, Bruder, & Luczak, 2010). Service science also assumes that the ambience at the service enterprise is an important aspect of service quality. The familiar instrument for analyzing service quality, SERVQUAL (Parasuraman, Zeithaml, & Berry, 1985), refers to it as "tangibles". Studies on the relevance of tangibles often refer to customer perceptions of background music (for an overview, see Nerdinger, 2011). In the questionnaire, ambiance is examined as follows:

- *Ambiance*: This scale refers to the quality of the spatial conditions of service delivery. It covers the customers' evaluation of cleanliness and neatness, as well as the subjective experience of spatiality.

It is assumed that a high quality ambiance is positively related to customers' work motivation.

As a final aspect of working conditions, emotions during service delivery are considered. Research on service work shows that emotions play an important role during service interaction (for an overview, see Nerdinger, 2011; Dunkel & Weihrich, 2013). In contrast to classic work in the field of industry and administration, interactive service work requires *emotion work* (Hochschild, 1983) and *sentimental work* (Strauss, Fagerhaugh, Suczek, & Wiener, 1982). While sentimental work means that workers influence the feelings of customers (or patients and clients), emotion work describes the employees' management of their own feelings. It is asserted that employees, through emotion work and sentimental work, create an emotional climate that may be considered as one aspect of customers' working conditions. It is further assumed that this emotional climate is related not only to customers' readiness to use the service in the future, but also to their work motivation. In the questionnaire, emotion climate is examined as follows:

- *Emotional climate*: In this scale, customers are asked how they experience the emotional climate, to what extent employees try to manage their own emotions, as well as understand and favorably influence customers' emotions.

In order to analyze the relationships between customers' working conditions and their willingness to perform work in their role as customers, one further scale that examines willingness to work was developed. This willingness means that customers are ready to take part in the process of service delivery to an extent that exceeds what is just merely unavoidable. Customers may contribute to the process of service delivery by taking over specific and genuinely useful activities like cleaning up their table after breakfast. Moreover, customers can also perform valuable emotion work and sentimental work (Dunkel & Rieder, 2003; Weihrich, 2011), for example by cheering up a frustrated service worker after having witnessed an unpleasant interaction with this worker and another customer. In the questionnaire, the customers' willingness to work is examined as follows:

- *Willingness to work*: Customers are asked whether they are willing to actively contribute to the process of service delivery to an extent that exceeds what is an avoidable. These contributions include instrumental work, as well as emotion work and sentimental work, and they refer to tasks for which employees are usually responsible.

4 Methods

The study was conducted in different German cities at Accor Hotels, which was one of the three partner companies in the research project *Professionalization of Interactive Work*. Accor Hotels owns standardized as well as non-standardized brands. While the standardized hotels comprise budget, economy and midscale brands, the non-standardized (or less standardized) hotels range from the midscale to the luxury segment. Standardized brands are especially useful for research on the process of outsourcing to the customer, because new forms of rationalization and standardization in the service industry often mean putting customers to work (McDonaldization, Ritzer, 1983, 2001). For the study at hand, five hotels from three standardized brands at different price-levels (from budget to midscale) were chosen. This meant that different "tasks" were expected from customers, depending on the hotel brand (Hoffmann, Menz, Hausen, Schill, & Schröder, 2012). For example, the Etap hotels (now called Ibis-Budget) provide only very basic services and expect that customers pay for their room in advance either at the lobby or via self-check-in with their credit card (if they arrive late). There is a very basic self-service buffet-breakfast. In contrast, the economy brand Ibis provides a lobby that is occupied around the clock and the rooms are paid for in the morning at the lobby. However, to date, many contributions of the customer to the process of service delivery are common at hotels of all the brands comprising the sample. For example, customers book their room through the Internet, serve themselves at the breakfast buffet and evaluate the service quality of the hotel with a questionnaire before they leave.

For the present study, customers of Accor Hotels completed the questionnaire on working conditions and on their role as working customers, resulting in 84 valid questionnaires (purged return rate: 43.7 %.). The questionnaire assessed customers' working conditions as described in the previous section, as well as their willingness to act as working customers. All scales comprise five points and range from almost never / not appropriate (1) to almost always / very appropriate (5). An overview of the scales, with a sample item and the reliability (Cronbachs α) for each scale is shown in Table 1.

In order to investigate the relationships between customers' working conditions and willingness to work, correlations were calculated and multiple regression analyses conducted.

5 Results

The results show that customers in the hotel are basically willing to act as working customers. The mean of the scale *willingness to work* is 3.69 (standard deviation: 0.57). Higher values indicate greater acceptance and the mean is clearly above the center of the scale. The high level of the customer readiness to contribute to service

Table 1 Overview of questionnaire scales on customers' working conditions and willingness to work

Scale	Example	Number of items	Cronbachs α
Control	Even in the case of special requests, employees try to find a solution	7	0.84
Disturbances	At the hotel, disturbing interruptions to my conversations with employees take place (e.g. by other employees or customers)	5	0.76
Information	At the hotel, customers get informed about everything important in a comprehensible way	4	0.76
Ambiance	The spatial design of the hotel is appealing	4	0.88
Emotional Climate	For the employees, it is really important that customers feel good at the hotel	4	0.84
Willingness to work	It happens that I take over tasks for which employees are actually responsible	10	0.75

delivery is also reflected in the frequencies: About one third of the customers (34.5 %) have values of 4.0 ("often / quite appropriate") or higher on the scale willingness to work.

The correlations show that there are indeed relationships between customers' working conditions and their willingness to contribute to the process of service delivery. All correlations except those for disturbances are statistically significant (see Table 2).

In the next step, multiple regression analysis was performed with those working conditions that showed significant correlations with the customers' willingness to work as predictors. The results demonstrate that control, information, ambiance and emotional climate indeed significantly predict the willingness to be working customers (adjusted $R^2 = 0.65$, see Table 3). Moreover, one significant single predictor, emotional climate, was revealed. Overall, the results confirm the relevance of customers' working conditions for their willingness to contribute actively to service delivery.

Thus, the study shows that concepts for the analysis of paid work are also important for the working customer. This confirms results from other studies on the customers' (or the users') work motivation (see Sect. 3).

The results also indicate that for customers at the hotel, the emotional climate is of particular importance for their work motivation. It seems that beside the usual features of work tasks, emotional aspects of the service interaction are important for customer willingness to actively participate in service delivery. This aspect has, to the best of our knowledge, not been included in previous studies on customers' or users' work motivation.

Thus, despite or maybe because of the distinct trend towards a standardization of work in the hotel business, more attention should be paid to emotions in service interactions. Employees should manage their own emotions and they should consider and take customers' emotions into account. With reference to research results

Table 2 Correlations between the customers' working conditions and their willingness to work

Customers' working conditions	Willingness to work
Control	0.35**
Disturbances	−0.04
Information	0.43**
Ambiance	0.37**
Emotional climate	0.77**

$*p < 0.05$, $**p < 0.01$

Table 3 Multiple regression on customers' willingness to work

Working conditions	Willingness to work
Adjusted R^2	0.65**
Beta-coefficients:	
Control	n.s.
Information	n.s.
Ambiance	n.s.
Emotional climate	0.71**

$*p < 0.05$, $**p < 0.01$

on emotion work and burnout however, emotional dissonance (the discrepancy between felt and displayed emotions) should be avoided. Emotional dissonance is known as a predictor of burnout (Zapf & Holz, 2006).

One practical result of the research project *Professionalization of Interactive Work* was the training program *Emofit*® as part of the doctoral dissertation of Isabel Herms (Herms, 2012). This training supports employees in managing their emotions in service interactions and preventing emotional dissonance. *Emofit*® was developed and put to the test in work for nursing homes for the elderly.

With reference to the results of the study at hand, *Emofit*® could well be adapted to the hotel business. If work is being outsourced to the customer, this should be done in a way that is acceptable and agreeable to customers. This means that a service option should be available for customers who are not able or willing to use the self-service. It also means that the working customer's work should be designed so that it is motivating. The study also shows that the management of emotions during service interactions seems to be an important aspect of all this.

However, the study has some limitations. It is cross-sectional, so that no causal influence of working conditions on customer work motivation can be tested. Moreover, it has a relatively small and specific sample, so that it is unclear, whether the results can be transferred to other hotels or even other industry sectors. From research in the care of the elderly for example, it seems that working conditions are less important for relatives' willingness to take over part of the instrumental work at homes for the elderly (Rieder, Schröder, Herms, & Hausen, 2012). One other limitation of this study concerns the employees. The focus of the study was on the working conditions of customers. However, the working conditions of *employees* and the question of whether their working conditions enable them to provide good working conditions for customers were not considered and cannot be covered. It is also not possible to discuss here, whether the trend towards the working customer is desirable from the perspective of society as a whole. With reference to the results presented, it seems that one aspect which is quite important for answering that question is whether enterprises should and can design favorable working conditions for customers and especially a favorable emotional climate. Hence, in the future, customers' working conditions should be taken into account systematically if service quality is addressed.

6 Key Conclusions and Learning Outcomes for the Tourism Industry

- Customers at hotels are to a considerable degree willing to serve as working customers.
- Customers' working conditions significantly predict the willingness to become working customer at the hotel.
- Enterprises in the hotel business, which outsource tasks to customers, should take into account customers' working conditions, especially the emotional climate.
- Training programs like Emofit® may help to empower employees to manage emotions during service interactions without risking emotional dissonance and burnout.
- In future studies, customers' working conditions should be taken into account systematically as aspects of service quality. Especially the role of emotional climate for customers' work motivation should be analyzed in greater detail.

Acknowledgements We thank Dr. Brian Bloch for his accurate and articulate editing of the manuscript. We also wish to thank Nadine Rauer for her support with the formatting of the manuscript and, last but not least, all the (working and non-working) customers who participated at the study.

References

Backé, E.-M., Seidler, A., Latza, U., Rossnagel, K., & Schumann, B. (2012). The role of psychosocial stress at work for the development of cardiovascular diseases: A systematic review. *International Archives of Occupational and Environmental Health, 85*, 67–79.

Barnard, C. I. (1940). Comments on the job of the executive. *Harvard Business Review, 18*(3), 295–308.

Chesbrough, H. W. (2003). *Open innovation. The new imperative for creating and profiting from technology*. Boston, MA: Harvard Business School Press.

Cova, B., & Dalli, D. (2009). Working consumers: The next step in marketing theory? *Marketing Theory, 9*(3), 315–339.

Dunkel, W., & Rieder, K. (2003). Interaktionsarbeit zwischen Konflikt und Kooperation. In A. Büssing & J. Glaser (Eds.), *Qualität des Arbeitslebens und Dienstleistungsqualität im Krankenhaus. Schriftenreihe "Organisation und Medizin"* (pp. 163–180). Göttingen: Hogrefe.

Dunkel, W., & Weihrich, M. (Hrsg.). (2012). *Interaktive Arbeit. Theorie, Praxis und Gestaltung von Dienstleistungsbeziehungen*. Wiesbaden: Springer VS.

Dunkel, W., & Weihrich, M. (2013). Interactive work: A theoretical and empirical approach to the study of service interactions. In W. Dunkel & F. Kleemann (Eds.), *Customers at work. New perspectives on interactive service work* (pp. 49–75). Houndmills: Palgrave Macmillan.

Gabriel, Y., & Lang, T. (2006). *The unmanageable consumer* (2nd ed.). London: Sage.

Gouthier, M. H. (2003). *Kundenentwicklung im Dienstleistungsbereich*. Wiesbaden: Deutscher Universitätsverlag.

Hackman, J. R., & Oldham, G. R. (1980). *Work redesign*. Reading, MA: Addison-Wesley.

Herms, I. (2012). Emofit® – Erprobung und Evaluation eines Trainings für Pflegekräfte zum angemessenen Umgang mit den eigenen Emotionen. *Plexus, 20*, 47–54.

von Hippel, E. (2005). *Democratizing innovation*. Cambridge, MA: The MIT.

Hirschman, A. O. (1970). *Exit, voice and loyalty. Responses to decline in firms, organizations and states*. Cambridge, MA: Harvard University Press.

Hochschild, A. (1983). *The managed heart. Commercialization of human feeling*. Berkeley, CA: University of California Press.

Hoffmann, A., Menz, W., Hausen, A., Schill, S., & Schröder, M. (2012). Interaktive Arbeit in der Hotellerie: zwischen Offenheit und Standardisierung. In W. Dunkel & M. Weihrich (Eds.), *Interaktive Arbeit. Theorie, Praxis und Gestaltung von Dienstleistungsbeziehungen* (pp. 219–258). Wiesbaden: VS-Verlag.

Hornung, S., Kleemann, F., & Voß, G. G. (2011). Managing a new consumer culture: „Working consumers" in Web 2.0 as a source of corporate feedback. In V. Wittke & H. Hanekop (Eds.), *New forms of collaborative innovation and production on the Internet. An interdisciplinary perspective* (pp. 131–152). Göttingen: Universitätsverlag Göttingen.

Kleemann, F., Voß, G. G., & Rieder, K. (2008). Un(der)paid innovators: The commercial utilization of consumer work through crowdsourcing. *Science, Technology & Innovation Studies, 4*(1). Retrieved from: www.sti-studies.de. October 10, 2008.

Leitner, K., & Resch, M. (2005). Do the Effects of Job Stressors on Health Persist over Time? A longitudinal study with observational stressor measures. *Journal of Occupational Health Psychology, 10*, 18–30.

Nerdinger, F. W. (2011). *Psychologie der Dienstleistung*. Göttingen: Hogrefe.

Nieuwenhuijsen, K., Bruinvels, D., & Frings-Dresen, M. (2010). Psychosocial work environment and stress-related disorders, a systematic review. *Occupational Medicine, 60*, 277–286.

Parasuraman, A., Zeithaml, V. A., & Berry, L. L. (1985). A conceptual model of service quality and its implications for future research. *Journal of Marketing, 49*(4), 41–50.

Prahalad, C. K., & Ramaswamy, V. (2004). Co-creation experiences: The next practice in value creation. *Journal of Interactive Marketing, 18*(3), 5–14.

Reichwald, R., & Piller, F. unter Mitarbeit von Ihl, C., & Seifert, S. (2009). *Interaktive Wertschöpfung: Open Innovation, Individualisierung und neue Formen der Arbeitsteilung* (2. überarb. Aufl.). Wiesbaden: Gabler.

Rieder, K. (2005). Ko-Produktion im Krankenhaus: Entwicklung eines Verfahrens zur Analyse der Handlungsbedingungen von Patientinnen und Patienten. *Zeitschrift für Arbeitswissenschaft, 59*(2), 111–119.

Rieder, K., Laupper, E., Dorsemagen, C., & Krause, A. (2008). Die Ausbreitung von Selbstbedienungstechnologien und die Konsequenzen im Alltag von Seniorinnen und Senioren. In E. Maier & P. Roux (Eds.), *Seniorengerechte Schnittstellen zur Technik* (pp. 168–175). Lengerich: Pabst.

Rieder, K., Matuschek, I., & Anderson, P. (2002). Co-production in call centres: The workers' and customers' contribution. In U. Holtgrewe, C. Kerst, & K. Shire (Eds.), *Re-organising service work: Call centres in Germany and Britain* (pp. 204–227). Aldershot, Hampshire: Ashgate.

Rieder, K., Schröder, M., Herms, I., & Hausen, A. (2012). Warum arbeiten die arbeitenden Kunden? In W. Dunkel & M. Weihrich (Eds.), *Interaktive Arbeit. Theorie, Praxis und Gestaltung von Dienstleistungsbeziehungen* (pp. 105–118). Wiesbaden: VS-Verlag.

Rieder, K., & Voß, G. G. (2010). The working customer – An emerging new type of consumer. *Psychology of Everyday Activity, 3*(2), 2–10.

Rieder, K., & Voß, G. G. (2013). The working customer – A fundamental change in service work. In W. Dunkel & F. Kleemann (Eds.), *Customers at work. New perspectives on interactive service work* (pp. 177–196). Houndmills: Palgrave.

Ritzer, G. (1983). The "McDonaldization" of society. *Journal of American Culture, 6*, 100–197.

Ritzer, G. (2001). *Explorations in the sociology of consumption: Fast food, credit cards and casinos*. London: Pine Forge.

Robles, G., Scheider, H., Tretkowski, I., & Weber, N. (2001). *Who is doing it? A research on Libre software developers*. Retrieved from http://widi.berlios.de/paper/study.pdf. October 10, 2008.

Schlick, C., Bruder, R., & Luczak, H. (2010). *Arbeitswissenschaft* (3. vollst. überarb. und erw. Aufl.). Berlin: Springer.

Schroer, J., & Hertel, G. (2007). *Voluntary engagement in an open web-based encyclopedia: Wikipedians, and why they do it*. Retrieved from http://www.abo.psychologie.uni-wuerzburg.de/virtualcollaboration/publications.php?action=view&id=44. October 10, 2008.

Strauss, A., Fagerhaugh, S., Suczek, B., & Wiener, C. (1982). Sentimental work in the technologized hospital. *Sociology of Health and Illness, 4*(3), 254–278.

Ulich, E. (2011). *Arbeitspsychologie* (6. Aufl.). Zürich: vdf.

Voß, G. G., & Rieder, K. (2005). *Der arbeitende Kunde. Wenn Konsumenten zu unbezahlten Mitarbeitern werden*. Frankfurt a.M: Campus.

Weihrich, M. (2011). Interaktive Arbeit – Zur Soziologie der Dienstleistungsbeziehung. In: Jeschke, S. (Hrsg.), *Innovation im Dienste der Gesellschaft*. Beiträge des 3. Zukunftsforums Innovationsfähigkeit des BMBF (S. 475–484). Frankfurt a.M.: Campus.

Zapf, D., & Holz, M. (2006). On the positive and negative effects of emotion work in organizations. *European Journal of Work and Organizational Psychology, 15*, 1–28.

Innovation for Volunteer Travel: Using Crowdsourcing to Create Change

Thomas Kohler, Anna Stribl, and Daniel Stieger

Learning Objectives

- Understand the challenges of volunteer travel
- Realize the necessity to innovate current business models in volunteer travel
- Explore how the community of *travel2change* works
- Demonstrate how crowdsourcing encourages collaboration between travellers and local communities
- Explain how business models in volunteer travel can leverage crowdsourcing effectively

1 Introduction

For school-leavers, students and early professionals it is becoming more common to take a gap year before starting a career. Some gap year students want to do community service at home, while others choose to travel or work abroad. In recent years a combination of travel and volunteer work has soared: volunteer tourism. Promoted as an opportunity to link holidays with a social, environmental or cultural purpose (Wearing, 2001), volunteer travel is generally situated within the field of alternative tourism and tends to have a positive connotation. However, critics argue that volunteer travel oftentimes merely benefits the travellers and fails to create a

T. Kohler (✉)
Hawaii Pacific University, Honolulu, HI, USA

University of Innsbruck, Innsbruck, Austria
e-mail: tkohler@hpu.edu

A. Stribl • D. Stieger
University of Innsbruck, Innsbruck, Austria
e-mail: a.stribl@outlook.com; daniel.stieger@uibk.ac.at

© Springer-Verlag Berlin Heidelberg 2016
R. Egger et al. (eds.), *Open Tourism*, Tourism on the Verge,
DOI 10.1007/978-3-642-54089-9_35

positive impact for local communities. Reasons range from ethical and cultural clashes, travellers arrogance and their ignorance of the local situation, lack of understanding for the real problems (especially on short-term placements) or one-sided volunteer trips that do not fit the environment (Sin, 2009). With the rising interest and popularity of volunteer travel and the growing number of volunteer travel providers, there is a need for innovation towards a more comprehensive approach to volunteer travel that truly benefits local communities. We propose that crowdsourcing can be a promising strategy for volunteer travel to tap into users' innovative potential, encourage interaction between travellers and local communities, and facilitate an open and transparent innovation process. To understand the full potential of crowdsourcing for volunteer travel, this case study investigates the community of travel2change—a platform to connect travellers and locals to create change (Travel2change, 2014).

2 Main Product Offering and Value Added

While volunteer travel was typically linked to charitable and non-profit organizations, the market structure has significantly changed over the past years (Benson, 2011). Attracted by the rapidly growing volunteer travel market, profit-making companies are pushing into the market to offer diversified volunteer travel programmes. Usually, everyone can participate in volunteer travel programmes, such as teenagers, students, postgraduates, families, corporate groups or retirees (Alexander & Bakir, 2011). The volunteer component of these programmes involves a wide range of activities, such as community development, education and teaching, environmental conservation, historic preservation, construction, medical aid or technical assistance (Brown, 2005). Volunteer travel providers are highly segmenting and targeting their service portfolio to different customer needs for all ages. Volunteer travel programmes can range, for example, from a 2-week volunteer adventure holiday in Costa Rica where volunteer travel becomes an easy adventure, all the way to a long-term volunteer placement in an orphanage in Cambodia that demands a great deal of altruistic motivation.

The value added depends upon the motivation of volunteer travellers for going abroad and the actual volunteer travel programme. There are volunteer travelers, who are primarily searching for leisure, fun and excitement (Sin, 2009), appreciate to explore the host country in both a comfortable and challenging way, to get to know local people and to have a good time during their volunteer travel placement. The key values provided for volunteer travellers, who want to actively contribute to local communities (Sin, 2009), are the opportunity to add a real purpose to their experience and to collaborate and interact with the local community rather than being a mere traveller. For locals, the value may be created by getting support from experienced and skilled travellers to solve certain problems in their community. The extent to which volunteer travel fosters sustainable development in local communities is closely linked to the business model of a volunteer travel provider and its programmes offered (Ingram, 2011).

3 Business Model and Need for Innovation

A business model explains the process of how an organization generates value (value creation) and the way it captures some of this value as profit (value capture) (Zott, Amit, & Massa, 2011). Volunteer travel providers create value as mediators between travellers and locals, bringing together two parties by considering their mutual expectations. For travellers they offer a portfolio of viable trips, assist in selecting appropriate programmes according to travellers' interests, establish the first contact between them and the local community in the destination and support them during the trip. For local communities volunteer travel providers present their offers and help to raise awareness and recruit volunteers.

However, profit-oriented companies in the volunteer travel market are built on a business model that capitalizes on volunteers' willingness to help but ends in rich profit streams (Magretta, 2002). The focus of volunteer travel providers has increasingly concentrated on the economic value added to the providers rather than on the social value captured for local communities in developing countries. As a result, the market of volunteer travel was partially transformed into a commercial business based on mass tourism (Tomazos & Butler, 2009). Rather than getting paid for their work, volunteer travellers are charged substantial fees for their volunteer placement, as the emphasis is rather on profit making than on volunteering and funding development programmes (Fee & Mdee, 2011). In the worst-case scenario volunteer travel providers exploit both volunteer travellers and local communities. The current business models of volunteer travel providers are to a great extent insufficient and do not benefit local communities in the long run. We suggest crowdsourcing-based business models to overcome the dilemma in volunteer travel.

4 Creating a Crowdsourcing-Based Business Model

The term "crowdsourcing" was coined by Jeff Howe (Howe, 2006). He describes crowdsourcing as the act of a company or institution taking a function once performed by employees and outsourcing it to an undefined (and generally large) network of people in the form of an open call. An organizer invites a targeted group of people to perform certain tasks in order to create value. With the maturation of new internet technologies—above all the emergence of social networks and collaboration software—this new form of value creation can be organized and orchestrated by means of online platforms.

With the rise of successful crowdsourcing initiatives (see Surowiecki, 2004; Howe, 2008), a crowdsourcing platform can act as the intermediary between volunteer travellers and local communities—without a commercial tour operator in between. This should empower both, volunteer travellers and local communities to create a collective impact, as they can directly communicate and collaborate via the platform.

To understand how business models in volunteer travel can leverage crowd-sourcing effectively, we present the case of travel2change. Travel2change's mission is to enable their community members to create change while travelling. By crowdsourcing the activities traditionally performed by volunteer travel providers, travel2change innovates the way volunteer travellers can connect with locals. Travel2change should inspire travellers to use their passion in order to share and discuss experiences together with local communities. Travelling becomes more meaningful and local communities benefit from travellers' activities.

Inspired by the power of collaboration, travel2change was launched as an online crowdsourcing platform in 2011. As shown in Figure 1, the travel2change process starts with an open call for local hosts to participate in challenges and for travellers to join meaningful travel experiences. Challenges can be at different stages of the innovation process—from idea creation, selection, pilot to scale. Local hosts and non-profit organizations submit experience ideas and thus create a portfolio of potential experiences. During the next stage, platform members can discuss, vote

Fig. 1 Travel2change web page (*Source*: Travel2change, 2014)

Table 1 The business model canvas—travel2change

Key partners	Key activities	Value propositions	Customer relationships	Customer segments
Stakeholders in the tourism industry including airlines, hotels and travel agencies	Provide platform where community connects and creates experiences	Making travel meaningful by enabling travelers to use their passion to create a positive impact during their trip	Travelers are active community members shaping experiences and sharing reviews	Responsible travelers who booked a trip and seek meaningful activities
Tourism agencies seeking to improve destinations	Inspire and support taking action	Making travel beneficial by enabling locals to find passionate travelers to work with	Network of local individuals and nonprofits who supply and shape projects	Locals (individuals and organizations) who benefit from travelers' support
	Key Resources		**Channels**	
	User profiles	Travel industry can improve destination offer	Crowdsourcing platform that builds connections and fosters collaboration	
	Experiences content			
	Platform technology		Ambassadors building network locally	

Cost structure		Revenue streams	
• IT		• Sponsored challenges	
• Marketing costs		• Sponsored content	
• Travel costs		• Travel partnerships	
• Grant expenses		• Technology licensing	

Source: Osterwalder and Pigneur (2009)

and refine experience ideas in order to make them more concrete and evaluate their viability. According to their interest, travellers can discover various experiences by means of searching and filtering mechanisms on the platform. Furthermore, they can directly get into contact with the local community. Next, it is about making the experience ideas happen. Reviews document the progress of an experience to make it sustainable and beneficial for local communities. Hosts and travellers can organize and support themselves by focusing on a specific theme. An example is the travel2change "Sports Challenge" that raises the question of how travellers can use sports to create a positive impact during their trip. The "Sports Challenge" is an open call to submit ideas that link sports and travel to create change. Both hosts and travellers co-create ideas, share and discuss experiences and specify how to realize them effectively. As a result travellers can join meaningful sports experiences provided by local hosts. Another example is the travel2change "Hawaii Challenge". Non-profit organizations and individual community members are invited to create and share meaningful travel experiences that benefit their local community, for instance a clean-up of hiking trails. Travellers can join the travel experiences and create a positive impact during their trip to Hawaii.

In the following we outline how travel2change integrates a crowdsourcing approach into the key elements of its business model (Osterwalder & Pigneur, 2009). We describe how travel2change creates, communicates, delivers and captures value (Table 1).

4.1 Customer Segments

Travel2change serves the two main customer segments of travellers and local hosts. Typical travel2change travellers can be profiled as follows: they are males and females in their twenties and early thirties, have an above average education (often university students, or recent graduates in their first job) with a low to medium income but increasing salaries. They are socially responsible, open minded, adventurous, enjoy travelling and seek personal satisfaction. They are extensive internet users and connected through social media and smart phones. Local hosts are the other side of the two-sided crowdsourcing platform. Locals can be individuals, groups or organizations located in the travel destination. Organizations are typically local grassroots non-profits. Locals show a deep understanding of their needs and problems combined with the drive to find solutions and improve the living conditions of the local community. They are open to host volunteer travellers and are optimistic to benefit from travellers activities.

4.2 Value Propositions

The core service of travel2change is the online platform that brings travellers and locals together around meaningful travel experiences. Travel2change helps travellers to (1) Find meaningful travel experiences that fit their itineraries and interests, (2) select a meaningful travel experience based on reviews and communication with the local host, (3) join a meaningful travel experience and (4) share reviews. Local hosts, such as non-profit organizations, can (1) raise awareness regarding the need they want to meet and draw attention to their mission, (2) develop their experience with the help of the travel2change community, (3) gain support and find travellers to support them.

4.3 Channels

Travel2change delivers the value proposition to its customers primarily online. The community platform is focused on providing a compelling user experience where knowledge can be shared and problems are solved collaboratively. It offers community functionality, interaction opportunities and a seamless integration with key social media channels. This allows travel2change to reach and co-create value with travellers and locals in ways that are interactive, fast and cost-effective.

4.4 Customer Relationships

The crowdsourcing approach of travel2change turns its users into active co-creators. Local hosts are not primarily recipients of aid, but are empowered to share their problems, showcase their challenges and lead a conversation about tourism development within their destination. Rather than consuming a trip designed by tour operators, travellers are enabled to co-create their own experience customized to their own passion, skills and interests.

4.5 Key Resources

The most important asset of travel2change is the vital community and the personal relationship with its most active key users, who are continuously creating valuable content on the platform. The online community allows travel2change to reach both travellers and local communities to foster social innovation through demand-driven, well-elaborated social and environmental experiences. Furthermore, travel2change built up technical capabilities to run the platform and steadily adapt to new requirements emerging. A strong focus is given to the integration of existing web-technologies.

4.6 Key Activities

The core activity of travel2change is to connect people to experiences in places around the world to create change. In doing so travel2change enables its community to create new experiences and aggregate existing ones, provide support (connections, information and resources) to move from idea to impact and encourage sharing of reviews. The supporting activities consist of community building (recruiting new members, providing editorial content to increase traffic, providing relevant resources) and platform building and management (improving design, adding features, fixing bugs, increasing usability and simplicity).

4.7   Key Partners

Various stakeholders in the travel industry are key for the success of travel2change. Travel companies are crucial to recruit a substantial numbers of travellers, who do not just travel, but travel2change. Universities, clubs and societies can serve as multipliers for marketing efforts. Due to the interest of governments and tourism authorities to create attractive destinations, the travel2change platform is a source of inspiration and a channel to create new solutions to challenges in a destination. Accommodation and transportation partners are particularly relevant to realize experiences. Local NPO's are crucial strategic partners to create and realize experiences according to local needs and circumstances in order to ensure sustainability and long-term impact.

4.8   Revenue Streams

One revenue stream results from partnering with organizations as sponsors of a travel2change challenge. The topic of the challenge is aligned with the CSR strategy of the sponsoring company or the mission of an organization. Organizations can tap into the global and active community to create and realize experiences that create change. The organization pays a fee to use the travel2change platform and provides the challenge reward. A second revenue stream comes from sponsored content where travel2change displays sponsored experiences along with user-generated content.

4.9   Cost Structure

The most important cost drivers are in the area of IT (server, licence costs and platform development costs), marketing (print and other promotion material), travel costs (team and project coordination) and grant expenses (supporting winning experiences and local non-profits).

5   Key Challenges for the Future

Regardless of the promising opportunities provided by crowdsourcing for volunteer travel, realizing it is not without challenges.

5.1   Engaging a Critical Mass of Users

One of the first challenges for crowdsourcing is building a crowd to sustain the business model. Many crowdsourcing initiatives are stillborn, because they fail to attract enough users who are willing and capable to co-create content. Marketplaces oriented platforms face similar issues: buyers want more sellers and vice versa. Travel2change started slowly, facing the critical mass problem that all crowd-sourcing platforms are confronted with. The engineered platform provides the base, but building the crowd is a time-intensive marketing challenge that requires resources and dedication. For travel2change to reach its potential, it is key that the users are engaged in a compelling process, appropriate incentives foster their motivation and collaboration is faciliated, so that the community collaboratively creates, refines and realizes meaningful experiences.

5.2   Ensuring Output Quality

User-generated content frequently suffers from poor quality. "Garbage in" will lead to "garbage out". In the context of travel2change volunteer travel experiences may not be ready for realization, not rooted in local problems or unsustainable. We recognize that travellers as the main content "consumers" should not necessarily be the ones creating them. Local non-profits have the necessary expertise, local knowledge and infrastructure to create high-quality experiences. To ensure that the experiences created by the community are effective and sustainable the crowd needs inspiration, guidance and support from the platform providers as well as mutual support from fellow users. Voting mechanisms and reviews contribute to quality assurance and ensure that the best experiences percolate to the top. Experience creators need to be guided through the innovation process and a refinement phase helps to improve the quality of experiences.

5.3   Going to Scale to Increase Impact

Travel2change started with a single idea competition in 2011. But it quickly turned out that this approach was limited to engage certain users around a particular theme or a specific location over a finite period. To foster social innovation, travel2change needs to move from the piloting and prototyping phase to diffusion and scaling (Deiglmeier, 2011). For the current iteration travel2change is implementing an on-going challenge and experience submission model, enriched by competitions that foster content creation. In addition, travel2change seeks to foster self-coordination where travellers can use their passion to travel with a purpose and locals can find passionate travellers to support them.

6   Key Conclusions and Learning Outcomes for the Tourism Industry

Travel2change envisions a world where everyone is inspired to use their passion to travel with a purpose and where local communities benefit from collaborating with travellers. Travel2change's hope is that travel changes lives for the better—for travellers, locals and our world. Crowdsourcing may lead to a more innovative and beneficial approach to volunteer travel. The case of travel2change holds valuable lessons for crowdsourcing in the tourism industry:

- *Travel changes lives:* Volunteer travel can be a transformational experience for both travellers and locals. However, travellers can currently only choose from a limited number of experiences that are costly to join and lack the ability to directly connect with local communities. Many local communities and grass-roots non-profits do not have the ability to market their offerings on a website. They have limited say in the experience creation and popular experiences for travellers are replicated. Innovation toward a more collaborative approach to volunteer travel is needed and crowdsourcing offers a promising pathway.
- *Volunteer travel should be fun:* While there are many opportunities that ask travellers to simply volunteer abroad, the most impact will occur if volunteer traveling is fun. Crowdsourcing helps to enable all users to create experiences that link their passion to travel with a purpose.
- *Collaboration leads to innovation*: Crowdsourcing brings travellers, local communities and organizations together to share fresh insights, uncommon ideas and new directions. The diversity of stakeholders coming together nurtures creativity and results in social innovation.
- *Sustaining participation is critical for the success:* Crowdsourcing only works when you have a crowd that is both willing and capable to perform the outsourced tasks. Building the crowd depends on the right incentives, a compelling experience and the benefits provided by the interactions. To activate participation travel2change has extended the opportunities for users to create content throughout the travel experience from planning to and sharing the experience, modularized the creation task and increased the interactivity of the user experience.

Successfully leveraging crowdsourcing for volunteer traveling is an on-going challenge, but a journey well worth the efforts, if in the end travellers and local communities come together to create meaningful change around the world.

References

Alexander, Z., & Bakir, A. (2011). Understanding voluntourism. A Glaserian grounded theory study. In A. M. Benson (Ed.), *Volunteer tourism. Theoretical frameworks and practical applications* (pp. 9–29). Abingdon: Routledge.

Benson, A. M. (2011). Volunteer tourism. Theory and practice. In A. M. Benson (Ed.), *Volunteer tourism. Theoretical frameworks and practical applications* (pp. 1–6). Abingdon: Routledge.

Brown, S. (2005). Travelling with a purpose: Understanding the motives and benefits of volunteer vacationers. *Current Issues in Tourism, 8*(6), 479–496.

Deiglmeier, K. (2011). *Ideas are not enough - Time to face the "Executioner"*. Online in the Internet. URL: http://csi.gsb.stanford.edu/ideas-are-not-enough. Retrieved March 31, 2014.

Fee, L., & Mdee, A. (2011). How does it make a difference? Towards 'accreditation' of the development impact of volunteer tourism. In A. M. Benson (Ed.), *Volunteer tourism. Theoretical frameworks and practical applications* (pp. 223–239). Abingdon: Routledge.

Howe, J. (2006). The rise of crowdsourcing. *Wired Magazine, 14*(6). Online in the Internet. URL: http://www.wired.com/wired/archive/14.06/crowds.html. Retrieved March 31, 2014.

Howe, J. (2008). *Crowdsourcing. Why the power of the crowd is driving the future business*. New York: Crown.

Ingram, J. (2011). Volunteer tourism: How do we know it is 'making a difference'? In A. M. Benson (Ed.), *Volunteer tourism. Theoretical frameworks and practical applications* (pp. 211–222). Abingdon: Routledge.

Magretta, J. (2002). Why business models matter. *Harvard Business Review, 80*(5), 86–92.

Osterwalder, A., & Pigneur, Y. (2009). *Business model generation* (A handbook for visionaries, game changers, and challengers). New Jersey: Wiley.

Sin, H. L. (2009). Volunteer tourism – "Involve me and I will learn"? *Annals of Tourism Research, 36*(3), 480–501.

Surowiecki, J. (2004). *The wisdom of crowds*. New York: Anchor Books.

Tomazos, K., & Butler, R. (2009). Volunteer tourism: the new ecotourism? *Anatolia an International Journal of Tourism and Hospitality Research, 20*(1), 196–212.

Travel2change. (2014). *About travel2change*. Online in the Internet. URL: http://travel2.change/about. Retrieved March 31, 2014.

Wearing, S. (2001). *Volunteer tourism: Experiences that make a difference*. Wallingford: CABI.

Zott, C., Amit, R., & Massa, L. (2011). The business model: Recent developments and future research. *Journal of Management, 37*(4), 1019–1042.

Further Open Tourism Examples and Cases

Philipp Allerstorfer, Kim Boes, Igor Gula, Zsofia Horvath,
and Emre Ronay

This book covers a number of case studies, thus providing several practical insights into the industry. However, there are numerous other examples related to Open Innovation, Crowdsourcing, Co-Creation and Collaborative Consumption in Tourism, that are worthy of being presented to the reader. We therefore collected, structured and edited a total of 51 examples, based on our contribution-utilization-matrix. Each example is structured in the same way, first by providing a brief description of the activity. The Idea, purpose and the outcome of the project are listed as well as the company/creator, the country and the website link, for one to pursue further information.

P. Allerstorfer
Johannes Kepler Universität, Linz, Austria
e-mail: philipp.allerstorfer@gmail.at

K. Boes
Bournemouth University, Bournemouth, UK
e-mail: kboes@bournemouth.ac.uk

I. Gula (✉)
MODUL University Vienna, Wien, Austria
e-mail: igor.gula@chello.at

Z. Horvath • E. Ronay
Salzburg University of Applied Science, Salzburg, Austria
e-mail: anna.horvath15@gmx.com; emre.ronay@gmail.com

© Springer-Verlag Berlin Heidelberg 2016
R. Egger et al. (eds.), *Open Tourism*, Tourism on the Verge,
DOI 10.1007/978-3-642-54089-9

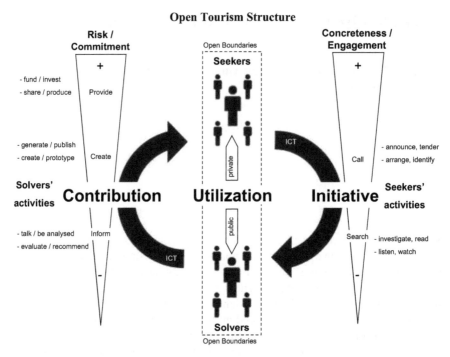

Fig. 1 Open tourism structure, see the first chapter of this book (Source: Own illustration)

1   Inform

1.1   Talk/be analysed

---

1. Smile land games

Description

Idea: The Tourism Authority of Thailand (TAT) launched a series of interactive Social Media games, branded under the name "Smile Land" that incorporate designs taken from the national icons of Thailand.[a] The games allow travellers to experience Thailand intuitively in an entertaining way. More than 200 points of interests can be discovered in the games, via the process of transforming into a virtual traveller coming to Thailand. During this journey, hidden treasures can be found at certain places and collected as tokens, which authenticate one's visit[b]

Purpose: The games are part of a digital marketing strategy initiated by the TAT. The target markets are young people using Social Media and smartphones. The TAT aims to reach one billion potential users worldwide and to enhance awareness of Thailand's tourism industry[c]

Outcome: Five interactive games that provide an entertaining perspective while raising awareness of Thailand have been developed. Potential visitors and travellers who are unfamiliar with Thailand, thus have the opportunity to partake in a pre-travel experience

---

(continued)

Country	Company/creator	Website
Thailand	Tourism Authority of Thailand (TAT)	http://www.smilelandgame.com/

[a]URL: http://www.tatnews.org/media-releases-2011/item/238-tat-launches-smile-land-games-on-social-networking-media, accessed on 18.08.2014
[b]URL: http://www.smilelandgame.com/gameinfo.php, accessed on 18.08.2014
[c]URL: http://www.thaitravelblogs.com/2011/06/tat-launches-smile-land-games-for-facebook-and-ipad/, accessed on 18.08.2014

1.2   Evaluate/recommend

2. ZAGAT
Description[a]
Idea: Zagat provides an information database, helping users to find various restaurants, ranging from the obscure noodle shop in New York, to the newest celebrity chef-owned restaurant in London. Zagat shows detailed ratings given to the restaurants. In addition, reviews and lists are displayed that are based on feedback from every day customers. This makes Zagat a reliable and accurate source of information to discover the most favourable places to eat and drink
Purpose: For every category that is being rated, surveys are conducted with regular and returning customers. The knowledge of these expert customers, their awarded points and ratings, and amusing quotes, offer internet users a comprehensive guide. The scoring system of Zagat is unique as it requires that the reviewer evaluates the restaurant according to separate components, based on a scale of 30 points
Outcome: Zagat has gained a lot of attention over the past few years. The Associated Press named Zagat as "the world's most influential travel and food guide", while The New York Times described it as "a necessity second only to a valid credit card"

Country	Company/creator	Website
State of New York, USA	Tim and Nina Zagat	http://www.zagat.com/

[a]URL: http://www.zagat.com/about-us, accessed on 18.08.2014

3. TripAdvisor
Description[a]
Idea: TripAdvisor claims to be the biggest travel website worldwide. The website enables users to plan their perfect trip based on the experiences of other travellers, and to share their own impressions. TripAdvisor manages websites with 23 other travel media brands and operates in 43 countries all over the world
Purpose: TripAdvisor provides reviews from travellers and a wide range of travel planning features, such as price comparison of various booking pages. The website provides a platform where travellers can retrieve information, recommendations and advice from other travellers, to plan their trip. Every minute, 60 more contributions are added to the database.[b]
Outcome: With more than 280 million visitors per month, over 100 million reviews, ideas and insights that cover more than four million accommodations, restaurants and attractions, TripAdvisor has become the largest travel community in the world

(continued)

3. TripAdvisor

Country	Company/creator	Website
State of Massachusetts, USA	Stephen Kaufer	http://www.tripadvisor.com/

[a]URL: http://www.tripadvisor.co.uk/PressCenter-c6-About_Us.html, accessed on 18.08.2014
[b]URL: http://www.tripadvisor.co.uk/help/gettingstarted, accessed on 18.08.2014

4. Tripwolf

Description[a]

Idea: Tripwolf is an online travel guide, which was founded in 2008. The travel guide is also available for mobile phones as an iPhone or Android app. The website comprises of up-to-the-minute information and high quality travel tips by combining mainstream travel information provided by travel guides such as Marco Polo and Footprint, with information provided by thousands of travellers located worldwide

Purpose: The user can browse through the website to find relevant information on destinations. For instance, information on thousands of points of interest, restaurants and hotels are available. In addition, users can create an individually customized travel guide which can be downloaded. Currently, more than 200 guides of the world's most beautiful destinations are available as in-app downloads. New guides are being added constantly

Outcome: The Tripwolf mobile travel map is currently one of the most successful personal travel guides on the market, with more than three million personal travel guides and around 1.6 million app downloads. The webpage is available in five different languages

Country	Company/creator	Website
Austria	Sebastian Heinzel	http://www.tripwolf.com/

[a]URL: http://www.tripwolf.com/en/page/about, accessed on 18.08.2014

5. Qype

Description[a]

Idea: Qype is Europe's leading consumer review site which was founded in 2006. It supports consumers who are seeking to make informed decisions on every day issues at home or on a trip. The idea revolutionized the way consumers were doing research and how they were deciding on which goods and services to patronize

Purpose: It provides a database with information that can be retrieved. New places can be discovered and shared. In addition, thorough and candid reviews are given based on restaurants, shops, hairdressers or even plumbers in more than 160,000 cities and towns around the world. The Qype App assists consumers by giving them instant access to reviews whenever they want

Outcome: Over three million reviews have been written and more than 900,000 places in Europe have been reviewed. The site is currently available in nine languages and attracts more than 15 million visits per month. It has over two million registered users in 166 countries. New content is uploaded every 10 s while every 7 s, a user conducts a local search via Qype

Country	Company/creator	Website
Germany	Stephan Uhrenbacher	http://www.qype.co.uk/

[a]URL: http://www.qype.co.uk/impressum, accessed on 18.08.2014

2 Create

2.1 Generate/publish

---

6. Wizard Istanbul

Description

Idea: WizardIstanbul.com is an online travel guide for people travelling to Istanbul. Its mission is to provide better Istanbul experiences. It offers useful and important information for people spending their time in Istanbul, which are created by the authors on the one hand, and insights and tips based on the questions which users asked about Istanbul on the other hand. WizardIstanbul.com has grown into a professional organisation consisting of 15 people

Purpose: People who "love Istanbul very much" come together and share their information, experiences and insights. Users can ask questions about Istanbul in selected categories. The questions can be asked via the website, Facebook or Twitter and will be answered within 30 min, 24 h a day. Users can also contribute to the website with their own texts and articles about Istanbul, and submit their impressions of Istanbul as well

Outcome: Crowdsourced online travel guide for Istanbul whose recommendations are based on the user-generated content

Country	Company/creator	Website
Turkey	Mehmet Cihangir	http://wizardistanbul.com/

---

7. "Global Youth Campaign", Fan photo of the week

Description

Idea: The destination New South Wales (NSW) conceptualized the "Global Youth Campaign"

Purpose: The "Global Youth Campaign" aims to get people together to talk about their experiences in New South Wales. Moreover, users can share their favourite places or secret spots online. The idea contributes to the promotion of NSW as a travel destination[a]

Outcome: Making use of Social Media platforms such as Facebook, users can upload their pictures which were taken at the destination. NSW would then choose the best fan photo of the week, and set it as wallpaper on NSW's Facebook profile[b]

Country	Company/creator	Website
NSW, Australia	Destination New South Wales	http://www.facebook.com/visitnsw

[a]URL: http://aboutourism.wordpress.com/2012/03/15/crowdsourcing-for-destination-marketing-make-it-personal/, accessed on 18.08.2014
[b]URL: http://www.facebook.com/visitnsw, accessed on 18.08.2014

---

8. Share your Washington

Description[a]

Idea: The campaign "Share Your Washington" can be traced back to the Washington Tourism Alliance of the State of Washington. The tourism industry is the fourth largest industry, which generates one billion in tax revenue per year and secures nearly 150,000 jobs in Washington

Purpose: The initiative was founded to support the tourism industry and it asked local people to share their favourite moments in Washington by uploading a picture of themselves and inviting their family and friends to visit Washington state

Outcome: A website, Facebook fanpage, YouTube channel and a video introducing the "Share your Washington" campaign and communicating the importance of tourism in Washington state

(continued)

were set up. Numerous pictures were uploaded to the website in addition to entries and discussions in numerous blogs

Country	Company/creator	Website
State of Washington, USA	Washington Tourism Alliance	http://www.shareyourwashington.com/ (offline) http://www.youtube.com/watch?v=5O5vpz_5VL8

[a]URL: http://aboutourism.wordpress.com/2011/04/29/crowdsourcing-tourism-campaigns-using-the-power-of-the-crowd/, accessed on 18.08.2014

9. Get social!—take the survey

Description

Idea: The Washington State Parks and Recreation Commission also started a survey to find out what type of stories users expect to see on the "Adventure Awaits" website as well as on the Washington State Parks Facebook fanpage

Purpose: The purpose of the campaign was to collect ideas for stories related to the Washington State Parks, uploaded by the users from all over the globe

Outcome: The campaign generated ideas and input for stories to be shared on the website of the Washington State Parks

Country	Company/creator	Website
State of Washington, USA	Washington State Parks and Recreation Commission	http://adventureawaits.com/2013/06/survey/

10. Secret d'ici/locals know

Description

Idea: In the summer of 2009 the Canadian Tourism Commission (CTC) encouraged locals to upload pictures of their most extraordinary experiences and favourite secret places all over Canada, onto the campaign website www.localsknow.ca or www.secretdici.ca. Air Canada sponsored the prize of one million Aeroplan Miles to entice Canadian residents to take part in the campaign and to support the CTC by uploading as many pictures and stories as possible within the given time frame[a]

Purpose: The purpose of the campaign was to give users an online platform to compile and share their great experiences and secret haunts in Canada with others

Outcome: In 2011, a new website and mobile application called "Explore Canada Like a Local" (ECLAL) was launched by the CTC, giving the consumers the possibility "to plot their journeys and share their tips before, during and after their stays in this country"
Moreover, within the mobile application, users can also search for points of interest, ranked according to the number of check-ins near the user's current location. The website was built on user-generated content, places and insights suggested by local people during the campaign described above[b]

Country	Company/creator	Website
Vancouver, Canada	Canadian Tourism Commission (CTC)	http://www.localsknow.ca/ http://www.secretdici.ca/

[a]URL: http://en-corporate.canada.travel/content/media_release/canadian-tourism-commission%E2%80%99s-%E2%80%9Clocals-know%E2%80%9D-campaign-inspires-canadians-discov, accessed on 18.08.2014
[b]URL: http://en-corporate.canada.travel/content/ctc_news/explore-canada-like-a-local, accessed on 18.08.2014

11. Thirty-five million directors

Description
Idea: "35 Million Directors" is a Crowdsourcing initiative of the Canadian Tourism Commission (CTC) that encouraged Canadians to participate in and contribute to a new video to promote Canada as a travel destination in international markets[a]
Purpose: The purpose of the campaign was to create an authentic promotion video with a "fresh and personal glimpse", using the expertise of millions of Canadians. Additionally, participants were invited to use Social Media in order to create awareness and generate publicity for their contributions and the campaign[b]
Outcome: The CTC received 65 h of video footage from a total of 6206 submissions. Eighty-two submitted videos were selected as winners and condensed into a new 2-min video clip promoting Canada.[c] The video has been published on YouTube and has reached almost one million views (1.5 million in the shorter version) at the time of analysis, thus being the most popular video of the YouTube channel "CANADA Explore|Explorez"[d]

Country	Company/creator	Website
Vancouver, Canada	Canadian Tourism Commission (CTC)	http://35milliondirectors.com/

[a]URL: http://www.brandchannel.com/home/post/2012/11/20/Canada-Travel-Crowdsourcing-112012.aspx, accessed on 18.08.2014
[b]URL: http://www.prnewswire.com/news-releases/canadians-invite-the-world-180137921.html, accessed on 18.08.2014
[c]URL: http://35milliondirectors.com/, accessed on 18.08.2014
[d]URL: http://www.youtube.com/user/canadiantourism/, accessed on 18.08.2014

12. L'effet Québec

Description[a]
Idea: The Quebec City Tourism Bureau (QTQ) and Cossette revealed a new microsite to raise the profile of Quebec City. On the website www.effetquebec.com, locals or any person who had resided in Quebec City were asked to share their ideas, hidden secret spots, or favourite places, activities or restaurants in the city with others
Purpose: The campaign targeted the domestic market and lasted for 6 weeks, ending on the 17th of June 2013. By utilizing locals' wisdom and tapping on their civic pride, it strove to portray Quebec City as a compelling and attractive destination
Outcome: The outcome of the campaign was a collaborative platform. The site offered weekly prizes such as hotel stays to its users. The strongest aspect was the implementation (or integration) of two Social Media platforms, Facebook and Twitter, which enabled simpler logins and users to give their rankings more quickly

Country	Company/creator	Website
Québec, Canada	Québec Tourism (OTQ)	http://effetquebec.com/

[a]URL: http://fredericgonzalo.com/2013/05/11/how-quebec-city-crowdsources-locals-to-promote-its-destination/, accessed on 18.08.2014

13. There is nothing like Australia

Description[a]

Idea: "There Is Nothing Like Australia" is a project under the auspices of Tourism Australia, meant to inform travellers more about the country. Australians share their personal stories about where they live and where they go on holidays in Australia. The provided content has been used by Tourism Australia to create an interactive map

Purpose: The goal was to provide a map for people interested in travelling to Australia, which was solely constructed based on authentic content

Outcome: The campaign generated a significant interest in the website and gathered a substantial amount of authentic content

Country	Company/creator	Website
Australia	Tourism Australia	http://www.nothinglikeaustralia.com/

[a]URL: http://www.nothinglikeaustralia.com/, accessed on 18.08.2014

14. Curators of Sweden

Description[a]

Idea: The "Curators of Sweden" is a project run by the National Board for the Promotion of Sweden (VisitSweden). Every week, a different user tweets on the official Twitter @sweden channel of VisitSweden. The curators have to register themselves on VisitSweden and are asked to suggest undiscovered places, recommend special events and share their opinions

Purpose: The curators give their own unique and individualized take on Sweden, on Twitter each week

Outcome: Community-generated content about Sweden is available online for interested users and potential visitors of Sweden

Country	Company/creator	Website
Sweden	National Board for the Promotion of Sweden	http://curatorsofsweden.com/ http://twitter.com/sweden

[a]URL: http://curatorsofsweden.com/about/, accessed on 18.08.2014

15. Visit Philly Guest Instagrammer

Description[a]

Idea: Greater Philadelphia Tourism Marketing, also known as VisitPhilly, handed over their Instagram account to chosen local photographers who were asked to take photos of one of the 14 neighbourhoods that were the focus of this campaign. The account was only given to long-term Instagram users in order to minimise the risks involved when handing over the account

Purpose: VisitPhilly used this campaign as part of Philadelphia's image building project

Outcome: Local community-generated photo content focusing on the whole region of Philadelphia

Country	Company/creator	Website
City of Philadelphia, USA	Greater Philadelphia Tourism Marketing Corporation (GPTMC)	http://instagram.com/visitphilly

[a]URL: http://press.visitphilly.com/releases/visit-philly-launches-guest-instagram-pinterest-programs, accessed on 18.08.2014

16. Share Wales

Description[a]

Idea: Visit Wales decided to support tourism businesses by strengthening social interaction between local residents, current visitors and potential customers, and to address their communities

Purpose: The vision is to provide assistance and support for tourism businesses when they have to deal with IT on the one hand, and to help them to interact with their guests and users on the other hand

Outcome: A website called "Share Wales" was set up to share content as well as essential information about current news, events and projects concerning the travel and tourism industry

Country	Company/creator	Website
Wales, UK	Visit Wales	http://www.sharewales.com/

[a]URL: http://www.sharewales.com/, accessed on 18.08.2014

17. Top 50—The Valleys Essentials

Description[a]

Idea: In 2011, over 4500 people in The Valleys voted for their favourite local places. The places were divided into five different categories: (1) Action and Adventure, (2) Castles and Sights, (3) Mining and Museums, (4) Sip and Scoff and (5) Walks and Drives. In each category, ten of the so-called "Valleys Essentials" were presented, including a map, a short description as well as pictures of some of the places

Purpose: The purpose of the campaign was to define the "Valleys Essentials" chosen by the visitors and users of The Valleys' website

Outcome: The Top 50 are a part of The Valleys tourism's online presentation and thus, its users can find out which are the most interesting places chosen by local people and how to get acquainted with their most beloved spots

Country	Company/creator	Website
Wales, UK	The Valleys, Visit Wales	http://www.thevalleys.co.uk/explore/our-top-10.aspx

[a]URL: http://www.thevalleys.co.uk/explore/our-top-10.aspx, accessed on 18.08.2014

18. The heart and soul of Wales

Description[a]

Idea: The Valleys also initiated another campaign called "The Hearth and Soul of Wales". Within this campaign, the tourism representatives of the Valleys were looking for answers to one simple question: "Why do you love The Valleys?"

Purpose: The purpose of the campaign was to find out what visitors and website users love about the Valleys and to produce user-generated content

Outcome: Sentiments from visitors and website users and reasons as to what they love about the Valleys were uncovered as well as ideas and input for the online presentation of content

Country	Company/creator	Website
Wales, UK	The Valleys, Visit Wales	http://www.thevalleys.co.uk/about/heart-soul.aspx

[a]URL: http://www.thevalleys.co.uk/about/heart-soul.aspx, accessed on 18.08.2014

19. It is more fun in the Philippines

Description[a]

Idea: Tourism officials in the Philippines invited users on Facebook and Twitter to create their own ads on their blogs and to share their fun tips with the world using the tagline "It's More Fun in the Philippines"

Purpose: The purpose of the campaign was to create a global tourism campaign for the Philippines without using many financial resources

Outcome: The tagline appears thousands of times on Facebook and Twitter and has generated positive word of mouth about the Philippines

Country	Company/creator	Website
Philippines	Philippines' Department of Tourism	http://itsmorefuninthephilippines.com/ thephilippines-fun-tips-from-locals/

[a]URL: http://nathanandrada.wordpress.com/2012/08/03/crowdsourcing-helps-promote-a-global-tourism-campaign-in-the-philippines/, accessed on 18.08.2014

20. Discover Ireland

Description[a]

Idea: Fáilte Ireland created "DiscoverIreland" on Facebook for tourists to share their favourite locations and activities with other readers. Tourism businesses already using Social Media promote this campaign on their Social Networks. People sharing their stories on this Facebook page had the chance to win weekly prices

Purpose: The purpose of the campaign was to encourage people to share personal stories about their favourite destinations, attractions and activities on the "DiscoverIreland" Facebook page

Outcome: A wealth of first-hand, authentic information was created by tourists for tourists

Country	Company/creator	Website
Ireland	Fáilte Ireland	http://www.facebook.com/discoverireland.ie

[a]URL: http://aboutourism.wordpress.com/2011/04/29/crowdsourcing-tourism-campaigns-using-the-power-of-the-crowd/, accessed on 18.08.2014

21. Louisiana calls all festival fanatics

Description[a]

Idea: Louisiana Travel asked its residents to visit festivals within the region and to post their experience on various Social Media networks. The so-called "Festival Fanatics" would combine their stories with other Festival Fanatics, shoot photos and videos and explain on blogs why they visited the festival and what they liked about it

Purpose: The purpose of the campaign was to use Social Media to share Louisiana's cultural offerings and to create positive word of mouth about Louisiana and its festivals on the web

Outcome: The "Festival Fanatics" resulted in a word of mouth promotion for Louisiana in various Social Media channels

Country	Company/creator	Website
State of Louisiana, USA	Louisiana Travel	http://www.facebook.com/LouisianaTravel

[a]URL: http://aboutourism.wordpress.com/2012/03/15/crowdsourcing-for-destination-marketing-make-it-personal/, accessed on 18.08.2014

22. My Cape Town holiday
Description[a]
Idea: Cape Town Tourism developed a Facebook game app where users could virtually experience Cape Town via their Facebook profile. The users could vicariously experience a 5-day holiday in Cape Town and explore the city's attractions and participate in activities. The more intense the exploration, the more in-depth information they received
Purpose: The purpose of the campaign was to promote the city of Cape Town globally via a Facebook game
Outcome: A significant number of Facebook users took part in the game between October and December 2012. Three users had the chance of winning an actual tour of the city of Cape Town

Country	Company/creator	Website
Cape Town, South Africa	Cape Town Tourism	http://www.facebook.com/CapeTown.Travel/app_ 464389300252127

[a]URL: http://www.capetown.travel/press_releases/entry/global-recognition-for-cape-town-tour isms-social-media-presence-with-travel;   http://www.facebook.com/CapeTown.Travel/app_ 464389300252127, accessed on 18.08.2014

23. "Global Youth Campaign", Unmapped Roadtrip
Description[a]
Idea: The destination New South Wales (NSW) conceptualized the "Global Youth Campaign". The idea behind the concept was to create a video diary blog with four participants, traveling around the destination for 30 days. They shared their trip on Social Media platforms to inform followers what they thought of the destination
Purpose: The participants travelled around NSW in a bus. The participants were Social Media experts, who filmed their adventures, posted, tweeted or blogged about them on Social Media platforms. These posts contributed to a more extensive promotion of the destination
Outcome: The campaign produced refreshing and authentic content and generated positive word of mouth about NSW as a destination

Country	Company/creator	Website
NSW, Australia	Destination New South Wales	http://www.facebook.com/visitnsw

[a]URL: http://aboutourism.wordpress.com/2012/03/15/crowdsourcing-for-destination-marketing-make-it-personal/, accessed on 18.08.2014

24. Crowdsourced battle for social media tourism symposium
Description[a]
Idea: Think! Social Media organised a Social Media Tourism Symposium which allowed the participant to decide which final destination the symposium should take place in. Via a Facebook app, users could vote for one of the four final destinations hosting the event
Purpose: To ask users where the symposium should finally take place
Outcome: The pre-promotion on Social Media created a buzz and thus an additional marketing campaign for the symposium that went viral

Country	Company/creator	Website
Vancouver, Canada	Social Media Tourism Symposium, Think! Social Media	http://www.sometourism. com/

[a]URL: http://sociallysorted.com.au/crowdsource-battle-for-social-media-tourism-symposium-case-study/, accessed on 18.08.2014

25. Tourism BarCamps

Description[a]

Idea: Barcamps are considered as an alternative to conferences, which provide a casual setting and let participants jointly set the agenda. In 2008, TourismusZukunft and the Catholic University of Eichstätt-Ingolstadt initiated such a Barcamp particularly for the tourism industry and then continued to host it as an annual event

Purpose: The Tourism BarCamp aims to bring a limited number of tourism professionals together. Among others, the target group includes leaders of tourism and hospitality businesses, representatives of DMOs, media and institutions of higher education. The purpose is to provide them with a setting which fosters discussions on trends and innovation

Outcome: In 2013, the Tourism BarCamp was successfully held for the sixth consecutive year and its capacity of approximately 120 participants was filled within a short time

Country	Company/creator	Website
Germany	TourismusZukunft, Catholic University of Eichstätt-Ingolstadt	http://www.tourismuscamp.de/

[a]URL: http://www.tourismuscamp.de/, accessed on 18.08.2014

26. Sauna from Finland

Description[a]

Idea: The "Sauna from Finland"[b] association is a network of companies related to the concept of sauna. Its goal is to consolidate the resources that different fields of business have, in order to strengthen the sauna concept and to collaboratively develop new ideas and business activities related to sauna

Purpose: The association includes sauna manufacturers, service providers as well as companies from the spa and tourism industry. The purpose is to enable them to share their expertise with each other. In regular meetings, they can think of new ideas, or jointly aim to realize them. In 2009, locals were also included in promoting and further developing the sauna concept, by submitting photos and personal stories to a contest initiated by a local newspaper

Outcome: A variety of innovative sauna products and experiences have already been developed within this network. Examples include Sauna Yoga, Sauna Retreat, Sauna of Silence and the Sauna Bar. Additionally, the concept of sauna has turned out to be a valuable branding strategy for the region of Central Finland

Country	Company/creator	Website
Finland	Sauna from Finland (community)	http://www.saunafromfinland.fi/

[a]URL: http://www.innotour.com/innovationCases/2010/10/developing-sauna-from-finland-concept-networking-and-co-operation-between-different-industries, accessed on 18.08.2014
[b]URL: http://www.saunafromfinland.fi/en/who-we-are/, accessed on 18.08.2014

27. Flinkster

Description[a]

Idea: Flinkster is a car sharing system initiated by Deutsche Bahn, the national German railway company. The idea is that cars are available on demand at no fixed costs, upon signing up on the Flinkster website and verifying one's registration at a Deutsche Bahn outlet

Purpose: Flinkster targets travellers arriving at train stations and airports, who are looking for a convenient way to continue their travels as well as people living in cities who occasionally need a car

(continued)

Outcome: With more than 800 car stations in 140 German cities, Flinkster is the largest car sharing provider in Germany and is further expanding to Austria, Switzerland and the Netherlands. Besides the web platform, a mobile application was set up. It facilitates the user in determining nearby locations and in directly booking cars, which can be done with a member card

Country	Company/creator	Website
Germany	Deutsche Bahn AG	http://www.flinkster.de/

[a]URL: http://www.flinkster.de/index.php?id=330&&f=3, accessed on 18.08.2014

28. INNOTOUR

Description[a]

Idea: The Centre for Tourism, Innovation and Culture of the University of Southern Denmark initiated INNOTOUR as an interactive web platform that should foster the exchange of ideas and provide resources related to innovation in tourism

Purpose: The purpose of INNOTOUR is to allow one to access and discuss various existing case studies of innovation in tourism as well as to contribute one's own case to the database. Its target groups include students and teachers of tourism management, who can benefit from the resources and interact on the forum or by using student blogs. Academics can add links to their publications and tourism professionals can use tools like the INNOWHEEL or an innovation checklist and present their company and products under the website's commercial section

Outcome: At the time of review, the online database contained more than 100 cases of innovation in tourism, articles and academic papers as well as various resources for innovation

Country	Company/creator	Website
Denmark	Centre for Tourism, Innovation and Culture, University of Southern Denmark	http://www.innotour.com/

[a]URL: http://www.innotour.com/about-innotour/, accessed on 18.08.2014

29. Advance tourism

Description[a]

Idea: Advance Tourism is an education program in Malta and Gozo, consisting of a series of workshops, mentoring sessions and an online community where participants are expected to actively contribute. The goal of the initiative is to improve the local tourism product

Purpose: The target group of Advance Tourism consists of senior and middle-level managers from the local tourism and hospitality industry. The purpose of Advance Tourism is to educate and support them in their engagement of life-long learning. The managers are then supposed to pass on their knowledge to their employees

Outcome: An interactive web platform was set up. At the time of review, approximately 1500 managers had already participated in the program and contributed to a lively online community dedicated to collaborative learning. Due to its current success, it is even likely that this community will continue to exist after the official end of the Advance Tourism program

Country	Company/creator	Website
Malta	Advance tourism	http://www.advance-tourism.com/

[a]URL: http://energise2-0.com/2012/03/13/advance-tourism-a-case-study-of-successful-crowdsourced-learning/, accessed on 18.08.2014

2.2 Create/prototype

30. KLM must see map
Description
Idea: The KLM Must See Map is a website that displays a customisable map of a chosen KLM destination. According to KLM, the goal of this campaign is not only to inspire people to make city trips, but also to expand the e-mail address database. However, as part of a "little act of kindness" strategy, KLM provides something in return for these e-mail addresses, a physical copy of the friend-sourced destination map[a]
Purpose: The purpose of the campaign is to enable users to create a personal destination map by adding their own points of interest for the next visit. Friends can be invited via Twitter, Facebook and e-mail, to incorporate their comments, recommendations and suggestions of must-see-places, onto the map. Additionally, a printout of the virtual map can be ordered free of charge[b]
Outcome: Advertisers admired KLM's ability to connect their customers' online and offline experience. A point of minor criticism was the delivery time of the print maps which took up to 3 weeks, making them impractical for spontaneous trips. Nevertheless, when the campaign was submitted to the Cannes Lions, users had already created more than 82,000 maps with almost eight tips per map on average. KLM's e-mail database had increased exponentially with more than 350,000 euros worth of addresses and they reported 16 % more city trips than in the previous year[c, d, e]

Country	Company/creator	Website
Netherlands	KLM Royal Dutch Airlines	http://mustseemap.klm.com; Video: http://www.youtube.com/watch?v=dosrsAy4ENY

[a]URL: http://www.brandchannel.com/home/post/2013/02/13/KLM-Must-See-Map-021313.aspx, accessed on 18.08.2014
[b]URL: http://www.youtube.com/watch?v=dosrsAy4ENY, accessed on 18.08.2014
[c]URL: http://www.brandchannel.com/home/post/2013/02/13/KLM-Must-See-Map-021313.aspx, accessed on 18.08.2014
[d]URL: http://blog.xeit.ch/2013/02/must-see-map-von-klm-verbindet-social-media-und-reale-welt/, accessed on 18.08.2014
[e]URL: http://winners.canneslions.com/entries/483726/klm-must-see-map, accessed on 18.08.2014

31. My Indonesian moment
Description[a]
Idea: The idea of the campaign was to solicit funny, dramatic or inspiring stories from travellers, in the form of writing or captured photographs, which were ultimately presented at the ITB travel fair. A jury selected the winner of a trip to Komodo, Indonesia[b, c]
Purpose: The goal of the campaign was to generate awareness towards the destination of Indonesia (particularly through the channels of Social Media and at the ITB in Berlin) by identifying unique places and experiences. Additionally, the contest provided a platform for exchanging and discussing travellers' favourite moments in Indonesia
Outcome: A Facebook page and website were set up for the contest. At the time of the review, the "My Indonesian Moment" community had 835 members, who submitted 1914 stories or photos and contributed more than 9000 evaluations as well as more than 7000 comments[d]

(continued)

Country	Company/creator	Website
Indonesia	KADIN Indonesian Chamber of Commerce and Industry	http://www.my-indonesian-moment.com/ (offline)

[a]URL: http://www.itb-kongress.de/media/itbk/itbk_media/itbk_pdf/praesentationen_2014/marketing_and_distribution_day_/Habibie-20140307--London.pdf, accessed on 18.08.2014
[b]URL: http://www.indonesia.travel/en/event/detail/653/my-indonesian-moment-photo-and-story-contest-win-a-trip-to-komodo, accessed on 18.08.2014
[c]URL: http://www.facebook.com/photo.php?fbid=10151355914672530, accessed on 18.08.2014
[d]URL: http://www.facebook.com/JaringIde?fref=nf, accessed on 16.04.2014

---

32. The most amazing show on earth

Description[a]

Idea: In 2011, the Tourism Authority of Thailand (TAT) launched a competition called "The Most Amazing Show on Earth". The aim of this campaign was to use the user-generated content and thus present amazing experiences from all over Thailand to other travellers

Purpose: The project consisted of two phases. In the first phase, TAT collected submissions of so-called "Amazing Moments" or unique stories from travellers who visited Thailand from all over the world. Users were able to upload their most memorable moments in the form of photo essays to the campaign website

Outcome: In the second phase, the TAT developed a seven-part film called "Hearing the Sunshine", inspired by the submissions described above and subsequently posted the film on its YouTube channel. Each of the film episodes was attached to a special region of Thailand and to experiences which pertained to that region. Moreover, the film allowed viewers to tag gifts related to each episode for a chance to win the gifts and have them sent to their homes

Country	Company/creator	Website
Thailand	Tourism Authority of Thailand (TAT)	http://www.mostamazingshow.com/ (offline) Videos: http://www.youtube.com/user/DiscoverThai

[a]URL: http://www.prweb.com/releases/2011/4/prweb8343598.htm, accessed on 18.08.2014

---

33. Your big break

Description

Idea: In the video competition "Your Big Break", the New Zealand Tourism Board invited young filmmakers to contribute a script for a 3-min short film presenting the spirit of New Zealand. After being selected, five of them got a chance to produce their own movie about New Zealand with the support of Academy Award-winning producer Barrie Osborne. The competition started on the 9th of December 2009. Four out of the five finalists were selected by an industry committee, but one of the five was the so-called "people's choice" finalist, who was chosen online by the crowd[a]

Purpose: The video competition ended on the 15th of January 2010. In the time between its launch on the 31st of November 2009 and its closure, the competition's website registered 250,000 visitors watching videos or reading scripts. The average user spent 3.5 min on the website. Around 1100 visitors from 30 countries took part in the competition and added their scripts for a 3-min short film about New Zealand[b]

Outcome: The completed short films from the five finalists went online on the 24th of February 2010. On the 5th of March 2010, the Academy Award-winning producer Peter Jackson selected the winner, and the winner's movie was presented on the US Independent Film Channel (IFC) before the IFC Independent Spirit Awards in the USA[c]

(continued)

Country	Company/creator	Website
New Zealand	New Zealand Tourism Board	http://www.your-big-break.com/ (offline) Videos: http://www.youtube.com/user/ YourBigBreakNZ

[a]URL: http://www.tourismnewzealand.com/news-and-features/latest-tourism-news/2010/01/new-zealand-set-to-star-on-silver-screen/, accessed on 18.08.2014
[b]URL: http://www.tourismnewzealand.com/news-and-features/latest-tourism-news/2010/01/ your-big-break-finalists-announced/, accessed on 18.08.2014
[c]URL: http://www.tourismnewzealand.com/news-and-features/latest-tourism-news/2010/02/ watch-the-your-big-break-films-for-yourself/, accessed on 18.08.2014

34. Visit Savannah video contest

Description

Idea: The Savannah Convention and Visitors Bureau (SCVB) conducted a video competition in fall 2011. It was announced on the SACV's website and on its Social Media platforms. The ultimate prize to win was $7500 (2nd place: $5000 and 3rd place: $2500)[a]

Purpose: The SACV received 15 video entries leading to the deadline of the contest and chose five finalists with the help of a specially set up task force. The videos from the finalists were published on the Facebook fanpage of the SACV's website "Visit Savannah". Consequently, the Facebook users had the possibility to vote "American Idol style" for each video once a day by clicking "Love it" or "Leave it" after watching it[b]

Outcome: The winner's video shows citizens of Savannah talking about their city, describing its diversity and persuading viewers to come to Savannah[c]

Country	Company/creator	Website
State of Georgia, USA	Savannah Convention and Visitors Bureau (SCVB)	http://savannahvisit.com/contact/video-contest (offline); Winner: http://www.youtube.com/ watch?v=ykh_C4Rx7-U

[a]URL: http://savannahvisit.com/contact/video-contest, accessed on 18.08.2014
[b]URL: http://savannahvisit.com/media-pr.php?doc_id=98, accessed on 18.08.2014
[c]URL: http://savannahvisit.com/media-pr.php?doc_id=101, accessed on 18.08.2014

35. Billboard writing contest

Description

Idea: In 2011, the Greater Philadelphia Tourism Marketing Corporation (GPTMC) started a billboard writing contest under the rubric of the "With Love, Philadelphia xoxo" campaign

Purpose: The GPTMC asked the participants to submit their own love letter, which if chosen, would be placed on a billboard along Philadelphia's I-95 route. The whole campaign was promoted on billboards on I-95 in Philadelphia, Route 30 in New Jersey and others as well as via Social Media and on a campaign website as a part of the visitphilly.com presentation. Moreover, the submissions could also be posted on Facebook or Twitter and the participants could hereby present their ideas and compare them alongside other competitors' ideas[a]

Outcome: Altogether, there were 2711 submissions from 42 states at the end of the competition, including one wedding proposal and three anniversary announcements. Finally, the winner was chosen by the GPTMC and his love letter line was placed on a billboard along Philadelphia's I-95 route, the main East Coast highway in February 2011[b]

(continued)

Country	Company/creator	Website
State of Pennsylvania, USA	Greater Philadelphia Tourism Marketing Corporation (GPTMC)	http://www.visitphilly.com/campaign/withlove/; Winner: http://c525832.r32.cf0.rackcdn.com/billboard-winner.jpg

[a]URL: http://press.visitphilly.com/releases/imagine-your-name-and-love-letter-on-a-philly-billboard, accessed on 18.08.2014
[b]URL: http://www.visitphilly.com/write-a-billboard-contest-winner/, accessed on 18.08.2014

36. "Brighter, Bolder, Better" ideas for travel

Description[a]

Idea: In 2010, Amadeus Corporation launched a global online competition called "Brighter, Bolder, Better" ideas for travel. It was designed to "find innovative ideas that would help transform the travel experience"

Purpose: The aim was to "listen to what the industry believes needs to be improved in terms of the all-round travel experience, recognising that good idea can come from anywhere"

Outcome: Unknown

Country	Company/creator	Website
Spain	Amadeus Corporation	http://www.amadeus.com/blog/16/12/launching-the-amadeus-brighter-bolder-better-ideas-for-travel-competition/ Video: http://www.youtube.com/watch?v=xZnUyY4hus0

[a]URL: http://www.amadeus.com/amadeus/x192006.html, accessed on 18.08.2014

37. Ninety-nine ideas Call for Pompeii

Description

Idea: In order to solicit ideas for developing the attractions in Pompeii, Italy, boosting the local economy and enhancing the tourism and cultural sector, the Ministry for Cultural Heritage and Affairs and the Municipality of Pompeii launched a competition, called "99 ideas Call for Pompeii"

Purpose: The organisers of the competition were looking for ideas fostering possible synergies between the area's major attractions, and focusing attention on the city, encouraging locals to participate in the development of innovative processes

Outcome: The competition was opened to all interested parties, professionals, academics and stakeholders in their individual capacity or as a member of an association. The competition ended on April 15, 2013. On July 29, 2013 the Evaluation Committee appointed the winners. There were five winning ideas, which can be found on the competition's website

Country	Company/creator	Website
Italy	Ministry for Cultural Heritage and Affairs and the Municipality of Pompeii	http://www.99ideas.it/site/ideas/en/home/ideas/for-pompeii.html

38. "My idea 2012" ideas competition

Description

Idea: The "My idea 2012" ideas competition was prepared, organised and executed in cooperation with the e-marketing department of the Slovak Tourist Board. The competition started on the 14th of May 2012 and ended on the 17th of June 2012

Purpose: The participants were invited to provide feedback on the Slovak Tourist Board's presentation of Slovakia at international tourism fairs. They could submit their input to already established promotions on the one hand, or generate new, alternative ideas for presentation of Slovakia on the other hand

Outcome: The ideas were submitted to the "My idea 2012" ideas competition via the Facebook application (1), via e-mail (145) and via Vyhravam.sk (189). Altogether, 259 participants took part in the ideas competition and sent 335 ideas. The input was submitted in various formats such as text, documents, pictures and presentations

Country	Company/creator	Website
Slovakia	Igor Gula, in cooperation with the e-marketing department of the Slovak Tourist Board	1st press release: http://www.sacr.sk/sacr/novinky/zapojte-sa-do-sutaze-moj-napad-2012-a-vyhrajte/ (in Slovak) 2nd press release: http://www.sacr.sk/sacr/clanky/vitazi-sutaze-moj-napad-2012/ (in Slovak)

39. "InnoWellen" ideas competition

Description[a]

Idea: The idea of the project was to enable and encourage stakeholders to collectively gather and select new ideas for the reconstruction of the public swimming pool "Wellenberg" in Oberammergau, Bavaria

Purpose: Creator Benjamin Kreitmeir aimed to present innovative ideas to the municipality of Oberammergau. Additionally, the project was an integral part of his Master thesis in Tourism Management, where he researched on how to include residents, local businesses, tourists and other stakeholders in the creation of ideas and decision-making process.

Outcome: A website and accounts in Social Media platforms were set up. A total of 38 ideas were submitted, out of which more than 80 % were considered as innovative by the municipality. One hundred and twenty-one votes were submitted, resulting in three winning ideas being identified, including a Caribbean-style water bar and a climbing wall for the public swimming pool. All results were gathered and published in a final report[b]

Country	Company/creator	Website
Germany	Bejamin Kreitmeir	http://www.innowellen.de

[a]URL: http://www.innowellen.de, accessed on 18.08.2014
[b]URL: http://www.innowellen.de/files/IDEEN-KATALOG.pdf, accessed on 18.08.2014

40. "#Wien2020" ideas competitions

Description[a]

Idea: In 2014, the Vienna Tourist Board organized the "Jetzt oder nie: Ihre Idee für #Wien2020" ("Now or never: Your idea for #Vienna2020") ideas competition. The competition started on the 18th of February and ended on the 18th of March 2014. The winner was selected by a jury and invited to spend a weekend in Vienna

Purpose: The purpose of the ideas competition was to invite people to submit their ideas and input for Vienna's new tourism strategy, called "Wien 2020" (Vienna 2020)

Outcome: 546 ideas were submitted in total. The ideas were further discussed by 2500 tourism experts invited to Vienna, as a part of a tourism strategy development

Country	Company/creator	Website
Austria	Vienna Tourist Board	http://2020.wien.info/

[a]URL: http://2020.wien.info/, accessed on 18.08.2014

41. Aloft Hotels of Starwood

Description[a]

Idea: Aloft Hotels (division of W Hotels and member of the Starwood Hotels and Resorts) made its virtual appearance in the form of "Second Life" in summer 2006, when it opened its virtual hotel. Aloft was the first hotel brand worldwide to implement a virtual property into a 3D computer-animated world

Purpose: The aim of the project was to gain feedback from customers on designs for rooms, restaurants and bars, and the hotel as a whole

Outcome: The first Aloft hotel based on the input and feedback submitted in "Second Life", opened in September 2008

Country	Company/creator	Website
USA	Starwood	http://www.virtualaloft.com/

[a]URL: http://www.businessweek.com/stories/2006-08-22/starwood-hotels-explore-second-life-first, http://www.virtualaloft.com/2006/10/aloft_to_open_in_second_life_n.php; accessed on 18.08.2014

3 Provide

3.1 Fund/invest

42. Up Greek tourism		
Description		
Idea: The "Up Greek Tourism" campaign was established to help Greek people understand the importance of Greek tourism on the one hand and to promote Greece as a tourist destination to the rest of the world on the other hand[a]		
Purpose: With the help of crowdfunding, "Up Greek Touris'" financed tourism promotion campaigns in London, Washington DC and New York		
Outcome: The first Crowdfunding campaign for London ran from the 1st of December 2012 to the 24th of December 2012 and generated £13,325 from 241 supporters. After that, an advertising billboard was displayed on the Piccadilly Lite 24 h a day for 2 weeks from the 31st of January to the 14th of February 2013. Similar billboards were crowdfunded and established in Washington DC as well as in New York, both promoting Greek tourism[b]		
Country	Company/creator	Website
Greek	Yorgos Kleivokiotis, Onic Palandjian and Stathis Haikalis	http://www.upgreektourism.gr/

[a]URL: http://www.upgreektourism.gr/about/, accessed on 18.08.2014
[b]URL: http://www.upgreektourism.gr/campaigns/, accessed on 18.08.2014

43. Cleaning Up the Yellow-Stone National Park		
Description[a]		
Idea: In March 2013, the National Park Service responsible for Yellowstone National Park discussed the use of crowdfunding to generate the resources necessary for cleaning up Yellowstone National Park due to federal budget cuts		
Purpose: Crowdfunding of resources for cleaning up Yellowstone National Park		
Outcome: Unknown		
Country	Company/creator	Website
State of Wyoming, USA	National Park Service	None

[a]URL: http://skift.com/2013/03/14/yellowstone-park-crowdsources-private-funds-to-clear-roads-following-sequester/, accessed on 18.08.2014

44. Investours		
Description[a]		
Idea: The idea of Investours is based on combining travelling and microfinancing. It aims to provide funds for small tourism businesses in developing countries, based on creating human networks and exchanging knowledge		
Purpose: The idea is to educate and mobilize travellers and micro-entrepreneurs across the world, to reshape educational tourism and to contribute to the global fight against poverty. Investours brings travellers funding interest-free loans face-to-face with aspiring micro-entrepreneurs. This merging of educational tourism and microfinance creates a network of socially responsible and empowered agents working towards global social change		
Outcome: Investours tries to combine the power of microfinance with the power of tourism to fight poverty. The company organizes "microfinance tours"—a new brand of goodwill tourism		

(continued)

that takes the whole small-loan concept and puts the power directly in the hands of the tourists. Instead of a bank making a decision about who gets a loan, strangers with minimal vested interest do

Country	Company/creator	Website
Mexico	Investours	http://www.investours.org/

[a]URL: http://www.innotour.com/innovationCases/2010/11/combining-travelling-and-microfinancing/, http://investours.org/about-investours/, accessed on 18.08.2014

3.2 Share/produce

45. #LoveCapeTown Campaign

Description[a, b]

Idea: "#LoveCapeTown" was a campaign conducted by the Cape Town tourism office as part of an award-winning e-marketing strategy focusing on using citizens and fans as ambassadors for the destination. In 2013, four international travel-bloggers were invited to Cape Town to share their experiences as iAmbassadors. In order to provide them with travel itineraries, locals were asked to contribute their expertise and recommend activities and hidden gems

Purpose: The campaign aimed at providing these guest travel bloggers with ideas for activities in Cape Town which they could experience and subsequently share via Social Media, with their followers around the world

Outcome: During the Twitter conversation between locals and iAmbassadors, the hashtag "LoveCapeTown" achieved already more than 145,000 impressions. In total, the conversation between locals and iAmbassadors led to approximately 23 million tweet impressions during the campaign. Furthermore, Cape Town Tourism was acknowledged as the organisation with the "Best overall use of Social Media" and given the SMITTY award[c]

Country	Company/creator	Website
Cape Town, South Africa	Cape Town Tourism	Blog entry by Cape Town Tourism: http://www.capetown.travel/blog/entry/i-ambassadors-in-cape-town-in-retrospect

[a]URL: http://www.capetown.travel/blog/entry/locals-show-they-know-cape-town-best-with-lovecapetown, accessed on 18.08.2014
[b]URL: http://www.capetown.travel/blog/entry/i-ambassadors-in-cape-town-in-retrospect, accessed on 18.08.2014
[c]URL: http://www.capetown.travel/press_releases/entry/global-recognition-for-cape-town-tourisms-social-media-presence-with-travel, accessed on 18.08.2014

46. Crowdsourced testing of local cellular networks

Description[a, b]

Idea: Regulations on cell towers aiming at protecting the scenic landscape of Hilton Head Island have prevented cell phone operators from extending their networks. However, since locals and tourists continued to demand for an improved network coverage, Hilton Head asked the RootMetrics company to crowdsource signal tests on the island to locals

Purpose: The goal was to gather data on signal coverage, thus enabling the town council to search for improvements together with network operators. The enhancement of the network coverage was demanded by locals, but there were also extraneous demands made to market Hilton Head as a destination for conferences and executive retreats

(continued)

Outcome: Volunteers used the RootMetrics smartphone app to collect more than 20,000 data points that were transformed into detailed maps. A task force made several recommendations to improve coverage while maintaining the aesthetics of Hilton Head, several of which were approved by the town council

Country	Company/creator	Website
Hilton Head Island, South Carolina (USA)	Hilton Head's town council	http://hiltonheadcell.com/

[a]URL: http://hiltonheadcell.com/, accessed on 18.08.2014
[b]URL: http://gigaom.com/2012/01/28/how-crowdsourcing-will-give-hilton-head-better-mobile-coverage/, accessed on 18.08.2014

47. Airbnb

Description[a]

Idea: Airbnb calls itself "a community marketplace for unique spaces". Airbnb was founded in August of 2008 in San Francisco and today, it is a community marketplace, where unique accommodations from around the world can be listed for free. Airbnb currently offers accommodation possibilities in 34,000 cities and 190 countries

Purpose: Airbnb serves as a platform where people from all over the world can market their extra space and thus offer others the possibility of having a unique travel experience

Outcome: Over 800,000 listings worldwide in more than 34,000 cities from 190 countries accommodated over 17 million guests at the time of analysis

Country	Company/creator	Website
State of California, USA	Nathan Blecharczyk, Brian Chesky and Joe Gebbia	http://www.airbnb.com/

[a]URL: https://www.airbnb.com/about, accessed on 18.08.2014

48. Couchsurfing

Description[a]

Idea: Couchsurfing is a global community of six million people from more than 120,000 cities connecting travellers with people willing to share their extra space (their couch) for free and to provide a true social travel experience. Couchsurfing was founded in 2004 in California, where the genesis of its idea can be traced back to

Purpose: The purpose of Couchsurfing was to generate a community creating unique travel experiences. "Couchsurfers" can stay at home with the other members of the community in whichever country or city they are visiting, or just join one of the events hosted by the local group of Couchsurfers

Outcome: A recent survey shows that the community consists of nine million people from more than 120,000 cities, with more than 430,000 organized events

Country	Company/creator	Website
State of California, USA	Casey Fenton, Daniel Hoffer, Sebastian Le Tuan and Leonardo Bassani da Silveira	http://www.couchsurfing.org/

[a]URL: http://www.couchsurfing.org/n/about, accessed on 18.08.2014

49. The Valleys Ambassadors

Description[a]

Idea: The latest project of The Valleys is called "The Valleys Ambassadors". The so-called "Community Tourism Ambassadors" are trained volunteers from across the Valleys who become "a welcoming host and source of information for their locality". The Valleys aim to train 200 local people as ambassadors promoting the region to visitors

Purpose: The purpose is to provide a unique travel experience for travellers to the Valleys by giving them the opportunity to meet with locals

Outcome: Many local people signed up to become host visitors

Country	Company/creator	Website
Wales, UK	The Valleys, Visit Wales	http://www.thevalleys.co.uk/about/heart-soul/valleys-ambassadors.aspx

[a]URL: http://www.thevalleys.co.uk/about/heart-soul/valleys-ambassadors.aspx, accessed on 18.08.2014

50. Visit a Swede

Description[a]

Idea: "Visit a Swede" is an initiative of the National Board for the Promotion of Sweden (VisitSweden). The website invites travellers to Sweden to meet with locals on their trip, because "the best way to experience Sweden is to meet the people". The idea is to connect travellers with local people, according to their likes and preferences

Purpose: The purpose is to provide a unique travel experience for travellers to Sweden by meeting with locals

Outcome: Over 10,000 Swedes signed up to host visitors

Country	Company/creator	Website
Sweden	National Board for the Promotion of Sweden	http://www.visitaswede.com/

[a]URL: http://www.visitaswede.com/, accessed on 18.08.2014

51. Travel2change

Description[a]

Idea: Travel2change is an online community of travellers and locals, with the aim to create a change. They believe that "travel changes lives"

Purpose: On the one hand, travellers can choose to travel in a way that maximally benefits the local communities they visit. On the other hand, locals from all over the world can host travellers, in order to gain their support

Outcome: On Travel2change one can join an already existing, on-going challenge/trip that is compatible with one's passion or skills, or one can create his/her own challenge/trip and connect with others in order to find supporters for one's challenge

Country	Company/creator	Website
State of Hawaii, USA	Travel2change (community)	http://www.travel2change.org/community/home

[a]URL: http://www.travel2change.org/community/static/about/, accessed on 18.08.2014

Index

Lightning Source UK Ltd.
Milton Keynes UK
UKHW02n0519251117
313304UK00008B/65/P